BRAZIL
THE DISPUTED RISE
OF A REGIONAL POWER

2003-2015

Collection « Inter-National »

dirigée par Denis Rolland,
Joëlle Chassin et Françoise Dekowski

Cette collection a pour vocation de présenter les études les plus récentes sur les institutions, les politiques publiques et les forces politiques et culturelles à l'œuvre aujourd'hui. Au croisement des disciplines juridiques, des sciences politiques, des relations internationales, de l'histoire et de l'anthropologie, elle se propose, dans une perspective pluridisciplinaire, d'éclairer les enjeux de la scène mondiale et européenne.

Série générale (dernières parutions) :

Salim TOBIAS PEREZ, *Religion, immigration et intégration aux Etats-Unis. Une communauté hispanique à New York*, 2015.
Daniel GRANADA DA SILVA FERREIRA, *Pratique de la capoeira en France et au Royaume-Uni*, 2015.
Patrick HOWLETT-MARTIN, *La coopération médicale de Cuba. L'altruisme récompensé*, 2015.
Maria Teresa GUTTIEREZ HACES, *La continentalisation du Mexique et du Canada dans l'Amérique du Nord. Les voisins du Voisin*, 2015.
Eric DICHARRY, *Théâtre, résidence d'artiste, médiation et territoire*, 2014.
Catherine DURANDIN et Cécile FOLSCHWEILLER, *Alerte en Europe : la guerre dans les Balkans (1942-1913)*, 2014.
Estelle POIDEVIN, *L'Europe : une affaire intérieure ? Ce qui change en Europe*, 2014.
Juliette MAFFRE, *La légalisation du mariage homosexuel en Argentine*, 2014.
Pierre-Philippe BERSON, *Sous le soleil de Chávez. Enquête sur le Venezuela d'Hugo Chávez*, 2014.
Mathieu CRETTENAND, *Le rôle de la presse dans la construction de la paix, Le cas du conflit basque*, 2014.
Pierre JOURNOUD, *La Guerre de Corée et ses enjeux stratégiques de 1950 à nos jours*, 2014.
Philippe SAUNIER, *Politique de la comptabilité publique*, 2014.
Laurent BORZILLO, *La Bundeswehr. De la pertinence des réformes à l'aune des opérations extérieures*, 2014.
Jean-Yves PARAÏSO, *La perception de la théologie latino-américaine de la libération en République Fédérale d'Allemagne. L'exemple du cercle d'étude « Eglise et libération » (1973-1978)*, 2013.
Edouard BOINET, *Hydropolitique du fleuve Sénégal. Limites et perspectives d'un modèle de coopération*, 2013.
Eric DICHARRY, *L'écologie de l'éducation. Un anthropologue à l'école du bertsularisme en Pays basque*, 2013.
Sébastien BARRERE, *Les Etats-Unis face au franquisme. 1936-1956, la croisée des chemins*, 2013.
Marc PAVE, *La pêche côtière en France (1715-1850). Approche sociale et environnementale*, 2013.
Marianne GUILLEMIN, *Femmes officiers de communication dans l'armée de Terre. Le parcours des combattantes*, 2013.
Ariane LANDUYT & Denis ROLLAND (org.), *Construire l'espace politique européen. Historiographies, politiques et territoires*, 2012.

PATRICK HOWLETT-MARTIN

BRAZIL THE DISPUTED RISE OF A REGIONAL POWER 2003-2015

Translation : Robert Burns, Patrick Howlett-Martin

Prologue by Celso AMORIM,

Preface by José Mauricio BUSTANI

L'Harmattan

First Published: L'Harmattan 2014, French edition.

5-7, rue de l'École-Polytechnique ; 75005 Paris

http://www.harmattan.fr
diffusion.harmattan@wanadoo.fr
harmattan1@wanadoo.fr

ISBN : 978-2-343-08073-4
EAN : 9782343080734

CONTENTS

PROLOGUE

Etymologycally prologue is what comes before the discourse. And so I shall not attempt to expand on the questions addressed in detail by the author in 400 richly informative pages with their comments and analyses. Nor do I believe I can add any new concepts to the preface written by Ambassador José Mauricio Bustani for the French edition, upon which this duly expanded and updated English edition is based.

As an active participant in the actions and events that took place during the period covered by Patrick Howlett-Martin, I would have one or two observations to make, without taking anything away from the general meaning of the book. I would say, for example, as regards Iraq, the author might have gone into greater depth on Brazil's role on the Security Council in the years 1998-99, when it proposed and chaired three panels on the situation in that country, which was overwhelmed by economic sanctions and under the constant threat of a devastating military attack. Brazil showed important leadership at the time, adopting an approach that would have a positive influence on how further initiatives were received some years later.

I had the privilege of writing the preface to the book by Hans von Sponeck (cited in this work) on the humanitarian disaster resulting from the coercive measures imposed on Baghdad on the eve of the first Gulf War. The outcome of these efforts was the replacement of the notorious UNSCOM, whose inspections increasingly seemed to be intended as provocations, by the more flexible UNMOVIC, led by Hans Blix. Under the leadership of the former Swedish Minister for Foreign Affairs, later head of the International Atomic Energy Agency, inspections moved forward and perhaps could have prevented the ill-fated unilateral military action against Saddam Hussein had an unfortunate sequence of events not intervened (chief among them the terrorist attacks on the Twin Towers on September 11 fueling the bellicose zeal of George W. Bush's first term), which sundered our hopes for a peaceful outcome. Blix resigned, UNMOVIC was disbanded, and Iraq was left virtually in ruins. No weapon of mass destruction was ever found. To a country in tatters, we bequeathed scorched earth and a terrorist movement far more destructive than anything seen before (and, contrary to the news we were fed, the Iraqi government had nothing to do with it). Brazil joined with other countries such as France and Germany in opposing any military solution without Security Council authorization, condemning the bombings and subsequent ground invasion. But at the time, when all seemed dominated by an apparently seamless unipolarity, these efforts were to no avail.

Another thing that shines forth in Howlett-Martin's work is how it reveals, in great detail, the density of diplomatic initiatives and processes in which Brazil was involved, especially in the years of President Lula's two terms in office.

From the fight against hunger and poverty (a program in which France was closely involved) to multilateral trade negotiations, and its unprecedented involvement in Middle East issues, in forging closer ties with Africa, and – priority of priorities – the uniting of South America, Brazilian diplomacy has not ceased to surprise supporters and critics alike (the latter principally within Brazil).

During this period, and marking a relatively novel element in Brazilian foreign policy, Brazil did not simply react to agendas put before it (such as the FTAA, discussed in this book) or seek, through alliances with other developing countries, to remedy distortions in ongoing negotiations (such as the WTO Doha Development Round). In Cancun, the creation of the G20-Developing Nations was an accomplishment of political boldness and fine diplomatic engineering. During the Lula administration, Brazil was a constant supporter of "new agendas", such as the South American Community of Nations, the forebear of UNASUL; the Summit of South American-Arab Countries (ASPA); rapprochement with African nations (Africa-South America Summit - ASA); and the institution of the IBSA forum, bringing together the great democracies of the three continents making up the Global South and the forerunner of the BRICS group.

In the three books I have published (Conversations with Young Diplomats; Short Narratives on Diplomacy; and Tehran, Ramallah and Doha) about this transformative time (as it was termed in *Foreign Affairs*), I discussed these diplomatic initiatives in what I would call "subjective" terms, i.e. from the perspective of one of the actors involved in developing the policy outlined by the President of the Federative Republic of Brazil. It is especially interesting to me to see how these initiatives are understood by a neutral observer (to the extent that it is possible to be totally neutral on political issues), which facts deserve greater attention, and how our actions and those of our counterparts are interpreted.

Another feature of this long and substantial text is that it does not merely analyze the attitudes and motivations of Brazilian diplomacy, it also describes in great detail the situations in the other countries with which we have had relations. The author thus presents a very broad overview of the world situation, giving readers the ability to reach their own conclusions about the soundness of our positions.

Howlett-Martin also goes beyond the Lula administration to address the situations arising during the subsequent government of Dilma Rousseff. I was Minister of Defense during much of her first term (August 2011 to December 2014). With her support, I sought to further some of the initiatives discussed in this book, such as our engagement in Haiti, the participation of our Navy in the United Nations Interim Force in Lebanon (UNIFIL), and the intensification of our actions within the Council of South American Defense, and regarding the South Atlantic Peace and Cooperation Zone (Zopacas). Revealing a keen discernment of the facts, Howlett-Martin puts the spotlight on specific military actions, such as Brazil's participation in naval exercises in the Gulf of Guinea and those in the IBSAMAR series.

While external factors may seem to have dampened Brazil's diplomatic efforts, the basic thrust has not changed. As I write this prologue, I note that Minister Mauro Vieira is working to expand and develop the line of action that was laid out just over a decade earlier. Short-term variations must not be confused with long-term historical trends. On my part, I am convinced that once the current economic recession is behind us and we have resolved the political crisis (caused to some extent by the recession), Brazil will regain its role at the forefront of major global issues, without setting aside the priority of South American unity (Latin American and Caribbean countries). And so we will rise to the vision expressed by the great San Tiago Dantas, theoretician of independent foreign policy in the early 1960s, to whom I refer at the end of my account of the Tehran Declaration, one of the books cited in the author's rich and extensive bibliography: Brazil must not limit itself to pursuing its own immediate interests but must work to contribute to the peace and prosperity of the entire planet.

Patrick Howlett-Martin turns an objective yet never disinterested gaze upon the adventure that Brazil's foreign policy (and – why not? – the "grand strategy" that also encompasses national defense) has represented at the dawn of the third millennium. Whatever your ideological background, you will come away from this book with a much more complete understanding of the people and events that have characterized what I call the "active and proud foreign policy" entrusted to me in December 2002 by President Lula. You may thus, without prejudice, formulate your own opinion of the value of the actions undertaken and the initiatives pursued during years marked by a wealth of achievements (and also, I must admit, moments of frustration). They were years marked by many controversies and disputes – principally with the Brazilian media. But I am confident that in the end you will agree with me that they were certainly not monotonous years. And as is clear from the reading (and not just the title), every new emergence meets with resistance.

Celso AMORIM

Brazil's Minister of External Relations (1993-1995 and 2003-2010),
Minister of Defense (2011-2015)

PREFACE[1]

Following *Le Brésil du Nord-Est* (2004), a work translated into Portuguese by a major Brazilian publishing house, French diplomat Patrick Howlett-Martin provides us with a new and pertinent resource for understanding Brazil: "*La Politique étrangére du Brésil: Une Émergence Contestée*". Reflected in this book is an entire life's experience acquired during the author's three diplomatic appointments in Brazil (Rio de Janeiro, Brasilia, Recife) coupled with his broad knowledge of the private sector in Brazil and in Latin America generally.

After examining the regional situation – the northeast in a state of flux, transmuting from a romanticized cliché to a hub of growth and social progress – Howlett-Martin traces out the general lines of the transformation underway in Brazilian foreign policy. The central theme leads from an analysis of Brazil's inner reality and its progress toward democracy, social justice and economic development to a better understanding of the country's role in the global reality via the roundabout route of its foreign policy. And this interpretation, as is always true when talking about states, must necessarily emerge from a study of the ideas and politics animating the public sphere.

Although he has more than three decades of experience in Brazil, Howlett-Martin has chosen to focus on a specific period: the presidency of Luis Inácio Lula da Silva, known simply in the traditional informality of Brazil as Lula. The other protagonist in this story is Celso Amorim, Minister of External Relations at the time. A large part of Brazilian transformation was clearly the fruit of how these two men responded to their times, of their ideas and their thoughts on Brazil, the external world and the interaction between them. It is due most of all to the fact that Lula and Amorim were perfectly in sync with the aspirations of the Brazilian people, their desire for peace, progress and – why not? – grandeur.

I personally experienced this period of less than 10 years as an insider, albeit most of the time assigned to missions abroad by President Lula. In spite of the skeptics and nostalgics, it was a time of absolutely extraordinary change, transformations of a breadth that the many prophets of (supposedly) smooth globalization in the 1990s not only failed to foretell, which is understandable, but even after they had taken place, were incapable of comprehending because they lacked the necessary conceptual tools.

In learning of the salient elements of foreign policy during the Lula years, the reader of this work by Howlett-Martin will be wise to bear in mind the transformations that were taking place outside of Brazil. The eight Lula-Amorim years (2003-2008) correspond to a period bracketed by two great upheavals in the global system. The first was the shock of the terrorist attacks

[1] To the French Edition (2014).

of September 11, 2001 and the ensuing political and strategic reaction of the superpower, grounded in a neo-conservative ideological foundation that led to the invasion of Iraq under false pretenses on March 19, 2003. It was in the aftermath that Lula won the election and took office.

The second upheaval, of an economic and diplomatic nature, started with the bankruptcy of Lehman Brothers on September 15, 2008, followed by the G-20 financial summit among chiefs of state and governments on November 15, 2008 and then the European sovereign debt crisis starting in 2010. It continues today in the prolonged stagnation of the central economies and the entry of large, formerly peripheral emerging countries into the decision-making process. Lula completed his second term during that crisis with a record approval rating. And he was rewarded by witnessing the victory at the polls of his chosen successor, Dilma Rousseff, his right-hand woman.

One can also frame the processes described by Howlett-Martin in their external context, comparing the Brazilian experience after the reestablishment of democracy in 1985 with the global transformations taking place under the name of globalization. Between the fall of the Berlin Wall on November 9, 1989 and the collapse of Wall Street on September 15, 2008, the international economy and reality had a certain ideological foundation. While now recognized as ultraliberal, free-market and extremist, at the time it was considered to be perfectly rational and non ideological.

With the benefit of hindsight, we now see that the entire period between the September 11 attacks and the financial crisis was characterized by a breakdown of regulation – "the deregulation of the world" in the words of Amin Maalouf – in the system, all taking place under the cover of normalcy and prosperity. In order to finance its transcontinental military forays and prolong its fleeting moment of uncontested hegemony, the superpower sought maximum leverage from the international monetary and financial system, stimulating speculative bubbles and setting the stage for the crisis that would inevitably follow.

Even the harshest critics of Lula and Amorim were forced to recognize that these two had foreseen these transformations many years in advance. One of the merits of Howlett-Martin's work is precisely that it helps us discern in these two men the sort of foresight that is the hallmark of a great statesman (and De Gaulle's appeal to the French nation in 1940 may be considered the greatest example of the 20th century).

While many were blinded by the neo-conservative, ultra-liberal ideology (if not by others), Brazil had the fortune of choosing – or rather, the Brazilian electorate may be credited with electing – leaders who had a relatively clear perception of the reality unfolding before them. They were prophetic, not in the sense that they were able to foresee the future, but in the Brazilian writer Nelson Rodrigues's concept of the prophet: he who sees what is evident before others do.

What were the ideological foundations of Brazilian actions in that period? Because there certainly were ideological foundations: recent history teaches us that it is precisely when we deny the dominance of a given ideology that its effects are manifested with yet greater force. But it is necessary to clarify the ideological premises of our own political action; this is the only way we can systematically contrast conjecture with facts and outcomes so that we can adapt our premises to better fit reality.

Howlett-Martin rightly points out that the writings and actions of Samuel Pinheiro Guimarães had an important influence on Brazilian foreign policy during the Lula years. I am quite ready to agree, especially because I count Pinheiro Guimarães as one of my friends (along with Lula and Amorim). We were both, at a certain point in time, marginalized in our diplomatic careers, kept out of positions of responsibility, treated as "ideologues" or worse, because we had dared to oppose two fundamentally ideological plans that we believed were detrimental both to Brazil and to all of humanity: for Pinheiro Guimarães it was the ultra-liberal Free Trade Area of the Americas, for me, the neo-conservative invasion of Iraq. Our critics had no idea that by sidelining us this way, they freed us from all obligations and facilitated our full cooperation with Lula and Amorim in the following stage of Brazilian foreign policy.

It may be too soon to write the definitive history of Brazilian policy in those years, and indeed this is not Howlett-Martin's goal. With time, the salient points of continuity between the foreign policy of President Lula and the historical project to build the Brazilian state will be easier to see, in contrast with whatever discontinuities may exist. Some may be surprised to learn – but not those who know him – that Pinheiro Guimarães is a specialist in and great admirer of the Baron of Rio Branco (José Paranhos), minister, philosopher and high functionary of foreign policy in the early years of the Old Brazilian Republic (1902-1912). His stature was such that it was obligatory for all diplomats returning from abroad to read his biography.

The foreign policy of President Hermes da Fonseca and the Baron of Rio Branco was not, and could not be, that of President Lula and Celso Amorim. The world had changed too many times over the ensuing century, and change is only accelerating, making it necessary to review and revise all the assumptions underlying political action at least once every ten years. But there is a certain underlying continuity constituting what we might consider the perennialism of the Brazilian state and nation.

I do not mean perennialism in the sense of immobility, but as an unwavering direction to the historical process. Over the course of a single human lifetime, this process led the son of poor illiterate farmers from the northeastern sub-region of Sertão (which was the subject of Howlett-Martin's first book on Brazil) initially to an education, graduating as a skilled worker from the National Service for Industrial Training (SENAI), then on to become a union leader, founder of a political party, candidate for president of the republic, finally elected on his fourth attempt. And it now leads to him becoming the subject of Howlett-Martin's second book.

And we have the impression that five centuries have passed between these two books; but this story unfolded over less than fifty years. The protagonist is a person endowed with exceptional qualities, but it is also a people, a nation, a state perpetually in the works, in which the sense of history – if I may borrow from Hegel – lies in constant progress toward democracy, social inclusion, the happy and harmonious coexistence of people of widely varying ethnicities and religious beliefs; and lastly toward the construction of a grand, original tropical civilization, without denying, but overcoming – definitively I hope – all the violence and injustice that this process might involve.

This is the Brazilian national project, or if you prefer, Brazilian ideology. There would be much to discuss here: the nature and role of the state, the economic paradigm, educational policy, race relations, environmental impact, defense strategy. And of course the great alliances and external constraints, "the overcoming of external vulnerabilities" so dear – and rightly so – to Pinheiro Guimarães; how to expand autonomy in decision-making (or the "policy space" theorized by post-liberal economists); how to create a "new world geography" in which the center and the periphery join into a multipolar collectivity that is as harmonious as possible; how to create, with our neighbors, a shared space of peace and development in South America, in Latin America and in the Caribbean, in the South Atlantic and beyond.

There is not, nor can there be, absolute agreement on all these questions among all players involved in the transformation of Brazilian foreign policy described by Howlett-Martin, much less in a constantly changing world. But all, and many of those who oppose this policy, identify with the Brazilian national project. Howlett-Martin provides us with a precious snapshot – with all the contradictions and controversies that characterize history seen close up – of this moment in Brazil's progress toward its goal of peace, prosperity and social justice.

José Mauricio BUSTANI
Brazilian Ambassador to the United Kingdom (2003-2008) and to France (2008-2015)
Director-General (1997-2002) of OPCW Organization for the Prohibition of Chemical Weapons (recipient of the 2013 Nobel Peace Prize)

INTRODUCTION

Brazil has long exerted a relatively discreet international influence despite taking an active role in multilateral debate, particularly in the United Nations (elected to the Security Council 10 times – equaled only by Japan – in spite of a long hiatus between 1968 and 1988[1]) and in multilateral trade negotiations.

During his two presidential terms (2003-2010) Luiz Inácio da Silva (Lula) implemented an ambitious foreign policy program. While in part continuing that of his predecessor, Fernando Henrique Cardoso (1994-2002), it is significantly more forthright, having a stronger ideological grounding and more clearly defined priorities. Having gained mastery in maintaining stability, Brazil is certainly no longer "on probation" – to quote Pedro Malan, Minister of the Economy during Cardoso's two terms as president – in the eyes of the international financial community. Brazil is now the primary recipient of foreign investment in Latin America, taking in a record 66.7 billion dollars in 2011[2] (64 in 2013, 62 in 2014).

Brazil is now the world's sixth world power, ahead of Great Britain, in terms of Gross Domestic Product (GDP), but it is ranked 84th in the UN Human Development Index, 73rd in terms of per capita GDP, 88th in the UNESCO education rankings, and 61st on the corruption index of the NGO Transparency International. Some 25 million families (43% of Brazil's population) live in unsanitary dwellings. One fourth of children between the ages of 4 and 17 do not go to school. The homicide rate among young Brazilians (15-24 years old) – 53 per 100.000 inhabitants – is one of the world's highest. The massive popular protests in June 2013 expressed the exasperation of the majority of Brazilians with the inadequacy of public services, increases in the cost of living, dim economic prospects and the lack of credibility of the elected leaders and political institutions, rife with recurrent episodes of corruption[3].

Very strong expansion and growth in exports, increasing by a factor of four since 2003, and improvements in the living standards of the most disadvantaged classes testified to the success of Brazil's economic policy. But the strong growth in 2010 (+7.5%) revealed major gaps in the economic system (deteriorating infrastructure, inadequate supply of qualified labor) and the weak growth observed subsequently in 2011 (+2.7%) and 2012 (+0.9%) signaled a loss of competiveness of Brazilian industry (27.2% of GDP in 1985; 14.6% in 2011). The Brazilian congress acknowledged the criticism and demands of the

[1]. 1946-47; 1951-52; 1954-55; 1963-64; 1967-68; 1988-89; 1993-94; 1998-99; 2004-2005; 2010-2011.

[2]. UN Economic Commission for Latin America and the Caribbean (ECLAC).

[3]. Luiz Inácio Lula da Silva, "The message of Brazil's youth", *International Herald Tribune*, July 17, 2013.

protesters and attributed most of the long-term proceeds expected from deep off-shore drilling to education and public health.

The former minister of external relations, Luiz Felipe Lampreia, emphasized in December 2000 that Brazil should have a role in international relations proportional to its size: "*It cannot be larger due to a series of limitations, the main one being its social deficit*"[1]. It is precisely the international impact of the social policies, partly inherited from the government of Fernando Henrique Cardoso, but considerably expanded by President Lula, that is now reestablishing the influence of Brazilian diplomacy. This influence cannot be separated from the charisma of its champion, Lula da Silva, from his origins, his union struggles, his political trajectory, his alliances on the continent, and his real impact on Brazilian diplomacy. And this in spite of a traditional Ministry of External Relations, better known in media and diplomatic jargon as Itamaraty, composed of accomplished diplomats graduating from the Rio Branco Institute, most of whom are conservative and rather averse to talk of alter-globalization, Third-Worldism, South-South dialogue and Latin American solidarity.

Lula's designated successor, Dilma Rousseff, whose election in 2010, was aided by the former president, did not make fundamental changes to this foreign policy. Reelected to a second term on October 26, 2014, the Brazilian president does not have the charisma of her predecessor and shows only minor interest in issues of foreign relations, doubtlessly deriving, in part, from her lack of experience and lack of an international network of personal contacts[2].

In spite of being reelected, Rousseff found herself weakened by the spontaneous protest movement in the country's principal cities in 2013 and by corruption scandals tainting her government (four ministers forced to resign) and the publicly owned oil company Petrobras. Rouseff was Chairwoman of the Board of Directors (2003-2010) of Petrobras while also serving as Minister of Energy in the Lula government (2003-2005), before being appointed chief of staff in June 2005 after José Dirceu resigned under a cloud of malfeasance. In February 2012, she appointed a close friend and company executive, Maria Das Graças Foster, as president of Petrobras. She was later forced to fire her in February 2015 due to the spreading corruption scandal.

Lastly, Rousseff found herself dealing with a growing deterioration of the country's finances: primary budget deficit (0.6% of GDP in 2014, the first since 2002), a surge in inflation (the Central Bank forecast average price increase of 9.3% in 2015), a deficit in the balance of trade since 2012 (3.9 billion dollars in 2014, when the cumulative surplus from the Lula years (2003-2010) had exceeded 260 billion dollars), stagnation in Gross Domestic Product (-2,5% forecast for 2015 as opposed to 4% annual growth under Lula), water and energy shortages in the country's industrial zone, damage from scandals regarding corruption in domestic investment, particularly in Petrobras affecting

[1]. *Jornal do Brasil*, December 17, 2000.

[2] In Brazil, as in Argentina,Colombia and Ecuador, re-election is permitted once, consecutively and again after 1-term gap.

the national oil company. Fifty-four figures in the echelons of power were the focus of a federal investigation into an extensive covert financing scheme[1] that would have benefited them as much as the Workers' Party.

The state-owned enterprise was also the target of legal action in the U.S. courts by the investment funds of eight countries, including the Melinda and Bill Gates Foundation, alleging that the company's losses on the New York Stock Exchange were partly the result of this financial scandal[2]. Brazil's principal private public-works companies top executives (from Odebrecht, Camargo Correia, Andrade Gutierrez...), were arrested in June 2015, and the object of judicial inquiries in various countries (Italy, Switzerland, Portugal, Peru, Ecuador, Panama)[3].

The non-governmental organization Transparency International ranks Brazil in 61st place out of 177 countries on its world corruption index for 2014. The best rankings for South America were earned by Chile and Uruguay (21st)[4]. An investigation by the Brazilian Public Security Forum and the Federal Graduate School of Law covering the year 2012 showed that only 27% of police investigations of white collar corruption resulted in charges being filed (and only 8.13% in the country's financial capital, São Paulo[5]).

This deterioration is occurring within an unfavorable international climate (decline in agricultural and mineral commodity prices, relative slowdown in the Chinese economy), further jeopardizing the country´s status, despite relatively stable foreign investment (62.5 billion dollars in 2014)[6]. However, investment will almost certainly drop off significantly in 2015: for the first semester of 2015, foreign direct investment is down 36% according to the latest report of the United Nations Economic Commission for Latin America and the Caribbean (ECLAC)[7]. From July 1 to September 15, 2015, the Brazilian currency, the *real*, lost 42% of its value with respect to the dollar[8].

---

[1] Paulo Paranagua, "Tremblement de terre politique au Brésil" (Political tremors in Brazil), *Le Monde*, March 8-9, 2015.

[2] *O´Globo*, "Fundos de pensão de oito países processam Petrobras nos EUA" (Penson funds from eight countries take Petrobras to court in the U.S.), May 21, 2015.

[3] Cleide Carvalho, Mariana Sanches, "Investigação internacional. Outros três países abrem auditorias contra Odebrecht após prisão do presidente da empresa" (International investigation: three more countries audit Odebrecht after arrest of company president), *O´Globo*, July 6, 2015.

[4] Corruption Perceptions Index, 2014.

[5] "A investigação e a persecução penal de corrupção e dos delitos econômicos: uma pesquisa empirica no sistema de Justiça Federal" (Investigation and prosecution of corruption and financial crimes: an empirical study in the federal court system), Forúm Brasileiro de Segurança Publica, Escola Superior do Ministerio Publico da União, 2012. Cf. Vinicius Sassine, "Crime sem castigo. Corrupção impune" (Unpunished corruption), *O´Globo*, August 16, 2015.

[6] Lucianne Carneiro, "Brasil sobe em ranking de investimento estrangeiro" (Brazil rises in foreign investment rankings), *O´Globo*, June 25, 2015.

[7] "Foreign Direct Investment in Latin America and the Caribbean", October 15, 2015.

[8] In seven of eight countries with flexible regimes in the region (Brazil, Chile, Colombia, Guatemala, Mexico, Paraguay, Peru and Uruguay), depreciationagainst the dollar reached an average 26,7% between July 2014 and July 2015 (Source: Trade and Integration Monitor, Inter-American Development Bank, October 2015).

The appointment of an Economy Minister who supports financial orthodoxy and austerity, Joaquim Levy, a graduate of the University of Chicago with experience in the International Monetary Fund and the Brazilian banking sector (the private bank Bradesco), and the accommodation of center and rightist parties in the new government in order to ensure a parliamentary majority have further isolated the President, leader of the Workers' Party (although originating in the Democratic Labor Party), which has lost seats in Congress (it holds70 out of 513 in the Chamber of Deputies). Rousseff has been weakened in Congress after the Attorney General indicated that the presidents of the Chamber of Deputies (Eduardo Cunha) and of the Senate (Renan Calheiros) would be named in the corruption investigations, along with numerous members of the governing coalition (Progressive Party, Brazilian Democratic Movement Party).

In this difficult situation, and in spite of real improvements in the standard of living of the disadvantaged portions of the population, in large part the legacy of Lula's social programs, it is clear that the historical deficiencies in Brazilian society have not been ameliorated and will continue to weigh on the country's image abroad: the concentration of revenues and endemic corruption[1] with an encephalitic federal government (39 ministries, 18,388 civil servants for the Office of the President of the Republic alone, 100.000 "trusted" employees [i.e. hired through unofficial channels] in the federal machinery); laborious transactions with political parties; continuing deterioration of public education[2]; the lack of serious and coherent family policies as seen by the gangs of juvenile delinquents in the cities and a high number of teenage mothers between the ages of 13 and 15; one of the world's highest homicide rates (29 per 100.000 inhabitants in 2013, twice as high as in certain northeastern Brazilian states[3]) – only 3% of crimes are solved and 0.5% of armed robbers are identified[4] –; geometric growth in the prison population with more than 700.000 detainees, with recent reports that the homicide rate in prison is greater than 167.5 per 100.000 inmates[5]. Brazil reached a new peak of violence in 2014 with more than 58.000 violent deaths, up nearly 5% from 2013. These are all factors that represent a serious handicap in the country's desire to assume a prominent role on the global stage.

---

[1] Merval Pereira, "Corrupção endêmica" (Endemic corruption), *O ´Globo,* July 29, 2015.

[2] Vanessa Barbara, "Another Defeat for Brazil´s Kids", *International New York Times,* June 25, 2015.

[3] The US has a rate of 4,7 and the UK stands at 1. See Mapa da Violenca 2014, cf. Gil Alessi "Com 56.337 homicídios em 2013 Brasil bate recorde histórico de homicídios" (Brazil breaks its record with 56.337 homicides in 2013), *UOL,* May 27, 2014.

[4] *O ´Globo*, July 22, 2015.

[5] Franco Ilimar, "Homicídios nas prisões" (Homicides in the prisons), Panorama político, *O ´Globo,* July 23, 2015.

CHAPTER 1

IDEOLOGICAL FOUNDATIONS AND PRIORITIES OF BRAZILIAN DIPLOMACY

The inspiration behind Brazilian foreign policy in the Lula years was Samuel Pinheiro Guimarães, secretary general of the Ministry of External Relations from 2003 to 2009, then Secretary for Strategic Affairs in the Office of the President with the rank of minister (2009-2010) and lastly, High Representative of Mercosur. He is the author of many works, including *500 Years in the Periphery*[1]. His most recent work, *Brazilian Challenges in the Age of Giants*, published in 2006, is dedicated to Celso Amorim. Minister of External Relations from 2003 to 2010 (briefly filling the role also in 1992-1993), Amorim is related to Samuel Pinheiro Guimarães and shares his ideas and convictions. He was Minister of Defense in the Rousseff government from August 2011 to December 2014. He did not join Lula's Workers' Party (Partido dos Trabalhadores) until 2009. He is close to the former Minister of External Relations (2011-2013), Antonio de Aguiar Patriota, who was also former Itamaraty Secretary General and former ambassador to Washington. Antonio Patriota, now Brazil's permanent representative to the United Nations, was an advisor to Celso Amorim while the latter was chief of the Brazilian delegation to the United Nations (1999-2001), and later succeeded him in October 2013. Lastly, the president's diplomatic advisor, Marco Aurélio Garcia, has been at Lula's side since day one. Exiled to Chile (at the time a militant in the Revolutionary Left Movement – MIR) and to France during the dictatorship (1970-1979), he was one of the founders of the Workers' Party (PT). He retained his functions under Dilma Rousseff.

According to this triumvirate (Amorim, Patriota, Garcia), the world system is composed of a small number of major political powers (the "center") who control the policy-making process, particularly by means of the Security Council (veto right); major economic powers hosting the principal international financial institutions (International Monetary Fund, World Bank) and accounting for some 80% of world GDP; and major military powers who have nuclear capabilities and advanced technology, who account for nearly all arms sales and whose defense budgets only continue to grow. Some states belong to all three categories, others do not, such as China, Russia, Germany and Japan.

Alongside these major powers we have "peripheral" states that have sufficient real potential (demographic, geographic, economic) to exert a significant regional influence. These include India, Argentina, Iran, Indonesia,

[1]. *Quinhentos Anos de Periféria, uma contribuição ao estudo da politica internacional* (Five hundred years in the Periphery: a contribution to the study of international policy), UFRGS, Porto Alegre, 1999.

Turkey, and South Africa. Brazil must forge political ties with these countries in order to contribute to the emergence of a multipolar world.

The United States is the principal obstacle to this nascent multipolarity in the international system. Deprived of the Communist menace, it now seeks new threats to justify its hegemonic position and military bases scattered across the globe: drug trafficking, religious fundamentalism, international migrations, rogue states, terrorism and now jihadism, not to mention China's ambitions in the South Pacific, where more than 85.000 American soldiers, seven aircraft carriers and 18 nuclear submarines are stationed[1]. Chinese claims to islands in the East China Sea (Senkaku or Diaoyu) and south China Sea (Spratly or Nansha, Paracels or Xisha) have a long legacy rooted in rights of sovereignty. With the exception of the Spratly Islands, they have a geographical basis corresponding to the local continental shelf[2]. They are now inflated by the United States to justify a new arms race (rearmament of Japan, regional treaties). Philippines, Brunei, Malaysia and Vietnam all dispute China´s historic claim to the Spratly Islands, but sending a guided destroyer in October 2015 into waters China considers its territory looks like a deliberate provocation from the United States, a reminiscence of nineteenth-century gunboat policy.

All these threats, potential or real, must be put in perspective. They are the result of U.S. hegemonic policy and not, as Washington would have it, preexisting causes necessarily demanding this policy.

The "global war on terror" is one of the centerpieces of the foreign and security policies of American administrations since the Reagan presidency, a policy amplified by the events of September 11, 2001 and the response by the Bush administration, a policy that President Obama has inherited without substantial revision. The strategy of intervention continues to inform this policy, although the accent, initially placed exclusively on military response and the notion of victory, has become more nuanced as illusions are stripped away by difficulties encountered on the ground, most notably in Afghanistan, Iraq and Somalia. It is now clear that the Iraq question was not originally an issue of terrorism: it has become an issue of terrorism precisely as a result of the invasion and occupation of the country. In 1982, the same year as the attack on Saddam Hussein that set the stage for the Dujail Massacre – the principal accusation that would see Saddam Hussein hanged high and short twenty-five years later – Iraq was removed from the list of terrorist states by the Reagan administration in order to allow U.S. arms dealers to sell weapons to the country to support it in its war against Iran. These sales were negotiated by Donald Rumsfeld, special U.S. envoy to the Middle East before becoming Secretary of Defense under George W. Bush.

---

1. *International Herald Tribune*, October 26, 2011.
2. Patrick Howlett-Martin, "Mer de Chine: Le problème de la délimitation du plateau continental" (The China Sea: the problem of delimiting the continental shelf), *Problèmes Politiques et Sociaux*, La Documentation Française, n° 88, August 1973.

This concept of war on terror, which has been adopted – to varying degrees and with only rare exceptions – by the traditional allies of the United States, does not draw a clear line between aggression and resistance. The case of the leader of the ANC, Nelson Mandela, who was included on the Pentagon's list of notorious terrorists until 1988, speaks volumes in this regard. As regards Luis Posada Carriles, the mastermind behind the 1976 bombing of Cubana de Aviación Flight 455 from Barbados to Jamaica that killed all 73 people on board, is openly enjoying the good life in Miami despite a request for extradition from the Venezuelan government pursuant to the treaty signed by the two countries.

The use of military action as the core of a security strategy has led to radicalization in Muslim countries (Afghanistan, Somalia, Yemen, Mali, Pakistan...). The *Livre Blanc sur la Défense et la Sécurité de la France*, published in 2013, openly sanctions this policy: *"the many military operations in which France has taken part in recent years (Afghanistan, Ivory Coast, Libya, Mali) prove that military action remains an important component of our [national] security"*. This approach is contested in Brasilia, where it is felt that security derives first and foremost from negotiation, mediation, and cooperation, and that a military response is not appropriate because it ultimately only generates more violence.

In her address before the 69th session of the United Nations General Assembly in September 2014, President Dilma Rousseff reaffirmed Brazil's opposition to military intervention, which she believes is incapable of removing the deep causes of international conflicts but instead engenders *"barbarism"*, referring to the emergence of extremist movements in the Middle East[1]. We must admit that most of the military operations initiated since 1999 are still underway and have not brought a solution to the conflicts (Kosovo, 1999; Afghanistan, 2001; Darfour, Iraq, 2003; Libya, Ivory Coast, 2011; Mali, Central Africa, 2013).

These conflicts have triggered an increasing flow of desperate, penniless refugees to the European Union, nearly a quarter of them young children and adolescents, at the mercy of unscrupulous handlers and subject in several countries to treatment upon their arrival reminiscent of the darkest years of Nazism (internment in concentration camps, forced expulsions, police brutality, tattooed forearms to facilitate identification...). And we must also mention the many lost to shipwrecks in the Mediterranean, providing a stark contrast to the luxury enjoyed by vacationers at the height of the European tourism season.

According to the UN High Commissioner for Refugees, António Guterres, in 2013 there were some 51 million people living as refugees or forced to leave their homes, one fourth of them from Syria and Iraq. And the numbers are only growing: in 2014, 60 million people were displaced. One third of the population of Lebanon is currently composed of Syrian and Palestinian refugees.

---

1. *O 'Globo*, September 24, 2014.

Brasilia stresses that the extreme violence and deadly attacks in Middle Eastern countries (Afghanistan, Iraq, Syria), the Arabian peninsula (Yemen), the Horn of Africa (Somalia), and sub-Saharan Africa (Mali, Central African Republic, Nigeria), predominantly attributed to fundamentalist Islamic movements, are not spontaneous acts generated locally but derive in large part from the aggressive policies of the United States and its allies across the globe and from a complex legacy of colonialization wherein the former colonial powers bear some responsibility.

Al Qaeda was created by combatants funded by Washington and Riyadh to fight against the Soviet occupation of Afghanistan. It has now penetrated into and expanded in Iraq, favored by the irrational and unjustifiable U.S. invasion of the country. The scope of the repression of the Sunnite majority, the use of arbitrary detention, the inexcusable practice of torture in prisons, the high number of civilian victims, the widows, widowers and orphans, the summary executions, the corruption of the power elites by American handouts in impoverished societies can only arouse extremely violent reactions against the occupiers and the imposition of a strict, orthodox, and heavy-handed interpretation of Islam. In this context, it is only religion that can stabilize an identity rooted in the local culture, tribal solidarity and customs, however retrograde or archaic they may be.

The emergence of the Islamic State of Iraq and the Levant (ISIL), whose leaders were once interned in the U.S. military prison at Camp Bucca, Iraq, is one of the outcomes. A similar trend has also led to the chaos in Libya, a country on the verge of civil war. As revealed by a *New York Times* investigation, the seven months of NATO bombings in 2011 killed a huge number of civilians[1], without mentioning the killing of Muammar Gaddafi under appalling circumstances.

In a February 2015 *New York Times* article, the new Emir of Qatar, Tamim bin Hamad Al Thani, commented on the rise of Islamic fundamentalism (some observers believe that Qatar is involved in some way in its development in Syria): *"As a Muslim, I can tell you that the problem isn't Islam: it's hopelessness. It's the kind of hopelessness that abounds in the Syrian and Palestinian refugee camps, and in war-weary towns and villages in Syria, Iraq, Yemen, Libya and Gaza. It's the hopelessness we see in the poorer neighborhoods of Europe's great cities, and, yes, even in the United States. And it is this hopelessness, which knows no state or religion, that we need to address if we are to stem the tide of terrorism[2]."*

China clearly emblemizes the syndrome with respect to its Uyghur minority (primarily Muslim in the Xinjiang Region), who have been subjected to harsh repression and discrimination. How else are we to explain the riots in July 2009 in the capital of the region, Ürümqi, that left nearly two hundred dead; the March 2014 knife attack that left some 30 people dead in the Kunming railway

---

[1]. C. J. Chivers, Eric Schmitt, "In Strikes on Libya by NATO, an Unspoken Civilian Toll", *The New York Times,* December 17, 2011.

[2]. "Qatar's message to Obama", *The New York Times,* February 24, 2015.

station, carried out by an Uyghur commando that included a pregnant woman[1]; and the attack on the Sogan coal mine at Baicheng (Xinjiang) where ethnic Uighurs fatally stabbed 50 Han Chinese during national celebrations to mark the 60th anniversary of the establishment of the Xinjiang Uighur Autonomous Region[2]?

The imbalance between civilian and military means inherent in the very concept of war (120 billion dollars in U.S. military spending in Afghanistan in 2011 as opposed to 2.5 billion in civil aid), has engendered growing hostility among the local populations and clear violations of international law (interference to put a favorable regime in power, imposition of values in conflict with local culture, indiscriminate use of targeted bombing using drones, nighttime raids by commando units accused of summary executions, killing of civilians including many children, grave violations of fundamental human rights in detention centers). Terrorism feeds off this violence. The American explanation for terrorism is not convincing. Investigations of the issue, such as that by Michael Bond, who studied 500 suicide attacks between 1980 and 2003 and published his findings in the British journal *New Scientist*, underscore the absence of fanaticism, religious extremism or poverty in the great majority of cases. What is highlighted instead are motives driven by dramas in the perpetrators' personal lives or by injustice and humiliation they have suffered, engendering a desire for vengeance and an openness to indoctrination within the tight-knit community of a brotherhood[3].

The 2009 U.S. defense budget was the highest ever recorded since the Second World War (663.255 billion dollars), greater than the combined budgets of China, Russia, Great Britain, France, Germany and Japan, and represents a 61% increase with respect to 2001. In 2012, the U.S. Congress approved a significantly higher budget (685.3 billion dollars, 43% of world military spending[4]) in spite of deficit-reduction regulations (Budget Control Act). In 2013, it rose to 716 billion dollars, seven times higher than the military budget of China, which the U.S. and Japan accuse of warmongering. Brazil's military budget is less than 5% of that amount. The world's major arms exporter (52% of world sales in 2011), the United States has 823 military bases scattered around the world[5] housing some 250,000 soldiers. According to the January 2, 2012 issue of the *Washington Post*, American special forces are engaged in 75 countries and comprise some 7,000 military personnel from 130 countries. In 2015, according to Special Operations Command spokesman Ken McGraw, U.S. Special Operations forces deployed to a record-shattering 147 countries–

---

1. *International New York Times*, March 25, 2015.
2. Jacobs Andrew, "Disturbed by Ethnic Tensions, China keeps Tight Lid on a Massacre", *International New York Times*, October 18, 2015.
3. "Terrorista suicida não seria fanático" (Suicide terrorist not fanatic), *O'Globo*, 13 May 2004 / Michael Bond, "The making of a suicide bomber", *New Scientist*, May 15, 2004 (www.newscientist.com).
4. SIFRI. Stockholm International Peace Research Institute, Yearbook, 2012.
5. In 2007 (717 in 2005). Source: Pentagon.

75% of the nations in the world, which represents a jump of 145% since the waning days of the Bush administration. With a military budget that equals half of all military expenditures for the rest of the world combined, U.S. militaristic global presence sends the message that violence is the ultimate solution to any dispute. *"The concentration of military power is a source of instability in the world system,"* emphasized Brazilian defense minister Celso Amorim in a speech before the National Defense and Foreign Affairs Commission of the Chamber of Deputies on November 27, 2012[1]. Thomas Jefferson, third U.S. president (1801-1809) had cautioned the rising nation: "*I hope our wisdom will grow with our power, and teach us that the less we use our power, the greater it will be*[2]."

In 2009-2013, the world's two largest arms exporters – the United States and Russia – increased sales by some 30% over the previous period (2004-2008). The principal importer in 2013 was India (14% of purchases); in 2014 it was Saudi Arabia[3]. Not one of the world's top 100 arms manufacturers is in Africa, and only one of them is in Latin America (Embraer in Brazil); two thirds are in Western Europe, the United States, and Canada[4]. In May 2014, President Obama announced the establishment of the Counterterrorism Partnerships Fund (CTPF): 5 billion dollars to support partner countries in the fight against terrorism[5], a multi-purpose term covering armed insurrections, rebellions, and resistance movements against occupational forces.

The NATO military budget has also been increasing in this period: 462.5 million dollars in 2011, up from 430 in 2010 and 408 in 2009[6]. But the U.S. sees this growth as insufficient, as stated initially by Secretary of Defense Robert Gates in June 2006 before the European NATO representatives in Brussels, and repeated in September 2011 by his successor, Leon Panetta[7]. The French defense budget for 2014-2019 is 189 billion dollars. The defense ministers of the principal European weapons-producing countries (Germany, Spain, France, Italy, United Kingdom, Belgium) established the Organization for Joint Armament Cooperation (OCCAR). Based in Bonn, OCCAR facilitates and manages cooperative armament programs. The NATO Secretary General introduced the concept of "*smart defense*" to optimize the military spending of member countries. With the Lancaster House Treaties (2010), France and the United Kingdom established close cooperation in developing joint defense and

---

1. "*We must recognize at this point that the concentration of power, especially military, is still an undeniable reality, and a source of instability in the international system.*" (*E preciso reconhecer, neste ponto, que a concentração de poder, especialmente militar, ainda é uma realidade inegável, e fonte de desestabilização no sistema internacional.*), Chamber of Deputies, Brasilia, November 27, 2012.

2. Letter to Thomas Leiper, 1815.

3. Source: Stockholm International Peace Research Institute.

4. Aude Fleurant, Sam Perlo-Freeman, "The SIPRI Top 100 arms-producing and military services companies, 2013", SIPRI Fact Sheet, December 2014.

5. *International New York Times*, May 29, 2014.

6. *The Financial Times*, June 22, 2011.

7. Steven Erlanger, "Panetta urges NATO unity on spending", *International Herald Tribune*, October 6, 2011.

security programs: nuclear capabilities, missiles, drones. There is a currently a clear overcapacity in the defense industry in Europe. This explains the feverish and competitive drive to find external markets, which is seen particularly vis-à-vis Brazil.

The inclusion of eastern countries in NATO has provided new prospects for the arms industry. It is no coincidence that the U.S. Committee to Expand NATO was chaired by Bruce Jackson, former Vice President for Strategy and Planning at Lockheed Martin. Poland, Romania and Bulgaria have already handed over their shopping lists to Washington. Three quarters of current NATO spending is borne by the United States. Eastern countries lacking NATO military bases are considered second-class members[1].

The conflict between Ukraine and Russia offers a pretext for advocates of re-armament. The loan of three French Rafale jets to Poland as reassurance to Warsaw against a possible Russian invasion and the reinstatement of the draft in Lithuania were scoffed at by Brasilia, where Russia, the world's eighth power, is considered to be a reliable partner that Europe should try to include rather than circumscribe.

However, the authorities fail to learn any lessons from hostile public opinion toward armed conflict and from the fact that military enlistment continues to decline despite the high unemployment rate. The United States has dangled the possibility of a fast lane to citizenship for the 30.000 foreigners wearing the uniform of the U.S. armed forces; the United Kingdom seeks recruits throughout the Commonwealth; Spain looks for its military personnel in its former colonies in South America; Russia draws on the former Soviet republics; France maintains its outdated Foreign Legion, formerly dedicated to colonial conquest, open to all comers. As for Israel, where three years of military service is obligatory for all, foreigners are recruited for 18 months if they meet a single ethno-religious criterion (the Mahal program is reserved to those who can claim to have "*at least one Jewish grandparent*"[2]).

The now massif use of undercover, "targeted" bombing campaigns by remote-controlled aircraft in Yemen, Pakistan, Ethiopia, Somalia, Iran and Saudi Arabia represents a violation of international law and a threat to civilians. According to the New American Foundation and the Bureau of Investigative Journalism, nearly twenty-five percent of the victims of drone attacks between January 2004 and August 2011 (2.588 recorded deaths) were innocent civilians, 174 of them children[3]. These summary executions engender growing feelings of hatred towards the United States and are cannot be separated from the resurgence in terrorism.

The former commander in chief of the U.S. forces in Afghanistan, General Stanley McChrystal (2009-2010), and the former head of the Pentagon's Defense Intelligence Agency, Lieutenant General Michael Klynn (2012-2014),

1. "NATO's Second-Class Members", *International New York Times*, August 22, 2014.
2. Lone Soldiers (www.fidf.org, and www.tsahal.fr).
3. *The Nation*, April 30, 2012.

now admit that drones generate more terrorists than they kill[1]. In Somalia, Yemen, Afghanistan and Pakistan, this type of execution – which has dramatic effects on the civilian population, who are under a constant threat, day and night, with no possible legal recourse – is carried out with complete impunity, in an extrajudicial manner, from well protected military bases. The targeted victims are no longer identified; according to the new Signature Strike Policy adopted by the CIA, it is the target's "*pattern of life activity*" that incriminates them. Controlled from some sixty bases scattered around the world, including some in the United States, the drones are flown by operators from private companies who are paid by the Pentagon and the CIA[2]. The United States have approximately 7.000 unmanned aerial vehicles (UAV) and currently use them in six countries, mainly where American military forces are not officially engaged. Classified as defense secrets, they cannot be the object of public debate or of investigation by journalists in the United States. The U.S. Senate may only speak about these drones behind closed doors. The journalist Abdulelah Haider Shaye was sentenced to 5 years in prison for having revealed the al-Majalah massacre in southern Yemen, where 41 civilians (including 21 children and nine women, 5 of them pregnant) were killed by a U.S. drone strike on December 17.2009[3].

In a report prepared by Philip Alston, former UN Special Rapporteur on extrajudicial, summary or arbitrary executions (2004-2010), and presented to the Human Rights Council in June 2010, the United Nations warned the United States on the use of these executions, which are a glaring violation of international law and set a dangerous precedent as access to drone technology spreads to other countries[4]. Even American citizens are not exempt from these "preventive" executions of civilians who have not been named in any preliminary investigation[5]. These drones foreshadow the lethal autonomous robots that are currently being developed by the United States, the United Kingdom, Israel and South Korea. In May 2013, the new UN Special Rapporteur on extrajudicial, summary or arbitrary executions, Christof Heyns, demanded an international moratorium on robots with "power to kill"[6]. There is a high-level support within the United Nations for serious control on lethal

---

[1]. David Alexander, "Retired general cautions against overuse of 'hated drones'", *Reuters*, January 7, 2013; "Retired US General: Drones causes more damage than good", *Al Jazeerah*, July 16, 2015.

[2]. Roger Cohen, "Of fruit flies and drones", November 13, 2009; James Risen, Mark Mazzetti, "Blackwater guards teamed with C.I.A. on raids", December 12, 2009, *International Herald Tribune.*

[3]. "Yemeni Reporter Who Exposed U.S, Drone Strike Freed from Prison After Jailing at Obama´s request", Democracy Now, July 25, 2013 (www.democracynow.org).

[4]. Charlie Savage, "U.S. should limit attacks by drones, U.N. asserts", *International Herald Tribune*, June 30, 2010.

[5]. Anwar al-Awaki and Samir Khan on September 1, 2011 and Anwar al-Awaki's 16-year-old son with five of his colleagues on October 14, 2011 in Yemen.

[6]. "U.N. expert calls for an end to production of armed robots", *International Herald Tribune*, May 31, 2013.

autonomous weapons (as happened to land-mines, sight-blinding laser weapons, cluster bombs). But a deal may not emerge fast enough to prevent devices from being deployed. The UK and the US are seeking to waterdown an agreement that only includes "emerging" technology. Brasil, like China, wants to discuss "existing and emerging technologies" as the current Phalanx[1] or the fighter jet CX49B[2] that can fly and strike on its own. Scientists, Human Rights organizations, the International Committee for Robot Arms Control have made pleas for a preemptive ban on offensive autonomous weapons; in July 2015 an open letter hosted by the Future of Life Institute[3] was signed by thousands artificial intelligence and robotics researchers calling for a ban on robots that select and engage targets without human direct intervention.

Lastly, the outsourcing of intelligence and security tasks in conflict zones to private companies whose leaders are, or have been, government officials underlies these generally unpunished violations. Dick Cheney, vice president to George W. Bush (2001-2009) and former U.S. Secretary of Defense (1989-1993), was Chairman and CEO of Halliburton from 1995 to 2000. Through its subsidiary Kellogg, Brown & Root, Halliburton received some 39 billion dollars in contracts from the Pentagon over a period of 10 years (2001-2011)[4]. Dick Cheney's wife, Lynne, sat on the board of directors of Lockheed Martin, the world's largest arms manufacturer, from 1994 to 2001. Mike McConnell, National Security Agency director under the Clinton administration from 1992 to 1996 and under the Bush administration from 2007 to 2009, returned to his role as vice president of Booz Allen Hamilton, which earns over half its revenues from government contracts. The current Director of National Intelligence under the Obama administration, James Clapper, is another Booz Allen alumnus. John O. Brennan, President Obama's Homeland Security Advisor and Deputy National Security Advisor, former CIA agent and current CIA director, is CEO of The Analysis Corporation, now known as Sotera Defense Solutions. Sheldon Adelson, controversial financial supporter of Republican candidate Ron Paul, is the founder of Palantir Technologies, a subcontractor for the CIA and the FBI on national security issues. George Schultz and Caspar Weinberger, prominent figures in former Republican administrations, have been executives at the Bechtel Group, which has a strong presence in Iraq. Robert Blackwill, former U.S. National Security Council Deputy for Iraq in the Bush administration, went on to become the highest paid lobbyist for Barbour, Griffith & Rogers in Iraq and Kurdistan. The head of Washington-based operations for Supreme Foodservice AG, a privately

---

[1]. A close-in weapon system for defense against anti-ship missiles.

[2]. unmanned combat air vehicule developped by Northrop Grumman.

[3]. The Future of Life Institute (FLI) is a volunteer-run research and outreach organization in the Boston area that works to mitigate risks of artificial general intelligence facing humanity. It was founded by MIT cosmologist Max Tegmark and Skype co-founder Jaan Tallinn among others, and includes cosmologist Stephen Hawking on the board of advisers.

[4]. David Vine, "The $385 Billion Military-Industrial Boondoggle You've Never Heard Of", *The Nation*, May 14, 2013.

owned Pentagon contractor for logistics services in Afghanistan, former Army Lieutenant General Robert Dail, was head of the Pentagon's Defense Logistics Agency from August 2006 to November 2008. General David Petraeus, former CIA director (September 2011 to November 2012) and former commander of the coalition forces in Afghanistan and in Iraq, has been the chairman of the KKR Global Institute for Kohlberg Kravis Roberts & Co. L.P. since May 2013.

Retired generals, speaking on behalf of the think-tanks of which they are members, defend the massive military interventions in Iraq and Syria in the media, neglecting to mention that they are on the payroll of the major arms dealers. General Jack Keane is chairman of the Board for the Institute for the Study of War, whose sponsors constitute a veritable who's-who of the arms industry (Raytheon, General Dynamics, Northrop Grumman, Palantir and others). He is a regular guest as military analyst on *Fox News*. He is a paid military advisor for Academi (formerly US Training Center, formerly Blackwater). He is also a generously compensated member of the board of directors of General Dynamics, like his fellow Marine James Mattis, and a partner in the venture capital firm SCP Partners, much involved in the defense industry. Retired general Anthony Zinni sits on the board of directors of the American branch of BAE Systems PLC[1]. In reality, they are all undeclared lobbyists for the arms industry.

The number of private military personnel in Iraq in 2010 has been estimated at between 30.000 and 50.000, making it at the time the world's second largest military force deployed on foreign soil after that of the United States (130.000) and well ahead of the UK (10.000). In Afghanistan, there are more private military personnel (113.491 in January 2012) than U.S. troops[2].

The information leaked by the young system administrator Edward Snowden, an employee of Booz Allen Hamilton working within the National Security Agency, on covert surveillance of governments, institutions, businesses and social networks (the Prism, Boundless Informant and X-Keystore programs), under cover of special legislation and the secretive Foreign Intelligence Surveillance Court, triggered strong condemnation from Brazilian president Dilma Rousseff, who canceled her official visit to the United States scheduled for October 2013. During the General Assembly of the United Nations, she proposed the establishment of regulations and multilateral control over the Internet, given its strong dependence on businesses located on U.S. soil. In liaison with the Los Angeles-based Internet Corporation for Assigned Names and Numbers (ICANN), whose executive director, Fadi Chenadé, visited her in Brasilia in October 2013.

The overt offering of political asylum to Edward Snowden, then in Moscow, by three South American states (Bolivia, Venezuela and Nicaragua) gave rise to a surreal episode: the forced landing in Vienna of the plane carrying

---

1. *The Nation,* September 16, 2014

2. Rod Nordland, "Perils of Afghan war shift to civilian contractors", *International Herald Tribune,* January 13, 2012.

Bolivian president Evo Morales, who was returning from Moscow after taking part in an international meeting of natural gas producing countries, after France, Italy, Spain and Portugal closed their airspace. The presidential plane was grounded for 24 hours, only being allowed to leave after Morales agreed to an inspection by Austrian police to ensure that Snowden was not on board[1]. Defined as *"confusion of a technical nature"* by French diplomacy, but doubtlessly related to the country's obsequence to NATO's integrated military command, this episode caused outrage and uproar in South America at this egregious affront to the dignity of the Bolivian president. The major leaders meeting at the UNASUL summit in Cochabamba, Bolivia, on July 3, 2013 all expressed their solidarity with Morales on this issue. President Dilma Rousseff did not take part in the summit; Brazil was represented by her diplomatic advisor Marco Aurelio Garcia. After meeting with President Morales during the United Nations General Assembly in September 2013, French President François Hollande declared the incident a "*closed case*", seriously underestimating the consequent loss of prestige to French diplomacy in the region.

Current international institutions, treaties and mechanisms are inspired and crafted by the United States and its allies to keep "marginal" countries in a state of dependence and subjection. A survey among fifteen European Union member states puts the United States in sixth position (after Israel, North Korea, Iran, Iraq and Afghanistan) on the list of countries posing the most significant threat to world peace[2].

The major powers seek to impose strict military disarmament policies on countries that are already disarmed. The Nuclear Non-Proliferation Treaty, the Missile Technology Control Regime (MTCR), the treaties outlawing chemical or biological weapons and those instituting nuclear-free zones (which do not preclude transit of weapons by the nuclear powers as was revealed during the 1982 Falklands War) are all obstacles preventing these marginal countries from achieving defensive autonomy.

The ousting of Brazilian diplomat José Mauricio Bustani from his post as director-general of the Organization for the Prohibition of Chemical Weapons (OPCW)[3] during Fernando Henrique Cardoso's government speaks volumes in this regard. Reelected to a second term (2001-2005), Bustani had invited Syria, Iran, Iraq and Sudan to join the organization and hoped to involve them in the investigation into the alleged presence of chemical arms in Iraq. This aroused hostility from the United States, which proved to be his undoing. John Bolton, undersecretary of state for arms control and international security, orchestrated

---

1. Evo Morales, "*Moi, président de la Bolivie, séquestré en Europe*" (Me, the President of Bolivia, detained in Europe!), *Le Monde diplomatique*, August 2013.
2. *Le Monde*, November 1, 2003.
3. Intergovernmental organization affiliated with the United Nations created in 1971 and based in The Hague. Its mission is to promote and verify adherence to the Chemical Weapons Convention, which prohibits the development, production, stockpiling and use of chemical weapons and requires their destruction. Washington has kept OPCW inspectors out of certain U.S. production centers for the purported reason of protecting industrial secrets.

a campaign of denigration against Bustani, who was removed from office in a secretive meeting without any further due process. John Bolton would go on to become U.S. ambassador to the United Nations (2005-2006). In its December 12, 2004 issue, the *Washington Post* reported that he had been behind the intense scrutiny of intercepted telephone calls by Mohammed ElBaradei, then director-general of the International Atomic Energy Agency (IAEA), seeking a pretext to prevent his election to a third term. ElBaradei received the Nobel Peace Prize in 2005. José Mauricio Bustani would be named Brazilian ambassador to the United Kingdom and later to France. OPCW received the Nobel Peace Prize in October 2013.

Certain important treaties, on the other hand, were not signed by the United States (3rd protocol on the Convention on Certain Conventional Weapons, 1980; Civil and Political Rights Act Abolishing the Death Penalty, 1989; Convention on the Prohibition of the Use, Stockpiling, Production and Transfer of Anti-Personnel Mines and their Destruction [Ottawa Treaty], 1997; Convention on Cluster Munitions, 2008), not ratified (Comprehensive Nuclear-Test-Ban Treaty, 1996; International Covenant on Economic, Social and Cultural Rights, 1976; Kyoto Protocol, 1997; Convention on the Elimination of All Forms of Discrimination Against Women, 1979; Convention on the Rights of the Child, 1990), withdrawn from (Anti-Ballistic Missile Treaty, 2002; Convention on Biological and Chemical Weapons, 2001; Optional Protocol to the Vienna Convention on Consular Relations, 1967, withdrawal in 2005) or signed with reservations (International Criminal Court, 2002[1] ; Convention on Chemical Weapons, 2007; Convention on Cluster Munitions, 2008).

The missile defense system advocated by Washington and endorsed by NATO[2], officially directed against the threat of ballistic missiles from Iran, a threat which Brazil regards as unfounded, is offensive to Russia and risks triggering a new arms race at a time when it is vital to further efforts at disarmament and nuclear non-proliferation. The United States unilaterally withdrew from the Anti-Ballistic Missile Treaty in December 2001 in order to implement this plan. The Americans refuse to commit to the future development of the system (number of interceptors, targeting, nuclear warheads, etc.) and their proposals appear willfully imprecise and of varying geometry.

There is one single security space, underscores Brasilia, and as a consequence it must be collective and include all countries in the region. The United States was the only member of the United Nations General Assembly to vote against the resolution to establish international standards for the import,

1. In July 2003, the United States suspended military aid to 35 countries (including Brazil) party to the International Criminal Court (ICC) and refusing to grant impunity to U.S. soldiers as demanded by Washington. In 2001, the Bush administration decided to strike the signature of the United States (dating to the Clinton administration) from the Rome Statute (1988), which established the ICC.

2. At the NATO summit in Bucharest, April 2-4, 2008.

export and transfer of conventional arms, approved by 153 countries on December 7, 2006. Only four (United States, Israel, United Kingdom, France) voted against the proposition to ban the use of nuclear weapons presented at the General Assembly of the United Nations in December 2012 by Cuba with the support of the non-aligned countries (179 votes in favor).

In Brasilia NATO is considered a "parallel" organization to the United Nations, which should have been disbanded after the breakup of the Soviet Union in December 1991. Instead, it has expanded to include most of the Eastern European countries, including the Baltic States – still recovering from the effects of Soviet domination – without consideration for Russia and, in contradiction to Article 5 of the Treaty, extended its operations well beyond its original vocation[1]. There were twelve member countries in 1949; there are twenty-eight in 2013. Originally defensive, it has now become an offensive organization with theatres of operations extending all the way to Iraq and Libya. It is in effect a military intervention force serving American interests. It has established cooperation agreements with Australia (April 2005), Mongolia (March 2012), New Zealand (June 2012), South Korea (September 2012), Japan (April 2013) and Colombia, during defense minister Juan Carlos Pinzon Bueno's visit to the organization's Brussels headquarters in June 2013. In May 2014, a technical agreement was signed with the African Union to strengthen its operational capabilities.

This holdover from the Cold War conflicts with international law because it envisages the use of military force without a resolution from the UN Security Council. It is anachronistic at a time when most conflicts are internecine rather than between states. France's return in 2012 to the NATO integrated military command, under American Secretary General Alexander Vershbow, was met with puzzlement in Brasilia, who recalled the much applauded speech by Chirac's foreign minister, Dominique de Villepin, at the United Nations on February 14, 2003, opposing the plans for war in Iraq. From Brasilia's viewpoint, the continued existence of the North Atlantic Treaty has quashed the faint hopes in Europe for the establishment of a third way and independent diplomacy.

Newly asserting its diplomatic status, Brasilia affirmed that coexistence demands understanding how one's actions may offend another. Instead of provoking a confrontation or designating a scapegoat, it is necessary to take a consensual approach, defending the idea of pluralistic, intercultural societies where people and their neighbors can live with their differences rather than using them to fan the flames of a bitter but bygone past. In Itamaraty parlance this policy is referred to as "*preventive diplomacy*".

The European Union now encompasses 28 member states, still traumatized for the most part by their past relations with the Soviet Union. They frequently cite the Georgian and Ukrainian crises as justification for adhering to campaign

[1]. Article 5: "*to restore and maintain the security of the North Atlantic area*".

against Russia and tilting European diplomacy toward the United States. The exclusive nature imposed by the EU in 2013 in an agreement for free trade with Ukraine, deemed hasty even nine years after the Orange Revolution, is seen as a mistake. The unabated deterioration of the internal situation, the ousting of the legitimately elected pro-Russian president in February 2014, American military aid to Kiev, the decision at the 65th NATO summit in September 2014 to create a 5.000-man *"rapid reaction force"* to counter any *"external"* aggression, NATO military exercises with the Polish army in September 2014, and the hopes to integrate Ukraine and Georgia into NATO, first aired at the April 2008 NATO summit in Bucharest, have all done little to calm tensions. General Mykhailo Kutsyn, the new Commander-in-Chief of the Ukraine Armed Forces, took part in the meeting of the Chiefs of Staff on May 21, 2014 in Brussels. The Assistant Secretary of State for Europe and Eurasian Affairs, Victoria Nuland, former diplomatic advisor to Vice President Dick Cheney and U.S. representative to NATO (G. W. Bush administration), stated to the National Press Club in Washington on December 13, 2013 that the United States had supported Ukrainian Non-Governmental Organizations to the tune of some 5 billion dollars after the country became independent in 1991 *"as they build democratic skills and institutions"*. According to our contacts, the sanctions imposed by Washington and the European Union against Russian individuals and businesses will have no effect other than to exacerbate the economic difficulties both for Ukraine and for European businesses.

Acceptance into the European Union tends to go hand-in-hand with acceptance into NATO, with the exception of the five countries that maintain neutrality (Sweden, Finland, Malta, Austria and Ireland). The two institutions are both based in Brussels. The Atlantic Alliance is mentioned in all treaties governing European institutions since the Maastricht Treaty signed on February 7, 1992: Amsterdam Treaty (1997), Treaty of Nice (2001), the European Constitution Treaty (signed in 2004 and abandoned in 2007), the Treaty of Lisbon (2007). It was not included in the Treaty of Rome, which instituted the European Economic Community in 1957.

It is clear that NATO allows the United States to command military interventions outside of UN control and international law, many of them outside of its geographical purview (Africa, Middle East). According to our contacts in Itamaraty, the grounding of Bolivian president Evo Morales' plane speaks volumes about Europe's military subordination to the United States. After De Gaulle withdrew France from NATO in 1966, ushering in 43 years of Gaullo-Mitterandism, France rejoined the NATO integrated military command in April 2009 under President Sarkozy.

The Atlantic Alliance is strengthening its position in Eastern Europe through the creation of six new command centers, a new headquarters in western Poland, and a tripling of intervention forces to 30,000 men. Announced at the Newport Summit in September 2014 as *"strictly defensive"* by NATO Secretary General Jens Stoltenberg of Denmark, these measures are seen by Brasilia as small steps in an escalating provocation of Russia, a nuclear power whose security interests should be better respected instead of being branded a rogue state that must be contained.

The eastward expansion of NATO announced at the Madrid summit (1994) and the planned inclusion of Georgia and Ukraine after the Bucharest summit (2008) went against promises made to President Gorbachev at the Malta summit (1989) not to extend NATO to include eastern bloc countries in return, according to the observers present at the Malta summit, for the withdrawal of Soviet troops and the reunification of Germany[1]. Of the 28 NATO member countries, 12 joined after the fall of the Berlin Wall in 1989. They point out in Brasilia that the inclusion of Poland, Hungary and the Czech Republic in 1999 coincided with the bombing of Serbia, a Russian ally, by U.S. air power under NATO cover.

The Georgian war and the issues of Abkhazia and South Ossetia set a precedent which should have been remembered in the approach to the Ukrainian crisis. In Brasilia's eyes, President Putin's warnings regarding the possibility of Ukraine joining NATO were sufficiently clear that the country could have been spared a war where civilians are the principal victims (5.600 dead and 13.000 wounded as of February 15, 2015 according to the United Nations) and that Kiev does not have the military capacities or financial resources to sustain[2].

The EU offer of an exclusive treaty, the saber-rattling tour of the armored convoy of 600 American soldiers returning from maneuvers in Poland, Estonia, Latvia and Lithuania known as Operation Dragoon Ride (part of Operation Atlantic Resolve), Poland's military spending program (43 billion dollars in 2013-2022, including the purchase of 238 cruise missiles to be delivered by the United States starting in 2017), the passage of a resolution to *"deepen military cooperation with the North Atlantic Treaty Organization with the objective of meeting the criteria for acceptance into it"*[3], the passage in the U.S. congress of the Ukraine Freedom Support Act in 2014[4], the threat of delivery of heavy arms to Ukraine by NATO supreme commander Philip Breedlove, and Ukraine's blockade of Transnistria in June 2015 do not appear to be measures designed to calm tensions.

1. Talk by Ambassador Jack Madlock at the National Press Club in Washington (see James Carden, "Legendary Ambassador delivers Some Straight talk in DC", *The Nation*, February 17, 2015).

2. Short speech by President Putin at the Valdai International Club in Sochi during the 11th plenary session of the Russian think tank on October 24, 2014.

3. Jean Pierre Stroobants, "L'Ukraine fait un pas vers l'OTAN" (Ukraine takes a step closer to NATO), *Le Monde*, December 26, 2014.

4. The act instituted, in particular, sanctions on the Russian company Gazprom and on Russian arms manufacturers that export to Syria (!), the delivery of defensive arms to Ukraine in 2015 to the tune of 350 million dollars, the designation of Ukraine, Moldavia and Georgia as "major non-NATO allies" in order to allow transit of arms, aid to the Ukrainian energy industry amounting to 50 million dollars (Ukraine is some 2 billion dollars in debt to Russia for its supply of natural gas).

Brazilian diplomacy sees Russia as a partner in efforts to build a multipolar world, a partner that bears the brunt of a policy of destabilization implemented by the world's major power going well beyond what is effectively at stake in Ukraine. And it sees the European Union, the majority of whose member states are NATO members, playing the role of sorcerer's apprentice. The Europeans have erred in neglecting their relations with Russia as regards the eastern republics (Armenia, Azerbaijan, Belarus, Georgia, Moldavia and Ukraine). Germany is clearly an exception in this regard, playing the Russian-economic-integration card after the period of *Ostpolitik*, particularly as regards energy. Gerhard Schröder, former German chancellor (October 1998 - November 2005), has been a member of the Gazprom board of directors since 2006. Exportations border on 50% of Germany's gross domestic product (24% in 1990); given the recession affecting the EU countries, keeping the door open to the East should be a priority for Berlin.

Ukraine is verging on bankruptcy: in February 2015 the 12-month inflation rate was 34.5%, the national currency had lost 70% of its value with respect to the dollar and the lending rate of the central Ukrainian bank is now one of the world's highest at 30%. Ukraine could only benefit from including Russia in any economic agreement. Russia is its main trade partner and creditor, and the country with whom it shares the deepest historical, cultural and social ties.

Crimea was ceded by the Soviet Union to the Ukrainian Soviet Socialist Republic in 1954 without consulting the local population, the majority of whom were pro-Russian. Its independence was declared by the local parliament in May 1992, and former president Yuri Meshkov was elected in January 1994 with 73% of the vote on a platform based on reunification with Russia. The territory was undergoing "Ukrainization": one fourth of its newspapers were published in Ukrainian, schools were set up offering lessons only in Ukrainian, and the separatist movements had practically disappeared both from within the Crimean political spheres and among the local population. This process of normalization was carried out successfully despite the reactions of the Russian nationalist factions (Duma resolution of July 1993 stipulating that Sevastopol was an integral part of Russia; statement in July 2001 by Moscow mayor Yuri Luzhkov during a visit to Crimea[1]) as long as Russian interests were taken into consideration (particularly the Sevastopol naval base, a sanctuary for Russian patriotism and symbol of Russian naval might since the time of the Tsars). President Vladimir Putin stated during a press conference in Sochi on December 16, 2005, that "*regarding the Crimea, no problem shall arise between Russia and Ukraine in the foreseeable future*"[2]. Russia is a signatory, together with the United States and the United Kingdom, of the Budapest Memorandum on Security Assurances (December 5, 1994) that guaranteed the integrity of

---

[1]. "Crimea is a Russian territory. It has always belonged to Russia and never to Ukraine", *Rossijskaya Gazeta,* July 31, 2001.

[2]. http://en.kremlin.ru/events/president/transcripts/23342

Ukraine in exchange for its denuclearization and its adherence to the Nuclear Non-Proliferation Treaty[1].

The thinking in Brasilia is that this rushed adhesion by Ukraine to the NPT, orchestrated by Brussels with the ultimate purpose of bringing it into the NATO fold, is what led to the crisis. Lviv and Donetsk have little in common; the Ukrainian nation had to be given time to come together. A statute inspired by Finland should have provided a model for a *modus vivendi*. Without question, the Organization for Security and Co-operation in Europe (OSCE), chaired in 2014 by Switzerland and including Russia as a member, should have played a more active role as mediator to push for the creation of a multi-ethnic confederation based on the Swiss model. Demonstrations in June 2006 in the Crimean port of Feodosia against NATO military exercises (Operation Sea Breeze) and the anti-NATO resolution of the Crimean Parliament constituted clear warnings. Like Chile, Argentina and Uruguay, Brazil has not signed on to the sanctions against Russia imposed by the United States and the European Union.

Our contacts in Brasilia expect that Crimea will return to Russia in keeping with its history. The conquest of Russia by the tsarist armies did not subjugate Ukraine, which did not exist at the time, but rather a Turkish vassal state. These lands were populated essentially by Russians. Ukraine, like Belarus, was an invention of the Soviet Union to gain two more votes in the United Nations. Kiev was once the capital of Russia. Crimea's annexation to Russia was largely favored by the population in the 2014 referendum called by the Crimean parliament. The population was not consulted when it was ceded to Ukraine in 1954 by the Khrushchev government.

Brasilia sees Russia as a vital partner in the resolution of many international issues; the imposition of sanctions is not conducive to dialogue. They penalize Russian and European businesses working in favor of integration and trade. This "exclusionary diplomacy" is a violation of international law. It constitutes an accusation against people who are stripped of any legal recourse.

Our Brazilian contacts were also puzzled by the suspension in March 2014 of Russia from the G8, the forum of the world's major economic powers within the circle of influence of the United States[2], a self proclaimed "international community" in spite of the fact that either of two non-members of this exclusive club, India or China, have a greater population and that there are 193 nations in the United Nations. They question the sense of the systematic anti-Russian policy promoted by the American government since *Ostpolitik* and the historic entente between presidents Reagan and Gorbachev, and they question the extent of U.S. interference in the Euromaidan demonstrations leading to the ouster of the democratically elected president

---

[1]. Article 1: "*to respect the independence and sovereignty and the existing borders of Ukraine*"; Article 2: "*to refrain from the threat or use of force against the territorial integrity or political independence of Ukraine*" (Budapest Memorandum on Security Assurances, Council of Foreign Relations, December 5, 1994).

[2]. United States, Canada, Japan, Germany, France, United Kingdom, Italy.

Viktor Yanukovych on February 23, 2014 in spite of the agreement with the opposition signed on February 21 and to a largely fictitious "democratic transition" dominated in reality by clan and oligarchical rule.

The leader of the governing party in the House, Andriy Parubly, co-founder of the radical nationalist, neo-Nazi party that would became Svoboda, was in Washington in February 2015 asking for military aid. Assistant Secretary of State for European and Eurasian Affairs Victoria Nuland, former U.S. ambassador to NATO (June 2005-May 2008) is married to a strongly anti-Russian neo-conservative, Robert Kagan, co-founder of the think-tank Project for the New American Century.

Without external interference, the conflict over the self-proclaimed republics of Donetsk and Lougansk will be at a lasting impasse, our contacts note, similar to the conflict over Transnistria.

Russia's goal is not the incorporation of these secessionist republics but rather – if they should become autonomous, decentralized, federal states – to monitor their future development particularly to prevent them from joining NATO and the possibility of it forming an alliance with the United States. Hunter Biden, son of the U.S. vice president, is one of the board members of the Ukrainian energy company Burisma Holdings. Ukrainian finance minister, Natalie Jaresko, appointed on December 2, 2014, is American, born in the Chicago suburb of Elmhurst. She has held a number of positions at the U.S. Department of State, the most recent as Chief of the Economic Section of the U.S. Embassy in Kiev. She is co-founder of the investment fund Horizon Capital. She was granted Ukrainian citizenship in a controversial expedited procedure. Her case echoes that of the French diplomat Salome Zurabishvili, granddaughter of Georgian immigrants, appointed Ambassador of France to Georgia in 2003 and Foreign Minister in Georgian President Mikhail Saakashvili's government (a post she held from March 2004 to October 2005) after an *ad hoc* law was passed to allow her to take Georgian citizenship. She is now a member of the group of experts who advises the committee in charge of sanctions against Iran in the United Nations Security Council.

The Brazilian diplomats who formerly took the organization of Europe as a model of integration for the Mercosur countries now criticize it. They cite the dysfunction in the Eurozone, built on an inconsistent array of social and fiscal legislation, the centralization of decision-making power in Brussels, and its lack of democratic legitimacy, evidenced in particular by the lack of legal standing for the Eurogroup and by the failure of popular referendums (in France and the Netherlands in 2005, in Ireland in 2008, and in Iceland in 2010). Other reasons include the rise of europhobic and nationalist groups, a growing disparity among member countries, a growing diplomatic dependence on the United States, and a confusion in relations with NATO that did not exist before the Treaty of Lisbon (1972).

Regarding Greece, they see the forgiving of its debt to European creditors to be inevitable. They see this debt (175% of GDP in January 2015, as opposed to 109% prior to the crisis) as being entirely unmanageable. They note with irony that one of the sources of Germany's prosperity is the partial forgiving of its debts following the Second World War at the London Conference in February 1953. Like Germany yesterday, this would be the best guarantee for Greece today against the establishment of fascist currents and the emergence of the latent Germano-phobia existing both in Greece and in southern Europe.

The recognition by the Italian High Court in June 2008 of the executive nature of the judgment in October 1997 by the Greek court in Livadeia awarding compensation to the families of the victims of a massacre by Nazi troops in the village of Distomo[1], a judgment confirmed by the Greek High Court (Aeropago) in May 2000, gives evidence of a growing disaccord in Europe. The German government filed a claim with the International Court of Justice, and in February 2012 the Court rejected arguments by Italy and Greece, citing German's immunity as a sovereign state according to international law. The sole dissenting opinion among the 15 magistrates was by the Brazilian judge, Antonio Augusto Cançado Trindade, who had sat on the ICJ since 2009[2].

Germany is responsible, along with France and the United States, for two thirds of the 216-odd billion dollars worth of weaponry sold to Greece between 1974 and 2011, and thus has some responsibility for the country's bankruptcy. In constant dollars, between 2002 and 2011 Greece spent 8.6 billion dollars per year on arms to ensure it could face up to the Turkish "threat", although the two NATO members should have been forcefully called to order instead of being allowed to expand their arsenals over the question of Cyprus. From 1994 to 2014, Greece was the world's eighth largest arms buyer, Turkey was fourth, while Brazil was in 22nd position. Greece's Air Force is equipped by the United States (166 F16s and 50 F4s) and France (43 Mirage 2000s), while its submarines are German (8 vessels). Greece has more fighter aircraft and submarines, and twice as many tanks, as Germany when its GDP in 2014 was only 7% of Germany's[3]. It dedicates 2.2% of its GDP to defense; Germany 1.2%; Brazil 1.5%[4]. Greece's per capita spending on arms from 1997 to 2011 was higher than Germany's on a year-by-year basis[5]. And these arms deals bore the taint of corruption, as illustrated by the 20-year prison term handed down in October 2013 to the former Greek Minister of Defense (1996-2001), Akis Tsochatzopoulos, and the heavy fines paid by the German companies Siemens and Ferrostaal. Until 2012, Greece was second only to Turkey as Germany's

---

1. On June 1, 1944 the village was sacked by the Germans and 218 civilians were murdered, most of them women and children. In 2007 the Swiss filmmaker, Stefan Haupt, filmed a documentary about the massacre, *Ein Lied für Argyris* (*A Song for Argyris*).

2. Juridictional Immunities of the State Germany v. Italy; Greece (intervening), Judgment of 3 february 2012.

3. 238 billion dollars v. 3.859 trillion dollars (source: IMF).

4. Source: Stockholm International Peace Research Institute. Military Expenditures Databases 2015.

5. 641 dollars v. 589 for Germany from 1997 to 2011. Per capita defense spending in Brazil for the same period was 188 dollars (Source: Stockholm International Peace Research Institute – 2015).

largest arms customer: 15% of German arms production went to Greece at the time[1]. Greek national debt is largely due to these ill-advised purchases of arms, arms that the country has never used. With creditors seeking settlement, this arms debt is the indirect cause for Greece's lack of social progress.

The German research center, Halle Institute for Economic Research, published a study on August 10, 2015 demonstrating that Germany has profited from the Greek crisis to the tune of 100 billion euros between 2010 and 2015[2].

Politically speaking, the powers of the Security Council and its updated concept of "threats to peace" make it possible to place certain countries under "neoprotectorates" with the support of NATO, whose revised strategy leads it into questionable interventions.

The Security Council holds a great deal of responsibility for the weakening of international law and in particular of the multilateral security system. Thus, two months after the invasion of Iraq, Resolution 1483 of May 22, 2003 legalized the occupation by the Anglo-American "authority" until a new Iraqi government could be formed[3]. On June 12, 2003, the Security Council voted to extend the exemption from prosecution before the International Criminal Court for American soldiers taking part in "peacekeeping operations". The Security Council should, according to Brasilia, include emerging countries among its permanent members: without their representation, its legitimacy will be increasingly contested.

On the political level, the powers of the Security Council and its renewed concept of "threats to peace" make it possible to place certain states under "neo-protectorates" with the support of NATO, whose revamped strategy leads it to engage in controversial interventions. There is only one security space, emphasizes Brasilia, and it must be by consequence collective and embrace all countries in the region. The United States was the only country to vote against the resolution by the General Assembly of the United Nations, adopted by 153 states on December 7, 2006 in favor of developing a treaty on the sale of conventional weapons. Only four countries (United States, Israel,

---

1. Helena Smith, "German hypocrisy over Greek military spending", *The Guardian*, April 19, 2012.

2. Geraldine Dany, Reint Gropp, Helge Littke, Gregor Von Schweinitz, "Germany´s Benefit From the Greek Crisis": *"The German public sector balance benefited significantly from the European/Greek debt crisis, because of lower interest payments on public sector debt. This is due to two effects: One, in crisis times investors disproportionately seek out safe investments ("flight to safety"), bidding down the returns on safe-haven assets. We show that German bunds strongly benefited from this effect during the Greek debt crisis. Second, while the European Central Bank (ECB) monetary policy stance was quite close to an "optimal" monetary policy stance for Germany from 1999 to 2007, during the crisis monetary policy was too accommodating from a German perspective, due to the emerging disparities across the Euro area. As a result of these two effects, our calculations suggest that the German sovereign saved more than 100 billion Euros in interest expenses between 2010 and mid-2015. That is, Germany benefited from the Greek crisis even in case that Greece defaults on all its debt (a total of 90 billion) owed to the German government via diverse channels (European Stability Mechanism [ESM], International Monetary Fund [IMF], or directly)".*

3. "ONU legaliza ocupação do Iraque" (the UN legalizes the occupation of Iraq), *O´Globo*, May 23, 2003.

United Kingdom, France) voted against the proposition banning the use of nuclear weapons presented to the United Nations General Assembly by Cuba in December 2012 with the support of the Non-Aligned Countries (179 votes in favor).

On the economic level, the international financial institutions have a mandate to promote (read: impose) neo-liberal policies of deregulation and structural overhaul in exchange for their aid. The weight of the United States in the International Monetary Fund and World Bank is excessive, given the current proportional stature of the American economy with respect to the world economy. With 17.67% of the vote, the United States can block any major decisions by the Fund, which must be passed with an 85% majority. A similar situation exists in the World Bank. The World Trade Organization, despite the rule of consensus that governs most of its resolutions, seeks to consolidate neo-liberal policies by creating a network of multilateral relations to lower customs tariffs, excluding the agricultural sector. The Free Trade Area of the Americas, consistently championed by the United States in the name of free trade across the two continents, would bring all of Latin America within the U.S. economic territory. Brazil has reason to fear this project because its business community will not be able to compete with North American industry and foreign investors will be discouraged from investing far from the main New World market unless some tariff and other protections are put in place.

The U.S. dollar enjoys excessive privilege. The world's financial resources do not fund the development of emerging countries nor that of new technologies. It all goes to supporting American consumption. The United States has a monumental budget deficit and resorts to massive injections of liquidity by the Federal Reserve. The offshore dollar system is about half the size of the U.S domestic banking industry compared with 10% in the fifties. Offshore dollar credit (bonds and loans) has risen from 28% to 54% of American GDP over the past decade[1]The attempt to replace the dollar with a more stable and neutral currency by China, Russia and Brazil in 2009 (IMF Special Drawing Rights) was rejected by the United States, which has veto power in the Fund. However, since the beginning of the third millennium, global growth is mainly driven by emerging countries (China, India, Brazil, Indonesia...). The creation of the New Development Bank by the five BRICS countries (Brazil, Russia, India, China and South Africa) and the establishment of the Asian Infrastructure Investment Bank in 2013 by China, which was joined by the principal European countries in 2015, are expressions of the desire to break free of U.S. hegemony in international financial institutions and the near monopoly of the U.S. dollar in financial transactions. Today, the share of China´s external trade conducted in yuan (Hong Kong left out of account) is less than 10%. This objective drives the growing use of the yuan in trade

[1] "The sticky superpower",*The Economist*, October 3, 2015.

between China and its Asian partners and the eventual creation of a common currency within the Eurasian Economic Union[1].

With Brazil running a record deficit in its balance of payments, the raising of interest rates by the Federal Reserve, expectedat the end of 2015, the devaluation of the yuan, and the strengthening of the U.S. dollar could have a disastrous effect as regards debts contracted in dollars by Brazilian businesses. The investment rate is falling: 16.5% of GDP in the second quarter of 2014, the lowest since 2006.

As a consequence, Brazilian foreign policy should focus on reducing the country's external vulnerabilities – political, economic, diplomatic and military – and work the resulting policies into the decision-making centers of the international system.

During Dilma Rousseff's first term as president, the Minister of External Relations, Luiz Alberto Figueiredo, a recognized expert in environmental issues, former Permanent Representative of Brazil to the United Nations (June-August 2013), appointed after Antonio Patriota's forced departure (after the blunder that allowed the escape of Bolivian senator Roger Pinto Molino, who had taken refuge in the Brazilian embassy in La Paz in May 2012), furthered President Lula's priorities of promoting South American unity and south-south cooperation.

However, personality differences between him and the Brazilian president led to his replacement in January 2015 (he has just been appointed Brazilian Ambassador to Washington) by a relatively unknown diplomat, Mauro Vieira, former Brazilian Ambassador to Washington, previously Ambassador to Argentina, former chief of staff for Celso Amorim. In spite of his two prestigious ambassadorships for Brazil, Vieira is cut out to be a cabinet member rather than a theoretician of international relations. He has published very little outside of a paper in 1992 on the liberalization of international trade. He appointed Sérgio Danese to the position of Secretary-General of Itamaraty. Former ambassador to Algeria (2005-2009), Danese is less ideologically assertive than his predecessor, Samuel Pinheiro Guimarães, leader of Brazilian diplomacy in the Lula years[2]. Former parliamentary attaché in Celso Amorim's office, he is well familiar with the workings of parliament and will doubtlessly be more valuable inside Itamaraty, which is facing serious budgetary problems, than in formulating and implementing foreign policy.

Dilma Rousseff showed thinly veiled contempt for Itamaraty in 2014, manifested as unusual delays in accepting the credentials of many new diplomatic heads in Brasilia (some had to wait nearly 12 months) and severe budget cuts (Itamaraty accounted for no more than 0.27% of the national budget in 2014, as opposed to 0.5% in 2003), in spite of the creation of 30%

---

1. Russia, Belarus, Kazakhstan, Armenia, Kyrgyzstan.

2. Sergio Danese, *A Escola da Liderança. Ensaios Sobre a Politica Externa e a Inserção internacional do Brasil* (The Leadership School: Essays on foreign policy and Brazil's inclusion on the international stage), Editora Record, São Paulo, 2009.

more diplomatic and consular posts during the Lula years[1] and an increase in the number of career diplomats from 1,084 in 2003 to 1,590 in 2014. Brazil's participation in trade fairs and economic missions has decreased significantly: 180 in 2013, 50 in 2014[2].

The country's diplomatic credibility has suffered. Brazil is significantly behind in its payments to many international agencies, to the point where it has lost its voting rights: this is the case, as of January 1, 2015, at the International Atomic Energy Agency (IAEA) and the International Criminal Court. And also in UNESCO, where Brazil is one of the major extra-budgetary contributors, its voting rights are threatened by a debt of 4.7 million dollars for the year 2013. Contributions to international organizations, where Brazil's arrears are estimated as of March 1, 2015 at some 340 million dollars, indeed no longer come from the Itamaraty budget (since 2009), but from the Ministry of Planning, Budget and Management. These shortfalls damage the image of Brazilian diplomacy. The *New York Times* recently published a long editorial harshly criticizing Brazilian foreign policy under Dilma Rousseff: "*While the other three large emerging economies, China, Russia and India, are pursuing muscular foreign policies, under Mrs. Rousseff's watch, Brazil's voice in the international arena barely registers above a whisper.")*[3].

---

[1]. André De Souza, "Corte de despesas nas representacões diplomàticas no exterior é de 50%" (Spending on diplomatic missions cut by 50%), *O'Globo,* January 23, 2001.
[2]. Isabel Fleck, "Itamaraty perde espaço no Orçamento" (Itamaraty loses ground in the Budget), *Folha de São Paulo,* December 25, 2014.
[3]. *International New York Times*, March 25, 2015.

CHAPTER 2

REDUCING POLITICAL VULNERABILITY

Mercosur, Latin America and the Caribbean

In August 1985, by initiative of Brazil, the Contadora Support Group[1] was formed to seek a negotiated solution to conflicts in Central America. This led to the creation of the Rio Group in 1986[2] and preceded the rapprochement with Argentina that was sealed with the Treaty of Integration, Cooperation and Development of 1988. At the same time, a zone of peace and cooperation of the South Atlantic (United Nations resolution 41/11 of October 27, 1986) was declared.

Political vulnerability was reduced by creating a political and economic pole in Latin America with a priority focus on Mercosur (southern common market) and its associate states (Chile and Bolivia in 1996, Peru in 2003) and a rapprochement between this pole and the countries exercising non-hegemonic leadership. This priority orientation to Latin America took concrete form in greater integration in trade (Mercosur, 1991), defense (Council of South American Defense, 2008), infrastructure (Initiative for the Integration of the Regional Infrastructure of South America, 2000; Mercosur Structural Convergence Fund, 2006), efforts against drug trafficking (South American Council to Combat Drug Trafficking, 2010) and diplomacy (Union of South American Nations – USAN, 2008).

It is part of a strategy whose premises were laid out with the democratization of Brazil as it emerged from military dictatorship (presidency of José Sarney, 1985-1990). The aim was to give more clout to a country burdened by difficult debt service negotiations and discredited in European eyes by its political repression and solidarity with the Southern Cone dictatorships (e.g. Operation Condor). The belief that Brazil could only consolidate its role on the international stage and that power could only be rebalanced with strong regional support is an old one. Hence:

- the agreement between Mercosur and the Andean Community (Ecuador, Bolivia, Peru and Colombia) in December 2003 and the unilateral concessions during the Lula presidency regarding trade with Argentina – seen as a vital trading partner – (particularly the antidumping mechanism put in place in 2006, known as the *Mecanismo de Adaptação Competitiva*) and with Uruguay; moderate official reactions to Bolivia's decisions to nationalize its energy

[1]. Including Mexico, Venezuela, Colombia and Panama.

[2]. Contadora Group plus Chile, Ecuador, Bolivia and Paraguay (1990). The Rio Group currently includes all the countries in Central and South America.

resources in 2006, which harmed Brazilian businesses and ran counter to the nationalist clamor in the major Brazilian media; the intervention to protect Bolivian integrity during the crisis associated with the call for autonomy by the Santa Cruz Department in 2008; the dismissal in 2013 of the Minister of External Relations, Antonio Patriota, by President Dilma Rousseff because of the help given to a Bolivian senator who had taken refuge in the Brazilian embassy in La Paz to reach Brazil;

- the subdued response to Ecuadorian threats to expel the major Brazilian companies (Petrobras, oil; Odebrecht, civil construction) and the final resolution of the crisis;
- the understanding manifested in response to Paraguay's pressure to renegotiate the terms of the treaty on the Itaipu hydroelectric plant;
- Brazilian diplomatic mediation in regional crises (Ecuador and Peru in 1998, Venezuela in 2002, Ecuador in 2005, Honduras in 2009, Colombia in 2010, Colombia and Venezuela in August 2015 principally with the support of Ecuador and Uruguay);
- Brazil's absence from the complaint against Argentina lodged with the World Trade Organization in March 2012 by forty countries, including Mexico, on administrative obstacles to imports (system of non-automatic import licenses, so-called *declaraciones juradas anticipadas de importación*)[1].

Brazil also took part in a workshop on alternative dispute resolution mechanisms with seven other countries (Argentina, Chile, Costa Rica, Honduras, Paraguay, Peru and Uruguay) organized by the Ibero-American Association of Public Prosecutors (AIAMP) as part of the European EuroSocial Program.

Brazil shares a border with nearly all countries in South America, the only exceptions being Ecuador and Chile. It intends to exercise a stabilizing role in Latin America and to promote respect for democratic institutions, although some of its initiatives to realize this ambition have encountered obstacles (diplomatic impasse in the Honduran crisis; hesitant approach to the issue of human rights in Cuba). The telegrams from the U.S. diplomatic representation to Brasilia between July 2006 and October 2009, the tenor of which was revealed by *Wikileaks*, evidence the negative reaction of Brazilian authorities to the defense and cooperation agreement between the United States and Colombia (particularly the stationing of American troops at seven Colombian military bases). The Brazilian chancellery reacted strongly – as did Bolivia, Nicaragua, Ecuador and Venezuela – to the announcement in June 2013 by Colombian President Juan Manuel Santos of cooperation and rapprochement between his country and NATO, a move that was viewed positively by U.S.

---

[1]. Janaina Figueiredo, "OMC: 40 paises abrem queixa contra Argentina" (WTO: 40 countries lodge complaint against Argentina), *O´Globo*, March 31, 2012.

Assistant Secretary of State for Western Hemisphere Affairs, Roberta S. Jacobson. At the same time, the Director of the Center for Defense Strategy Studies of the Union of South American Nations (USAN), Alfredo Forti, announced the creation of a military school ("Escuela Suramericana de Defensa") to train officers from the twelve member countries using concepts and methods proper to their continent.

In August 2009, a special summit was convened in Bariloche, Argentina, to discuss the regional security implications of the use of Colombian military bases by North American forces. Brazil stressed on that occasion that the initiative was not compatible with declarations by Colombian authorities stating that armed resistance in their country had decreased significantly. Brazil sustained that violence in Latin America grew out of social problems that could not be resolved by military force. The issue of drug trafficking is at the heart of this debate.

The Merida Initiative (2007-2010), part of U.S. efforts to combat drug trafficking, and its extension beyond 2010 (Caribbean Basin Security Initiative, Central American Regional Security Initiative), is considered to be an attempt to reestablish close relations between the police and armed forces of Mexico and Central American and Caribbean nations (El Salvador, Guatemala, Honduras, Panama, Haiti, Dominican Republic, Belize, Costa Rica) under the pretext of fighting drug trafficking. Most of the funds earmarked for the Merida Initiative (3 billion dollars, half going to Mexico) are used to buy arms and for police training by American instructors, particularly at the International Law Enforcement Academy (*Academia Internacional para el cumplimiento de la Ley* – ILEA) created in 2006 in El Salvador, to consolidate relations and affinities and, in the final analysis, to reinforce repressive regimes. Most of the funds are ostensibly earmarked for the modernization of the armed forces; in truth they remain in the United States to finance arms purchases.

The war against drug trafficking, conducted in the region for some 20 years by the United States, has coincided with an escalation of violence in most Central American and Caribbean societies, excluding only Costa Rica, Nicaragua and Cuba. This growing militarization, fed by an inflow of American-made arms freely sold along the entire U.S.-Mexican border, has triggered hostile reactions. President Evo Morales expelled the Drug Enforcement Administration (DEA) from Bolivia, and attempts to decriminalize the production, sale and consumption of drugs are noted, particularly in Paraguay, Uruguay and Guatemala.

Brazil responded to plans to establish a North American military presence in Paraguay in 2006 – purportedly to better control the Argentina-Brazil-Paraguay border, seen as being exposed to threats of terrorism and drug trafficking because of the presence of a Muslim community that was viewed with suspicion – with the creation in 2005 of an Intelligence Center at Foz de Iguaçu to share information and analyses with its two neighbors.

Brazil also responded to wiretapping of the public oil company Petrobras and the principal Brazilian institutions by implementing a regional digital strategy. The Minister of Defense, Celso Amorim, was in Buenos Aires in September 2013 with the director of the army's digital defense center (*Centro de Defensa Cibernética*) to lay the groundwork for regional cooperation. After failing to obtain the explanations and apologies she had demanded of President Obama regarding the covert surveillance of herself and primary Brazilian institutions revealed by the young system administrator and IT analyst Edward Snowden, President Dilma Rousseff met in a closed-door session with former president Lula and the chair of the Workers' Party, Ruy Falcão, where she decided to cancel her official visit to the United States scheduled for October 23, 2013. She invited her BRICS partners to require social networks to record their data locally so that they would be protected by national legislation.

President Lula and his Cuban counterpart, Fidel Castro, were the forces behind the creation of the São Paulo Forum in 1990, anxious to "console" the leftist Latin American movements following the 28th Soviet Communist Party Congress in July 1990 and the collapse of the regime. Uniting left-wing political parties and non-governmental organizations close to the Alter-globalization movement, meeting every two years since its inception in a different city in South America, it met in its 18th session in Havana in April 2013, inaugurated by the head of the department of international relations of the Cuban communist party, José Ramon Balaguer, former Cuban ambassador to Moscow. The chair of the Brazilian Workers' Party, Ruy Falcão, took part in the discussions. The first Social Movement Coordination Assembly (*Asamblea de Articulación de Movimientos Sociales*) took place in May 2013 in São Paulo under the auspices of the Bolivarian Alliance for the Peoples of Our America (ALBA) with representatives from the social movements of 22 countries in South America and the Caribbean. The 19th session of the Forum took place in La Paz, Bolivia in August 2014.

Brazil is also one of the founders of the Union of South American Nations (USAN), created in Cuzco, Peru in 2007. Its first summit in December 2008 brought together the heads of state of the major Latin American countries[1], while neither the United States nor the European Union was invited. Its first Secretary-General was the former president of Argentina, Néstor Kirchner (May - September 2010). The organization went on to be headed by the former Minister of Foreign Relations for Colombia, Maria Emma Mejia (2011-2012) and then by the former Minister of Foreign Relations and of the Economy of Venezuela, Ali Rodriguez, former Venezuelan ambassador to Havana and Marxist militant in his youth in the Venezuelan Revolutionary Party (*Partido de la Revolución Venezolana).*

---

[1]. USAN: Argentina, Bolivia, Brazil, Chile, Colombia, Ecuador, Guyana, Paraguay, Peru, Surinam, Uruguay, Venezuela.

USAN is the successor to the South American Community of Nations, which was boycotted by the president of Argentina when it was created in 2004 because he saw it as an instrument of Brazilian hegemony. Headquartered in Quito, the 12-member Union established the Council of South American Defense to better communicate the defense budgets and priorities of the member states, defuse mutual suspicions and coordinate security policies. Five working groups of experts (energy, infrastructure, finance, social policies, education) meet regularly to develop shared initiatives to facilitate regional integration.

Brazilian diplomacy worked hard to develop regional instruments to better affirm its role as a regional power as part of its strategy to join the club of world powers.

Brazil sponsored Venezuela's entry into Mercosur, which was approved by the Brazilian senate in December 2009, and entertained cordial relations with President Chávez, the *bête noire* of the principal Brazilian media. Lula foreign policy advisor Marco Aurélio Garcia predicted that Chávez would leave a mark on Venezuelan politics as Perón had once marked Argentine politics[1]. Former president Lula recently wrote a column in the *New York Times* that was particularly flattering to the former Venezuelan president[2]. Brazil vehemently opposed the April 2002 coup against Chávez and his temporary replacement by Caracas trade organization leader Pedro Carmona. It was behind the creation of the Group of Friends of Venezuela (United States, Spain, Portugal, Mexico and Chile) for the reestablishment of democratic institutions in the country. Brazil played a determining role here, particularly by convincing, as reported by Celso Amorim[3], the Venezuelan president to accept the participation of the Spanish government under Aznar, which had initially recognized the attempted coup several months earlier. Itamaraty points out that Hugo Chávez had taken part in 15 uncontested elections since 1998 and won 14 of them, and that the percentage of Venezuelans living below the poverty threshold had dropped from 55% at the time of his election in 1998 to 18% in 2011. The former Brazilian Minister of External Relations, Antonio Patriota, expressed concern over the extreme political polarization in Venezuela after the election of Nicolás Maduro, especially the lack of dialogue between the opposition and the ruling party. He felt that the admission of Venezuela to Mercosur should help consolidate democracy in the country.

After the recent discovery of extensive deep offshore oil fields (to which Brasilia attributes the reactivation of the U.S. Fourth fleet), and prior to the fall in oil prices and the Petrobras scandal, Brazil had hoped to join Venezuela in OPEC. Meeting in extraordinary session, the Mercosur parliament termed the redeployment of the Fourth Fleet, which had been disestablished in 1950, as "*pointless*" and "*inopportune*" and reiterated that the United States had yet to sign

---

1. Interview in the monthly *Piaui*, no. 30, 2009.
2. *The New York Times*, March 6, 2013.
3. "*Breves Narrativas Diplómaticas*" (Brief diplomatic narratives), Benvirá, São Paulo, 2013.

the United Nations Convention on the Law of the Sea[1], unlike 160 other countries. In September 2010, Brazil unilaterally extended its exclusive economic zone to the maximum limit of 350 nautical miles specified in the Montego Bay Convention.

Brasilia deplores President Obama's recent designation of Venezuela as a "*U.S. national security threat*" and supports the mediation mission undertaken by USAN in March 2015 to ease internal tensions and ensure normal institutional relations. The deteriorating economic situation (inflation at 68.5% in 2014) and the tightening of control by the regime (opposition leaders Leopoldo Lopez and Antonio Ledezma detained in February 2015) are viewed with concern. Our contacts question the compatibility of President Nicolás Maduro's plan for extraordinary legislative powers that would allow him to govern by decree with the legislative elections planned for December 2015.

Former president Lula has remained quite close to the Chávez circles. In June 2015 he received the following dignitaries at the institute in São Paulo named after him: the president of the Venezuelan national assembly, Diosdado Cabello, and the ministers of the Economy, Rodolfo Marco Torres, and Industry, José David[2]. President Dilma Rousseff stated her opposition to the sanctions announced by President Obama on March 9, 2015 against members of the Venezuelan regime (freezing of assets, denial of visas): "*We Latin American and Caribbean countries do not accept unilateral measures, preludes to coups-d'état, or isolationist policies. We know that such measures are counterproductive, ineffective and unfair. We therefore reject the adoption of any sanctions against Venezuela*[3]."

It was Brazil to insist that Cuba be allowed back into the Organization of American States in 2009 after being ostracized for 47 years, and it was a Brazilian initiative, according to Celso Amorim, that Cuba added its name to the list of signatories to the Treaty of Tlatelolco for the Prohibition of Nuclear Weapons in Latin America and the Caribbean. At its 67th session in 2012, the United Nations General Assembly voted for the 21st consecutive year to lift the U.S. embargo on Cuba (188 votes in favor; 3 votes against – United States, Israel and Palau). That unilateral embargo had been in place since 1962, and was rendered even more severe by the Torricelli Law (Cuban Democracy Act – 1992), which, among other things, prohibited travel to Cuba by U.S. citizens and family remittances to Cuba, and the Helms-Burton Act (1996), which extended the embargo to foreign firms trading with Cuba. In April 2012, the Florida legislature passed a bill excluding companies having interests in Cuba from participating in public procurement, undermining the Brazilian public works firm Odebrecht, which had infrastructure projects in Miami and Mariel

---

1. Drafted in 1982, entered into force in 1994.

2. Sérgio Roxo, "Número 2 do chavismo se encontra com Lula em SP" (Chávez no. 2 meets Lula in São Paulo), *O'Globo*, June 11, 2016.

3. "*Nós, países latino-americanos e carabenhos, não admitimos medidas unilaterais, golpistas e politicas de isolamento. Sabemos que tais medidas são contraproducentes, ineficazes e injustas. Por isso, rechaçamos a adoção de quaisquer tipo de sanções contra a Venezuela*", *O'Globo*, June 11, 2015.

(Cuba). Odebrecht was forced to file a lawsuit in Miami federal court in order to continue its work in the Cuban port, explaining that it is carried out by a Cuban subsidiary.

In 1982, during the Reagan presidency, Cuba was arbitrarily added to the blacklist of state sponsors of terrorism, blocking access to international financing. It remained on the list until President Obama announced in April 2015 that he would remove it. Cuba was not an invitee to the annual summit of the Organization of American States – at this point by its own wishes – nor to the Summit of the Americas, a gathering instituted in 1994 by initiative of the United States. Brazilian diplomacy had stressed that the sixth Summit of the Americas, held in Cartagena, Colombia on April 14 and 15, 2012, would be the last one without Cuban participation. Ecuadorian president Rafael Correa boycotted the meeting because of Cuba's absence.

In September 2014, during a meeting of the working group in charge of organizing the seventh Summit of the Americas (Panama, April 10-11, 2015), the chairman of the group, Panama's Deputy Minister of Foreign Affairs, announced that the Havana authorities had been invited.

The resumption of diplomatic relations between the United States and Cuba, announced on December 17, 2014 by President Obama, contrasts with the deterioration of relations between Washington and Venezuela, Cuba's main ally in the region.

In December 2011, Brazil contributed to the constitution of the Community of Latin American and Caribbean States (CELAC), a political forum consisting of 33 sovereign countries. The United States and Canada are not members. Brazil's major concern, according to Celso Amorim, was the inclusion of Mexico (a signatory to the NAFTA Treaty) and Cuba in the same regional institution. CELAC is the culmination of diplomatic currents running counter to the United States and manifesting themselves in different ways, particularly regarding the North American Free Trade Area (NAFTA) treaty, the Summit of the Americas, and the Organization of American States. Cuba held the pro tempore Presidency in 2013, assisted by a troika composed of the previous president (Chile), the following president (Costa Rica) and the pro tempore President of CARICOM (Haiti). During a press conference in Quito on May 2015, Ecuadorian president Rafael Correa, president pro tempore of CELAC, asserted that this organization should be the true regional forum, the OAS being *"totally under the influence of the hegemonic powers"*, an allusion to the United States and Canada[1].

In Brasilia in April 2010, President Lula organized the first summit between Brazil and CARICOM, an organization founded in 1973 (Treaty of Chaguaramas): 12 of the 14 member countries are also members of the Commonwealth of Nations. The second summit was held in Paramaribo

1. "'La OEA es insalvable'. Correa llamó a darle um impulso a la Celac" ('The OAS cannot be saved': Correa calls for boost to CELAC), *Pagina12*, May 13, 2015.

(Surinam) with Dilma Rousseff among the participants. The presidents of the Dominican Republic, Venezuela and Equatorial Guinea took part in the Port of Spain Summit in July 2013. The Caribbean islands under the dominion of France (Martinique, Guadeloupe, Guyana) and the Netherlands (Curação, Saint Maarten) have applied for status as associate members. With generous funding from the European Regional Development Fund (ERDF), they have established autonomous regional cooperation. Martinique will soon establish a diplomatic seat in Belem (Brazil) and Havana (Cuba). This group of states (14 states plus Montserrat) represents 7% of the votes at the United Nations and 45% in the Organization of American States (OAS).

The Venezuelan-sponsored Petrocaribe alliance – building refinery infrastructure and providing oil at preferential payment conditions to 19 countries in Central American and the Caribbean – has brought the countries in the region closer to one another, particularly as regards public works projects. The ALBA Caribe fund was created within the Petrocaribe framework to combat social exclusion and inequality, while the ALBA Alimentos fund supports farming and food security.

Brazil holds observer status at the Association of Caribbean States, a consultatory body with a modest budget numbering 25 states. It was founded in Cartagena, Colombia with the main areas of cooperation laid out in the Merida Declaration (Venezuela) in 2001: sustainable development, regional integration and cooperation, natural catastrophe response, environmental integration of the Caribbean Sea. The organization's 6th summit took place in Merida, Mexico, in April 2014. A Caribbean Sea Commission was established by UN resolution. It is chaired by Costa Rica and its work is funded by Finland. The Commission has yet to take a position on the transportation of nuclear wastes from Europe to Japan via the Panama Canal.

The legacy of past divisions, the tensions inherent in the process of integrating asymmetrical economies, nationalist demands and energetic indigenist movements have all engendered a certain prudence with regard to a continent-sized state whose potential for hegemony is feared. An Argentine economist recently pointed out that, by itself, the Brazilian National Bank for Economic and Social Development (BNDES) had lending and subsidy power for Brazilian enterprise equal to all the credit available in the Argentine national economy[1]. Financing of Brazilian public works companies at cut rates (2.79% to 8.61% per year) by this bank totaled 11.9 billion dollars between 2007 and 2014[2]. The principal beneficiary countries, receiving 80% of the total financial assistance, were Venezuela, Argentina, the Dominican Republic, and Angola[3]. Brazil's GDP is six times that of Argentina (although they are equivalent *per capita*) and more than a hundred times that of Bolivia.

---

1. *Valor Económico*, January 14, 2012.

2. Financing is extended to countries that commit to selecting a Brazilian company in the procurement process; 70% of the funding went to a single company, Odebrecht.

3. *O'Globo*, July 22, 2015.

The President of Uruguay, José Mujica (2010-2015), does not share this opinion and speaks in favor of a "mobilizing hegemony": *"What we are seeking to achieve with the expansion of Mercosur is to bring together all of Latin America. We understand that we should move towards a more homogeneous group, but we lack the needed thrust of the most powerful*[1]*."*

On April 28, 2011, Colombia, Chile, Peru and Mexico, signatories to a free-trade agreement with the United States and Canada, created the Pacific Alliance, uniting some of the countries bordering on the Pacific and excluding Brazil. This bloc currently lacks international legal status, a permanent governing body and its own independent budget. Mexico is the only country to have ratified the framework agreement. Panama and Costa Rica may soon join the treaty, which currently includes as local observers within the region (Ecuador, El Salvador, Honduras, the Dominican Republic, Uruguay and Guatemala), while other observers include Canada, France, Portugal Australia and Japan.

In July 2013, Brazil expressed its opposition to Uruguay's plans to join the organization, formulated by Vice President Danilo Astori in May during the 7th summit of the Alliance in Cali. In the end, President Mujica aligned with the Brazilian position to maintain exclusive moorings within Mercosur. Following the meetings of ministers in Cartagena on November 1 and in Santiago on November 24, 2014, Mercosur has made overtures to the Pacific Alliance.

Chile and Peru were engaged in negotiations on the Trans-Pacific Partnership, spearheaded by the United States, whose chief diplomat termed it as the "*Pacific Dream*" in analogy to the "*American Dream*"[2]. Brasilia saw this as a resurgence of the neo-liberal policies of the Organization for Economic Cooperation and Development (OECD) of the 1990s, hashed out behind closed doors, to maintain a favorable investment climate for foreign enterprise. The presidents of Peru (Ollanta Humala) and Chile (Sebastian Piñero) took part in the Asia-Pacific Economic Cooperation (APEC) summit in Bali in October 2013. The APEC forum includes 21 countries, three of which are Latin American: Chile, Peru and Mexico. Joined by Mexico in 2011, Chile and Peru also take part in negotiations for the Trans-Pacific Partnership (TPP), which includes 12 countries – with Japan joining at the last hour – of the 21 in APEC, and which aims to contain China. In May 2013, the Chilean Minister of Foreign Affairs, Alfredo Moreno, would only discuss it in a closed session of parliament, citing a non-disclosure clause[3], and the head of the Chilean delegation, Rodrigo Contrera, resigned in June 2013 because he disagreed with the general lines of the project (especially with the extension of pharmaceutical

[1]. André Danza, Ernesto Tulbovitz, "*Una oveja negra al poder. Confesiones e intimidades de Pepe Mujica*" (A Black Sheep in Power: Confessions and intimacies of Pepe Mujica), Editorial Sudamericana, Buenos Aires, 2015.

[2]. Speech by John Kerry, U.S. Secretary of State, at the Tokyo Institute of Technology, Tokyo, April 15, 2013.

[3]. *Verdade Ahora*, June 11, 2013.

patents, the foreign investment protection measures, and the institution of private *ad hoc* courts in place of the national courts and the World Trade Organization). Parties to that agreement are Singapore, Brunei, Vietnam, Malaysia, Australia, New Zealand, Japan, Canada and the United States.

Brazil's candidacies for a place in international institutions (World Trade Organization, Inter-American Development Bank) have not received regional support commensurate with the country's stature in international trade negotiations and its claim to a permanent seat on the Security Council (opposed by Colombia and Argentina).

Kirchner's Argentina has made overtures to Venezuela with the hope, in part, to counterbalance Brazil's weight in Mercosur. But Venezuela has become an important partner to Brazil: trade between the two countries has increased sevenfold over the past decade, reaching six billion dollars in 2012, with a 4 billion dollar trade surplus in favor of Brazil. Brazilian investments in Venezuela are estimated at 20 billion dollars[1].

Lastly, Brazil is principally responsible for the impasse in negotiations on the Free Trade Area of the Americas, despite the Miami compromise (November 2003), which pared back the content and scope of the agreement (a two-track system with common and balanced set of rights and obligations applicable to all countries and the option for plurilateral agreements for countries wishing to take higher levels of commitments) and the Monterrey (2004) and Mar del Plata (2005) summits. At the time, the United States accounted for some 25% of Brazilian exports; in 2011 that figure was less than 10%. The trend is shared across all of Latin America: the United States took in one fourth of all exports in 2000 and only one seventh in 2010. Brazil's trade surplus with the United States (5 billion dollars in 2002) gave way to a trade deficit (-5.6 billion dollars in 2012 according to Brazilian sources).

Our contacts frequently mention Mexico as an example. Despite the implementation of a free trade agreement with the United States and Canada (NAFTA), nearly half the country's population lives in poverty: 53 million people in 2010 according to estimates by the Monterrey Institute of Technology. Violence has become endemic: 105.682 kidnappings in 2012 – nearly 300 a day – and 4007 disappearances have been registered by the National Institute of Statistics and Geography (INEGI)[2]. More than 11% of the Mexican population lives in the United States, half of them without visas, providing cheap labor for the North American economy[3]. Apprehensions by US border authorities exceeded 486.000 in 2014 in spite of the US recession and expanded border security[4]

---

[1]. *O 'Globo*, May 10, 2013.

[2]. National inquiry 2013 (*Encuesta Nacional de Victimización y Percepción sobre Seguridad Publica. Envipe 2013*). Instituto Nacional de Estadística y Geografía (www.inegi.org.mx).

[3]. *The Nation*, January 23, 2012.

[4] *The Guardian*, October 14, 2015.

Following the now classic pattern in developing countries, the lowering of customs tariffs facilitates sales of subsidized U.S. grain and has forced some two million farmers to abandon their fields, many of them attempting to emigrate to the United States. Mexico now imports corn. Between 2002 and 2011, Mexico's trade deficit reached 72 billion dollars; in the same period Brazil recorded a surplus of 330 billion dollars. Mexico is a marginal partner in Brazil's foreign trade, accounting for less than 1.3% of its exports in 2014, most of them being absorbed by the United States (80%).

The same phenomenon is observed in Colombia, signatory in 2012 of a free-trade agreement with the United States. Colombian farmers went on strike in August 2103 (and were brutally repressed) in spite of the structural, rather than political, nature of the crisis in rural zones. A curfew had to be imposed in the towns in the impoverished outskirts of Bogotá: Ciudad Bolívar, Suba, Soucha and Rosa. Rubén Dario Lazarralde, a graduate of the University of Miami, is Chief Executive Officer of Indupalma, one of the private groups in the African palm oil market. It owns some 427.000 hectares of land in Colombia (156.000 ha in 2000), a sector where farm workers went on strike for 100 days in 2013[1]. His appointment as Minister of Agriculture and Rural Development is considered a strange choice at a time when farming is at the heart of negotiations with the Revolutionary Armed Forces of Colombia (FARC) in the peace process initiated in Havana in 2012 and finally concluded in September 2015.

Samuel Pinheiro Guimarães, then chair of the Itamaraty think tank (Institute of Research in International Relations), owes his dismissal in March 2001 by the Minister of External Relations in the Cardoso government, Celso Lafer, to his public opposition to the Free Trade Zone. President Fernando Henrique Cardoso would eventually be swayed by the arguments of the man who would become the mentor for Brazilian diplomacy in the Lula years: the opening up of trade accentuated asymmetries among the regional economies and did not remove the tariff barriers used and abused by the United States to protect its domestic market (antidumping legislation, compensatory rights, subsidies and grants, phytosanitary measures, etc.), which Washington made clear were not negotiable. And we must not forget the importance of competition from European Union industry once the common external tariff is abrogated in Mercosur. The High Representative of Mercosur, named in February 2015, the Brazilian federal deputy Florisvaldo Fier (President from 2008 to 2009 of ParlaSul, the Mercosur parliament), underscored the constant opposition to Mercosur by the United States in his comments in July 2015[2].

---

1. *Prensa Fensuagro, "Trabajadores de la Palma, esclavos siglo 21"* (Palm Oil Workers: 21st century slaves), YouTube, September 19, 2013.

2. Dario Pignotti, "Florisvaldo Fier, "El Mercosul siempre disgustó a EE.UU" (Florisvaldo Fier, high representative of the Brazilian government to Mercosur: "Mercosur always angers U.S."), *Página12*, July 17, 2015.

Brazil demanded concessions on access to the North American market for sensitive products (ethanol, for example: after 30 years of effort, it finally obtained the abrogation of import taxes and subsidies in December 2011) but did not make efforts in many other sectors (industrial property, services, standards). The United States, on the other hand, demanded concessions in these sectors and referred topics directly regarding Brazil (dumping, export subsidies) to the World Trade Organization. In April 2010, the World Trade Organization deemed U.S. subsidies to its cotton producers illegal and authorized Brazil to impose tariffs amounting to a total of 829 million dollars on U.S. goods. A bilateral agreement that year finally ended the eight-year dispute.

The refusal of the United States to open its markets to agricultural *products from Brazil (particularly orange juice, meat and sugar)* undermined the position of a pro-FTAA lobby led by representatives of the private sector and, within the Brazilian government, by the ministers of agriculture and foreign trade, whose priorities are out of sync with Itamaraty.

The former minister of Development, Industry and Foreign Trade in the Fernando Henrique Cardoso government, José Botafogo Gonçalves, judged the priority given to Mercosur as exaggerated, marginalizing Brazil in the free-trade negotiations currently underway. This is also the opinion of the president of the Association of Foreign Trade ("*Associação do Comércio Exterior do Brasil*" – AEB), José Augusto de Castro, for whom Mercosur has "*ceased to be a trade agreement and has become an ideological agreement*"[1]. This critical stance is generally echoed in the main Brazilian media[2], which are aligned with North American business circles. President Rousseff's Minister of Strategic Affairs, Roberto Mangabiera Unger, Harvard professor, who exercised a similar function during Lula's second term (October 2007 – June 2009), favors a reorientation of priorities toward a partnership with the United States and bilateral agreements rather than Mercosur[3]. This reorientation of trade policy toward the United States is supported by the major Brazilian media, the powerful Federation of Industries of the State of São Paulo (FIESP) and nostalgic diplomats, such as the President of the Brazil-United States Council of Industries, Rubens Barbosa, former Brazilian Ambassador to Washington (1999-2004), a prolific writer who frequently contributes columns in major newspapers in favor of this reorientation. They underlined that America remains the world´s economic hegemon even as its share of the global economy has fallen. The Uruguayan president, José Mujica, denounced this lobby centered in the economic capital of the country, São Paulo, and pushing for rapprochement with the United

---

1. *O´Globo*, February 15, 2003.

2. "O autismo da política de comércio exterior" (The autism of foreign trade policy), editorial in *O´Globo*, February 26, 2013.

3. Eliane Oliveira, "Mangabeira: Mercosur é corpo sem espírito e foco deve ser EUA" (Mangabeira: Mercosur is a body without a soul, focus should be on the USA), *O´Globo*, 9 mai 2015.

States at the cost of stronger regional integration: "*The principal obstacle to uniting all of Latin America is the São Paulo's bourgeoisie*"[1].

The establishment of the European Economic Community introduced some friction into the traditionally harmonious trade relations with Europe (with rare exceptions such as the "lobster war" with France in 1961-1963) because of discriminatory preferences introduced by Articles 131-136 of the Treaty of Rome conferring privileged status on former French and Belgium colonies in Africa. Relations with the principal European countries were later normalized in bilateral agreements, but cooperation between Brazil and the EEC remained limited in spite of the agreement signed in 1997. The first summit meeting between the European Union, Latin American and Caribbean (UE-LAC) heads of state in Rio de Janeiro in 1999 resulted in the establishment of a committee to negotiate easing of trade restrictions. To date, a total of six EU-LAC summits have been held. While a 20-year treaty (Cotonou Agreement) was signed with the countries of the Caribbean (and Africa and the Pacific Group of States) in June 2000, and an association agreement was signed in May 2010 with Central American countries at the Madrid Summit, as regards negotiations with the EU, Mercosur has yet to achieve success.

It would be with Brazil that a strategic partnership was established at the Brazil-EU summit in July 2007[2]. The European Union is Brazil's fifth trading partner while Brazil represents less than 2% of EU trade. The balance of trade in goods has been running a deficit for the European Union for the past twelve years. Brazil's position on the Mercosur-European Union negotiations may be altered by pressure from the Brazilian private sector if the Brazilian currency continues to depreciate. At the Mercosur-EU summit in Brasilia in January 2013, President Dilma Rousseff and the President of the European Commission, José Manuel Barroso, agreed to resume negotiations. In Brussels during the summit between the European Union and the Community of Latin American and Caribbean States (CELAC) in June 2015, President Dilma Rousseff, confronting stagflation (stagnation + inflation) expressed her hope for an agreement as soon as 2015, emphasizing that trade between the two blocs had grown from 90 billion dollars in 2000 to 267 billion dollars in 2014 and should be codified and consolidated in the future[3]. Among Mercosur

---

[1]. The bourgeoisie of São Paulo, "*El principal obstáculo que tenemos para unir a toda Latinoamérica es la burguesia paulista*", in *"Una oveja negra al poder. Confesiones e intimidades de Pepe Mujica"* (A Black Sheep in Power: Confessions and intimacies of Pepe Mujica), Andrés Danza, Tulbovitz (p.278), Editorial Sudamericana, Buenos Aires, 2015.

[2]. The European Union established what were termed "strategic partnerships" with the United States, Japan, Canada, India, Russia, China and South Africa.

[3]. Fernando Eichenberg, "Dilma pressiona por acordo entre Mercosul e EU" (Dilma pressing for agreement between Mercosur and EU), *O 'Globo*, June 11, 2015.

countries, Argentina was certainly the most hesitant regarding the agreement[1]. In any case, no result is expected prior to the Argentine presidential election (October 2015).

The announcement of free-trade negotiations between the United States and the European Union doubtlessly influenced Brazil's decision in this regard as did the negotiations between Canada and the European Union.

For the time being, Brazil favors Mercosur, which received 12% of its exports in 2011 (excluding Venezuela), placing it ahead of the United States. Most importantly, it took in close to one fourth of Brazil's manufacturing output. The volume of trade within Mercosur has developed considerably over the past twenty years: 20 billion dollars in 1998; 39 billion in 2007; 62 billion in 2011[2]. But Brazil's share of exports has diminished slightly in recent years (13.7% in 2007; 12.7% in 2011). Brazil is currently working to bring Ecuador into Mercosur, having overcome the differences that marred relations between the two countries in the period 2008-2010 and has implemented new infrastructure projects (the Manduriaco hydroelectric project, in which Odebrecht was once again involved). Surinam and Guyana have been admitted as associate members. A candidate since December 2012, Bolivia joined Mercosur in March 2015.

However these investments are still limited in proportion to Brazil's share of its economy (65% of Mercosur GDP) and trade. With its main trade partner, Argentina, which sells 21% of its exports (42% of its industrial exports) to Brazil and 82% of its automobile production in 2010, Brazil is only the fourth largest investor. In March 2013, the Vale do Rio Doce mining company threatened to withdraw investments of some 5.9 billion dollars, Brazil's largest foreign investment, in a potassium mine (Rio Colorado, Mendoza Province) employing 6.000 miners. Marco Aurélio Garcia, presidential foreign policy advisor, offered to act as a mediator during Dilma Rousseff's visit to Buenos Aires in April 2013.

The Mercosur Structural Convergence Fund (FOCEM) was a Brazilian initiative, and Brazil is its principal contributor. FOCEM seeks to smooth out imbalances among the economies of the member countries and develop interregional infrastructure. For example, the Brazilian Development Bank (BNDES) is financing, to the tune of 400 million dollars, the construction of a highway connecting the Brazilian state of Acre to the Pacific. Argentina and Brazil have a similar profile as regards trade in grain; they are among the world's top soy and corn exporters. Argentina exports 80% of its production, Brazil 40%. But the contribution of these exports to the national budget is

---

[1]. Federico Kucher, "Timerman adelantó que no habrá acuerdo Mercosur-Unión Europea por ahora. Em suspenso hasta que haya garantias" (Timerman said no Mercosur-EU agreement yet: suspended while awaiting guarantees), *Página12*, June 11, 2015.

[2]. Ministry of External Relations, June 2012 (Comercio Exterior Mercosur. Ministerio das Relações exteriores).

greater in Argentina, the taxes (*retenciones*) applied to them correspond to 45% of the budget.

Brazil is a prudent member of the new Latin American financial architecture composed of the Bank of the South (created in 2009 with headquarters in Caracas and capital of 20 billion dollars) and the Southern Monetary Fund, whose aim is to control capital flows and resolve specific trade imbalances, the Latin American equivalent of the International Centre for Settlement of Investment Disputes (ICSID), which is a member of the World Bank Group. Bolivia and Ecuador withdrew from ICSID in 2007 and 2008, respectively.

Former president Fernando Henrique Cardoso wrote in one of his books that if forced to choose between friendship with Argentina, regional integration and a seat on the Security Council, he would not hesitate to opt for Brazil's regional partner[1]. However, the leaning toward Argentina, leitmotif in Brazilian presidencies since 1980, has not found easy consolidation or a mutual and durable entente. The importance of trade (Brazil is Argentina's largest customer and largest supplier), the intensity of political dialog, the shared vigilance regarding the democratic process on the continent, and convergence in the realm of world government (greater voice for emerging countries in international economics and finance) do not prevent the expression of a deep reluctance rooted subconsciously in every Argentine – deriving, no doubt, from the conviction of a missed historical opportunity, in a country so humanly and naturally well endowed, with pro-European intellectual and cultural leanings – because of the growing disparity between their economies and respective fields of diplomacy. The World Economic Forum competitivity rankings for 2012-2013 places Argentina in 94th position among 144 countries, far behind its main regional partner (48th). The bitter realization of the diverging evolution of these two countries over the past fifty years underpins the current reluctance of Argentine leaders to envisage a seat for Brazil on the Security Council as the sole representative of Latin America.

The Security Council

Cordell Hull (1871-1955), 1945 Nobel Peace Prize laureate, U.S. Secretary of State during the Second World War, wrote in his memoir that President Roosevelt was in favor of a permanent seat for Brazil on the Security Council[2]. But Stalin considered Brazil to be a natural ally of the United States, which also wanted to see China (under Chiang Kai-shek) on the Council.

Brazil first requested a permanent seat on the United Nations Security Council in 1989 during a speech by President Sarney before the United Nations. Brazil and India opposed the proposal by the working group in 1992 of a quick fix allowing only Germany and Japan to join the Council. Brazil and

---

1. Fernando Henrique Cardoso, *A Arte da politica. A Historia que vivi* (The Art of Politics: History that I Lived), 2006.

2. *The Memoirs of Cordell Hull*, Hodder and Stoughton, London, 1948.

India wanted to see the entry of developing countries, while accepting, at least in the initial stage, that these new permanent members would not have veto rights.

"*We must be realistic*", says Celso Amorim, pointing out that China would never admit Japan to the Security Council with veto powers, Russia would not admit Germany, nor would the United States concede veto rights to developing countries[1].

Brazil defended this position within the United Nations Blue-Ribbon Panel (High Level Panel on Threats, Challenges and Change) of 15 experts organized by Kofi Annan, chaired by the Brazilian diplomat João Clemente Baena Soares, former Secretary-General of the Organization of American States. The fact remains that Celso Amorim has continued to point out the "*total lack of transparency*" that he sees as characterizing talks among the permanent members of the Security Council, the five members with veto rights refusing to engage in these talks in the great majority of cases[2].

Outside of the 59th General Assembly of the United Nations in September 2004, President Lula united with the German Minister of Foreign Affairs (Joschka Fischer), the Prime Minister of India (Manmohan Singh) and the Prime Minister of Japan (Junichiro Koizumi) to found the G4 group of nations and push for a reform of the Security Council. In July 2005, the Group proposed a resolution to reform the Council by increasing the current number of members: six permanent seats without veto rights (two for Africa, two for Asia, one for Eastern Europe, one for Latin America and the Caribbean) and four alternating non-permanent seats covering the same geographical areas. The project was supported in particular by France, but it ran into opposition from the U.S. representative John Bolton[3], which probably caused Japan to announced its withdrawal from the G4 in January 2006. Germany opposed the American intervention in Iraq and lost the support of the United States. The German example demonstrates, according to our contacts in Itamaraty, the anachronistic structure of the Security Council: more than twenty years after the end of the Cold War, Germany, albeit in the top ranks of all other organs of world governance, occupies a secondary position in the United Nations, in virtue of Article 107 of the UN Charter, known as the "enemy states clause" and now fallen into disuse, even though it is the third largest financial contributor to the regular and peacekeeping operations budgets after the United States and Japan.

---

1. Celso Amorim, *Conversas com jovems diplomatas* (Conversations with young diplomats), Ed. Benvira, São Paulo, 2011.

2. "A declaração de Teerã: oportunidade perdida?" p.91, in *"Teerã, Ramalá e Doha, memórias da política externa ativa e altiva"* (Tehran, Ramallah and Doha – Memories of an Active and Generous Foreign Policy), 2015.

3. John Bolton, *Surrender is not an option: defending America at the United Nations and abroad*, Threshold, New York, 2007, p.213-215.

While the United States recognized and supported India's claim (speech by President Barack Obama on November 9, 2010 in New Delhi) doubtlessly with the intention of countering China, it has yet to speak out in favor of Brazil's entry as permanent member, in spite of insistence on this point by the Brazilian media during the U.S. president's visit to Brasilia in March 2011. Argentina, Brazil's main regional partner, has not recognized Brazil's claim and seeks the suppression of veto right and the adoptions of resolutions by consensus within the Security Council.

A reform of the Security Council, after the rearrangements instituted in 1965 (Resolution 1990 that expanded the Council from 11 to 15 members and the majority from seven to nine votes, without altering the veto rights of the five permanent members), is confronted with this impossible problem: how to give greater representativeness to an institution that receives 25% of its funding from the world's premier power (39.89% in 1945), which contributes 27% of its peacekeeping forces, when one of the objectives of the reform is to contain military supremacy and hegemony? In terms of value, Brazil is the 11th contributor to the budget of the Organization and the 13th to its peacekeeping missions.

CHAPTER 3

REDUCING ECONOMIC VULNERABILITY

Brazil seeks to reduce its economic vulnerability by accessing new markets to improve its balance of payments. It seeks a "*new economic and commercial geography*" in the words of President Lula. Hence the recent interest in the Middle East and non-Portuguese Africa, an initiative inherited by President Dilma Rousseff. She appointed former President Lula as her special envoy and head of the Brazilian delegation to the African Union summit in Equatorial Guinea in June 2011.

Arab Countries

President Lula's tour of five Arab countries[1] in December 2003 was the first by a Brazilian head of state. Lebanese president, Emile Lahoud, and the king of Morocco, Mohammed VI, made official visits to Brasilia in 2004; Algerian president, Abdelaziz Bouteflika, followed suit in 2005. Another visit by a Lebanese president (Michel Suleiman) would take place in 2010.

A first summit between Arab and South American countries, a Brazilian initiative, was held in Brasilia in May 2005 with 33 countries in attendance (all countries from the Arab world, excluding Israel but including Yemen and Djibouti), the Arab League and the UNASUL representatives. The resulting Brasilia Declaration testified to a shared vision of regional current issues: the establishment of a nuclear-weapon-free zone in the Middle East; the establishment of an independent Palestinian State according to 1967 borders; the withdrawal of Israel from the Occupied Territories; reaffirmation of the pivotal role of the United Nations in the reconstruction of Iraq; and the condemnation of American sanctions against Syria.

A second took place in Doha, Qatar in March 2009. A third summit was scheduled for Lima in 2011, but was postponed due to the developments associated with the Arab Spring. It was finally held in October 2012. An action plan for South America was adopted at this meeting, coordinated by the Arab and South American Library and Research Center (bibliASPA), located in São Paulo. The Ministers of Culture of Arab and South American countries met on two occasions, in February 2006 in Algiers and in May 2009 in Rio de Janeiro. The IV ASPA Summit of heads of state and government is scheduled for November 2015 in Riyadh, Saudi Arabia.

These ministerial gatherings offered Brazil a new opportunity – and Turkey a resumed opportunity – for influence in the Middle East. Brasilia feels that the

[1] In Egypt, Syria, Lebanon, Libya, United Arab Emirates.

United States, France and Great Britain have too long worked to prop up unpopular regimes in the region at the cost of democracy, favoring a status quo instead of political openness, motived by economic interest (oil, arms, etc.), clientelism, and the fear of a fundamentalist Islamist takeover, whether through violence or elections.

A free trade agreement is being negotiated with Jordan and with the Gulf Cooperation Council states. After Israel (2007) and Egypt (2010), Mercosur signed a trade agreement with the Palestinian National Authority in Montevideo during the 42nd summit, which was the first one to feature the participation of Ecuadorian president Rafael Correa. Agreements should soon be signed with Lebanon and Tunisia. A defense cooperation agreement was signed with Dubai when the emir – who is also the Prime Minister of the United Arab Emirates – visited Brasilia in May 2014.

Brazil has held observer status at the Arab League since 2003 and maintains embassies in 17 of the 22 League countries (excluding Yemen, Bahrain, Comoros, Djibouti and Somalia). President Lula traveled to Israel, the West Bank and Jordan in March 2010. The Secretary General of the Arab League visited Brazil three times during Lula's presidency.

Trade between Brazil and the Arab countries increased from 5.48 billion dollars in 2003 to 19.58 billion in 2010[1] and to 28.83 billion dollars in 2012 with a slight but stable surplus for Brazil (in 2013 trade totaled 25.42 billion dollars[2]). Bilateral trade with the United Arab Emirates grew from 550 million dollars in 2003 to 2.6 billion dollars in 2013.

In March 2012, Mubadala, an investment and development company situated in Abu Dhabi (United Arab Emirates), acquired a 2-billion-dollar share in the private Brazilian oil group, EBX (5.63% of group stock). The financial woes of the group's president, Eike Batista, whose assets were seized by the Brazilian courts, and the bankruptcy of his principal companies led the Arab investment fund to cut its losses by accepting a 10% share in the mining company MMX as part of a receivership arrangement and reorganization of the holding company. The fund, controlled by the hereditary Prince Mohammed Bin Zayed Al Nahyan, now holds a 65% stake in the harbor terminal currently under construction near Rio de Janeiro, Porto Sudeste[3].

In October 2014, the former Minister of Foreign Relations, Luiz Alberto Figuereido, and Eduardo Santos, then Secretary General of Itamaraty, organized a meeting in the Egyptian embassy in Brasilia of 18 ambassadors from Arab countries, constituting the Council of Arab Ambassadors to Brazil, whose senior member is the representative from Palestine, Ibrahim Alzeben.

---

1. Source: Brazilian Ministry of External Relations, *Política Externa*, vol. 20, August 2011.

2. Brazil-Arab News Agency, Arab-Brazilian Chamber of Commerce, October 24, 2014 (www2.anba.com.br).

3. Mariana Sallowicz, Oscar Naiana, "O fundo que controla o que restou do império X" (The fund that controls what remains of Empire X), *O Estado de São Paulo*, June 8, 2015.

There is a significant and perfectly integrated Arab community in Brazil (10 million Brazilians are of Arab ancestry). This community is larger than its counterparts in Guyana and Suriname, which are members of the Organization of Islamic Cooperation, which is headquartered in Jeddah (Saudi Arabia) and numbers 57 states. Brazil requested observer status in 2011. When Israel attacked Lebanon in July 2006, Itamaraty ordered the evacuation of more than 3,000 Brazilian nationals, principally to Adana in Turkey.

There is no evidence of Islamophobia in Brazilian society. One does not see the controversies witnessed in France regarding the use of the burka and veil, or the secularism imposed in public spaces, schools and universities. There is nothing like the censorship enacted in Switzerland in the referendum prohibiting the construction of minarets. In its approach to the Arab world, Brazil can boast a model of religious syncretism, tolerance and integration, one that is free of a colonial past and dependence on foreign oil and massive arms contracts. In July 2012, Itamaraty organized an international conference in Brasilia titled "Side by Side – Peacebuilding in the Middle East: A Role for the Diasporas"[1]. Invitees included Middle Eastern intellectuals and representatives of the Jewish and Muslim communities in Brazil and the Mercosur countries.

Africa

The first Africa-Latin America summit, a Brazilian initiative, took place in Abuja (Nigeria) in November 2006. The second summit was held in Venezuela in September 2009. The 3rd South America-Africa summit, attended by President Dilma Rousseff and former president Lula, took place in Malabo (Equatorial Guinea) in 2013. The proposal to create a trust fund (which had already been advanced at the Margarita summit in Venezuela) to which all countries would contribute, especially the major ones (Algeria, South Africa, Nigeria, Angola, Brazil, Venezuela, Argentina), was again addressed but no significant decision was reached. Equatorial Guinea affirmed its grant of 30 million dollars for a solidarity fund to be managed by FAO (Food and Agriculture Organization of the United Nations). The 4th summit is planned for 2016 in Ecuador.

President Lula had organized a Brazil-Africa cooperation and trade forum in March 2003 in Fortaleza (state of Ceará). During the African Union summit in Sirte (Libya), where he was invited as guest of honor in July 2009, Lula pledged to develop a food assistance program for African countries. The first Brazil-Africa forum on food security, rural development and the fight against hunger with the ministers of agriculture and the Director General of FAO, took place in Brasilia in May 2010. Extending its *Bolsa Família* social welfare program, Brazil provides some 2.4 million dollars to projects in Ethiopia, Malawi, Mozambique, Niger and Senegal. An Africa-Brazil program for social

[1]. "*Lado a lado – a construção da paz no Oriente Médio, um papel para as diásporas.*"

development, inspired by cooperation between Brazil and Ghana in this realm and also supported by the United Kingdom, was implemented in March 2008 with the participation of six African countries[1].

The Brazilian Cooperation Agency, affiliated with the Ministry of External Relations, now provides 60% of its credit to Africa, where it participates in projects in 18 countries. The Brazilian Corporation of Agricultural Research (*Empresa Brasiliera de Pesquisa Agropecuária* - EMBRAPA) has opened a regional office in Accra, Ghana. A vocational training center has been inaugurated in Equatorial Guinea. A model cotton farm has been established as a joint venture with Mali. A cooperative water management project was implemented with Benin, Angola, Mozambique, Guinea and Cape Verde following the Africa-Brazil-Bahia Forum on this issue in Salvador (Bahia) in December 2008. Brazil has proved willing to help African countries benefit from its experience in school meal programs. An agreement was signed in this regard in August 2013 with FAO, whose Director General is Brazilian.

Equatorial Guinea, the only Spanish-speaking country in Africa, has recognized Portuguese as an official language in order to be accepted into the Community of Portuguese Language Countries, created by Brazilian initiative in July 1996 and headquartered in Lisbon[2]. Inspired by the Francophone Space, this group was proposed in 1989 during a cultural gathering in the state of Maranhão to which President Sarney, a native of that state, had invited the presidents of Portugal, Angola, Mozambique, Equatorial Guinea, Cape Verde, and São Tomé and Principe. However, beyond cooperation projects to fight AIDS and institute centers for vocational training and public administration, the Community has little substance.

In spite of this, cultural exchange and cooperation within the group has been very fertile. An international meeting titled "Conference of Intellectuals of Africa and the Diaspora" was organized in Salvador, Bahia, Brazil in July 2006 by Lula's minister of culture, Gilberto Gil in response to a suggestion by the President of Senegal, Abdoulaye Wade. A cultural cooperation program has been implemented with Ivory Coast and Senegal. A host of artistic events celebrating African descent have been organized in recent years: the 6th edition of the Latin American Women's Festival (Brasilia, July 2013), the 8th Africa-Brazil Culture of African Descent Prize (São Paulo, May 2013), 7th Brazil, Africa and Caribbean Black Cinema Festival (Rio de Janeiro, December 2013), 2nd Afro-Latino and Caribbean Meeting (Salvador, 2010), Latin American and Caribbean Women's Festival (Brasilia, July 2013). Brazil was the guest of honor at the Annual Lagos Black Festival in Nigeria in October 2013.

Brazil has opened 19 new embassies in Africa since 2002 (bringing its current total on the continent to 37). Over the course of his two presidential terms, Lula made twelve official visits to Africa. Brazil-Africa trade is

---

1. Angola, Ghana, Mozambique, Namibia, Kenya, Tanzania.

2. The Community includes: Angola, Cape Verde, Equatorial Guinea, Mozambique, Portugal, East Timor and São Tomé.

developing quite significantly (5 billion dollars in 2002; 26 billion dollars in 2008; 39 billion dollars in 2012), constituting an export market that is larger than Germany and Japan. Brazil's principal trading partner in the region is Nigeria (with trade in 2012 on the order of 9 billion dollars). Brazil helped fund the first public university in Cape Verde, created in April 2005. Three thousand Cape Verde students are enrolled in the Brazilian university; some 500 São Tomé families benefit from the Brazilian federal welfare program *Bolsa Família.*

The Oswaldo Cruz Institute (Fiocruz), a prominent Brazilian healthcare research center, opened a facility in Mozambique in October 2008 where Brazil is working to build an anti-retrovirus production unit. The Africa-Brazil Conference on AIDS was held in Belém in May 2010 with five English-speaking countries attending (Botswana, Ghana, Kenya, Tanzania and Zambia). One adult out of five in Africa is a carrier of HIV. Sub-Saharan Africa alone accounts for 69% of the world's AIDS cases. One million two hundred thousand Africans die each year from the disease.

In 2011, Brazil signed 53 cooperation agreements in the field of healthcare with 22 countries on the African continent. In the realm of medicine, Cuba is the only Latin American country with more extensive cooperation projects with Africa.

With its BRIC partners China and India, Brazil offers an advantageous alternative to the African countries, which find themselves engaged in an overly exclusive dialog with the former colonial powers. Africa was the source of 2.8% of direct foreign investments in 2011 (approx. 42 billion dollars), with a growing portion from developing or transitioning countries (53% in 2001)[1]. The Indian Import-Export Bank offers easy terms to sub-Saharan countries and takes in 1,600 African students each year. In July 2012, China, which has a volume of trade with Africa on the order of 200 billion dollars, announced a pledge to increase its prime rate lending by 20 billion dollars in 2013-2018. Zambia offers an example of this tripartite aid: in 2010, China provided foreign direct investment of 57.8 million dollars for the construction of nine field hospitals; India provided credit lines of 125 million dollars for the construction of a hydroelectric plant; Brazil invested massively in the Konkola copper mines and the Brazilian firm Vale do Rio Doce initiated a joint venture with the South African mining company Rainbow, with an investment on the order of 400 million dollars for mineral prospecting.

At the fifth Tokyo International Conference on African Development (TICAD), held every five years, Japan provided preferential financing, however this public aid was not relayed via the private sector, which is reluctant to invest in Africa, an exception only being made for South Africa.

However, the slowing of economic growth in Africa countries in 2011 (falling to close to half the rate in 2010 according to the UN Economic Commission for Africa) due to the recession in the European Union countries,

[1] Report on World Investment, UNCTAD, June 2012.

Africa's main economic partner, marked the limits to this trade. Exports from sub-Saharan African countries to the United States fell by 33% in 2012 (49.7 billion dollars[1]) with respect to the previous year (74 billion dollars) in spite of a measure approved by Congress in May 2000 and extending until 2015 to sustain African economies by facilitating access to the American market to those countries that continued to move toward a market-based economy (Africa Growth and Opportunity Act). In truth, African exports to the United States derive principally from three countries (Nigeria, Angola and South Africa) with oil being the main commodity. Regarding purchases, following the scheme that has become traditional in many developing countries, including Cuba, we see a significant portion of imports of grain and food products benefiting from overseas subsidies, making the costs much more advantageous within a free-trade framework than if they were locally grown.

The structure of trade with Brazil is also concentrated on just a few countries (Nigeria, Angola, South Africa) and investments go to a relatively small number of companies and markets: oil (Petrobras: Nigeria, Cape Verde, Tanzania, São Tomé), mining (Vale do Rio Doce: Zambia, Guinea, Liberia, Mozambique, South Africa), infrastructure (Odebrecht: Angola, South Africa, Botswana, Congo, Djibouti, Gabon, Mozambique, Liberia), rolling stock (Marco Polo: South Africa).

Brazil increased its lines of credit to Angola in 2004, particularly to allow completion of the Capanda hydroelectric plant, a project in which the Brazilian firm Odebrecht participated. That same year, Brazil canceled Mozambique's debt, amounting to 331 million dollars. The Brazilian hydrocarbon exploration firm Petrobras made its largest foreign investment (2.3 billion dollars) in Nigeria, Brazil's premier trading partner in the region (9 billion dollars in 2012, of which 8.4 billion going to Nigerian crude oil imports). In May 2012, during a seminar on Africa organized in Rio de Janeiro by the public development bank BNDES, the private Brazilian bank BTG Pactual announced the creation of an investment fund worth one billion dollars to co-finance the priority projects in the Programme for Infrastructure Development in Africa (PIDA), led by a group of multilateral institutions.

Brazil has also provided support to Namibia to delimit an exclusive economic zone and train officers in the Namibian navy.

Brazil helped bring the Community of Latin American and Caribbean States (CELAC), created in Caracas in December 2011, closer to Africa. This rapprochement was facilitated by Cuba in its role as *pro tempore* president in 2013. Instrumental here were the close relations Cuba had developed with many African countries (19 African countries have opened embassies in Havana) through its support for independence and anti-Apartheid movements and its exemplary cooperation initiatives in the medical field since the 1960s[2].

---

1. U.S. Department of Commerce (International Trade Administration).

2. Patrick Howlett-Martin, "*La Coopération médicale internationale de Cuba : l'altruisme récompensé*" (Cuba's international medical cooperation: altruism repaid), L'Harmattan, Paris, 2015.

President Dilma Rousseff took part in the 50th anniversary of the Organization of African Unity (African Union) in Addis Ababa in May 2013. The union includes 53 countries with Haiti as an observer member. Madagascar, Egypt and Guinea-Bissau were suspended temporarily but have been readmitted; the Central African Republic remains suspended. The Brazilian president and the Cuban representative (Estaban Lazo Hernández, president of the National Assembly of People's Power) were the only authorities from the Americas invited to speak on that occasion.

It was Rousseff's third trip to Africa in three months. While there, she announced the cancellation of the debt of 12 African countries, totaling 900 million dollars, most of it dating to the 1970s and renegotiated. Speaking before the senate in July 2013, she endorsed amnesty and rescheduling of the debts contracted by the Republic of the Congo (Congo-Brazzaville), the Democratic Republic of the Congo (Congo-Kinshasa), Sudan, Gabon, Zambia, Tanzania, Ivory Coast and Equatorial Guinea, bringing it down to a total of 787 million dollars[1]. Brazil forgave 80% of the 352.6 million-dollar debt owed by the Republic of the Congo and rescheduled the rest. Brazil's opposition party and media reacted very negatively to this controversial measure, claiming that it benefited contested regimes whose leaders were known for their corruption and nepotism[2]. Debt forgiveness allowed Brazil's public development bank (BNDES) to resume financing of Brazilian businesses operating in those countries (financing is granted to countries that commit to including Brazilian companies in invited tenders).

Brazilian relations with Africa, characterized by particular historical circumstances associated with a dramatic phenomenon that still exerts an immense impact on Brazilian society today – slavery – and which were somewhat handicapped by Brazil's loyalty to Portugal up to the Carnation Revolution (*Revolução dos Cravos*) of April 25, 1974, certainly go well beyond mercantile or humanitarian considerations. Africa sees itself reflected in Brazil's emergence and is proud of its contribution. Testifying to the emotion that marked the official visit by President Lula and his ministers to the World Social Forum in February 2011 in Dakar, Gilberto Gil composed a song in French emblemizing these relations:

---

1. Million dollars: Congo-Brazzaville (352.6), Tanzania (236.9), Zambia (113.4), Sudan (43), Gabon (24), Congo-Kinshasa (4.7), Equatorial Guinea (12), Ivory Coast (1.2).

2. "Paises pobres, presidentes ricos. Ditadores perdoados" (Poor countries, rich presidents. Dictators pardoned), *O'Globo*, August 4, 2013.

La Lune de Gorée[1]

La lune qui se lève
Sur l'île de Gorée
C'est la même lune qui
Sur tout le monde se lève

Mais la lune de Gorée
A une couleur profonde
Qui n'existe pas du tout
Dans d'autres parts du monde
C'est la lune des esclaves
La lune de la douleur

Mais la peau qui se trouve
Sur les corps de Gorée
C'est la même peau qui couvre
Tous les hommes du monde

Mais la peau des esclaves
A une douleur profonde
Qui n'existe pas du tout
Chez d'autres hommes du monde
C'est la peau des esclaves
Un drapeau de Liberté

From the 16th to the 19th century, four million men and women were transported to Brazil and enslaved. Segregation still lies at the heart of the socioeconomic inequality in this country of 191 million, where 7.6% are black and 43.1% of mixed race. After the *tropicalismo* of the 1960s and the concepts of "cultural anthropology" and "racial democracy" so dear to Jorge Amado, Brazil has embraced the movements of black people in the Caribbean and Central America and takes part in the principal regional events: World Summit of Afro-Descendants (Honduras 2011, Panama 2012); International Forum on Afro-Descendants and the Decolonialization of Memory (Venezuela 2012); Afro-Latin and Caribbean Encounters (Cuba 2012).

Brazilian diplomacy has yet to take a stand in the debate over reparations relating to slavery that characterized the 34th CARICOM summit held in July 2013 in Port-of-Spain. Four Caribbean states (Antigua, Jamaica, Barbados, Suriname) instituted commissions to assess the means of compensation that would be asked of the former colonial powers (Great Britain, France and the Netherlands) that profited from the slave trade. A council led by the Prime Minister of Barbados, Freundel Stuart, was set up to address this issue during the CARICOM summit. The fifteen Caribbean nations created a Reparations Commission in 2013, chaired by Barbados historian Hilary Beckles, Vice Chancellor of the University of the West Indies, whose book *Britain's Black Debt: Reparations for Slavery and Native Genocide*[2], published in 2012, was an important reference work for CARICOM. The consultancy firm for the

1. The Moon of Gorée: *The moon that rises / over the Isle of Gorée / is the same moon that rises / over the entire world / But the moon of Gorée / has a deep color / that exists nowhere else / in any other part of the world / It is the moon of slaves / the moon of anguish / But the skin that covers / the bodies on Gorée / is the same skin that covers / all people of the world / But the skin of the slaves / has a deep anguish / that exists nowhere else / in other people of the world / It is the skin of slaves / a banner of liberty!*
2. University of the West Indies, 2012.

Caribbean Community is Leigh Day, who obtained a judgment from the Supreme Court in June 2013 against the UK amounting to 305 million dollars in compensation for the torture and killings of more than 100,000 rebels in the Mau-Mau uprising during the Kenyan "Emergency" of 1952-1960.

We must also take into account the strong penetration in Africa since 1992 of the Brazilian Universal Church of the Kingdom of God *(Igreja Universal do Reino de Deus)*, founded by the evangelist Edir Macedo in an impoverished suburb of Rio de Janeiro in 1977. Hundreds of Brazilian pastors from the church have lived in Africa, initially in the Portuguese-speaking countries (mainly Angola and Mozambique) and later also in South Africa, Botswana, Kenya, Uganda and in French-speaking Africa. Controlling, as in Brazil, local television and radio networks, and running charitable and social services associations, the development of this sect is overshadowing the influence of American protestant churches. The event organized by the Universal Church in September 2011 in the national stadium in Maputo, Mozambique, with 42,000 people in the stadium, another 30,000 gathering outside, and Prime Minister Aires Ali and Justice minister Maria Benvida Levy in attendance, testifies to the influence of this Brazilian church. But in Africa the Universal Church does not seek to enter the political arena, as it has in Brazil: Pastor Marcelo Crivella, nephew of Edir Macedo, a missionary in Africa in 1993 and 1994, has been reelected to his senate seat for the state of Rio de Janeiro and has served as a minister in the Rousseff government (February 29, 2012 – May 17, 2014).

The Brazilian president responded sternly to the intervention of the French armed forces in Mali – the deployment of 4,000 troops in the north of the country leading to the killing of 700 islamist militants – seeing "*colonial temptations*" in it. She commented that the armed intervention against Muammar Gaddafi's regime had *"opened a Pandora's box"*.

Brazilian media did not fail to point out the support provided by the United States on that occasion, specifically: the equipping of the African-led International Support Mission to Mali (AFISMA) from U.S. logistics facilities in Freetown (Sierra Leone); intelligence sharing; and the installation of a drone base in Niger, whose uranium mines are exploited by French interests, with some one hundred military personnel[1].

According to our contacts, who spoke with caution, the alliance of islamists with Tuareg tribes in northern Mali, particularly Ansar al-Dine ("defenders of the faith"), led by Iyad Ag Ghaly, and the Azawad National Liberation Movement, the brutal hostage-taking at the Tigantourine gas facility in Algeria by islamist terrorists under the command of Algerian Mokhtar Belmoktar in January 2013, the kidnapping of tourists and foreigners for ransom money, and the May 2013 suicide attacks on a military base in Agadez and on a French mining company in Arlit, in northern Niger, all relate to the still unresolved

[1]. Michael Gordon, Eric Schmitt, "U.S. weighs plan to share information with Algeria", *International Herald Tribune*, February 28, 2013. Scmitt Eric, "Drones in Africa reflect U.S. shift", *International Herald Tribune,* July 11, 2013.

issue of conflicts in the Sahel and to the military intervention in Libya. The majority of the jihadis detained in Bamako belong to northern Malian ethnic groups (Songhai, Fula, Hausa)[1] who have been marginalized following French colonization, and are not foreign fighters. The first war of independence in northern Mali (the first Tuareg rebellion, centered in the Adrar des Ifoghas region), led by Elledi ag Alla, whose father and older brother were executed by the French army in 1954, dates to 1963. Al Qaeda, now held responsible for all evils, had not yet been founded. The rebellion was swiftly and harshly put down by the Malian president Modibo Keïta, who would later be overthrown in a coup d'état in November 1968. The second rebellion began in 1990. However the new Malian president, General Moussa Traoré, was inclined to recognize the legitimacy of the rebels' territorial claims on Mali (formerly the French Sudan) and Niger: traditional Tuareg leadership from Kidal and Ménaka thus gained a presence in parliament. The Tamanrasset Accords (January 1991), the National pact (April 1992), and the World Peace Flame ceremony (March 1996) all sought to integrate the Tuaregs and the Arabs of Azawad into Malian society. The effort did not succeed.

The UN peacekeeping mission to Mali (MINUSMA), deployed to assume partial responsibility from the French contingent (Opération Serval), numbered close to 6.000 soldiers in December 2014, the great majority of them African. Its budget for 2013-2014 was 600 million dollars. Equipment, transportation and logistic support were all primarily provided by the United States.

The United States has spent more than 550 million dollars after the establishment of the U.S. Africa Command (2008) to train West African armies to fight islamist terrorists. More than 19 billion dollars worth of arms were sold to sub-Saharan Africa in 2010. Mainly as part of the Africa Contingency Operations Training and Assistance program (2013), the armies of 35 African countries are trained by American instructors. There have been some one dozen joint military exercises organized under the guidance of the United States since 2013. These exercises have included the participation of a number of non-African countries (Belgium, France, Norway, the Netherlands, Turkey, Italy and others), mostly with colonial background. For example, in 2014 exercises were carried out under the codenames *African Lion* (Morocco), *Western Accord* (Senegal), *Central Accord* (Cameroon), and *Southern Accord* (Malawi), and, annually since 2005, *Flintlock* (in Chad, Niger, Nigeria, Cameroon, and Tunisia). Only two sub-Saharan countries did not take part in the U.S. operations: Eritrea and Zimbabwe.

This training and these exercises have raised legitimate concerns in Brasilia, given the consequences of similar initiatives on Latin American armed forces in the 1970s and '80s, leading to coups and violent repression, and the recent high desertion rate observed in the Malian army, which has been trained since 2008

---

1. "L'avenir judiciaire incertain des djihadistes arrêtés au Mali" (Legal fate uncertain for jihadis arrested in Mali), *Le Monde*, April 8, 2013.

by the United States. The attrition rate over a period of three months (January-April 2012) in an army of 22,000 soldiers fighting combatants numbering in the hundreds speaks volumes in this regard. The instigator of the coup d'état against President Amadou Toumani Touré was the U.S.-trained officer, Amadou Haya Sanogo. Also trained by the United States is the strongman of Burkina Faso, the lieutenant colonel Yacouba Isaac Zida, and the controversial president of Ruanda, Paul Kagamé, who got his training at the Command and General Staff College in Fort Leavenworth.

Joint military exercises have been staged in northwest Africa since 2006. One recently took place on the Mauritanian border (in the cities of Nema, Kiffa and Ayoun) with soldiers from Senegal, Burkina Faso, Chad, Niger and Nigeria, and 250 North American instructors, with the support of officers from France, Italy, the Netherlands and Spain. The United States maintains three bases: in Djibouti, Ethiopia and Burkina Faso. Great importance is attributed to military assistance with only modest support for civil governance: the European Union has allocated credit worth 28 million dollars to improve the legal system in Mali, where corruption is corroding civil institutions; Brazil has put a similar program in place for Tanzania and Guinea.

The president of the European Commission, Jean Claude Junker, announced the creation of an emergency aid fund for Africa in September 2014. Eritrea, the source of 7% of immigrants surveyed in Europe in 2015, might have received 200 million euros in aid but Brussels refused to provide it to Asmara because of the repressive nature of Isaias Afewerki's government, which has held power since independence in 1993[1].

Our contacts believe that a truly effective response to real emerging threats cannot be of military nature. The time of military expeditions is over, as is that of the presidents who were formerly soldiers in the French army (Omar Bongo in Gabon, 1967-2009; Gnassingbé Eyadéma in Togo, 1967-2005), in spite of their succession by their sons (Ali Bongo Ondimba in 2009, Faure Eyadéma in 2005, respectively). These colonial throwbacks keep things from changing, as in Libya or Mali, but they cannot solve the problems underlying the above threats. On the contrary, these military interventions – which result, due to budget limitations, in the creation (by attrition and replacement) of national armed forces with low morale, no regard for the rule of law, and low-paid soldiers and officers sorely tempted by the opportunities offered by corruption and coups d'état – can only engender more violence. There have been three coups d'état in Mali (1991, 2002, 2012) and many in neighboring states: four in the Central African Republic (1965, 1981, 2001, 2003); two in Niger (1996, 2010); five in Burkina Faso (1966, 1980, 1983, 1987, 2015); two in Guinea (1996, 2010); six in Benin (between 1963 and 1972), four in Mauritania (1978, 1984, 2005, 2008), and eight in Nigeria (January 1966, July 1966, 1975, 1976, 1983, 1985, 1990, 1993), and the list is only partial. There have been 85 successful coups d'état in

[1]. John Aglionby, "EU seeks €200m aid agreement with Eritrea", *Financial Times*, September 17, 2015.

Africa in the past fifty years, most of them commanded or supported by foreign powers external to the continent.

Costa Rica is certainly a unique case: the absence of an army was written into its constitution in 1949[1], but it is clear that armed violence in Africa derives predominantly from the legally constituted armies. The Southern Sudanese army has 745 generals[2]. As Victor Hugo once said: "*Wars have all sorts of pretexts, but the cause is always the same: the army. Eliminate the army and you eliminate the war*[3]."

The radicalization of the islamist movements in Somalia (Al-Shabaab), Nigeria (Boko Haram), the Central African Republic (Séléka), movements that spring up in the most disadvantaged regions and in states ranked among the world's most corrupt[4], is proportional to the brutal repression to which these rebellions are or have been subjected. With the exception of Cape Verde and Botswana, there is no African country ranked among the top fifty least corrupt nations in the Corruption Perception Index[5].

Some sixty corpses of partisans or Boko Haram militants, bearing signs of torture, were deposited every day during the second quarter of 2013 at the Maiduguri hospital by the Nigerian army and the para-military forces ("Joint Task Force") for lack of space at the local morgue[6]. In conditions such as these it can come of no surprise to behold appalling abuses such as the killing on July 6, 2013 of 29 students at a school in Potiskum[7] and of more than 50 students at the Gujba College of agriculture in Yobe State by Boko Haram gunmen during the night on September 29, 2013.

"Haram" comes from the Arabic for "forbidden" and "Boko" in the Hausa language means "fake" and has become a synonym for Western education, emblemizing the group's view of Western influence as a sin. Its founder, Mohammed Yusuf, was arrested and then killed while in Army custody on July 30, 2009. Amnesty International has recently painted a distressing picture of the widespread use of torture by Nigerian police[8].

The particularly brutal islamist rebels in the Central African Republic belonging to the Séléka movement ("coalition" in Sango), founded in June 2012 by former self-appointed president Michel Am-Nondokro Djotodia, who hails from the disadvantaged and neglected north of the country, ended the

---

1. Title I, Article 12: "The Army as a permanent institution is abolished." (*Se proscribe el ejército como institución permanente*).
2. Alex Waal, Abdul Mohammed, Handmaiden to Africa's Generals, *International New York Times*, August 15, 2014.
3. Lausanne Peace Conference, September 4, 1869 ("*Les guerres ont toutes sortes de prétextes mais n'ont jamais qu'une cause: l'armée. Ôtez l'armée, vous ôtez la guerre"*). Transparency International, Corruption Perceptions Index 2013.
4. Transparency International, Corruption Perceptions Index 2013
5. Transparency International Corruption Perceptions Index 2013.
6. Adam Nossiter, "Bodies Pour In as Nigeria Hunts for Islamists", *New York Times*, May 7, 2013.
7. "Islamist militants accused in deadly attack on school", *International Herald Tribune*, July 8, 2013.
8. "Welcome to hell fire: Torture and other ill-treatment in Nigeria", Amnesty International, September 18, 2014.

dictatorship of François Bozizé (2002-2013) in March 2013. Michel Djotodia, trained in the former Soviet Union, was the first Muslim to govern a predominantly Christian country. Former president Jean-Bédel Bokassa (1966-1979), a generous friend of former French president Valéry Giscard d'Estaing (1974-1981), did convert temporarily to Islam, but purely for opportunistic reasons in order to receive funding from Libyan leader Muammar Gaddafi, who famously paid the bill (20 million dollars) for Bokassa's absurdly lavish imperial coronation in Bangui on December 4, 1977. He was overthrown in a coup d'état orchestrated and executed by France on September 23, 1979 while on an official visit to Tripoli.

The killings at the Westgate shopping mall in Nairobi by Al-Shabaab militants on September 21, 2013 (67 dead) are linked to the repression exercised in Somalia since 2011 by Kenyan troops. In 2006, after 15 years of war in Somalia, the United States opposed the rise to power of a moderate islamist governing body, the Union of Islamic Courts, and the progressive implementation of a system based on the *sharia.* The Bush government seized the assets of Somalia's most important private group, al-Barakaat, which was suspected of providing support to terrorists in Somalia. The group's banking system (*hawala*) was essential to the survival of the population through remittances from Somali expatriates. Certain employees of this banking system have been detained at Guantanamo without any proof of wrongdoing, including Mohammed Sulaymon Barre, a Somali banker arrested in Pakistan. It was not until February 17, 2012 that the United States lifted its ban on this now debilitated network.

The U.S. encouraged the brutal invasion of Somalia by Ethiopian troops, a country that is predominantly Christian and traditionally hostile to Somali Muslims, which caused more than 16,000 civilian casualties, and two years later the intervention by Kenyan forces, then part of the African Union Mission to Somalia (AMISOM), with the support of Ugandan and Burundian troops, trained and financed by the United States, particularly by Bancroft Global Development, which is headquartered in Washington and provides training to private armies[1].

The car bomb attacks of August 7, 1998 on the U.S. embassies in Nairobi (213 dead, some 4,000 wounded) and Dar es Salaam (11 dead, 85 wounded), killing mainly local civilians, clearly expressed the standards of violence as the systematic execution in Kenya of 148 Christian students at the Garissa University College on April 2, 2015 by gunmen claiming affiliation with Al-Shabaab. The Union of Islamic Courts became radicalized mainly around the militants of Al-Shabaab ("the youth" in Arabic) whose leaders Aden Hashi Farah Ayro and Ahmed Abdi Godane, the secretary general of the Executive Council of the Islamic Courts Union, were killed by U.S. drone strikes, in 2008

[1]. Katharine Houreld, "Bancroft Global Development, U.S. group Advises African Troops in Somalia, *Associated Press*, October 8, 2011.

and 2014 respectively. The looting of the Westgate Mall by Kenyan soldiers while they were supposedly battling terrorists, as reported by the *New York Times*, gives an idea of how they must have behaved in Somalia[1].

The contrast observed in sub-Saharan Africa between the amount of violence (very high) and the incarceration rate (the world's lowest) does not fail to surprise. In South America, the average incarceration rate is 200 detainees for every 100,000 inhabitants (274 in Brazil); for countries in the Sahel (Mali, Mauritania, Burkina Faso, Niger, Ivory Coast, Chad, Benin), the average rate is 50 per 100,000 inhabitants. The highest rates are found in Nigeria (320) and Somalia (136)[2].

The rushed organization of elections in Mali in July 2012 (with date decided and announced tellingly in Paris by the French president) so that the country would be eligible for international aid, without first assuring the bases for governing a country where 80% of the population is illiterate and where 3,200 soldiers from the former colonial power are still stationed, is seen by Brasilia as a recipe for failure. The elections will merely instate the same politicians that plunged the country into the morass in which it now finds itself and international aid will only feed into the traditional system of corruption. Mali is 127th (out of 177, ranging from the least to the most corrupt) on Transparency International's Corruption Perception Index[3].

According to our contacts, a true response must necessarily take the form of a political, economic and social approach that seeks to respond to the demands of islamist movements and of nomadic populations and involve them in the exercise of decentralized power. The nomadic tribes obey local chiefs on the basis of complex hierarchies. Nomads view the state as a foreign power that has been imposed upon them since colonial times and that designates leaders that are generally disregarded. There is an urgent need to respond, through tribal leaders, to the basic needs (health, food, education) of the adherents to the radical movements that have grow out of religious fundamentalism, something that finds fertile ground in the poverty and ignorance of marginalized populations bound by tribal alliances or ethnic ties inherited from their elders and who survive generally within a milieu of illegal trade and trafficking. In dealing with the abhorrent Lord's Resistance Army (LRA) led by the enigmatic Joseph Kony, the International Committee of the Red Cross was certainly not able to prevent the enlistment of child soldiers by this militant group, but did achieve significant improvement in aid to the victims of the conflict in northern Uganda[4].

---

[1]. Jeffrey Gettleman, Nicholas Kulish, Josh Kron, "Thievery Comes After Carnage at Kenya Mall", *New York Times*, October 3, 2013.

[2]. International Centre for Prison Studies, 2012 (www.prisonstudies.org).

[3]. Corruption Perceptions Index, 2013.

.[4] Teresa Whitfield, "External Actors in Mediation", Centre pour le Dialogue Humanitaire (Geneva), February 2010.

Starting with its first summit in Durban in 2002, the African Union established the Peace and Security Council to mediate conflict and crisis situations in Africa. Algerian diplomat Ramtane Lamamra was appointed to lead it and was reelected during the 19th meetings of heads of state in Addis Ababa in July 2012[1]. This mediation is indispensable to prevent the extreme violence that has characterized Africa since the colonial era.

Is the modern-day violence in Africa inseparable from colonial violence? Does it have such a different cause from the Marxist-Leninist rebellions of the Cold-War years, which were brutally put down and their leaders executed? Are not the jihadi movements the heirs of past violence and humiliation and do they not feed off the same miseries?

The answer is complex. The roots are indubitably similar and the extreme violence that characterizes the stem is certainly shared. The British repression of the Mau-Mau revolt, a tribe belonging to the Kikuyues minority in Kenya, between 1952 and 1960 (victims estimated at 100,000-200,000) was finally recognized in June 2013, with retribution of 20 million pounds sterling. But Germany refused to compensate the few descendants of the 50,000-odd Hereo and Namaqua rebels exterminated between 1904 and 1907 by the *Schutztruppe* (German colonial troops) and the survivors imprisoned in the Shark Island concentration camp in Namibia, where Dr. Eugen Fischer conducted scientific experiments foreshadowing those of his colleague Josef Mengele in the Birkenau camp[2]. In March 2014 the University of Freiburg agreed to give up some twenty skulls of people who had been decapitated in prison in the name of science, but hundreds are still in Germany. In August 2015 Zimbabwe president Robert Mugabe demanded the return of the skulls of the leaders of the First *Chimurenga* (the Ndebele and Shona insurrections against administration by the British South Africa Company during the late 1890s), taken home by British troops as war trophies and now exhibited at the London Museum of Natural History[3].

The brutal repressions in French Somaliland in the 1930s; the 1947 insurrection in Madagascar (90,000 dead); violence in Senegal (Thiaroye massacre) and Algeria (Setif and Guelma massacres) in the 1940s, and against the Bamileke people of Cameroon in the 1950s; the deaths of an estimated 6 million persons on the private property of the king of Belgium, now the Democratic Republic of the Congo; the slave trade; apartheid in South Africa tolerated for too long, if not condoned, by the West and Israel; the slaughter in

---

1. Handbook of African Union Practitioners, vol. 3, "Managing Peace Process Towards more Inclusive Process", June 1, 2013.

2. Benjamin Madley, "From Africa to Auschwitz. How German South West Africa Incubated Ideas and Methods Adopted and Developed by the Nazis in Eastern Europe", *European History Quarterly*, Vol.35, 2005.

3. David Smith, "Robert Mugabe tells Natural History Museum to return human skulls", *The Guardian*, August 13, 2015.

Biafra (2 million killed between 1966 and 1970)... Do these not figure somehow in the historiography of current violence[1]?

Is the wanton and uncontrolled use of drones by the American army to fight Al-Shabaab in Somalia, a campaign on which Washington has spent more than one billion dollars, completely unrelated to the killing of 20 Christians in November 2014 and the summary execution of more than 100 Christian Kenyan students at the Garissa University College in April 2015? According to the United Nations[2], some 260,000 people in Somalia, half of them children under the age of 5, died of hunger between 2010 and 2012, a period when nearly one billion dollars in military spending flowed into the country to maintain the African Union's peacekeeping mission and Ethiopian occupation troops.

The examples of Guinea Bissau and Liberia are quite eloquent in this regard: development, education and social justice are worth much more than the holding of elections in societies marked by an appalling illiteracy rate. More than 20 million euros were dedicated by the international community to elections in Guinea Bissau in February 2014, while the power of the army and the plotters behind the April 2012 coup d'état remains fully in place and the social indicators are among the most alarming on the continent (10% infant mortality; life expectancy of less than 46 years; place 168th for literacy according to the United Nations Development Programme).

Brazilian diplomats who have served in Africa see expanding literacy, providing access to decentralized health services, slowly developing uncorrupted public institutions, reducing the armed forces, limiting foreign interference as the only way to address current problems. The fact that healthcare workers in an anti-polio vaccination campaign in the city of Kano (Nigeria) could be targeted by islamist militants testifies to the deep distrust of the West[3], to the trauma of experimental vaccination campaigns under colonial rule, whose victims have yet to be counted, and to issues associated with the fact that in the past, medical care was provided by evangelical churches in a predominantly Muslim country. And we must also mention the vicious acts violence targeting Muslims (the attack on the grand mosque in Kano in December 2014 that killed 120[4]). Nigeria is the largest economy in Africa, with annual oil revenues of some 52 billion dollars while 70% of its population lives on less than a dollar a day. It is in 144th place in Transparency International's

---

1. Cf. the conference organized by the Free University of Brussels and the University of Southern Brittany in Lorient, France in November 2014, ("Massacres and repression in the colonial world. Archives and fictions in the service of historiography or official speeches"). A Brazilian researcher from the Federal University of Juiz de Fora, Fernanda do Nascimento Thomaz, took part in the conference.

2. Robyn Dixon, "U.S. counter-terrorism measures and Islamist militants contributed to the nearly 260 000 deaths in Somalia's 2010-1012 food crisis", *Washington Post*, May 2, 2013.

3 "Gunmen attack polio aid workers in Nigeria", *International Herald Tribune,* February 9-10, 2013.

4 "Attaque meutrière de Boko Haram dans la grande mosquée de Kano" (Deadly attack by Boko Haram in the grand mosque of Kano), *Le Monde*, December 1, 2014.

corruption rankings for 2013 (Somalia, in 177th place, is the most corrupt)[1]. Angola, one of Africa's richest countries, is also one of its most corrupt (153rd). Following a recent on-site investigation, the *New York Times* illustrated the disastrous condition of public health in Angola, particularly the appalling number of children dying of malnutrition[2], laying ultimate blame on endemic corruption. With the exception of Cape Verde and Botswana, there is not a single African country in the top 50 (i.e. least corrupt) countries on Transparency International's Corruption Perception Index[3].

According to our contacts, the approach to Africa taken by India, China and Brazil – countries without military bases or a past colonial presence in the region – must be taken as a model. Since 2005 and the 6th Ministerial Conference of the World Trade Organization in Hong Kong, Brazil has been forging closer ties with four of the most disadvantaged African cotton-producing countries (Mali, Togo, Benin, Burkina Faso) in their fight against U.S. subsidies. In 2008 a cooperative relationship was established between these countries and the Brazilian Corporation of Agricultural Research (EMBRAPA). Officials in Brasilia are well aware of the contrast between the breadth of the problems and needs and the meagerness of Brazilian financial and diplomatic resources in the region. The first summit between Brazil and countries in the Economic Community of West African States (ECOWAS) took place in Cape Verde in July 2010 (Sal Island). China has built and equipped some thirty hospitals in Africa over the past ten years. More than 2.000 Chinese workers helped build the new mosque of Algiers, covering 22.000 m².

It is difficult to convince Brazilian diplomacy that the bonds created during the colonial era have left a host of interconnections across a great range of fields – university education, agricultural research, currencies, healthcare, immigration, the arts, military agreements – and entail specific responsibilities on the part of the former ruling powers, but that this may offer a way out. In any case, this was the message conveyed by France – a country that owes 15% of its current population and its demographic growth to African immigrants – in sharing its reflections on a past era with the Brazilian chancellery.

Certainly, Brasilia recognizes that – in the absence of a functioning Malian army capable of officially ensuring the "integrity" of Mali before the "Islamist peril" – a response is demanded to the taking of hostages, the violence committed by rebels (revealed by a number of sources, including Canadian journalist Amanda Lindhout, who was held for 460 days[4]) whose code of honor derives from an archaic interpretation of Islam and a radical interpretation of *sharia* law, and to the smuggling taking place under cover of the Azawadi Declaration of Independence (April 2012), all which has certainly been

---

1. Transparency International, Corruption Perceptions Index 2013.
2. Adam Ellick, Nicholas Kristoff, "The World's Deadliest Place For Kids", "Corruption is Killing Children in Angola", *International New York Times,* June 24, 2015.
3. Transparency International. Corruption Perceptions Index 2013.
4. *A House in the Sky*, Scribner, Simon & Schuster, New York, 2013.

aggravated by the fall of the Gaddafi regime, resulting in the return to the country of former soldiers from the Libyan army and a host of jobless people. They observe that such an intervention later received the support of the Security Council, which authorized the establishment of an African support mission (AFISMA, Resolution 2085 of 20 December 2012) and a peacekeeping force stabilization mission (MINUSMA, Resolution 2100 of 25 April 2013) directed by a Special Representative. They believe nevertheless that this reaction should have come from African and Arab countries within the context of mediation and not in the form of a French expeditionary force, which is already excessively represented in Africa (10,000 French soldiers in addition to United Nations and European Union missions), divided among nine countries (Cameroon, Ivory Coast, Djibouti, Gabon, Guinea, Mali, Senegal, Chad, Central African Republic), on a bilateral basis independently of MINUSMA and MISCA (African-led International Support Mission to the Central African Republic). And it has brought the nearly inevitable abuses that come with occupation forces, such as the violent mistreatment and rape of children who had taken refuge at the M'Poko airport in Bangui by French soldiers. This was revealed by Anders Kompass, a Swedish civil servant at the Office of the High Commissioner for Human Rights[1], and reported in *The Guardian* in April 2015. The perpetrators of the abuses have yet to be punished while the author of the report has been fined for revealing them[2]. Similar conduct was reported in Haiti in 2011 by the Uruguayan contingent of UN peacekeeping forces. However the incriminated soldiers were tried and sentenced by a Uruguayan court and President José Mujica recalled the entire contingent within 24 months[3].

Brasilia sees French interventions as the expression of a major power's global strategy to control regions rich in minerals. The intervention in Mali would have been motivated, in reality, by the need to protect the uranium mining areas in neighboring Niger that supply the French nuclear reactors, which provide three fourths of the country's energy. As regards the argument that France, because most of its immigration comes from Africa, is a receptive host country that has overcome its colonial past, we note that the 21 million Latin-American immigrants living in the United States (14% of the population) have hardly had any effect on U.S. policy towards their home region since the Monroe Doctrine, a region John Kerry referred to as "*our backyard*" while speaking before the U.S. House Foreign Affairs Committee[4].

---

1. Director of field operations at the Office of the High Commissioner for Human Rights (Geneva).
2. "UN aid worker suspended for leaking report on child abuse by French troops", *The Guardian,* April 29, 2015 (www.theguardian.com).
3. Jamil Chade, "ONU investiga abusos sexuais por tropas no Haiti" (UN investiages sexual abuse by troops in Haiti), *O Estado de São Paulo,* June 12, 2015.
4. In response to a question put to him by New York Representative Gregory Meeks, Kerry stated: "*We have some issues obviously with Argentina [...] which we need to work through, but the western hemisphere is our backyard, it is critical to us*").

Doubtlessly worse is the observation generally shared by Brazilian diplomats who are familiar with Africa of the limited room for maneuver of French diplomacy, which no longer has the financial resources to maintain a truly independent African policy, given the developing security risks throughout Africa associated with the growth of Islamist fundamentalism and drug trafficking, and the priority given to an armed response over the imperatives of development. They underline the alliance with the United States, which is expanding its bases and military support points in what was once the domain of French foreign policy, the annual benefits of American largess in the form of the "Presidential Drawdown"[1], and the implementation of strategic groups (Sahel Military Planning Group, African Multilateral Strategic Group).

U.S. engagement in favor of French intervention is very significant: beyond operational cooperation in intelligence gathering, air transport and aerial refueling, the United States have provided some 200 million dollars as of December 31, 2013 for operations in Mali and 100 million dollars for those in the Central African Republic. Washington has announced the establishment of a fund to finance regional projects in Africa. Brasilia acknowledges the efforts by the African Union to institute its own intervention forces (the African Standby Force with Rapid Deployment Capability) in order to avoid having to resort to hiring South African mercenaries[2], but points out that most financing comes from non-African countries and that, unlike the UN peacekeeping forces, the soldiers come from countries having a strategic stake in the conflicts. As underscored in a recent report by the Norwegian Institute of International Affairs, the African Union stabilization missions are composed primarily of military personnel (the ratio of civilian to military personnel is much lower than that in UN missions[3]).

Brasilia also stresses that the African Union has lost credibility by repeatedly naming contested figures to its presidency: Muammar Gaddafi in 2009, then in his 40th year in power (Lybia); Teodoro Obang in 2011 after 32 years at the helm (Equatorial Guinea); Robert Mugabe in 2015, in power since 1980 (Zimbabwe). It has also failed to condemn the growing efforts by African heads of state to amend the constitutions of their countries to extend their terms in office: ten have recently succeeded[4]. A parliamentary report on French policy in the 21 French-speaking countries in Africa, written by Deputy Philippe Baumel and published in May 2015 – and somewhat censored after its release by the President of the Commission for Foreign Affairs – underscores the relative growth in French military expenditures in Africa with respect to credit for

---

1. 50 million dollars for Operation Serval (Mali) and 60 million dollars for Operation Sangaris (Central African Republic) in 2013.

2. Adam Nossiter, "Mercenaries battle rebels in Nigeria", *International New York Times,* March 13, 2015.

3. Strategic Options for the Future of African Peace Operations 2015-2025, Seminar Report (Cape Town 17-18 December 2014), Oslo, Norwegian Institute of International Affairs, Oslo, 2015.

4. David Zounmenou, "AU must prevent third-term bids from destabilising Africa", Institute for Security Studies, June 11, 2015.

development (which is constantly decreasing) and observes that "*the French Minister of Defense has become the Minister of African Affairs*".

Starting with the Africa-South America Summit in Abuja (2006) and the Luanda Declaration (2007), Brazil has sought to revitalize the South Atlantic Peace and Cooperation Zone, which was created by the UN General Assembly in 1986 on Brazil's initiative. Its overtures to the 21 countries on Africa's west coast that are parties to the Declaration and the naval cooperation agreements recently established with Angola, Mozambique, South Africa, Namibia, Saõ Tomé and Príncipe, and Cape Verde are in line with the development of its submarine program (ProSub), with which France and Germany are associated, and with the South-South approach it promotes and defends in the south Atlantic (IBSAMAR exercises with India and South Africa, the creation of the Council of South American Defense). The main concern, according to the Brazilian defense minister, Celso Amorim, is to prevent unlawful activities (mainly drug trafficking) that could serve as a pretext for external intervention. Brazil took part in naval exercises in the Gulf of Guinea in April 2014 (Obangame Express) with 19 other nations, including 8 other non-African states (Belgium, France, Germany, the Netherlands, Portugal, Spain, Turkey, the United States). But it is reluctant to go further in its cooperation with the United States and it prefers to base its participation in surveillance operations in the Gulf of Guinea on a bilateral agreement (Portugal, Mozambique, Angola) rather than one with the European Union and the United States.

The IBSA Dialogue Forum (India, Brazil, South Africa)

One of the most visible aspects of these diplomatic overtures was the creation of the IBSA Dialogue Forum in June 2003, by which Brazil sought to implement solidarity policies in trade, development, science, technology, and food security with India and South Africa. The first IBSA summit was held in Brasilia in September 2006. South Africa joined the BRIC countries at the Hainan, China summit in April 2011.

Since 2004, newly industrialized and developing countries have been Brazil's main customers by value of agricultural products (62% of agricultural exports v. 38% for developed countries). The drop in exports to developed countries (particularly the United States, the European Union, and Japan), traditional outlet markets for Brazil's farm products, is a continuing trend (these countries bought 77% of Brazilian agricultural exports in 1990; 54% in 2003; 48% in 2005; 38% in 2009).

The European Union now purchases 28% of Brazilian agricultural exports (down from 41.5% in 2003)[1]. The principal customers are now Russia, China, India, Egypt, North Korea, and Saudi Arabia. Along with the European Union,

[1] Source: Brazilian Ministry of Agriculture and Fishing. Office of the Secretary for International Relations, 2010.

China has been Brazil's leading trade partner and its primary export market since 2009, and was its primary investor in 2010 (17.2 billion dollars v. 6.2 from the United States). Brazil is the world's number one meat exporter and Russia and Iran are its primary customers in this market.

In May 2004, the three countries instituted the IBSA Fund for the Alleviation of Poverty and Hunger, administrated by the United Nations Development Programme (UNDP) with an annual contribution of 1 million dollars from each country. As of today, Haiti, Equatorial Guinea, Palestine, Laos, and Burundi have benefited from this tripartite initiative.

The IBSA Forum's agenda focuses on issues of multilateralism, particularly reform of the UN Security Council, conservation of biodiversity, and the development of South-South cooperation and trade. During President Lula's visit to India in January 2004, Mercosur signed a preferential trade agreement with India.. Joint naval exercises have been conducted in the southern Atlantic every year since 2010 (IBSAMAR). IBSA has instituted a Joint Defense Working Group tasked with establishing cooperation in military science, technology and engineering.

BRICS Countries

Taking form in 2001 based on an acronym coined by Goldman Sachs (originally BRIC – Brazil, Russia, India, and China – with South Africa joining in 2011) the association lacks a permanent secretariat or shared institutions and is actually a rather disparate group in spite of its media appeal. BRICS countries account for half of all economic growth over the past decade. They represent 40% of the world population and 20% of gross world product. However, the per capita GDP in these countries are some of the world's lowest: Russia is 71st, Brazil 94th, South Africa 96th, China 105th, and India 142nd[1]. Public debt as a percentage of GDP is highest in Brazil (68.5% on December 31, 2012) with the others following in this order: India (66.8%), South Africa (39%), China (23%), and Russia (10.9%).

The BRICS countries have shown real but unequal economic growth since 1990: Russia and Brazil have grown much less than India or China. Forecast growth in GDP for 2015 is, respectively, -1.5% and -2.7% for Brazil and Russia, and +7.5% and +7.1% for India and China.

China's contribution to gross world product rose from 1.6% in 1990 to 6.5% in 2008; Brazil's remained stagnant at approximately 2.8%, while Russia's shrank from 2.4% to 1.1%[2]. A comparable trend is observed in the contribution of these countries to world trade. Brazil's remained stable during the period at around 1,3%; China´s increased from 1,6% to 7,7%. More than half of Brazilian exports to the other BRICS countries are dyads of staples and

[1]. Source: CIA World Factbook 2015.

[2]. Source : World Development Indicators, ECLAC.

raw materials (soybeans and iron ore to China; soy oil and copper ore to India; sugar and beef to Russia). While the profile of Brazilian trade has not changed significantly, China has made considerable modifications to its industrial base and exports (textile products and home appliances in the 1990s; computers, telecommunications, and automobiles in the 2000s).

Brazil's rate of internal investment is the lowest among the BRICS countries at less than 18% of GDP. On the other hand, it receives a significant portion of foreign investment (65.3 billion dollars in 2012), higher than Russia (51 billion) and India (26 billion) and trailing only the United States and China. The country's investments abroad, going mainly to developed countries (42% to Europe) and Africa (25%), have decreased significantly over the past decade while those of China and Russia have practically tripled. India has remained the largest investor in the least developed countries (LDC), followed by China and South Africa.

The BRICS group's share of world trade more than doubled between 1990 and 2008, going from 10% to 22.6%. Trade within the BRICS increased by 28% between 2001 and 2008 according to data from the International Monetary Fund, reaching 230 billion dollars at the end of the period. In 2011 it was 282 billion dollars and nearly tripled in 2013 to 850 billion dollars[1]. The BRICS countries received 38% of global foreign investments in 2011[2].

The BRICS countries work together essentially on issues of world trade; their relations are more nuanced or even divergent on other issues of importance (world government, climate, disarmament, nuclear non-proliferation, the Middle East, etc.). Brazil and South Africa are members of the Cairns Group[3], which works towards reform in agricultural trade; China and India are members of the G33 group of developing countries, whose principal objective is the protection of small farming establishments. It remains that the BRICS countries operate within the logic of a slow but inevitable gestation of a new world order, as also evidenced by the Shanghai Cooperation Organisation[4] and the Eurasian Economic Union[5].

---

[1]. José Alfredo Graça Lima, "VI Cúpula do BRICS: Perspectivas e Resultados" (6th BRICS Summit: prospects and results), *Cadernos de Politica Exterior*, FUNAG, Ano 1, N°1, Brasilia, 1st semester 2015.

[2]. "World Investment report", UNCTAD, June 2012.

5. Established in 1985, the group includes 19 agricultural exporting countries, including 9 Latin-American countries (Argentina, Brazil, Bolivia, Chile, Costa Rica, Guatemala, Paraguay, Peru, and Uruguay), which seek the reform of European Union common agricultural policies instituted in 1962 and the North American farming subsidies program (United States Export Enhancement Program) established in 1985, which they feel discriminate against the developing world.

[4]. Created in 2001 from the nucleus of the Shanghai Five (Russia, China, Kazakhstan, Turkmenistan, Kyrgyzstan), the Shanghai Organization also includes Uzbekistan, India and Pakistan. It is a military, financial and political organization. Its 15th summit took place in Ufa (Russia) in concomitance with that of the BRICS.

[5]. Created in 2014, the financial organization includes Russia, Armenia, Kazakhstan and Belarus. It has signed free-trade agreements with Ukraine, Moldavia, Uzbekistan and Vietnam.

During the second BRIC summit in Brasilia in April 2010, the presidents of development banks signed an agreement in principle – still quite loosely defined – on cross-financing in national currencies, and the Federation of the Industries of the State of São Paulo (FIESP) organized a seminar of some 350 businessmen. Brazil sought to bring private enterprise into a process that was essentially between governments.

The South African Minister of Trade and Industry stated on that occasion that the "*tectonic plates of the world economy are in motion*". Celso Amorim had pointed out that the BRICS countries did not claim to be the elite of developing countries, emphasizing that "*We will not replace one aristocracy – the G8 – with another.*" The third BRICS summit, held in New Delhi in March 2012, established a major stock market index, BRICSmart, in Mumbai, involving the markets of São Paulo (Bovespa), Hong Kong (HKEx), South Africa (JSE) and Russia (Micex-RTS). Lastly, during the 5th summit in Durban (South Africa), a development bank was instituted with overall funds of 100 billion dollars: China has pledged to contribute 41 billion, South Africa 5 billion and Brazil, Russia, and India 18 billion each.

The New Development Bank, announced at the conclusion of the 6th BRICS summit in Fortaleza (Brazil) on April 16, 2014 and whose vice president is Brazilian (Paulo Nogueira Batista) and president is Indian (Kundaput Vaman Kamath), proposed an ambitious alternative to the American and European-dominated world financial institutions that are no longer considered to be representative of the new world order. BRICS countries accounted for 21% of world GDP in 2013 but held only 10.3% of voting rights at the International Monetary Fund[1].

The equal sharing of responsibilities within the new institution (headquartered in Shanghai) between India (Executive President), Brazil (Chairman of the Board of Directors) and Russia (Chairman of the Board of Governors) contrasts with the structure of the International Monetary Fund and the World Bank, which are obligatory conduits to the Bank for International Settlements.

The New Development Bank currently has capital of 50 billion dollars and should go into operation in 2016. The 100 billion dollars (Contingent Reserve Arrangement) mentioned above will allow the parties to forestall short-term balance of payment pressures and generally strengthen their financial stability. But the new bank aims to go beyond the vocation of a typical development bank, such as the European Investment Bank, the Development Bank of Latin America (Corporación Andina de Fomento – CAF) or the Chiang Mai Initiative. It seeks to impose limits on the excessive privilege of the U.S. dollar, currently the reserve currency for more than two thirds of world countries. The enormous deficit in the U.S. balance of payments and the quantitative easing policy of the Federal Reserve are considered to be prejudicial to emerging

[1]. *Financial Times*, September 30, 2014.

countries. Wealthy countries seek to devalue their currency and extend credit (both by lending directly to banks, such as the Bank of Japan and the European Bank, at preferential rates and by buying bonds like the Federal Reserve Bank and the Bank of England do). Given the convertibility among major currencies (dollar, pound, euro, yen), the actions of central banks has a disproportional effect on the economies of developing countries. China, which holds 3.66 trillion dollars in reserves and 1.6 trillion in U.S. Treasury Bonds, has signed swap agreements with some twenty countries in order to be able to use the yuan as reserve currency. The support given to the vulture funds by the Federal Court of Manhattan in the case of the Argentinian debt dating to the country's bankruptcy in 2001 and the European Union's threats to exclude Russian banks from the SWIFT system have tended to push developments in this direction.

These measures include a component for cooperation in the realm of energy: the Energy Alliance. The Alliance will include a fuel reserve bank and an institute of energy policy. It aims to stand counter to the Intercontinental Exchange (ICE), which is dominated by Western oil companies (BP, Shell, Total, ENI, etc.) and associated with such institutions as Goldman Sachs and Morgan Stanley. This BRICS project unites PetroChina (one of the world's largest oil & gas companies, ahead of Exxon Mobil), Gazprom (Russia) and Petrobras (Brazil). It also aims to bring in public corporations such as the National Iranian Oil Co., Petroléos of Venezuela, Sonatrach of Algeria, Petronas of Malaysia, and YPF of Argentina. This effort has also witnessed the drafting of a gas contract worth over 400 million dollars between Gazprom and CNPC of China, complemented by an agreement between VTB, Russia's second largest financial institution, and the Bank of China for payment in local currency, both signed on May 20, 2014.

The BRICS group countries have considerable financial reserves, placing them at the top of world rankings: with 3.549 billion dollars, China is the leader of the entire category, followed by Russia in 4th place globally (561 billion dollars), Brazil in 6th (371 billion dollars), India in 10th (287 billion dollars), and South Africa in 32nd position (55 billion dollars)[1].

When all is said and done, the BRICS countries constitute an informal forum for consultation and coordination without a strong shared identity, with a varying economic agenda based on issues of the moment rather than bona fide long-term solidarity strategy and a shared diplomatic thrust favoring multilateralism.

Russia is an economic power that has been in decline over the past twenty years. It has little presence in Latin America (with the exception of Venezuela), focusing its priorities on Central Europe (Georgia, Ukraine, Kosovo...), Syria, and its strained relations with NATO and the United States. It is certainly a global player however, and the inversion of power relations with China, affecting its stature in Asia, has led the country to seek external partners.

---

1. *O'Globo*, March 26, 2013.

Ultimately, it regained influence in Latin America mainly through military cooperation (Venezuela, Brazil), energy (Bolivia), and the implementation of an independent policy at a time when its historical partners (Spain, France, Portugal) have aligned with American interests (the diplomatic incident arising from the "seizure" of Bolivian president Evo Morales' plane, adumbrations of a military intervention in Syria, and joint bombing campaigns in Iraq and Libya). The visit to Moscow by the Brazilian president in December 2012, and that by Russian Prime Minister Dimitri Medvedev to Brasilia in February 2013, were intended to boost modest trade volumes (six billion dollars in 2012, one third of Russia-Latin America trade). Brazilian beef exports are limited by strict non-tariff barriers to trade. As confirmed in the seminar organized in Saint Petersburg in September 2013 by the Latin America Institute of the Russian Academy of Sciences, the Russia-Latin America relationship has become more pragmatic, based more on economic interests, but shared concerns have helped consolidate it (multilateralism, non-recourse to military force, the Falklands, Libya, Syria, Iran, the Cuba embargo).

Regarding the Ukrainian question, Brazil takes a critical view of the overthrow of an elected president, Viktor Yanukovych, corrupt or not, following the pro-European street protests by demonstrators of different persuasions, but some of them allied with movements on the extreme right. The election of a pro-EU president, Petro Poroshenko, and the signing of an agreement of association in principle on June 27, 2014 with the European Union were judged precipitous given the ongoing conflict in the northeast of the country. Brasilia does not believe that the economic sanctions imposed by the European Union and the United States will have any effect whatsoever on local politics or lead to the isolation of Russia. German trade with Russia in 2013 was a quarter of total Brazilian trade, some 106 billion dollars; one fourth of European natural gas supplies come from Russia.

Russia's historical birthplace is Kiev (capital of Russia from the 9th to the 12th century); a large part of the Ukrainian population is Russian. The Crimea was given to Ukraine in 1954 by the Secretary General of the Communist party, Nikita Khrushchev. The people were not consulted. In this regard, the referendum held by the parliament of the autonomous region of Crimea, revealing that a huge majority of the population favored rejoining Russia, was seen as a step forward by Brasilia.

Brazilian Defense Minister Jacques Wagner, who represented President Rousseff at the ceremonies in Moscow on May 9, 2105 to commemorative the 70th anniversary of the victory of Soviet troops against Nazi Germany, defined the boycott of the ceremonies by the major European heads of state (only the Czech president, Milos Zeman, was in Moscow for the occasion) as an error and an obstacle to seeking a mutually agreeable solution to the Ukrainian question. Among BRICS countries, only Brazil was not represented by a head of state[1].

Brazil's anti-imperialist and non-aligned diplomatic stance brought India closer to Lula and to the "Bolivarian revolution", both countries sharing skepticism of the principles of liberal economics (India is constitutionally a "socialist republic"). China, India's number two trade partner and number one for Brazil, is a growing influence, a power in the process of gestation. India and Brazil, like South Africa, are intermediate powers, significant on the regional level, active in multilateral issues, anxious to respond to the interests of developing countries, but with limited international influence.

When former president Lula went to Buenos Aires in September 2015 to support the candidacy of Daniel Scioli in the presidential election, the latter requested Brazil's help in allowing Argentina to join the BRICS[2]. President Cristina Kirchner had been a special guest at the BRICS summit in Brasilia in December 2010. In 2014 she received Russian president Vladimir Putin and Chinese president Xi Jinping in Buenos Aires.

Russia's disputes with the European Union and the United States have moved Moscow to reconsider its relations with China and India. The agreement signed in May 2014 between the Russian company Gazprom and the China National Petroleum Company regarding the construction of a pipeline to provide Siberian natural gas to China (a gargantuan project estimated to cost 400 billion dollars over 10 years[3]), the Chinese company's participation in developing the Vankor oil field in eastern Siberia, and statements by Chinese authorities offering a guarantee of financial aid in the event of a further devaluation of the Russian currency are all expressions of this rapprochement. The contracts signed (regarding the supply of twelve nuclear reactors and critical military supplies) in December 2014 during Vladimir Putin's visit to India, accompanied by the head of government of Crimea, now Russia's 86th region, and India's refusal to support the sanctions imposed on Moscow by the United States and the European Union all work in favor of a partnership termed "*stratégic and incomparable*" by Indian prime minister, Narenda Modi[4].

---

[1]. Wagner had stated that the marriage of a close friend had kept Dilma Rousseff in Brazil. The wedding of the cardiologist Roberto Kalil, attending physician for the Brazilian political class, on May 8 was a high profile affair with the participation of the leaders of the major Brazilian political parties and many celebrities in the lavish event, which could not fail to call to mind Kalil's first wedding, in 1980, when one of the godfathers was the general João Figueiredo, president of the dictatorship.

[2]. Nicolás Lantos, "Intentan reinstalar em la region las politicas neoliberales que nos llevaron al fracaso y el hambre" (Attempt to reinstate the neoliberal policies that brought us disaster and hunger), *Página12*, September 10, 2015.

[3]. Andrew Kramer, "Gazprom agrees to build pipeline to China", *International New York Times*, November 11, 2014.

[4]. Isabelle Mandraud, Julien Bouissou, "Poutine cherche des débouchés en Inde" (Putin seeks outlets in India), *Le Monde*, December 5, 2014

It is, to say the least, premature to expect from the BRICS any fundamental changes to world financial and economic governance. Less than 3% of BRICS foreign investments remain within the group, another 5% goes to Africa while 40% goes to developed countries, according to a March 2013 study by the United Nations Conference on Trade and Development[1]. The Fortaleza Declaration adopted at the closure of the 6th BRICS summit in July 2014 reaffirmed the themes dear to Brazilian diplomacy of multilateralism, dialogue, mediation and peaceful conflict resolution, and strongly condemned economic sanctions that violate international law. The presence of all the heads of state of the countries in the region at the outreach meeting organized alongside the summit represented a success for Brazilian diplomacy and proof of the appeal of the BRICS group in Latin America.

India's test of a long-range missile in April 2012 – part of a military development program implemented progressively since 1983, now bringing Shanghai and Beijing within range – was clearly a warning to China. This gesture reveals the strains in current relations among BRICS countries and belies their apparent willingness to share influence in world governance.

Indeed, there is an inherent irony when regimes characterized by deep social inequality and endemic corruption take a stance defending the legitimate principle of greater democratization in world governance.

China

Brazil's defense of its international interests and formulation of an independent foreign policy are recent developments in its diplomacy. Its emergence as an influential player – as a mediator, when all is said and done – is concomitant with the development of a strategic partnership with China, a partnership that is part of multilateral solidarity efforts (Seattle, Doha). Brazil leverages this South-South cooperation against the North in the international arena with the goal of achieving more equitable trade arrangements and structural reform of major international institutions (Security Council, World Bank, International Monetary Fund). Brazil views China as an essential partner in its efforts to establish itself as an international power in a world that both Brasilia and Beijing want multilateral. The joint statement issuing from Dilma Rousseff's visit to Beijing in April 2011 underscores "*the comprehension and support for Brazil's ambition to play a more preeminent role in the United Nations*". President Xi Jinping made an official visit to Brasilia in July 2014. Brazil supports the candidacy of China as president of the G20 in 2016.

In an interview with a correspondent from *O'Globo* at the Davos forum in January 2012, economist Joseph Stiglitz stated that for Brazil, what happens in China is more important than what happens in the United States[2]. The number

---

[1]. Lydia Polgreen, "BRICS join to create own development institution", *International Herald Tribune*, March 28, 2013.

[2]. *O'Globo*, December 20, 2010.

of countries for which America is the biggest export market has dropped between 1994 and 2014 from 44 to 32. Over the same period, the figure for China has risen from 2 to 43[1].

In the space of a few years, China has become Brazil's main trading partner and investor (77.95 billion dollars in trade in 2014, with the United States trailing at 62.02 billion)[2]. Termed "*strategic*", the partnership proposed by Beijing during president Jiang Zemin's visit to Brasilia in 1994 – with Venezuela being added in 2001 and Mexico and Argentina in 2004 – is beginning to bear fruit in terms of investment. In 2010, China committed to investing between 12 and 20 billion dollars in industry (steel, infrastructure, energy, oil, mining). A significant portion of these investments will be used to ensure provisions of iron ore. Examples include the acquisition by Wuhan Iron and Steel (WISCO) of a 21.52% share in MMX Mineração for 400 million dollars, the construction of a steel plant costing 4 billion dollars in the Açu harbor complex near Rio de Janeiro, and the acquisition of the Brazilian mining company Itaminas by a Chinese conglomerate in March 2010 for 1.2 billion dollars.

As in Venezuela, loans from the Chinese Development Bank are linked to a guarantee of oil supply: for the Venezuelan public oil company, PDVSA, 20 billion dollars and 300.000 barrels of oil per day; for Petrobras, 10 billion dollars and 200.000 barrels of oil per day from 2010 to 2019. The public company Sinopec (China Petroleum and Chemical Corporation) acquired a 40% share of the Spanish company Repsol's Brazilian arm in October 2010 for 7.1 billion dollars, and Sinochem obtained 40% of the Norwegian State Oil consortium for offshore Brazilian oil prospecting for the price of 3 billion dollars. Loans from the Chinese Development Bank are also linked to the purchase of equipment and to investments in industry, as in the case of the company Huawei, which received a loan of one billion dollars over a period of ten years for its research and training center in Campinas (state of São Paulo).

According to Charles Tang, president of the Brazil-China chamber of commerce, inward investments in Brazil in 2012 reached 30 billion dollars, nearly all going to the mining and energy industries, ranking Brazil alongside Venezuela as the greatest beneficiary of Chinese investments in Latin America[3] and fourth in the world after Australia, the United States and Canada. But it is difficult to assess the exact value of these investments because the lion's share transit through the local tax havens (Cayman Islands, British Virgin Islands) according to data from the Chinese Ministry of Trade. But the fact remains that since 2005, Latin America has displaced Asia as the principal recipient of

---

1 "The sticky superpower", *The Economist*, October 3, 2015.

2. "Brazilian Trade Balance. Consolidated Data. 2014", Brazilian Ministry of Development, Industry and Foreign Trade (*www.desenvilvimento.gov.br)*

3. According to the United Nations Economic Commission for Latin America and the Caribbean, Chinese investments in Latin America amounted to 15.3 billion dollars in 2010 and 22.7 billion dollars in 2011.

Chinese investment. China is currently the world's third largest investor after the United States and Japan[1].

China became a member of the Inter-American Development Bank (IBD) in 2008. Working with the IBD, the Chinese public bank for international trade negotiated the creation of a fund in *yuan* worth one billion dollars for infrastructure, after having negotiated a loan in September 2011, partly in *yuan*, worth 200 million dollars to finance trade with Latin America. The February 2012 bulletin of the North American analysis center, Inter-American Dialogue[2], estimated a total of 75 billion dollars of Chinese credit issued to Latin America since 2005 (37 billion in 2010 alone), more than the amount extended by the World Bank, the IBD and the U.S. Ex-Im Bank, and generally at more advantageous conditions. The bulk of credit went to Brazil, Venezuela, Argentina, and Ecuador, two thirds going to the oil sector. China made no investments in healthcare, education, public administration, or the environment, which are the favored sectors for the World Bank and the Inter-American Development Bank. In 2009-2010 Latin America accounted for half of all Chinese loans in the world, estimated by the *Financial Times* at 110 billion dollars[3].

The Chinese economic presence in the Caribbean is growing and the investments are diversified: tourism, sports infrastructure, harbor infrastructure (Bahamas), sugar cane and road infrastructure (Jamaica), sports facilities (Grenada). In Central America, the most favored partner is Costa Rica, the only state on the isthmus to recognize the People's Republic of China (all others maintaining diplomatic relations with Taiwan). In June 2013, President Xi Jinping visited the country and signed contracts with a value of more than 2 billion dollars, equivalent to nearly 4% of Costa Rican GDP. Ecuador receives Chinese investment for the ambitious project for the Pacific Refinery (costing an estimated 12 billion dollars), but at a high interest rate (7% annually to be paid off in eight years).

During the first decade of the new millennium, bilateral trade rose from 2 billion to 56 billion dollars. In 2014, the figure was 77.95 billion, not differing greatly from the 77 billion in 2011. This stagnation is attributed to a slowing in growth of the Chinese economy and a fall in raw material prices. Close to one fifth of all Brazilian exports went to China in 2011 (in 2000 the figure was 6%). China doubled the portion of its sales to Brazil between 2005 and 2010 (from 7.3% of Brazilian imports in 2005 to 14.5% in 2010 and 16.3% in 2014)[4].

---

1. United States, 329 billion dollars; Japan, 123 billion dollars; China, 84 billion dollars. Source: UNCTAD.

2. Research center based in Washington DC focusing on Latin America and the Caribbean, with funding from public and private foundations, governments and governmental agencies (Canada, Chile, Guatemala, Mexico, Sweden, USAID) and multilateral organizations (OAS, IBD, and others).

3. *Financial Times*, January 17, 2011.

4. "Brazilian Trade balance. Consolidated Data. 2014", Brazilian Ministry of Development, Industry and Foreign Trade (*www.desenvolvimento.gov.br*).

Brazil accounts for 2% of Chinese foreign trade; China for some 15% of Brazil's.

The value of the principal exports (sugar, soy, meat, iron ore) increased much more than their volumes. Hence, in 2010, the value of Brazilian exports (201 billion dollars) registered a 31% increase over the previous year, while overall volumes only increased by 14%. Exports of iron ore, which represents 16.35% of Brazil's sales to China, increased in value by 75% and in volume by 18.16%. This means that trade with China has enjoyed exceptional economic circumstances thanks to high commodity prices, but is characterized by a North-South "center-periphery" relationship, in the expression used by the mentor of Brazilian diplomacy during the Lula years, Samuel Pinheiro Guimarães.

According to a study by the Brazilian Federation of Industries published in February 2011, one Brazilian company in four is negatively impacted by competition from Chinese products, particularly in tailored and prêt-à-porter clothing, metallurgy, footwear, optics, and toys. Regarding the toy industry, there are practically no more national-level toy manufacturers in Argentina, Uruguay, and Brazil. Brazil lost some 13,000 jobs in three years (2007-2010) in this sector according to the president of the Brazilian toymakers association (*Associação brasileira dos fabricantes de brinquedos* - ABRINQ)[1]. It is estimated that 20.000 Brazilian textile workers lost their jobs in 2011. In 2012, two thirds of clothing imported by Brazil came from China. Prior to 2005, Brazil imported practically no clothing from China. Brazil is the world's third largest cotton exporter after the United States and India. Its exports of this commodity increased by a factor of five in the period 2001-2011.

Brazil's industrial apparatus suffers from Chinese competition, which benefits from an unrealistic exchange rate (undervalued *yuan* and clearly overvalued *real* on January 1, 2013), questionable customs and trade practices (under-invoicing, smuggling, forgeries passing through Paraguay, which has still not recognized the People's Republic of China, subsidies to Chinese exporters), glaring disparities between social security and benefits, which are real and maintained in Brazil yet flouted in China, much to the disadvantage of Brazilian industrialists (healthcare and pension benefits paid by employers in Brazil may be equal to a worker's salary whereas in China they do not even amount to 15%), and, it is true, inadequacies in Brazilian production (excessive tax burden, inadequate infrastructure). Of the 121 antidumping actions undertaken by Brazil before the World Trade Organization in 2000-2010, more than two thirds regarded China.

Brazilian industrial production remained virtually stagnant in 2011 with respect to the previous year (+0.3%). Its contribution to Gross Domestic Product is steadily decreasing (less than 15% in 2011).

---

[1]. *O 'Globo*, December 20, 2010.

One of the rare joint industrial projects – the building of aircraft in China by the Brazilian company Embraer in Harbin, organized in 2003 – has to grapple with the growing strength of Chinese competitors in this sector and is increasingly threatened in spite of China's purchase of 60 Embraer 190 jets (40 for Tianjin Airlines and 20 for the Industrial and Commercial Bank of China – ICBC) announced in July 2014 during President Xi Jinping's visit to Brasilia.

As regards cooperation in the aerospace sector, which began in 1988 with the construction of two earth observation satellites launched from the Chinese base in Shanxi, very little progress has been made due to the yawning gap that now separates Brazilian and Chinese aerospace research and development capabilities.

This trend will only grow stronger with the changes China is bringing to its industrial base and its export capabilities. The repeated attempts to buy the Brazilian technology company Positivo – the only significant, if not sole, enterprise in this field in Brazil – by Chinese firms is part of a more sophisticated diversification strategy, as witnessed by Lenovo's acquisition of IBM's personal computer business in 2005, TCL Corporation's joint venture with the French Thomson SA in November 2003, Nanjing Automotive's acquisition of the British MG Rover in 2005, Greely's acquisition of the Swedish Volvo in 2010, etc. The Chinese automobile industry has already set up shop in Uruguay and in Brazil (Jac Motors in Salvador de Bahia, and Cherry in Goiana). Sales of Chinese automobiles on the Brazilian market tripled in a single year (2011). They are still a small minority (less than 1% of the market), but the pace of growth prompted the Brazilian government in October 2011 to double the existing importation duty (35%) to provide an incentive to the Chinese automakers to shift production to Brazil.

Chinese competition is growing on Brazil's traditional turf: Latin American countries and Portuguese-speaking countries in Africa. Two thirds of Brazilian companies surveyed in the study by the Brazilian Confederation of Industries cited above stated that they had lost parts of their third-party markets to Chinese competitors. At the 4th Forum on China-Africa Cooperation in Sharm el-Sheikh in November 2009, China committed to opening its markets to African exports and, most importantly, to the most disadvantaged countries on the continent. Brazil's special relationship with its former colonial overlord, Portugal, did not prevent the China Three Gorges Corporation from acquiring, in December 2011, a majority share in one of Portugal's largest business groups, Energias de Portugal (EDP), which produces and distributes electricity in six Brazilian states. This acquisition had been a coveted goal of the Brazilian utility companies CEMIG and Electrobras.

The penetration of Chinese firms into Central America and the Caribbean does not raise similar issues of competition for Brazil, which, with the exception of Cuba has a relatively meager presence in the region. Chinese diplomacy is pursuing different objectives in a region where most countries still have not recognized the People's Republic of China: in the Caribbean, these include Haiti, Belize, Saint Lucia, Saint Kitts and Nevis, and Saint Vincent and the Grenadines. As regards Mexico, its relations with Beijing are very unbalanced (a negative balance of trade of 51 billion dollars for Mexico in 2012) and it only competes with Brazil in the realm of cooperation on offshore oil prospecting: the Chinese Export-Import Bank granted a line of credit on the order of one billion dollars to the Mexican state-owned petroleum company Pemex.

The Economic Commission for Latin America and the Caribbean (ECLAC) conducted a comparative analysis of gains and losses for the major export products on the BRICS markets between 1995 and 2008. The study concluded that Brazil had made market gains of 13 billion dollars with respect to its partners (China, Russia, India), a pittance when compared to China's gains in the same period (512 billion dollars), mainly in the North American, Asian and European markets.

These comparisons are difficult to make given that the relevant currency exchange rates varied in different ways. While China and India did not modify their foreign exchange regimes between 1993 and 2008, the Brazilian economy witnessed three exchange regimes and the introduction of a new currency (the *real* in 1994). During this period, the trend in exchange rates was relatively stable for the *yuan* and the *ruble*, but quite erratic for the *real*. The foreign exchange market has been unified in India and China since 1994; it would not be until 2005 that the same happened for Brazil. In March 2008, Brazil eliminated its last controls on currency repatriation.

In the North American market, Brazil feels the pressure of Chinese competition directly. China doubled its share of North American imports between 2000 and 2008, from 8.3% to 16.1%, while Brazil's portion remained stable at approximately 1.4%. The balance of trade with the United States, traditionally positive for Brazil, became negative starting in 2009. Its trade deficit with the United States is the largest registered by Brazil in its international trade relationships: 8.15 billion dollars, higher than Nigeria (7.1 billion), Germany (6.1 billion), South Korea (5.4 billion) and India (2.9 billion). This deficit derives, in part, from the significant decrease in the share of manufacturing products in Brazilian exports to the United States (77% in 2001; 45.3 % in 2011)[1].

Relations with China are complex. Beyond exponential growth in trade and investments, China provides Brazil with freedom of maneuver on the diplomatic level, particularly regarding the United States, the European Union and the multilateral relations that the country could not have hoped for without the help of Chinese economic demand during the years of the Lula presidency. For example: in August 2013, Brazil's trade deficit with the United States for the previous 12 months, setting a historical record at 10.6 billion dollars, was

[1]. Source: Foreign Trade Association, *O'Globo*, February 23, 2012.

partly compensated by the trade surplus with China in the same period (8.2 billion dollars).

But China's growing influence in Latin American countries (particularly Ecuador, Cuba, Bolivia, Venezuela, and Uruguay) in terms of both trade and investment, significantly alters the economic and geopolitical weight in the region exerted by the United States and, to a lesser extent, Brazil. Brazil's share of imports in Latin America shrank from 11% in 2008 to 9.7% in 2011[1]. China's share grew in the same period: 11.6% in 2008; 13.4% in 2012. China's presence is generally well accepted on the diplomatic level to the extent to which it is not seen as having hegemonic designs. The fact remains that this growing presence brings the risks of a dependency relationship that may become delicate in the event of a reversal of economic trend. When Argentina chose to resort to antidumping measures in its trade with China, Beijing threatened to boycott imports of Argentine soybeans. Some 80% of Argentina's exported soy crop goes to China[2].

The issue of trade with China is of course not unique to Brazil. France asked the European Commission for reciprocity measures regarding in particular public tenders, which are relatively open in the European Union, but sealed off to foreign businesses in China, which has yet to subscribe to the WTO agreement on public markets. France also pushed for the enactment of legislation by the European Union to favor European business, following the model of the U.S. Buy American Act. A report solicited by the French government and published in March 2012 underscored the underhanded competition by Chinese products, where intellectual property rights are not always honored, safety norms are not in line with European legislation, environmental requirements are ignored and social security is but rudimentary[3]. The fact remains that the European Union is the second largest exporter to China (after Japan), and some 33,000 European businesses have facilities in the country, earning income estimated at 180 billion euros, something which is obviously not the case with the industries of the major Latin American countries.

Multilateral Trade Negociations

Until the 1980s, the Brazilian economy developed under the shelter of protectionist tariffs. Based on steel, the automotive industry and ship building, it benefited from a strong domestic market and the central role of the state, particularly in the form of generous financing from the state banks (Caixa Economica Federal, Bank of Brazil, National Bank of Economic and Social Development). The Brazilian economy grew at an average annual rate of 7.5%

---

1. Source: International Monetary Fund, *O 'Globo*, May 22, 2013.
2. *O 'Globo*, July 21, 2010.
3. Yvon Jacob, Serge Guillon, "*En finir avec la mondialisation déloyale !*" (Enough of unfair globalization!), Ministry of the Economy, Finance and Industry, Paris, 2012.

from 1947 to 1980, however at the cost of high indebtedness. The Brazilian Constitution, adopted in 1988, continued an economic system characterized by significant state control, the near monopoly of state-owned businesses that ensured tariff protections for the domestic market, and very heavy taxation that did little to even out deep social inequalities. The adoption of the *Plano Real* and the common external tariff ushered in with Mercosur significantly reduced import taxes and began to open up the domestic market. Privatization and foreign investment during the 1990s marked Brazil's integration into the world market, confronting it with the crises in Mexico (1994), Russia (1998), Argentina (1999) and the United States (2008).

Brazil took bold positions in negotiations during the WTO Doha Development Round in November 2001, most significantly with the creation of the G20 finance ministerial meetings in 1999, which was considered more representative than the G8 (65% of world population and 90% of its wealth as opposed to 13.5% of the population and two thirds of the wealth [1]).

In Cancún during the 5th Ministerial Conference of the World Trade Organization (September 2003), Brazil coordinated a group of 21 countries, including India, China, Mexico, South Africa, and Indonesia, that no longer wanted to see agricultural trade liberalized. Since the 1950s and the GATT treaty, the European Union and the United States have not wanted to discuss the issue of agricultural subsidies, which countries in the South see as having a negative impact on their exports.

After the impasse in negotiations at the Cancún Conference, the participation of the G20 was fundamental, under the urging of Brazil and with the support of the developing countries in the G77. The objective was to develop an agenda regarding the limits that could be tolerated for domestic agricultural subsidies, now hierarchized, and the concept of "double proportionality" mentioned in the Hong Kong Declaration (2005) on industrial products to better account for the degree of development of each country. Although they have differing interests, an alliance between Brazil and India is inevitable according to our contacts in Itamaraty, as seen in the shared position firmly assumed by both countries at the Potsdam Conference in 2007.

On behalf of the G77, Brazil, India, China, Peru, Mexico, and Cuba are seeking to strengthen the institutional status with the United Nations of the High-Level Committee on South-South Cooperation. The Committee traces its

---

[1] The G20 included the G8 countries (Germany, Canada, the United States, France, Italy, Japan. the United Kingdom, Russia) plus South Africa, Argentina, Brazil, Australia, China, South Korea, India, Mexico, and the European Union. The presidency is held on a rotating basis (France in 2011; Mexico in 2012; Russia in 2013; Australia in 2014; Turkey in 2015). The meeting agendas are prepared by the state holding the presidency. In Cancún, Brazil assembled a group of twenty-one countries, known as the "Trade" G20, which was first formed in Geneva in August 2003 during the preparatory meetings to the Cancún Conference. Pressure from the United States prompted many countries to withdraw from the group (Colombia, Peru, Uruguay, Guatemala). The group currently has 19 members (5 Africa countries, 6 Asian countries, 8 Latin American countries). Russia, admitted to the G8 in 1994, was excluded in 2014.

origin to the Buenos Aires Plan of Action for Promoting and Implementing Technical Cooperation among Developing Countries (1978) and meets every two years. Its 18th session took place in May 2014. The G77 advocated transforming it into the United Nations Office for South-South Cooperation, with more resources and more personnel.

The São Paulo Protocol was negotiated in Brazil in December 2010 by seven southern countries (Cuba, South Korea, India, Egypt, Indonesia, Malaysia, Morocco) and Mercosur within the framework of the Generalized System of Preferences of the United Nations Conference on Trade and Development. Its entry into force requires parliamentary approval by at least four of its member countries (currently only Cuba, India and Malaysia have done so). The Protocol aims to reduce tariff barriers by some 20% and invites the least developed countries to join on a non-reciprocity basis.

South-South trade accounted for 21% of world trade in 2009. Three quarters of this trade takes place in Asia. In the period 1995-2009 it grew at a rate (+14%) greater than that of total world trade (+9%). The conclusion of the third round of negotiations in the Global System of Trade Preferences (GSTP) in December 2010 provided further stimulus for South-South trade. The first two rounds (1986-88 and 1991-98) had only produced limited results. Legally linked to the GATT, the São Paulo round began in 2004 during the UNCTAD meeting in São Paulo and its conclusions were approved in the ministerial meeting in Foz de Iguaçu (Brazil) in December 2010.

When it was founded, the G20 was a group of twenty finance ministers and central bank governors proposed by the G7/G8 with the aim of preserving the international financial system through facilitating dialogue between developed and developing countries. Boosted by the 2008 crisis, the G20 progressively moved from the margins to the center of the world decision-making process and was consecrated at the Pittsburgh summit as the principal forum for international economic cooperation. Brazil held the presidency of the G20 at that time. There were six G20 summits between November 2008 and November 2011. Under Brazil's initiative, the Financial Stability Forum, created in 1999 with the G20 and including Switzerland, Hong Kong, Singapore, Australia and the Netherlands in addition to the G7, was expanded to include developing countries. Shortly after the Washington summit, the Forum was transformed into the Financial Stability Board with all members of the G20 plus Spain. It developed along the lines of the Basel Committee on Banking Supervision. However, while the G20 has replaced the G8 on questions regarding trade and finance (it is now represented on the Basel Committee and the International Organization of Securities Commissions) it has no significant influence on defense or security governance.

As regards Brazil, its influence is more significant within the multilateral organizations dedicated to development (Economic and Social Council, United Nations Conference on Trade and Development) than it is in the financial institutions created at Bretton Woods, with the exception of the Inter-

American Development Bank. Brazil has shown a capacity to unite large coalitions of developing countries around agricultural issues, in spite of conflicting interests (for example, India and Argentina), on the basis of shared opposition to the traditional North-North scheme of international trade.

Brasilia took a dim view of British Prime Minister David Cameron's calls at the Davos Forum in January 2012 to replace the Doha Round with bilateral agreements. Generally based on reciprocity, these agreements are seen in Brazil as being disadvantageous to developing countries due to the asymmetries among the parties.

In May 2013, a Brazilian diplomat, Roberto Carvalho de Azevêdo, was elected Director-General of the World Trade Organization (WTO). The first Latin American to lead the organization since its founding in 1995 (Marrakech Agreement). Brazil's Ambassador in Geneva, supported by the BRICS group, he was chosen over the former Mexican minister of trade, Herminio Blanco Mendoza, one of the architects of the North American Free Trade Agreement (NAFTA) who enjoyed the backing of the United States and the European Union. A specialist in agricultural issues, Azevêdo's main task is to revitalize the Doha Rounds, which have been at a standstill since 2008, particularly over the question of agricultural subsidies, and move them forward on a more realistic and mutually beneficial basis. After his election, he expressed concern over the proliferation of regional agreements and trade preferences[1].

His candidacy was wholly in keeping with the priorities of Brazilian diplomacy in favor of greater representation of emerging countries in international organizations. Brasilia points out that elections to the World Trade Organization are open, competitive, and based on merit, unlike the "*scandalously anachronistic*" convention by which the presidency of the World Bank is reserved to a North American national and that of the International Monetary Fund to a European national. In 2005, the Brazilian candidate, the diplomat Seixas Corrêa, had to concede defeat to the former European Commissioner for Trade, Pascal Lamy.

Brazil has taken part since 1995 in 106 disputes, acting as plaintiff in 25 of them. The most significant of these cases heard by the Dispute Settlement Body involved subsidies to the aeronautical industry (Canadian Bombardier v. Embraer, which ended in a bilateral agreement in 2007); to the sugar industry (action by Brazil-Australia and Thailand against the European Union, obliging the European Commission to amend its rules in 2006); to the cotton industry (against North American subsidies, ending favorably in an arbitration agreement for Brazil in 2009 and in the signing of a bilateral agreement in 2010); to the importation of used tires (on the initiative of the European Union), which forced Brazil to revise its exceptional rules in favor of Mercosur, judged discriminatory; for the exportation of orange juice to the United States.

---

[1]. "*Protectionismo está se alastrando*" (Protectionism is spreading), *O 'Globo*, May 9, 2013.

Excluding the United States and the European Union, which are responsible for more than half of the cases heard between 1995 and 2012, Brazil is, along with Canada, the country that has taken the greatest initiative in these disputes (7% of the total). The Minister of Development, Industry and Foreign Trade, Fernando Pimentel, a companion in Dilma Rousseff's revolutionary militancy right from the start, stated at a reception for Egyptian president Mohamed Morsi, organized by the president of Brazil in May 2013, that protectionism was "*a concept used by rich countries when they want to penetrate the markets of other countries*"[1].

Brazilian trade unions pushed for the introduction of fair labor clauses in international negotiations, such as the clauses included as non-binding recommendations in the Havana Charter (Article 7)[2]. President Fernando Henrique Cardoso had already criticized asymmetrical globalization in his address to the 56th General Assembly of the United Nations in 2001, declaring his support for equitable globalization, a difficult goal given the disparities in social security standards, labor laws and political systems. The urgent need for international fair labor legislation is underscored by the series of disasters in Bangladesh clothing factories (fire at Tazreen Fashion in the Ashulia district of Dhaka causing the deaths of 112 workers in November 2012; the fire at Smart Garment Export in January 2013 killing eight workers; the collapse of the Rana Plaza building in April 2013, where 1127 workers lost their lives; the fire in May 2013 at Tung Hai Sweaters that killed eight people), where products are manufactured for major brands (Asics, Hennes&Mauritz, WalMart, Gap, Carrefour, Benetton, El Corte Inglés...) under appalling working conditions. With China, Bangladesh is the world's major clothing exporter: 60% of its production goes to Europe, 25% to the United States.

Recent labor inspections in Brazil have revealed working conditions bordering on slavery for Bolivian immigrants in garment factories on the outskirts of São Paulo, an ill-conceived response by certain Brazilian industrialists to the myth of "Asian competitiveness". The same phenomenon has been observed in Argentina, where there are hundreds of clandestine textile factories exploiting imported labor (generally from Bolivia) in the Flores and Floresta districts of the capital[3].

Among G20 members, Brazil has one of the most protected domestic markets (68th among the 75 largest economies). Its international openness rating is 9.6% (for comparison, France's is 22%). Its foreign trade (imports and exports), on the order of 480 billion dollars in 2011, is equivalent to 10% of its GDP. Brazilian trade amounts to some 1.4% of world trade, the same percentage as in 1985 (2.6% in 1950). It was the world's 22nd largest exporter in 2011 (20th in 1970), with 1.33% of world exports. Its trade surplus (close to

---

1. *O 'Globo* , May 9, 2013.

2. United Nations Conference on Trade and Employment, Havana, Cuba, November 21, 1947 to March 24, 1948, leading to the creation of the World Trade Organization.

3. Raúl Dellatore, "Del taller clandestino a la gran vidriera" (Sweatshop with big windows), *Pagina12,* May 3, 2015.

47 billion dollars in 2006) has been falling constantly (29.79 in 2011; 19.39 in 2012; 2.28 in 2013; and into the negative numbers in 2014 at -3.95 billion dollars)[1]. The surplus was essentially the result of two items (soybeans and iron ore) sold to two countries (China and Argentina). Essential products account for nearly half of its receipts (22% in 1995), a rather high proportion. Manufactured goods represented less than 19% of exports to developed countries (United States, Japan, European Union) but close to 47% of sales to Latin American countries in 2010. Their portion of exports has also been falling constantly (55.1% in 2005; 39.4% in 2010; 35.6% in 2014). The most negative trade balances in 2014 were with Nigeria (-8.5 billion dollars) and the United States (-7.9 billion dollars). The largest surpluses have been with Venezuela (3.4 billion dollars) and China (3.3 billion dollars)[2]. The first two supplier and customer countries are China (15%) and the United States (12%). Brazilian exports of manufactured goods amounted to less than 0.7% of world trade in this class of commodities in 2013[3].

There is a high level of tariff protection for intermediate goods in Brazil, a legacy of the traditional policy of discouraging importation. These tariffs were preserved when the common external tariffs were established – 10-16% for intermediate goods and -18-20% for consumer goods – comforting national monopolies but compromising the international competitivity of the country's businesses (particularly in cellulose paper and the chemical and steel industries). At the December 2011 Mercosur summit in Montevideo, the decision was taken to increase import duties on some one hundred supplementary products until 2014 within the framework of common external tariffs.

The penetration of imported intermediate products remained stable in Brazil from 2000 to 2006. As regards information technology (computers in particular), Brazil has the highest import duties in the world (currently 16%, down from 30% in 1999) when its partners in the region, with the sole exception of Venezuela (5%), have eliminated them. Nevertheless, essentially as a result of appreciation in the value of the national currency up to 2014, the portion of imported products consumed by households has increased significantly, growing from 14% in 2003 to 23.7% in 2008[4].

In May 2011, Brazil presented a proposal to the WTO Working Group on Trade, Debt and Finance (WGTDF) calling for an analysis of the impact of exchange rates on international trade. That year, the Brazilian Finance Minister Guido Mantega decried what he called "*currency wars*", particularly the practice of "quantitative easing", whereby a central bank buys financial assets, which generally lowers currency prices. Such practices have been implemented in the United States, Japan, the United Kingdom and, recently, by the European

---

1. "Brazilian Trade Balance. Consolidated Data. 2014", Brazilian Ministry of Development, Industry and Foreign Trade (*www.desenvolvimento.gov.br)*

2. *O 'Globo*, May 4, 2015.

3. Plano Nacional de Exportações 2015-2018 (www.desenvolvimento.gov.br)

4. *Valor Económico*, February 13, 2009.

Central Bank, whose president, Mario Draghi, is the former vice president of Goldman Sachs (2002-2005). This practice is judged to be harmful to the real economy over time because it favors banks and stock market speculation and obliges the state to promote privatization, in which the banks are now the prime contractors.

Within the framework of the G20, Brasilia was reluctant at the St. Petersburg summit to extend to 2016 the "standstill clause" devised in Toronto to preserve the status quo, seeing it as being unbalanced, with subsidies given more favorable treatment than customs duties.

In its trade relationships, Brazil suffered then a significant revaluation of its currency (+48% with respect to the dollar between 2008 and 2011) as a result of high interest rates, some of the highest in the world, which provide a partial explanation for the massive influx of foreign capital. During the first half of 2014, the *real-dollar* exchange rate decreased significantly (-14%), a trend that was accentuated in the first half of 2015 (-28%). In order to prevent capital flight and contain inflation, the interest rates were raised to a level that was not consistent with spending on public services (health, education) envisaged in response to the street protests of June 2013. The high amount of foreign investment (64 billion dollars) in the period August 2013-August 2014 included a significant portion of speculative capital attracted by the high interest rates (over 14% per year in June 2015) and exchange rate protection offered by the Brazilian Central Bank. Brazil's balance of current accounts shows a strong deficit (3.5% of GDP)[1].

Given the decreasing share of manufactured goods in exports and the rapid growth of imports, recourse to protectionist measures appears inevitable unless the national currency is significantly devalued. A recent report by the World Trade Organization underscores that, among the G20 countries, Brazil, along with India and Russia, was the country that imposed the most restrictive trade measures in the period from October 2010 to April 2011. The *Brasil Maior* program was implemented in August 2011, constituting in effect a series of measures to decrease importation (reimbursement of taxes and special financing to exporters; customs policies designed to protect automakers producing in Brazil; reduction in salary taxes in sectors offering employment; reduction in interest rates, etc.). It was regarded by the local media as a short-term palliative to the real problems of Brazilian industry. In July 2015, the Brazilian president unveiled an ambitious export plan, "*Plano Nacional de Exportações*". Starting from the observation of a reduction in trade of goods and services as a portion of GDP, less than 28% in 2013 when Brazil's principal BRICS partners saw figures above 50%, the plan embodied the somewhat theoretical and resolutely optimistic prospect of a short-term increase in exports to priority countries[2].

---

[1]. Miriam Leitão, Ciranda Cambial, *O 'Globo*, August 24, 2014

[2]. *Plano Nacional de Exportações* 2015-2018, July 7, 2015 (www.desenvolvimento.gov.br)

The worsening of the balance of trade in 2013 and the growing deficit in service accounts and revenues (-24 billion dollars in 2009; -54 billion dollars in 2010; -70 billion dollars in 2013; -90.9 billion dollars in 2014) are not likely to encourage Brazil to reconsider these measures. All things considered, this protectionist strategy benefits foreign businesses that have set up shop in Brazil. It has not prevented Brazil from being one of the world's principal import markets: for example, the average annual growth in French exports to Brazil in the period 2000-2012 is more than 10% and U.S. exports to Brazil have grown from 11.21 billion dollars in 2003 to 42.4 billion dollars in 2014[1].

Access to the Brazilian public procurement market is limited, and Brazilian companies benefit from a 25% preference margin for national companies, even if the procurement in question is funded internationally. Brazil is not a signatory to the Agreement on Government Procurement, negotiated under the auspices of the World Trade Organization, and is thus exempt from its rules. Enacted on January 1, 1996, this Agreement was not signed by any South American country (Argentina, Chile, Colombia and Panama have held observer status since 1997) and only by one country in the Non-Aligned Movement.

The laborious negotiations between Mercosur and the European Union since 1999 for greater openness to trade have produced no result due to the differences in the processes of integration, disparity in trade flows and the economic heterogeneity of the main sectors. Resumed in 2014, they have the alluring backdrop for Brasilia of opening negotiations between the United States and the European Union, continuation of negotiations between Canada and the European Union, and the establishment of the Trans-Pacific Partnership.

Itamaraty is opposed to the creation of arbitration mechanisms, envisaged in treaties negotiated behind closed doors, entrusted to private courts (investor-state dispute settlement). Multinational corporations and investors would now enjoy the same status as sovereign countries within a framework of privatized justice. It would be used by major corporations to take action against governments whenever they feel that the decisions made – even with the goal of protecting public health or the environment – run counter to their interests.

The lawsuit filed within the framework of the North American Free Trade Agreement by Lone Pine Resources against the Canadian government, which imposed a moratorium in 2013 on hydraulic fracturing in the Saint Lawrence watershed, provides a clear picture of the risks implicit here[2]. So do the suits filed in the late 1990s against South Africa by 38 American and European pharmaceutical laboratories to protect their monopoly on retroviral medicines at a time when 8,000 deaths were being recorded per day from AIDS in the state; those by the Philip Morris company challenging Uruguay's and Australia's public health policies; by the Pacific Rim Mining Company in a case before the

---

1. Source: United States Census Bureau. Trade in Goods with Brazil 2015.

2. Joyce Nelson, "Corporate Coup d'État. Those Crappy Trade Deals", *Counterpunch*, February 13-15, 2015.

International Center for Settlement of Investment Disputes of the World Bank demanding 301 million dollars from El Salvador, which terminated its gold prospecting contract because of pollution caused by the company; by the Swedish group Vattenfall contesting Germany's decision to phase-out nuclear power, demanding 4 billion euros in damages; by Bechtel against Bolivia regarding the privatization of water imposed by the World Bank (Cochabamba Water Revolt).

The most momentous cases before the World Bank's arbitrage body are those regarding Occidental Petroleum's suit against Ecuador (1.77 billion dollars) and Exxon's against Venezuela (1.6 billion dollars). Even if the countries win their cases, the legal costs are very high: El Salvador has spend more than 13 million dollars so far, more than its annual environmental budget[1].

These free trade treaties are also meeting with increasing opposition in the United States, particularly from Congress and trade unions, because of their negative impact on employment. They reward businesses that delocalize production to countries with the laxest tax, social security and environmental regulations. The U.S. trade deficit with the 23 partners who have signed a free-trade treaty amounted to 180 billion dollars in 2013, of which 51 billion regards manufactured goods. The deficit in the U.S. balance of trade with Mexico has exceeded 50 billion dollars every year since 2010[2]. According to the U.S. Department of Labor, some 845,000 workers lost their jobs as a result of the North American Free Trade Agreement and three out of five of them could only find replacement work at lower wages[3]. In truth, protectionism has historically helped economies develop, it favors internal growth.

Labor legislation in the United States is less generous than its Brazilian counterpart (Brazilian workers enjoy 13 months of wages, 4 weeks paid vacation, four to six months paid maternity leave, five days paid paternity leave, and universal healthcare although deficient). Brasilia acknowledges American competitiveness but views the asymmetry in social legislation as representing a bonus for the U.S. Furthermore, the clout of trade unions in Brazil might help maintain a certain equilibrium between productivity gains and salary gains. A recent study by the economist Elise Gould shows that while productivity in the United States increased by 64.9% between 1979 and 2013, hourly wages grew by only 8%[4]. The decline of unions in North American private enterprise, where only 7% of workers are unionized, may be a factor in close to 33% of wage inequality. For example, in the construction industry, in current dollars,

---

1. Manuel Pérez Rocha, "When corporations sue governments", *The New York Times,* December 3, 2014.

2. 66.32 billion dollars in 2010; 64.58 in 2011; 61.71 in 2012; 54.48 in 2013; 53.82 in 2014. Source: United States Census Bureau. Trade in Goods with Mexico 2015.

3. Ben Beachy, "Ten Tall Tales on Trade", *Counterpunch*, January 29, 2015.

4. Elise Gould, "2014 Continues a 35-Year Trend of Broad-Based Wage Stagnation", Economic Policy Institute, February 19, 2015.

hourly wages in 2013 are less than they were in 1973, largely as a consequence of a decrease in union representation in this sector (40% unionized in 1973, 14% now)[1].

A significant portion of international trade takes place between multinationals, tentacular enterprises whose interests often differ from those of national businesses and consumers. The Trans-Pacific Partnership (TPP), which has been in a process of negotiation since March 2010 among twelve countries[2], provides an apt illustration of this issue: negotiations have been conducted under the greatest secrecy as regards public representatives, while more than 500 banks and businesses have been included in the discussions. The North American chief negotiator, Michael Froman, is an executive from Citigroup. The principal directors of banks headquartered in New York signed a letter to New York legislators on May 1, 2015 encouraging them to vote in favor of the TPP. The signatures on the letter include those of Kenneth Jacobs (Lazard), Kenneth Chenault (American Express), Lloyd Blankfein (Goldman Sachs), Jamie Dimon (JP Morgan), Ajay Banga (MasterCard), James Gorman (Morgan Stanley), and Michael Corbat (City Group)[3]. This treaty was put on a fast track through the Senate ("presidential fast track negotiating authority for trade agreements"), eliminating the possibility of amendments or filibusters. One should note that Robert J. Stevens, member of the Monsanto Board of Directors since 2002, former executive director of Lockheed Martin, the premier U.S. defense supplier which doubled stock price over past two years according to Fortune 500 (2015), was appointed by President Obama in 2012 to the Advisory Committee for Trade Policy and Negotiations. The trade deal, reached in Atlanta in October 2015, is seen as a challenge to China´s growing dominance in the Pacific region.

The emergence of Brazil and the difficulties of inter-bloc dialogue have led Brussels, since 2005, to favor bilateral relations with Brazil. A partnership termed "*strategic*" was implemented at the Lisbon summit (July 2007), joining other strategic partnerships signed by the European Union with the United States, Canada, Japan, Russia, China, India and Mexico. It remains to be seen whether the reform of European Union common agricultural policy with, particularly, the elimination of export subsidies and quotas (expected in 2015, for sugar in particular) will serve to revitalize Brazil-European Union dialogue.

Brazil has not signed on to the U.S. Department of State's "Pathways to Prosperity" initiative of 2007, uniting 14 American countries with the Inter-American Development Bank, the Organization of American States, and the Economic Commission for Latin America and the Caribbean. It currently holds observer status. With the sixth annual congress taking place in Cali,

---

1. Nicholas Kristoff, "The Cost of a Decline in Unions", *International New York Times*, February 20, 2015.

2 Australia, Brunei, Canada, Chile, Japan, Malaisia, México, New Zeland, Peru, Singapore, United-States and Vietnam.

3. Zach Carter, "Republican Billionaires love Obama´s Trade Deal", *Huffington Post*, May 5, 2015.

Colombia in October 2012, the initiative has sought to better distribute the benefits of growth among four sectors, or pillars, entrusted to the various member countries: small businesses (Honduras), exchange rates, (Costa Rica, Chile), labor (Uruguay), trade (Peru, United States). The fact remains that 2.5% of Latin Americans hold 50% of the wealth of South America.

The associations linked with the business communities in the United States (Coalition of Services Industries) and Europe (European Services Forum) joined together in the Global Services Coalition lobby, outside the framework of the World Trade Organization, to promote a draft agreement on trade in services (the Trade in Services Agreement), which was revealed on June 3, 2005 in documents published by *Wikileaks*. Some twenty countries[1], the European Commission, and seven Latin American countries took part in these negotiations to accelerate privatization in all sectors and prevent public re-appropriation of a privatized business enterprise. State-owned monopolies will be prohibited (education) and limits will be placed on the exclusive public management of services (water, healthcare, public transportation, etc.). None of the BRICS countries have yet participated in these negotiations, the seventh round taking place behind closed doors inside the Australian embassy in Geneva.

The relatively good economic performance recorded in Latin America during the first decade of the new millennium cannot mask the structural fragility of its economies. Volatility in growth, typical of commodity exporting countries, is partly to blame for stagnation in Brazil and in the region in world trade, contrasting with the growing share held by Asian countries.

Intellectual Property

Brazil has taken a leadership role among developing countries as regards intellectual property and public health measures within the framework of the Doha Development Round. It achieved an important goal in Paragraphs 4-6 of the Doha Declaration on the TRIPS Agreement (Agreement on Trade Related Aspects of Intellectual Property Rights) and Public Health, which grant member countries flexibility with respect to patent rights in order to protect public health. The compromise of 30 August 2003 provided exporting countries the ability to waive territorial patent rights.

Brazil proposed an "action plan for development" in September 2004 with Argentina and the support, notably, of Iran and Kenya, to change the mode of action of the World Trade Organization, accused of unduly favoring patent holders and developed countries. This proposition was opposed by the United States.

---

1. Australia, Canada, Chile, Colombia, South Korea, the United States, Hong Kong, Iceland, Israel, Japan, Liechtenstein, Mexico, Norway, New Zealand, Pakistan, Panama, Paraguay, Peru, Switzerland, Taiwan, Turkey.

In March 2010, the WTO's Intellectual Property Group met, on request by Bolivia, to envisage the creation of a working group having the goal of facilitating access to generic medicines for countries not having a pharmaceutical industry. However, no decision was made regarding a working group to amend Paragraph 6 (compulsory licenses) because of opposition from the United States.

Faced with the issue of the cost of medicines distributed free of charge within the framework of public health programs (AIDS in particular), Brazil has used the threat of compulsory licenses on a number of occasion to put pressure on foreign laboratories (Roche and Merck have proven to be more amenable than Abbott). Currently, only Efavirenz medications developed by the Merck Laboratories, which contain an AIDS/HIV cocktail, have been the object of a compulsory license (in 2007), while Abbott Laboratories' patent for Kaletra was annulled by a Brazilian judge in 2012. Brasilia has stated that close to 90% of the anti-AIDS budget of the Brazilian Ministry of Health goes to "North American multinationals" that produce eight of the fifteen drugs in the anti-AIDS cocktail (the other seven are generic) that Brazil distributes free of charge within its borders and in certain African countries (Cape Verde, Mozambique).

In March 2010, Brazil and India took legal action before the World Trade Organization against the European Union in response to the seizure in European ports of generic medicines en route from India to Brazil. Having failed to shift the dispute to the TRIPS Council in October 2009, the European Union deliberately blurs the distinction between generic and counterfeit medicines to justify holding the generic medicines from India and is developing a new legal framework with the support of Japan and the United States. This stance has been harshly criticized by Oxfam[1]. In September 2011 before the United Nations, President Dilma Rousseff advocated greater flexibility in honoring patents for medicines for treating non-transmissible chronic ailments such as hypertension, diabetes, cancer and respiratory disorders.

Along with South Africa, Argentina, China, India, Cuba, Singapore (representing the Association of South East Asian Nations – ASEAN), Bolivia, and Norway, in March 2013 Brazil came out in favor of a permanent waiver for the poorest countries regarding the TRIPS Agreement. It hopes for a modification of the Agreement (Article 29) in order to combat bio-piracy, making it obligatory to reveal the origin of the genetic resources that go into making a patented invention and, if applicable, to share profits and benefits. It is supported in this effort by China, India, Nigeria, Tanzania, Peru, Bangladesh, Pakistan, and Nepal; the United States strongly opposes this action.

India is one of the world's largest producers of generic medicines, trailing only the United States and China, and the world's largest exporter: it exports some 10 billion dollars worth of medicines every year, mainly to developing countries. The association "Médecins Sans Frontières" (Doctors Without

[1]. Article by Oxfam America representative Rohit Malpani. Source: *O Globo*, June 8, 2010.

Borders) points out that 80% of the generic anti-AIDS drugs that it has provided to some 170.000 patients in Africa come from India. While India has recognized pharmaceutical patents since 2005, it does not recognize patents for pharmaceutical products or ingredients produced prior to that date. The pharmaceutical giant Novartis recently went before the Indian Supreme Court to defend its leukemia drug Gleevec, which costs on the order of 70.000 dollars for one year of treatment, as opposed to 2.500 for a generic medicine manufactured in India[1]. But in its judgment of April 1, 2013, the court ruled that Gleevec had been produced since 1993 and could not benefit from the Indian law adopted in 1995. Sales of Gleevec brought Novartis revenues of some 4.7 billion dollars in 2012. In April of 2013, 120 physicians and specialized researchers signed an article in the journal *Blood* of the American Society of Hematology protesting the prohibitive costs of treatment with the drug and questioning the morality of pharmaceutical laboratories that asked such prices.

Of the 1.2 billion people living in India, only one fourth have health coverage and thus the availability of generic medicines is vital. Following the refusal in 2012 of physicians at the Memorial Sloan-Kettering Cancer Center in New York to treat their patients with the drug Zaltrap because of its high price, Sanofi cut the price by half. In May 2013, the Global Alliance for Vaccines and Immunization (GAVI), funded in part by the Bill and Melinda Gates Foundation, pressured Merck Laboratories and GlaxoSmithKline to significantly reduce the price of their vaccines against cervical cancer (Gardasil and Cervarix) for vaccination programs in the most disadvantaged countries. According to GAVI CEO Seth Berkley, this should make it possible to vaccinate 30 million young women in 40 countries by the year 2020. In spite of this price reduction (from 130 dollars to 5 dollars), "Médecins Sans Frontières" considers the price still too high, pointing out that the production costs of each vaccine are less than twenty-five cents and that the research has been funded for fifty years by U.S. taxpayers via the National Institute of Health. Brazil and other countries in South America had obtained a price reduction (to 13 dollars) for these vaccines negotiated by the World Health Organization.

Production of generic anti-AIDS medicines in Brazil is generally limited to state-owned laboratories and to the domestic market. However, aid in generic medicines has been in place since 2002 for several hundred patients under Brazilian care in Angola, Cape Verde, Botswana, and São Tomé. The Brazilian government has committed to participating in the creation of a pharmaceutical laboratory to produce anti-retrovirus medicines in Mozambique. A partnership agreement with Nigeria to produce anti-retrovirus medicines was signed in 2005. The publicly owned Oswaldo Cruz Foundation (FIOCRUZ) for research and development in biomedical sciences does not yet have the capacity to produce the complete range of anti-retrovirus drugs. Representatives of the

[1]. *International Herald Tribune*, March 7, 2012.

foundation pointed out the high cost of registering patents and of legal costs for small laboratories, including those engendered by "patent trolls", companies that misuse patents as a business strategy, oftentimes preferring to profit through litigation rather than product sales.

The high level of development of the pharmaceutical industry, in Brazil as in India, has been acquired by countries that did not initially observe intellectual property rights. This tends, in many ways, to slow development. Additionally, a definitive exemption to Article 66.1 of the TRIPS Agreement must be implemented to favor the least-developed countries[1].

In April 2013, the British Office of Fair Trading accused the pharmaceutical giant GlaxoSmithKline of secretly paying small rival labs (Alpharma, Generics, Norton Healthcare) to delay release of generic medicines in order to favor GSK's monopoly position with its drug Seroxat (paroxetine), sold in the United States under the name of Paxil. Once a generic arrives on the market, the price falls by 70-80%. The Supreme Court of the United States heard a similar case regarding Solvay Pharmaceuticals, its brand-name drug Androgel, and its agreement with the generic drug company Actavis. In 2005, the European Commission levied a heavy fine against the drug company AsraZenica for having delayed the release of a generic drug competing with its anti-ulcer medicine Losec. In June 2013, European Commissioner for Competition, Joaquín Almunia, announced that the Danish pharmaceutical company Lundbeck was fined 94 million euros for having delayed, starting in 2004, the release onto the market of a competing generic medicine (Citalopram) until its own stocks had been depleted. A Chinese laboratory that has succeeded in producing and delivering an anti-Ebola drug in large quantities, based on the North American drug ZMapp, currently undergoing testing in Sierra Leone, now finds itself facing a lawsuit for patent violation[2].

The Bolivarian Alliance for the Peoples of Our America (ALBA) implemented a mechanism in August 2013 to guarantee provisions of basic medicines among the eight member countries (ALBAmed, Regulatory Center for Medicines). Mercosur has taken inspiration from this mechanism and implemented a purchasing center for the most costly medicines with the support of the Pan American Health Organization[3]. The Trans-Pacific Partnership trade deal, if approved by the elected legislators of the 12 countries concerned, will extend patent protection for brand-name drugs preventing similar and much cheaper generic drugs. It will affect health-care budgets and drug access in all signatories countries, especially the poorest ones (Vietnam, Peru, Malaysia). According to a report released in October 2015 by Citizens for

---

[1]. An extension to the transitional period (10 years, expiring January 1, 2006) may be granted for a "duly motivated request".

[2]. Sheri Fink, "A Chinese Ebola Drug Raises Hopes, and Rancor", *International New York Times*, June 11, 2015.

[3]. Lígia Formenti, "Mercosul fará compra conjunta de remédios" (Mercosur to buy medicines jointly), *O Estado de São Paulo,* June 12, 2015.

Tax Justice and the US Public Interest Research Group Education Fund[1], of the 30 Fortune 500 companies with the most money held in off-shore tax-havens, 9 are pharmaceuticals companies (Pfizer, Merck, Johnson and Johnson, Proctor & Gamble, Amgen, Eli Lilly, Bristol-Myers- Squibb, AbbVie Inc., Abott Laboratories)[2].

Global Financial Governance: the World Bank and the International Monetary Fund

Following the commitments undertaken at the G20 meeting in Pittsburgh in September 2009, the membership of southern countries in the World Bank was increased to 47.19%. Brazil's share rose from 2.06% to 2.44%. The United States' share remained unchanged at 16.85%.

In 2012, for the first time in its history, the election of the president of the World Bank, traditionally held by an American, witnessed the nominations of candidates from developing countries (former Colombian Minister of Finance and Agriculture, José Antonio Ocampo; current Nigerian Minister of Finance, Ngozi Okonjo-Iweala). At its third summit, held in New Delhi in March 2012, the BRICS group emphasized that the presidency of the World Bank should be chosen through a democratic process and that the Bank should change its current role as mediator between North and South to one where it promotes true partnership on issues of development. Former Brazilian Finance Minister Guido Mantega declared that the candidate must be chosen according to merit and not on the basis of nationality[3].

The Economist, the *Financial Times* and Nobel Economics laureate Joseph Stiglitz all came out in favor of the Nigerian candidate. In spite of the fact that the Colombian candidate withdrew from the race prior to the election, the U.S. candidate, a Korean American, Jim Yong Kim, was chosen by the 25 members of the board. The president must gain an 85% majority from the Board of Directors, where the voting power of each member is based on its share of contributions to the Bank; the United States has a share of 15,85%, giving it the power to block any unfavorable decision and virtually guaranteeing the election of an American.

According to our contacts at Itamaraty, the World Bank should be reformed based on the model of the main regional banks, where the allocation of voting power does not favor the largest shareholders but treats all member countries equally. At a time when the World Bank and the International Monetary Fund

---

1. CTJ is a Washington D.C. based advocacy think tank founded in 1979 dealing primarily with federal tax policy. PIRG is an independent, non-partisan group that works for consumers and for the public interest; it was proposed in the book *Action for a Change* (1971) by Ralph Nader and Donald Ross.

2. "*Offshore Shell Games 2015. The Use of Offshore Tax Havens by Fortune 500 Companies*", (Table 2. Top 30 Companies with the Most Money Held Offshore), October 6, 2015.

3. *Prensa Latina*, Brasilia, April 5, 2012.

are turning to emerging countries for support in alleviating the financial crisis afflicting many developed countries, this sort of monopoly power is deemed anachronistic. According to the annual report of the United Nations Development Program (UNDP) for the year 2013, between 2000 and the third quarter of 2011, world cash reserves grew from 1.9 billion dollars to 10.1 billion dollars, much of it due to the reserves built up by emerging and developing countries (6.8 billion dollars) during this period. Companies originating in the South represented less than 4% in the Global Forum 500 classification; in 2011 they were 22%.

All things considered, the profile of the new leader of the World Bank, Jim Yong Kim, and his experience in public health, particularly with the programs of the World Health Organization regarding HIV, malaria and tuberculosis, and with his own NGO "Partners in Health", could presage a shifting of priorities towards reducing poverty, which was indeed the institution's original purpose.

While the portion of the world's population living below the poverty threshold (two dollars per day) has decreased significantly in percentage terms, the number of people living below this line is the same as it was in 1981, some 2.5 billion people, accounting for demographic development. A large part of these people live on the outskirts of large urban agglomerations and local authorities do not have the means to ensure the minimum necessary infrastructure without the financial support of the World Bank. According to statistical data published by the International Monetary Fund in May 2013, 0.5% of the world's population holds 35% of global wealth. The 400 richest Americans have an accumulated wealth of two trillion dollars, equal to Russia's Gross Domestic Product[1].

The dynamic "Economically More Developed Countries" (EMDC) benefited in theory from a shift in IMF quota shares of over 6%[2], decided at the Meeting of Finance Ministers and Central Bank Governors in Gyeongju, South Korea in October 2010. However, this decision has yet to be heeded. The US Congress has failed to approve the reform on four occasions since 2010. The BRICS countries referred to this commitment in the final communiqué on their work at the New Delhi summit, linking their complementary financial support requested by the IMF in order to double its intervention funds to the effective implementation of the Gyeongju decision. During Egyptian President Mohamed Morsi's visit to Brasilia in May 2013, Dilma Rousseff once again emphasized the urgency of changes in the IMF's quota and voting system.

BRICS countries represent 27% of world GDP but only hold – assuming that the 2010 reform is actually implemented – 14% of the votes in the IMF (10 % prior to October 2010); the European Union generates 20% of world

---

[1]. Stéphane Lauer, *Le Monde.fr*, September 16, 2013 (citing an investigation by *Forbes* magazine).

[2]. Quota shares are allocated based on the decision of an 85% majority, thus necessarily with the agreement of the United States, which holds a 17.67% voting share in the IMF and 15.85% in the World Bank.

GDP but controls nearly one third of IMF votes. The Netherlands and Belgium currently hold a high share of votes in the IMF than Brazil (2.08% and 1.86% versus 1.72%); Belgium has nearly three times the voting power of Nigeria (1.86% versus 0.72%).

Brazil has requested the modification of certain methods of calculation used by the IMF, considering them to be outdated and prejudicial to emerging countries (such as the calculation of public deficits and the exclusion of investment expenditures, especially in infrastructure).

Shortly after his inauguration on January 1, 2003, President Lula voluntarily proposed a budget surplus before debt payments of 4.25% of GDP (the previous government had stuck to the 3.75% mandated by the IMF). He maintained and met this objective until 2007. The loan from the International Monetary Fund was repaid in advance (15.5 billion dollars in December 2005) and the agreement was not renewed. Currently, some 80% of government debt is owed to enterprises in Brazil which are thus anxious to avoid a depreciation in the national currency yet intervening sharply in July and August 2015. Brazilian public debt has little exposure to variations in the exchange rate (less than 5 %).

The country had significantly improved its investment ranking during the Lula years but Standard & Poor´s downgraded Brazil´s bonds in September 2015 from investment-grade to "junk". In spite of a decrease in economic growth, Brazil is ranked third or fourth globally, after China (and Hong Kong), the United States, and Canada in terms of foreign investment. According to the World Investment Report by the United Nations Conference on Trade and Development (UNCTAD), the inflow of foreign investments rose to 65.3 billion dollars in 2012. The country's foreign exchange reserves amounted to some 371 million dollars at the end of 2012. This brought improvement to Brazil's stature and credibility in the eyes of international financial institutions as long as the fragile balance of its accounts was not called into question.

President Lula has always demonstrated a certain hostility towards the IMF, which he criticizes for having maintained policies that have often had disastrous social consequences for developing countries, victimized by what amount to veritable diktats imposed by the institution. Nevertheless, Brazil agreed to lend some 10 billion dollars to the IMF in January 2009. The former Brazilian representative to the IMF, Paulo Nogueira Batista, abstained from the vote to support Greece with a 1.7 billion dollar loan in August 2013, contrary to the wishes of Finance Minister Guido Mantega, believing that Greece could not provide sufficient guarantees of repayment. Appointed to his post in 2007 by Mantega, Nogueira Batista feels that the IMF is quite indulgent when it is a question of loans to European countries, in stark contrast with the severity that has been observed historically in its relations with Latin American countries[1].

---

1. *O´Globo*, August 2, 2013.

It is clear that the dynamic axis of the market economy is currently shifting toward the Asian Pacific while European countries are losing their preeminence among the world's economic powers. This also means that they are displacing emerging countries as major borrowers from the International Monetary Fund, and thus as its major debtors. Many emerging economies vowed that they will never borrow from the IMF again.

It is symptomatic that Portugal, which requested a 78 billion dollar loan from the European Union in 2011 and is now in a severe recession, is now turning to Brazil: the number of Portuguese requesting work visas in Brazil rose from 52.900 in 2010 to 328.860 in 2011[1]. This calls to mind the words of the writer Luis Felipe Castro Mendes: "*If Portugal is Brazil's past, Brazil is Portugal's future*". Itamaraty is currently studying a mechanism to facilitate and incentivize the repatriation of qualified Brazilians residing abroad: more than 2.5 million, one half in the United States, one third in Europe and one tenth in Japan[2].

The emerging institutions of Latin America (Development Bank of Latin America – CAF, established in 1970, including 18 countries and 14 private banks; Bank of the South-*Banco del Sur*, created in 2007), the Development Bank, and the Reserve Fund of the BRICS group of countries are all elements of South-South cooperation, gradually reworking the financial architecture of the world. This is also accomplished by a number of initiatives, such as the Shanghai Cooperation Organization, tracing its origins to the Shanghai Five in 1996 (China, Russia, Kyrgyzstan, Kazakhstan, Tajikistan, with Uzbekistan joining in 2001); the Chiang Mai Initiative, launched following the Asian crisis in 1997 and now multilateralized; the Arab Monetary Fund, created in 1976 by the members of the Arab League; the Regional Cooperation Fund of the Reserve Bank of India to favor South Asian countries; and the Asian Infrastructure Investment Bank, a Chinese initiative headquartered in Beijing with 27 founding member countries as of March 30, 2015, including eastern Asian countries, countries in the Middle East (Qatar, Saudi Arabia, Jordan, Kuwait, Oman) and Europe (Germany, France, United Kingdom, Switzerland, Italy, Luxembourg), with the United States taking a hostile stance.

Brazil rallied to the support of Argentina's proposal to create a UN commission on debt restructuring. In September 2015 the General Assembly of the United Nations, on Argentina's initiative, adopted by a vote of 136-6[3], the ethical principles governing debt restructuring to prevent speculative vulture funds, which invest in distressed securities and then sue the debtor country in U.S. courts for a larger amount than the purchasing price[4].

---

1. *International Herald Tribune*, March 15, 2012.

2. *O ´Globo*, February 17, 2013.

3. The European Union abstained. Nay votes were cast by the United States, the United Kingdom, Germany, Japan, Canada, and Israel.

4. Tomás Lukin, "Se puso um limite a los piratas del siglo XXI" (Limit placed on 21st-century pirates), *Página12*, September 13, 2015.

CHAPTER 4

AFFIRMATION ON THE GLOBAL SCENE

Beyond its rapprochement with the large emerging countries in multilateral trade negotiations, Brazil's demand for a permanent seat on the United Nations Security Council, placing it within the larger framework of a reform of world governance, has led it to take a series of initiatives that go well beyond the regional sphere in its diplomatic influence.

Innovative financing and UNITAID

Since President Lula's first term in office (2003-2006), Brazil has sought to persuade the major industrialized nations, with mixed results, to allocate new multilateral financial resources to help in the fight against poverty, hunger and infectious disease (AIDS, malaria, tuberculosis). Following up on the proposition presented by Lula during his speech before the General Assembly of the United Nations on September 20, 2004, the "Declaration on Innovative Sources of Financing for Development" was presented during the 2005 General Assembly, with the co-sponsorship of Algeria, Germany, Chile, and Spain. A central drug-purchase facility (UNITAID) was created at the UN conference on AIDS on June 2, 2006. It has an annual budget on the order of 300 million dollars, two thirds of it from an innovative levy on airline tickets. France is the largest contributor (197 million dollars in 2010). Its financial support between 2006 and 2014 (close to 1,4 billion dollars) amounts to some 58% of total contributions. Thirty countries, twenty of them African, take part in UNITAID, but only fourteen provided financial support in 2010 (Spain, France, United Kingdom, Norway, Luxembourg, Chile, Brazil, South Korea, Congo, Guinea, Mali, Madagascar, Mauritius), along with the Bill and Melinda Gates Foundation. Brazil pledged to provide 11 million dollars in 2011. Originally in favor of a tax on arms sales, Brazil rallied to the French proposition to levy a tax on airline tickets[1]. The chairman of the UNITAID Executive Board is a former French Minister of Foreign Affairs, Dr. Philippe

[1]. In 2008-2009, the five permanent members of the Security Council earned some 30.5 billion dollars from arms sales, two thirds going to the United States and Russia (source: Stockholm International Peace Research Institute – www.sipri.org). Taxing arms sales would have generated significantly more resources than the airline ticket levy. UNITAID funds are much less than those going to the U.S. PEPFAR fund (President's Emergency Plan for AIDS Relief), initially announced at 45 billion dollars for the period 2008-2013, but reduced by some 20% by the Obama administration. The North American fund works on a bilateral basis with a group of 88 countries, of which 15 are priority. Ambassador Eric Goosby coordinated the program from June 2009 to November 2013, when he was succeeded by current coordinator, Ambassador Deborah Birx.

Douste-Blazy, and the Executive Director since October 2014 is the Argentinian sociologist, Lelio Marmora.

The UNITAID drug purchase facility is managed by the Global Fund to Fight AIDS, Tuberculosis and Malaria, created in 2001. The Fund receives three quarters of its financing from G8 countries and is currently managed by the Colombian banker Gabriel Jaramillo, president of the Santander Bank in Brazil from 1999 to 2008. The Fund has received some 26 billion dollars between 2001 and 2013. The largest sources of state funding come from the United States (8.53 billion dollars), France, Japan, Germany, the United Kingdom, and the European Union. Aid to Brazil for its anti-AIDS policy was suspended in November 2010 because Brazil was not honoring its financial commitments to the Fund.

Brazil made a first modest contribution (1 million dollars) to the Global Alliance for Vaccines and Immunisation (GAVI) in 1973. GAVI represents a group of public and private organizations. Its major supporters are the United Kingdom (5 billion dollars since 2000), the Bill and Melinda Gates Foundation, France, Norway, Italy, and the United States.

Climate and the Environment: Climate Change Aid Fund to Low-Income Countries

Following the lines of the Green Fund suggested by Mexico in 2008, and with the support of South Africa, India, and China, Brazil championed the creation of a fund to aid the poorest countries at the Copenhagen Conference in 2009, laying out a number of non-negotiable points for Southern countries. Commitments to reduce greenhouse gas emissions had to be voluntary for these countries (i.e. not subject to a binding pledge and review system). International control must not be exercised over non-funded initiatives by industrialized countries, a concern relating to the green economy in developing countries that fear "environmental protectionism" by industrialized countries. Developed countries must pledge, in writing, not to impose trade barriers using climate protection as a pretext.

The only agreement emerging from the conference, rather theoretical in nature, was to limit global warming to less than two degrees centigrade in the coming century. Brazil supported the Tuvalu proposal to limit warming to 1.5 degrees. This proposal was also supported by a group of African states and by the islands in the Alliance of Small Island States (AOSIS)[1]. Its position has developed significantly over the years. In Copenhagen, Brazil proposed to achieve 2005 emissions levels by 2020 (1.700 tons of CO_2 per year), representing a reduction of 36-39% for Brazil.

---

[1]. The Alliance of Small Island States was created in 1990 as an intergovernmental organization to address the issues of global warming. It is composed of 39 member countries, including Cuba and Haiti, and 5 observers. It represents 20% of the members of the United Nations.

The Copenhagen Green Climate Fund was placed under the direct control of a council of 24 countries – developed and developing – created at the Conference. Starting in 2020, the council would mobilize 100 billion dollars per year (of which 30 were expected from the European Union, the United States, and Japan between 2010 and 2012) in aid to emerging countries, including compensation through the REDD mechanism (Reducing Emissions from Deforestation and forest Degradation). This was an ambitious objective given the economic crisis facing the presumed donor countries.

After laborious negotiations at the Durban Conference (November 28 - December 9, 2011), developed and developing countries accepted the obligation to reduce greenhouse gas (GHG) emissions starting in 2020, based on norms to be developed and adopted prior to 2015. It is clear that the two major sources of these emissions (China and the United States), responsible for 43% of global GHG emissions, have to commit to reducing their emissions as early as possible. The United States has pledged to achieve by 2020 emission reductions of 17% with respect to 2005 levels, in line with the directives of the Copenhagen Conference (December 2009).

As coordinator of the G77 on the future of the Kyoto Protocol, Brazil worked to harmonize the different viewpoints in preparation for Rio+20 (June 13-22, 2012), the fifth major UN conference on the environment (after Stockholm 1972, Rio de Janeiro 1992, Johannesburg 2002, and Copenhagen 2009).

Brazil is a vital international actor in climate and biodiversity issues because of the enormous importance of the Amazon Basin. It embraces one fifth the world's renewable freshwater reserves. It is also the world's fourth-largest consumer of fresh water, after the United States, China, and India. Although it is relatively energy-independent and almost all of this energy derives from hydroelectric sources, it is nevertheless a significant source of greenhouse gases as a result of the cutting and burning of the Amazonian forest (hardwood market, expansion of croplands, expansion of livestock raising). According to the Netherlands Environmental Assessment Agency, Brazil was responsible for 5% of world GHG emissions in 2010, less than Russia (6%), India (8%), and especially China (26%), the United States (18%) and the European Union (14%), but more than Japan (4%), Indonesia (4%), Mexico (2.5%), Canada (2.5%), and South Africa (2%).

In 1998, the Brazilian government created a Fund for the Amazon with the goal of collecting some 20 billion dollars by 2020 to complement the compensation made under the REDD-plus mechanism. As of January 1, 2010, there was less than 200 million dollars in the Fund. Norway was the first donator[1].

---

[1]. Norway pledged to contribute one billion dollars by 2015, with the condition of being able to monitor achievement of annual objectives.

In the period 2000-2010, some 175.000 km^2 (an area larger than England) of the Brazilian Amazon was deforested[1]. The pace of deforestation has since decreased but is still considerable.

In December 2009, Brazil enacted binding climate legislation (*Política nacional de mudanças climaticas*) with special emphasis on deforestation and polluting industries. This led to the establishment of an interministerial committee on climate change, the creation of a National Climate Change Fund in the Ministry of the Environment and an Innovation Fund for the Environment by the National Bank for Economic and Social Development (or Brazilian Development Bank, BNDES) with 70 million euros to finance companies that develop programs to generate their own electricity. However, a certain amount of skepticism is generated by this legislation, which is subject to consensual negotiations among all parties. The implementation of these funds has been delayed. In the year 2011, 13% of the financing provided by the Brazilian Development Bank went to renewable energy projects[2]. In spite of the prosecution of the principal polluters (e.g. Petrobras, Compagnie Sidérurgica Nacional, Votorantim) and the heavy fines imposed by the courts, no payments have yet been made.

Itamaraty is opposed to REDD on issues of sovereignty. Presented by a coalition of tropical states led by Costa Rica and Papua New Guinea during the 2005 United Nations Climate Change Conference (including the 11th Conference of the Parties – COP11), this mechanism aims to co-finance efforts to protect forests. A consensus has taken form (REDD-plus) regarding financial aid to developing countries that meet one of the following criteria: reduction in carbon emissions resulting from deforestation or forest degradation; increase in forest reserves; conservation management of the forest. But there is some disagreement on the means for achieving these goals. Brazil does not support the carbon credits market, favoring instead the establishment of a compensatory fund by developed countries. It defended this position at COP12 in Nairobi in 2007 and at COP20 in Rio de Janeiro in 2012. Peru's request for some 200 million dollars in international contributions to reduce deforestation falls within this framework. Honduran forests received 50 million euros in October 2013 from the European Union's Forest Law Enforcement Governance and Trade (FLEGT) Action Plan. Honduras and Guyana are the only Latin American countries to have benefited from this program. Ecuador had sought 3.6 billion dollars to preserve the Yasuni National Park, an UNESCO biosphere reserve since 1989 but lying over oil reserves estimated at 800 million barrels. After the failure of the Yasuni Ishpingo-Tambococha-Tiputini (ITT) Initiative, designed to keep the oil in the ground in exchange for international contributions, the Ecuadorian government gave the green light to drilling, saying "*the world has failed us*".

---

1. *O 'Globo*, June 12, 2010.

2. Jacques Marcovitch, "Como avançar na Rio+20" (The way forward from Rio+20), *Política Externa*, May 2012.

With the help of the Ford Foundation, which is particularly active in Brazil, a pioneering program (*Reserva Extrativista* – extractive reserve) was implemented to favor indigenous populations whose lives and livelihoods depend on the forest. The program is administered by the Chico Mendes Institute for Biodiversity Conservation, the Brazilian Ministry of the Environment's administrative arm, created in 2007. This program may serve as a model for Indonesia and South Africa.

The Amazon Cooperation Treaty[1] fostered an international organization in 1998 which has been headquartered in Brasilia since 2002. However the country has limited its sphere of action to some extent. Former president of the World Trade Organization, Pascal Lamy, declared his support in 2005 for international management of shared public assets, among which he included the tropical forests, a position apparently shared by Peter Mandelson, then European Commissioner for Trade. Some 400.000 km^2 of forests have been destroyed since the Treaty was signed. According to the Hadley Centre for Climate Prediction and Research, operating within the UK Met Office, if the current rate of global warming continues, the Amazon rainforest will be totally gone by 2080[2].

The resignation of the Minister of the Environment, then a close Lula associate, Marina Silva, Green Party candidate in the October 2010 presidential election and of the Brazilian Socialist Party (PSB) in the October 2014 election; the many scandals brought to light by the federal police, including corruption charges against the former director of the Brazilian Institute of Environment and Renewable Natural Resources (IBAMA); the imprisonment in 2011 of 83 high officials, among them the former Governor of the State of Mato Grosso and his secretaries of the Environment and Climate Change, responsible for one third of illegal deforestation since 1989; the adoption in August 2012 of a new and more liberal draft of the Forestry Code, granting amnesty to violators[3]; the arrest by federal police in April 2013 of the Secretaries of the Environment in the State of Rio Grande do Sul and the city of Porto Alegre with some fifty officials under the accusation of fraud; the imprisonment in April 2015 of the Commissioner for Environmental Protection in the State of Rio de Janeiro (DPMA) on corruption charges; and, lastly, the proposal to amend the constitution to eliminate executive authority over the definition and delimitation of indigenous territories, which stirred heated protests by thousands of Indios in the Brazilian capital on October 2, 2013, have all done little to encourage international donations.

---

[1]. Signed in Brasilia in July 1978 by eight states: Bolivia, Brazil, Colombia, Ecuador, Guyana, Peru, Suriname, Venezuela. The Secretary-General is the former Ambassador of Suriname to Brasilia, Robby Ramlakhan.

[2]. Rubens Ricupero, "A Amazonia e a Rio+20" (The Amazon and Rio+20), *Politica Externa*, May 2012.

[3]. Paulo Adario (Greenpeace). "Sorriso amarelo na Rio+20" (A yellow smile at Rio+20), *O 'Globo*, April 30, 2010.

After this amnesty to violators, the pace of deforestation seems to have increased. According to the satellite-based deforestation monitoring and alert system (*Sistema de Alerta de Desmatamento*), from August 2012 to June 2013, the rate of deforestation increased by 103% (a total of 1.838 km^2 deforested) in relation to a similar period one year earlier[1]. The Justice Minister condemned the parliamentary maneuver, but Dilma Rousseff's administration has proven to the slowest at delimiting and protecting indigenous lands since the presidency of José Sarney (1985-1990).

The major industrialized countries are more strongly in favor of the implementation of a global organization or an international agency for the environment: Brasilia takes a dim view of this proposition, fearing an "internationalization of the Amazon". Brazil would rather see the adoption of a global code of the forest with fewer legal constraints than that envisaged by the World Forestry Congress in Durban in September 2015. It is in favor of compulsory contributions to the United Nations Environment Programme, which are still voluntary. This financing mechanism is designed to respond to supplementary needs regarding climate, ecological forest management, mercury, and biodiversity issues but is currently rendered ineffective by the reluctance of the major contributors (i.e. the United States). Brazil has also expressed support for a dual approach, addressing both the environment and the social issues associated with it.

The Executive Secretary for the Convention on Biodiversity of the United Nations for 2012-2016 is the Brazilian Braulio Ferreira de Souza Dias, Secretary for Forest Biodiversity in the Brazilian Ministry of the Environment. During working meetings of the United Nations Convention on Climate Change, Brazil presented an ambitious plan for substantial reduction of greenhouse gas emissions associated with the Amazon Basin by 2020. At the Climate Conference in Durban in December 2011 (COP17), Brazil broke with its BRICS partners China and India by supporting European Union efforts to set 2015 as the year for a binding global agreement on climate.

However, twenty years after the United Nations Conference on Environment and Development (Rio Summit) in 1992, after the institution of the World Social Forum (Porto Alegre, 2001), a rallying point for the alter-globalization movement, and just after hosting the Rio Earth Summit 2012, proposed by Lula in 2007, Brazil ranked 62nd among countries of relevance in the fight against atmospheric pollution. This is certainly better than its BRIC partners (Russia, 69th; China 121st; India 123rd), but not enough to give it credibility internationally[2]. Emissions of greenhouse gases, approximately half of which arise from deforestation, increased by 62% between 1990 and 2005. At the Copenhagen Conference in December 2009 (COP15), Brazil was questioned by representatives of the Green Party in the European Parliament

[1]. Míriam Leitão, "Desmatamento continua" (Deforestation continues), *O Globo*, July 17, 2013.

[2]. Source: Environmental Performance Index, 2010, Yale and Columbia Universities.

about the increase in carbon dioxide emissions (+75% in the State of Rio de Janeiro) caused by the startup of a production facility belonging to the Brazilian steel company Companhia Siderurgica Nacional, which was privatized in 1993. Created in the early 1940s, CSN set aside large tracts of land for employee housing and facilities, land which it actually uses to store hazardous materials (e.g. lead, cadmium, benzene) that have become a worrisome source of contamination for neighboring populations[1].

Brazil refused to participate in the meeting of the Inter-American Commission on Human Rights of the Organization of American States held on October 26, 2011 and addressing plans for the Belo Monte hydroelectric plant. Furthermore, in a gesture of irritation, it withdrew the candidacy of the former Secretary for Human Rights in the Lula administration, Paulo de Cesar Vannuchi, as its representative on the Commission. Since that date, Brazil has no representative in the OAS. The nomination of Guilherme Patriota – brother of Antonio, former Minister of External Relations and currently Permanent Representative of Brazil to the United Nations – in May 2015 was rejected in a secret vote by the Senate. This marks the first time in Brazil's history that a diplomat in high standing has been rejected by the Senate, an action that Celso Amorim qualified as a gesture of ill will by the senators towards President Rousseff[2]. However, it was defended by the leader of the opposition party in the Senate (PSDB), Cassio Cunha Lima, on the basis of the overly favorable stance vis-à-vis Venezuela expressed by the diplomat during hearings in the Chamber.

Located on the Xingu River within the Xingu National Park, this hydroelectric plant is part of a complex of six dams approved by the Brazilian Congress in July 2005 and scheduled to go into operation in 2019. It has met with opposition from the alter-globalization movement, from the principal NGOs and the indigenous communities, who are concerned about the impact of the project on the populations living along the river. The World Commission on Dams[3] has expressed a negative opinion of this project, recalling the unfortunate experience of the Balbina Dam near Manaus, built between 1975 and 1986 and flooding 2.700 km^2 of Amazon forest. The Belo Monte dam (in Altamira) is expected to flood more than twice that area. It will be the world's third-largest dam by generating capacity, behind the Three Gorges Dam and the Itaipu Dam on the border with Paraguay.

Brazil has earmarked more than two thirds of its energy budget (67.3%) in the period 2010-2020 for oil and gas prospecting. Investments in new and

---

[1] Flávia Milhorance, "Envenenados, solo, água e ar trazem riscos à saúde" (Poisoned soil, water, and air pose health risk), *O 'Globo*, May 25, 2015.

[2] Personal conversation, Rio de Janeiro, July 3, 2015.

[3]. A commission created in April 1997 by the World Bank. It is composed of 12 members, including two Brazilians, José Goldemberg, former Minister of Science and Technology, and Achim Steiner, director of the United Nations Environment Programme. Its report and recommendations were published in 2000 (WCD 2000 – "Dams and Development: A New Framework for Decision Making").

alternative energy sources for the same period represent less than 7% of that budget. The scenarios for developing the recently discovered deep off-shore oilfields will doubtlessly increase emissions of greenhouse gases. According to the ten-year energy plan, *Plano Decenal de Energia*, the increase in the share of renewable energy in the country's energy portfolio will be less than 1% (going from the current 45.6% to 46.3%), despite Brazil's membership in the Global Bioenergy Partnership (GBEP[1]) created in 2007. The report published in March 2012 by the Organization for Economic Co-operation and Development (OECD) forecast a 50% increase in greenhouse gas emissions by 2050 if more ambitious policies are not put in place. Fossil fuels (oil, coal, national gas) are still expected to provide 85% of energy at that time.

More than thirty years ago, Brazil decided to develop its production of biofuels deriving from sugar cane. Until 2010, it was the world's largest exporter of ethanol. Ninety percent of its automobiles are flexible fuel vehicles, burning a mixture of gasoline and ethanol. Ethanol – of which Brazil is among the world's major producers – produces five times less greenhouse gases than petroleum-based fuels. On the international level, Brazil has found itself faced with heavy duties imposed by the United States (until 2011) and the European Union, and this has given rise to disputes. It has also had to answer critics claiming that biofuels result in a reduction in land dedicated to food crops and will lead to an increase in the price of agricultural food products. Brasilia sought to differentiate between corn-based biofuels (the mainstay in the United States, the world's largest producer), which consume seven times as much energy in the transformation process into ethanol as sugar cane or palm oil, the prime producers of the latter being Malaysia and Indonesia. In 2010, 40% of the United States corn crop (138 million tons, 15% of world production) was used to produce ethanol at a cost of 6 billion dollars. Working with the specialized agency EMBRAPA[2], the Brazilian authorities drafted a sugar-cane cropland development plan that would spare the Amazon forest. However, in May 2013, the Senate's Environmental Commission – chaired since February of that year by one of the country's principal soybean producers, *bête noire* of ecologists, Blairo Maggi, former governor of the State of Mato Grosso (2003-2010) – approved the extension of sugar cane cultivation into the Amazon. The consequence would be an advancement of the frontiers of stock-raising operations and an increase in the deforestation rate.

The Environmental Performance Index, developed by the Universities of Yale and Columbia, the World Economic Forum, and the European Union,

---

[1]. Instituted in March 2006, GBEP includes the G8 countries plus Brazil, China, India, Mexico, and South Africa. It was originally chaired by former Italian Minister of the Environment, Corrado Clini. Its current chair is Francesco La Camera, former Director-General for Sustainable Development at the Italian Ministry of the Environment. The co-chair is Brazilian diplomat Mariangela Rebuá. It currently numbers 23 member and 22 observer countries. The major international organizations are participants.

[2]. *Empresa Brasileira de Pesquisa Agropecuaria* - Brazilian Agricultural Research Corporation.

ranks countries on the basis of their environmental performance. In 2012, Brazil was placed relatively well at 30th, well ahead of its BRICS partners (Russia 106th; China 116th; India 125th; South Africa 128th), partially because of the wealth of biodiversity in the Amazon rainforest. The rural exodus, the demographic expansion of destitute populations, and burgeoning urbanization have led to an alarming outcome: 44% of households do not have access to safe drinking water and 80% of their wastewater goes untreated. In the period 2000-2010, bracketing the Lula presidency, the rate of provision of basic sanitation to homes was slower than it had been in the previous decade[1].

On the whole, performance on environmental protection during the Lula years is somewhat mixed and Brasilia has little possibility to use it as leverage in international fora. This is evidenced by Brazil's low prestige after the resignation of Marina Silva, a member of Brasilia's political elite, as Minister of the Environment (the Ministry receives less than 1% of the federal budget); the liberalization of genetically modified organisms (soy in 2003, corn in 2007), with responsibility for inspections not in the hands of the Ministry of the Environment but in those of an interministerial commission (*Comissão Tecnica Nacional de Biosegurança*) associated with the office of the president; and the continuation of deforestation at a rate of some 17.500 square kilometers per year (2000-2010) despite the creation in 2003 of a permanent interministerial commission[2].

It is true that the deforestation rate in the Amazon appears to have dropped off by some 75% (27.000 km² deforested in 2004; 6.200 km² in 2011[3]; 4.571 km² in 2012[4]), but it still remains high. Indeed, it would increase in 2013 (5.891 km², an increase of 29% according to the National Institute for Space Research – INPE) and again in 2014. The pace has decreased but even at this rate the destruction of the Amazon forest is an inevitable outcome. Brazil is not a signatory to the New York Declaration on Forests, produced during the Climate Summit in September 2014 attended by some 120 heads of state. The non-binding Declaration calls for halving deforestation rates by 2020 and eliminating deforestation altogether by 2030. India and China also declined to sign the initiative, which is supported by 34 countries, including the United States. During her official trip to the United States (June 30 - July 2, 2015), the Brazilian president pledged to stop illegal deforestation by 2030, renewing this commitment during her speech before the United Nations General Assembly in September 2015, without being in a position to state the pace or extent of legal deforestation. This was a commitment that had already been made in

[1]. Cássia Almeida, Seima Schmidt, Letícia Lins. "Censo mostra que metade do país ainda não tem esgoto; avanço foi mais lento que nos anos 90" (Survey shows that half of households are not connected to the sewer system and that the rate of progress in this regard is lower than during the 1990s), *O 'Globo*, April 30, 2011.

[2]. *Grupo de Trabalho Interministerial Permanente para o Controle e Redução do Desmatamento na Amazonia.*

[3]. Source: National Institute for Space Research (INPE) in Agostinho Vieira, *O 'Globo*, May 3, 2012.

[4]. *O 'Globo,* June 6, 2013.

December 2008, when the National Climate Change Plan (*Plano Nacional sobre Mudança de Clima*) was published, but little had been done to follow up.

One of the effects of deforestation is a significant loss in biodiversity, which is aggravated by the fact that soy farmers make wide use of genetically modified seed. Prohibited in Brazil in 1999, GMOs were authorized in 2003 by President Lula under pressure from farmers in the south of the country who had illegally acquired Monsanto seed stock in Argentina. Brazil is one of the world's largest soybean growers, with production in 2012 of 81 million tons. Currently, 88% of soy is produced from genetically modified seed stock. Non-genetically modified soybeans have proven to fetch higher prices on the export market, particularly in Japan, where they are used to make *tofu.* Today, 60% of corn and 50% of cotton are grown from genetically modified seed stock. A bill introduced in 2008 by Deputy Luis Carlos Heinze, representative of the State of Rio Grande do Sul, was approved in April 2015 by the Chamber of Deputies. It proposed to reinstate a domestic law (*Lei de Biosegurança*) that required genetically modified products to be labeled as such[1]. To date, 64 countries have laws requiring labeling of GMOs, including 4 in Central and South America (Ecuador, El Salvador, Bolivia, Peru).

The contradictions between the National Energy Development Plan (2008-2017) and the National Climate Change Plan underscore the complexity of the associated issues, the difficulty of presidential arbitrage, and the weight of heritage. Thus, Brazil is the leading consumer of pesticides per capita at 5 liters per year (1 billion liters in 2013, some 20% of global demand), a heritage of the 1970s when farmers could only obtain credit by purchasing pesticides; with monocultures, the concentration of agricultural lands, and the use of genetically modified crops all leading to increased pesticide use. More than 40% of the pesticides used in Brazil are in the glyphosate (Monsanto's Roundup) family. In March 2015, the International Agency for Research on Cancer found this chemical to be a "*probable carcinogen*". However, the Brazilian Public Health Agency (*Agência Nacional de Vigilância Sanitária*) has classified it as benign since 1984 (assigning it a value of 4 on a scale of 5, from most to least carcinogenic, when the World Health Organization has given it a 2)[2], despite the request submitted by the Attorney General that it be banned[3].

Brazil is the world's third largest producer of asbestos. Between 1975 and 2005, the Brazilian market consumed five million tons of asbestos. In spite of the growing number of deaths from mesothelioma, caused by exposure to asbestos in 80% of the cases recorded by the Brazilian Ministry of Health, and the fact that asbestos has been classified as a carcinogen since 1977 by the International Agency for Research on Cancer (IARC), a limb of the World

---

1. Sérgio Matsuura, "Senado debate fim de rótulo transgênico" (Senate debates GMO labeling), *O 'Globo,* May 23, 2015.

2. IARC's Report on Glyphosate, Monographs, Volume 112, March 20, 2015.

3. "Polêmica. Ministério Público quer banir glifosato do Brasil" (Conflict over prosecutor's attempt to ban glyphosate in Brazil), *Canal Rural,* April 17, 2015.

Health Organization, asbestos has still not been banned in Brazil[1]. In December 2007, the Brazilian Supreme Court voided the law enacted in the State of São Paulo against the use or transportation of asbestos in a suit brought by industrialists[2]. Brazilian asbestos producers sued a researcher at the biomedical research institution FIOCRUZ in February 2012 for having published a scientific paper stating the dangers of asbestos. It would not be until August 2013 that the Ministry of Labor took legal action against the Eternit company, which had operated a plant in Osasco in the State of São Paulo from 1943 to 1993, for not having honored a commitment made in 2009 to provide medical care to its former employees suffering the effects of asbestos exposure. At the same time, the Court of Appeals of Turin sentenced the CEO of the Swiss Eternit Group, Stephan Schmidheiny, to 18 years in prison and fines totaling 20 million euros to the Region of Piedmont and 30 million euros to the city of Casale Monferrato, where the main Italian plant was located.

The Guanabara Bay cleanup project (Rio de Janeiro), begun in 1994 with the help of the Japan International Cooperation Agency (JICA) and the World Bank and on which some 1.5 billion dollars had been spent as of January 1, 2014, has failed to achieve any of its objectives regarding both treatment of contaminated water and reduction in pollutant sources.

We may mention a number of other serious environmental issues:

– Lead contamination in the city of Santo Amaro (State of Bahia), characterized in a study by the University of Bahia as the world's most heavily lead-contaminated city. The source of this disaster is a French company, Peñarroya, whose production facility operated through its subsidiary, the Brazilian Lead Company (*Companhia Brasileira de Chumbo* - COBRAC). The Deputy for the Workers' Party in Bahia, Emiliano José, led a delegation of French journalists on a visit of the site in September 2005;

– The contamination between 1974 and 2002 of the environment and thousands of employees at a pesticides plant in Paulínia (State of São Paulo), belonging originally to Shell Oil and then to BASF;

– Mercury pollution from a gold prospecting operation. In spite of the Minamata Convention on Mercury established by the United Nations Environment Programme and signed by 147 countries in October 2013, Brazilian negotiators were quite reluctant to halt this operation, citing the heavy social consequences of a prohibition (10% of gold prospecting is conducted by independent prospectors known as *garimpeiros*, concentrated principally in the Amazon basin and numbering in the hundreds of thousands).

In spite of its diplomatic efforts in international environmental policy, where it hopes to take the leadership role among Southern countries, Brazil has difficulty reconciling its international stance with the oftentimes laborious

[1]. *O 'Globo*, February 16, 2012.

[2]. Cássia Almeida, "Supremo decide suspender lei contra o amianto" (The Supreme Court decides to suspend anti-asbestos law), *O 'Globo*, December 21, 2007.

implementation of its own domestic policies to protect the surrounding environment. In addition to the obstacles imposed by its export paradigm (industrial agriculture, extension of the boundaries of farmland) and social issues (sanitation, waste management, shortcomings in the educational system), Brazil must cope with powerful political lobbies, endemic corruption (facilitated by the complexities of three levels of government – federal, state and municipal), and excessive ministerial compartmentalization.

The issue of indigenous peoples speaks volumes in this regard. In spite of the rights recognized and preserved in the 1988 Constitution and Brazil's ratification in 2002 of Convention 169 of the International Labour Organization regarding indigenous and tribal peoples, there has been no stop to agrarian conflicts. According to the Indigenous Missionary Council for Indigenous Peoples (CIMI), an arm of the Catholic Episcopal Conference, 676 Indios were murdered between 2003 and 2012, most of them in the State of Mato Grosso do Sul[1]. This is double the number recorded during Fernando Henrique Cardoso's presidency (1995-2002)[2]. Financing for the Brazilian governmental agency responsible for indigenous peoples (FUNAI) was reduced by half during Dilma Rousseff's tenure[3]. Brazil's indigenous communities include close to a million people representing 305 distinct ethnic groups and 274 languages distributed over 12% of the country's land. Major demonstrations by these peoples took place in October 2013 to protest parliamentary adumbrations of constitutional amendments to open up indigenous lands to economic exploitation.

The issue of indigenous peoples is a complex one that both unites Brazil with its neighbors (12 of the 17 countries that have ratified Convention 169 are in Latin America) and exposes it to criticism. We must also mention the agrarian conflicts in June 2013 resulting in the murder of Indios in the State of Mato Grosso do Sul, one of Brazil's most prosperous farming areas. These were caused by territorial limits that violated the indigenous people's legitimate rights (according to the Indigenous Missionary Council of the Catholic Church, more than 700 Indios have been killed in Brazil since 2003, the great majority in the State of Mato Grosso).

Many rural leaders and militants in the Landless Movement have also been killed, at times triggering an international outcry (Chico Mendes in December 1988; the American Dorothy Stang in February 2005; Maria and José Claudio da Silva in May 2011, to whom the United Nations paid homage on February 9, 2012; the Spaniard Gonzalo Alonso Hernández in August 2013). The Pastoral Land Commission, associated with the Catholic Church, lists 458 activists who were murdered between 2000 and 2012, most of them in the States of Pará and Rondônia.

---

1. *O 'Globo*, June 28, 2013.
2. *O 'Globo*, June 8, 2013.
3. Report by the Brazilian Court of Audit (*Tribunal de Contas da União*), April 2013.

According to the British NGO Global Witness, which has produced a list of 908 rural leaders killed worldwide between 2002 and 2013, Brazil alone accounts for nearly half[1], but over those last 12 years, they have been only 10 successful prosecutions in Brazil. Paraguay and Brazil are the countries with the world's most concentrated landholdings: in Paraguay, 80% of the land is owned by 2% of the population; in Brazil, less than 1% of rural landowners own 43% of the land.

Regarding the construction of the Belo Monte Dam on the Xingu River (State of Pará) – which earned Brazil an injunction from the OAS Human Rights Commission on behalf of the indigenous peoples because of the devastation consequences for riverside communities and for the social equilibrium of the town of Altamira, now rife with drug trafficking and prostitution – the chief of the Kaïapo people, Raoni Txucarramãe, traveled to Paris in September 2011 to promote his autobiography, with a preface by Jacques Chirac[2], and to submit a petition signed by 100.000 people opposed to the dam.

The issue of indigenous peoples – one keenly followed by the media and public opinion, of great concern to a large number of non-governmental organizations, publicized by renowned artists and musicians, and studied and popularized by preeminent ethnologists and geographers – invariably puts Brazilian diplomacy on the defensive. Because of Brazil's many shortcomings, which represent a major handicap in its multilateral approach to environmental and humanitarian issues, and in spite of widespread support for the indigenous cause among Latin American countries, Brazil has failed to set a standard in this regard. An investigation by the newspaper *O´Globo* published on July 19, 2015, reported that 90% of the schools in indigenous communities do not have access to drinking water and that 41% of them are without electricity[3].

The appointment of senator Katia Abreu in January 2015 as Minister of Agriculture is not likely to reduce that handicap. Abreu is president of the Confederation of Agriculture and Livestock, a powerful pro-agribusiness lobby, awarded the "Golden Chainsaw" (*Motoserra de Ouro*) prize in 2010 by the indigenous leader Sonia Guajajara for its initiatives to undermine the fundamental rights of indigenous peoples. Sonia Guajajara is coordinator of Brazil's Association of Indigenous Peoples (*Articulação dos Povos Indigenas do Brasil* – APIB). She took part in a demonstration on March 14, 2014 in Paris in support of indigenous peoples and denounced amendments proposed in the Brazilian Parliament that she says are aimed at transferring the executive authority (FUNAI) provided in the constitution for delimiting and approving indigenous lands to Congress[4].

---

1. "Deadly Environment. The Dramatic Rise in Killings of Environmental and Land Defenders (01/01/2003-31/12/2013)" Case Study Brazil p.19 (www.globalwitness.org).
2. *Raoni. Mémoires d´un chef indigène*, Jean-Pierre Dutilleux, Éditions du Rocher, Paris, 2011.
3. Renata Mariz, "Tragédia escolar indígena" (Indigenous school tragedy), *O´Globo*, July 19, 2015.
4. *Observatoire des Multinationales*, March 13, 2014.

Human Rights

Respect for basic rights

It was by initiative of President Lula that the Group of High Authorities on Human Rights (RAADH[1]) was created within Mercosur. The Group held its 23rd session in Montevideo in June 2013. Brazil has played a constructive and generally praised role on the United Nations Human Rights Council since its creation in 2006, and was elected to represent the Latin American and the Caribbean States on three occasions. However, the Brazilian media have found much to criticize: administration of internal affairs characterized by the inefficient management in 2011 of a Commission of Inquiry into crimes committed during the years of the military dictatorship (1964-1985) and the amnesties of 1979; one of the world's highest rates of homicides involving firearms – 23 per 100.000, and 80 per 100.000 within the age group 18-24 (more than 50.000 murders are recorded each year, less than 8% of them solved[2]); the world's third largest prison population (approximately 700.000, of whom 217.000 awaiting trial); an appalling 195.000 non-executed arrest warrants; the recurring use of torture by police, prison guards, and the military[3]; and a certain ambiguity in Brazil's diplomatic relations.

On an official visit to Havana in March 2010, President Lula equated Cuban political prisoners with common criminals, shortly after the death of the dissident Orlando Zapato Tamoyo following an 80-day hunger strike. Visiting Havana in February 2012, his successor, shortly after the death of another dissident, Wilmar Villar Mendoza, also as a result of a hunger strike, expressed no solidarity with Cuban political prisoners nor concern about the conditions of their incarceration. Indeed, Rousseff limited herself to allusions to the iniquities of the Guantanamo prison and recommends for a multilateral approach to the issue of human rights. According to the Brazilian Committee for Refugees (CONARE), 133 Cubans live in Brazil as political refugees. Since the late 1980s, Brazil has abstained on votes at the United Nations regarding the issue of human rights in Cuba. From Dilma Rousseff, who had experienced dictatorship and torture in her youth, one would expect a more nuanced position for Brazil on this issue.

Brazil's procrastination in directly condemning violation of human rights in Cuba has been attributed to the respect for the Cuban Revolution on the part of the political elites in the Workers' Party and by the entire Latin American left. It is held up as a model, a symbol of dignity and of resistance to imperialism under the lash of the trade embargo imposed since 1962 by the world's number one power and its boycott on investments and financing

---

1. *Reunião de Altas Autoridades em Direitos Humanos do Mercosul.*
2. Cassio Brúno, "Crimes sem castigo" (Unpunished crimes), *O'Globo*, May 9, 2011.
3. Antônio Werneck, Barbara Marcolini, Vera Araújo, "Nem lei consegue impedir tortura no país" (No law can stop torture in this country), *O 'Globo*, July 12, 2015.

(Cuban Democracy Act in 1992, Helms-Burton Act in 1996) and victimized by terrorist plots by Cuban exiles funded and sponsored by the United States. The examples are numerous: the Bay of Pigs invasion in 1961; bombing of Cubana de Aviacion Flight in 1976 with 73 persons on board, with the mastermind behind the operation living in Miami; and bomb attacks on Havana hotels. We may also mention the incentives program by the U.S. Department of State known as the "Cuban Medical Professional Parole Program", aiming to poach Cuban physicians from projects benefiting third-party countries, and the development of a roadmap for a post-Castro transition government (Commission for Assistance to a Free Cuba) during George W. Bush's second term in 2004, with Washington believing it must quickly be imposed externally.

Most of the leaders of Brazilian left-wing political parties took refuge in or were exiled to Cuba during the military dictatorship. Many Brazilian intellectuals and artists obtained some of their education or training in Cuba. Some sixty current Brazilian filmmakers got their training at the School of San Antonio de Los Baños and at the Cuban Institute of Cinematographic Art and Industry (ICAIC). Furthermore, in a profoundly unequal society such as Brazil's, the respect for the basic human rights of home, healthcare, and public education that has characterized Cuban society would serve as an incentive to tolerance and indulgence for the progressive elites[1]. More than three fourths of Cubans own their homes, although comfort is not always guaranteed; 98% have access to running water and electricity. The number of doctors *per capita* is one of the highest in the world (more than six physicians per 1.000 inhabitants; Brazil has fewer than two[2]). Each year the Cuban government welcomes 10.000 scholarship holders from Africa and Latin America. Since its inauguration in 2009, the Latin American School of Medicine, based in Havana, has trained 24.486 doctors from 83 countries at no cost, some 3.000 of them from Africa. Cuba is an active participant in the public health programs funded by Venezuela, preeminent among which is "Operación Milagro" against blindness and cataracts (more than three million patients selected from poor communities have undergone operations free of charge by Cuban doctors in Latin America since 2008)[3].

This performance clashes with the social reality of Brazil. One would have to witness the much applauded speech by former President Lula in Havana during the World Equilibrium conference in February 2013, dressed significantly in the red shirt of the Venezuelan Bolivarians as he paid homage to the Cuban Revolution, to grasp the fervid esteem felt for Cuba. Uruguay

---

[1] Claudia Wasserman (University of Rio Grande do Sul), "A recepção da Revolução Cubana no Brasil: a historiografia brasileira" (Regard for the Cuban Revolution in Brazil: Brazilian historiography), *Estudos Interdisciplinarios América Latina y el Caribe*, Vol. 12, No. 2, 2007 (University of Tel Aviv).

[2]. *O 'Globo*, April 8, 2012.

[3]. Patrick Howlett-Martin, "*La Coopération médicale internationale de Cuba. L'altruisme récompensé*" (Cuba's international medical cooperation: altruism repaid), L'Harmattan, Paris, 2015.

forgave Cuba's debt, 31.5 million dollars, in June 2015, justifying the action because of the medical aid (particularly in ophthalmology) provided by Cuba since 2007.

These considerations have their share of merit. But in truth, human rights have never been a top priority in Brazilian diplomacy. It was not until 1977 that Brazil joined the United Nations Commission on Human Rights, created in 1946[1]. It took Brazil ten years to recognize the jurisdiction of the Inter-American Court of Human Rights (during the presidency of Fernando Henrique Cardoso in 1988) and twenty-seven years after the end of the dictatorship to establish a commission of inquiry into disappearances (and murders) carried out by the military regime. Indeed the latter initiative was only implemented under pressure from the OAS Commission on Human Rights and only with repeated assurances that it was merely a question of information and not of judicial retribution. As regards the amnesty commission established on August 28, 2001 by the Ministry of Justice, it was 28 years after the fact before it finally approved provision of psychological support for the victims (*Clinicas* project implemented in April 2013)[2].

This issue has never been addressed in more than a marginal way by the Brazilian diplomats I have encountered over the course of my career. During the dark years of the military dictatorship in Argentina, and when international organizations (e.g. Amnesty International, the Inter-American Commission on Human Rights) had brought to light the thousands of disappearances and kidnappings, a dozen of them Brazilian nationals, my fellow diplomats at the Brazilian embassy and consulate in Buenos Aires, all graduates of the Rio Branco Institute, were always quite reticent and reserved in meetings they attended at European embassies, and the question of taking measures against the authorities or police was never broached. Not even the case of Brazilian musician Francisco Tenório Cerqueira Junior could spur them to action. An icon of the *bossa-nova* who had come to Buenos Aires during a tour with Vinicius de Moraes, their colleague at Itamaraty, a poet and musician in his spare time, Cerqueira was kidnapped off the street after leaving his hotel (the Normandie) to buy cigarettes and was never seen again. One of his torturers, Claudio Vallejos, former member of the Naval Intelligence Service, who admitted participating in the kidnapping during an interview with a Brazilian magazine in Rio de Janeiro in 1986, was expelled from Brazil. He revealed that the Brazilian embassy had been informed of the death of the musician, which happened while he was being tortured at the Escuela Superior de Mecánica de la Armada (Navy Petty-Officers School of Mechanics – ESMA) on March 25, 1976, and of the delivery of his body to the local morgue. This information was never passed on to Cerqueira's family. The Argentine government eventually

---

1. In 2006 it was replaced with the United Nations Human Rights Council, a subsidiary body of the General Assembly.

2. Elenice Bottari, "Vítimas da ditadura terão assistência psicológica" (Victims of dictatorship to receive psychological aid), *O 'Globo*, April 20, 2013.

paid compensation to the family. It is thanks to an Argentine parliamentarian, Raul Puy, that a commemorative plaque was finally put up on the façade of the Hotel Normandie. In February 2012, the Brazilian press again mentioned the presence of Vallejos in Brazil, in the State of Santa Catarina, where he had lived for 25 years, and his interrogation on January 4, 2012 for a number of cases of fraud, prior to his extradition to Argentina in March 2013. It was not until April 2013, through the mission to Buenos Aires of the National Truth Commission (*Comissão Nacional de Verdade*), that Brazil finally officially requested information from the Argentine authorities on acts of violence against Brazilian nationals between 1964 and 1985.

The newspaper *Correio Brazilense* published a series of articles on Itamaraty's "secret service", the *Centro de Informações do Exterior* (CIEX). Between 1966 and 1985, CIEX cooperated with the military regime by keeping records and reporting on Brazilian political exiles. The archives to which journalist Claudio Dantas was given access contained files on 64 of the 380 activists murdered and/or disappeared during the years of the dictatorship.

The election of the evangelical pastor Marco Feliciano as president of the Senate Human Rights Commission in February 2013 aroused a great deal of protest. Congress enacted a series of measures in July 2013 to prevent the use of torture by the police (*Sistema Nacional de Prevenção e Combate a Tortura*), but thirteen of the twenty-seven Brazilian states have no such program despite federal directives adopted in 2007 (*Plano Nacional de Direitos Humanos* – PNDH)[1] and the law of April 7, 1997 providing prison sentences for those who use torture.

A mix of complex sociological factors, inherent to Brazilian society, underlie this attitude: violence as the exclusive purview of the State and the police in a profoundly unequal society, where no eyebrows are raised at the torture of blacks, indios, poor people, thieves and drug dealers; the lack of any ethic of respect for human life, as testified by crimes committed with unspeakable brutality and cruelty; and a certainty of impunity leveraged by the apparatus of repression and white-collar crime. The use of torture by police is often mentioned in mass-circulation newspapers. Recent examples include torture in the commissariats in the State of the Amazonas and in the prisons of João Pessoa, capital of the State of Paraiba, denounced by the Church[2], in the police station in Curitiba in July 2013[3], and in October 2013 in the police station in Rio de Janeiro's largest *favela*[4]. The reports by United Nations special

[1]. Cassio Brúno, Juliana Castro, "Em 13 estados não há plano para direitos humanos" (Thirteen states without human rights programs), *O'Globo*, March 16, 2013.

[2]. Cleide Carvalho. "Policiais do Amazonas são accusados de tortura" (Police in Amazonas accused of torture), *O'Globo,* April 29, 2012. / "Pastoral denuncia tortura em presídio da Paraiba" (Church denounces torture in prison in the State of Paraiba"), *O'Globo*, May 1, 2012.

[3]. *O'Globo*, July 24, 2013.

[4]. Elenice Bottari, Fábio Teixeira, Gustavo Goulart, "Presos PMs acusados da morte de Amarildo. Inquérito contém depoimentos de 22 pessoas torturadas" (The police officers accused

rapporteurs are illuminating in this regard (Nigel Rodley in 2000, Asma Jahangir in 2003, Leandro Despouy in 2004, Hina Jilani in 2005, Philipp Alston in 2007, Gulnara Shahinian in 2010[1], and the Working Group on Arbitrary Detentions in 2013).

In August 2013, the Brazilian press reported that 20 years after the Candelária massacre (six street children and two adults were murdered on the night of July 23, 1993 as they slept next to the Candelária Church in Rio de Janeiro) no one had been sentenced for the killings. Of the 65 children who survived the massacre, 43 had subsequently been murdered, 10 were in in jail and 5 had died of AIDS[2]. In spite of the fact that Brazil has ratified the International Convention for the Protection of All Persons from Enforced Disappearance, adopted by the General Assembly of the United Nations on December 20, 2006, the press frequently reports instances of kidnappings by police, although the phenomenon is difficult to quantify because of the lack of official data. In the States of Rio de Janeiro, São Paulo, Minas Gerais, Goias, and Parana, youths have been arrested by police in front of witnesses and never seen again[3].

Among the principal Latin American countries suffering repression and dictatorships, Brazil is one of the few that have not reviewed their amnesty laws or opened, to date, any judicial inquiries into the fate of the victims and the identities of the torturers. The National Truth Commission (*Comissão Nacional da Verdade*), finally implemented by Congress in September 2011 after repeated motions by the Inter-American Commission on Human Rights regarding the cases of 62 deaths and disappearances during the Araguaia Guerrilla War (1972-1974)[4] had very limited authority, no budget of its own, and a very small staff (seven people and a maximum of 24 months of limited activities). The members were not named until May 2012, more than eight months after the Commission was created. During the inauguration ceremony in Brasilia, the daughter of Deputy Rubens Paiva, who was arrested at his home on January 20, 1971 and never seen again, was asked to speak but ultimately prevented from doing so. The coordinator of the Commission is Paulo Sergio Pinheiro, who is also the Chairman of the International Commission of Inquiry for Syria.

One gets an idea of the indifference or unwillingness to know in Brazilian society from an editorial in the newspaper *O 'Globo*, a generally middle-of-the-road publication, about the Commission: "*Some of the dead and disappeared whose fates are being investigated by the Truth Commission did not take up arms in favor of*

---

in the death of Amarildo are in prison. Investigators heard the testimony of 22 torture victims), *O 'Globo*, October 5, 2013.

1. Their reports may be found on the following site: www.ohchr.org/english/bodies/chr/special/countryvisitsae.htm#brazil

2. *O 'Globo*, August 5, 2013.

3. Gustavo Uribe, Marcelo Fiuza, "Os amarildos do Brasil. Drama vivido pelos parentes do pedreiro da Rocinha é comum a outras famílias do país" (The drama for the relatives of the Rocinha mason shared by other local families), *O 'Globo,* August 18, 2013.

4. Sentence of November 24, 2010, Gomes Lund and others case.

democracy, but merely to replace one dictatorship with another"[1]. The media have reported on dissention within the Commission, as evidenced by the resignation of two of its members, and on the criticism by the families of the victims. This offers a key to the restrictive nature of its mandate. The federal courts have cooperated only to the point of issuing a *habeas corpus* in favor of the former commander of the torture facility[2] during the 1970s in São Paulo, Colonel Alberto Brilhante Ustra, so that he could stand mute before the public hearing to which he was summoned by the Commission in May 2013.

The institution of this Commission was met with the publication of a manifesto signed by 350 retired officers, including 44 generals, and among them Maynard Marques de Santa Rosa, who was relieved of his functions by the Minister of Defense in February 2010 for having publicly labeled the Commission as the "*slander commission*". The manifesto was also a source of embarrassment for the Defense Minister, Celso Amorim: former director of the Brazilian state-funded movie production and distribution company Embrafilme (1979-1982), he was removed by the military dictatorship in 1982 for having authorized the distribution of Roberto Farias's movie *Para Frente Brasil*, which exposed the use of torture.

The Inter-American Court of Human Rights stated in 2012 that the Brazilian Truth Commission did not eliminate the country's obligation to determine the truth and assign individual responsibilities via judicial inquiry. International law requires prosecution of those who violate human rights. All international conventions are aligned in this regard (Convention on the Prevention and Punishment of the Crime of Genocide, 1948; European Convention on Human Rights, 1959; International Covenant on Civil and Political Rights, 1966; American Convention on Human Rights, 1969; Convention against Torture and Other Cruel, Inhuman or Degrading Treatment or Punishment, 1984; International Convention for the Protection of All Persons from Enforced Disappearance, 2007). Two researchers from the University of Minnesota conducted a comparative analysis showing that the rule of law was significantly strengthened in the 14 Latin American countries that had taken the initiative to persecute past abuses[3].

The Inter-American Court of Human Rights and the European Court of Human Rights (1959) have emphasized that only criminal prosecution offers an effective remedy to violations. The amnesty laws work against this by perpetuating a culture of impunity. It was by order of the Inter-American Court that the Brazilian federal prosecutor (*Ministerio Público Federal*) established a working group in March 2012 dubbed "Transition Justice" (*Justiça de Transição*) bringing together the States of Rio de Janeiro, São Paulo, Rio Grande do Sul,

---

1. *O 'Globo*, May 19, 2012.
2. DOI-CODI (*Destacamento de Operações de informações - Centro de Operações de Defesa Interna*).
3. Kathryn Sikking, Carrie Walling Booth, "The Impact of Human Rights Trials in Latin America", in *Pratica de direitos humanos*, Reis Rocha (org.), São Paulo, 2010. Originally published in the *Journal of Peace Research*, Volume 44, 2007.

Santa Catarina and Pará to study the possibility of initiating judicial investigations of human rights violations committed during the military dictatorship in spite of the amnesty law, an initiative mocked by one of the justices of the Brazilian Supreme Court.

In Brazil and many other Latin American countries, amnesty laws were considered a necessary and inevitable evil in order to establish the rule of law during the delicate transition process and put an end to state-of-emergency rule: 40% of the amnesty laws enacted during the period of the military regime are still in force. But these laws are generally repealed for the sake of justice and fairness to the victims once democratic institutions have been restored. A number of truth commissions have been instituted since 1970: Bolivia, 1982; Argentina, 1983; Uruguay, 1985; Chile, 1986; El Salvador, 1992; Ecuador, 1996; Guatemala, 1999; Panama and Peru, 2001; Paraguay, 2004; Brazil, 2011; Venezuela, 2013. Colombia too decided, in August 2014, to establish an ad hoc commission titled "Historical Commission on the Conflict and its Victims" with the support of the Revolutionary Armed Forces (FARC).

To this day, only Brazil and Ecuador have failed to take legal action in this regard. The Ecuadorian Truth Commission submitted its report in 2010. Which means that Brazil stands out for its inaction, with the exception of some parsimonious, and now capped, indemnity. The Brazilian Supreme Court (*Tribunal Superior Federal*), responding to a petition from the Lawyers Guild, refused to review the 28 August 1979 Amnesty Law, enacted under the military regime, exempting state agents, members of the armed forces and police, and opponents of the regime from prosecution for crimes committed between 1961 and 1979. This law was approved by a vote of 206 against 201 in a parliament where one third of the deputies had been appointed by the military.

Many Latin American countries have prosecuted these crimes without having repealed their amnesty laws (e.g. Chile, Panama, Peru); others, including Guatemala, Honduras, the Dominican Republic, and Suriname, enacted amnesty laws more than twenty years after the fact with the clear aim of protecting torturers and criminals. In May 2013, Mexico created a commission of inquiry into disappearances (estimated at 26.000 between 2006 and 2012), but without naming the guilty parties or having an independent budget. The government of José Mujica (Uruguay), a former Tupamaro who spent 15 years in a military prison, has been unsuccessful in its repeated attempts to repeal the amnesty law enacted by the dictatorship on December 22, 1986, whose abrogation was voted down in referendums in 1989 and 2009. The law he decreed in October 2011 to eliminate the statute of limitations for crimes committed under the dictatorship was judged unconstitutional by the Supreme Court in January 2013. Uruguyan new president, Tabaré Vázquez, announced on his first day in office earlier this year 2015 an investigation into the military dictatorhip of 1973 to 1985.

The winding course of the process in Guatemala, a country ravaged between 1962 and 1966 – 200.000 dead or disappeared – by the armed forces of the former dictator Efraín Ríos Montt (1982-1983), accused of having ordered the massacre of the Mayan Ixil people, illustrates the limitations of taking judicial action fifty years after the events in question. In August 2013, the Argentine Defense Minister, Agustin Rossi, revealed the existence of a secret fund to help former military officers elude justice or escape from prison.

Argentina during the Kirchner presidency stands as a model in these efforts: 500 military men and police have been sentenced, one thousand are in detention, and 900 have been arraigned to date[1]. Prosecution has also been extended to judges, business leaders, religious figures, unionists, and journalists accused of abetting torturers.

Argentina and Peru are among the few countries that, in spite of a painful past, have undertaken the fight against the proponents of oblivion by studying reports and testimony and distributing them to all schools and universities ("*Nunca Más*" in Argentina; "*Yuyanapaq*" – "do not forget" in Quechuan – in Peru), and by converting the secret torture and detention centers into museums to memory and contemplation (in 2004, during the presidency of Nestor Kirchner, the Navy Petty-Officers School of Mechanics [ESMA] was transformed into the Space for Memory and for the Promotion and Defense of Human Rights). The Chilean courts recently prosecuted 17 military officers implicated in the murder of singer-songwriter Victor Jara in 1973 and of the photographer Rodrigo Rojas[2].

Kirchner's Argentina has clearly established itself as a reference for these efforts in Latin America. Some 30 years after the savage repression wrought by the *Junta* of General Videla, Admiral Massera and Brigadier Agosti (1976-1980), the Argentine courts are prosecuting the now elderly torturers. The action of these courts has been cited in Spain by the families of the victims of Franco´s repression (1936-1975), during which 114.000 people disappeared and thousands of newborns were kidnapped. The families have demanded that Spanish authorities extradite some twenty former agents of this repression and open a mass grave in the Guadalajara cemetery, where Franco's victims were buried[3]. However, the Argentine magistrate (Maria Servini de Cubría) was thwarted by a demurrer from the Rajoy government, which defended the amnesty law enacted on October 15, 1977[4]. The teams of Argentine medical examiners assigned to the task continue to try to identify the bodies and bones of the deceased, in respect for the memories of the families. But in Spain this

---

1 "Cristina Kirchner en primera persona" (Cristina Kirchner in her own words), interview with the Argentine president by *The New Yorker* on March 11, 2015, reproduced in *Pagina12*, July 13, 2015.

2 Bernardo Tabak, "Reviravolta na historia, Revelações da ditadura" (Historical twist: revelations of dictatorship), *O´Globo*, July 25, 2015.

3. Natalia Junqueira, "La justicia argentina pide que se abra uma fosa del franquismo em Guadalajara" (Argentine courts order opening of Francoist grave in Guadalajara), *El País*, February 21, 2014.

4. "España volvió a rechazar extraditar a lós imputados por genocidio. El gobierno de Rajoy, firme com la impunidad franquista" (Spain again refuses to extradite those accused of genocide. Rajoy's government stands by Francoist impunity), *Página12*, April 22, 2015.

task is carried out under modest conditions, some 40 years after the death of the Dictator, by the *Associación por la Recuperación de la Memoria Histórica,* an association of volunteers and helpers[1]. Judge Baltasar Garzon was suspended on May 14, 2010 by the General Council of the Judicial Power of Spain (*Consejo General del Poder Judicial*) for having ignored a 1977 amnesty law when he authorized the exhumation of 19 unmarked mass graves, including one thought to hold the remains of the poet Federico Garcia Llorca, and the identification of the bodies[2]. He was later declared honorary resident of Argentina by President Cristina Kirchner.

The Brazilian Ministry of Justice and the Commission of Inquiry of the State of Rio de Janeiro, which were denied access by the army in August 2013 to the facility used to torture detainees in the military police headquarters during the years of the dictatorship, have pressed for the classification and preservation of the facility so that it can be made into a place of memory of political repression[3]. On December 10, 2014, the Brazilian Truth Commission submitted its 4,300-page report giving the names of 434 dead or disappeared people, a higher number than envisaged because the Commission, not wanting to offend the military as an institution, did not focus exclusively on the years of the dictatorship but extended its investigation back to 1946. A list naming 377 torturers or people with clear responsibilities in the chain of command leading to disappearances and torture was included as an appendix to the report.

Countries in the region continue to send their officers to be trained at the U.S. Army School of the Americas in the United States, now renamed Western Hemisphere Institute for Security Cooperation, located in Fort Benning, Georgia. Chile granted authorization to the U.S. South Command in April 2012 to open a training center in Concón (Fuerte Aguayo), near Valparaiso, for soldiers tasked with urban peacekeeping, and misused anti-terrorism laws at the expense of the indigenous Mapuche community.

All things considered, the truth commissions that have been instituted have completely skirted the issue of United States responsibility in the repressions. On March 10, 1999, President Clinton offered apologies during his official visit to Guatemala, stating that his country's engagement alongside the Guatemalan security forces, accused of murdering some 200.000 people during thirty years of war but mainly in the period 1979-1983, was "*a mistake*"[4]. But the interference by the United States following the coup d'État that overthrew the elected president Jacobo Arbenz (1951-1954) was not mentioned during the trial of General Efraín Ríos Montt, the Guatemalan military officer most closely associated with the repression. After seizing power in a coup d'État in March 1982, he was received at the White House later that year (December 4) by

1. http:// memoriahistorica.org.es
2. Juzgado Central de Instrucción N°5. Audiença Nacional. Sumario 53/ 2008 E, Madrid, November 18, 2008.
3. *O 'Globo*, August 21, 2013.
4. *Washington Post,* March 11, 1999.

Ronald Reagan, who characterized him as being "*totally dedicated to democracy*". Like the principal generals in the Guatemalan armed forces, Montt was on the CIA payroll, as revealed by the agency's own archives[1]. The principal perpetrator of repression in El Salvador, Colonel Nicolás Carranza, Deputy Minister of Defense (1979-1981) and chief of police (1983-1984) has been a U.S. citizen and resident since 1991, like former officer Pedro Barrientos Nuñez, who tortured and killed Victor Jara in the stadium of Santiago in 1973.

The Truth Commission (*Comissão da Verdade*) established by the legislative assembly of the State of São Paulo has had access to the records of visitors to the facility for torturing political prisoners during the period of the military dictatorship. In February 2013, it questioned U.S. consular officials and the Federation of Industries of the State of São Paulo (FIESP) regarding the regular visits by their representatives recorded in the archives[2]. Financing of the repression by FIESP was mentioned by Dilma Rousseff's ex-husband, Carlos Araújo, her *compañero* in the Revolutionary Armed Vanguard (*Vanguarda Armada Revolucionaria Palmares*), jailed and tortured, like Dilma, between 1970 and 1972, during his testimony in March 2013 before the Commission.

A review of Brazilian voting behavior at the United Nations on questions regarding China (2004), Chechnya (2003-2004), Zimbabwe (2002-2004), Darfur (2006), and North Korea (2009) evidences a propensity for abstention, justified by a desire for an "equidistant" approach, presented as being constructive and non-punitive. Brazil restated its proposal for a yearly global report on human rights around the world to the United Nations in 2005, originally submitted before the full Assembly in March 1998 by the Secretary of State on Human Rights of the Cardoso government. The goal of the proposal was to prevent the polarizing effect of an investigation targeting a single country due to reasons of urgency. It was to be *"a global report to be prepared by an impartial team of UN experts [...] based on multilaterally defined criteria and parameters*", in the words of Amorim during his speech at the inaugural session of the Human Rights Council on June 19, 2006 in Geneva, Switzerland.

Brazil abstained from voting on a resolution before the UN General Assembly in November 2010 condemning the human rights situation in Iran, despite the rigorous and detailed indictment by lawyer Shirin Abadi, 2003 Nobel Peace Prize laureate, presented in June 2008 during the 8th session of the Human Rights Council: massive application of the death penalty, even for minors; detainment in secret facilities for months without charges filed; flouting of rights of gathering and meeting. On March 24, 2011, Brazil voted in favor of a resolution proposed by the United States before the Human Rights Council to designate a Special UN Rapporteur in Iran.

Celso Amorim defended the implementation of concrete actions that he felt were more effective than censure and mentioned Brazil's contribution of

---

1. Elizabeth Alkin, "Guatemala Trial leaves out U.S. role", *International Herald Tribune*, May 18-19, 2013.
2. *O 'Globo*, February 19, 2013.

1 million dollars in aid to protect women from sexual violence in the Democratic Republic of the Congo and its appeals to the Iranian president on behalf of the Frenchwoman Clotilde Reiss, who was arrested in Iran in July 2009 and not freed until March 2010, and of the American Sarah Shourd, who was arrested in 2009 and freed in September 2010[1].

The Universal Periodic Review (UPR) instituted in 2007 by the Human Rights Council of the United Nations, headquartered in Geneva, works well for Brazilian diplomacy, which considers it to be a constructive approach. What country has sufficient moral authority on human rights to judge another? During the 8th session of the UPR in April 2008, Brazil received and immediately accepted 15 recommendations.

The joint communiqué published after Rousseff's official visit to Beijing in April 2011 illustrates Brazil's cautious approach to the issue of human rights: "*The two parties will strengthen bilateral consultations on the issue of human rights and share experiences and practices*". What experiences and practices are being referred to here? Since 1989 and the suppression of demonstrations in Tiananmen Square in Beijing, China has been subjected to an embargo on weapons and sensitive materials. The new provisions in the Chinese criminal code submitted during the plenary session of the National Congress in April 2012 (Article 73) allow imprisonment for up to six months in secret detention centers, for security reasons. Hu Jia, one of China's highest profile activists for human rights, awarded the Sakharov Prize in October 2008 by the European Parliament, has termed this the "*KGB clause*". Imprisoned from 2008 to 2011 – like his colleagues, the intellectual Liu Xiaobo, Nobel Peace Prize laureate, arrested in 2008 and sentenced to 11 years in prison and whose wife, Liu Xia, has been under constant state surveillance since 2010, and his brother-in-law, Liu Hui – Xiaobo was sentenced to 11 years in prison in June 2013 for having signed an internet petition in favor of a constitutional democracy in China. The poet Liao Yi Wu, was imprisoned, tortured and humiliated from 1990 to 1994 and is now a refugee in Berlin. The journalist Shi Tao has been imprisoned since 2004, and the militant Liu Ping was jailed in March 2012 and again on April 27, 2013 for the crime of having asked the political elites to declare their wealth[2]. The international press has recorded testimony of torture in some 350 "re-education camps", where criminals can be imprisoned for up to four years without a trial, as can members of the religious movement Falun Gong and those who file too many petitions, and "rumor-spreading" internauts[3]. The Chinese bishop, Shi Enxiang, ordained in 1947 and passing away in February 2015, spent most of

---

[1]. Celso Amorim, *Conversas com jovems diplomatas*, Ed. Benvira, São Paulo, 2011.

[2]. Didi Kirsten Tatlow, "No news from activist in China, group says", *International Herald Tribune*, March 20, 2012.

[3]. Bruce Pedroletti, "Les suppliciés de Masanjia" *(Torture in Masanjia), Le Monde, May 10, 2013.* Andrew Jacobs, "Worker say labor camps in China used torture", *International Herald Tribune*, June 12, 2013.

his life in Chinese prisons because of his allegiance to the Vatican[1]. The Tibetan monk Tenzin Delek Rinpoche died in a Chinese prison cell in July 2015 while serving a life sentence based on questionable charges.

The adoption of a resolution regarding the rights of older persons (discrimination, social security, healthcare, violence) by the UN Human Rights Council during its 21st session in June 2012 was a Brazilian and Argentine initiative. Brazil declared its support for the adoption of a legally binding document. This policy falls within the framework of the so-called Brasilia Rules regarding access to justice by vulnerable persons, adopted at the 14th Ibero-American Judicial Summit, which took place in the Brazilian capital in March 2008.

During the 28th session of the Intergovernmental Council of the UNESCO International Programme for the Development of Communication (IPDC), the director of the program presented a Plan for the Safety of Journalists, which was developed through consultations with member countries, the principal NGOs and the media. However, it was not possible to adopt the Plan because of opposition from Brazil, India, Pakistan, Cuba, and Venezuela. The Brazilian delegation had raised a procedural point by stating that UNESCO did not have the authority to issue such a document. In truth, records for these countries – and we must add Honduras and Russia – in the years 2010-2011 show a high number of imprisoned or murdered journalists. Brazil is tied for fifth place with Russia in this sad list, with five murdered journalists[2]. According to the Committee to Protect Journalists, "*at least seven Brazilian journalists were killed in direct relation to their work between January 2011 and November 2012, making the nation one of the world's deadliest for the press*"[3]. Since 2006, a total of 372 journalists have been killed around the world in the line of work, and in 80% of these cases, the perpetrators have not been brought to justice. In March 2013, two journalists working for the newspaper *Vale do Aço*, Rodrigo Neto and Walgney Carvalho, were murdered for their investigation of a dozen murders and disappearances that occurred in Ipatinga (State of Minas Gerais) between 1992 and 2013. The police have been implicated but no one has yet been charged. In May 2013, the non-governmental organization Reporters Without Borders ranked Brazil 108th out of 179 countries in terms of freedom of the press. The suppression of street protests in São Paulo by the police in June 2013 did not spare journalists who were simply doing their jobs: seven journalists from the newspaper *Folha de São Paulo* were hit by rubber bullets and two of them received severe facial wounds. The associations of journalists (Reporters Without Borders, Committee to Protect Journalists, National Association of Journalists) reported

---

[1]. Chinese Catholics seek answers to bishop's fate, *International New York Times*, February 14-15, 2015.

[2]. Mexico, 18; Pakistan, 16; Honduras, 13; Iraq, 11; Brazil, 5; Russia, 5, Afghanistan, 4. During the two years 2010-2011, 127 journalists were killed, the great majority outside of war zones in their own countries, and 85% after having received threats (Source: UNESCO, March 2012).

[3]. "Attacks on the Press: Journalism on the World's Front Line", Committee to Protect Journalists, 2013 Edition.

on the brutal actions of the police during the demonstrations. The Brazilian Association of Broadcasting presented its annual report at the 43rd general assembly of the International Association of Broadcasting (IAB) in Rio de Janeiro in October 2013: five journalists murdered in 2013, six in 2012, 136 cases of aggression against journalists in 2013 as opposed to 51 in 2012, most of them by police[1]. Fifteen journalists were killed in Brazil in 2014[2].

The Brazilian Minister of External Relations, Antonio Patriota, was present with his Argentine and Ecuadorian counterparts at the meeting in May 2013 of the states parties to the American Convention on Human Rights (adopted in 1969) in Cochabamba (Bolivia) to evaluate the option of moving the headquarters of the Inter-American Commission on Human Rights, currently in Washington D.C., to Latin America. The United States and Canada are not parties to the Convention and were not invited. The Commission is chaired by Paulo Vannuchi, former Secretary for Human Rights of the Lula government (2005-2010), elected in June 2013. His candidacy had been suspended in 2011 by Brazil, which had not appreciated the interference of the Commission in the dispute engendered by plans for the Belo Monte Dam. Vannuchi's term expires on December 31, 2017. The Court is composed of 7 judges having 4-year terms, with the possibility of being re-elected once; 4 judges were re-elected in June 2015 (Argentina, Costa Rica, Chile, Ecuador) joining the three judges whose terms end at the end of December 2017 (Brazil, United States, Saint Lucia). A new role, dedicated to equality of opportunity and rights, should soon be given to Ideli Salvati, formerly a former minister in Dilma Rousseff's cabinet from 2011 to 2015. Salvati is currently advisor to the Secretary General, Luís Almagro, who is the former Minister of Foreign Affairs of Uruguay (2010-2015).

Only 21 members of the Organization of American States (OAS) have recognized the jurisdiction of the Inter-American Court of Human Rights (IACHR, associated with the Inter-American Commission on Human Rights), founded in 1979 and based in San José, Costa Rica. Unlike the European system, where oversight power of the execution of judgments is in the hands of the Committee of Ministers of the Council of Europe, the IACHR has sole oversight over the execution of its decisions. In September 2012, Venezuela denounced the Inter-American Commission on Human Rights, and many other Latin American countries (Nicaragua, Bolivia, Ecuador) have taken their distance from this organization, which has accomplished exemplary work in Latin America over the past twenty years.

This hostility – strongly shared by Brazil – of the ALBA countries, and especially Ecuador and Venezuela, toward the Commission, which they accuse of not having shown the same diligence in addressing the issue of human rights in the United States and Canada and not having raised the issue of the Guantanamo Bay detention camp, has not affected the remarkable work carried

[1]. *O 'Globo*, October 14, 2013.

[2] *O 'Globo*, Sociedade, p.22, May 4, 2015.

out by the Court in a strongly polarized political context and relying on a controversial mode of financing.

In November 2014, the Dominican Republic expressed its desire to withdraw from the jurisdiction of the Court, which it had recognized since 1999. It did not accept the Court's judgment of the expulsion of people of Haitian descendence born in the Dominican Republic but lacking a birth certificate as discriminatory. Some 200.000-300.000 Haitians live in the Dominican Republic without proper documents. Since June 2015 more than 87.000 Haitians and Dominicans of Haitian descent have fled the Dominican Republic under the threat of deportation and fear for their lives.

A number of factors have compromised the ability to approach the global situation via a constructive, universal critique, within the framework of the Kantian categorical imperatives implicit in the domain of human rights:

– the Kafkaesque detention center that has been in operation for over 10 years at the Guantanamo Naval Base;

– the killings committed by United States Marines in near total impunity, with the squad leader principally responsible for the November 2005 killings of 24 unarmed Iraqi civilians in Haditha (including 10 women and children ages 1, 3, 4, 5 and 8), Sergeant Frank Wuterich, granted a plea bargain that allowed him to avoid any prison time (and he was honorably discharged from the United States Marine Corps in 2012);

– the torture and humiliation of Muslim detainees by their American jailers in Iraq and Afghanistan, widely reported in mainstream media and treated in a less-than-outraged manner by President Obama[1] before the Senate published a voluminous report (6.700 pages) in 2014, revealing the alarming extent of the use of torture by the Central Intelligence Agency (CIA)[2] and the psychological assistance provided to torturers by psychologists James Mitchell and Bruce Jessen from the American Psychological Association[3];

– the euphemism for torture ("*enhanced interrogation techniques*") used in official memorandums to cloak political responsibility and shield officers, coined in August 2002 by the legal advisors John Yoo, Jay Bybee, and Alberto Gonzales (Yoo is currently a professor of law at the University of Berkeley, Bybee is a federal judge on the U.S. Court of Appeals, and Gonzales, former U.S.

---

1. "*We tortured some folks*", *The Guardian,* August 1, 2014 *(www.theguardian.com).* Despite the broad extent of torture revealed in a host of reports ("Torture at Abu Ghraib", Annals of National Security, Seymour Hersh), in violation of the Federal Torture Act and UN Convention against Torture, only one person has been convicted: CIA agent David Passaro, for the torture of Abdul Wali, who was killed by Passaro on June 21, 2003 (see "Anatomy of an Interrogation", *RetroReport*, April 20, 2015).

2. Senate Select Committee on Intelligence Report. Central Intelligence Agency´s Detention and Interrogation program, December 2014. The report is 6.000 pages long; only 528 pages, extensively censored, have been made public.

3. *International New York Times,* editorial, "Psychologists Who Greenlighted Torture", July 10, 2015; James Risen, "Psychologists Shielded U.S. Torture Program, Reports Finds", July 10, 2015.

Attorney General from February 2005 to September 2007, is currently Dean of Belmont University College of Law in Nashville, Tennessee);

– the targeted executions by remote-controlled drones and their "collateral damage" in the form of civilian deaths;

– the abductions of political leaders and militants in Europe organized by the CIA and their secret transfer (*"extraordinary rendition"*) to prisons in third-party countries where they may be interrogated using methods worthy of the Gestapo and the failure of the European legal system to prosecute the perpetrators[1]. In the words of former CIA agent Robert Baer: "*If you want a serious interrogation, you send a prisoner to Jordan. If you want them to be tortured, you send them to Lybia. If you want someone to disappear – never to see them again – you send them to Egypt*[2]."

The non-governmental organization Open Society published a report in February 2013 listing 54 countries that participate in the program[3]. Above all, these actions, which have not been confronted and whose authors have not been duly prosecuted, have completely undermined any credibility in criticizing the violation of basic rights in another country. And this is all the more true when the few people who do stand up to expose the use of torture are prosecuted and sentenced to imprisonment, such as CIA officer John Kiriakou, imprisoned in the United States from February 2013 to February 2015[4].

It takes all the cynicism of U.S. diplomacy to prepare a yearly report on human rights (the Annual Country Reports in Human Rights Practices) when there are detainees who have been held for 14 years at the Guantanamo detention center without charges or trial and subjected to degrading treatment, one of them being Shaker Aamer, a Saudi citizen who is still detained in spite of the fact that he was cleared for release in 2007. The efforts of British Prime Minister Cameron and other parliamentary representatives to gain his release (Aamer wants to go to the UK to join his wife and children) have been to no avail[5].

While representing only 5% of world population, the United States has 25% of its prisoners. There are more African American adults under correctional control today — in prison or jail, on probation or parole — than were enslaved in 1850, a decade before the Civil War began. It is the only country in the world (with Papua New Guinea) that does not grant paid maternity leave[6]. More than

1. The kidnappers of Egyptian cleric Abu Omar in Milan in 2003: some twenty people, including the local CIA base station chief Robert Seldon Lady, who were convicted *in abstentia* on November 4, 2009 by Italian judge Oscar Magi and sentenced to eight years in prison.

2. Extraordinary Rendition, *The Guardian*, August 31, 2011.

3. *International New York Times*, editorial "Partners in rendition: Many countries, including leading democracies, are complicit in America´s brutal treatment of terror suspects", February 19, 2013.

4. John Kiriakou, "I Went to prison for Exposing the CIA´s Torture Program. Why Are the People Responsible for It Walking Free?", *The Nation*, May 20, 2015.

5 Jeremy Corbin, David Davis, Andrew Mitchell, Andy Slaughter, "Obama´s Slap in Britain´s Face", *International New York Times*, June 7, 2015.

6 Laura Addati, Naomi Cassireri, Katherine Gilchrist, *"Maternity and Paternity at work: Law and practice across the world"*, International Labour Organization, 2014.

40% of employees in the private sector (some 44 million people) do not have paid sick leave. As regards federal employees, starting only in 2017 they will be granted seven days of paid sick leave per year[1]. According to government data, the United States has 4.4 percent of the world's population, but over 40 percent of all civilian-owned guns[2]. In 2013 there were approximately 357 million firearms in this nation of 319 million people.This includes military-style assault weapons, of which it is estimated there are about 3.75 million in private hands. The U.S. society is the most weaponized modern society in the world. Police forces, in particular, have been outfitted with full riot gear, submachine guns, armoured vehicles, and other lethal weapons imported from the battlefields of Iraq and Afghanistan. Hundreds of people are killed each year by U.S. Police forces, mostly Black people, over 700 already in 2015 (up to October). The U.S. has been voted as the most significant threat to world peace through a global survey conducted by the Worldwide Independent Network of Market Research and Gallup at the end of 2013.

Brazil has been a member of the International Court of Justice, the primary judicial branch of the United Nations whose main function is to settle legal disputes among member countries, since its creation in 1946. It is composed of 15 judges, including one Brazilian judge, Antonio Augusto Cançado Trindade, elected to serve from 2009 to 2018. He has been a professor since 1979 at the Rio Branco Institute, the training venue for Brazilian diplomats.

In June 2002, Brazil ratified the Rome Statute, the treaty that established the International Criminal Court (ICC) in 1998. The Court prosecutes four core international crimes, including crimes against humanity. The ICC is based in The Hague (Netherlands). The Court is currently recognized by 123 countries, including all countries in Latin America and the Caribbean, excluding Haiti and Cuba. Neither China nor India have signed the Rome Statute; Russia, Israel, and the United States have signed but not ratified it. In December 2001, the U.S. Congress passed a law exempting U.S. citizens and military personnel from prosecution by the Court. The American Service-Members' Protection Act, better known to its detractors as the "Netherlands Invasion Act", authorizes the President of the United States to use military force to free U.S. service members detained by the ICC[3].

The Court is composed of 18 judges, three of whom represent Latin America and the Caribbean (Argentina, Dominican Republic, Trinidad and Tobago), elected in 2013 to nine-year terms. The President of the Court is the Argentine judge Silvia Alejandra Fernández de Gurmendi. Africa is represented

---

1 Gregory Korte, "Obama to Propose Paid Sick Leave for American Workers", *USAToday*, January 15, 2015; Peter Baker, "Obama Orders Federal Contractors to Provide Workers Paid Sick Leave", *New York Times*, September 7, 2015.

2 *The Washington Post*, May 10, 2015.

3. *"Authority to free members of the Armed Forces of the United States and certain other persons detained or imprisoned by or on behalf the International Criminal Court"*. American Service-Members´ Protection Act - Title II, Section 2008.

by three judges (from Botswana, Nigeria, and the Democratic Republic of the Congo) and the prosecuting attorney, from Gambia, while Europe is represented by 8 judges (from Belgium, Italy, United Kingdom, Czech Republic, France, Poland, Germany, and Hungary) and the court clerk, from the Netherlands.

The Brazilian judge, Sylvia Helena de Figuereido Steiner, was allowed to sit on the court until the end of the trial over which she was presiding, in keeping with its statutes. She served on the Commission on Human Rights of the Order of Attorneys of Brazil (OAB) and on the Peace and Justice Commission of the São Paulo archdiocese. As she sees it, one of the Court's challenges is to find an equilibrium between the notions of justice and peace without compromising the principles laid out in the Rome Statute. The ICC should be a last resort. National jurisdictions should take precedent; hence the importance of working the Rome Statute into national legislation.

To date, the Court's judgments have exclusively regarded Africans, with the exception of war criminals from the former Yugoslavia and the Special tribunal for Lebanon that prosecuted the assassination of Rafic Hariri, former Lebanese prime minister, on February 14, 2005. Granted that Gaza is not a state and that the United States are not parties to the Court, Celso Amorim deplores the fact that the Court has not expressed an opinion regarding the civilian deaths in the Gaza Strip or the Guantanamo Bay detention camp, focusing its decisions on non-European violators, almost all of them African and generally on the other side of the political fence from Western powers[1].

Brasilia is very reticent on the concept of "Responsibility to Protect" (R2P), which it sees as giving free rein to any intervention that can be masked with a humanitarian label, as we have seen in the Libyan crisis[2]. The former Australian Minister of Foreign Affairs, Gareth Evans (1988-1996), who showed little compassion for the Timorese suffering under Indonesian repression when he was in charge of Australian diplomacy, has now become the champion of R2P in the think tank "Global Center for the Responsibility to Protect", based in New York and including among its members the former UN Secretary General Kofi Annan of Ghana. The resolution adopted by the Non-Aligned Movement in Kuala Lumpur in February 2003, shortly after the invasion of Iraq, raised the alarm about the improper use of the so-called right to humanitarian intervention, which is absent from the Charter of the United Nations and from international law. The fear is that it will be used as cover to legitimize illegal interventions, without the express authorization of the UN Security Council, against independent, nationalist regimes. The examples are not lacking:

---

[1] Celso Amorim, "O Brasil e o Oriente Médio" (p. 254) in *Teerã, Ramalá e Doha, memórias da política externa ativa e altiva,* 2015.

[2] See the paper by the Itamaraty diplomat, Senise Paes Leme João Marcos, "*A responsabilidade de proteger antes e depois da intervenção na Líbia: uma perspectiva brasilend*" (Responsibility to protect before and after the intervention in Libya: a Brazilian perspective), Itamaraty, Rio Branco Institute, no. 686, 2011.

Mosaddegh in Iran, Arbenz in Guatemala, Goulart in Brazil, Allende in Chile, Jean Bertrand Aristide in Haiti, Manuel Zelaya in Honduras, Gaddafi in Libya, Mohamed Morsi in Egypt, Bashar al-Assad in Syria, all to the great distress of the civilian population.

During the NATO summit in Chicago in May 2012, which should have confirmed the withdrawal of the troops in the International Security Assistance Force, under NATO command since August 2003, signs were put up enjoining NATO to persevere in Afghanistan *("NATO Keep the program going!")*. They were financed by Amnesty International, which had been promoting improvements in the condition of women in Afghanistan since 2003 and told to ignore Afghan abuse of boys, so called "*bacha bazi*"[1], an initiative that aptly illustrates the complexity of the Western concept of Responsibility to Protect, where violence and intervention are used to protect or to ignore human rights[2].

In 2011, President Dilma Rousseff introduced the complementary concept of "Responsibility while Protecting" (RwP), observing that this responsibility can only be exercised within the framework of the United Nations and in strict adherence to its initial mandate (alluding to the intervention in Libya)[3].

The Fight against Poverty

Brazil has become a landmark in the fight against poverty. According to the Getulio Vargas Foundation, more than 20 million Brazilians have risen out of poverty between 2003 and 2009. This achievement is an international reference in spite of a social situation which is still problematic: according to the government, 16.2 million Brazilians still live below the poverty threshold[4].

Social inclusion programs (*Bolsa Escola* in 1997, *Bolsa Familia* in 2003) benefited some 23.9 million people in 2013 with monthly support of 142 *reals* (approximately fifty dollars in 2013). This money is granted on condition that the children go to school and are vaccinated. A report by the United Nations Food and Agriculture Organization (FAO) published in October 2013 states that Brazil had attained the following millennium goal within its borders: "halve, between 1990 and 2015, the proportion of people who suffer from hunger". Brazilian social programs have been an inspiration for Chile (*Puente* program launched in 2002), Peru (*Junto* program, 2005), Bolivia (*Bono Juancito Pinto*, 2006), and Argentina (*Asignación Universal por Hijo*, 2009). A 2012 study by

---

[1] Literally "playing with boys"; cf. the documentary by Jamie Doran and Najibullah Quaraishi ("The dancing boys of Afghanistan", 2010) and the interview with Nazer Alimi, director of the UNICEF-funded Youth Information and Contact Center in Mazar-e-Sharif (*Frontline*, March 25, 2009).

[2] See Neve Gordon, Nicola Perugini, *The Human Right to Dominate,* Oxford Studies in Culture and Politics, 2015.

[3] See "The protection of civilians in armed conflict and Brazil´s responsibility while protecting", Passarelli Hamann Eduarda, Norwegian Peacebuilding Resource Center, NOREF, October 2012.

[4]. Demétrio Weber, "O tamanho da miséria extrema" (The scale of extreme poverty), *O´Globo*, May 4, 2011.

the Inter-American Development Bank in 18 countries in the region found that 130 million people were receiving aid in 2010, four time more than in 2001[1].

President Lula was an inspirational force behind the adoption in 2004 of the voluntary Right to Food Guidelines by the FAO with the support of 188 countries, and the Action against Hunger and Poverty, cosponsored by France, Chile, and Spain and supported by 110 countries. Graziano da Silva, elected as Director General of FAO in 2012 over the former Spanish Minister of Foreign Affairs, Miguel Angel Moratinos, is the former Minister of Food Security in the Lula government, responsible for Lula's Zero Hunger Program (*Fome Zero*) in 2003-2010.

Brazil joined in supporting the World Food Programme (WFP) in 2007 with a contribution of 1.1 million dollars. In 2012 it was the tenth largest supporter with an estimated contribution of 82 million dollars. In 2011 Brazil established food stocks of 710.000 tons for the WFP, with 25,000 tons of rice going to Cuba in December 2012. Brazil's most important international aid project regards the cultivation of cotton in four African countries (Burkina Faso, Benin, Chad, Mali). Brazil extended the benefits of the *Bolsa Familia* program to some families in Kenya with the support of the UK Ministry of International Development and Malawi. The Malawian project manager was invited to Brasilia for an internship at the Center of Excellence in the Fight against Hunger, inaugurated in November 2011 with the support of the WFP. The Center currently has partnerships in Mozambique, Timor, and Haiti. Its director is Daniel Balaban, who developed a school lunch program for 45 million Brazilian children during the Lula presidency and is a member of the board of directors of the North American Global Child Nutrition Foundation, with aid programs principally in Angola.

According to a 2012 study by the Brazilian Institute of Applied Economic Research (IPEA), Brazil dedicated 1.4 billion dollars to international cooperation projects between 2005 and 2009 (including its participation in international organizations) and 80 million dollars to humanitarian aid.

Given the composition of its agricultural exports, Brazil profits from speculation on the agricultural food products that account for 75% of world food consumption (wheat, rice, corn), where prices have increased significantly. Over the past ten years, the price of corn on the international market has increased by 63%, that of wheat has doubled, while rice prices have increased by a factor of five. Brazil has profited from these quotations while also lamenting the disastrous impact of these increases on the billion people around the world who live in conditions of extreme poverty. The fact that 10 multinational corporations control 85% of world food trade only adds to the complexity of the situation. Imported legumes, fruit and poultry cost one third as much as their local equivalents on the markets of Dakar, Abidjan, or Bamako. As regards the European Union, which broadly subsidizes its farmers,

---

[1]. *O'Globo*, May 12, 2013.

worsening conditions for the 35.8% of Africans who suffer chronic malnutrition, it is indirectly responsible for the emigration of Africans pushed to despair, as witnessed by the tremendous hardships and risks (some 12% are lost at sea) they are ready to endure to reach the Island of Lampedusa. In 2013, an estimated 30.000 African refugees arrived on Lampedusa, most of them from Somalia and Eritrea, more than twice the number registered in 2012, revealing the breadth of the distress among the populations in the Horn of Africa. Jean Ziegler, UN Special Rapporteur on the Right to Food (2000-2008), paints a harsh picture in his book *Destruction massive. Géopolitique de la Faim*, published in 2011 and translated into Portuguese in Brazil in July 2013[1].

Brazil is in favor of the creation of a global fund for the protection of the poorest, which was recommended in May 2013 by the UN Special Rapporteurs on the Right to Food (Olivier de Schutter) and on Extreme Poverty and Human Rights (Magdalena Sepúlveda). The fund would be financed through donations from developed countries. But Brasilia would prefer to see this fund managed via the UN (FAO, ILO, UNFPA) rather than by the World Bank, which excludes Cuba. The United Nations Population Fund (UNFPA) has dedicated 6.5 million dollars in aid to Cuba for the period 2014-2018.

According to the United Nations Development Program (UNDP), the Human Development Index (HDI) has improved proportionally in Brazil, which stood in 79th place in 2014 out of a total of 187 countries. Brazil is faced with growing internal violence (51.000 murders in 2012; 58.000 in 2014), in line with the general image of Latin America, Central America and the Caribbean (with the exception of Cuba and Costa Rica), where homicide rates are among the highest in the world (23 per 100.000 inhabitants as opposed to the world average of 6.9, with rates in some countries greater than 50 per 100.000 inhabitants and greater than 100 for the 18-24 age group). Brazil alone accounts for 11% of world homicides; more than two thirds are black or mulatto and more than half are young (15-29 years old). Of the 50 most dangerous cities in the world in terms of homicide, 19 are in Brazil[2].

The *per capita* incarceration rate in Central America and the Caribbean are among the highest in the world at more than 400 per 100.000 inhabitants (Belize, El Salvador, Costa Rica, Panama, Cuba). Brazil is fourth in the world for number of detainees. There is some correlation between these rates and the social and economic exclusion of poor populations, but the situations are often much more complex (drug trafficking, illegal immigration, white collar crime, easy access to weapons, corruption in institutions, excessive impunity, further corruption of detainees in prison facilities that are veritable schools for criminality).

Nevertheless, the land of the "American Dream", the United States, which still exerts a strong fascination for a large part of poor, generally rural South

---

1. Jean Ziegler, "*Destruição em Massa. Geopolitica da Fome*", translated by José Paulo Netto, Editora Cortez, 2013.

2 *Business Insider*, "The 50 Most Violent Cities in the World", January 23, 2015.

American immigrants, is world leader for number of detainees (2.239.731, of whom 7% are non-nationals) – nearly one fourth of the world's prison population –, number of prisons (4.575) and *per capita* incarceration rate (716 per 100.000)[1]. We see the same discrimination between blacks and whites as in Brazil in terms of incarceration rate: young blacks are the principal victims – and perpetrators – of homicides and blacks are six times more likely to be incarcerated than whites[1].

UNSTAMIH- Haiti

After hedging for some time, in June 2004 Brazil accepted command of the peacekeeping forces deployed under the United Nations Stabilization Mission in Haiti (UNSTAMIH). In November 2011 it provided some 2.200 military and civilian personnel to the total peacekeeping contingent of 12.500. This would be the fifth successive United Nations mission to the island.

Brazil had already participated in a number of peacekeeping operations, particularly in Angola (with a thousand military personnel between 1989 and 1999) and Mozambique (200 soldiers in 1993-1994). Brazil holds the naval command as part of UNIFIL in Lebanon, with one warship and 200 stationed soldiers, and also takes part in missions in Sudan (UNISFA and UNMISS), Liberia (UNMIL), Cyprus (UNFICYP), Timor (UNMIT), Ivory Coast (UNOCI), and the Democratic Republic of the Congo (MONUSCO). In this last country, the UN mission has directed since April 2013 by the Brazilian general who had served in Haiti, Carlos Alberto Cruz. Furthermore, a number of Brazilian military personnel joined the UN observer mission in Syria in April 2012.

Peacekeeping operations are not envisaged in the United Nations Charter; they have developed as a sort of *ad hoc* tool, the great majority of them in Africa authorized by the Security Council.

Brazilian reluctance in this regard, as revealed in private interviews, is of two orders: the operations are seen as a form of imposition – the decisions are made by the countries on the Security Council while most of the contingents come from Southern countries; and the instrument, which has expanded considerably, suffers from serious problems of management and would benefit from establishing tighter relations with regional organizations. Latin America provides 70% of the UNSTAMIH contingent in Haiti.

Brazil's agreement to participate in the UN mission to Haiti doubtlessly rests on its ambition to gain a permanent seat on the Security Council (without veto rights). This participation was encouraged by French foreign relations, whose role regarding Haiti is somewhat ambiguous. It still turns a deaf ear to repeated entreaties to reimburse Haiti the debt imposed in 1825 as a "highway

[1] Pew Research Center, Drake Bruce, "Incarceration gap widens between whites and blacks", September 6, 2013 (*www.pewresearch.org*).

tax" on the road to independence: 90 million gold francs to indemnify the rich colonial plantation and slave owners for the loss of their human capital, a debt that Haiti paid off to French banks at exorbitant interest rates into the 1950s and that has been a major factor in crippling the country's economic development [1].

The Brazilian military command in Haiti, sensitive to maintaining socio-economic order, is relatively well regarded and appreciated by the local population. Zilda Arns Newmann, a leader in Brazil's humanitarian efforts, founder and coordinator of *Pastoral da Criança* (Pastoral Care for Children), an organ of the National Conference of Bishops of Brazil, died in the Haitian earthquake on January 12, 2010.

The earthquake cut into the cohesion and domain of the Brazilian command. The United States refused to place the 10.000 troops it sent to Haiti under Brazilian command, and took direct control of the Port-au-Prince airport.

In August 2011, Brazilian Defense Minister Celso Amorim said he was in favor of reducing the peacekeeping contingent and progressive Brazilian disengagement from the UN mission, which had become embroiled in a series of incidents, aggravated in the eyes of the local population by the diplomatic immunity enjoyed by the peacekeepers (e.g. dubious suicide of a 16-year-old Haitian Gérard Jean Gilles on one of the mission's police bases; cholera epidemic attributed to the Nepalese contingent; abuse of young Haitians by Uruguayan and Brazilian soldiers).

Impunity is a relatively ambiguous notion in a country that received Jean-Claude Duvalier after 25 years of golden exile on the French Riviera. With his father, François "Papa Doc" Duvalier, Jean-Claude Duvalier was responsible for the killings of 30.000 Haitians during the thirty years of a family regime of terror. In January 2012, an examining magistrate dismissed charges against Jean-Claude Duvalier of crimes against humanity by 22 victims.

Papa Doc's grandson, François Nicolas Duvalier is now a civil servant in the presidential palace. His father Jean-Claude returned to Haiti in 2011, where he enjoyed a life of luxury in his estate in Piétonville, a suburb of Port-au-Prince, with his longtime companion Veronica Roy. Roy is the granddaughter of Paul Magloire, president of Haiti from 1950 to 1956. Jean-Claude finally received a warrant ordering him to appear before the Port-au-Prince Court of Appeals on February 28, 2013. He died in the comfort of his home of a heart attack on October 4, 2014.

A cholera epidemic broke out in October 2010, killing over 8.000 Haitians and infecting some 650.000 (approximately 5% of the population). The United Nations was slow in recognizing the extent of and responsibility for this epidemic. Cuban epidemiologists working as part of mission to Haiti had clearly

---

[1] "M. Sarkozy, rendez à Haïti son argent extorqué" (Mr. Sarkozy, give Haiti back its extorted money), *Libération*, August 16, 2010.

pointed out the similarities between the cholera bacteria brought to the island by the Nepalese contingent in October 2010 and those implicated in the epidemic. It took the United Nations four months to decide to send independent medical experts to the island in February 2011 and earmark an estimated 284 million dollars in 2012 to cope with the disease[1], of which only a small amount has actually been disbursed. The United Nations has refused to pay indemnity to the families of the victims, claiming immunity from its Charter and from the Convention on the Privileges and Immunities of 1946. In June 2013, the Secretary General was questioned about this by members of the U.S. Congress, who demanded that he grant compensation to the victims' families and make a public apology. This is a position privately shared by the Brazilian command: immunity must not be confused with impunity.

President Lula traveled to Port-au-Prince three times during his two terms; his Minister of External Relations, Celso Amorim, went there ten times. President Dilma Rousseff made an official visit to the island in February 2012. The UN dedicates an average of 800 million dollars per year to maintain its mission to Haiti. In December 2012, the Inter-American Development Bank organized a forum of investors from 29 countries in Port-au-Prince as part of the events surrounding the inauguration of the Caracol Industrial complex. Brazilian companies have yet to take part. Most investments have arrived through the Haiti Action Network, an element in the Clinton Global Initiative, founded by the former U.S. president, who was co-chair in 2010 of the Interim Haiti Reconstruction Commission. Clearly a redemptive initiative, given the serious impact that foreign investment had had on Haitian food production (rice, poultry) during the Clinton administration, when Haiti was forced to buy subsidized North American rice and meat, not to mention oil supplies to the military regime – in theory under embargo – by the Texaco Oil Company. All in all, the failure of international aid may be chalked up to blindness. After obtaining documents through the Freedom of Information Act, the U.S. press revealed that less than 1% of this aid went to NGOs and Haitian institutions. The money from USAID, estimated at 1.5 billion dollars, went mainly to private American firms based in Washington D.C.[2] The American Red Cross is not able to provide precise answers regarding how 500 million dollars from donations was used now that it has withdrawn from the country: one third of the money apparently went to intermediaries[3].

In its program to fight the extreme poverty of the shanty towns in Port-au-Prince ("Ede pèp"), Haiti has taken inspiration from the Brazilian social aid

---

1. Deborah Sontag, "For Haiti, aid brought a disaster", *New York Times*, *International Herald Tribune*, April 2, 2012.

2 Jake Johnston, "Is USAID Helping Haiti to Recover or US Contractors to Make Millions?", *The Nation*, January 21, 2015.

3 Justin Elliott, "How the Red Cross raised half billion dollars for Haiti and built six homes", *ProRepublica*, June 3, 2015; Laura Sullivan, Mitzy-Lynn Hyacinthe, "In Search of the Red Cross's $500 Million in Haiti Relief", *NPR Radio*, June 3, 2015.

program *Brasil sem miseria*, implemented in 2011 by Dilma Rousseff in the *favelas* on the urban outskirts. During the visit to Brasilia of Haitian Prime Minister Laurent Lamothe in May 2013, discussions included a cooperatively based strategic partnership, and trade and investment agreements (mainly in textiles and bio-ethanol), and several memorandums of understanding were signed. Former president Lula met with the Haitian prime minister in São Paulo during this visit. However, the political situation in Haiti has prompted rather harsh criticism from Brazilian diplomats: the country has certainly inherited a great burden, and the earthquake has certainly only made matters worse, but social and ethnic divisions persist and underlying tensions threaten an obsolete and challenged economic model, one brought into being by a self-obsessed oligarchy that is highly dependent on foreign non-governmental organizations with independent and diverging agendas. The largest favela in Port-au-Prince, the Corail refugee camp, has grown from 7.000 to 200.000 inhabitants in three years. "*Haiti is the international community's latest failure, because the catastrophe is not the earthquake itself, but the incapacity to respond to it*" stated filmmaker Raoul Peck, former Haitian Minister of Culture (1996-1997), author of the critical documentary *Fatal Assistance* presented at the Berlin Film Festival in 2013 and winner of the Best Documentary prize at the Trinidad & Tobago Film Festival that same year.

The replacement of Hillary Clinton by John Kerry as Secretary of State, the disappearance of Hugo Chávez, concerns in the Dominican Republic about the growing drug trade and the establishment on the island of Mexican cartels, the less conciliatory approach of its principal donors (Canada in particular), the decay of internal security, and rampant corruption have prompted Brazilian diplomats to paint a depressing picture of the situation in Haiti and to advise gradual disengagement. In 2016, UNSTAMIH is expected to include 7,000 police officers and soldiers. The report published by the Secretary General in March 2013 and the annual report of the NGO Save the Children issued in May 2013 provide an inventory of the persisting human rights issues, in spite of large sums of money flowing in from abroad: impunity, forced evictions from refugee camps, and child slavery (according to UNICEF, 300,000 children, known locally as *restavek*, live under conditions bordering on slavery[1]). More than 1.5 million Haitians suffer from serious food shortages. Haiti has the world's highest maternal mortality rate (one mother out of 83 dies from pregnancy-related causes). Close to 80% of the population is illiterate.

President Martelly, elected in 2011 with the support of the United States, is committed to recreating an army, citing security issues and unemployment and mentioning the sum of 95 million dollars to accomplish the task. Former president Jean-Bertrand Aristide, victim of two coups d'état (1991, 2004) dissolved the army in 1995, following the example of Costa Rica, in order to ensure political stability and prevent killings (5.000 people were killed during his

1. Julian Vigo, "Child Trafficking and Adoption in Haiti", *Counterpunch*, September 17, 2013.

exile from 1991 to 1994). Over the course of its history, Haiti has experienced 32 coups d'état and only three democratic transitions of power.

The situation at the beginning of 2015 was one of grave institutional crisis: members of parliament and mayors of the main cities in office past the end of their terms, a decaying judiciary, massive interference by the United States.

The Haitian question has helped strengthen ties between Brazil and the Caribbean Community (CARICOM). This rapprochement took concrete form in the Brazil-CARICOM summit organized by President Lula in Brasilia on April 26, 2010, following the Latin America-Caribbean summit for Integration and Development, also organized by Brazil, in December 2008. Following this summit, Brazil opened four new diplomatic missions in the region: Dominica, Antigua and Barbuda, Saint Christopher and Nevis, Saint Vincent and the Grenadines. The most recent Brazil-CARICOM summit took place in September 2013 in Paramaribo (Suriname). The 14 CARICOM countries (excluding Montserrat) represent 7% of the votes at the United Nations and close to half of those in the Organization of American States (OAS).

One of the unexpected consequences of Brazil's engagement in Haiti was the arrival of thousands of Haitian refugees in Brazil in 2011. Estimated to number 4,000 that year, these undocumented and penniless immigrants were not expelled. They were granted a residence permit for humanitarian reasons, along with a work permit. On January 14, 2012, the Brazilian government decided to place a cap of 100 on the number of monthly visas issued to Haitians hoping to settle in Brazil. However, during the first quarter of 2013, more than 1.700 Haitians entered Brazil illegally via the State of Acre. Close to 10% of the population of the state capital, Rio Branco, is now Haitian. In April 2013, the National Council on Immigration decided to eliminate the cap in order to disincentivize illegal immigration. Although it is coping with a difficult social situation, Brazil has taken a tolerant approach, breaking with the European Union's "Return" immigration directive adopted on June 18, 2008 and contrasting with the arbitrary measures, denounced by the Brazilian press, to which Brazilian citizens have been subjected since 2010 on their entry into Spanish territory.

An investigation by the U.S. Committee for Refugees and Immigrants evaluating 52 host countries in 2009 gave Brazil honors as the only country to receive the top scores in each of the analyzed criteria (repression/physical protection, detention/access to courts, freedom of movement and residence, right to earn a livelihood)[1]. In 2015, the State of São Paulo inaugurated a receiving facility for undocumented immigrants (*Centro de Integração da Cidadania do Imigrante*), who are estimated to number close to a million in the state and represent a significant portion of its prison population according to the Secretary of Justice, Eloisa de Souza Arruda.

[1]. World Refugee Survey 2009.

The Brazilian media has reported on degrading work conditions for many immigrants in the coal, refrigeration and civil construction industries along with – something rare here – the first cases of xenophobia[1].

In September 2013 a meeting was organized under the auspices of the International Immigration Office between the Director of Political Affairs of the Haitian Foreign Affairs Ministry and the Itamaraty Immigration Director with the goal of improving cooperation and the coordination of immigration flows. According to a study by Professor Duval Fernandes of the Pontifical Catholic University of Minas Gerais, in December 2014 there were 50.000 Haitian immigrants in Brazil.

The Honduran crisis

It is clear that Honduras holds no geopolitical importance for Brazil. But the seizure and forced exile of the democratically elected president, Manuel Zelaya, by the armed forces on June 28, 2009 prompted a strong reaction from Brazil (including asylum and a platform from which to speak for Zelaya in the Brazilian embassy in Tegucigalpa after he re-entered Honduras covertly).

While the United States, Peru, and Colombia recognized the new president, Porfirio Lobo Sosa, who emerged as the victor from the November 2009 election, Brazil and other members of the Union of South American Nations (USAN) did not. Brazil was also outspoken in opposing the re-admission of Honduras to the Organization of American States, as urged by the United States[2]. In March 2012, 94 members of the U.S. House of Representatives delivered a letter to the Secretary of State, Hillary Clinton, demanding the suspension of military aid to Honduras because of the deteriorating situation in the country and lack of judicial response. This aid was to double by 2013, according to statements by Vice President Joe Biden during his official visit to Tegucigalpa on March 6, 2012, contravening the Leahy Law (named after Vermont Senator Patrick Leahy, who sponsored it), which prohibits military aid to countries that violate human rights with impunity. The Soto Cano Air Base, where some 600 U.S. troops are stationed, costs American taxpayers 89 million dollars per year.

In January 2012, the lawyer José Ricardo Alves was murdered for having disclosed the mistreatment and torture inflicted by police on prisoners in the Tela prison to the local newspaper *El Tiempo*, raising the total number of lawyers killed since 2009 to 74; in February 2012, 360 prisoners died in a deliberate fire in the Comayagua prison; in March, the journalist Fausto Evelio Hernandez was murdered, bringing the total number of journalists killed in Honduras in the previous twenty-four months to 18, one of the highest

[1] Such as attacks on Haitian refugees in São Paulo in August 2015 (cf. Leonardo Guandeline, Mariana Sanchez, "Haitianos: OEA acompanha investigação" (Haitians: OAS aids investigation), *O 'Globo*, August 11, 2015).

[2]. Speech by Secretary of State Hillary Clinton in Lima in June 2010.

numbers recorded by UNESCO in the world. The Rector of the National Autonomous University of Honduras, Julieta Castellanos, whose 22-year-old son was murdered by the police in 2011, presented a report in December 2012 stating that 149 people had been killed by the police since the election of Porfirio Lobo Sosa. Ebed Yanez was 15 years old on May 26, 2012, when he was murdered by a Honduran special forces unit that had been trained and equipped by the United States. Honduras's second-largest city, San Pedro Sula, is now ranked as the world's most violent city with a homicide rate of 169 per 100,000 inhabitants, ahead of Acapulco, according to a study by the Mexico-based Civic Council for Public Security and Criminal Justice (*Consejo Ciudadano para la Seguridad Pública y Justicia Penal*) of cities with more than 300,000 inhabitants. The top twenty cities on this dismal list are – with the sole exception of New Orleans – all in Latin America, six of them Brazilian (Maceió, João Pessoa, Manaus, Fortaleza, Salvador, Vitória). The United Nations Latin American Institute for the Prevention of Crime and the Treatment of Offenders (ILANUD) released a damning report in 2013 on the prison system in Central America, and particularly in Honduras (overcrowding, deaths, violence).

This country has never gotten back on its feet since it let itself be used as a U.S. military base against the Sandinista regime in Nicaragua. U.S. military aid to Honduras went from 4 million dollars in 1981 to 77 million in 1985, without including the parallel financing, unknown to the U.S. Congress, via the Iran-Contra Affair, with the involvement of Israeli and Argentine officials. In 2012, Honduras received 67.4 million dollars in military aid. The perpetrators of the coup d'État against President Manuel Zelaya, the generals Romeo Váquez Velásquez and Luís Prince Suazo, are former students of the U.S. Army School of the Americas, as are their forebears, the military dictators Juan Melgar Castro (1975-1978) and Policarpo Paz Garcia (1978-1982), and the Army Chief-of-Staff, General Luis Alonso Discua (1990-1996), the top commander of the infamous Battalion 3-16, responsible for numerous acts of violence, kidnappings and murders. The Honduran newspaper *La Tribuna* reported that private security firm Triple Canopy, founded by veteran U.S. Army Special Forces soldiers and merging with Academi (formerly Blackwater), recruited and trained a thousand South American mercenaries at the Lepaterique military base to serve in Iraq[1]. This project, which included the participation of the Peruvian armed forces, was meant to compensate the loss of Dominican Republic, Honduran, El Salvadoran, and Nicaraguan forces, which had joined the American offensive in June 2003 but later withdrew (with the exception of El Salvador) following the exit of Spain in April 2004.

Can the current violence in Latin America, a region with 10% of the world's population, 30% of its homicides, a homicide rate 4 times higher than the world

---

[1] Cesar Uco, "Latin American Mercenaries Guarding Baghdad's Green Zone", December 28, 2005 (wsws.org).

average, be separated from past acts of violence? Can we draw a line between the oppression and repression described by the Guatemalan writer Miguel Angel Asturias in *Los ojos de los enterrados* (The Eyes of the Interred), the financial support provided by the CIA and the United States for the death squads in Central America and the generals in charge of the fight against "subversion", responsible for the deaths of hundreds of thousands of people in the 1970s and '80s, and the alarming homicide rates we see today in Honduras, El Salvador and Guatemala?

Honduras is now the most violent country in Latin America, with most of its people (67.4%) living below the poverty threshold in 2012, according to the "Social Panorama of Latin America 2012" prepared by the Economic Commission for Latin America and the Caribbean (ECLAC). Between 1997 and 2012, 250,205 Hondurans were expelled for having entered the United States illegally[1].

This current crisis brings to mind the fundamental role played by Brazilian diplomacy during the Bolivian and Ecuadorian crisis of 2005 and during the coup d'état against President Chávez in 2002, with the creation of the "Group of Friends of the Secretary General of the OAS for Venezuela[2]", an essential component in easing tensions, and the calling of an abrogative referendum that put an end to the crisis. One gets an idea of the long road taken by Brazilian diplomacy since 1965, when it sent a contingent of one thousand soldiers to help U.S. troops invade the Dominican Republic.

Without altering its pro-U.S. stance, Honduras has since normalized relations with its most hesitant neighbors: President Lobo Sosa participated in the first summit of the Community of Latin American and Caribbean States (CELAC) in December 2011, rejoined the Venezuelan Petrocaribe program, and normalized relations with Ecuador in May 2013. In an ironic twist, the new president, U.S.-educated Juan Orlando Hernández, elected in November 2013, could run for a second term if the Supreme Court, which he has largely manipulated, judges unconstitutional the articles of the Honduran Constitution that forbid abrogating the clause prohibiting a second term, a question that had led to the ousting of the earlier president Manuel Zelaya (2006-2009).

[1] José Meléndez, "Se dispara número de deportados em 2014" (number of deportees skyrockets in 2014), *El Universal*, December 27, 2014.

[2]. Brazil, Chile, Spain, United States, Mexico, and Portugal.

Disarmament and Nuclear Non-Proliferation

Disarmament

In November 1995, Celso Amorim, then Brazilian Representative to the United Nations, took part in the Canberra Commission on the Elimination of Nuclear Weapons. The Commission report was published in August 1996 and presented before the United Nations the following month and to the World Disarmament Conference in Geneva in January 1997. The outcome of thinking by diplomats representing their countries at the United Nations and/or in Geneva[1] and by noted personalities[2], and of contributions from civilian organizations, researchers, and a great number of institutions, the report recommended the implementation of a program to eliminate nuclear weapons starting in 1997. It constituted the basis for Brazilian disarmament policy, a terrain where Brazil was as active as it was powerless. The president of the Non-Proliferation Review Conference – held in 2005 and ending at an impasse – was the Brazilian diplomat Sergio de Queiroz Duarte, who was later named United Nations High Representative for Disarmament Affairs, a post he held until February 2012.

Brazil was behind the creation of the New Agenda Coalition in 1998 with eight member countries[3], formalizing a number of demands for the five nuclear powers with permanent seats on the Security Council and signatories to the Non-Proliferation Treaty: the undertaking of a real, verifiable and irreversible tiered disarmament process in compliance with Article VI of the NPT; the ratification of the Nuclear Test Ban Treaty (it has yet to be ratified by the United States and China); the non-modernization of their nuclear arms during the process of their total elimination; and to take all nuclear weapons off their current "maximum alert" status[4]. The initiatives of the New Agenda Coalition are supported by non-governmental organizations joined together in the Middle Powers Initiative.

In April 2010, President Lula had commented wryly on the recent Russia-United States agreement (Strategic Arms Reduction Treaty – START): "*I would ask the U.S. President Obama, what the meaning is of the agreement he recently signed with Russian President Dimitri Medvedev on the decommissioning of nuclear warheads.*

---

[1] Britt Thevron for Sweden, Qian Jiadong for China, Ryukichi Imai for Japan, Nabil Elaraby for Egypt, Jayantha Dhanapla for Sri Lanka, Richard Butler for Australia.

[2] Michel Rocard, French Prime Minister from 1988 to 1991; Robert McNamara, Secretary of Defense in the Kennedy and Johnson administrations and former President of the World Bank; George Lee Butler, Commander-in-Chief of the U.S. Strategic Air Command from 1991 to 1992; the renowned oceanographer Jacques-Yves Cousteau; and Joseph Roblat, 1995 Nobel Peace Prize laureate.

[3]. New Zealand, Sweden, Egypt, Ireland, South Africa, Mexico, Brazil, Slovenia. Slovenia left the group when it joined NATO.

[4]. President Obama recently confirmed that the maximum alert status will be maintained in the new armed forces strategy (Nuclear Posture Review).

Decommissioning what, exactly? Because if it is a question of decommissioning that which is already obsolete, it makes no sense. I too have a box of medicines at home and throw away the ones that have expired[1]."

Any agreed disarmament obviously is only of relative value. In order to get the treaty ratified by Congress, President Obama promised the Republican party that 210 billion dollars would be spent over the period 2011-2021 to modernize the country's nuclear arsenal[2].

Global military expenditures increased in real terms by 45% between 1998 and 2008, going from 847 billion dollars to 1.126 trillion dollars, with increased spending mainly coming from the United States[3], which has 5.000 nuclear warheads, half of them deployed. The four French nuclear submarines have been armed with a new generation of nuclear missiles (M51) since 2010 (at a cost of 8 billion dollars)[4] and, starting in 2015, 200 kt thermonuclear warheads known as "*têtes nucléaires océaniques*" (ocean-going nuclear warheads) will progressively be installed. Great Britain's four nuclear submarines will be decommissioned in 2022 and replaced with three nuclear submarines each carrying 24 new Trident missiles (at a cost of 30-40 billion dollars)[5], which will make it possible to reduce the number of nuclear warheads by 20% starting in 2020. One of these missiles can carry eight 455-kt warheads (each one 32 times more powerful than the Hiroshima bomb). France and Great Britain signed a 50-year military cooperation agreement in 2009 on nuclear technology and warheads. In March 2009, President Dimitri Medvedev announced a rearmament plan aiming to increase the combat capabilities of the strategic nuclear forces by 2020, taking form mainly in the construction of eight nuclear submarines each having a capacity of 24 nuclear missiles. Prime Minister Vladimir Putin estimated the cost of this rearmament at 76.8 billion dollars[6]. Russia's BRICS partner, India, has announced a program to modernize its nuclear weapons at an estimated cost of 50-80 billion dollars over five years. The call for tenders regards 126 fighter aircraft[7]. In April 2012, India tested a long range missile (5.000 km), bringing Shanghai and Beijing within range, at an estimated cost of 480 million dollars, heralding growing militarization in Asia

Japan is obliged by its Constitution (Article 9) to "forever renounce war as a sovereign right of the nation and the threat or use of force as means of settling international disputes". However, it announced an increase in its military budget in 2015, citing the "*expansionist policies*" of Beijing in the China Sea, with

---

1. *Vou perguntar ao presidente dos Estados Unidos, Obama, qual é o significado do seu acordo recente com o presidente russo Dimitri Medvedev sobre a desativação das ogivas nucleares. Desativar o que? Por que se estamos falando de desativar o que já estava vencido, não faz sentido. Eu também tenho na minha casa uma caixa de remédios e vou tirando os que estão vencidos* (Source: *El País*, May 9, 2010).

2. *International Herald Tribune*, editorial, October 31, 2011.

3. Stockholm International Peace Research Institute (www.sipri.org).

4. *Le Monde*, January 18, 2005.

5. *International Herald Tribune*, editorial, October 31, 2011.

6. Source: Rossyiska Gazeta, February 20, 2012, cited in *O 'Globo*, February 21, 2012.

7. *International Herald Tribune*, February 1, 2012.

Prime Minister Shinzo Abe qualifying the ratcheting up of his own country's military capabilities as "*proactive pacifism*".

At the 65th NATO summit in Wales on September 5 and 6, 2014, the heads of state or government committed to pegging their defense budgets at 2% of GDP, with 20% allocated to the purchase of new weaponry. In 2014, only Estonia and Greece had a defense budget equal to 2% of GDP. The European Commission announced in January 2014 that spending on the manufacture and purchase of weapons systems would be considered an investment rather than an expenditure.

Norway represents an example *a contrario*: for 20 years it has pursued a policy aimed at lessening the violence of "asymmetrical" conflicts. While Brazil signed and ratified the Ottawa Treaty (Convention on the Prohibition of the Use, Stockpiling, Production and Transfer of Anti-Personnel Mines and on their Destruction – 1997), it did not adopt the Wellington Declaration in February 2008 and boycotted the Convention on Cluster Munitions in Dublin the following May, where 109 countries accepted the final text of the Convention. The reason for this was doubtlessly to protect its industries that exported to Zimbabwe, Malaysia, Iran, Iraq, and Saudi Arabia. It has been very difficult to obtain information about these industries from the Brazilian authorities. A bill to prohibit manufacture of cluster munitions introduced in the Brazilian parliament in 2012 failed to pass.

Brazil is not a participating state in the Wassenaar Arrangement (1996), which includes 41 countries (including Argentina and Mexico in Latin America) with the aim of establishing consensual controls on the exportation of conventional weapons. However it is part of the group of international experts of 28 countries (also including, among Latin American countries, Argentina, Cuba, Costa Rica, Colombia, and Mexico) to whom the Secretary General of the United Nations has assigned the task of developing an international treaty on trade in conventional weapons. It voted in favor of the Arms Trade Treaty (ATT) submitted to a vote before the General Assembly of the United Nations on April 2, 2013, as did most Latin American countries (with Bolivia, Cuba, and Nicaragua abstaining). Three countries voted against the ATT: Iran, Syria and North Korea. Signed by Brazil on June 3, 2013, this treaty will not go into force until it has been ratified by 50 countries. It is limited to regulating trade in weapons, not their production. Drones are not included. The United States signed on September 25, 2013.

During his second term in office (2006-2010), President Lula set forth a National Defense Strategy (*Estrategia Nacional de Defesa*) with the aim of creating an industrial and technological foundation for the defense program. The stated purpose was to better protect the Amazon Basin and the 9.000 km of coastline, where deep offshore oilfields had recently been discovered. Brazil's defense budget amounted to 3.3% of the federal budget in 2010 but has shrunk significantly since: 1.3% in 2014[1] at 31.74 billion dollars (half of the defense budget of France or Great Britain[2]). Among the BRICS countries, Brazil has the lowest military budget. During his instatement ceremony as Minister of Defense, Celso Amorim underscored that "*a peace-loving country like Brazil must not be mistaken for a disarmed country.*"

Cooperation with France, involving technology transfers, is part of this strategy. Brazil ordered four Scorpène submarines from France (to be delivered between 2017 and 2022, partially built in Brazil by Odebrecht and Arsenaux français-DCNS as a joint venture with the Brazilian Navy [ProSub], which has been contested locally because it was established without a public procurement process) and plans to built its own nuclear submarine by 2025. This contract, worth a total of 6.7 billion euros, includes cooperation in the construction of a shipyard and a new submarine base on the Island of Madeira (Itaguaí), south of Rio de Janeiro, inaugurated by President Rousseff on March 1, 2013. The technology transfer will regard the hull of the nuclear submarine but not its reactor. Through its Brazilian subsidiary Helibras, the European firm Eurocopter will furnish 50 EC-725 helicopters costing a total of 1.85 billion euros. However, the helicopters in question are plagued with technical flaws, particularly with the gearbox, which prevents them from being put at the service, according to our contacts, of the Brazilian president.

Agreements were signed by presidents Lula and Sarkozy worth some 12.8 billion dollars, if brought to fruition. France is now the second largest supplier of arms to Latin America (25% of sales; 6.3 billion dollars in 2006-2009) and Brazil is its principal customer.

In a private conversation, former president Lula explained why he had left the choice of multi-role combat aircraft for the Brazilian Navy to his successor, Dilma Rousseff, despite his own publicly professed (2010) preference for the French proposal: a call for tenders for 120 aircraft, of which the first lot of 36 Dassault Rafale planes is estimated to cost six billion dollars. He would have been disappointed with the attitude taken by France regarding Brazilian mediation in the Iran question, when the French president, Nicolas Sarkozy, had personally encouraged it. In the end, it was the Swedish offer (JAS 39 Gripen by SAAB) that won out; a contract worth 5.4 billion dollars.

The president of the Brazilian aerospace conglomerate Embraer stated to the press on December 14, 2011 that it would dedicate a greater proportion of its business to military projects in coming years (at the time they constituted 15% of business volume). A growing competitor in the civil aviation market, Embraer contends with Bombardier of Canada for the title of world's third-largest aircraft maker and is Brazil's fifth largest exporter. It is currently the only South American firm ranked among the world's top 100 arms producers (in 62nd place)[3].

---

1 Source: World Bank.

2 Stockholm International Peace Research Institute – SIPRI, military expenditure database, 2015.

3. SIPRI, Top 100 arms producing companies, 2013.

In January 2012, the company announced it had won a bid for the delivery of 20 Super Tucano aircraft to an American airline company, triggering a lawsuit by rival Hawker Beechcraft and unfavorable reactions from Republican leaders in Congress, leading the White House to suspend the order in February 2012.

In 2007, Washington had opposed the sale of Embraer Super Tucano aircraft bearing U.S. technology to Venezuela on a contract signed with President Chávez on August 25, 2005 worth some 170 million dollars. Venezuela then turned to Russia and purchased more highly sophisticated equipment (costing four billion dollars). This produced a critical reaction in the Brazilian media against the designs for regional hegemony ascribed to the Venezuelan president.

The United States is opposed to any technology transfer within the framework of the Brazilian space program even if the Brazilian Senate were to ratify the Technology Safeguards Agreement signed by the two countries in April 2000. President Lula eventually had to take the proposal off the Senate agenda due to opposition from a majority of the senators. The agreement provided for ceding a part of the Alcantara base to exclusive U.S. control. In spite of the Missile Technology Control Regime (MCTR), which Brazil joined in 1995[1], the United States prohibited Brazil from allocating resources that might derive from the sale of a part of the VLS rocket launch-pad base, operated until 2015 with the support of Ukraine after the tragic accident of August 2003 that cost the lives of 21 Brazilian scientists. After the revelations by Edward Snowden, sales of aerospace equipment, especially satellite imaging equipment, from the United States, are viewed with suspicion. As regards components subject to U.S. export regulations (International Traffic in Arms Regulation), a satellite imaging system may only be exported if equipped with a shutter preventing its use at certain times and in certain geographical zones, such as above Israel.

Historically, Brazil perceives threats and risks in terms of economic vulnerabilities. In geopolitical terms, Brazil is a stable country. It has no territorial claims or disputes with its neighbors since the Treaty of Petrópolis (1903), which involved an exchange of territory with Bolivia, giving Brazil the former Bolivian territory of Acre. But it has 15.600 km of terrestrial borders, of which 11.000 km are in the Amazon.

Brazil has long advocated a self-reliant model of economic development as regards industry, with a predominant role for the state. It has played a leadership role in North-South negotiations and in multilateral negotiations (e.g. UNCTAD, GATT). It had not manifested any aspiration to become a military power until the period of the military dictatorship, when it rejected the Nuclear Non-Proliferation Treaty in 1968 and signed a nuclear agreement with Germany in 1975. When a democratic regime was established (1985) and a new

---

1. A voluntary agreement established in 1987 with the signatures of 34 countries.

constitution adopted (1988), Brazilian diplomacy made efforts, as the country regained credibility, to better integrate into the international community and there to play a greater, consensual role both in South America (creation of Mercosur) and in multilateral mechanisms. With the arrival of Lula as president, this strategy of integration was realized thanks to reestablished financial and economic stability, the marked autonomy of its diplomacy, and the charisma of its leader on the international scene, which was seduced by this orator of humble origins and affirmed social concerns, as comfortable in the company of major powers as he is with a farmers' union in the *sertão* in northeastern Brazil. According to many sources, this serene and consensual diplomacy lacks a solid military, the traditional *appanage* of a great power.

Beyond the legitimate desire to master the entire nuclear process and defend borders that are almost continental in scale, it is difficult to assess the real military ambitions of this country. It is a country marked by a tradition of consensus and resistance to any regional hegemony, but having as one of its principal diplomatic objectives the assertion of a progressively greater role on the international scene with the goal of altering world governance, which it sees as inequitable, by changing its structures, institutions, and power relationships. According to the Stockholm International Peace Research Institute (SIPRI), in 2014 Brazil was the world's 23rd exporter of conventional weapons, accounting for some 0.1% of the world arms market (excluding handguns) and its 21st weapons importer[1]. During the Lula years, Brazil's military spending increased by more than fourfold, going from 8.39 billion dollars in 2003 to 36.93 billion in 2011[2], placing the country in 11th position globally for military spending (5% of the U.S. defense budget). In a bold prediction, the U.K. Defence Minister said that the Brazilian defense budget will reach 97 billion dollars in 2045, moving it up to 6th place globally[3].

Brazil must cope with the classic problem of influence and power. It is clear that much of its participation in major ongoing debates will depend on its structural reforms, its fiscal adjustments, its economic growth, the preservation of its biodiversity, the integrity of its elites and its institutions, and the development of its social policy prior to that of its military capabilities. These capabilities are currently almost laughable, and increasing them does not appear to be a high priority in Brazilian society, considering the enormous and overshadowing social problems it faces. This, of course, is not the position of the armed forces, and the United States never fails to encourage rearmament during bilateral meetings, as clearly illustrated by the telegrams from the American ambassador in Brasilia, obtained from *Wikileaks* and published by the *New York Times*. In a telegram dated January 30, 2007, U.S. Ambassador to Brazil, Clifford Sobel, reiterated the words of General Jorge Armando Felix, member of the Institutional Security Cabinet of the Office of the President,

---

[1] Stockholm International Peace Research Institute – SIPRI, arms transfer database, 2015.

[2] Stockholm International Peace Research Institute- SIPRI- Military Expenditure Database, 2015.

[3] Global Strategic Trends Out to 2045, United Kingdom Ministry of Defense, July 15, 2014.

according to whom, "*Brazil must be willing to modernize and deploys its forces for international operations and confront the prospect of body bags returning to Brazil*[1]."

Nuclear Non-Proliferation

Brazil accepted the amendments to the Treaty of Tlatelolco, signed in 1967, which prohibits nuclear arms in Latin America and the Caribbean (signed by the 32 countries in South and Central American and the Caribbean, with Cuba signing in 2002). The treaty does not explicitly prohibit the transit of nuclear arms. The nuclear powers having permanent seats on the Security Council signed the text (Protocol II) declaring an interpretation whereby transit is allowed.

It is written into Brazil's Constitution, adopted in 1988 (Article 20-XXIII), that all nuclear activities within its boundaries shall be exclusively for peaceful purposes.

In 1997, close to thirty years after it was originally signed, Brazil joined the Nuclear Non-Proliferation Treaty (NPT) after much hesitation, feeling it was discriminatory. It ratified it in 1998. On September 14, 2002, speaking before the officers of the Superior War School, based in Rio de Janeiro, Lula declared: "*This treaty would only make sense if all countries that already have nuclear weapons gave them up*[2]."

During President Lula's trip to Washington in June 2003, the Brazilian Minister of Science and Technology, Roberto Amaral, pointed out in an interview with the BBC that Brazil could not abandon its pursuit of scientific knowledge and technical mastery of nuclear fission. The Vice President, José Alencar, stated in May 2010 that he felt it had been "*a mistake*" to sign the treaty because of the "*respect*" commanded on the international level by the possession of nuclear arms[3]. Luis Felipe Lampreia, Minister of External Relations when Brazil ratified the NPT (administration of Fernando Henrique Cardoso), whom I met recently in Rio de Janeiro on the occasion of the release of his memoir of five decades as a Brazilian diplomat[4], instead justified the decision on the grounds of avoiding a costly arms race with Argentina, given that Brazil was not faced with any military threat.

The two countries only signed the NPT after establishing the Brazilian-Argentine Agency for Accounting and Control of Nuclear Materials (ABACC), imposing very strict mutual controls, every bit as rigorous as those in the Additional Protocol of the NPT currently bearing the signatures of 98 countries. Brazil is not one of them, it judges the Protocol to be overly

---

[1]. Telegram from Clifford Sobel, January 30, 2007, *Wikileaks*.

[2]. "*Só teria sentido esse tratado se todos os países que já detêm armas nucleares abrissem mão das suas*". Source: *Folha de São Paulo*, September 15, 2002.

[3]. *O 'Globo*, March 20, 2010.

[4]. *O Brasil e os ventos do mundo – Memórias de cinco décadas na cena internacional* – Editora Objetiva – Rio de Janeiro, June 2010.

intrusive. Inspectors from the International Atomic Energy Agency now have highly restricted access to the centrifuges in the Rezende nuclear plant, which are monitored via environmental sampling and small observation ports. As regards assurances pertaining to the uranium enrichment facility in Aramar (State of São Paulo), an agreement should soon be finalized with the Agency. Currently, only a dozen countries with significant nuclear capabilities have not signed the Additional Protocol. Brazil will sign the Protocol only on condition that the nuclear powers effectively implement disarmament as defined in the Non-Proliferation Treaty[1].

After being suspended for more than 25 years, construction has resumed on the third nuclear power plant. It is scheduled to go into operation in 2018 instead of 2016, with a power of 1.350 Megawatts. A part of the nuclear agreement signed with Germany in 1975, work on the plant was interrupted in 1986 following the Chernobyl accident, in spite of the fact that much of the equipment and materials had been delivered and that storage and maintenance costs were in the neighborhood of 20 million dollars per year. The question of the nuclear wastes stored provisionally on site remains critical and a solution must be found in the next two years according to experts. None of the Brazilian diplomats I have spoken to have a response to this question, which presupposes the adoption of specific legislation and the choice of a site for the construction of a waste storage facility, which is extremely costly (work on the Bure facility in France, scheduled to be completed in 2025, has been estimated at 36 billion euros[2]).

The agreement with Germany envisages the construction of eight waste processing facilities. The French company Areva, which absorbed the nuclear business line of Siemens, is in charge of the worksite with German financing of 1.4 billion euros. The Brazilian nuclear program provides for five additional power plants by 2030, but given the opposition it has encountered it is expected that this number will be reduced. During Dilma Rousseff's visit to Moscow in 2012, the possibility of Russia participating in the program was broached, as confirmed by the assistant manager of the state-owned company Rosatom, Kirill Komanov, when he visited Brasilia in June 2013. Brazil did not participate in the BRICS meeting on cooperation on nuclear power that took place alongside the 7th International Forum on Nuclear Power in Moscow in June 2015. The cooperation agreement signed in June 2000 with Russia mentioned the possibility of cooperation in the peaceful use of nuclear power (Article 7) but no initiative to this effect has yet been taken.

---

[1] "Brazil will not sign the additional protocols to the Non-Proliferation Treaty broadening its restrictions unless the nuclear powers make progress on the central premise of the Treaty: their own nuclear disarmament", (*O Brasil não aderirá a acréscimos ao Tratado de Não-Proliferação de Armas Nucleares destinados a ampliar as restrições do Tratado sem que as potências nucleares tenham avançado na premissa central do Tratado: seu próprio desarmamento nuclear*), in Presidência da República, Estratégia Nacional de Defesa (2008).

[2] Pierre Le Hir, "Le retour raté des déchets nucléaire dans la loi Macron" (The failed return of nuclear wastes in the Macron Law), *Le Monde*, December 6, 2014.

The negative experiences with the publicly owned French company Areva, now close to bankruptcy[1], in the construction of the Olkiluoto nuclear plant (with costs rising from 3 to 8 billion euros between 2003 and 2005) and with the French largely state-owned EDF in the Flamanville plant, whose cost has skyrocketed from the 3.3 billion euro initial quote in 2007 to 9 billion euros today[2], are not likely to inspire Brazil to return to this energy source. Nor, of course, will the Fukushima accident of 2011, which has left high levels of radioactive contamination four years after the event[3], especially given the fact that the Brazilian plants are located along the coast of one of Brazil's most scenic tourist areas, in Angra dos Reis Bay, 200 km from Rio de Janeiro.

A judicial inquiry was initiated in July 2015 to investigate corrupt administration by the CEO of the state-owned corporation Eletronuclear that manages these plants, Vice Admiral Othon Pinheiro da Silva, appointed by President Lula in 2005. Educated in nuclear sciences at the Massachusetts Institute of Technology, Silva was in charge of the Parallel Nuclear Program (*Programa Nuclear Paralelo*) in the 1970s, a military program to develop uranium enrichment technology outside of the nuclear agreement with West Germany.

Nuclear power currently provides 2.2% of Brazilian energy. The country's hydroelectric potential is such that an alternative source can be expected to become an issue only after c. 2030. Argentina, which has three operating nuclear power plants (providing 10% of the country's electricity), plans to build three new plants with the cooperation of China and Russia[4].

In March 2012 the president of Eletronuclear (Eletrobas Termonuclear S/A) announced a curious initiative: the construction on the site of the three nuclear plants in Angra dos Reis of a memorial dedicated to the victims of nuclear power plant accidents in the world.

Brazil is seeking to establish a bilateral uranium enrichment consortium with Argentina. It is apprehensive regarding Argentina's intention to develop an enrichment facility in its own territory, hoping to be the only country to master this technology in the region. Following Rousseff's visit to Buenos Aires in April 2011, a nuclear agreement was signed to share engineering for two research reactors modeled after the 20 MW Open-Pool Australian Lightwater reactor (OPAL), delivered by the Argentine company INVAP in June 2000. At any rate, Brazil opposes the creation of an international institutional instrument (such as the Zangger Committee, a multilateral export control body for nuclear technologies and materials created in 1971 and composed of 36 countries, Brazil not being a party) that would allow the Security Council to assess

[1] Michel Villette, "Areva ou les promesses intenables du nucléaire" (Areva or the impossible promises of nuclear power), *Le Monde*, March 13, 2015

[2] *Le Monde*, March 12, 2015

[3] Pierre Le Hir, "A Fukushima, l'interminable décontamination" (Neverending contamination at Fukushima), *Le Monde*, March 11, 2015.

[4] "La Alianza nuclear con Rusia y China" (Nuclear alliance with Russia and China), *Página12*, June 1, 2015.

compliance with Article II of the NPT (the International Atomic Energy Agency does not have a formal mandate to verify such compliance).

The proposal for an international uranium enrichment facility presented by Russia and the United States in 2007, with units to be sited in their respective territories, known as the Kennebunkport Initiative, is seen by Brasilia as a way to benefit the current suppliers (United States Enrichment Corporation – USEC; European Gaseous Diffusion Uranium Enrichment Consortium – EURODIF, a subsidiary of Areva; Urenco Group, with UK, Dutch and German ownership; Tenex-Tekhsnabexport, a Russian company). In spite of excess installed capacity, reprocessing in an international facility is dimly viewed not only by Brazil but also by countries such as Canada, Australia, and Jordan, all having uranium ore deposits and seeing themselves as potential suppliers for a market that is expected to grow. In agreements on civil nuclear power signed by the United States, technology transfer is contingent on the renouncement by the recipient of uranium enrichment or reprocessing. This is the case in agreements signed with Bahrain in March 2008; with the United Arab Emirates in April 2008; with South Africa in May 2008; and Qatar, also in 2008. Since 2009, the Obama administration has negotiated less binding agreements with Jordan and Vietnam, both countries having uranium reserves.

In 1981 Brazil provided purified uranium produced by the Institute for Nuclear Power Research of the University of São Paulo for the Osirak reactor in Iraq, which was later bombed by the Israeli Air Force. From 1979 to 1990, Brazil provided Iraq with yellowcake (*urania*) from the Poço de Caldas mine, which belongs to the state-owned company Nuclebras. A team of some twenty Brazilian technicians led by Hugo de Oliveira Piva, president of the Brazilian Center for Aerospace Technology (now Aerospace Technology and Science Department), were in Baghdad in late 1989 to work on the development of a ballistic missile.

Brazil has the world's sixth largest uranium reserves (310.000 tons). The enrichment of locally produced uranium is only profitable above ten gigawatts (the equivalent of a dozen nuclear reactors). Given the current situation (two nuclear power plants and a third under construction), Brazil imports nuclear fuel from Urenco, holding its enrichment facility in reserve. But it plans to increase its enrichment capacities and develop the uranium hexafluoride (UF6) production process to supply the third plant after 2018[1].

Speaking before the United Nations in September 2011, Dilma Rousseff argued for the extension of the mandate of the International Atomic Energy Agency (IAEA) to ensure that the nuclear arsenals of the major powers would also be subject to inspections, and not just the civil nuclear power plants in developing countries. The Brazilian representative to the IAEA conference on nuclear security (July 1-5, 2013 in Vienna) asked that disarmament benchmarks be introduced into the Agency's three-year security program.

---

1. *O'Globo*, January 19, 2011.

The U.S. doctrine on non-proliferation was announced in December 1993 by the Secretary of Defense in the Clinton administration, Lee Aspin. The United States and the United Kingdom bombed Iraq in 1998 without authorization from the Security Council and also bombed a suspicious facility in Sudan which later turned out to be the Al-Shifa pharmaceutical factory, an error which had dramatic consequences given that it was the principal medicine producer in a country ranked 154th on the United Nations Human Development Index in 2010. In March 2003 the United States and the United Kingdom invaded Iraq without Security Council authorization with the official excuse of eliminating the country's weapons of mass destruction. On June 7, 1981, Israel bombed the Osirak nuclear plant in Iraq, which had been supplied by France, after an earlier failed attempt at sabotage on April 6, 1979 in La Seyne-sur-Mer, where it was built. In September 2007, the Israeli Air Force destroyed a suspected nuclear reactor in the Deir ez-Zor region of Syria. Counter-proliferation efforts are conducted outside of multilateral forums.

The Obama administration established a new strategy for nuclear arms (Nuclear Posture Review 2010-2018), apparently reducing the role of atomic weapons in the U.S. defense strategy. The United States pledges not to use nuclear weapons against a non-nuclear country that has signed the Non-Proliferation Treaty and has met all its obligations thereto. This does not exclude their use against China, Russia, India, Pakistan, North Korea, non-state entities, or NPT signatories who have not fulfilled the obligations laid out in the treaty, without designating an arbitration body to rule on the effective fulfillment of said obligations, leaving Washington free to interpret it as it deems fit.

Nuclear non-proliferation can only be defended within the framework of total nuclear disarmament. Joseph Rotblat (1908-2005), 1995 Nobel Peace Prize laureate, the only scientist to have quit the Manhattan Project on the grounds of conscience (1945) before the first bomb exploded over Hiroshima, pointed out the "*impossibility of a world order being maintained indefinitely on the basis of a handful of nations that possess nuclear weapons when all others are forbidden from acquiring them. The alternative to a world without nuclear weapons is not 'business as usual', it is a world where a great number of states will end up gaining a nuclear capability. And then it is inevitable that sooner or later the dissuasion will cease to be effective and nuclear arms will be used.*"

Similarly, Brazilian diplomacy insists on the need to set as the ultimate objective the elimination of nuclear weapons. It bases this position on a somber assessment of the status quo of non-proliferation and the NPT, stressing that there is no alternative to the effective implementation of Article VI on nuclear disarmament. The Community of Latin American and Caribbean States (CELAC) gave its support to the proposal put forth by Cuba and the Non-Aligned Movement against the use of nuclear weapons. The proposal was adopted in December 2012 by the General Assembly of the United Nations by a vote of 179 to 4 (the nays being the United States, Israel, France, and the United Kingdom).

Celso Amorim believes that countries with nuclear weapons are not working seriously to eliminate them: a situation leading to instability with potentially dire consequences[1]. This explains the impasse at the most recent conference of the parties held in New York from April 27 to May 22, 2015, tasked with assessing the NPT every five years. The United States, Canada, and Great Britain opposed the Egyptian proposal calling for a calendar for a denuclearized Middle East and refused to endorse the final communiqué[2], as they had done in the past (1980, 1990, 1995, and 2005 sessions). A parallel declaration, titled "*humanitarian pledge*", was signed by 108 countries, including Brazil and all Latin American countries. In this document, the signatories "*committed themselves to working for the prohibition and elimination of nuclear weapons*"[3].

It represented a further declaration issuing from a series of meetings on the humanitarian consequences of the use of nuclear arms organized since 2013 (Oslo, March 2013; Nayarit, February 2014; Vienna, December 2014) and generally boycotted by the nuclear powers on the Security Council. The Vienna meeting was attended by 158 countries, with China, France, and Russia all absent.

President Richard Nixon contemplated dropping two nuclear bombs on North Vietnam in November 1969[4]. He had also envisaged using them against North Korea, according to documents obtained from the U.S. National Security Archives[5]. Geoff Hoon, Defense Secretary in the Blair government (1999-2005) threatened their use on a number of occasions[6]. During the Falklands War, Margaret Thatcher had mentioned their possible use when demanding that François Mitterrand give her the code for the Exocet missiles that France had sold to Argentina, one of which struck and sank the destroyer Sheffield, killing 20 British seamen[7]. President George W. Bush asked Congress in 2003 to fund nuclear tests for earth-penetrating tactical nuclear devices of less than 5 kt (the Hiroshima bomb "Little Boy" was 12.5 kt) won approval for a budget of 20 million dollars[8].

And we must not forget the hydrogen bombs lost at sea or on land as a result of aircraft accidents (Tybee Island collision on February 5, 1958; Mars Bluff incident on March 11, 1958; Palomares B-52 crash on January 17, 1966;

---

1. Interview with Celso Amorim by Martin Granosvsky, *Pagina 12*, September 16, 2013.

2 "Lost Opportunity on Nuclear Disarmament", editorial, *International New York Times*, June 3, 2015.

3 Richard Norton-Taylor, "Nuclear disarmament? Forget it", *The Guardian*, June 2, 2015.

4. *Time Magazine*, July 29, 1985.

5. *O 'Globo*, July 9, 2010.

6. "*Saddam can be absolutely confident that in the right conditions we would be willing to use nuclear weapons*", BBC News World Edition, February 2, 2003.

7. Tam Dalyell, *Thatcher's Torpedo*, Woolf ed., London, 1983; *Daily Mail*, April 12, 2010; John Follain, *The Sunday Times*, November 20, 2005; Ali
Magoudi, *La psychanalyse de François Mitterand*, Marin Sell éd., Paris, 2005.

8. Nick Anderson, "Senate OKs Study of Nuclear Arms", *Los Angeles Times*, September 17, 2003.

Thule Air Base B-52 crash on January 21, 1968). Files declassified in April 1993 reveal that U.S. scientists carried out more than 2.000 radiation and plutonium ingestion tests and experiments on civilians[1]. This disclosure prompted President Clinton to issue a public apology and institute the Advisory Committee on Human Radiation Experiments, which published its report on October 3, 1995[2].

The United States had originally excluded the idea of nuclear disarmament because of the purported superiority of the Soviet Union in conventional arms. Even though the United States has now achieved unquestionable superiority in this regard, nuclear disarmament remains a utopia. In Europe, France, a declining power with respect to non-nuclear Germany, does not want it; in the Middle East, Israel cites its special threatened status in a hostile environment; China, one of the few allies of North Korea, is in a good position to understand the respect commanded by the possession of nuclear arms in international relations. In January 2007, former U.S. Secretaries of State George Shultz and Henry Kissinger, former Secretary of Defense Bill Perry, and former senator Sam Nunn published a document in favor of nuclear disarmament, which they saw as the only guarantee of non-proliferation. The document would clearly have had more clout had the signatories not all been retirees[3]. The former Vice Chairman of the Joint Chiefs of Staff and former Commander of the U.S. Strategic Command, General James Cartwright, also waited to retire before supporting a study in May 2012 arguing that U.S. nuclear forces could be considerably reduced without compromising national security[4]. The former Prime Minister of the Netherlands (1982-1994), Ruud Lubbers, has only now disclosed the existence of 22 U.S. nuclear bombs stored on the Volkel base.

"A nuclear-weapon-free world" is a slogan seen with increasing frequency in international forums. President Obama advocated it during a speech in Prague in 2009. The Security Council approved a resolution in September 2009 setting the objective of a world completely free of nuclear weapons (Resolution 1887). However, in its instructions to its representatives to the relevant international institutions, the French Ministry of Foreign Affairs expressly forbade any mention or formulation of the concept of "total nuclear disarmament". France is one of the few European Union member states to defend nuclear deterrence and the use of nuclear weapons, as we heard in President François Hollande's speech on February 19, 2015 at the Istres-Le Tubé Air Base. "*I would like to recall here that France may, as a last resort, underline its willingness to defend its vital interests*

---

1. Eileen Welsome, "*The Plutonium Files: America's Secret Medical Experiments in the Cold War*", Random House, New York, 1999.

2. "*Human Radiation Experiments*", Presidential Advisory Committee on Human Radiation Experiments, Oxford University Press, 2006.

3. *Wall Street Journal*, January 4, 2007.

4. Study published by the organization Global Zero on May 22, 2012 and signed by Richard Burt, former negotiator on nuclear issues, Thomas Pickering, former U.S. Ambassador to Moscow, General Jack Sheenan, former U.S. representative to NATO, among others (*International Herald Tribune*, May 16, 2012).

through a warning of nuclear nature, with the aim of re-establishing deterrence. The definition of our vital interests cannot be restricted to the national scale[1]."

Germany, which has abandoned nuclear power for civilian uses, is in favor of the withdrawal of American nuclear weapons stationed on its territory. It is supported in this stance by Belgium, the Netherlands, and Luxembourg, but Berlin has hardly expressed any haste to get rid of them. The B61 nuclear bombs at these American arsenals were modernized in May 2012 at a cost to German taxpayers of 250 million euros[2]. In early 2010 these countries, with Norway joining them, had urged discussions on withdrawal of these weapons at a time when many of them had renounced civil nuclear energy (Germany, Austria, Switzerland) and when the principle of deterrence had become anachronistic in Europe, despite the rear-guard action by France, Poland, the Baltic States and NATO Secretary General, Fogh Rasmussen of Denmark.

The United States has 240 nuclear warheads in Europe[3], certainly within the NATO framework, but based on bilateral agreements (Italy, 90; Turkey, 90; Belgium, 20; Netherlands, 20; Germany, 20). The U.S. Atlantic Council think tank, led by the former security advisors of Presidents Ford, Bush senior, and Clinton, is conducting a campaign against efforts by the European countries in question – actually rather low-keyed – for the withdrawal of nuclear arms installed in Europe under the auspices of NATO[4].

The Comprehensive Nuclear Test Ban Treaty, adopted by the General Assembly of the United Nations in September 1996 and signed that year by the United States (Clinton administration), has not been ratified by the U.S. Congress. The U.S. Senate rejected ratification in October 1999 by a narrow margin (51-48), the first security-rated treaty in 80 years not to be ratified by the Senate. The National Academy of Sciences published a report in March 2012 which concluded that the United States no longer needed to conduct nuclear tests for scientific purposes[5]. China, Iran, Indonesia, Israel, and Egypt have also not ratified the treaty; North Korea, Pakistan, and India have not signed it. To date, 153 countries have signed, but the treaty has not gone into force because of an annex that lists 44 countries whose signature and ratification are indispensable. India had agreed to sign in 1998 on condition that the United States presented a timetable for the destruction of its nuclear stockpile, complying with the progressive disarmament described in Article VI of the Non-Proliferation Treaty.

---

1 "*Je veux rappeler ici que la France peut, en dernier ressort, marquer sa volonté à defendre nos intérêts vitaux par un avertissement de nature nucléaire ayant pour objectif le rétablissement de la dissuasion. La définition de nos intérêts vitaux ne sauraient être limitée à la seule échelle nationale*", *Le Monde*, February 21, 2015.

2. John LaForge, "German Bomb Sharing Confronted with Defiant Instruments of Disarmament", *Counterpunch*, August 9-11, 2013.

3. *International Herald Tribune*, May 3, 2010.

4 "NATO-Based Nuclear Weapons are an Advantage in a Dangerous World", *The Washington Post*, August 18, 2014.

5. *International Herald Tribune*, April 2, 2012.

The relative stability, or rigidity, of the international institutions created in the aftermath of World War II constrains newly emerging actors who question the representativeness of these institutions and the legitimacy of certain international agreements that have been imposed by the principal powers instead of being negotiated within a multilateral context, such as the Non-Proliferation Treaty.

Originally, all atomic energy was to be subject to international control, and access to nuclear technologies for peaceful purposes was to be regulated by international safeguards. The Baruch Plan of 1946 and Dwight Eisenhower's "Atoms for Peace" initiative of 1953 already posed the principle that nuclear power for peacetime use should be subject to international control in order to prevent proliferation. During debate at the World Disarmament Conference in Geneva in March 2013 on the proposed treaty prohibiting the production of fissile material for nuclear weapons, the permanent representative of Brazil, Antonio José Vallim Guerriero, acting on behalf of the New Agenda Coalition (Egypt, Mexico, Ireland, New Zealand, South Africa, Sweden), a group constituted in 1998, spoke in favor of the elimination of nuclear arms and the establishment of a nuclear-free zone in the Middle East. However, he made no mention of the existing stocks that many delegations – Switzerland in particular – believed should be covered by the treaty if it was to be a tool for disarmament and not simply an instrument for non-proliferation (only prohibiting production).

Some states have given up their nuclear programs (Taiwan in 1970, South Africa in 1991, Libya in 2004). North Korea, faced with what it believes is a nuclear threat from the United States, feels it has a legitimate need for a deterrent capability.

During the presidency of Fernando Henrique Cardoso, Brazil established diplomatic relations with North Korea (2001), opening an embassy in Pyongyang in 2009. Only 25 countries have embassies in the North Korean capital. Two of them are Latin American: Brazil and Cuba. However, unlike Cuba, which has a longstanding political rapport with North Korea, particularly as regards military cooperation, dating to common struggles in Africa, Brasilia has only distant relations with the regime of Kim Jong-un. During the 1970s, North Korea aided insurrection movements in Brazil (particularly the People's Revolutionary Vanguard – *Vanguardia Popular Revolucionária*[1]). A trade agreement was signed in 2006; in 2012, Brazil was Pyongyang's 13th trading partner. The Minister of Foreign Affairs of the Democratic People's Republic of Korea (DPRK), Pak Ui-chun, was in Brasilia in May 2009 to ask his counterpart, Celso Amorim, for help from the Brazilian company Petrobras in off-shore oil drilling. The Brazilian minister had invited the DPRK on that occasion to sign the Comprehensive Nuclear-Test-Ban Treaty. Brazil condemned the North Korean nuclear test on February 12, 2012, which violated Security Council

[1]. *O Estado de São Paulo*, September 15, 2009 (*Estadão.com.br*).

resolutions, and expressed hopes for the establishment of a denuclearized zone on the Korean peninsula.

The Security Council reiterated its resolutions against the North Korean nuclear program and its ballistic missile program (Resolution 825 of May 11, 1993 that calls on the DPRK to reverse its withdrawal from the Non-Proliferation Treaty; Resolution 1540 of April 28, 2004; Resolution 1695 of July 15, 2006; and Resolution 1718 of October 14, 2006) and imposed an embargo on the transfer of sensitive weapons and technologies. Since the end of World War II more than 9,000 missiles have been launched (five by North Korea) and 2,000 nuclear tests have been performed (three by North Korea). The North Korean threat must be put in perspective. Brasilia feels that the ostracism imposed on this atypical regime (power handed down in a paternal lineage for three generation, a disconcerting personality cult, and extreme militarization) will not lead to appeasement. The U.S. military bases in South Korea that have remained closed to inspectors from the International Atomic Energy Agency, and the military maneuvers carried out each year near the North Korean coast using stealth bombers carrying nuclear weapons are taken as provocations by the Pyongyang regime. According to Brasilia, the denuclearization of the Korean peninsula must be an essential objective of the United Nations, deterrence being, under current conditions, North Korea's main concern, and not the adoption of additional sanctions that have proven to be counterproductive, given the particular characteristics of the regime in power in Pyongyang. The journalist James Rosen, working for *Fox News*, reported in June 2009 that U.S. intelligence services feared that the imposition of sanctions by the United Nations would only prompt North Korea to carry out more new nuclear tests. Stephen Kim, former State Department analyst, suspected of being James Rosen's source, was charged with violating the counter-espionage law and sentenced to 13 months imprisonment in February 2014.

The first region declared off-limits to nuclear arms was Antarctica in 1959, followed by Latin America and the Caribbean (Treaty of Tlatelolco in 1967), Oceania-South Pacific (Treaty of Rarotonga, signed in 1985, not yet ratified by the United States or France because it prohibits the transit of nuclear weapons), Southeast Asia (Treaty of Bangkok in 1995, not ratified by the United States, going into force in 1997), Africa (Treaty of Pelindaba in 1996, coming into effect in 2009), Central Asia (Treaty of Semipalatinsk in 2006, coming into effect in 2009), to which we must add New Zealand (1987), Austria (1999), and Mongolia (2000).

The Egyptian proposal for a denuclearized zone in the Middle East was originally introduced before the 17th General Assembly of the United Nations, presented again by Iran at the 29th session in 1974 (Resolution 3263), and thereafter at each session of the General Assembly. Security Council Resolution 1687, which ordered Iraq to give up its weapons of mass destruction and was exploited by the United States and the United Kingdom to justify their invasion of Iraq, also called for the establishment of a nuclear-free zone in the Middle East. Resolutions adopted each year by the General Assembly of the United Nations since 2005 have supported the creation of a denuclearized zone in the Middle East. The most recent is UN General Assembly Resolution A/RES/68/27, adopted on December 5, 2013.

The United Nations planned an international conference on this theme in Finland in 2012, but it was postponed. A forum on the question was organized in Vienna on November 21-22, 2012. In September 2013, Arab member countries introduced a new non-binding resolution demanding the ratification by Israel of the Nuclear Non-Proliferation Treaty; 54 states voted against the resolution, 43 in favor, the others abstained or did not take part in the vote. All States in the Middle East except Israel are parties to the Treaty on the Non-Proliferation of Nuclear Weapons and have undertaken to accept comprehensive Agency safeguards.

Israel developed its first nuclear weapon after France delivered a Marcoule reactor, which went into operation in 1963 in Dimona, with the semi-covert cooperation of France and South Africa. France declared this type of reactor obsolete in 1984. Very little information is available on the Israeli nuclear program in spite of revelations made in 1986 by a former technician at the Dimona facility, Mordechai Vanunu to the British newspaper *The Sunday Times*. Vanunu was later lured into a trap in Rome by a an agent of Mossad, Israel's counter-espionage service, kidnapped, and sentenced in Israel to 18 years in prison, 11 of them spent in solitary confinement. Released in 2004, he lives in Israel, where he remains subject to harsh restrictions on his speech and movement[1].

Brazil took part in Conference on the Humanitarian Impact of Nuclear Weapons in Oslo (March 4-5, 2013). It was boycotted by the five nuclear powers on the Security Council and by Israel. India and Pakistan took part. A follow-up meeting was organized in Nayarit (Mexico) in February 2014 with 146 nations in attendance. Countries having experienced nuclear disasters gave their testimony (Japan, Marshall Islands, Kazakhstan, Belarus, New Zealand, Ukraine, Algeria). The participants recommended the destruction of nuclear arsenals in keeping with Article VI of the NPT. They met again in Vienna in December 2014. There is an anti-nuclear lobby in Brazil run by some one hundred Japanese survivors of Hiroshima and Nagasaki living in Brazil (the so-called *hibakusha*)[2].

The mobilization of civil society on the issue of the consequences of nuclear accidents and, of course, the much more devastating impacts of the use of nuclear weapons, meets with the obstructionism adopted by nuclear powers when confronted with any disarmament initiative. Negotiations for a treaty to

---

[1] Hounan Peter, *The Woman from Mossad: the Story of Mordechai Vanunu and the Israeli Nuclear Program*, Frog Books, Berkeley, 1999.

[2] Zupello Maria, Watts Jonathan, "Brazilian Hiroshima survivors campaign against new push for nuclear power", *The Guardian*, August 5, 2015.

prohibit the production of fissile material, originally announced in 2010, have yet to begin. Brazilian diplomacy feels that the NPT Review Conference, attended by the nuclear powers, is absolutely not the proper forum for achieving tangible results on nuclear disarmament.

The Middle East

Brazil is strongly opposed to what it considers illegitimate interventionism on the part of the major Western powers and the obsessive recourse to sanctions that often have dramatically negative consequences on civilian populations. Iraq and Afghanistan are eloquent examples of the consequences of this interventionist policy: deterioration of drinking water and electricity supply, compromised hospitals and the resurgence of treatable diseases (polio[1]), families broken up, flows of refugees and exiles, and threats to the civilian population (more than 600.000 civilians estimated killed in Iraq since the U.S. occupation and two million children orphaned in Afghanistan). Four of the six top countries in terms of numbers of refugees are in the Middle East (Palestine, Afghanistan, Syria, Iraq[2]). In July 2015 Prime Minister David Cameron could complain publicly about the high number of refugees and asylum seekers flooding into the United Kingdom (25.000), but as of January 2015 Lebanon has 1.4 million refugees, Jordan 1 million and Turkey 1.62 million, numbers that grow month by month[3].

The intervention in Libya has become a total fiasco: a country without a central government, torn apart by armed factions, whose sovereignty is mocked (bombings attributed to Egypt; capture by U.S. commandos in October 2013 of Abu Anas Al-Libi, accused of planning the 1998 U.S. Embassy bombing in Nairobi, Kenya; kidnapping of Ahmed Abu Khattala in June 2014 by the U.S. Armed Forces under suspicion that he had been involved in the 2012 attack on the U.S. diplomatic compound in Benghazi that killed four people, including Ambassador Christopher Stevens). Between January 1 and August 31, 2014, more than 120.000 immigrants have passed through Libya and been received by the Italian Navy (three times more than in the same period in 2013) and some 2.800/3.000 have died crossing the Mediterranean (four times more than in 2013)[4].

This poorly organized flow of undocumented immigrants, whose numbers have swelled in 2014 and the first half of 2015, partially as a result of Western military interventions in Somalia, Libya, Afghanistan, Iraq, Syria, and Mali – or

---

1. Rod Nordland, "Afghan polio surges, provoking alarm", *International Herald Tribune*, January 19, 2012.

2. The other two are in Africa: Sudan and Somalia. The 4.9 million Palestinians do not figure in the statistics of the Office of the United Nations High Commissioner for Refugees (UNHCR) because they are recorded by another UN agency (United Nations Relief and Works Agency for the Near-East –UNWRA).

3 Source: 2015 UNHCR Country Operations Profile.

4 *International New York Times*, September 18, 2014.

by their allies (Saudi Arabia in Yemen and Israeli in the Gaza Strip) – has a direct relation to the emergence of extreme rightist parties in many European countries (e.g. France, Denmark, Hungary, the United Kingdom, Sweden, Switzerland, Poland). It has occurred in concomitance with the opening of intra-European borders following the Schengen Agreement, which facilitated the movement of workers from less developed countries (Romania, Bulgaria, Kosovo) and sparked xenophobic and islamophobic reactions. It is voiced as fears of a worsening of the economic crisis and unemployment levels in countries that have traditionally been generous to immigrants and refugees who are predominantly Muslim, and in those European countries that are receiving a growing flow of undocumented immigrants from Kosovo, a country that has yet to be recognized by five EU member states and whose young people, who are overwhelmingly Muslim, face unemployment rates on the order of 40%[1]. And then there are the Romani, nomadic communities originating in northern India and the object of segregationist policies and expulsion in many European countries. France has distinguished itself in this realm (9.500 expulsions in 2013; 19.000 in 2013; 13.483 in 2014[2]).

During an episode of 60 Minutes (on CBS) on May 12, 1996, Madeleine Albright, then Secretary of State in the Clinton administration, was questioned by journalist Lesley Stahl on sanctions against Iraq. According to a report by UNICEF, these sanctions have led to the deaths of five hundred thousand children, several times the number of casualties in Hiroshima. Albright responded that the price was certainly high but still worth paying[3]. Tony Blair's Secretary of Defense had similar comments in a radio interview on the fate of Iraqi children killed by cluster bombs used by the British army.

Targeted attacks now deliberately disregard the presence of children: to kill a Ezedeen Al-Quassam militant (Essa al-Batran), Israel bombed on July 31, 2010 his home in the Nuseirat refugee camp in Gaza, also killing his five children. Having targeted Nizar Rayan, a leader in the Islamist movement, the Israeli Air Force destroyed his home on January 2, 2009, killing his eleven children[4]. In its assassination of Libyan general El Khweldi El-Hamedi, NATO forces killed thirteen civilians, including three of his grandchildren.

An editorial in the December 3, 2012 issue of the magazine *Military Times*, which is owned by Gannett Company, the largest American media holding company, stated that Afghan children can be targeted by NATO forces because the Taliban use them as accomplices in their operations[5]. In the Afghan village of Uwshi, an 8-year-old girl detonated a bomb near a police station and was the

---

[1] Alison Smale, "They fought for land and now flee", *International New York Times*, March 9, 2015.
[2] *International New York Times*, "France´s War on the Roma" (editorial), September 4, 2015.
[3] "*We have heard that half million children have died. I mean that´s more children than died in Hiroshima. Is the price worth it ?*" - Albright: "*I think, this is a very hard choice, but the price, we think the price is worth it.*"
[4] Khalil Ashraf, Ahmed Burai, "Israeli strike kills a top Hamas leader in Gaza", *Los Angeles Times*, January 2, 2009.
[5] Bob Dreyfuss, "The US military approves bombing children", *The Nation*, December 4, 2012.

only casualty[1]. During the Gaza offensive in 2009, Israeli soldiers used a 9-year-old Palestinian boy in Tel al-Hawa as a sniffer dog to find disguised bombs[2].

Like terrorist attacks, military operations kill more hapless children than they do armed enemies. In Baghlan, Afghanistan, a terrorist attack on November 6, 2007 killed fifty-nine school children[3]; on July 9, 2009 another attack in Kabul killed sixteen children, aged 8-12[4]. In Pakistan, 132 children were shot to death by Taliban gunmen in the Army Public School in Peshawar on December 16, 2014. By the end of the second Israeli offensive in the Gaza Strip (December 2008-January 2009), three hundred and thirteen children had been killed, according to a report by Amnesty International[5]. During the third Israeli offensive, officially in response to the killing of three Israeli teenagers, the United Nations reports that 551 children were killed and 3.374 wounded between July 8 and August 26, 2014[6]. The Israeli humanitarian organization B'Tselem is forbidden by national authorities to read the names and the ages of the young victims on the air[7]. In Gaza as in Sderot, 75% of children between the ages of 4 and 15 suffer from Post-Traumatic Stress Disorder. UNICEF estimates that 425.000 children need psychological treatment in Gaza after the Israeli offensive of July 2014.

Mention of the deaths of four Palestinian children killed by an Israeli missile in June 2014 while they played ball on a Gaza beach in front of dozens of journalists lodged at the Al-Deira Hotel, resulted in NBC correspondent Ayman Mohyeldin being relieved of his functions[8]. Over the course of the last 14 years, more than two Palestinian children are killed every week by the Israeli army[9]. A typical six-year-old Palestinian child has already lived through three wars. UNICEF has recorded 1500 orphans in the Gaza Strip.

A recent report by the non-governmental organization Defense of Children International-Palestine corroborated the study published by UNICEF in February 2013: nearly one fourth of Palestinian children between the ages of 12 and 17 detained in Israeli prisons are in solitary confinement, the great majority of them for stone throwing, which can bring a sentence of up to 20 years. An estimated 8.000 young Palestinians have been arrested and charged (again

---

1 Joshua Norman, "8-year-old Afghan tricked into suicide bombing", *CBS News*, June 26, 2011.

2 Anshel Pfeffer, "Two IDF soldiers charged with using 9-year-old human shield in Gaza war", *Haaretz*, March 11, 2010.

3 Tahir Quadiry, "Suicide bomber kills 50 in northern Afghanistan", *Reuters*, November 6, 2007.

4 Abdul Waheed Wafa, Alan Cowell, "Truck blast in Afghanistan leaves at least 24 dead", *The New York Times*, July 9, 2009.

5 Report on the Gaza war, August 25, 2009.

6 United Nations Office for the Coordination of Humanitarian Affairs.

7 Harriet Sherwood, "Israel bans radio advert listing names of children killed in Gaza", *The Guardian*, July 24, 2014.

8 Joe Coscarelli, "4 Palestinians Children Killed in Israeli Air Strike Right in Front of Reporters", *New York News and Politics*, July 16, 2014. Aged 9 to 11, they all belonged to the same family: Ahed Atef Bakr, Zakaria Ahed Bakr, Mohamed Ramez Bakr, Ismael Mohamed Bakr.

9 Noam Chomsky, "Nightmare in Gaza", in *On Palestine*, (Chapter 9), Haymarket Books, Chicago, 2015.

mainly for stone throwing) since 2000 with the arrests most often taking place in their homes at night, methods reminiscent of Argentine military squads in 1976-1980[1]. According to the Israeli NGO B'Tselem, 12 children and minors were shot dead by Israeli soldiers in East Jerusalem and the West Bank in 2014 for throwing stones[2]. However, UN Secretary General, Ban Ki-moon did not include Israel (or Hamas) on the list of countries that violate the rights of children as defined by the United Nations, in spite of recommendations by Leila Zerrougui, Special Representative of the Secretary-General for Children and Armed Conflict[3].

In May 2012 in Houla, near the town of Homs, pro-Assad Syrian militiamen methodically killed 32 children, cutting their throats or shooting them in the head[4].

The infant mortality rate in the refugee camps near the Afghan capital are some of the highest in the world: 144 per 1,000 children under the age of 5. This means that one child in seven does not live to see his or her fifth birthday. Rod Norland, a correspondent for the *New York Times* in Kabul, listed the names of the twenty-two children under the age of 5 who died of cold in these camps during the month of January 2012[5].

According to the United Nations, in the sole year 2014, 710 children were killed in Afghanistan, 679 in Iraq, 368 in Syria, 167 in Darfur (Sudan), and 557 in the Gaza Strip[6]. The Bureau of Investigative Journalism has kept track of 389 targeted U.S. drone killings in Pakistan from 2004 to August 1, 2014, with total casualties in the thousands, including 200 children[7].

It took seven years for sergeant Frank Wuterich, leader of the patrol that executed seven children and their mothers in Haditha, Iraq in 2005, to be sentenced (essentially by a slap on the wrist). The charges finally reduced through a plea bargain process from murder to "*negligent dereliction of duty*" and he was demoted in rank and docked two thirds of his pay for three months, while all other members of the platoon either had charges dropped or were acquitted[8].

There is a somber space in the Baghdad morgue known as the "room of the absent", where the images of hundreds of unidentified children, their faces

[1] Olivia Becker, "Israel is Holding Even More Palestinian Children In Solitary For Throwing Rocks", *Vicenews*, May 15, 2014.

[2] Isabel Kershner, "Israel Considers Ammunition to Counter Palestinian Stone Throwers", *International New York Times,* September 2, 2015.

[3] "U.N. Keeps Israel, Hamas Off Children´s Rights Blacklist; Raps Israel Army", *International New York Times,* June 8, 2015.

[4] Neil Mac Farquhar, Hwaida Saad, "Many children among victims in Syria attack", *International New York Times,* May 26, 2012.

[5] Rod Nordland, "Driven away by a war now stalked by winter's cold", *International New York Times,* February 3, 2012.

[6] United Nations Report, "Children in Armed Conflict", June 8, 2015.

[7] Source: Bureau of Investigative Journalism (www.thebureauinvestigates.com)

[8] "Anger in Iraq after plea bargain over 2005 massacre", *The New York Times,* January 24, 2012.

generally bloodstained, are projected on four screens so that the relatives or neighbors can identify them and pray for them in their numbered graves in the adjacent cemetery[1].

What can we expect when children, the most precious part of our life, are killed or abused, except more grief, hatred and violence? What can we hope to reap from fields sown with so much sorrow and despair? What alternative means of redress is offered to Gaza resident Tawfik Abu Jama, the only survivor of an Israeli bombing raid on July 20, 2014 that killed 26 members of his family, including his wife and his eight children[2]?

Brutal military interventions, causing untold humiliation and engendering an unquenchable thirst for vengeance in countries such as Iraq, Libya, Somalia, Afghanistan, and Yemen that are already hostile to the United States and to most of the NATO countries because of historical conflicts and profound cultural and religious differences, upset delicate sociological and religious equilibria that have been achieved over a long history, of which the occupying forces may know nothing, or otherwise ignore, deride or deny. How could a country like Iraq, cradle of the first civilizations (Sumer, Assyria, Babylonia), once the center of the Sunni Muslim world, have been directed from May 11, 2003 to June 28, 2004 by the likes of a Lewis Paul Bremer III? According to the report by Stuart Bowen, Special Inspector General for Iraq Reconstruction, under Bremer's stewardship of the Occupation Authority of Iraq, 8.8 billion dollars disappeared, the principal museum art collections were stolen, and religious animosity and conflict were reawakened (among Sunnites, Shiites, Kurds, and Christians), the latter still having disastrous consequences throughout the region both within and outside of the Iraqi borders. This gives us some idea of the ignorance and contempt to which this country has been subjected.

Three hundred and fifteen suicide attacks were recorded in the Middle East from 1980 to 2003; since 2003 they number in the thousands. Young Muslims (from Belgium, France, Denmark, Germany, Canada...) join the *jihad* in Somalia, Algeria, and Syria. They metamorphose into terrorists in the name of a cause that will continue to motivate followers as long as it continues to appear legitimate and without alternative in their eyes. This cause is amplified by a growing Islamophobia, the persistence of the Palestinian drama, and the Kafkaesque detention and torture centers and systems that have recently been instituted. It is fueled by repeated military operations on Islamic soil, particularly drone strikes, the indiscriminate deaths of innocents raining down from the sky, leaving a seething wake of injustice and humiliation. They include young Americans, such as the imam Anwar al-Awlaki, the first United States citizen to be targeted and killed in a drone strike (on September 30, 2011 in Yemen), the Tsarnaev Brothers, authors of the Boston Marathon bombing, and

[1] Rod Nordland, "Driven away by a war now stalked by winter's cold", *International New York Times,* February 3, 2012.

[2] Report of the United Nations on war crimes during the July 2014 Israeli offensive.

Ibragim Todashev, shot dead by an FBI agent, perhaps the victim of an unfortunate friendship. Others are British, such as Parviz Kahn, or Michael Abedolajo and Michael Adebowale, both of Nigerian descent, who killed a British soldier in London in May 2013[1]; Danish, such as the man who attempted to kill journalist and author Lars Hedegaard in January 2013[2]; Canadian, such as the young Xristos Katsiroubas and Ali Medlej, killed while participating in an assault on an Algerian base in January 2013[3]; French, such as Mohammed Merah, who attacked French soldiers and Jewish civilians in Toulouse and Montauban in March 2012; or Australian such as the 15 year-old Farhad Khalil Mohammad Jabar of Iraqi-Kurdish background who fatally shooted in Sydney on October 2015 police accountant Cheng Curtis.

With a community estimated at 10 million persons of Arab descent, Brazil has so far been spared this turmoil, apart from the detention by Israeli authorities in 1986 of a young Brazilian woman, Lamia Maruf, accused of killing an Israeli soldier (David Manos) and released in 1997, and the current drama of the young Brazilian Islam Hamed, a Hamas sympathizer, in a Palestinian National Authority jail in Nablus since 2002 for having thrown stones at Israeli soldiers[4]. His release hangs on the granting of safe conduct by the Israeli authorities, who oppose his return to Brazil. A young Brazilian, Kaique Luan Ribeiro Guimaraes, 18 years old, a convert to Islam, was arrested in Bulgaria in December 2014 on suspicions that he was bound for Syria and extradited to Spain, where his family has lived since 2006.

Article 22 of the Covenant of the League of Nations states that there are colonies that have ceased to be under the sovereignty of the states that formerly governed them and "*inhabited by peoples not yet able to stand by themselves under the strenuous conditions of the modern world*"[5]. This article regards Mesopotamia (Iraq) and the Levant (now composed of Syria, Lebanon, Jordan, Palestine, and Israel) as well as other regions. It was thus up to the United Kingdom and France to decide when the Arab and Kurdish populations were ready for independence. The conflict in the region exists within this neocolonialist framework: the "savage wars of peace" mentioned by Rudyard Kipling in his poem *The White Man's Burden*. Bombardments, blockades, sanctions, invasions, occupation: if the foreign powers – Turkey, France, the United Kingdom and the United States principally – had left these regions to their own devices, their development would certainly have been less fraught. Sectarian conflicts were not entirely absent from the region before European colonialism, but the

---

1. John Burns, Alan Cowell, "2 appear in court in soldier´s killing", *International Herald Tribune*, June 4, 2013.
2. Andrew Higgins, "Denmark´s Muslims follow a new script", *International Herald Tribune*, January 28, 2013.
3. Ian Austen, "Canada identifies 2 attackers on gas plant in Algeria", *International Herald Tribune*, April 4, 3013.
4 Richard Furst, "*Piora estado de saúde de brasileiro em greve de fome na Palestina*" (Brazilian hunger striker's health deteriorating in Palestine), *O ´Globo*, June 16, 2015.
5 Covenant of the League of Nations.

colonial occupation manipulated ethnic and religious differences in the service of its imperial goals. Oil was central then as it is today. In Syria the French used the Alawites and other minorities against Sunni majority; the British established in Irak a Sunni minority dominance.

The brutal violence exhibited now by combatants in the jihadi movement and particularly by the Islamic State of Iraq and the Levant (ISIL) has grown out of this heritage. This violence may seem less incomprehensible if we put it in the context of some hard, revealing data: an estimated 600.000 Iraqi civilians have been killed following the invasion and occupation of Iraq; 500.000 children died between 1991 and 1998 as a result of sanctions imposed against the regime of Saddam Hussein[1]. Hans Von Sponeck, the former United Nations Humanitarian Coordinator in Iraq from November 1998 to February 2000 when he resigned from his position for that he judged were genocidal punishing policies that had only one goal, regime change, has written a remarkable book about the devastation brought up by the sanctions[2]. In Afghanistan since 2003 more than 250.000 civilians have been killed[3].

In 2014 alone, more than 1.2 million people were forced into refugee status; and the appalling figures continue in 2015 (more than 4 million Syrian refugees). The 71 decomposing Syrian bodies found in a smuggler´s abandoned truck in Austria and the drowned body of three-year-old Alan Kurdi washed up on a Turkish beach have shocked the West and should weigh heavily on its conscience, given its fundamental role in their misfortune. But The media consistently cloak the responsibility of the West and its proxies for initiating and expanding wars in Afghanistan, Iraq, Libya, Syria, Yemen and the Horn of Africa; those fleeing are denied their legitimate status as refugees of war and more often labeled "*migrants looking for work*".

According to United Nations data: 900 Palestinian children were killed between 2000 and 2007; in the space of 7 weeks (July 7 - August 12, 2014), 2,131 Palestinians were killed by the Israeli armed forces, 66% of them women and children[4]; from July 3, 2013 to January 31, 2014, 3.248 people were shot and killed in Egypt by the police, 80 of them while in prison; between March 2011 and August 2015, more than 250.000 Syrians were killed, 15% of them women and children[5]. There are an estimated 5 million orphans in Iraq; 2 million in Afghanistan. Drone strike victims in Pakistan alone are estimated at 2.440 to 3.949, many of them civilians[6] who remain nameless as long as they are Muslim, but recorded when they are Western victims of collateral damage, as was the case of two hostages, the American Warren Weinstein and the Italian

---

[1] UNICEF, Iraq Child and Maternal Mortality Survey, 1999.

[2] "*A Different Kind of war. The U.N. Sanctions Regime in Iraq*", Barghan Books, New York, 2006.

[3] Study by Physicians for Social Responsability (the largest physician-led association in the US), March 2015.

[4] United Nations Office for the Coordination of Humanitarian Affairs.

[5] UNICEF, Iraq Child and Maternal Mortality Survey.

[6] Bureau of Investigative Journalism (www.thebureauinvestigates.com)

Giovanni Lo Porto, abducted in 2012[1], both victims of the same drone strike in Pakistan in January 2015. Before them, there was the case of the young Scottish aid worker, Linda Norgrove, killed in October 2010 by "friendly fire" in the form of a grenade.

President Obama used a curious expression dating to the 19th century to explain the fatal inexactitude of the new military technologies: *"the fog of war"*. It was coined by Carl Von Clausewitz in his book *Vom Kriege* (1832, with an English translation published with the title *On War* in 1873 by Princeton University)[2]. He revealed on that occasion something that specialists and many observers already knew: the victims are not identified by name, they are not "targeted killings", in most cases the American authorities have not identified their targets. They are killed on the basis of suspicious "patterns of behavior"[3]. The principal humanitarian organizations (Amnesty International, Human Rights Watch, European Center for Constitutional and Human Rights, Open Society Foundation, Human Rights Clinic, and others) sent an open letter to President Obama on May 13, 2015 demanding that explanations and compensation be proffered for the deaths of civilian victims of drones, providing the examples of a dozen such deaths between 2009 and 2014[4].

History teaches us that extremism is born out of foreign invasions and repression. In the 19th century, the Caliphate of Mascara, led by Abd al-Quadir, rose up against French colonization of Algeria; "Mahdi" Muhammad Ahmad in Egypt against the Ottoman Empire and the British Crown; the Islamic State of the Caucasus (Chechnya, Dagestan) against the armies of tsarist Russia. They were all movements led by religious leaders, promoting *sharia*, and all were repressed with extreme violence without any analysis of the causes that led to the birth of the movements.

During a speech before the General Assembly of the United Nations in September 2011, President Dilma Rousseff spoke out against military interventions, arguing that they only aggravate conflict, generate new cycles of violence, and nurture terrorism[5].

During the Paraty Book Fair (State of Rio de Janeiro) in 2013, the Egyptian poet Tamin al-Barghouti, son of the Palestinian poet Mourid Barghouti, who

---

[1] Marjorie Cohn, *Drones and Targeted Killing: Legal, Moral and Geopolitical Issues*, Olive Branch Press, 2015.

[2] "*War is the realm of uncertainty; three quarters of the factors on which action is war is based are wrapped in a fog of greater or lesser uncertainty*" (*On War*, Book 1, Chapter 3, Princeton University Press).

[3] Shane Scott, "Drones Strikes Reveal Uncomfortable Truth: U.S. Is Often Unsure About Who Will Die", *International New York Times*, April 23, 2015.

[4] Ali Gharib, "Human Rights Groups to Obama: Investigate All Civilian Victims of Drone Strikes", *The Nation*, May 13, 2015. Sarah Knuckey, Balquees Mihirig, Bassan Khawaja, Surya Gopalan, "Ten More Strikes the Obama Administration Should Immediately Acknowledge and Investigate", Justesecurity, April 28, 2015 (www.justesecurity.org)

[5] "*The world suffers today from the painful consequences of interventions that aggravated existing conflicts. They allowed terrorism to penetrate into places where it previously did not exist, gave rise to new cycles of violence and multiplied the number of civilian victims.*" Dilma Rousseff speaking before the 66th UN General Assembly.

had been invited to the 2006 edition of the same fair, and the Egyptian writer Radwa Ashour granted a long interview with the Brazilian newspaper *O 'Globo*, in which they stated: "*We have much to learn from Brazil, and from Latin America in general. A region that has succeeded in achieving the goals it has set forth: breaking free from U.S. hegemony, independence, economic development, social justice. In truth, we hope that one day, we the Arabs, Iranians, and Turks, to become a part of the BRICS so that we may fight together for a fairer and more just world*[1]."

Afghanistan

The infant mortality rate in the refugee camps near the Afghan capital is 144 per 1.000, one of the highest in the world, despite humanitarian aid of 3.5 billion dollars and development aid estimated at 58 billion dollars from 2000 to 2010[2]. The number of civilian deaths from the violence in Afghanistan has increased constantly since 2005 at a rate of 8% per year[3]. Even if it proves that a significant portion of these victims were killed in attacks by the Taliban, in spite of the code of "good conduct" to protect civilians announced in 2009 by the former Taliban leader Mullah Mohammed Omar[4], the fact remains that the deaths are directly related to the occupation of the country by foreign troops, the great majority of them from North America[5].

The number of Afghan refugees seeking asylum increased by more than 33% from 2010 to 2011 (35,700 in 2011). According to the annual report of the United Nations High Commissioner for Refugees, the number of Afghan refugees in 2012 was 2.6 million, 1.6 million hosted in Pakistan and 870.000 in Iran[6]. These figures conflict with the soothing words by NATO Secretary General Anders Fogh Rasmussen on the situation in Afghanistan. A significant portion of these refugees, on the order of 46%, are children or unaccompanied adolescents.

Widespread and profound resentment is growing among rural Afghan populations towards the occupying powers, who are held responsible for the deterioration of security within the country. Their list of complaints is long and justifiable: night-time raids by American and NATO forces and their collateral damage to the civilian population, which the UN representative in Kabul condemned insistently before leaving in September 2008, as did the Afghan

1. Pedro Sprejer, "Ecos da primavera. O vigor da poesia, da praça Tahrir aos destroços da guerra na Síria" (Echoes of spring. The vigor of poetry, from Tahrir Square to the destruction of the war in Syria). Interview with Al-Barghouti, *O 'Globo*, April 27, 2013.
2. *International Herald Tribune*, February 6, 2012.
3. *International Herald Tribune*, February 10, 2012.
4. 55% in 2008; 80% in 2012, according to a report from the United Nations Assistance Mission in Afghanistan (UNAMA).
5. "Rights advocates shift their focus to Taliban abuses", *International Herald Tribune*, February 11, 2011.
6. Ami Sedghi, "UNHCR 2012 refugee statistics; full data", *Theguardian.com*, June 19, 2013.

president, Hamid Karzai on numerous occasions[1]; the abusive treatment of Taliban detainees, such as the young Sayid Mohammed, who was arrested in November 2012 by the American Special Operations A Team and held on the base in Nerkh (province of Wardak) before his tortured and mutilated corpse was found in May 2013 two hundred meters from the edge of the base[2]; the lack of respect for the dead exhibited by North American and Australian troops, as illustrated in troubling photographs in mass circulation newspapers; the summary execution of Afghan civilians as a sporting pastime for American soldiers[3]; detention of militants and suspects on the Guantanamo base without charges or a trial since their capture in 2001, violating all rules of international law; the destruction in the Israeli fashion of thousand of houses suspected of being traps or sheltering insurgents[4]; financial support from NATO for bona fide warlords having no popular support or accountability to Afghan institutions to help protect convoys and troops[5]; and the indiscriminate attacks by the Taliban and their allies, responsible for the majority of the civilian victims according to the UN Mission to Kabul. It is obvious to everyone that thousands of Afghan civilians killed during the conflict would still be alive if their country had not been invaded.

The urban population dwells in a society where corruption has become a plague at all levels of government and civil administration. The confirmation by the Afghan president himself, in October 2010 following revelations by the *New York Times*, of envelopes hand-delivered to him personally from neighboring governments, including six million dollars in cash from Iran, and the arrest of Ahmad Zia Massoud, Vice President of Afghanistan from 2004-2009, by the customs authorities of the United Arab Emirates while in possession of 52 million dollars[6], speak volumes on the moral stature of the political class in power in Kabul. As revealed by the *New York Times* in May 2013[7], the CIA has given the Afghan president a monthly cash "salary" since 2003 amounting to a total of some 10 million dollars to date. What credibility or moral authority can he have in condemning the CIA operation on April 7 in the province of Kunar that accidentally killed 17 Afghan civilians, 12 of them

---

1. Sam Allison, "Grim view of Afghan risks and missteps", *International Herald Tribune*, September 15, 2008.

2. Rod Nordland, "Afghans say American led rogue unit", April 14, 2013 / "Body of missing Afghan is found near ex-US base", May 22, 2013. / "Afghan experts try to put names to torture victims", May 30, 2013, *International Herald Tribune*.

3. Taimoor Shah, Alessa Rubin, "Rogue US soldiers on the run", *International Herald Tribune*, October 5, 2010. / Charlie Savage, "Court hears case of army 'kill team' in Afghanistan", *International Herald Tribune*, October 4, 2010.

4. Carlotta Gall, "Battling to win hearts, minds and war", October 18, 2010 / Taimoor Shah, Rod Nordland, "U.S. destroying Afghan buildings", November 17, 2010, *International Herald Tribune*.

5. Dexter Filkins, "With US help, warlord builds empire", June 7, 2010. / "US is said to fund Afghan warlords", June 23, 2010, *International Herald Tribune*.

6. Scott Shane, Mark Mazzetti, Dexter Filkins, "Afghan corruption undercuts U. S. efforts", *International Herald Tribune*, December 3, 2010.

7. Editorial, "Ghost Money", May 3, 2013, *International Herald Tribune*.

children[1]? The NGO Transparency International, which monitors governmental corruption in the world, places Afghanistan as the world's third most corrupt country after Somalia and Myanmar. The special envoy of the monthly *Le Monde diplomatique*, Louis Imbert, described a similar inflow of cash to the Taliban[2].

Aware of their growing unpopularity and the senselessness of their presence, many countries announced a progressive withdrawal: the Netherlands in 2010, Germany and Canada in 2011, Poland in 2012. Others maintain their presence, based on their transatlantic bonds[3] and a controversial authorization from the United Nations, but seek to keep their troops far from the conflict zones so as not to accentuate hostile public opinion to this war at home.

Since 2009, a year witnessing a significant surge in foreign armed forces (123.000 soldiers, including 100.000 U.S. troops within the NATO contingent; 26.500 U.S. troops in the operation "Enduring Freedom", which marked the beginning of the occupation), there has been a resurgence in attacks[4] and a growing number of victims.

During eight years of the Bush presidency (2001-2008), 1.049 Coalition soldiers were killed; in less than five years of the Obama presidency, 2.240 have lost their lives[5]. Violence breeds violence. According to the *New York Times*, the number of civilian victims increased by 61% from 2010 to 2011[6], in a ratio of 60-40 as follows: 60% are killed by rebels because they are accused of collaborating with the enemy or are victims of collateral damage; 40% are killed by the International Security Assistance Force (ISAF) during their night-time raids or bombardments, and increasingly at roadblocks. Indeed, things reached the point where the Commander of the U.S. Forces Afghanistan (USFOR-A), Stanley McChrystal, admitted in June 2009 that success should be measured not in how many Afghans are killed, but in how many are spared[7]. It has been estimated that each civilian killed prompts 20 militants to take up arms. General McChrystal, dismissed in 2010 for speaking too freely to journalists, estimated that the deaths of civilians, regardless of who is to blame, has undermined the credibility of the intervention[8]. The tribal councils (*ulama*) in the province of Wardak organized demonstrations against night-time raids by the U.S. Special Operations Troops and the disappearances and abductions following in their wake, demanding the withdrawal of "*occupying forces*" and transfer of control of

---

1. Rod Nordland, "Karzai faults C.I.A, in fatal strike", *International Herald Tribune*, April 20-21, 2013.
2. Louis Imbert, "D´où vient l´argent des talibans ?" (Where do the Taliban get their money?), *Le Monde diplomatique*, September 2010.
3. Japan is bound by a security pact with the United States and did not send troops.
4. Rod Nordland, "Afghan violence reverses again", *International Herald Tribune*, August 30, 2010.
5. iCasualties.org
6. *New York Times*, November 28, 2011.
7. *International Herald Tribune*, June 3, 2009.
8. "*Because of civilian casualties I think we have just about eroded our credibility here in Afghanistan*", Sean Naylor, "McChrystal: Civilian deaths endanger mission", *Army Times*, May 30, 2010.

the Bagram prison to the Afghan armed forces[1]. In February 2013, President Karzai himself instructed the Afghan armed forces by decree not to request air or drone support from the American forces[2].

The use of drones to kill Taliban leaders and militants along the border between Afghanistan and the Pakistani region of Waziristan, or, in Afghanistan, to eliminate men who are suspicious by virtue of their age ("Military Age Male" – MAM), has aroused the rage of civilian populations, who consider themselves to be the first victims of these summary and uncontrollable executions. An American website (The Long War Journal) keeps an updated list of these air attacks: 117 air attacks in 2010 with 801 Taliban killed and 14 civilian casualties; 64 air attacks in 2011 with 405 Taliban killed and 30 civilian casualties. However, the site only identifies 18 Taliban leaders killed in 2010 and 10 killed in 2011, fueling the controversy over this type of operation.

The Pakistani Foundation for Fundamental Rights estimates that 170 of the people killed in North Waziristan are Taliban; its director, the lawyer Mirza Shahzad Akbar, estimates that civilian casualties are in the range of 2.800-3.000 since 2008. In April 2012, the Pakistani president Asif Ali Zardari demanded a halt to these operations during an interview in Islamabad with the U.S. Special Representative for the region, Marc Grossman, repeating a demand formulated in 2008 by the Pakistani parliament. Flights were suspended by the United States in December 2011 following the killing by mistake of 24 Pakistani soldiers at two checkpoints in Pakistan. They were resumed in January 2012. In April 2012, a missile fired from a drone destroyed a girls' school in the capital of North Waziristan, Miranshah, killing three civilians[3]. Shahzad Akbar, who took the case of the victims' families to the Supreme Court of Peshawar, went to Washington with the help of humanitarian associations on April 28, 2012 to testify at an international conference on the use of drones. He pointed out that the Pakistani army had sealed off access to the targeted zones (the north of Waziristan in particular), and information was only emerging slowly, delaying action by the judicial authorities.

"*The Hydra's heads grow back quickly and in increasingly radical forms,*" commented an Itamaraty diplomat during a private conversation. This is also the point of view expressed in an opinion column in the *New York Times* by two former advisors to the presidents Jimmy Carter and Bill Clinton with the suggestive title "Assassination season is open". They decried the fact that a *de facto* end had been put to the prohibition against political assassinations adopted in 1976 during the Ford presidency[4].

A researcher at the University of Chicago, Jenna Jordan, published a study in 2009 that found that the assassination of the leaders of a religiously-based

---

1 *International Herald Tribune*, March 18, 2013.

2. *The New York Times*, February 16, 2013.

3. *Press TV*, April 29, 2012.

4. Joel McCleary, Mark Medish, "Assassination season is open", *International Herald Tribune,* April 14, 2010.

terrorist group tends to increase the likelihood that this group will survive. These assassinations are counter-productive, the following generation tends to be more motivated, more radical, more persevering, and more respected and emulated by their peers[1]. The emergence of a particularly brutal, hardened, violently anti-American jihadi movement in Iraq and Syria provides the clearest support for the conclusions of Jordan's study. To this we must add the young French, British, Portuguese, Russian, Moroccan, Australian, German and even American nationals who expatriate and join the islamist cause, their numbers swelling into the thousands in 2014.

Since 2001, some 2.340 American soldiers have been killed and 19.000 wounded in Afghanistan, with several thousand of the latter now dependent on the care of their families or suffering from mental disorders[2]. The sons and daughters of other countries have also been lost: 444 Britons, 158 Canadians, 86 French, 54 Germans, 48 Italians, 43 Danes, 38 Poles, 34 Spaniards[3], but also several thousand Afghan civilians and 25-30 thousand real or presumed Taliban militants[4]. More than 130.000 people disabled, mainly because of landmines, including 40.000 amputees among the civilian population according to Afghan governmental sources, and these figures are considered to be significantly underestimated[5].

And the numbers are only increasing: according to a report by the United National Assistance Mission in Afghanistan (UNAMA) published on July 30, 2013, civilian casualties increased by 23% during the first six months of 2013 (1.319 as opposed to 1.158 in the same period in 2012) and the number of wounded civilians increased by a similar proportion (2.533 v. 1.976 for the same period in 2012)[6]. According to Emanuele Nannini, director of the Italian NGO Emergency, which runs two hospitals and some forty clinics in Afghanistan, the number of casualties increased by 12% in 2014 with respect to the previous year[7]. According to the United Nations, the number of Afghan children and Afghan women killed in the first half of 2015 increased by 13%

[1]. Jenna Jordan, "When Heads Roll: Assessing the Effectiveness of Leadership Decapitation", *Security Studies*, December 2009.

[2] Dave Philipps, "In Unit Stalked by Suicide, Veterans Try to Save One Another. Members of a Marine battalion that served in a restive region in Afghanistan have been devastated by the deaths of comrades and frustrated by the V.A.", *International New York Times,* September 19, 2015.

[3]. iCasualties.org

[4]. Very loose estimates based on combining data from the United Nations Assistance Mission in Afghanistan, Human Rights Watch, *The Guardian*, Mark Harold (University of New Hampshire), and the Afghan Commission on Human Rights. The study published in March 2015 by Physicians for Social Responsibility increased the number of civilians estimated to have been killed since 2003 to 220,000.

[5] Rod Nordland, "Maimed Defending Afghanistan, Then Neglected", *International New York Times*, May 2, 2015.

[6]. Ahmed Azam, "Afghan civilian war casualties rise", *International Herald Tribune*, July 31, 2013.

[7] Rod Nordland, "For Afghans the Fighting Now Knows No Season", *International New York Times*, November 28, 2014.

and 23%, respectively, with respect to the same period in 2014[1]. Civilian casualties, attributed in a ratio of three to four to insurgents, are particularly women and children. An investigation by an American agency with the support of the Universities of Princeton and Stanford, and the London School of Economics underscores the geometric increase in attacks on Coalition forces following the deaths of civilians, regardless of who was directly to blame for their deaths[2]. And we should also add the losses among the Pakistani military, which are greater than those among Coalition forces in Afghanistan with the Taliban mounting new attacks in Peshawar and in the Tirah Valley in Khyber, and along the Afghan border, and the attacks against Shias in Quetta, capital of the province of Balochistan. A recent report published in March 2015 estimates the number of civilian casualties in Pakistan since 2003 at 80.000[3].

What has been achieved in Afghanistan? A country in tatters with a social fabric and infrastructure devastated after three decades of conflicts, with an illiteracy rate around 80%, a country that the United Nations puts in 173rd place (out of 177 countries) on the Human Development Index (HDI), where 20% of the children will not live to see their fifth birthday according to a report by the World Bank, where opium production has increased significantly (185 tons in 2001; 8.000 tons in 2012) with 1.5 million addicts (45% women and minors) as illustrated in the 2009 documentary film *Addicted in Afghanistan* by Jawed Taiman and as admitted by the government spokesman, Zalmai Afjali, in 2010. Russia, where 30.000 people die each year from problems associated with Afghan heroin, recently confronted the leaders in Kabul, whom all observers agree are complicit in the drug trafficking that the Taliban had suppressed while they were in power (1996-2001). Following the invasion by Coalition forces, the amount of land dedicated to poppy cultivation tripled, covering some 200.000 hectares in 2013[4].

One of our contacts at Itamaraty pointed out the similarity with the final years of the South Vietnamese government. It all fits. Widespread administrative corruption, feeding on financing designated as humanitarian aid, aid for development, and military aid that are totally out of proportion to the dimensions of the country's actual administrative infrastructure (120 billion dollars per year in U.S. military spending in Afghanistan; four billion dollars in humanitarian aid in 2010). The prolongment of the war and its failure to achieve its ends, attributed to the sanctuary offered to the Taliban by the tribal

---

[1] Sune Engel Rasmussen, "Afghanistan: sharp rise in women and children casualties in first half of 2015", *The Guardian*, August 5, 2015.

[2]. Luke Condra, Joseph Felter, Radha Iyenga, Jacob Shapiro, "The Effect of Civilian Casualties in Afghanistan and Iraq", *The National Bureau of Economic Research,* Working Paper N° 16152, Cambridge, July 2010.

[3] Body Count. "Casualty Figures after 10 years of the 'War on Terror'", Physicians for Social Responsibility (www.spr.org), March 2015.

[4] Testimony Before the Senate Caucus on International Narcotics Control. Future U.S. Counternarcotics Efforts in Afghanistan, Report. Special Inspector general For Afghanistan Reconstruction (SEGAR), Statement by John F. Sopko, Washington, January 15, 2014.

areas and by the Afghanistan-Pakistan borderlands (in Vietnam, the sanctuaries in Laos and Cambodia ended up being invaded by U.S. forces, leading to the metastases of the Khmer Rouge and the Pathet Lao, while in the Middle East we have the Islamic State of Iraq and the Levant – ISIL).

In Afghanistan, a local army was established with the task of taking over operations from the foreign forces (counterpart of Vietnamization) but it has suffered from a high desertion rate (47%)[1]. The election fraud in Afghanistan in 2009 echoes that in Vietnam in 1971. The My Lai Massacre has many correlates in Afghanistan[2]: Sergeants Calvin Gibbs, David Bram and Robert Bales are the direct heirs of William Calley[3]. The massacre of over 2000 Taliban prisoners at Sheberghan by General Abdul Raslud Dostum's forces, involving CIA personnel and US Special Forces, was never investigated by the Bush administration. The napalm strikes in Vietnam have their Afghan counterpart in "Willy Pete", the white phosphorus used by American troops in their assault on the city of Fallujah. The Pentagon Papers leaked by Daniel Ellsberg in 1971 share a kinship with the thousands of classified documents on the conflict from 2004-2009 revealed by *Wikileaks* and published by the *New York Times*, *The Guardian* and *Der Spiegel.* The bombing by the U.S. warplanes of a fully operational hospital in Kunduz, Afghanistan on the night of October 3, 2015 killing 22 people including 12 members of the volunteer medical staff of Doctors Without Borders, remember the U.S. bombing of Hanoi´s Bach Mai hospital on December 22, 1972, when 28 medical staff members were killed among the civilian casualties.

According to our contacts, the departure of the American forces will leave Afghanistan to the same fate as Vietnam: the collapse of the central administration governing essentially no more than the capital, like the house of cards in Saigon, the return of the Taliban to power, or at least a pro-Pakistan, fundamentalist Pashtun regime and exile for the more fortunate collaborators – that is, the most corrupted – in the United States or Dubai, where the top Afghan authorities have their luxury second homes, many on the seafront at Palm Jumeirah.

Brazil and Chile were the only Latin American countries invited to the International Conference on Afghanistan on June 12, 2008 in Paris, a French initiative. They did not commit to providing aid, which amounted to some 20 billion dollars for the period 2009-2013 as decided at the Conference, the

---

[1]. Elisabeth Bumiller, "U.S. outline big goals for Afghan forces", *International Herald Tribune*, August 25, 2010.

[2]. Charlie Savage, "Court hears case of army 'kill team' in Afghanistan", *International Herald Tribune*, October 4, 2010. / "Army charges 6th soldier over Afghan civilian deaths", *International Herald Tribune*, May 19, 2011. / "U.S. gives $50 000 payments to survivors of fatal rampage", *International Herald Tribune*, March 26, 2012.

3. Sergeants Calvin Gibbs, Robert Steven and David Bram and nine soldiers are responsible for murdering Afghan civilians for sport in 2010; Sergeant Robert Bales murdered 16 Afghan civilians, including nine children, in two separate attacks on March 11, 2012 in the province of Kandahar.

lion's share coming from the United States (51%). Our contacts at Itamaraty note that Arab countries are practically absent (their contributions do not exceed 2%). France's contribution (106 million euros) puts it in 16th place among donors, far behind Norway (786.5 million euros), Germany (660.6 million), and Denmark (430 million). Foreign military, humanitarian and economic aid amounted in 2011 to 97% of Afghan Gross Domestic Product according to the World Bank, setting the stage for a severe recession after the foreign powers withdraw[1]. An editorial in the *New York Times* in October 2014 underscored the fact that the United States has spent some 104 billion dollars in Afghanistan following the invasion – not counting military aid (the war price tag is totalling $ 715 billion according to the U.S. Congress). In current dollars, that is more than all the Marshall Plan aid money to 16 European countries after the Second World War.

Brasilia does not believe in the democratization of a country such as Afghanistan. Fair and open elections are impossible because of security risks, widespread corruption, and local traditions. The fraud revealed during the 2009 presidential election provides clear testimony in this regard. The voting process is distorted by ethnic influences on voting behavior. Elections are not a mechanism that can facilitate the emergence of institutional mechanisms suited to this country. Common sense would dictate postponing this type of selection process. A national and centralizing approach is not appropriate in a country where social issues are managed locally, at the tribal or community level, by councils of elders, the *shuras*, by negotiation, consensus or arbitrage, rather than by the police or national institutions. The European Union Police Mission in Afghanistan (EUPOL), tasked with training the local police force, is doomed to failure (1.400 Afghan police officers were killed in 2010[2] and the desertion rate is on the order of 30%). And so is the militarization of the occupation. At the Chicago Summit in May 2012, the United States asked its NATO partners to guarantee, for ten years beyond 2014, the date forecast for troop withdrawals, yearly military aid of 4.1 billion dollars, two thirds to be provided by the United States.

Our contacts feel that U.S. and NATO armed forces should not have maintained a residual presence in Afghanistan beyond their envisaged withdrawal in 2014. This has made it impossible for the Afghan administration to resume negotiations with the Taliban and can only prolong hostilities. These negotiations are a source of conflict and suspicion between Kabul, Islamabad and Washington, as witnessed by the Afghan president's opposition to the opening of a Taliban office in Dubai, the abduction by the American army of the Taliban leader Latif Mehsud, negotiating partner of the Afghan president, in the province of Logar, and the release from a Pakistani prison of the Taliban

---

1. Graham Bowley, "Afghans brace for the occupation´s end", *International Herald Tribune*, February 2, 2012. *Eurasianet*, February 28, 2010.

2. *International Herald Tribune*, February 16, 2011.

leader Abdul Ghani Baradar upon request from the Afghan president[1]. For the time being, the country is totally dependent on foreign aid, which provides for the essential budget and a tidy sum for the president. This situation has parallels with the period after the Soviet withdrawal in the 1990s. On September 28, 1997, President Najibullah was tortured and killed by the Taliban and hung up on display in Kabul as a warning.

The political compromise struck between the rival candidates in the election to choose a successor to Hamid Karzai was immediately seized upon to secure an agreement to ensure that American and NATO troops would remain beyond December 31, 2014 and that annual military aid of 5.1 billion dollars would continue to flow until 2017. Washington had not allowed direct negotiations between Karzai and the Taliban, negotiations which Brasilia felt were essential in achieving an end to hostilities[2]. Since 2001, the one inescapable conclusion of Brazilian diplomacy has been that only a power-sharing arrangement with the Taliban can provide the hope of ending the war. The largest war in American history (14 years) will keep getting longer. Current foreign troops level of roughly 10.000, along with the full capacity of airstrikes will remain in place according to president Obama up to 2017.

The Afghan Minister of Agriculture, Mohammad Asif Rahimi, expressed hopes in February 2010 to see the Brazilian Agricultural Research Corporation (EMBRAPA) engaged in the development of agriculture in Afghanistan[3]. But Brazil did not wish to enter into a cooperative arrangement with a government totally dependent on foreign support for its survival and not able to govern beyond the capital. It has reluctantly taken in Afghan refugees. In January 2012, the Brazilian press revealed their wretched situation, working in a factory near the federal capital owned by the company Sadia, which exports halal chicken to Arab countries.

Iraq

According to UNICEF, the mortality rate for children less than 5 years old increased from 56 per 1,000 births in 1984-1989 to 131 per 1,000 in 1994-1999 as a result of sanctions[4]. According to Oxfam, 43% of Iraqis live below the poverty threshold (less than 1 dollar a day), and 70% of the population lacks regular access to drinking water (50% in 2003)[5].

Violence in Iraq, which had shown a diminishing trend in 2010-2012, with an average homicide rate of 300 people per month[6] (3,000 people per month in

---

1. *The Washington Post,* October 10, 2013.
2 "Karzai-Taliban talks deepen U.S. mistrust", *International New York Times,* February 5, 2014.
3. Milan Rai, *War Plan in Iraq*, p. 176. Voir éd. 2002.
4. Tim Arango, "Wave of attacks shakes Iraq", *International Herald Tribune,* April 19, 2012.
5. Damin Cave, "Oxfam seeks more aid in bleak report on Iraq", *International Herald Tribune,* July 31, 2007.
6. Sabrina Tavernise, "Mix of trust and despair helped turn the tide", *International Herald Tribune,* October 25, 2010.

2005[1]), increased significantly in 2013. In 2013, after the first decade of hostilities, the average number of Iraqi civilian casualties per month was on the order of 700-1.000, most of them victims of the indiscriminate bomb attacks that are the currency of sectarian rivalries. Vice President Tariq al-Hashimi, a Sunnite Muslim, was accused by Prime Minister Nuri Kamal al-Maliki, a Shi'ite, in December 2011 of employing hired killers. Al-Hashimi took refuge in Qatar. A massacre of Sunni demonstrators by government forces took place in the town of Hawija in May 2013, killing 33 civilians[2].

The Iraq invasion in 2003, which instated a pernicious system promoting nepotism and sectarian divisions, eventually led to full blown civil war between the Shi'ites, Sunnis and Kurds, all to the advantage of extremist elements close to Al-Qaeda, which had no foothold in Iraq during Saddam Hussein's reign. The radical Sunnite wing, allied with Al-Qaeda, gained strength after U.S. troops withdrew and gave its support to the development of Jabhat al-Nusra in Syria, then spearheading armed opposition to the Assad regime. It was led by a veteran of the Iraqi resistance, Abu Mohammad al-Julani.

Over 600.000 Iraqi civilians are estimated to have lost their lives in this war[3], a number that is certainly underestimated. More than 4.480 American soldiers lost their lives and 36.000 were wounded, not to mention the high suicide rate among active duty soldiers and veterans, a suicide rate 14 times that of all Americans[4]. It is difficult to estimate the number of Iraqi refugees in Europe, but they number in the hundreds of thousands. According to the United Nations High Commissioner for Refugees, there are more than two million in neighboring countries (Syria, Jordan, Lebanon). As part of its program to grant visas to Iraqis who collaborated with the occupying forces (Special Immigrant Visa Program), the United States has issued some 74.000 visas and 62.000 applications are pending.

---

1. Source: *Wikileaks*, "Organisation mondiale de la santé, Iraqi Body Count", *Le Monde*, October 25, 2010.

2. Tim Arango, "33 are dead after Iraqi forces raid Sunni camp", *International Herald Tribune*, May 24, 2013.

3. *The Guardian*, March 28, 2007, citing a study by Johns Hopkins University in Baltimore. Close to 500.000 according to a study published in October 2013 by the University of Washington, Johns Hopkins University, and Simon Fraser University (Canada), and the Iraqi Ministry of Health ("Mortality in Iraq associated with the 2003-2011 War and Occupation: Findings from a National Cluster Sample Survey by the University Collaborative Iraq Mortality Study"). More than 700.000 according to Richard Falk, United Nations Special Rapporteur on human rights in the occupied Palestinian territories since 2008 (*The New World Order* <richardfalk.worldpress.com>). More than a million according to a study published in March 2015 by Physicians for Social Responsibility (www.psr.org).

4 Dave Philipps, "In Unit Stalked by Suicide, Veteran Try to Save One Another", *International New York Times*, September 19, 2015.

In February 2005, the Brazilian judicial system opened an inquiry into the recruitment of Brazilian soldiers for missions in Iraq by security companies based in the United States[1].

The application of "smart" or "targeted" sanctions against individuals, their families, or institutions is also opposed by Brasilia because they are based on insufficient evidence. These completely extra-judicial blacklists created by Resolutions 1333 and 1390 have lasting effects on the lives of hundreds of people and their families (e.g. freezing of assets, travel restrictions, monitored movements). Representatives of the United Nations enjoy diplomatic immunity and cannot be prosecuted for rights violations, not even by the representative's own country of citizenship. There is no fund to compensate victims of illegal sanctions. The unsuccessful and repeated initiatives by the Swedish government between 2001 and 2006 to remove three totally innocent citizens from the United Nations sanctions list (Resolution 1267/99) and of the Belgian government in favor of the president of the Global Relief Foundation, an Islamic charity organization, illustrate the often arbitrary and discretionary nature of these sanctions. Applied without any judicial procedure or indictment in violation of European and international conventions on human rights, these measures have been the subject of seminars organized by governmental and non-governmental organizations in Interlaken, Bonn, Berlin and Stockholm, earning a hostile reaction from the United States.

As regards the night-time raids by the occupation forces, they call to mind the commandos of the Argentine military junta: no criminal liability before local courts, no accountability to any authority, local witnesses considered discredited *a priori*[2]. The comparison with the repression witnessed in Latin America is by no means gratuitous. In March 2013, upon completing a 15-month study with the BBC Middle East desk, the British newspaper *The Guardian* revealed that the American officers who organized the death squads in El Salvador in the 1980s, responsible for 30.000 murders and 9.000 disappearances in a country with six million inhabitants, and the *Contra* rebels in Nicaragua, responsible for the deaths of 15.000 civilians, were assigned a mission in Iraq involving the creation of 15 secret interrogation and torture centers for the Iraqi police and the establishment of paramilitary commando units recruited from among the Shi'ites to quash the Sunni insurrection. One of them, former colonel in the Special Forces, James Steele, reported directly to the Secretary of Defense, Donald Rumsfeld; the other, Reserve Colonel James Coffman, was the main

[1]. Rodrigo Rangel, "Os mercenarios brasileiros" (Brazilian mercenaries), *O'Globo*, February 6, 2005. / "Recrutamento sob investigação" (Recruitment under investigation), *O'Globo*, February 10, 2005.

[2] Mark Mazzetti, Nicholas Kulish, Christopher Drew, Serge Kovalevski, Sean Naylor, John Ismay, "SEAL Team 6: A Secret History of Quiet Killings and Blurred Lines", *International New York Times*, June 6, 2015.

advisor to David Petraeus when he was the Commanding General in Iraq (2007-2008), before being appointed Director of the CIA (2011-2012)[1].

Murder, torture, collateral damage, rape: the daily report from American soldiers in Iraq, revealed by *Wikileaks* and in the media, show a troubling banalization of military violence, most of whose victims are civilians. Thus, early one morning in August 2011, the spiritual leader of the Al Rufait tribe, Sheikh Hameed Hassan, handcuffed and blindfolded, was summarily executed after having been abducted from his home in the middle of the night by a mixed American-Iraqi commando unit[2]. The Haditha Massacre in 2005, where 24 civilians were executed; the Mahmudiyah rape and killings in 2006, where four U.S. soldiers gang raped a 14-year-old girl and then killed her and her entire family; and the summary execution of 17 Afghan civilians at their homes, most of them women and children, by a sole rogue American soldier are not isolated incidents, and their prosecution by the U.S. military justice system has tended to be more the exception than the rule[3]. *Wikileaks* reviewed over 14.000 reports from soldiers revealing 603 Iraqi civilians killed by the U.S. Army as opposed to 120 insurgents, a ratio of nearly five to one. The private security firm Blackwater, founded by a former U.S. Navy SEAL, admitted to having paid a million dollars to Iraqi authorities in December 2007 to cover up the unjustified killing of 17 Iraqi civilians in Nisour Square in Baghdad on September 16, 2007[4].

According to our contacts in Brasilia, as a result of events like this, after the nearly unanimous solidarity expressed following the events of September 11, 2001, the war in Iraq has significantly eroded the influence and appeal of the United States in the world. This influence has been even more severely compromised in Latin America, given the history of its relations with the United States, with the Iraq war bringing home a host of outstanding issues. It is symptomatic that the ambassador of the United States in Iraq in 2004-2005 was John Negromonte, who commanded the military operations of the *contras* in their fight against the Sandinista government in Nicaragua while he was American representative to Honduras (1981-1985), also administrating the center of detention and torture where 200 religious workers and human rights activists disappeared. The United States was condemned for this in 1984 by the World Court in a case brought by Managua. The CEO of the most powerful American company in Baghdad (Science Applications International Corporation) is Roberto Rabelli, implicated in the *contra* scandal in 1987.

---

1. Dorrit Harazim, "O passado bate à porta" (When the past knocks at the door), *O'Globo*, March 10, 2013.

2. Tim Arango, Duraid Adnan, "As deadline nears, U.S. still deeply engaged in Iraq", *International Herald Tribune*, August 2, 2011.

3. David Johnston, "Inquiry into abuses ends with no U.S. civilian indictments", *International Herald Tribune*, December 20, 2006.

4. Mark Mazzetti, James Risen, "Blackwater Said to have planned Iraq bribes", *International Herald Tribune*, November 12, 2009.

The authorized use of torture or interrogation techniques that amount to the same thing by the 21st century's greatest democracy, and the effort put into imprisoning combatants without any local judicial authority and transferring them to secret detention facilities, in keeping with the tradition of totalitarian regimes, *"hidden partners in the Bush Doctrine"* as they were described in the Brazilian press[1], call to mind the excesses committed by the military dictatorships in the Southern Cone in the name of liberal democracy, inspired by the methods of the French army in Algeria. To this we must add the embedded journalists and the reporters killed by American forces: Tareq Ayyoub killed by a U.S. missile in his office at Al-Jazeera on April 8, 2003; Taras Protsyuk of Reuters and José Couso of Telecinco killed by American tank fire on the terrace of the Hotel Palestine in Baghdad; Namir Noor-Eldeen and Saeed Chmagh working for Reuters, mown down by a helicopter on July 12, 2007, accompanied by the laughter of their assailants in the helicopter with comments such as "nice" and "good shooting", a stomach-churning scene that moved the young soldier Bradley Manning, then 23, to give the video and thousands of documents to *WikiLeaks*, earning him a 35-year sentence in 2013 and a dishonorable discharge from the army.

The provision of sophisticated weaponry to Iraq announced by Washington in November 2011, including 18 F-16 combat aircraft and tanks, at a price of 11 billion dollars, is a gamble given the ambitions for autonomy of the Iraqi minorities (Kurds, Sunnis). Like the sales of Russian and Iranian arms (25 Sukhoi Su-25 jets in 2014), they will consolidate the sectarian Shi'ite armed forces, but not necessarily strengthen democracy in the country, as our contacts in Brasilia point out. A well founded concern when we know that, since the emergence of the Islamic State of Iraq and the Levant (ISIL), a portion of these arms were taken from the Iraq army or sold on the black market. After Mosul fell in June 2014 in a battle fought by a thousand rebels against 30.000 Iraqi soldiers, 2.300 Humvee armored vehicles, 52 M198 Howitzer artillery pieces, 40 M1 tanks, and 74.000 machine guns fell into rebel hands[2].

Iraqi Prime Minister Nouri al-Maliki (in office from 2006-2014) refused to sign the Status of Forces Agreement, which aimed to grant immunity to U.S. soldiers and prolong the U.S. military presence *ad infinitum*, and made overtures to Tehran. The United States removed him from office, citing an excessively sectarian approach that favored the Shi'ite majority. The Sunnite opposition is marginalized, the victim of anti-terrorist legislation (Section 4 of the Terrorism Act) permitting the arrest and detention without warrant of anyone suspected of being or having been a Ba'athist. It was radicalized in December 2012 after demonstrations in the provinces of Anbar and Nineveh demanding the liberation of 4.500 women captives – it later being revealed that they were the

---

1. *"Sócios ocultos da Doutrina Bush"*, in Magnoli Demétrio, "Leis da Tortura", *O'Globo*, December 28, 2006.

2 Peter Van Buren, "Dude, Where is my Humvee? Iraq losing equipment to Islamic State at staggering rate", *Reuters*, June 2, 2015.

victims of violence and rape in prison[1] – were brutally suppressed and most of the leaders killed. A minority in Iraq (20% of the population), the Sunnites could opt for an alliance with the Islamist combatants fighting the Bashar al-Assad regime in neighboring Syria, where the Sunni community makes up 60% of the population.

It is clear that the American intervention in Iraq, the repression taking place in the country and the widespread corruption (even the U.S. Ambassador to Iraq, Zalmay Khalilzad [2003-2005], was accused of corruption) all foster the emergence of increasingly radical and more virulently anti-Western elements. The growing presence in Iraq of an armed Islamist movement, part of it arriving from neighboring Syria, one that is particularly brutal, as witnessed by the execution of two American journalists, James Foley and Steven Sotloff, with videos of the act spread across the Internet, and the British hostage David Haines, kidnapped and dressed in the orange jumpsuit reserved for detainees at the Guantanamo base, is the direct consequence of the American intervention in Afghanistan and Iraq. It is a "*by-product of the invasion and occupation*", to cite the expression used by the Brazilian president during a press conference in New York in September 2014[2], a view shared by the Iranian president, Hassan Rouhani, in his speech before the 69th General Assembly of the United Nations. A phenomenon that has its parallels with the emergence of the Khmer Rouge, originally a minority Maoist rebellion, led by Pol Pot. After the violation of national sovereignty in 1973 and U.S. bombing raids causing some 500.000 deaths, the Khmer Rouge transformed into an extremely violent movement, responsible for the deaths of an estimated 2 million people between 1975 and 1979, a quarter of the country's population.

The invasion and occupation of Iraq by the United States profoundly disrupted traditional society and incited the people to seek an identity-preserving response to foreign aggression that followed upon years of repression under the Ba'ath regime, eight years of war with Iran (1980-1988), and sanctions imposed by the international community. And they sought it in the most extreme interpretations of Islam and *sharia* law. The aerial bombardments in Iraq started again in September 2014 by a new "international coalition" (eight countries and the United States) – this time including France, whose policy of non-intervention from the days of Jacques Chirac had aroused admiration in Brasilia – were considered by Brazilian diplomacy as the expression of the impasse into which the United States had led this country. The bombing raids, violating international law, not authorized by a UN Security Council resolution, and subject to no constraints of accountability, generated yet more damage, deaths, orphans, widows, and hatred. According to the NGO Airwars, the coalition conducted more bombing raids from January 1 to August

---

[1] "'No One is Safe', The Abuse of Women in Iraq's Criminal Justice System", Human Rights Watch, February 6, 2014.

[2] *O Globo*, September 24, 2014.

20, 2015 than it had in the previous eight years combined (3.945 as of August 24, 2015)[1].

One should visit the U.S. embassy in Baghdad, the largest embassy in the world, a veritable fortress that cost 790 million dollars to build[2] and more than 1 billion dollars per year to maintain (not including the salaries of 1.000 agents and 5.000 employees), to understand that the U.S. intervention in this country is not intended as a short-term affair and that the methods applied so far will only engender more resistance and more violence.

Brazil maintained close relations with Saddam Hussein's Iraq. In the early 1970s, Brazil was the world's 7th largest importer of oil. With the energy crisis, Brazil turned to Iraq, becoming its third trading partner in 1977. In 1980, Iraq provided 40% of Brazilian oil imports. The Brazilian public works companies were particularly active in Iraq, one example being the construction of the Baghdad-Akashat railroad in 1978-1983 by the company Mendes Junior for 1.2 billion dollars. Iraq was then the largest customer of the Brazilian arms industry. It is no coincidence that the Brazilian ambassadors to Baghdad in those years were generals in the army (Samuel Alves Correa, Alacy Frederico Werner). There were some 5.000 Brazilian expats in Iraq at the beginning of the 1980s[3]. Relations were suspended after the invasion of Kuwait by Saddam Hussein in August 1990, and Brazil diversified its sources of supply (Venezuela, Angola, Mexico) and developed its own oil resources. The Brazilian state-owned oil company, Petrobras, discovered a promising oil field in Majnoon, where reserves are estimated at 10 billion barrels. The Iraqi government awarded a license to a consortium composed of Royal Dutch Shell and Petronas, a Malaysian state-owned company. Iraq repaid Brazil investments (300 million dollars) and agreed in 1979 to provide Brazil with 150.000 barrels of oil per day for 15 years at a special price. Brazil is currently absent from Iraqi oil exploration, which is now principally in the hands of American corporations (Halliburton, Baker Hughes, Weatherford, Exxon Mobil, Hunt Oil).

Iraq has been one of Brazil's main trading partners, buying uranium from the Nuclear and Energy Research Institute (IPEN) for the Osirak reactor, which was provided by France. Between 1979 and 1990, Brazil exported lightly enriched uranium oxide (yellowcake). A group of 23 Brazilian military engineers led by the head of the Aeronautics Institute of Technology (ITA), Hugo de Oliveira Piva, provided assistance to Baghdad in the construction of a ballistic missile. When the first Gulf War broke out, there were more than 250 Brazilian workers, technicians and engineers in Baghdad[4]. Brazil protested vehemently

---

[1] airwars.org

[2] Walter Hickey, "The US Embassy in Baghdad cost a staggering $750 million", *Business Insider*, March 20, 2013.

[3] Seme Taleb Fares, "The Oil Pragmatism: the Brazil-Iraq Relations", *Revista Brasileira de Politica Internacional*, Vol. 50, July-December 2007.

[4]. Luiz Alberto Muníz Bandeira, *As relações perigosas: Brasil-Estados Unidos*, Ed. Civilização Brasileira, Rio de Janeiro, 2010.

before the United Nations in 1981 against Israel's air raid on the Osirak nuclear reactor, which France had provided to Iraq, characterized by Sérgio Correa da Costa, Permanent Representative of Brazil to the Unied Nations (1975-1983) as "*a flagrant breach of international law*" and of *"the principles on which the Security Council is based*"[1].

A Brazilian engineer, João José Vasconcellos Junior, who was working on the construction of an electrical plant for the Brazilian firm Odebrecht, was abducted in January 2005 in Iraq and killed. Shortly after this abduction, and the tragic police killing of the young Brazilian electrician Jean Charles de Menezes on the London underground in July 2005, a specialized department was created in Itamaraty to provide assistance to the Brazilian expat community (*Subsecretaria-Geral das Communidades Brasileiras no Exterior*). Brazil closed its diplomatic mission in Baghdad in 1991; it was reopened in 2012.

Brasilia points out the enormous cost of the invasion and occupation of Iraq, estimated at between 3 and 4 trillion dollars, financed through loans. In 2003, Donald Rumsfeld, then U.S. Secretary of Defense, estimated the cost at 50 billion dollars[2]. The U.S. debt rose from 6.4 trillion dollars in March 2003 to 10 trillion dollars in 2008 (prior to the financial crisis): at least one fourth of this is attributable to the Iraq war. And the war has also had a significant cost for the international community. In March 2003 a barrel of oil cost about 23 dollars; the average price in 2011 was 140 dollars. Part of this increase was certainly attributable to the war.

The Arab Spring: Yemen, Libya, Syria, Tunisia, Egypt

Brasilia sees the Egyptian example as being emblematic of the impasse reached through support for single-leader, dictatorial regimes by the world's major democracies in order to prevent the installation of Islamic governments, which are unfairly labeled as being fundamentalist. Countries that could have exerted an influence in generating more openness, greater liberalization of governments on the basis of historical relations – following the example of France in the Maghreb or other parts of Africa – and have the necessary leverage, have not taken action in this direction. One fourth of the foreign students in French universities come from the Maghreb. Most of France's international cooperation projects, in terms of credit, and its public development aid, are oriented to this part of the world and to former French colonies in Africa, for whom France is a major trading partner. But Paris continues to provide support to controversial regimes: in Gabon, where the Bongo clan has been in power for 40 years; in Niger, whose president, Mamadou Tandja suspended civil liberties to stay in power; in Cameroon,

---

[1] Ramiro Saraiva Guerreiro (Brazil´s Foreign minister at the time), *XXXVI Sessions of the United Nations General Assembly, 1981. The Voice of Brazil in the United Nations*, FUNAG, Brasilia, 1995.

[2]. Nicholas Kristof, "One minute in Iraq = $380,000", *International Herald Tribune*, October 25, 2006.

where the dictator Paul Biya, in power since 1982, is warmly received in Paris as was the Mauritanian general Ould Abdel Aziz just after his coup d'État; and we must also add Denis Sassou-Nguesso in Congo-Brazzaville and Teodoro Obiang Nguema Mbasogo in Equatorial Guinea and Egypt´s Abdel Fattah al-Sissi. The forced resignation of the French Minister of Foreign and European Affairs, Michèle Alliot-Marie, because of her controversial relationship with the fallen Tunisian dictator, is symptomatic of these ingrained choices.

It is the fear of seeing the rise to power of popular, nationalist regimes subscribing to Islam, whether through elections or other means, that explains, certainly along with other interests, this nonsensical support for strongmen that has continued for close to three decades: in Egypt for Hosni Mubarak; in Tunisia for Zine-el-Abidine Ben-Ali; in Yemen for Ali Abdullah Saleh; in Algeria since 1999 for Abdelaziz Boutlefika; not to mention support for the royal families in the Persian Gulf (al-Khalifas in Bahrain since 1783; al-Thanis in Qatar since 1825; al-Sauds in Saudi Arabia since 1932).

After 30 years of Mubarak and 50 billion dollars in U.S. aid, more than three quarters of it military, more than one third of Egyptian men and more than half of Egyptian women are illiterate.

After 33 years under the leadership of Ali Abdullah Saleh, **Yemen** is the poorest of the Arab states, where 50% of the population lives below the poverty threshold and, according to the World Health Organization, one third have no access to healthcare[1]. After a long convalescence in Saudi Arabia from an attempted bomb attack, the former president returned to Yemen declaring that the Arab Spring was stillborn. The regime was dissolving, led by his former lieutenant, Abdu Rabbu Mansour Hadi, who took to his heels before the Houthis rebellion and sought refuge in Saudi Arabia. The situation was quite complex and attacks on mosques, condemned by the Brazilian Foreign Ministry, claimed hundreds of lives. It is a cauldron of tribal allegiances, sectarian divisions, and geo-strategic rivalries. The majority of the Muslim population is Shi'ite, unjustly accused by Riyadh of playing into Iran's hand. The former president, Ali Abdullah Saleh, who has not lost all hopes of placing his son Ahmed at the helm, struck an alliance with the Houthis, who were disgruntled about their marginal role in the country's government. A portion of the national guard, commanded by Ahmed until 2014, allied itself with the Houthis, who had seized some of the weapons that have been supplied by the United States since 2006 (more than 500 million dollars of arms and equipment between 2006 and 2014 according to the Pentagon). The extremist Islamist groups take advantage of this confusion to extend their influence in the south of the country; the military base in the port city of Al Mukalla fell into their hands in January 2015.

[1] Mohammed Ali Kalfood, Kareem Fahim, "Medical Need Climbs Alongside Death Toll in Yemen", *International New York Times*, May 27, 2015.

Brasilia is of the opinion that the bombing campaign against Yemen by the Saudi Air Force and its allies (excluding Oman) in the Gulf Cooperation Council – causing more than 8.000 civilian deaths according to the World Health Organization, hundreds of them women and children – only exacerbates an already confused situation, rendered problematic by the emergence of Islamist currents affiliated with al-Qaeda, to which the Houthis are resolutely opposed, and by semi-covert interference by the United States, in particular the resumption of drone strikes commanded by an American military detachment, whose presence was revealed in March 2015 when they had to evacuate due to the worsening security situation, a deterioration to which they largely contributed.

Cori Crider, who heads the abuses-in-counterterrorism team at the human rights charity Reprieve, condemns this covert war waged by the United States: "*We are constantly told that US drones are surgically precise. But any weapon – especially a remote-controlled one – is only as accurate as the intelligence behind it. At least 38 people died before a CIA strike finally killed this man. Who were the rest? How many lives did we take in the effort to assassinate al-Wuhayshi*[1]*? How many have we driven into the arms of militants with the 38 others we killed? The secret drone war conceals a mountain of hidden costs, and the idea we can bomb our way out of the problem of terrorism is short-sighted and, ultimately, false*[2]."

The US has launched, presumably from inside and outside Yemen (Djibouti, Saudi Arabia), over 106 drone strikes in Yemen since Obama took office and has killed more than 800 individuals identified as "*militants*" and also 80 civilians, according to the New America Foundation.

Brasilia believes that the causes of the conflict are local and should be resolvable without external intervention, despite the profound differences between the north and the south of the country, with two states now outlined (the Yemen Arab Republic in the north and the People's Democratic Republic of Yemen in the south), which Brazil recognized in 1984 and which were joined in 1990 under the leadership of Ali Abdullah Saleh, then president since 1978 of North Yemen. This is also the view of the UN Special Advisor on Yemen, the Moroccan Jamal Benomar (2013-2015), who resigned his post in April 2015.

Brazil is part of the Friends of Yemen group created in January 2010 and including 39 donor countries, the main one being Saudi Arabia, to help what is one of the world's poorest countries. The group held its eighth summit in September 2014 in New York in concomitance with the General Assembly of the United Nations. It is co-chaired by the United Kingdom, Saudi Arabia, and Yemen. Brazil, which does not have an embassy in Yemen, is the only South American country in the group. President Dilma Rousseff received the young Yemeni journalist Tawakkol Karman, co-recipient of the Nobel Peace Prize in 2011, in Brasilia in November 2012. Karman belongs to the opposition party

---

[1] Leader of al-Qaeda in Yemen, killed in a U.S. drone strike in June 2015.

[2] Black Ian, "Death of al-Qaida leader masks reality of drone strikes: they don't bring stability", *The Guardian,* June 16, 2015.

al-Islah, the local offshoot of the Muslim Brotherhood, hostile to President Saleh.

The use of cluster bombs by the Saudi Air Force[1] has not evoked an official Brazilian response. Brazil, like the United States, Russia, and China, is not a signatory to the Convention on Cluster Munitions, which prohibits the use of these weapons. It went into force in August 2010 and as of March 2015 has been signed by 108 countries. Colombia, Bolivia, Peru, Chile, Paraguay, and Uruguay are the only South American countries to have signed the Convention. But Brasilia points out the irresponsibility of heavily arming a country that is in the hands of a dynastic regime characterized by repression and oppression. According to the Congressional Research Service, between October 2010 and October 2014, the United States has delivered some 90 billion dollars worth of weapons to Riyadh[2].

On December, 2013, a US drone strike against a wedding procession, a convoy of 11 cars that was bringing the bride and family members to the groom´s hometown of Aquabat Za´j, near Rad´a, killed at least 12 men and wounded 15 others. Human Rights Watch has published a report based on research in Yemen from January 11 to 16, 2014 on this attack. Unamed US and Yemeni government officials told the media that all those killed were "*militants*[3]. A Saudi airstike on a livestock market in province of Lahj killed 50 civilians in July 2015[4]. On September 28, 2015 the Saudi Arabian airforce obliterated a wedding party, killing at least 131 civilians, including 80 women, huddled under a desert tent. Calls for an independent and international enquiry by UN commissioner Zeid Ra´ad al-Hussein, former Jordan ambassador to the United States, were blocked by Saudi Arabia with American support[5]. The United Nations Human Rights Council adopted by consensus in September 2015 a flawed resolution largely drafted by Arabia Saudita that shuns the investigations in reported abuses and alleged violations by all sides to the conflict[6]. An inquiry will be provided by exiled government of Abdu Rabbu Mansour Hadi.

The coalition´s commander, Saudi prince Muhammad bin Salman, who at age 30 is the youngest and least experienced defence minister on the planet. He is the king, 79-year-old Salman bin Abdul Aziz Al Saud´s, favourite son. The Saudi led war in Yemen was launched on the pretense of reinstalling the exiled government of Yemeni president Hadi. The real aim of the Saudi bombing is to

---

[1] Kareem Fahim, "Saudi-Led Group Said to use Cluster Bombs in Yemen", *International New York Times*, May 3, 2005.

[2]. Christophe Blanchard, "Saudi Arabia: Background and U.S. Relations", Congressional Research Service, April 29, 2015 (www.crs.gov).

[3] "*A Wedding That Become a Funeral. US Drone Attack on Marriage procession in Yemen"*, Human Rights Watch, February 2014.

[4]. Shabeen Kareem, "Deadly airstrike hits market in Yemen", *The Guardian*, July 6, 2015.

[5]. "Situation of human rights in Yemen. Report of the United Nations High Commissioner for human rights", Human Rights Council, September 7, 2015.

[6] Cumming-Bruce Nick, "Saudi Objections Halt U.N. Inquiry of Yemen War", *International New York Times*, September 30, 2015.

destroy Yemen´s Houthi Shia rebels which Saudi Arabia considers as Iranian proxies. The war has led to the death of more 4.500 Yemenites, half of them civilians.

While our contacts do not hazard a prediction of the future of these regimes, they expect the moderate Islamic movements, close to the Muslim Brotherhood, long proscribed, to take power after winning at the polls, in spite of their lack of international recognition. Islam is a synonym of jurisprudence, culture and national tradition and offers a means of differentiation, of self-affirmation against the wealthy West and the local corrupt despots. What Islam represents today for the young people who constitute the great majority of the population of these countries and who seem to live with a deep abiding sense of injustice certainly represents the key to future developments. Brasilia does not believe that any Arab country can escape the Islamist experience. The Pew Research Center, an American think tank based in Washington, published a study in 2013 of 39 Muslim countries in which the majority of the 38.000 people surveyed hoped for the establishment of *sharia* law rather than a Western secular model[1].

The Arab world is not what it used to be in the 1950s or '60s. Neither are America or Europe. If it cannot be toned down, **Islamophobia** will arouse increasingly violent reactions in the Muslim world. Beyond the issues that have nourished the debate on Islam (the burqa, caricatures of the Prophet, terrorist plots, plans for a mosque at Ground Zero, burning of the Qur'an, campaign against *sharia*, the ad campaign on buses in Washington DC with a photograph of Adolf Hitler with the grand mufti of Jerusalem, Haj Amin al-Husseini and the words "*Islamic Jew-Hatred: it's in the Quran*", expulsion of Muslim girls from a school in the French town of Charleville-Mézières because of their unusually long dresses[2]), there is a real increase in anti-Muslim discrimination and Islamophobic acts.

According to statistics from the Equal Employment Opportunity Commission, an agency of the U.S. federal government that fights discrimination in the workplace, the number of complaints from Muslims in the United States has doubled in five years. The U.S. judicial system is rife with Islamophobia, as witnessed by the differences in sentencing of American citizens for similar indictments depending on whether they are of "pure stock" or of Arab descendance and Muslim faith. A comparison of the 5-year sentence for Timothy Joiner[3] by a Pennsylvania court and the life imprisonment in solitary confinement handed down to the student Ahmed Abu Ali by an

---

[1]. *O´Globo,* May 4, 2003.

[2] Alissa Rubin, "French School Deems Teenager´s Skirt an Illegal Display of Religion", *International New York Times*, April 29, 2015.

[3] "Timothy Joiner Sentenced to 5 Years in Jail for Army Militia Plot", *Huffington Post,* January 22, 2013.

Alexandria (Virginia) court for a confession extracted after two years of torture in a Saudi prison speaks volumes in this regard[1].

The number of reports recorded in the United Kingdom by the British organization Tell MAMA (Measuring Anti-Muslim Attacks) increased by a factor of 15 from 2011 to 2012. The murder of the British soldier Lee Rigby in the Woolwich district of London on May 22, 2013 triggered a wave of anti-Islamism, taking form in the desecration of a dozen mosques and a resurgence in attacks on the Muslim community, who constitute 5% of the British population (some 2.7 million)[2]. Islamophobia was accentuated in the Netherlands following the murder in 2002 of the populist leader Pim Fortuyn and in 2004 of the film-maker Theo Van Gogh. In Germany, it crystallized around PEGIDA (Patriotic Europeans Against the Islamisation of the Occident). The number of Islamophobic acts recorded by the Collectif Contre l'Islamophobie, founded in France in 2003, have multiplied[3], especially after the murder of 12 journalists at the satirical newspaper *Charlie Hebdo* on January 7, 2015 by two French brothers of Algerian origin (Saïd and Chérif Kouachi).

This attack gave rise to solidarity movements in the principal French cities and among French expat communities, with banners bearing a slogan (*Je suis Charlie*) in defense of freedom of speech, which was not the actual issue at hand. The real issue was the repeated insults in the form of degrading images and acts of the Prophet which had already earned the increasingly Islamophobic magazine an arson attack in November 2011 and violent demonstrations in the Muslim world in September 2012 for the publication of another obscene image of Muhammad. When the Danish broadsheet *Jyllands-Posten* published caricatures on February 8, 2006, demonstrations in the Arab world led to a total of some fifty deaths[4]. When the Nigerien president, Mahamadou Issoufou, marched at the head of the procession next to the French president, 45 Christian churches were sacked in his country.

Henri Roussel, one of the founders of *Hara-Kiri*, predecessor of *Charlie Hebdo*, banned because of offense to the deceased President De Gaulle, published a story on the tragedy, arguing that it had been a chronicle foretold given the insults and obscenities circulated by this satirical magazine against a religion that constitutes, in many countries and in the disinherited suburbs of the major French cities, the only moral support, the only source of dignity, for marginalized and humiliated communities[5]. This view is shared by the Brazilian diplomats I have spoken with. And this is why 200 authors opposed the

---

[1] Esam Al-Amin, "Ten Years of Hell. The Harrowing Tale of Ahmed Abu Ali", *The Nation*, June 28-30, 2013.

[2] Vivian Oswald, "Ataques islamofóbicos disparam após morte de soldado britânico" (Islamophobic attacks increase after death of British soldier), *O Globo*, May 29, 2013.

[3] CCIF Annual Report, 2015 (www.islamophobie.net)

[4] "Caricatures: dix ans de fièvre planétaire" (Caricatures: ten years of planetary fever), *Le Monde*, January 9, 2015.

[5] Henri Roussel, "Delfeil du Ton", *Le Nouvel Observateur*, January 2015; see also the book by the historian Emmanuel Todd, *Qui est Charlie?*, éditions du Seuil, Paris, 2015.

decision by the PEN American Center to award the Freedom of Expression Courage Award to the magazine *Charlie Hebdo*, declaring that freedom of the press must be defended but insults to a religion should not be rewarded[1]. In these conditions, the Muhammad Art Exhibit and Contest organized in Garland, Texas in May 2015 to award the best caricature of the Prophet was an absurd provocation. It incited two American citizens, Elton Simpson, a Muslim convert, and Nadir Hamid Soofi, to carry out a terrorist attack, where they were the only victims thanks to the prompt response of the local police.

In Egypt or Yemen, in Somalia or Afghanistan, the intervention by foreign powers risks radicalizing these reactions. Examples include the Saudi attacks on Yemen with the support of the United States, the destabilization of Somalia wrought by the orchestrated invasion by Ethiopian and Kenyan troops (16.000 civilian casualties between 2006 and 2008), or the continuing annual military aid to Egypt of 1.3 billion dollars to nourish an encephalitic military and prolong its hold on power.

This interference, like the continuing Palestinian drama, can only arouse hostile reactions by populations weary of these conflicts where they are the principal victims and extreme reactions by armed groups declaring their allegiance to an orthodox and fiercely anti-Western Islam, a shared trait which, like the repression inflicted upon them, guarantees them kinship and the appearance of unity.

The influence of the Qur'anic schools (Wahhabism and Salafism) financed and run by Saudi Arabia, which prides itself for its missionary role in the region, certainly helps nourish this fundamentalist Islam. The perpetrator of the suicide attack that killed 27 worshippers at a mosque in Kuwait City in June 2015, Fahad Suleiman al-Abdulmoshen Gabbaa, was Saudi, as were 15 of the 19 terrorists in the September 11, 2001 attacks.

Thus, in Yemen where radical Islamic movements have been the object of severe repression and their leaders frequently targeted in drone strikes (the U.S. Treasury Department has put popular mullah Abdul Majeed al-Zindani on its "Specially Designated Global Terrorist" list), the situation tends to generate more radicalization. The Yemeni journalist Abdulelah Haider Shaye, who reported on the Al Ma'jalah cruise missile attack on December 17, 2009 (41 civilian casualties, including 14 women – five of them pregnant – and 21 children, the youngest only two years old), which was presented in the press as a Yemeni Air Force attack on militants, was arrested and sentenced to five years in prison. Nasser al-Awlaki, former rector of the university of Sanaa and former Yemeni Minister of Agriculture and Fishing, has never received a

[1] The authors include: the Americans Taiye Selasi, Rachel Kushner, Teju Cole, Francine Prose, and Joyce Carol Oates; the Canadian Michael Ondaatj; the Australian Peter Carey; the Indians Siddharta Deb and Padma Vendrakaman; the Pakistani Kamila Shamsie; the Moroccan Hedi El Kholti; the French Héléne Cardona, and others. Francine Prose (president of the PEN Club from 2007 to 2009) stated, *"I admire Charlie Hebdo's courage. But it does not deserve a PEN award"*, *The Guardian*, April 28, 2005.

response from the Pentagon explaining the U.S. drone attack on his 16-year-old grandson, an American citizen, on October 14, 2011. He was killed along with five of his friends while they were dining peacefully on the terrace of a Yemeni restaurant[1].

As regards Bahrain, a Saudi "protectorate", what could we expect from Isa bin Sulman al-Khalifa, who succeeded his father (in power since 1960) in 2002 after training in the British military school in Sanhurst and the U.S. Army Training and Doctrine Command at Fort Leavenworth, Kansas? It is currently the only country in the region to support the Saudi effort to create a Federation of Gulf States to ensure the continuity of the monarchy system, which has been unnerved by the popular demonstrations in favor of greater openness in the political process. In the study by the U.S. think tank cited above, the great majority of Muslims surveyed say they are in favor of democracy and against authoritarian regimes.

Turkey is always cited as a model by Western democracies, a secular state with a majority Muslim population, but it is kept on the sidelines. The European Union does not want Turkey as a full member state. Turkey made the mistake, blinded by its conflict with Greece, of joining NATO in October 1951 and thus lost its trump card, now finding it difficult to negotiate – doubtlessly with few illusions – its entry into the European Union, which it has sought since April 14, 1987. Its constructive role in partnership with Brazil in the Iranian nuclear issue has not been recognized. Regarding the Libyan question, Turkey was marginalized in spite of being the first state to fund the rebels. As regards Syria, Turkey is accused of colluding with the jihadis, smuggling both weapons and foreign fighters into Syria, which does not want to see the development of a Kurdish resistance, the only real force opposing Bashar al-Assad's regime along with the Islamic State (ISIL). Most of the nearly half-million refugees who entered Europe by sea between January and September 2015 arrived via Turkey. Ankara has received over 2 million Syrian refugees, now scattered across the country (only 270.000 are living in camps near the border). In addition to the 8 billion dollars the Turkish government said it is spending on humanitarian aid for refugees, instability has cost Turkey huge losses in revenue from trade and tourism.

These were the principal issues mentioned during private interviews in Brasilia, with Itamaraty diplomats generally sharing similar opinions. The accent is placed on the inappropriateness of both the means and the objectives vis-à-vis the local customs and culture. The imposition of a parliamentary democracy in a land where divisions fall along tribal, ethnic, or religious lines is seen as being doomed to failure. Priorities should be placed on civil governance, the slow maturation of democratic institutions, the fight against corruption, and the development of the educational system. The biggest problem is the discrediting of the concept of liberal democracy, imposed and propped up by expeditionary

[1] Nasser Al-Awlaki, "Death by drone", *International Herald Tribune*, July 19, 2013.

corps in a country with archaic, patriarchal structures where Islam is the sole refuge of dignity in the face of social and military humiliation wrought by foreign powers who are at the root of the corruption of local elites.

The Brazilian press provided broad coverage of the book by BBC journalist Humphrey Hawksley, *Democracy Kills: What's So Good About the Vote?*[1], which calls into question the democracy advocated by Western powers that supported and still sustain authoritarian regimes in Africa and the Middle East and do not recognize elections unless the outcomes are deemed advantageous to their national interests: examples include the parliamentary elections in Iran in 1951, putting power into the hands of a popular, nationalist leader, Mohammed Mosaddegh, who was overthrown in a coup d'état orchestrated by the CIA in 1953; the Gaza Strip, where Hamas won the majority of seats in 2006; Lebanon, with Hezbollah duly represented in Parliament and in the government since June 2011; in Algeria in 1991, where the elections gave a majority to the Islamic Salvation Front before they were annulled after the first round by a coup d'état, carried out with France's blessing and ushering in a decade marked by some 200.000 killings; in Tunisia, with the challenge to the legitimately elected and moderate Islamic Ennahda Movement, with the pretext of the murder of two members of the opposition (Mohammed Brahmi, Chokri Belaid), attributed to the Ansar al-Shariah movement and provoking stronger condemnation among Western powers than the assassination in November 1999 in Algiers of the number three of the Islamic Salvation Front, Abdelkader Hachani; in Egypt, with the overthrow of President Mohamed Morsi, elected in June 2012, in a coup d'état on July 3, 2013 that did not meet with condemnation from the United States or its allies, who were happy to thwart the Muslim Brotherhood's claim to power. Representing moderate Islam, the Brotherhood has been denied a role in political life for more than sixty years. Banned again in 2014, its assets have been seized and its leaders persecuted, some imprisoned for life, others have received death sentences on trumped up charges[2]. Former president Morsi was sentenced in April 2015 to twenty years in prison for "inciting deadly violence" and a court at the police academy sentenced him to death in May 2015 along with over one hundred Muslim Brotherhood leaders, including the movement's spiritual guide, Mohammed Badie, for having "escaped from the Wadi Natroun prison on January 28, 2011 to help in the revolt against President Mubarak[3]". Mohammed Badie's only son, Ammar, was killed during a demonstration in Cairo on August 16, 2013. The Prosecutor General of Egypt, Hisham Barakat, who issued the death sentences, was killed in a car bombing on June 29, 2015. There are hundreds of detainees,

---

1. Adriana Carranca, Interview with Humphrey Hawksley, *"A democracia está em decadência"* (Democracy is in decline), *O Estado de São Paulo*, February 14, 2010.

2 "Egypt´s hunger strikers", *International New York Times*, September 25, 2014.

3 Jared Malsin, "Egyptian Court Sentences Ousted President Morsi to Death", *International New York Times*, May 16, 2015 / "In Egypt, Deplorable Death Sentences", Editorial, *International New York Times*, May 18, 2015.

whose principal crime was believing in democracy, now subject to torture and dying during hunger strikes.

In June 2011 Celso Amorim participated as keynote speaker in the Cairo International Democratic Transition Forum, along with the then former president of Chile, Michelle Bachelet. The Forum was organized by the Egyptian Prime Minister, Essam Sharaf, to compare and contrast various models of democratic transition. Brazil had laid out a number of ambitious plans in light of what it believed would be a strategic partnership with Cairo[1]. Dilma Rousseff had received President Morsi in Brasilia in May 2013. On that occasion she declared: "*I am confident that in Egypt, as in Brazil during the 1980s when it underwent a similar process, the winds of democratization will usher in an economic plan that will bring both social and political innovation*"[2].

Of all the countries touched by Arab Spring uprisings (Egypt, Bahrain, Libya, Yemen, Syria), Tunisia is the only one that not reverted to a dictatorship, thanks to a small army that chose to stay out of the political turmoil and to a religious homogeneity (99% of the population is Sunni muslim). President Dilma Rousseff had a meeting with president Moncef Marzouki in the margin of the 3rd Summit of South America-Arab Countries (ASPA) in Lima on October 2012. For the Brazilian government the Nobel Peace Price 2015 awarded to Tunisian National Dialogue Quartet represents not only the role played by the Quartet in the Tunisian political transition process but also "*a victory for those who, throughout the world, stand for dialogue, tolerance and democracy*"[3].

Libya

While Brazil voted to suspend Libya from the United Nations Human Rights Council and for an arms embargo against the Gaddafi regime (Consensus Resolution 1970), it abstained, along with Germany, Russia, India, and China, on UN Security Council Resolution 1973 of March 17, 2011. It saw this latter resolution as going beyond the request of the Arab League (the creation of a no-fly zone over Libya) and giving free rein to military options at a time when Brazil was working with its BRICS partners and the African Union to impose a cease-fire and seek a negotiated solution that would ensure the protection of the civilian population.

More than 30,000 Libyans died during seven months of bombing by an essentially tripartite force – France, Great Britain, United States – which clearly favored the rebels. "*The most successful mission in NATO's history*", in the

---

[1] See the paper by Itamaraty diplomat Guimarães Amaral Rubem, "*O Egito no fim da era Mubarak: saudade, renovação política e esperanças de democracia. Perspectivas para as relações Brasil-Egito e a política externa brasileira para o Oriente Médio*" (Egypt at the end of the Mubarak era: nostalgia, political renewal and democratic hopes. Prospects for Brazil-Egypt relations and Brazilian foreign policy in the Middle East), Thesis no. 621, Itamaraty, Rio Branco Institute, 2011.

[2]. *O 'Globo*, May 9, 2013.

[3]. www.itamaraty.gov.br.

imprudent words of NATO Secretary General, Anders Fogh Rasmussen, a Dane, in Tripoli in October 2011[1].

French president Nicolas Sarkozy's eagerness to support a military intervention with the purported aim of protecting the civilian population contrasts with the reception offered to the Libyan president when he visited Paris in December 2007 and signed major military agreements worth some 4.5 billion euros along with cooperation agreements for the development of nuclear energy for peacetime uses. The contracts that Libya seemed no longer willing to pursue focused on 14 Dassault Rafale multirole fighter jets and their armament (the same model that France wanted to sell to Brazil), 35 Eurocopter helicopters, six patrol boats, a hundred armored vehicles, and the overhaul of 17 Mirage F1 fighters sold by Dassault Aviation in the 1970s[2].

We must recall that in 1986, when the U.S. was bombing Syrian military sites, France, Italy, and Spain refused to allow American F111s access to their airspace.

The major oil companies (Occidental Petroleum, State Oil, Petro-Canada...) working in Libya helped Libya pay the 1.5 billion dollars in compensation that the Libyan regime had agreed to pay to the families of the victims of Pan Am flight 103[3]. At the time, the compensation was intended to be one of the conditions for Libya to be reaccepted into the community of international relations.

The principal Libyan investment funds (LAFICO-Libyan Arab Foreign Investment Company; LIA-Libyan Investment Authority) were shareholders in many Italian and British corporations (Fiat, UniCredit, Juventus, the Pearson Group, owner of the *Financial Times*, and the London School of Economics, where Gaddafi was addressed as "*Brother Leader*" during a video conference in December 2010 and his son Saif was awarded a PhD in 2008). The New York investment bank Goldman Sachs was sued in 2014 by a Libyan fund (Libyan Investment Authority) which had lost more than 1.2 billion dollars between January and April 2008 after the American firm took a commission of 350 million dollars for investing their money in highly speculative derivatives[4].

Muammar Gaddafi had been received with full honors by the major powers some months earlier: in addition to the reception in grand style in Paris, where he was a guest for five days in 2007, he was received in Spain in December 2007, in Moscow in October 2008, and in Rome in August 2010, two years after accepting the Italian gift of 5 billion dollars as compensation for the Italian occupation of Libya from 1913 to 1943. And also of note are the five trips to Tripoli in three years by former British Prime Minister Tony Blair, a

---

[1] "NATO chief Rasmussen 'proud' as Libya mission ends", *BBC News*, October 31, 2011.

[2]. *Agence France Presse*, December 11, 2007.

[3]. *International Herald Tribune*, March 24, 2011.

[4] Jeremy Anderson, "Goldman to reveal income linked to Libyan lawsuit", *International New York Times*, November 25, 2014.

paid senior advisor to the investment bank JPMorgan Chase[1]. Former French president Nicolas Sarkozy was received in Tripoli in July 2007, where he announced the beginning of a partnership for the installation of a nuclear power plant in Libya. On that occasion, the Brazilian press had reported on commitments by the European Union to facilitate access to the European market for Libyan agricultural exports[2]. Libya was invited by the NATO Chiefs of Defense to the Maritime Commanders' Meeting (MARCOMET) in Toulon on May 25-28, 2008.

Brasilia noted the coincidences in approach with the time of Saddam Hussein: the Iraqi leader was invited to Paris in June 1972 and September 1975; an agreement was signed in June 1977 for the sale to Baghdad of 32 Mirage F1 combat aircraft. A coincidence that didn't do either of them any good in the long run.

During the war, where it quickly became evident that the French-British intervention, under cover of NATO, could not succeed without American air support[3], Arab military leaders (veterans of Afghanistan and members of the Libyan Islamic Fighting Group, with ties to Al-Qaeda) helped overthrow Gaddafi. One of the principal military leaders of the rebellion, Abdel Hakim Belhadj (a.k.a. Abu Abdullah al-Sadik), then Tripoli Security Chief, had been arrested in Bangkok in 2004, tortured by CIA agents, and delivered to Gaddafi's Abu Salim prison. He is now the main ISIL leader in Lybia. Jaballah Matar was kidnapped from his home in Cairo by the CIA in 1990 and then handed over to Libyan officials[4] Documents seized after the death of Gaddafi reveal close cooperation between Libyan, American (CIA), and British (MI6) intelligence services[5].

Under Gaddafi, Islamic terrorism was virtually non-existent. Prior to the U.S. led bombing campaign in 2011, Libya had the highest Human Development Index, the lowest infant mortality and the highest life expectancy in all Africa. Today Lybia is a wrecked state.

In January 2012, three months after the end of hostilities, the United Nations High Commissioner for Human Rights, Navi Pillay, reported the widespread use of torture, summary executions, and rape in Libyan prisons. At the same time, the organization Doctors Without Borders decided to withdraw from the prisons in Misrata because of the ongoing torture of detainees[6]. More than 1.500 Libyan refugees drowned in the Mediterranean while attempting to seek a safe haven from the fighting. In March 2012, the European Council lamented the indifference and inaction of NATO forces with regard to ships in

---

1. *The Telegraph*, March 23, 2012.
2. *O 'Globo*, July 26, 2007.
3. Norway, Canada, Italy, Denmark, and Belgium provided secondary air support.
4 Souad Mekhennet, Eric Schmitt, "Libyan rebels seek to shed El Qaeda past", *International Herald Tribune*, July 19, 2011.
5. Rod Nordland, "Files note close CIA ties with Qaddafi spy unit", *International Herald Tribune*, September 5, 2011.
6. *International Herald Tribune*, January 28-29, 2012.

distress, where 62 refugees who lost their lives in March 2011 might have been saved.

These complex and controversial situations have inspired a measured approach to the Libyan conflict by Brazil, in line with the positions of its BRICS partners, particularly South Africa, whose president, Jacob Zuma – in spite of the fact that his country was the only BRICS member to vote in favor of Resolution 1973 – spared no effort in finding a solution to the conflict, acknowledging the Libyan leader's aid to the African National Congress during the darkest days of apartheid.

Brazil opened an embassy in Tripoli in the early 1970s when the country was highly dependent on oil imports, motivated by the same concerns that drove it to seek a rapprochement with Saddam Hussein's Iraq in the same period. The Brazilian public works companies (Andrade Gutierrez, Queiroz Galvão) and the state-owned oil company Petrobras withdrew from Libya in 2011 because of the fighting. Brasilia recognizes the progress made by Libyan society after Gaddafi's rise to power, in infrastructure development, public health, and, a particularly difficult issue in all Muslim countries, women's rights. A good many leaders in Lula's Workers' Party looked favorably on the pan-African projects "guided" by Libya, perhaps judging them as somewhat utopian, especially the creation of an African central bank, currency unit, and monetary fund. However, the responsibility of the Libyan leader for acts of terrorism, the embargo imposed by the UN in 1992, and U.S. hostility towards the regime induced Brasilia to keep its distance from this country, which President Lula visited in 2003. He was received by Gaddafi in his tent, not far from Tripoli. Also invited to the official reception were the former president of Algeria, Ahmed Ben Bella, and the Sandinista leader Daniel Ortega. The Brazilian president met on two subsequent occasions with the Libyan leader, whom he held in high esteem: in concomitance with the Africa-South America summit in Abuja in 2006, and during the 13th African Union summit in 2009 in Sirte. Lula's diplomatic advisor, Marco Aurelio Garcia, bore a personal message from the Brazilian president to Muammar Gaddafi in 2007. Along with Ecuador, Brasilia backed Venezuela's March 2011 proposal for international mediation to seek a peaceful resolution to conflicts within Libya and thus avoid foreign intervention, later also supporting similar efforts by the South African president.

Brazil indirectly recognized the National Transition Council in 2011, now confined to the towns of Baida and Tobruk, near the Egyptian border. But it did not take part in the meeting of the Friends of Libya in New York in September 2011: 22 states, the great majority of them NATO members, along with Australia, Japan, and pro-West states (Bahrain, Jordan, Kuwait, Morocco, Qatar, United Arab Emirates) but not one African country, other than Morocco. In April 2013, Brasilia received a Libyan delegation led by Vice Prime

Minister Abdusalam Al-Mahdi Al-Quadi, who expressed a wish to re-establish bilateral cooperation[1].

The NATO intervention in Libya, involving most member countries under a humanitarian pretext, set an unfortunate precedent for efforts to resolve the Syrian crisis: the attack by French and British warplanes on the Warfallah tribe, who remained faithful to Muammar Gaddafi, and on the convoy carrying the Libyan leader and one of his sons, leading directly to Gaddafi's death under deplorable circumstances. The images by videographer Ali Algadi and journalist Tracey Sheldon provide a graphic account of the Libyan leader being dragged from a drain pipe on October 20, 2011 and killed shortly thereafter. These circumstances belie the pseudo-humanitarian nature of the military intervention and tarnish the image of the "Libyan Spring"[2].

The death of U.S. Ambassador to Libya, J. Christopher Stevens and one of his aides in a fire set in the U.S. Consulate in Benghazi in September 2012, revealing the breadth of CIA activities, in which the Consulate served as a façade; the car bomb attack on the French Embassy in Tripoli in April 2013; the escape of 1,200 detainees from the Benghazi prison; the murder of the human rights lawyer Abdel Salam al-Mismari in July; and the attack on the Swedish Consulate in Benghazi in October all highlighted the inability of the central government to gain control over the security situation in Libya as it was overrun by heavily armed militias. In July 2013, Libyan Prime Minister Ali Zeidan threatened to bomb Libyan ports in the Benghazi region that were in the hands of militias who were profiting by exporting the oil now under their control. In October, the Prime Minister was kidnapped by 150 armed men in the center of Tripoli and held for six hours to protest the abduction on Libyan soil of Abu Anas al-Libi in a secret American airport operation. Al-Libi was accused of being one of the leaders of Al-Qaeda and later died while in custody in the United States.

The year 2015 began with Libya bereft of all institutions. Lacking any central government, it is ruled by a motley group of coalitions vying for power, based in Tripoli (Farj Libya, which controls the central bank), Benghazi (Shura Council, consisting of Ansar al-Sharia, facing off against the Libyan National Army of the renegade general Khalifa Hiftar), and in Tobruk-Bayda (offshoot of the National Transition Council, enjoying international diplomatic recognition after the June 2013 elections).

The security and health situation for the civil population is near disastrous. When I visited the country in 1994 it was a model for public health and education, and boasted the highest *per capita* income in Africa. It was clearly the most advanced of all Arab countries in terms of the legal status of women and families in Libyan society (half of the students at the university of Tripoli were women). The aggression against the presenter Sarah Al-Massalati in 2012, the

---

1. Marcos Carrieri, "Libyan minister discusses return of Brazilian companies", *Brazil-Arab News Agency*, Arab-Brazilian Chamber of Commerce, April 17, 2013.

2. Borzou Daragahi, "Call for probe into Libyan Civilian Deaths", *Financial Times*, May 14, 2012.

poet Aicha Almagrabi in February 2013, and the women's rights activist Magdalene Ubaida, now in exile in London, bear grim testimony to their legal status in post-Gaddafi Libya. The city of Benghazi is now semi-destroyed; schools and universities are closed[1].

Libya has become a hub for illegal trafficking, particularly of African emigrants under conditions reminiscent of the slave trade. According to Global Initiative Against Transnational Organized Crime, the refugee smuggling market in Libya was worth 323 million dollars in 2014. It is the theatre of fratricidal clashes between rival factions financed and armed by a series of sorcerer's apprentices (Saudi Arabia, Egypt, and the United Arab Emirates in favor of General Hiftar on the one side, Qatar, Turkey, and Sudan supporting Farj Libya on the other). Among them, minority but heavily armed militias rise up in allegiance to the Islamic State of Iraq and the Levant (ISIL), the authors of the grisly decapitation of 21 Egyptian Christian workers on the beach near Sirte in February 2015. This act was certainly meant as a reprisal for the unilateral bombardments by the Egyptian Air Force in 2014 in spite of condemnation by Qatar, close ally of the former Egyptian president, Mohamed Morsi, elected in June 2012 but overthrown in a military coup by General Abdel Fattah al-Sisi on July 3, 2013, who then became self-proclaimed marshal. The recruitment by the CIA on its Benghazi base[2] of combatants from the city of Derna for the conflict in Syria, fief of the Islamists (Al-Bittar brigade), against President Bashar al-Assad, has inescapable parallels with the recruitment in 1979, again by the CIA, of the *mujahedeen* against the Soviet Union in Afghanistan, with all the consequences that we are well familiar with, and particularly the birth of Sunni jihadism.

The Brazilian Ambassador to Libya is currently housed in Tunis because of the lack of security in Tobruk, and to take an equidistant position with respect to a government installed in Tobruk, which Brazil recognizes as legitimate, and a rival administration in Tripoli, with which Brasilia hopes to maintain a dialogue. Although Brazilian diplomacy supports the United Nations Special Representative Bernardino Leon in the search for a settlement to the crisis through dialogue, it invests little hope in this effort. Indeed, Bernardino Leon was not even allowed to leave the airport at Tobruk upon his arrival. The armed factions are consolidated at the east and west extremes of the Libyan coastline. A general who has been stationed in the United States for 27 years commands a motley coalition with military backing from Egypt, the United Arab Emirates and Saudi Arabia while Islamist groups claiming allegiance to ISIL and well entrenched in Sirte and Derna are able to spread their influence thanks to the institutional crisis.

---

[1] Abdel Sharif Kouddous, "Report from the Front: Libya's Descent Into Chaos", *The Nation*, February 25, 2015.

[2] Seymour Hersh, "U.S. Effort to Arm Jihadis in Syria. The Scandal Behind the Benghazi Undercover CIA Facility", *Global Research*, *Washington's Blog*, April 15, 2014.

Gaddafi, leader of the Libyan revolution, the *Jamahiriya*, in power from 1969 to 2011, gave a warning to Europe in an interview with French journalist Laurent Valdiguié of the *Journal du Dimanche* on the eve of the NATO intervention, in words that now seem prophetic: "*If one seeks to destabilize [Libya], there will be chaos, Bin Laden, armed factions. That is what will happen. You will have immigration, thousands of people will invade Europe from Libya. And there will no longer be anyone to stop them. Bin Laden will base himself in North Africa [...]. You will have Bin Laden at your doorstep. This catastrophe will extend out of Pakistan and Afghanistan and reach all the way to North Africa*[1]."

In the first five months of 2015, more than 50.000 undocumented immigrants have reached Italy from sub-Saharan Africa via Libya; 1.791 of them lost their lives at sea[2]. Prior to the initiation of hostilities, 1.5 million sub-Saharan Africans worked in Libya in generally menial jobs (oil industry, agriculture, services, public sector).

Syria

The joint communiqué published on March 8, 2011 at the conclusion of the 7th IBSA forum with India, Brazil, and South Africa, countries involved in the 2007 Annapolis Conference on the Israeli-Palestine conflict, mentioned the willingness of these three countries, all then non-permanent members of the Security Council, to cooperate on finding a solution to the conflict. In August 2011, an IBSA mission went to Damascus to meet with President Bashar al-Assad and his Minister of Foreign Affairs, Walid al-Muallem. The principal international humanitarian organizations called upon the Ministers of Foreign Affairs of the three countries in a joint letter dated August 4, 2011 to raise awareness about the repression in Syria at the IBSA forum, which met in Pretoria on October 17, 2011. Nevertheless, in October 2011 Brazil abstained, along with its IBSA partners, on the resolution against Syria, having received President Assad on an official visit in July 2010 (President Lula visited Damascus in December 2003). China and Russia vetoed the resolution, chastened by the earlier experience in Libya. Brazil saw the expression "*targeted measures*" in reference to Syria as being unnervingly reminiscent of the "*all necessary measures*" applied to Libya to legitimize NATO's military intervention and impact on the Libyan civil war.

Brazilian diplomacy, having learned from experience, erred on the side of caution as regards the positions it should have defended in solidarity with the Arab League and Turkey (humanitarian corridor, exclusion zone at the border to receive civilian refugees and displaced populations). It was very reluctant to support coercive measures that would be admissible according to Chapter 7 of the UN Charter and concerned about the distinction of meaning now existing between the notions of "*peacekeeping*" and "*peace enforcement*". It placed emphasis on the principle of non-intervention and the peaceful resolution of differences,

---

[1] *Journal du Dimanche*, March 5, 2011 (www.lejdd.fr)

[2] Source: International Organization for Migration and the European Commission.

taking seriously the threat of civil war in a country subjected to reckless interference.

It gave its support, exactly as did Argentina, to the proposals of the Arab League and to mediation by the United Nations, originally in the hands of Secretary General Kofi Annan and then, after he was thwarted, in those of the Algerian Lakdar Brahimi. The major Brazilian media criticized this position on Syria, where more than 7.500 civilian casualties, including 500 children, had been recorded as of March 1, 2012 according to the Chair of the Independent International Commission of Inquiry on the Syrian Arab Republic, Brazilian diplomat Paulo Sergio Pinheiro, former Secretary for Human Rights in the government of Fernando Henrique Cardoso (1995-2002). The number of casualties has increased significantly since that date: more than 200.000 dead and six million people displaced, half of them children, four million people living as refugees abroad in August 2015. The country's GDP fell by 35% in one year; its reserves decreased by two thirds; the Syrian currency has lost more than three fourths of its value; the war damage is considerable.

While Brazil favors extending the mandate of the Commission of Inquiry on Syria, it did not support Switzerland's proposal to give jurisdiction to the International Criminal Court to judge the perpetrators of flagrant human rights violations during the conflict. To date, Costa Rica is the only country in Latin America to support the Swiss initiative. The National Coalition for Syrian Revolutionary and Opposition Forces, in exile, headed until July 2013 by an American citizen of Syrian origin (Ghassan Hitto) who had spent most of his life in Texas, did not seem very representative of the forces engaged within the country against the Assad regime. Brutality and abuses are reported in the media and underscored in the latest report on violations of human rights in Syria published by the Commission of Inquiry on September 11, 2013. The report paints a distressing picture of the violations committed by the armed forces in the country, with half of the victims being civilians. The killing of one of the commanders of the Free Syrian Army, Kamal Hamani, in August 2013 by Islamist combatants testifies to the profound divisions within the opposition.

Brasilia is on guard regarding the growing proportion of radical Islamist groups within the circle of influence of Al-Qaeda among the rebels, many of whom have fought the American troops in Iraq and now represent the most hardened and fiercely determined units. Since September 2013 they are united in the "Alliance for an Islamist State": some 6.000 volunteers, generally Sunnite (Jabhat al-Nusra, Jaish al-Muhajireen wal Ansar, Islamic State of Iraq and the Levant) along with many thousands of foreign fighters, young Islamists coming in from all countries[1], such as the American Nicole Lynn Mansfield and the Briton Ali al-Manasfi, who died fighting in May 2013. The perpetrator of

[1]. Christophe Cornevin, "L'inquiétant profil des djihadistes français en Syrie" (The unsettling profile of French jihadis in Syria), *Le Figaro*, September 14-15, 2013.

the attack on the Jewish Museum of Belgium in Brussels on May 24, 2014 that killed four people was a 29-year-old French student of Algerian origin who had spent over a year in Syria, Mehdi Nemmouche. One of the two Kouachi brothers responsible for the attack on the journalists at the Parisian offices of the French satire magazine *Charlie Hebdo* had just returned from Yemen. Regardless of whether they win or lose their struggle against President Bashar al-Assad, it is perfectly legitimate to ask the question: what will become of them, what will they do next?

Speaking in private conversations, our contacts in Brasilia often point out the inconsistencies in French diplomacy. In September 2007, President Nicolas Sarkozy received Muammar Gaddafi lavishly for a five-day visit, graciously allowing the Libyan leader to set up his tent in the gardens of the official residence in Marigny. And in 2008, he extended a personal invitation to the Syrian leader, Bashar al-Assad, to watch the military parade celebrating Bastille Day on July 14. This contrasts with the feverish activism in favor of military interventions to overthrow their regimes. They also mention the about-face regarding military intervention in Iraq, initially ruled out by President Jacques Chirac but now implemented – albeit in half measures – by President François Hollande (deployment of 600 ground troops and the nuclear-powered aircraft carrier Charles de Gaulle with 2,500 marines as part of the "Chammal" operation[1], more than 200 air raids between September 2014 and August 2015[2]). And we must now add the intervention in Syria, which violates international law, has not been authorized by the Security Council, and was not requested by the Syrian government. French Prime Minister Manuel Valls legitimizes the action by invoking the concept of pre-emptive defense introduced by U.S. President George W. Bush, with the disastrous consequences we are all familiar with[3].

The limited provision of arms to the Syrian opposition – excluding the generous supplies from Qatar and Saudi Arabia –, which rests on a dubious distinction between "moderates" v. "extremists" and "defensive" v. "lethal" arms, quite eloquently testified to a shared concern: a repeat in Syria of the Taliban experience in Afghanistan. By seeking to support armed opposition, the United States and its allies prolong the conflict, exacerbate inter-faith tensions (Sunnite-Shi'ite-Christian), and destabilize the region, leading, most notably, to the growing involvement of Russia, the Hezbollah and Iran, for whom Assad's Syria is the principal ally. Brazil fears that the country will collapse in spite of increasing Russian support for the Syrian government (resumption of military

---

[1] Nathalie Guibert, "La France envoie discrètement des renforts à Bagdad" (France quietly sends reinforcements to Baghdad), *Le Monde*, February 20, 2015.

[2] Airwars.org

[3] "*We are striking Daesh (ISIS) in Syria because this terrorist organization prepares and organizes attacks in France from Syria, from these sanctuaries. We are therefore acting in self-defense, which article 51 of the United Nations Charter permit us to do*", in (Breden Aurelien, "France Says It Has Struck at ISIS in Syria"), *International New York Times*, September 26, 2015.

supplies, expansion of the Lattakié air base, Russian air raids) in keeping with the statement by Russian Foreign Affairs Minister Sergey Lavrov on the occasion of the 70th General Assembly of the United Nations in September 2015: "*We don't feel any affection to anyone in the region, but we are firmly convinced that we cannot allow Syria to collapse as a State*[1]." The least thing the country needed was to become the site of a proxy war between the United States and Russia.

The inclusion of the military arm of Hezbollah on the European Union list of terrorist organizations by the European Council in July 2013 is merely an exercise in semantics given that the group has won seats in the Lebanese parliament, has ministers within the government, and receives aid from the European Union. The move has been criticized by two-term Lebanese Prime Minister, Nagib Mikati. Brasilia sees Hezbollah as a unified force, originally a resistance network for Shi'ite families against Israeli invasion – along the lines of the *basiji* in Iran (paramilitary volunteer militias), whose emblem it borrowed (a yellow flag) – that has developed a broad social solidarity network. Exclusion and ostracism have never helped resolve conflicts and it would be better to work to enforce the commitments made in the Baabda Declaration on June 12, 2012, urging the Lebanese political forces to distance themselves from the Syrian conflict to help preserve the fragile stability in the country rather than suspending the arms embargo to Syria, as was decided by the European Union on May 27, 2013.

The Syrian president wrote a letter to the BRICS countries (Brazil, Russia, China, South Africa) in March 2013 on the occasion of the Durban Summit to urge their support. The final declaration produced by the Summit stated that the agreement reached in Geneva in June 2012 at the conference organized by the United Nations and the Arab League for a transition government must serve as a framework in negotiations and prevent military escalation of the conflict[2]. Brazilian diplomacy advocates the constructive approach championed by the Syria Contact Group, which included Egypt, Iran, Saudi Arabia, and Turkey in 2012, the United States and Russia declining to take part. Brasilia supported the second Geneva Conference on Syria proposed by Russia and the United States in May 2013 and taking place in January 2014. The initiative also enjoyed the support of the Special Joint Representative of the Arab League and the United Nations. The G-20 meeting in St Petersburg in September 2013 found Brazil's position on Syria shared by the other BRICS members and by the European Union: any military intervention in Syria, on whatever pretext, must be clearly and unequivocally authorized by the United Nations Security Council. Brasilia stressed that the people's hopes for a democratic government must also be taken into consideration, without any foreign military influence, which can only worsen the already precarious living conditions of the civilian population. After seven weeks of NATO bombing in the former Yugoslavia –

---

[1] TASS, Russian News Agency, September 29, 2015.

[2]. "Assad recorre a Brics contra terroristas" (Assad turns to BRICS against terrorists), *O'Globo*, March 28, 2013.

military operations that were not authorized by the Security Council – the civilian toll was 1.200 killed and 4.500 wounded. On April 30, 2015, in the Syrian village of Bir Mahli in the Aleppo Governorate, on the east bank of the Euphrates – a village I found peaceful and hospitable in 1972 when I participated in an archaeological dig at the Citadel of Aleppo – more than 50 civilians were killed by Coalition bombs, including 31 children and 19 women[1]. The NGOs Airwars and McClatchy have challenged the Pentagon about these blunders. And we must also add the deaths of 18 civilians in Harem on November 5 and 50 in Al-Bab on December 28, 2014; of 70 civilians in Hawija on June 2, 13 in Kafr Hind on July 28, and 11 in Atmeh on August 11, 2015. With 2.449 air attacks in Syria between September 2014 and August 20, 2015, the only civilian deaths publicly acknowledged by the Pentagon (Centcom) on May 21, 2015 were those of two 5-year-old girls[2].

The great majority of Latin American countries, with the exception of Guatemala, Honduras, and Panama, sided with Secretary General of the Organization of American States in opposing military intervention in Syria. Unanimously condemning the use of chemical weapons, they came out in favor of an arms embargo and urgent mediation by the Security Council. Luiz Alberto Figueiredo argued in favor of a total arms embargo for Syria (applied to all nations, including Turkey and the Gulf monarchies). He believed that the current flow of arms could only lead to more violence[3].

Brasilia notes that the Commission of Inquiry on Chemical Arms led by the UN High Representative for Disarmament Affairs, Angela Kane, met in Damascus in August 2013 to take action on the official request by the Syrian government to investigate the March 19 chemical attack on the village of Khan al-Assal in northern Syria, which it attributed to the armed rebels. This position appears to have been shared by Carla del Ponte, member of the Independent International Commission of Inquiry on the Syrian Arab Republic. The request was made the day after the attack but the United States delayed the inspection, seeking to extend the scope from *"investigate all massacres"* to *"investigate all alleged violations of international human rights law since march 2011 in the Syrian Arab Republic"*. Once the mission was in place, it refused to continue it as requested by the Assad government. The Syrian Representative to the United Nations, Bashaar Jaafari, reiterated the fact that Israel was not yet a party to the Chemical Weapons Convention.

There is a long list of precedents (acts whose perpetrators have yet to be punished) that banish any moral pretext cited to justify armed reprisals for the use of sarin gas on August 21, 2013. Launched, according to the conclusions of

---

[1] Anne Barnard, "Strikes on Syria Tied to Deaths of 52 Civilians", International *New York Times*, May 2, 2015.

[2] "Six months after deadly Syrian air raid US finally concedes it killed two children", *Airwars.org*, May 21, 2015.

[3]. "Brasil defende embargo de armas convencionais" (Brazil in favor of embargo on conventional weapons), *O Globo*, September 17, 2013.

the United Nations inspectors' report, from the Syrian government positions, the gas killed a thousand people, including 300 children in the Ghouta area in Syria.

The precedents include: the use of Agent Orange (contaminated with dioxin) by the American Army in Vietnam from 1961 to 1975, leading to the birth of some 150.000 handicapped children, according to the Vietnamese Red Cross, with lasting effects for 3 million Vietnamese and for many American veterans of the war; the use of mustard gas and sarin by Iraq in its war against Iran, with Tehran's protests at the time falling on deaf ears but confirmed by CIA archives and by the former assistant Defense Intelligence Officer stationed in Baghdad, Rick Francona[1]; radiation poisoning by depleted uranium, a highly toxic waste product of nuclear reactors, used in Coalition munitions in Iraq, responsible, according to the World Health Organization for a significant increase of birth defects, cancer and leukemia as reported by journalist Lisa Holland and aired on the British *Sky News* on September 1, 2009; the cluster bombs used in the Iraq War[2]; and the white phosphorus bombs used by Coalition troops in the Fallujah offensive (Iraq) in April and November 2004, and by the Israeli armed forces when they invaded Lebanon (2006) and the Gaza Strip (2007-2008)[3].

There are above all strategic decisions that underlie the threat of intervention, particularly relating to the Iranian question, which is ubiquitous[4].

According to our contacts, the way out of the conflict – beyond the signing and ratification by Syria of the 1993 Chemical Weapons Convention and the destruction of its chemical arsenal in keeping with Security Council Resolution 2118 of September 27, 2013 and urged by Russia – necessarily involves global negotiations with all relevant parties. These include Iran, which has elected a moderate president, Hassan Rouhani, and Hezbollah, whose principal supporter is Bashar al-Assad's Syria. Ironically, we now look to experts from the Organization for the Prohibition of Chemical Weapons (OPCW) – which was excluded from Iraq and its Director General, José Bustani, a Brazilian diplomat, ousted by the Bush administration in 2002 because he called for international weapons monitors in Iraq, impeding the U.S. push for war – to

---

1. Shane Harris, Matthew Aid, "Exclusive: CIA Files prove America Helped Saddam as He Gassed Iran", *Foreign Policy*, August 26, 2013.

2. The international treaty prohibiting the use of cluster munitions was adopted in 2008, signed by 152 countries and ratified by 83. The United States, Brazil, Israel, Russia, China, and Pakistan are among those who have not signed the treaty. The United States has still not signed the Ottawa Treaty outlawing anti-personnel mines (1997). The Treaty has been signed by 32 countries, with Brazil joining in 1999.

3. Peter Popham, Anne Penketh, "US Intelligence classified white phosphorus as chemical weapon", *The Independent*, November 25, 2005; Sigfrido Ranucci, "Fallujah: the hidden massacre", *Radiotelevisione Italia* - RAI, April 4, 2007; Paul Wood, Mustafa Khalil, Michael Tait, "White Phosphorus in Gaza: the victims", *The Guardian*, February 19, 2009.

4. On the *ABC* program "This Week", President Obama stated: "*My suspicion is that the Iranians recognize they shouldn't draw a lesson that we haven't struck [Syria], to think we won't strike Iran.*" Anne Gearen, William Booth, *Washington Post*, September 15, 2013.

oversee the destruction of the Syrian chemical weapons arsenal, which was necessary to prevent a further war from breaking out in the Middle East.

Similar causes tend to produce similar effects. The United States was behind the emergence of the Taliban in Afghanistan in the 1980s, propping them up as an opposition force to counter the Soviet troops that had invaded the country. The Sunni warlords in Iraq were generously compensated – to the tune of more than 300 million dollars in Operation "Anbar Awakening", led by General David Petraeus in 2007 – and imprudently armed so they could fight against the factions allied with Al-Qaeda. A minority in Iraq, Sunni Arabs are the largest population group in Syria. The country's borders have no relation to history or geography, race or ethnicity, but were drawn out on paper during French-British negotiations (Sykes-Picot secret Agreement of May 16, 1916). Foreign powers (including the United States, Russia, Saudi Arabia, Qatar, Turkey, Iran, Israel, Pakistan, France, and the United Kingdom) have defended, financed, and exacerbated rivalries among opposing factions and in so doing have exposed themselves to unpredictable reactions. The government of Bashar al-Assad, like those of Saddam Hussein or Muammar Gaddafi, is the guarantor of a stability that certainly may be contestable, but has the merit of being relatively institutionalized and favored by the civilian population, who face historical, cultural and religious tensions that must be contained and not exacerbated. This is true even after the severe repression of the Muslim Brotherhood in Aleppo and Hama in 1982.

During a television interview in June 2013, former French Foreign Affairs Minister Roland Dumas revealed that the United Kingdom was training Syrian rebels two years before the beginning of the revolt against Bashar al-Assad. According to diplomatic telegrams revealed by *WikiLeaks* and the *Washington Post*, and confirmed as authentic by U.S. Department of State spokesperson Mark Toner, between 2006 and 2010, the United States spent some 12 million dollars to support the Syrian opposition forces[1].

As our contacts see it, it makes no political or cultural sense to turn to the oil barons of the Gulf, who are among the Western arms industry's biggest customers and tend to be distinguished by the repressiveness of their regimes, to fight the Shi'ites.

Brasilia does not understand Qatari politics. The country hosts U.S. military bases. It has a television channel, *Al-Jazeera*, which provided relatively impartial coverage during the Second Gulf War but is judged to be anti-American. It has close ties with Hamas in spite of their differences regarding Syria. It is one of the few Arab countries to have maintained economic representation in Tel Aviv (along with Egypt and Jordan) up until the invasion of the Gaza Strip by the Israeli army in August 2014. It hosted the second Arab-Latin America summit, after the breakdown of talks in Morocco.

---

[1] "U.S. Admits funding Syrian opposition", *CBC News*, April 18, 2011.

Celso Amorim attributes this heterogeneity to the diverging personalities of Sheikh Hamad Bin Khalifa, whom he sees as being rather in favor of dialogue with Damascus and Tehran, and of the Prime Minister, Hamad Bin Jassim (2007-2013), who has also served as Minister of Foreign Affairs (1992-2013), from the same family but with strong ties to the United States (he is a member of the Brookings Institution)[1]. Jassim was removed from his functions – also as president of the Qatar Investment Authority – when the new Emir, Sheikh Tamin Bin Hamad al-Thani, came to power, succeeding his father in 2013.

The Caliphate of the leader of the Islamic State of Iraq and the Levant (ISIL), Abu Bakr al-Baghdadi, former detainee of Camp Bucca, like many of his lieutenants (Abu Louay, Abu Kassem, Abu Jurnas, Abu Shema), constitutes the backbone of the armed opposition to President Bashar al-Assad, complemented by other factions, all jihadis – Kurds apart – and Shi'ite, fiercely hostile to the United States (Jabhat al-Nusra, Ahrar al-Sham, Islamic Front, Khorasan...). More than 100.000 Iraqis have been detained arbitrarily in Abu Ghraib prison and Camps Bucca, Cropper and Taji under appalling conditions, as seen in shocking photographs hastily censored by General Antonio Taguba, who was sent by President Obama to investigate the abuses. To fight this movement – which was initially aided and funded by Saudi Arabia, cradle and apostolate of Wahhabism, the source of much of the ideology of the leaders of the Caliphate, and by Kuwait, Qatar, and even Turkey, allies of the United States, but now financially weaned thanks to the oil field that it controls in the northeast – it is necessary to provide support to the government of Bashar al-Assad, which its former sponsors and Washington are trying to overthrow.

The Syrian National Council is recognized as the legitimate government of Syria by only seven countries in addition to the United States and the European Union (France, United Kingdom, Libya, Tunisia, Spain, Bulgaria, and Turkey) and does not represent any of the armed factions fighting against the Syrian president. The National Coalition for Syrian Revolutionary and Opposition Forces (Syrian National Coalition), founded in November 2012 and dominated by the Muslim Brotherhood, is rife with internal divisions depending on allegiances either to Qatar or to Saudi Arabia, both of whom provide some funding. The moderate Free Syrian Army has lost all its credibility since 2013 and its leader, General Abdal Ilah al-Bashir, who deserted the Syrian army in 2012, acknowledged that his movement was financed and directed by the CIA. As for the Sunnites, both in Syria and Iraq, they fear the established power more than they do the militants and fighters of the Caliphate.

Certainly, Syrians would doubtlessly prefer a regime change, but they are attached to secularism and to the right of women to take part in social and economic life. They are aware of the fundamentalism animating the opposition to the current government and the catastrophe awaiting the country from this

[1] Celso Amorim, "O Brasil e o Oriente Médio" (p. 248), in *Teerã, Ramalá e Doha, memórias da política externa ativa e altiva,* 2015.

suicidal, unresolvable conflict. And they know they are the principal victims. As underscored by Paulo Sergio Pinheiro, Brazilian Chairman of the United Nations panel investigating human rights abuses in Syria, "*every decision – whether to visit a neighbor or go out to buy bread – has potentially become a life-and-death decision*[1]". Syria has suffered enormous harm, on the order of 140 billion dollars according to United Nations estimates. It is not clear whether Syria will ever be able to re-establish itself. This might be, according to Brasilia, the goal of the U.S.-Israeli plan in Syria: insuring its effective dismemberment.

The bombings of the Syrian oil and gas fields by the U.S. Air Force and Navy in order to limit the oil revenues available to the Caliphate have driven the repressive Gulf oil barons into an adventitious coalition, in flagrant violation of international law, which can only discredit a possible moderate opposition to the Assad regime. The planned training of thousands of "moderate" combatants[2] (seen in Brasilia as mercenaries) by the U.S. Army at training camps in Jordan and Turkey will be of little effect if we are to judge by the disaster of Mosul. There, 1.500 ISIL fighters routed 100.000 men in the regular Iraqi army who had been trained by the United States. The U.S. had more than 500 military bases in Iraq and a detachment of 166.000 soldiers, but there were only 3.100 of these trainees, spread out over six bases, in July 2015. General Lloyd J. Austin III, the head of the United States Central Command told a Senate committee in September 2015 that only four or five Syrians trained by the American military to confront the Islamic State remained in the fight, acknowledging that a 500-million-dollar program to raise an army of Syrian fighters had gone nowhere[3].

Under cover of a war on terrorism and jihadism, the air raids by the United States and France, and interventions by the Gulf States (Saudi Arabia, Qatar, Bahrain, United Arab Emirates), Israel, and Jordan, are inevitably going to spill over and force a regime change in Damascus, exactly as happened with Saddam Hussein's Iraq and Muammar Gaddafi's Libya. Russia has stepped up its aid to Syria over the past few month to bolster the position of president Bashar al-Assad forces against Islamists rebels. The bombing of targets in Homs and Alepo by Russian air forces was approved by the Russian parliament after president Assad approval. The only alternative to the Caliphate, as Brasilia too sees it, is the Assad government. Without it, we will have another Iraq, Yemen, Libya...with the same results: the emergence of extremists vying for power, the country's institutions in tatters, and further horrific suffering of the civilian population, half now displaced or forced into perilous exile (more than 4 million Syrians now live in exile, half of them taking refuge in Lebanon and

---

[1] Karen Yourish, Rebecca Lai, Derek Watkins, "Death in Syria", *International New York Times*, September 14, 2015.

[2] Matthew Rosenberg, "U.S. Trains Syrian Rebels in Jordan to Fight ISIS", *International New York Times*, May 7, 2015.

[3] Helen Cooper, "U.S. Says Rebel It Trained Surrendered Materiel in Syria", *International New York Times*, September 25, 2015.

Turkey, less than 10% in the European Union in 2015, sparking xenophobic, and especially Islamophobic, reactions in many European countries). Approximately one fifth of the Syrian refugees are children or adolescents under the age of 17[1]. The Gulf States financing armed opposition to the Assad regime have not, as of September 30, 2015, taken in a single refugee from Syria[2]. As of September 1, 2015, the United States – which takes in an average of 70.000 refugees every year and plans to raise this number to 85.000 in 2015 and to 100.000 in 2016 – has only accepted 1.800 Syrian refugees, justifying this on the basis of the risk that there may be jihadi terrorists among them[3]. Canada and Australia are no more generous, with 1.074 and 2.200 Syrian refugees, respectively, as of August 31, 2015. Australian Prime Minister Tony Abott stated that only "*persecuted minorities*" would be accepted, an allusion to the Christian minorities, whereas other asylum seekers of the Muslim faith (particularly *rohingas* from Myanmar and *bengalis*) are considered to be economic migrants with thousands confined to prison camps on the islands of Manus and Nauru. In Australia, the institution looking after refugees has been somehow militarized. Peter Dutton, the minister for Immigration and Border Protection is a former police officer; Michael Pezzulo, the Secretary of the Department of Immigration and Border Protection comes from the Department of Defence; the Australian Border Force Commissioner, Roman Quaedvlieg, was the Chief Police Officer of Australian Federal Police. In October 2, 2015 the government secretly flied a pregnant Somalian refugee out of Australia to escape a court injunction[4]. As regards European Union policy (Dublin Regulation), applications by asylum seekers (with fingerprints) are registered in the first country of contact. In other words, southern European countries find themselves coping with massive inflows of refugees to islands of Lampedusa (Italy) and Lesbos (Greece) and forced to improvise a quota policy (Slovakia, Hungary, Romania, and the Czech Republic are not signatories to the EU policy agreement) regarding some 120,000 refugees, less than one fourth of the refugees recorded in 2015[5].

The United States is the principal donor to the support program for Syrian refugees (3RP Regional Refugee and Resilience Plan), providing close to 40% of funds collected as of August 31 by the office of the United Nations High

[1] "Syria Situation 2015", UNHCR.

[2] With the exception of Yemen, no Gulf State has signed the UN Convention relating to the status of Refugees (1951) or the additional "Bellagio" Protocol (1967), signed as of April 30, 2015 by 142 countries, including Brazil.

[3] David Herszenhorn, "Many Obstacles Are Seen to U.S. Taking in Large Number of Syrian Refugees", *International New York Times,* September 4, 2015.

[4] Ben Doherty, "Australia secretly flies pregnant refugee out of country before hearing", *The Guardian,* October 16, 2015.

[5] 477.906 refugees recorded as of September 15, 2015 (216.054 in 2014), three quarters of them from Syria.

Commissioner for Refugees[1]. However, as of that date, only 41% of the funds budgeted for 2015 have been received, placing the UNHCR in a very tense budgetary situation with regard to actual needs.

There are some 3 million people of Syro-Lebanese descent in Brazil, most of them Christians, who view President Bashar al-Assad as the protector of Christians in Syria. The Syrian president met with representatives of this community in São Paulo during his official visit to Brazil in June 2010. Brazilian diplomacy is inspired by prudence. It believes that the Syrian leader and the Alawite clan to which he belongs must be integrated into future political system rather than excluded. The preservation of the principal Syrian institutions (army, courts, administration) must be a priority objective in order to prevent the institutional collapse observed in Iraq and Libya. Assad´s crime is not that he is a dictator and a ferocious repressor of any form of opposition to his regime (for that matter, not unlike the West´s close regional allies on the Arabian peninsula, the Saudis and the Gulf monarchies), the problem with the Assad regime in Syria is that it has long been a bastion of resistance against U.S. hegemonic designs on the region dating back to the invasion of Iraq.

The Syrian conflict has been particularly disastrous for Palestinian refugees. According to the Commissioner General of the United Nations Relief and Works Agency for Palestinian Refugees in the Near East (UNRWA), Pierre Krähenbühl, 80% of the 580.000 Palestinian refugees in the 13 Syrian camps have been forced to move. He says that the Yarmouk refugee camp, which provided a home to 150.000 Palestinian refugees before the outbreak of war (18.000 today), has become "*an apocalyptic city scape, where women have died in childbirth for lack of medicines and children have reportedly starved*[2]".

As in Iraq and Libya, military intervention will put an end to secular administrations that are tolerant and respectful of religious diversity, where the quality of healthcare and schools, and the level of emancipation of women are much better than what we see in the regimes installed by the United States to succeed them. Saddam Hussein's Vice President and Minister of Foreign Affairs, Tariq Aziz, was a Christian. One of the spiritual guides of Ba'athism in the 1940s, which extended during the following decade into Jordan, Lebanon, and Iraq, and that counted among its devotees Saddam Hussein and Hafez al-Hassad, was a Syrian Christian, educated at the University of Paris, Michel Aflaq. He served as Minister of Education in Syria in 1950. He spent a brief period of exile in Brazil (1966-1968). His mausoleum in Baghdad was desecrated by American troops and converted into a supermarket.

The spiritual leader of the Greek Orthodox Church of Antioch and All the East lived in Damascus. Patriarch Ignatius IV (Hazim) (1920-2012) and his successor, John X (Yazigi), were both born in Syria. Many early Catholic popes

---

[1] As of August 31, 2015, the principal donors are: United States (160 million dollars), Sweden (80), United Kingdom (53), Netherlands (45), Norway (44), Denmark (28), and Australia (24), *Syria Situation 2015. 3RP Regional Refugee and Resilience Plan*, UNHCR.

[2] "In Need of Aid But Hungry For Peace", UNRWA, March 30, 2015.

were born in Syria (Anicetus, John V, Sisinnius, Costantine, Gregory III). While the Syrian Constitution dictates that the president must be Muslim, 10% of the population were Christians, most of them orthodox, who were well integrated into Syrian society. Their peaceful coexistence with the Muslim community was a point of reference. Anxious to maintain harmonious relations, they did not engage in proselytism nor did they accept converts from Islam. They often made their careers in the army. They are now victims, like many other minorities (Druze, Kurd, Armenian...) of ethnic and religious rivalries exacerbated by a brutal civil war. A number of bishops were kidnapped in Aleppo in April 2013; the Franciscan father, François Murad of the Custody of the Holy Land, was killed in the convent of Ghassanyah in June 2013. There are practically no more Christians in the city of Homs, which had a Christian community of more than 160.000 before the war. The religious leader of the Druze, Sheikh Wahid al-Balous, was killed in an attack with 27 of his followers in September 2015 in As-Suwayda. The Druze make up 5% of the Syrian population.

Although it was invited, Brazil did not take part in the international forum on Syria in Montreux in January 2014. It was a multilateral forum with invitations going to 34 countries, the kind of format favored by Brazilian diplomacy. In a private conversation, Celso Amorim characterized it as "*an incomprehensible absence*"[1].

On request from Damascus after President Lula's visit in December 2003, Brazil has played a role as mediator between Syria and Israel, particularly in working toward a peace pact between the two countries and the return of the Golan Heights to Syria[2]. On December 3, 2003, Brazil voted in favor of Resolution 58/23 of the General Assembly of the United Nations, returning the Golan Heights to Syria.

In the Kobani (Ayn al-Arab) enclave in northern Syria, the Kurdish People's Protection Units (Yekîneyên Parastina Gel – YPG), the Syrian branch of the Kurdistan Workers' Party (Partiya Karkerên Kurdistanê – PKK), which the United States considers a terrorist organization, have held their own against the Caliphate. Brasilia sees the Kurdish question as now one of the major components of the confusion, raising genuine concerns, shared by Tehran, because of the interference of the United States and Israel in the attempts to establish an independent Kurdish state in northern Iraq having control of Iraq's principal oil resources but characterized by profound internal rivalries, particularly vis-à-vis Turkey. It was Ankara's repression of the Kurdish rebels in the 1990s that put Turkey at the top of the list of arms buyers from the United States, which accounted for 80% of its military equipment. The importance gained by the Kurdish armed forces in the fight against the Islamic State is a further source of concern for Ankara. Turkey seems more focused on targeting

---

[1] July 3, 2015, Rio de Janeiro.

[2] Amorim Celso, *Teerã, Ramalá e Doha, memórias da política externa ativa e altiva*, Benvirá, ed. Saraiva, São Paulo, 2015.

the Kurds than it is on targeting ISIL. Longstanding tensions with Turkey´s Kurdish population have broken out into open war. Some 32 leftist Kurdish activists were killed in July 20, 2015 in the border town of Suruc and on October 10 a peace demonstration in Ankara organized by the Kurdish-led leftist People´s Democratic Party (HDP) was bombed, allegedly by Islamists, killing more than 100 people and wounding hundreds more.

Egypt

Destabilized by the supporters of the former regime, as witnessed by the dissolution of an elected Parliament in 2012 where his Freedom and Justice party along with the ultra-conservative islamist Al Nour party had won a majority of seats, and by hostile media campaigns, President Mohamed Morsi was confronted by enormous street protests erupting across Egypt on June 30, 2013 calling for his resignation. The military stepped in three days later to remove him from office.

Following the coup d'état, the pro-Morsi protestors, who quite legitimately decried the flagrant violation of law, were the victims of savage repression (more than 1,000 dead in Nahda and Ramses squares and at the Rabaa al-Adawiyya and Fatah mosques, the great majority killed by bullets on August 14, 15 and 16, 2013[1], many of them adolescents, such as Asmaa, the daughter of the islamist leader, Mohamed el-Beltagy, and several journalists Michael Deane of *Sky News*, Habiba Ahmed Abd Elaziz of *Gulf News*, Ahmed Abdel Gawad of *Al-Akhbar*, Mosab El-Shami of *Rassd News Network*[2], not to mention the murders of 38 islamist leaders on August 20 as they were being transferred to the Abu Zaabal prison). Female demonstrators were forced to submit, by order of the general who had seized power, to humiliating tests of virginity. A witch hunt was organized against all the leaders of the movement, who were brought before military tribunals. The great majority of the 25 provincial governors were replaced by generals allied with the former dictator, Hosni Mubarak (1981-2011).

More than 65 journalists were arrested. This did not stop Germany, acting on a request by Egyptian authorities, from arresting *Al-Jazeera* journalist Ahmed Mansour on June 20 in Berlin. The authorities claimed that he had been sentenced in abstentia in 2014 to 15 years in prison for having "*tortured an Egyptian lawyer in Tahrir Square*"[3]. The Egyptian president had just made an

---

1. "Military Madness", editorial, *International Herald Tribune*, August 16, 2013.

2 "All According to Plan. The Rabá Massacre and Mass Killings of Protesters in Egypt", Human Rights Watch Report, August 12, 2014.

3 Melissa Eddy, David Kirkpatrick, "Al Jazeera Journalist Held in Germany Awaits Verdict on Egyptian Arrest Warrant", *International New York Times*, June 21, 2015.

official visit to Germany, during which the Siemens Group announced the signing of an equipment contract worth 8 billion dollars[1].

More than 20,000 people were imprisoned. President Mohamed Morsi, held in total isolation since his arrest on July 4, 2013, appeared before the Criminal Court of Cairo in January 2014, where he was held in a soundproof glass cage[2]. The court handed down a death sentence for Morsi and 122 members of the Muslim Brotherhood, many of them in abstentia, including one of the spiritual leaders of the movement, Sheikh Yusuf al-Qaradawi, president of the International Union of Muslim Scholars, a prolific and well respected author among the Muslim world, who had been living in exile in Qatar for 30 years before returning to Egypt after the fall of Mubarak in 2011. Moderate and respected leaders such as Ahmed Maher, Mohammed Abdel, and Emad Shahin were imprisoned and sentenced to death. Young protesters were killed, such as 32-year-old Shaima al-Sabbagh as she went to place a wreath of flowers in Tahrir Square, or abducted and detained. Secretary of State John Kerry incautiously declared during a visit to Pakistan in 2013 that the Egyptian army was "*restoring democracy in Egypt*"[3].

The government is now led by a 79-year-old Prime Minister, Hazem al-Beblawi, the former finance minister of the caretaker government, which is dominated by the military since Mubarak's resignation. He resigned in October 2011 to protest the killing of 27 Christian demonstrators by the army, an episode known as the Maspero Massacre. The Vice President, Mohammad ElBaradei, Nobel Peace Prize Laureate, resigned from the caretaker government set up after the coup d'état and chose exile to dissociate himself from the repression that had not spared journalists from the United States (Mick Deane of *Sky News*), Dubai (Habiba Ahmed Abd Elaziz of *X-Press*), and Qatar (Peter Greste, Mohamed Fadel Fahmy, and Baher Mohamed of *Al-Jazeera*, who was sentenced in August 2015 to 3 years in prison on the basis of unjust criteria). According to a prison census conducted by the New York-based Committee to Protect Journalists on June 1, 2015, Egypt was holding a record 18 journalists behind bars.

Saudi Arabia and the United Arab Emirates have pledged 8 billion dollars and Kuwait 4 billion dollars for the new government[4]. This prize for the coup from conservative monarchies that threatened the "Arab Spring" (the Morsi government benefited from financial aid from Qatar, Turkey, and the European Union) and the reluctance of the United States and its allies to take any retaliatory action are an eloquent testimony to the meagerness of hopes for

---

[1] He was freed several days later. See Ben Knight, "Germany frees Egyptian journalist Ahmed Mansour", *The Guardian*, June 22, 2015.

[2] "Egypt court controls voice of Morsi with a glass cage", *International New York Times*, January 29, 2014.

[3] Michael Gordon, Kareem Fahim, "Kerry Says Egypt's Military Was 'Restoring Democracy' in Ousting Morsi", *International New York Times*, August 1, 2013.

[4]. Robert Worth, "Monarchies in Gulf to write giant check for Egypt", *International Herald Tribune*, July 11, 2013.

democratization in Egyptian politics. Three months after the coup, President Obama announced that the United States would recalibrate its military aid, suspending, in particular, the delivery of heavy equipment (planes, helicopters, tanks). However, on his visit to Cairo on June 22, 2014, John Kerry provided reassurance to the Egyptians. A large portion of American aid goes to financing weapons purchases from major U.S. corporations (e.g. General Dynamics, Lockheed Martin). The European Union pledged 90 million dollars in financial aid to the new regime and the High Representative of the European Union for Foreign Affairs and Security Policy, Catherine Ashton, showed incredible poor taste by spending her 2013 Christmas vacation with her family in Luxor while repression was rampant throughout the country.

It was after an official visit to Paris in November 2014 by the new Egyptian president, installed after Morsi's ouster and a sham election, that France announced, in February 2015, its premier trade agreement, worth 5 billion euros, involving the sale of Dassault Rafale fighter aircraft, the exact models that Brazil had declined in favor of the Swedish company Saab[1]. The announcement was blazoned on official communiqués, echoing a similar enthusiasm expressed when a deal was made with Libyan leader Muammar Gaddafi after his visit to Paris in December 2007 for 14 Rafale planes, a deal that ultimately came to nothing. It should be noted that the Egyptian Air Force already had 220 American F-16 fighter aircraft and that Egypt is only able to remain afloat economically thanks to financing from Saudi Arabia and the United Arab Emirates. Sweden, the world's 11th arms exporter, suspended its sales to Saudi Arabia in March 2015, citing the country's failure to respect human rights after the female Swedish Minister of Foreign Affairs, Margot Wallsröm, was forbidden from speaking at the meeting of the Ministers of Foreign Affairs of the Arab League, to which she had been invited by the Secretary General, Nabil el-Araby. In September 2015, French President François Hollande announced the sale to Egypt of the two Mistral-class landing ships originally built for the Russian navy but their sale canceled in September 2014 because Russia´s involvement in Ukraine and mounting pressure from NATO to call off the sale[2].

The military coup, the incarceration of thousands of sympathizers of the Muslim Brotherhood, including the former president elect, Mohamed Morsi, who was warmly received in Brasilia in May 2013, did not prevent the Conference of Investors from responding to an invitation by the Egyptian president, Marshal Abdel Fattah Al-Sissi, to a meeting in Sharm el-Sheikh in March 2015 with 22 heads of state. The meeting concluded with the signing of

---

1. Dominique Gallois, "La vente du Rafale au Caire bouclée en un temps record" (Sale of Rafales to Cairo secured in record time), *Le Monde*, February 14, 2015.

2 Frane refunded Russia 1 billion dollar for the cancellation.

contracts announced as being worth a total of 34 billion euros[1]. Brazil was represented by a second-tier diplomat sent by Itamaraty.

Working with the World Food Programme and by request of Egyptian authorities, Brazil studied ways to implement a cooperation project involving school meals after representatives of a similar program in Brazil (*Programa Nacional de Alimentacão Escolar*) had completed their mission to Cairo in March 2015.

Brasilia is opposed to outlawing the Muslim Brotherhood, which it considers to be a moderate group that has been excluded for too long from Egyptian politics. It is now subject to repression even though its charity work, hospitals and social programs have done much over the years to improve the social climate in Egypt.

The strongman behind the putsch, General Abdul Fattah al-Sissi, appointed Minister of Defense by President Morsi in 2012, got his education at the Army War College in Pennsylvania. He is a member of a privileged and wealthy caste, rubbing shoulders with the powerful for over sixty years. He now commands an army of 450.000 men with a budget that is no longer under Parliamentary control and administers 40% of the country's economy. Each year, 500 Egyptian officers receive training in the United States. However the benefits are by no means evenly distributed: despite American aid estimated at 50 billion dollars since 1979, one fourth of the Egyptian population is illiterate[2].

This situation is unacceptable to Brasilia, and to virtually all the South American governments, traumatized after long years of oppression and repression by military coups carried out by former pupils of the U.S. Army School of the Americas (now the Western Hemisphere Institute for Security Cooperation). Originally operating in Fort Gullick, Panama, in 1984 it was expelled and is now located near Columbus, Georgia in the United States. It provides training for high-level military officers.

Venezuela, which experienced an attempted coup in 2002, withdrew its ambassador from Cairo as a gesture of protest and said that it would submit a motion to the United Nations on behalf of the Bolivarian Alliance for the Peoples of Our America (ALBA) against the repression exercised by the Egyptian army. But the ALBA countries did not sign the joint declaration issued on March 7, 2014 before the United Nations Human Rights Council United by 27 countries, including 24 EU member states, the United States, Japan, and Turkey, expressing concern regarding the extent of repression, an initiative that Brasilia viewed as being "*hypocritical*".

According to our contacts in Itamaraty, of greater concern are the lessons that will be drawn from the Egyptian impasse by the islamist groups which were ready to accept democratic rule and those that are dedicated to armed struggle. The car bomb that killed the Prosecutor General of Egypt, Hisham

---

1. Hélène Sallon, "Le monde investit en masse dans l'Égypte de Sissi" (The world invests en-masse in Sissi's Egypt), *Le Monde*, March 17, 2015.

2. Thomas Friedman, "Tell me how this ends well", *The New York Times*, April 20, 2015.

Barakat, who issued the death sentence against Morsi and the main leaders of the Muslim Brotherhood in sham trials[1], and the resurgence of attacks in the northern Sinai illustrate the perils to Egypt of the repression wrought by Abdul Fatta al-Sissi, who declared his willingness in June 2015, given the absence of a Parliament since 2012, to rework the legal code by means of decree-laws in order to "*accelerate the pace of executions*"[2]. The aberrant alliance with the army discredits liberalism and secularism in the Arab world. The people will discover at their own expense that it will only serve to reintroduce the same neo-liberal politics and put the same elite back in power, and the supporters of the Muslim Brotherhood who do not choose exile and manage to avoid incarceration will become radicalized and presented to us in the mainstream press as "*terrorists*".

Israel and Palestine

In the sole month of November 2009, Brasilia received a succession of presidents: Shimon Peres of Israel, Mahmoud Abbas of the Palestinian National Authority, and Mahmoud Ahmadinejad of Iran. President Lula traveled to Israel, the West Bank, and Jordan in March 2010. In April 2010, the president of Lebanon, Michel Suleiman, was welcomed in Brasilia.

Israel was not on the itinerary of Lula's first visit to the Middle East in 2003 (Syria, Lebanon, United Arab Emirates, Egypt and Libya). Israel did not want to appear anxious to prevent the Brazilian president from visiting Arafat in Ramallah in return for the Palestinian leader's visit to Brasilia in 1998. Lula's speech in Damascus in December in favor of a return of the Golan Heights to Syria had irritated the Israeli Foreign Ministry. Aluf Ben, political reporter for *Haaretz*, observed: "*Actually, Israel cares little about what Brazil thinks, it is hardly one of our priorities*"[3].

During Lula's official visit to Egypt in December 2003, Nabil Shaath, chief negotiator for the Palestinian National Authority, had urged that a Brazilian diplomatic mission be opened in Ramallah (it was inaugurated in 2004) and that a special envoy be appointed for the region. This post went to the diplomat Affonso Celso de Ouro-Preto, Celso Amorim's chief of staff while he was the Minister of External Relations in the government of Itamar Franco (1992-1994). In 2005, Brazil organized a mission to observe the Palestinian elections. A Palestinian technical mission visited Brasilia in 2008 to study the Brazilian electronic voting system. The following year a technical cooperation agreement was signed between Brazil and Palestine.

---

[1] According to Mohamed Elmessiny, who monitored the trial for Amnesty International, the defense was not authorized to argue its case, witnesses were not heard, and some of the defendants were tried in abstentia. See Patrick Kingsley, "Egyptian Judge Sentences 720 Men to Death", *The Guardian*, April 28, 2014.

[2] Patrick Kingsley, "Egyptian president to change Law to allow faster executions", *The Guardian*, June 30, 2015.

[3] *BBC Brazil*, December 4, 2003.

The Palestinian question commands a certain consensus within the BRICS group. The Palestinian Minister of Foreign Affairs, Riad Malki, was invited to the BRICS summit in Brasilia in March 2010. The BRICS countries voted during the 65th session of the General Assembly in favor of Resolution 272 to strengthen the United Nations Relief and Works Agency for Palestinian Refugees in the Near East (UNRWA). The resolution passed 123 votes to one (Israel). The BRICS unanimously supported the membership of Palestine in the United Nations and UNESCO. In her speech before the General Assembly in 2011, President Dilma Rousseff expressed her "*regrets at not being able to welcome Palestine, from this rostrum, as a full member in the United Nations*"[1].

Brazil, Argentina, Bolivia, Guyana, Peru, Ecuador, Chile, Suriname, and Uruguay all recognized the Palestinian state between December 2010 and March 2011 within the 1967 borders. With the sole exception of Colombia, all Latin American countries have recognized Palestine. Cuba, Nicaragua, and Costa Rica recognized it in 1988; Venezuela in 2009. As of May 15, 2015, 135 countries have recognized Palestine. Brazil recognized the Palestine Liberation Authority in 1979, the second country in Latin America after Mexico (1975). Chile was the first Latin American country (Cuba aside) to open an embassy in Ramallah (2002), followed by Brazil in 2004. Mahmud Abbas was invited to Brasilia in May 2005 to take part in the first Summit of South American-Arab Countries. He visited five countries in the region in November 2009 (Brazil, Chile, Argentina, Paraguay, Venezuela). Brazil recognized the Palestinian state within the 1967 borders after President Lula's visit to Ramallah on December 3, 2010, leading the way for Argentina (December 6) and 11 other Latin American countries. The president of the Palestinian National Authority, Mahmoud Abbas, was present at the presidential inauguration of Dilma Rousseff in Brasilia on January 1, 2010. On that occasion, he symbolically laid the first stone of the Palestinian embassy. Bolivia and Venezuela broke off diplomatic relations with Israel in January 2009 in protest over the invasion of Gaza. But, unlike Venezuela, Bolivia, and Nicaragua, Brasilia is allegedly trying to observe a balanced policy.

Under the government of General Ernesto Geisel (1974-1979), Brazil came out in favor of Resolution 3379 of the General Assembly of the United Nations, adopted on November 10, 1975[2], considering Zionism to be "*a form of racism and discrimination*", sponsored by Muslim countries and Cuba. Oil certainly must have figured into this choice. Geisel had served as president of Petrobras and Brazil was seeking to forge closer ties with Arab countries after the oil crisis of 1973 and to reframe its relations with the United States. Geisel

---

1. "*Lamentar não poder saudar desta tribuna, o ingresso pleno da Palestina no Organização das Naciones Unidas*", in Luiza Maria Barroso de Aguiar, *Posição dos Brics diante da questão da Palestina*, BRICS Policy Center, January 2012.

2 It was revoked in December 1991 (Resolution 46/86 sponsored by 90 countries including Brazil).

defended his choice as a personal conviction[1], as reiterated by his Minister of Foreign Affairs, Azeredo da Silveira, in his memoirs[2]. In December 1991, during Fernando Collor de Mello's presidency, Brazil co-sponsored Resolution 46/86, repealing Resolution 3379.

During his official visit to Israel, President Lula refused to bow before the tomb of Theodor Herzl, champion of modern political Zionism, during a ceremony that had not been part of the official program. Celso Amorim explained that it would have been particularly inopportune to do so, given that the Israeli colonies were growing at the expense of Palestinian interests[3]. In a gesture of ill humor, the Israeli Minister of Foreign Affairs, Avigdor Lieberman, boycotted the official dinner offered by President Shimon Peres.

Israel's role as a purveyor of munitions to the military dictatorships (Argentina 1976-1978; Chile, 1974-1978; Guatemala, 1977; Nicaragua, 1979; Honduras, 1980-1985) and its voting in lockstep with Washington against the progressive forces in Latin America and the rule of law have certainly contributed to a certain coldness of the Latin American countries toward Israel.

Three successive military regimes in Guatemala and sweeping campaigns against indigenous Indians (with an estimated 40 000 Guatemalan Indians killed since 1978) had the benefit of Israeli techniques, experiences and hardware. By 1982, nine of the 17 Aravat Aircraft delivered by Israel had been mounted with gun pods. The Galil became Guatemala´s standard rifle. In late 1984, Galil rifle were manufactured in Guatemala under licence. Honduras was one of Israel´s first arms customers in Central America. Between 1975 and 1977, this poorest country in the region after Belize bought 20 French used super-Mystère fighter planes from Israel, some equipped with Israel-made Shafrir heat seeking missiles. "*I owe to Israel my essence, my human and military achievements*", said Colombian indicted drug dealer Carlos Castano (1965-2004), the former leader of the largest right-wing paramilitary force in South America (Autodefesas Unidas Colombia- AUC), trained in the 1980´s in Israel, in his ghost written autobiography[4].

The entry of the Israeli army into Lebanon on June 6, 1982 (causing the deaths of 20.000 Palestinians and Lebanese), the brutal invasion of the Gaza

---

[1] "*I am still convinced that Zionism is a form of racism. I am not an enemy of the Jews as regards their religion; I am very tolerant… But Judaism is transmitted along the maternal line. That's not racism? Is that not how race is transmitted? Why can I not say this out loud to the world? How is it reprehensible?..*" in Norma Breda Dos Santos, (ed.) *Brasil e Israel : diplomacia e sociedades*, Universidade de Brasilia-EdUnB, 2000, ("*Estou convencido atè hoje de que o sionismo é racista. Não sou inimigo dos judeus, inclusive porque em matéria religiosa sou muito tolerante...O judaismo se transmeite pela mãe.O que é isso? Não é racismo? Não é uma raça que assim se perpetua?*")

[2] Matias Spektor (ed.), *Azeredo da Silveira. Um Depoimento* (*Azeredo da Silveira: testimony*), Fundação Getulio Vargas, Rio de Janeiro, 2010.

[3] Celso Amorim, "O Brasil e o Oriente Medio" (p. 272), in "*Teerã, Ramalá e Doha, memória as política externa ativa e altiva*", Editora Saraiva, São Paulo, 2015.

[4] Molina Aranguren Mauricio, "*Mi Confesión. Carlos Castaño revela sus secretos*", Editorial La Oveja Negra, Bogotá, 2001.

Strip on January 3, 2009 (17 Israeli casualties, 1.400 Palestinian casualties, including 400 children) and new offensives in 2012 and 2014 have only exacerbated these reservations. When Evo Morales broke off diplomatic relations with Israel, he publicly demanded that the Israeli Prime Minister, Ehud Olmert, be summoned before the International Criminal Court and that Shimon Peres return the Nobel Peace Prize he won in 1994.

On December 16, 2011, Brazil sent 8.5 million dollars to Ramallah via the United Nations Development Program (UNDP) for reconstruction in the Gaza Strip. With its BRICS partners, it financed a sports center in Ramallah, but was not able to implement a project to build a hospital in Gaza because of opposition from Israel, in spite of the fact that Celso Amorim went to speak personally, but in vain, with the Israeli Prime Minister, Benjamin Netanyahu[1]. Brazil is among the 10 largest sources of aid to Palestine (Gaza and the West Bank). Its contribution, estimated at 25 million dollars over the next five years, nevertheless represents a very small percentage (less than 1%) of total international aid to Palestine. In 2007, some one hundred Palestinian refugees from Jordan were received in Brazil. Brazil's artistic community has taken up the cause of Palestine. After her 2009 documentary (*Budrus*) on the construction of the Israeli West Bank barrier and the coalition between Palestinians and progressive Israelis, the filmmaker Julia Bacha produced a short film titled *My Neighborhood* on the Israeli pacifist resistance movements, presented at the Tribeca Festival in New York in April 2012.

Ray Dolphin, Representative in the occupied Palestinian territories for the United Nations Office for the Coordination of Humanitarian Affairs (OCHA), painted a distressing picture of the situation in the West Bank and the Gaza Strip in June 2008. He reported that 50% of the population in the West Bank and 80% in the Gaza Strip lived below the poverty threshold; 29% of the population in the occupied territories was unemployed (35% in Gaza). And the situation is only getting worse: in 2010, the unemployment rate in Gaza was over 45%[2]. A growing number of Palestinians depend on aid: 75% of the population of Gaza after the Israeli military operations and air raids in August 2014. Studies conducted by OCHA bring out the fact that the problems are generated both from the expansion of colonies and their access routes and by the construction of the security wall around a portion of the occupied territories. The repercussions on agriculture and water supply are very negative, and the sealing off of Gaza since June 2007 and repeated air raids by the Israeli Air Force have almost completely destroyed its industrial and manufacturing base. The *per capita* GDP in Gaza is less than 2,000 dollars; in Israel it is over 38,000 dollars.

All visitors (restrained by Israel to journalists and NGO members) who spend time in the Gaza Strip come back shocked and appalled at the stark and

---

[1]. Celso Amorim, "Brazil and the Middle-East", *The Cairo Review of Global Affairs*, May 14, 2012.
[2]. "United Nations Relief and Work Agency", *International Herald Tribune*, June 15, 2011.

unconscionable contrast between the wealth of Israeli society and the Palestinians' lack of even the most elementary infrastructure or the liberty to circulate freely in their own territory, where they are subject to continuing and humiliating Israeli checks and inspections, whereas on roads reserved exclusively for Israeli settlers, circulation is unfettered. Chief of Staff of the Israeli Defense Forces in 2002, Moshe Ya'alon publicly stated that "*the Palestinians must be made to understand in the deepest recesses of their consciousness that they are a defeated people*". According to the United Nations Children's Fund (UNICEF), there are more than 1,500 orphans now in Gaza.

The young journalist Anat Kamm was arrested in April 2010 for having published documents regarding the premeditated murder of Palestinian militants by the Israeli armed forces[1]. Young American Jewish pacifists were killed or crippled for life by Israeli soldiers only slightly older than them for having taken part in demonstrations against the Israeli occupation (Rachel Corrie in March 2003 in Rafah; Tristan Anderson in March 2009 in Nilin; Emily Henochowicz in May 2010 in Qualandia; Furkan Doğan on board the Mavi Marmara in May 2010). None of the lawsuits presented by the families of the victims to the Israeli courts have been successful.

In July 2011, according to Israeli data[2], some 5.300 Palestinians were in Israeli prisons. Since the occupation of 1967, the number of Palestinians jailed in Israeli prisons was estimated at 750.000 by Richard Falk, United Nations Special Rapporteur on the Palestinian territories, close to 40% of the Palestinian males in Gaza and the West Bank[3]. During the six years of his mission, Falk never received authorization from Israel to enter the Palestinian territories; he was arrested on December 14, 2008 upon his arrival in Tel Aviv and expelled from the country.

Israeli law allows incarceration for six months without charges, and this prison term may be renewed indefinitely, with no formal accusation or conviction. This prolonged detention in Israeli prisons has led many Palestinians to take desperate measures (suicide, hunger strikes). Two Palestinian detainees (Khader Adnan and Mohammed Allan) were released in 2015 after a hunger strike lasting more than 55 days. But Mohammad Allan was arrested again several weeks later when he was discharged from the hospital where he had been convalescing[4].

Leonid Eidelman, president of the Israeli Medical Association, asked membership not to participate in the force-feeding of prisoners, which had been approved by the Knesset in July 2015. Some one hundred Palestinian

[1] Rashid Khalidi, *International Herald Tribune*, January 9, 2009.

[2] Israeli Prison Services, cited in *The Nation*, September 22, 2011.

[3] Richard Falk, "Report of the Special Rapporteur on the Situation of Human Rights in the Palestinian Territories Occupied since 1967", 2014.

[4] "Israel puts Palestinian back in custody after hunger strike", *International New York Times*, September 17, 2015.

detainees are currently on a hunger strike to protest the administrative procedure that allows their indefinite imprisonment without a sentence.

Throwing stones at the Israeli armed forces can now get you 20 years in prison[1]. The bill was introduced to the Knesset by deputy Nissan Slomiansky of the right-wing Zionist party "Jewish Home", which is also the party of the former Justice Minister, Rabbi Eli Ben-Dahan, who qualified stone throwing as an "*act of terrorism*"[2]. Between 500 and 700 Palestinian minors are detained each year in Israeli jails, 93% of them for stone throwing according to the Israeli NGO B´Tselem[3]. Some 8.000 minors have been sentenced by Israeli military courts and jailed between the year 2000 and August 1, 2015, 22% of them in solitary confinement[4]. In July 2014, B´Tselem reported – with videos to back them up – the arrest of a 5-year-old Palestinian by Israeli soldiers for stone throwing; in October 2014 the arrest of a deaf-mute and developmentally-disabled 12-year-old to the jeers and insults of Israelis from the nearby Kyriat Arba settlement[5]. UNICEF issued a disturbing report on the methods of arrest and detention of Palestinian children, which concludes: "*Ill-treatment of Palestinian children in the Israeli military detention system appears to be widespread, systematic and institutionalized*"[6]. And to this we must add the high number of Palestinian adolescents summarily killed for stone throwing by Israeli soldiers and officers and recorded on the B´Tselem website[7].

Humanitarian organizations record 40 Palestinian adolescents killed in 2014 by the Israeli army for stone throwing[8]. The most recent, on July 2, 2015, Muhammad Hani al-Kasba, age 17, was killed near the Qalandia refugee camp by Colonel Yisrael Shomer, just like his two brothers, Yaser and Samer, 12 and 16, respectively who were killed in 2001[9].

In April 2012, Israel prevented 1.200 pacifist activists from reaching the West Bank as part of a solidarity initiative to finance an international school in

---

[1] Kate Shuttleworth, "Palestinian stone throwers could face 20 years in jail", *The Guardian*, November 4, 2014 / Robert Tait, "Israel introduces controversial 20-year jail sentences for stonethrowing", *The Telegraph*, January 22, 2015.

[2] Ezra Hezki, "Knesset Approves Harsher Punishments for Rock Throwing", *Arutz Sheva, Israelnationalnews.com*, July 21, 2015.

[3] Harriet Sherwood, "The Palestinian children – alone and bewildered – in Israel´s Al-Jalame Jail. Special report: Israel´s military justice system is accused of mistreating Palestinian children arrested for throwing stones", *The Guardian*, January 22, 2012.

[4] Olivia Becker, "Israel Is Holding Even More Palestinian Children In Solitary For Throwing Rocks", *news.vice.com*, May 15, 2014.

[5] "Soldiers detain developmentally-disabled child", Hebron, October 19, 2014, B´Tselem, press release, October 20, 2014.

[6] "Children in Israeli military Detention", UNICEF, February 2013 (www.unicef.org)

[7] Muhammad Quadus (15 years old) and Usayed Quadus (17 years old) on March 20, 2010 in Iraq Burin near Nablus; Samir Awad (16 years old) on January 15, 2013 in Budrus; Nadim Nawarah (17 years old), Muhammad Salameh (16 years old) in Bitunya on May 15, 2014; Iman Jamil Dweikat (17 years old) near Nablus on December 28, 2014, and the list goes on.

[8] Isabel Kershner, "Israeli Military Kills Palestinian Teenager in West Bank", *International New York Times*, December 29, 2014.

[9] Alison Deger, "Palestinian teen killed on way to pray in Jerusalem", *Mondoweiss*, July 3, 2015.

the city of Bethlehem. Dozens of these activists, including Israeli pacifists, were detained by the police. The Israeli Minister of Defense, Moshe Ya'alon, stated that the 43 Israeli military intelligence reservists who refused to adopt the methods used by Israel against the Palestinians would be "*treated as criminals*"[1]. This situation underscores – especially after the dramatic boarding of the peaceful Turkish ship Mavi Marmara in May 2010 by the Israeli Navy in international waters – Israel's determination to keep this humiliated, downtrodden people in a permanent state of isolation, of quarantine.

On December 20, 2010 during a ceremony honoring the Brazilian armed forces, President Lula stressed that as long as the United States exercised "tutelage" over the Middle East peace process, it would remain at an impasse and that the only solution was to extend negotiations to all relevant parties in the region (Iran, Syria, Hamas, Palestinian National Authority...): "*Peace in the Middle East is not the exclusive purview of America*", he stated.

Noam Chomsky stated his opinion in February 2012 that "*serious negotiations would have to be under the auspices of some neutral party, preferably one that commands some international respect, perhaps Brazil*"[2].

The United States cannot be both judge and plaintiff, as illustrated eloquently by the American veto to the UN Security Council resolution condemning the extension of Israeli settlements – 5.000 Israeli settlers in 1981, 650.000 today – when this veto went against America's official position.

The influence of the pro-Israel lobbies in the United States (American Israel Public Affairs Committee, American Jewish Committee, Zionist Organization of America...) makes it difficult for the United States to take an objective approach to the Palestinian question, despite the more nuanced positions of younger organizations (such as J Street, founded in 2008 by Jeremy Ben-Ami). Leaders of the Republican and Democratic parties and more than half of the members of Congress were present at the annual convention of the American Israel Public Affairs Committee. Congress members who express some doubts about Israeli politics are ostracized and their reelection hopes put in doubt: examples include Paul Findley in 1982, Earl Hillard in 2001, Cynthia McKinney in 2002[3]... In June 2015, the U.S. congress would only extend the controversial Trans-Atlantic Trade and Investment Partnership (TTIP) to countries that agreed to abandon the boycott campaign against Israel. In Congressman Peter Roskam's words: "*The bipartisan TPA provisions I authored are simple: if you want free trade with the United States, you can't boycott Israel*[4]".

---

[1] *Financial Times*, September 16, 2014.

[2]. Noam Chomsky, *The Nation*, February 14, 2012.
(www. thenation.com/print/article/166271/imperial-way).

[3] Paul Findley, *"They Dare to Speak Out: People and Institutions Confront Israel's Lobby"*, Lawrence Hill Books, Westport, 1989.

[4] Rebecca Shimoni Stail, "Landmark anti-BDS Law passes final Senate legislative hurdle", *The Times of Israel*, June 25, 2015.

Many figures in the American administration border on a double allegiance[1]. Rahm Emanuel, Chair of the Democratic Congressional Campaign Committee and of the House Democratic Caucus, Obama's White House Chief of Staff, and currently Mayor of Chicago, is a former member of the Israel Defense Forces. Israeli Ambassador to the United States, Ron Dermer was born in the United States and is a U.S. citizen, like his predecessor, Michael Oren (2009-2013), and like the Secretary General of the Israeli Ministry of Foreign Affairs, Dore Gold, born in Hartford, Connecticut, educated at Columbia University, appointed to his current post in May 2015 by Benjamin Netanyahu, who controls the budget of the Ministry[2]. American magnate Sheldon Adelson, a prominent donor to the Republican Party and electoral supporter of the Israeli prime minister, owns three Israeli newspapers: *Maariv* (Evening), *Makor Rishon* (Primary Source) and *Israel Ha Yom* (Israel Today). The Israeli paper *Haaretz* reported in May 2015 that the American philanthropist, Irving Moskowitz, had purchased a large amount of land in the West Bank to found a new Jewish settlement[3].

There is no record of an Israeli advisor of Arab or Palestinian descent. The era of the "Arabists" from the Ivy League universities[4] has come to a close[5]. This certainly saved President Obama, when he went to visit the President of the Palestinian National Authority in the Mukataa of Ramallah in March 2013, the trouble of paying homage before the tomb of Yasser Arafat. Whatever opinions may exist regarding this leader, he is considered by all Palestinians to be the father of the nation, just as Mahatma Gandhi is for the Indians or David Ben-Gurion for the Israelis.

In August 2014, when the Israeli bombing of the Gaza Strip was meeting with increasing international criticism because of the high number of women and children being killed, out of 495 congresspeople (House and Senate), only eight voted against emergency supplementary military aid of 225 million dollars to Israel. On that occasion, Pentagon spokesman Vice Admiral John Kirby disclosed the existence of a permanent stockpile of American weapons in Israel worth some one billion dollars[6].

This Israeli operation, dubbed "Protective Edge", inspired the Brazilian president to characterize the Israeli intervention as "*disproportionate*", and Itamaraty to vigorously condemn the "*disproportionate use of force*", call back its

---

1. James Petras, Henry Veltmeyer, *The Power of Israel in the United States,* Clarity Press, 2006.

2 The U.S. Supreme Court overturned the prohibition against dual citizenship in 1967 in a case brought by an Israeli citizen of Polish origins (Afroyim v. Rusk) rendering unenforceable the Bancroft Treaties, bilateral agreements which sought to limit dual citizenship following naturalization.

3 Judah Ari Gross, "US millionaire hid purchase of West bank property", *The Times of Israel,* May 28, 2015.

4 Harvard, Yale, Pennsylvania, Princeton, Columbia, Brown, Dartmouth, Cornell.

5 See Robert Kaplan, "*The Arabists*", Free Press, New York, 1996.

6 "U.S. Restocks Israel's Ammunition Supplies Hours After Condemning Attack On a UN School in Gaza", *AFP*, July 30, 2014.

representative in Tel Aviv for consultations, and summon the Israeli Ambassador to the Ministry of External Relations. This reaction by Brazilian authorities led to a diplomatic row, leading the spokesman for the Israeli Ministry of Foreign Affairs, Yigal Palmor, to qualify Brazil as an "*economic and cultural giant but a diplomatic dwarf*".

There are no pro-Israel lobbies in Brazil that speak out so openly. The Jewish community generally avoids public statements on the Palestinian question so as not to upset the cohesion and peaceful relations it enjoys with other faiths in Brazilian society and with the government. But they remain alert, as marked by the demonstrations organized to protest the official visit of Iranian president Ahmadinejad to Brasilia in November 2009, which represented, in the words of the Brazilian Israelite Confederation, "*an offense to the Jewish community*". Business groups (Klabin, Bloch, Feigl, Safra...) run by powerful and openly Zionistic families from providing major financial support to the Jewish state in the past. The CEO and owner of the Bloch publishing house (now closed), Adolpho Bloch (1908-1995) was given an doctorate *honoris causa* by the Weizmann Institute and his right-hand man, Zevi Ghivelder, was the president of the Brazilian Zionist Union and Editor-in-Chief of the only Yiddish language weekly published in Rio de Janeiro. Edmond Safra (1932-1999) and Lily Safra (Safra Group, Republic National Bank of New York) have multiplied their donations to synagogues, and Jewish schools and hospitals in Israel and Europe. The current Brazilian Minister of Defense, Jaques Wagner, appointed in 2015, former Governor of the State of Bahia (2007-2014) and former Minister of Labor in the Lula government (2003-2006), is a Polish Jew whose family escaped the Nazi persecution and took refuge in Brazil. He was a very early activist in the Brazilian Zionist movement. He is one of the founders of the Workers' Party and of the main national trade union center in Brazil (Central Única dos Trabalhadores – CUT).

The evangelical churches, which support Israel both in Brazil and in the United States, took a dim view of the president's condemnation of the invasion of the Gaza Strip by the Israeli army and sent a delegation to Itamaraty to express this disagreement. A significant number of members of parliament, 73 in 2015, are members of these churches and the reelected senator for the State of Rio de Janeiro, Marcelo Crivella, was a minister in Dilma Rousseff's government from February 2012 to March 2014. He authored a bill that would have established November 29 as a day to celebrate Brazil-Israel friendship. It was approved by Parliament but President Rousseff vetoed it in July 2013, on the date established by the United Nations to celebrate solidarity with the Palestinian people. She proposed the date of April 12 (in reference to the establishment of diplomatic relations between the two states on April 12, 1951).

The inauguration ceremonies of the monumental temple of the Universal Church of the Kingdom of God in the Temple of Solomon in São Paulo in 2014, with seating for 10.000 and president Dilma Rousseff in attendance, featured the Israeli national anthem. But the evangelical members of parliament, associated with different churches and different political parties are not, apart from certain social issues (civil marriage, abortion) a homogeneous pressure group and, to date, have virtually no influence on foreign policy. The president of the Chamber of Deputies, Eduardo Cunha, an avowed evangelist, was received on June 2, 2015 by the Israeli Prime Minister, Benjamin Netanyahu, on the occasion of a parliamentary mission to Tel Aviv. Guests of the Israeli government, the mission was composed of eleven deputies, Pastor Everaldo Dias Pereira, candidate in the presidential election of 2014, and representatives of the Brazilian Jewish community[1].

Regarding discussion of the Palestinian question, Brazil prefers the conference model represented by Annapolis in November 2007, where forty countries participated, including India, Brazil, and South Africa. Sponsorship by countries outside of the region in question that are non-hegemonic and multi-ethnic (examples of religious and racial coexistence) and that have good relations with all parties are the best way to facilitate negotiations. Along with five other countries[2], Brazil took part from March 1957 to June 1967 in the First United Nations Emergency Force stationed in Sharm el-Sheikh and Gaza. This period thus witnessed some 3.300 Brazilian soldiers deployed to Gaza, a territory that had been under Egyptian administration from 1948 to 1956.

The commitments undertaken in Annapolis regarding a roadmap for stopping the expansion of settlements in exchange for a United States offer of 3 billion dollars in military aid and F-35 fighter aircraft to Israel were not maintained. Construction resumed in Jerusalem and in the West Bank at a rate unprecedented since 2000 and, as planned, compromise the viability of a Palestinian state. The security barrier that separated Israel from the West Bank cordoned off 10% of the Palestinian territory and constituted an "*annexation in disguise*" according to the Israeli human rights organization B'Tselem. It is still necessary to assess the real extent of Palestinian territory free of Israeli interference and military control, which is doubtlessly less than 40% of the area currently assigned to them. As regards the settlements, if the policy of encouraging Jewish immigration *(Aliyah)* is not limited, it can only lead to further expansion.

General De Gaulle once lucidly observed:

> "*Israel now organizes an occupation in the territories it has captured that can only be accompanied by oppression, repression and expulsion; and in turn it will qualify the resistance against it as terrorism. [...] We witnessed the emergence of a warlike Israeli state resolute in its desire for expansion. And then the action it takes to double its population through immigration leads us to think that the territory acquired would not long suffice and it would be given to seizing every available opportunity to grow*"[3].

---

[1] Daniel Carvalho, "Comitiva de Eduardo Cunha vai a Israel e tem reunião com Netanyahu" (Eduardo Cunha's group goes to Israel for meeting with Netanyahu), *Estado de São Paulo*, June 3, 2015.

[2] Canada, Denmark, India, Sweden, Yugoslavia (Finland and Indonesia withdrew from the force in 1957, and Colombia in 1958).

[3] Charles de Gaulle, *Discours et Messages*, volume 5, January 1966-April 1969, Plon, Paris, 1970.

According to a report by the Israeli organization "Shalom Achshav" (Peace Now), 2014 witnessed an increase on the order of 40% in the number of new buildings in the West Bank settlements. Following the ceasefire of August 26, 2014, Israel annexed some 500 hectares in the Gush Etzion area south of Jerusalem. The number of requests for tenders regarding new construction had tripled since 2011[1]. In 2014, 26.500 Jewish immigrants arrived in Israel in the *Aliyah*, an increase of 30% with respect to the previous year[2]. A Jew who arrives in Israel has more rights than a Palestinian who was born there into a family that has lived there for generations.

Israel offers the opportunity to young non-Israeli Jews to join the combat units assigned to the occupied territories as part of the *Mahal* program. It consists of 14-18 months of service with the Israel Defense Forces (IDF). This program has raised no eyebrows in Brussels or in the European capitals.

The Israeli ambassador to Paris organized a meeting at the Grande synagogue de la Victoire on May 26, 2014 with a Tsahal officer (the Israeli army) stating that individual recruitment appointments were available[3]. The official website of these foreign soldiers enlisted in the Israeli army, "Lone Soldiers", registered 2.562 soldiers in the year 2013. The largest contingents were from the United States (740), Russia (393), Ukraine (280), and France (236). The numbers for Brazil and Argentina were 35 and 34, respectively[4]. Approximately 40% of them had fought in the last Israeli offensive in Gaza, with the death of two American soldiers (Max Steinberg, Nissim Sean Carmeli) and one French soldier (Jordan Bensemhoun).

In its January 14, 2014 issue, the *Jerusalem Post* reports that the French Ambassador, Patrick Maisonnave, publicly congratulated the "*courageous enlistment of young French people in the Israeli army*" without questioning the legitimacy of such an arrangement. If a non-Israeli French citizen feels justified, on the basis of his membership in the Jewish community, to enlist in an occupation force judged illegal by United Nations territorial resolutions, could not a non-Palestinian Frenchman, in the name of his Muslim faith or in virtue of his Arab origins, also find it legitimate to fight alongside the Palestinians against the illegal expansion of Israeli colonies in Palestinian lands? Which of these choices is more legitimate within the spheres of international and French law?

---

[1] "West Bank Settlements Housing Starts Rise by 40%", *The Jerusalem Daily Forward*, February 24, 2015.

[2] Source: The Jewish Agency for Israel.

[3] Union Juive Française pour la Paix-UJFP, "Alerte: la grande synagogue de Paris appelle à la guerre sainte!" (Attention: the Grand Synagogue of Paris calls for holy war!), May 24, 2014 (*www.ujfp.org/spip.php?article3240)*

[4] Lone Soldiers Program. Friends of the Israel Defense Forces. See also Julie Watson, Bem Nuckols, Tami Abdollah (A.P.), "How many Americans have joined the Israeli military?", *The Christian Science Monitor*, July 22, 2014.

The appointment of former British Prime Minister Tony Blair in June 2007 as head of the Quartet[1] – nicknamed *"Bush's poodle"* by the media, Blair was enlisted by the U.S. Secretary of State, John Kerry, in May 2013 to coordinate a program of investments in Palestine – was, according to our contacts, an unfortunate choice. Going against his own party (five ministers resigned) and Parliament on the invasion of Iraq (vote of March 18, 2003), which was the object of a commission of inquiry[2], he is widely discredited in the region. Disclosures made in October 2010 by his sister-in-law, Lauren Booth, who converted to Islam, confirm the contempt felt among the Muslim community[3] for this eager broker for British Petroleum in Israel in 2007, for J. P. Morgan in Tripoli from 2008 to 2010, for the Anglo-Swiss group Glencore in Qatar, and for the Mubadala Investment Fund in Abu Dhabi. After eight years at the helm of a fruitless and scarcely credible mission, he resigned in May 2015. He now directs the European Council on Tolerance and Reconciliation[4], working with Moshe Kantor, president of the European Jewish Congress, and the former Spanish Prime Minister José Maria Aznar, who founded the pro-Israel lobby "Friends of Israel Initiative" in 2010 along with other international figures, including John Bolton. The controversial former representative of the Bush administration to the United Nations, advisor to the Jewish Institute for National Security Affairs, a pro-Israel think tank based in Washington D.C., as Undersecretary of State, John Bolton was behind the ouster of the Brazilian diplomat José Bustani form the Organization for the Prohibition of Chemical Weapons. To reach a resolution to the Palestinian question, he supported the three-state solution: Gaza ceded to Egypt and the West Bank divided between Jordan and Israel[5].

We are still awaiting the conclusions of the inquiry assigned to the former Permanent Secretary of Northern Ireland, John Chilcot, by former British Prime Minister Gordon Brown on the engagement in Iraq in 2003, an inquiry estimated to cost 9 million euros and whose publication has been postponed several times. A leaked memo from former U.S. secretary of State, Colin Powell, written in March 2002, seems to prove that Tony Blair decided war in Iraq was inevitable from early 2002, before seeking a vote in parliament[6].

---

1. Comprising the United Nations, the United States, the European Union, and Russia, the Quartet on the Middle East was created at the 2002 Madrid Conference. From that date until December 1, 2011, it has met 47 times to seek a solution in negotiations on the Palestinian question.

2. John Burns, "U.K. war inquiry focuses on Blair", *International Herald Tribune*, November 25, 2009.

3. Fernanda Duarte, "Uma conversão embaraçosa para Blair" (Blair's awkward transformation), *O'Globo*, October 26, 2010.

4 Non-governmental organization founded in 2008 by Aleksander Kwasnievski, president of Poland from 1995 to 2005, and Moshe Kantor, president of the European Jewish Congress.

5 John Bolton, "The Three State Option", *Washington Post*, June 5, 2009.

6 Tisdall Simon, "There is no doubt about it: Tony Blair was on the warpath from early 2002", *The Guardian*, October 18, 2015.

The Palestinians depend on the good will of the Israeli government for virtually all economic questions: natural resources, currency, trade in goods and services in the country and with other countries, taxes, planting and harvesting, wells and reservoirs, roadways. Excluding the roads reserved exclusively for Israelis, the road network is deplorable and permanently subject to checkpoints. The trip from Hebron to Ramallah, a thirty minute trip for an Israeli who can pass through Jerusalem, takes three hours on poorly maintained roads for a Palestinian, who is forbidden from passing through Jerusalem. According to the United Nations, there are 490 Israeli checkpoints in the West Bank, constituting borders that have nothing to do with the green line established in the armistice of 1949. It is a system that makes any foreign investment highly risky. Even Palestinian vital records (births, weddings, deaths...) are kept by Israeli authorities.

In Zone C, covering 61% of the richest land in the West Bank in terms of natural resources, under Israeli civil and military administration, Palestinians are not allowed to erect any buildings, whether for residential, industrial or commercial use. Generally speaking the Palestinians cannot develop any lands located within three kilometers from the Israeli border (44% of Gaza), nor can they fish beyond three nautical miles from the Gaza coast. The population density in Gaza is on the order of 4.000 inhabitants per km^2 (344 in Israel) and the population growth rate is one of the highest in the world (2.91% per year in 2014, more than twice that of Brazil).

As regards the Gaza Strip, it is under quarantine, subjected to a blockade against trade by land or sea at the arbitrary discretion of Israel, after having been the victim in recent years of three invasions by the Israeli military: in 2009 (Operation "Cast Lead"); 2012 (Operation "Pillar of Defense"); and 2014 (Operation "Protective Edge").

Over the space of 22 days in 2009 (December 27, 2008 – January 18, 2009), 1.434 Palestinians were killed, of which 1.259 were civilians and 288 were children; Israeli casualties totaled 3 civilians and 6 soldiers. Between November 14 and November 21, 2012, 103 Palestinian civilians were killed, 30 of whom were children; 4 Israeli civilians were killed[1]. According to UN data, over the course of 50 days in 2014 (July 8-August 26), 2.251 Palestinians were killed, including 1.462 civilians (551 children) and 11.231 were injured, including 7.000 women and children. Israeli casualties were 67 soldiers and 6 civilians, including one child. As a result over 9.000 Palestinians have been killed and over 73.000 injured since 2000. This is reported to the world as acts of self-defense on the part of Israelis. Such an assertion is hard to sustain when one sees the lopsided kill and injury ratio between Palestinian and Israeli victims.

According to the United Nations, in 50 days of the Israeli offensive in the Gaza Strip, 24 schools were leveled and 112 damaged, 15 hospitals and 43 healthcare centers were destroyed, and 20-30% of the water supply network

[1] Jon Donnison, "Gaza baby only knew how to smile", *BBC News*, November 26, 2012.

was compromised[1]. More than 200 businesses and 300 shops were destroyed in the already decimated industrial fabric of Gaza. According to the president of the Association of Palestinian Businesses, economic targets were deliberately chosen, an opinion shared by the United Nations Special Rapporteur for the region, Robert Serry. It is estimated that 50% of the working age population of Gaza was left unemployed after the Israeli intervention. More than 18.000 homes were destroyed and 108.000 people are now homeless according to the United Nations. In an interview with a journalist from the Associated Press in June 2015, the director of the UNDP Programme of Assistance to the Palestinian People, Roberto Valent, estimates that given the pace of the Israeli importation authorization process, it will take 30 years to rebuild the buildings destroyed during the Israeli offensive[2]. By mid-May 2015, not a single destroyed building had been rebuilt. At photography exhibition in São Paulo in 2014 illustrating the situation experienced by Palestinian refugees, Paz Fernandez, External Relations and Projects Officer for the United Nations Relief and Works Agency for Palestine Refugees in the Near East (UNRWA) stated: "*There is an international blockade on Gaza. All economic activity has ceased; it is like living in prison. In 2000, some 80.000 Palestinians depended on humanitarian aid from the Agency. Now 800.000 of them do, out of a population of two million*"[3]. The International Organization for Migration has counted more than 3.000 Palestinians who have taken refuge in Italy during the third quarter of 2014, one thousand of them from Gaza. This does not include the 400 who lost their lives at sea in their attempt to reach the Italian peninsula.

Exile appears to be the only possible way out for a population where two thirds of its members are refugees, but this is obviously only an option if they are able to leave the territory, something which is possible only for the luckiest among them, and for the Christian minority. In a report published in July 2015, the United Nations Conference on Trade and Development (UNCTAD) forecast that by 2030 the Gaza Strip would no longer be habitable[4].

The risk here is that the poor people of Gaza, without a future, without hope for a resolution to their problems, constantly humiliated, will be tempted by the islamist movements and swell the ranks of an armed resistance along the lines of Hezbollah, alongside the regular forces of the Palestinian National Authority and Hamas, not to mention the all-consuming, suicidal temptation of the Caliphate (ISIL). The principal risk is the sort of radicalization witnessed in

---

[1] "Report on UNCTAD assistance to the Palestinian people. Developments in the economy of the Occupied Palestinian Territory" (35), July 6, 2015.

[2] Karin Laub, Fares Akiam, Edith Lederer, "AP Interview: Gaza rebuilding moving at snail´s pace", *Associated Press*, June 25, 2015.

[3] Thais Folgosi, "Palestina: uma tragédia que parece não ter fim" (Palestine: a tragedy that seems to have no end), *Brasileiros*, February 4, 2015.

[4] "*If the current blockade and insufficient levels of donor support persist, even with a reversion to the status quo that prevailed before the latest military operation, Gaza will become economically unviable*". Report on UNCTAD assistance to the Palestinian People. Developments in the economy of the Occupied Palestinian Territory (61), July 6, 2015.

Iraq, with Hamas no longer in control: according to press information, more than 40 Salafist militants or leaders have been killed by Hamas in the Gaza Strip[1]. The stabbings by young Palestinians are a predictable outgrowth of endless brutality from Israeli settlers and security forces combined with discrimination, marginalization, constant humiliation and injustice.

Contrary to what was envisaged in Tel Aviv, in spite of the considerable damage caused by the bombardments, the majority of Gazans still support Hamas. According to a survey by the Palestinian Center for Policy and Survey Research in September 2014, 80% of the population of Gaza supports Hamas and, for the first time in eight years, the leader of Hamas, Ismail Haniyeh, would win an election against Mahmoud Abbas in the West Bank. In student council elections in April 2015 at Birzeit University in Ramallah, the list of candidates associated with Hamas (Islamic Wafaa) won the majority of seats against Fatah.

The continuation of cooperation on security with Israel, reaffirmed explicitly on June 18, 2014 in a speech in Jeddah by the president of the Palestinian National Authority, was received very negatively by the Palestinians, as was his perceived lack of solidarity with the people of the Gaza Strip, an area he has not visited since the Israeli attack. The Palestinian Council now seems to want to reject this outsourcing of security, which is particularly unpopular in the West Bank and brings to mind the darkest years of collaboration in occupied France during the Second World War

The Gaza Strip was particularly affected by the coup against Egyptian president Mohamed Morsi on July 3, 2013. It is estimated that 1.200 people crossed the border between Egypt and Gaza every day at the Rafah Border Crossing before that date; afterwards the number fell by 80%. Currently, more than 15.000 Palestinians are on a waiting list to be admitted into Egypt according to the EuroMid Observer for Human Rights, including physicians and students holding scholarships to foreign universities. At the beginning of the year 2015, the border crossing only allowed traffic into Gaza; and inhumane and arbitrary treatment was meted out at the border crossing to Palestinians seeking to return home. The investment program entailing 4 billion dollars over three years announced by John Kerry at the World Economic Forum in May 2013 has yet to be finalized. The commitment by donors meeting at the Cairo Summit in October 2014 to provide 5.4 billion dollars to Palestine, 3 billion of which earmarked for the reconstruction of Gaza, announced by Norwegian Foreign Affairs Minister Boerge Brende, had only barely begun to materialize one year after the hostilities[2]. As of mid-May 2015 only 27% of

[1] Majd Al Waheidi, Isabel Kershner, "Hamas Forces Kill Leader of Islamic Splinter Group in Gaza", *International New York Times*, June 2, 2015.

[2] "Donors pledge $5.4 bn for Palestinians at Cairo Summit", *BBC News*, October 12, 2014.

these monies had been made available[1]. Meanwhile, the United States provided aid to Israel of 3.15 billion dollars in 2013, renewed yearly.

Brazil and nine other countries in Latin America (Argentina, Bolivia, Chile, Cuba, Ecuador, Nicaragua, Peru, Uruguay, Venezuela) are among the sixty nations that sponsored the proposition before the United Nations to upgrade Palestine to non-member observer state, which passed on November 29, 2012 (Resolution 67/19). Panama was the only country in Latin America to follow the lead of the United States and Israel in voting against the resolution. Six other countries joined them: Canada, Czech Republic, Marshall Islands, Micronesia, Nauru, and Palau. Among the 41 abstentions, four were in Latin America: Colombia, Guatemala, Haiti, Paraguay.

The United States' threat to use its veto currently poses an obstacle to the admission of Palestine, now recognized by 135 countries, as a fully endowed member state of the United Nations.

The prospect opens of Palestine becoming a signatory to the Rome Statute of the International Criminal Court. On January 21, 2009, Palestine issued a declaration of acceptance of the jurisdiction of the ICC to *"investigate crimes committed in Palestine since July 2002"*.

Unlike the countries in ALBA, Brazil seems little interested in the general debate on human rights in the Palestinian and Arab territories that have been occupied since 1967 within the framework of the United Nations Human Rights Council (Item 7 on the agenda of the universal periodic review concerning Israel scheduled for October 29, 2013, which was postponed because of Israel's refusal in May 2012 to collaborate). It also rarely takes part in the interactive dialogue with the Special Rapporteur on this question[2]. It has not stated a position regarding the movement to boycott Israeli enterprises that operate in the occupied territories. It has not adopted the French position of prosecuting those advocating a boycott. In February 2010, French Attorney General, Michèle Aliot Marie, signed a directive ordering public prosecutors to take legal action against anyone urging consumers to stop buying Israeli products. Hundreds of activists were then brought before the courts (most of their cases were dismissed). This initiative – unique in Europe – astonished Brazilian diplomats: how could a nation prosecute its own citizens for organizing a campaign to fight for observance of international law and Security Council resolutions? Israel's parliament, the Knesset, enacted legislation in 2011 forbidding any initiative promoting a boycott of Israeli products or products produced in Israeli settlements in the West Bank. This movement (Boycott, Divestment and Sanctions), initiated in 2005, has not attracted important Brazilian personalities, with the exception of Francisco Whitaker Ferreira, co-

---

[1] "Report on UNCTAD assistance to the Palestinian people. Developments in the Economy of the Occupied Palestinian Territory", July 6, 2015.

[2] Edmond Sanders, "Israeli law targets boycott campaigns", *Los Angeles Times,* July 12, 2011.

founder of the World Social Forum, winner of the Right Livelihood Award[1] bestowed by the Swedish Parliament in 2006, and a city councilman in São Paulo with the Workers' Party. Union organizations close to the Workers' Party and non-governmental organizations in the collective *Frente em Defesa do Povo Palestino* (Palestinian People's Defense Front) pride themselves on having convinced the governor of the State of Rio Grande to back out of an agreement signed in December 2014 with the Israeli company Elbit Systems when the company's president, Bezhalel Machlis, visited Porto Alegre in April 2013. But the Israeli firm provides equipment for the Embraer KC-390, the 53 recently upgraded Northrop F6EM/FM fighter aircraft, the Guarani tank, etc. The Brazilian artists Caetano Velloso and Gilberto Gil[2], were subject to repeated pressure from abroad to cancel their concert in Tel Aviv in July 2015, and the Brazilian press published letters addressed to Caetano Velloso by Roger Walters, former leader of Pink Floyd, urging a boycott[3].

In June 2015, the rector of the public Federal University of Santa Maria (27.000 students) in the State of Rio Grande do Sul, issued a circular letter in response to a request from a pro-Palestinian association (*Comité Santamariense de Solidariedade ao Povo Palestino* – Committee of Santa Maria for Solidarity with the Palestinian People), ordering that Israeli teachers and students in master's programs at the university be reviewed to ensure that their specialties are not associated with possible bellicose acts against the Palestinian people in the occupied territories[4]. This action was soon the object of an inquiry by the Brazilian public prosecutor. The university defended itself against any accusations of anti-Semitism by pointing out that the policy regards nationality and not religion. This distinction is not accepted in Tel Aviv, where any manifestation of hostility toward the Israeli government is illegitimately considered to be an anti-Semitic act. On U.S. universities campus Israel advocacy groups have been at the forefront of campaigns to pressure universities to investigate and censor pro-Palestine activists.

During my appointment to Buenos Aires in the worst years of the dictatorship and repression (1976-1980), I learned of this ambiguous distinction

---

[1] Considered to be a sort of alternate Nobel Prize, the Right Livelihood Award has been assigned to different categories of recipient since 1980. Among the Brazilian winners of this prize, some are associated with the church (Leonardo Boff in 2001, Erwin Karaütier in 2009) and some with the cause of indigenous peoples and the environment (José Lutzenberger in 1987). Among Israelis, there are pro-Palestinian humanitarians (Arna Mer Khamis in 1993, Rachel and Uri Avnery in 2000, Physicians for Human Rights in 2010) as well as Mordechai Vanunu, Israeli scientist who leaked information about the Israeli nuclear program and was abducted in Rome by Mossad agents and imprisoned for 18 years, 11 of them in solitary confinement. In 2014, the Palestinian lawyer, Raji Sourani, founder of the Palestinian Center for Human Rights, won the award.

[2] Arrested and exiled during the dictatorship (December 1968 – May 1972), Gilberto Gil was Minister of Culture during the Lula presidencies (2003-2008)

[3] "Boicote a Israel", *O'Globo*, June 30, 2015.

[4] Sonia Racy, "*A pedido, universidade do sul investiga presença de israelenses*" (By request, southern university investigates Israelis), *Estado de São Paulo*, June 3, 2015.

embodied by the Israeli Ambassador, Ron Nergard. When Jewish Argentine citizens were victims of the repression (kidnapping, torture, disappearance, murder, fraud, dispossession)[1], many of them for the simple reason of being Jewish, Israeli diplomats were invariably absent from the meetings held with the principal European and American diplomats on the question of violation of human rights. Only the Rabbi Marshall Meyer attended those meetings. He was a regular guest at the French embassy and sought to call the attention of the media and North American organizations (particularly the American Jewish Committee) to the disappearances, fully aware of the powerful and dangerous anti-Semitic currents then flowing through Argentine society (the armed forces, the police, the nationalist and Catholic extreme right). The local Jewish organizations and the Israeli embassy refused to recognize and publicly condemn these currents, even in response to the disappearance of Israeli citizens[2] and the abduction and torture of the owner and editor of the newspaper *La Opinion*, Jacobo Timerman, father of Argentine Minister of Foreign Affairs, Hector Timerman (2010-2015).

Jacobo Timerman described the long and painful anti-Semitic interrogations he was subjected to in a book published in 1981[3]. The testimony of French people of Jewish origin who disappeared for some time after being arrested by armed men claiming to represent the police and freed after being tortured by their captors is categorical: being Jewish is always an aggravating factor[4]. The Israeli Ambassador, Ron Nergard, said that he was not the ambassador of the Jews but the ambassador of Israel and refused to issue visas to Argentine Jews that were considered to be too far left on the political spectrum, and thus the ones in greatest danger, much to the despair of the local representative of the Jewish Agency, Daniel Recanati. Unlike the concern manifested by Prime Minister Ben-Gurion at the upsurge in attacks on the Jewish community in Argentina after a coup d'état unseated Peron in September 1955, prompting the dispatch to Buenos Aires of the chief of the Israeli secret service, Isser Harel, Israeli authorities hardly showed any such solidarity during the repression of many Argentine Jews by the military dictatorship. However, a number of Israeli citizens were among the disappeared, including the daughter of an officer of the *Delegación de Asociaciones Israelitas Argentinas* (DAIA), who was 17 when she was abducted from her home, not to mention the Jewish leaders subject to arbitrary and brutal incarceration (including Amnòn Rudin of the Jewish Agency for Israel, Jaime Pompas, former president of the Jewish Community of Cordoba). It was not until March 1978 that an Israeli newspaper (the March 29

[1] Some 1.500 Jewish citizens of Argentina were victims of the repression between 1976 and 1980 and since then recorded as disappeared.

[2] Amnon Rudin of the Jewish Agency, Jaime Pompas, former president of the Jewish community of Cordoba, Mauricio Weinstein, son of the president of the Commission on Disappeared Jews created in Buenos Aires in 1978.

[3] Jacobo Timerman, *Prisoner without a name, cell without a number*, University of Wisconsin Press, 1981.

[4] Testimony of Anita Jarolavsky, arrested on April 29 and freed May 7, 1976, and of Raymond Franck, arrested on May 9 and freed on May 24, 1976.

issue of *Haaretz*) first mentioned the issue of disappeared Jews in Argentina[1]. When the Israeli Minister of Foreign Affairs went to Buenos Aires in 1982, he refused to receive a delegation of parents of the disappeared; this happened again in 1984, when the former president of Israel, Yitzhak Navon, came to participate in the 11th congress of the local Jewish organization DAIA *(Delegación de Asociaciones Israelitas Argentinas*). The DAIA, which Jacobo Timerman equates in his memoirs with the *Judenrat*, reproached the Jewish Movement for Human Rights, led by the rabbis Marshal Meyer and Herman Schiller, for its role in support of the disappearances, seeing its initiatives as constituting a threat to the Jewish community. Shulamit Aloni (1928-2014), former Minister of Education and Culture in Yitzhak Rabin's government (1992-1993) and member of parliament, told the newspaper *Haaretz* on May 24, 2006 that she had never succeeded in getting the Knesset to debate the sale of Israeli arms to the Argentine military junta. It is estimated that some 1 billion dollars in Israeli weaponry was sold to Argentina during the dictatorship (1976-1983)[2]. Federal police inspector, Peregrino Fernandez, a repented torturer, revealed during his public confession that the economic adviser of the Israeli embassy in Buenos Aires, Herlz Inbar, provided courses in counter-insurrection to the chiefs of staff of the Argentine army during the dictatorship. We cannot rule out that these arms contracts may have reined in any thoughts of intervention – granted that such truly existed – by the Israeli government to aid the Jewish victims of repression by the military junta. It is indubitable however that the embargo on arms sales to Argentina imposed by the Carter administration (1977-1981) because of human rights violations prompted Israel and European countries – Germany and France in particular – to satisfy the requests presented by the Argentine military. This no doubt sent an ambiguous message to the junta and weakened the effectiveness of actions by the principal consulates in favor of their disappeared citizens. Israel was clearly not alone in this. These arms sales reinforced the junta's hold on power at a time when the military leaders found themselves thwarted on the diplomatic level by their paradigm, the United States, who had trained these very military leaders[3].

The main expressions of support and solidarity with the South American Jewish community during the years of military repression came from U.S. Jewish organizations, particularly the American Jewish Committee, which sent a delegation to Buenos Aires in 1979 and 1981. The solidarity committees that came together in Israel in 1977, particularly to promote a boycott of the Soccer World Cup recommended by the writer Marek Halter, were essentially due to

[1] An Israeli journalist, Marcel Zohar, published a book (in Hebrew) on this question in 1990: *Let my people go to hell: treachery in blue and white*, Citrin Publishing House, Tel Aviv.

[2] Aharon Kleiman, *A Double-Edged Sword. Israeli Defense Exports in the 1990s*, (pp. 233-235), 1972.

[3] Between 1950 and 1970 an estimated 2,808 Argentine officers were trained in the United States, mostly at the School of the Americas (then in the Panama Canal zone) and at Fort Benning (Georgia). Two generals in the military junta, Leopoldo Galtieri and Roberto Viola, were among the trainees.

the efforts of Argentine exiles. These committees did not receive even the slightest support from rightist parties in Israel, nor from the Israeli communist party, which had been particularly active in the situations in Chile and Uruguay in 1973 and 1974, respectively. Anti-Semitism, on the other hand, is invariably reported and denounced by Tel Aviv when it works against Israeli interests.

Marco Aurelio Garcia, former member of the Brazilian Communist Party, living in exile in Chile and France during the military dictatorship, and one of the founders of the Workers' Party, one of the mentors of Brazilian diplomacy since 2002, has this to say of Israel:

> *"Is Israel not a terrorist state when it bombs two UN schools and kills dozens of children? If it is not terrorism it is certainly a war crime. We must cease this hypocritical diplomacy. The Jews must get out of the habit of considering any criticism to be an attack on the existence of Israel. Israel consistently supported the Apartheid regime in South Africa. It provided constant support to the Somoza dictatorship in Nicaragua, and to Salazar in Portugal. Do not come to me now seeking to play the good guys*[1]*."*

On the initiative of the Israelite Federation, a demonstration of some one thousand people was organized in Rio de Janeiro in July 2014 to support Israel during its bombing campaign in the Gaza Strip. The majority shareholder in the Klabin Group (cellulose), Israel Klabin, former mayor of Rio de Janeiro (1979-1980), had accused the Minister of External Relations, Luiz Alberto Figueiredo, in an open letter titled "Itamaraty offends the State of Israel and us Jews"[2] when Brazil summoned its ambassador for consultation during the deadly Israeli offensive on Gaza, an offensive characterized as "disproportionate" by Itamaraty. The Brazilian minister emphasized in his response: "*Criticizing the actions of a government does not mean criticizing a country or a people. I cannot accept the confusion between these things*[3]."

In August 2015, a campaign was launched by the Union of Engineers in Rio de Janeiro to urge the Organizing Committee for the August 2016 Olympic Games to break off its contract with the Israeli company ISDS (Israel Security and Defense Systems) for security at the Games. Founded in 1982 by Leo Gleser, former Mossad agent, the company is accused of having collaborated with the military dictatorships in Central America (Honduras, Guatemala, El Salvador)[4] and to have supplied the teargas and eavesdropping equipment used

---

[1]. Interview in the monthly *Piaui*, no. 30, 2009: "*Quando Israël bombardeia duas escolas da ONU e mata dezenas de crianças não é terrorismo? Se não é terrorismo então é crime de guerra. Temos que para com essa diplomacia de punhos de renda. Os judeus têm que perder o habito de achar que qualquer crítica é uma manifestação contra a existência de Israël...Israël apoiou durante todo o tempo o regime do apartheid na Africa do Sul. Apoiou todo o tempo a ditadura de Somoza na Nicaragua, e a de Salazar, em Portugal. Não venham agora querer bancar os bacanas para o meu lado.*"

[2] "*Ofensa feita ao Estado de Israel e a todos nós judeus, pelo Itamaraty*" (Offense to the State of Israel and all us Jews by Itamaraty), source: Beit Lubavitch – Rio de Janeiro (www.pletz.com).

[3] "*Acho apenas que criticar as ações de um governo não quer dizer criticas um país ou um povo. Não aceito que essas coisas se confundam*", source: Beit Lubavitch - Rio de Janeiro (www.pletz.com)

[4] Cf Yorsi Melman, "How did a nature-loving boy who dreamed of reforming the world grow up to be Colonel Gleser?", *Haaretz*, March 30, 2006.

against the Brazilian embassy in Tegucigalpa when president Manuel Zelaya took refuge there (September 21, 2009 - January 27, 2010)[1].

The fact remains that the growing Islamophobia in Europe, which so far has not touched Brazil, is accompanied by a resurgence of anti-Semitism, often veiled as criticism of the Israeli government. This new form of anti-Semitism certainly grows out of the historical religious anti-Semitism of the Catholic right and the anti-Semitism of the nationalist groups represented in the army and in far right movements, but it is increasingly fueled by the alarming repression of the Palestinian people by the Israeli army.

The anti-Semitism traditionally seen among the armed forces and extreme Catholic and nationalistic right is now expressed episodically within movements on the left. Here, all things considered, it is expressed as a stance against Israel and not against Jews, such as in the *quebracho* Argentina´s movement. A similar trend may be observed in Brazil, although to a lesser degree.

In Europe, the most violent expression of anti-Semitism do not originate anymore exclusively with the European Christians and far-rightists responsible for the worst atrocities against the Jews (the Inquisition, expulsions, pogroms, the Shoah...) but are animated principally by young immigrants or children of immigrants, generally of North-African origin and Muslim faith.

This resurgence is feared by many Jewish intellectuals who are critical of Zionism[2]. Repeated attacks on synagogues, desecration of Jewish cemeteries, attacks on Jewish institutions and museums, attacks on Jews on public streets, kidnapping for ransom (such as the young Ilan Halimi tortured and murdered in France in January 2006), a Jewish couple attacked in their home in the Paris suburbs in December 2014 and the wife raped, the taking of Jewish hostages and killing of four in a kosher supermarket in January 2015, Jewish children killed in March 2012 in the Ozar Hatorah Lyceum in Toulouse, including Myriam Monsonego, 8 years old, whose killer chased her to shoot her in the head point blank in the style of the *Einsatzgruppen (SS)*, and the counterpart of these anti-Semitic attacks, the Islamophobia of the young Israelis who abducted 16-year-old Muhammad Abu Khdeir on July 2, 2014, beat him and burned him alive, and those who set fire to a humble Palestinian dwelling in the West Bank on July 30, 2015, burning to death 18-month-old Ali Saad Dawabsheh, his father Saad and his mother Riham, and leaving his 4-year-old brother Ahmad in critical condition with major burns.

South America has been largely spared these extreme acts, with the exception of Argentina, stricken by the attacks on the Israeli embassy on

---

[1] José Antonio Felicio (Secretary-General for International Relations of the Unified Workers' Central [Central Única dos Trabalhadores – CUT] of Brazil and President the International Trade Union Confederation), "Por um espírito olímpico coerente: Não a ISDS" (In keeping with the Olympic spirit: no to ISDS), *Le Monde Diplomatique Brasil*, March 18, 2015.

[2] See David Myers, "Was There a Jerusalem School? Reshaping the Past", *Studies in Contemporary Jewry*, Vol. X, 1994 / Schumel Feiner, "The Jewish Enlightenment", Jewish Culture and Contexts, University of Pennsylvania Press, 2011.

March 17, 1992 (29 dead) and the bombing of the Asociación Mutual Israelita Argentina (AMIA) on July 18, 1994 (85 dead). The authors and motives for these attacks are still unknown. The distinction between anti-Semitism and hostility toward the Israeli government for its policy regarding the Palestinians is not uniform. Thus the demonstrations in January 2009 in front of the Israeli embassy in Argentina to protest the Israeli offensive in the Gaza Strip was seen by some as the expression of "disguised anti-Semitism"[1], and by others as the legitimate condemnation of the Jewish colonial state's approach to the Palestinian question[2], a dichotomy also observed in Brazil, but in subtler forms. President Dilma Rousseff expressed her dissatisfaction in September 2015 with the appointment of Dani Dayan, leader of the Yesha Council, the federation of Jewish colonies in the West Bank, as Israeli ambassador to Brasilia. A group of 56 Brazilian members of parliament signed and delivered a petition to the Israeli government stating that the choice was inopportune given Dayan's positions in favor of Israeli settlements in the Occupied Territories[3], which are diametrically opposed to those taken by Brazilian diplomacy.

Brazil joined the UNRWA Advisory Commission in 2014, the first country in Latin America to do so. It makes a yearly voluntary contribution of 8-9 million dollars to the Agency. Brazil began receiving Palestinian refugees from the Ruweished camp (Jordan) in 2007 and currently hosts 117 of them. Aid consisting of 11.500 tons of rice delivered shortly before the start of the Israeli offensive in 2014 alleviated food shortages among 1.2 million Palestinians in the Gaza Strip. Between 2007 and 2014, Brazil agreed to provide 10 million dollars to the Agency to aid the Palestinians, in addition to donations of rice[4].

Unlike its populous Syrian community, which has recently taken in a large number of Syrian refugees, Brazil's Palestinian community is not numerous. Palestinians are the largest Arab community in four countries in Latin America: Peru, Chile, Honduras, and El Salvador. The last three countries abstained (along with their regional neighbors Colombia, Argentina, and Mexico) from the vote at the General Assembly of the United Nations on November 29, 1947 on the partitioning of Palestine. Brazil, which presided over the Assembly, and 12 other countries in Latin America voted in favor[5]. However, citing the occupation of Jerusalem and the failure to observe UN resolutions regarding Palestinian refugees abstained from the vote to allow Israel to join the United States on May 11, 1949 and did not establish diplomatic relations with the country until 1952.

---

[1] Daniel Goldman, Alejandro Dujovne, "Antisemitismo disfrazado" (Disguised anti-Semitism), *Página12*, January 30, 2009.

[2] Ezequiel Adamovsky, "Uso político del antisemitismo" (The political use of anti-Semitism), *Página12*, February 9, 2009.

[3] André De Souza, "Indicação de embaixador israelense em Brasilia gera polêmica" (Appointment of Israeli ambassador to Brasilia stirs controversy), *O 'Globo*, September 24, 2015.

[4] According to Paz Fernandez of the UNRWA, cf Thais Folgosi, "Palestina: uma tragédia que parece não ter fim" (Palestine: a tragedy that seems to have no end), Revue *Brasileiros*, February 4, 2015.

[5] Cuba was the only country in the region to vote against it.

In October 2011, Palestine achieved full member status in UNESCO. In response, the United States suspended financial support to the organization (22% of the UNESCO budget). UNESCO was forced to cancel its training programs in Iraq and Afghanistan, which were particularly important to Washington (literacy programs for Afghan police, training of judicial authorities in Iraq, rural sanitation and irrigation projects in Iraq, development of a database of subsurface drinking water reserves in Iraq in collaboration with NASA, etc.). The United States withdrew from UNESCO between 1985 and 2003.

Between 2004 and 2008, more than two thirds of arms sales by the United States, the world's largest weapons supplier, went to the Middle East (207 fighter aircraft and 5.000 guided missiles), principally to Israel and the United Arab Emirates. In the same period, 40% of arms sales by France, the world's fourth supplier, also went to the Middle East. Arms purchases in this region increased by 62% in the period 1998-2007, mainly in the Gulf states and the United Arab Emirates[1]. Russia sold arms worth a total of 4.7 billion dollars to Syria in 2007-2010, financing a good deal of these sales. This is twice the value of arms sold in 2003-2006[2]. Since the 1979 Camp David Accords, Egypt has received yearly military aid from the United States of some 1.3 billion dollars[3], which was not suspended after the coup d'état against President Mohamed Morsi. The most recent Global Peace Index (2013) of the Institute for Economics and Peace, headquartered in Sydney, Australia, ranks the United States in 99th position and Israel in 150th.

As regards the European Union, our contacts in Itamaraty were somewhat reserved. The European Union has lost influence by refusing to recognize the perfectly legitimate electoral victory of Hamas in January 2006 and to engage in any dialogue with its leaders in spite of developments within the organization (Fatah-Hamas Mecca Agreement, Riyadh Summit, Palestinian State within 1967 borders). Following the U.S. lead, the EU classified Hamas as a terrorist organization and has kept its assets frozen since 2000. The European Union should have made an effort to reconcile with the Palestinians, unite Gaza with the West Bank, and forge stronger ties with local organizations (including the recognition of Hamas, which is particularly popular in the Gaza Strip), encouraging all parties to abide by international law. The European Union now operates in the shadow of the United States as an outsourcer for humanitarian aid. Brasilia has a hard time understanding the lack of reaction and failure to demand compensation when the humanitarian facilities financed by European funds are destroyed by the Israeli army; more than one hundred dwellings in 2014 according to the United Nations Office for the Coordination of Humanitarian Affairs, with a similar number destroyed in 2013.

---

1. SIPRI, Stockholm, April 2009.
2. Richard F. Grimmett Report, 2012.
3. *International Herald Tribune*, March 17-18, 2012.

The new strictly bilateral measures adopted on June 28, 2013 to prohibit any money from the EU budget going to cooperation or trade with Israeli institutions sited in the territories occupied since 1967 are considered largely marginal in their effect given the 40 billion dollars in trade in 2011, boosted by a European Union association agreement signed in 1995. There is also the particularly generous research and innovation agreement signed on June 8, 2014 (Horizon 2020 Program) with a budget on the order of 70-80 billion dollars between 2014 and 2020 that should benefit Israeli industries that produce security equipment in the occupied territories (Motorola Israel, Aeronautic Defense Systems, Israel Aerospace Industries)[1].

Hamas has organized an efficient network of charitable associations to assist a humiliated and distressed population. Its victory in the 2006 election cannot be separated from the radicalization of Palestinian society in response to the Israeli occupation and blockade, nor can its birth in December 1987 at the start of the first Intifada. The cofounder and spiritual leader of Hamas, Ahmed Yassin, a quadriplegic since the age of 12 and nearly blind, was assassinated by Israel on March 22, 2004. The Security Council condemned the assassination in a resolution authored by Brazil and Algeria with the support of France, Russia, and China, but the United States exercised its veto right. Yassin's successor, Abdel Aziz al-Rantissi, was also assassinated. The current leader, Khaled Mashal, was the victim of an attempted poisoning by two Mossad agents while he was in Jordan. King Hussein immediately demanded that Israeli Prime Minister Benjamin Netanyahu turn over the antidote, and it took the intervention of U.S. President Bill Clinton to compel him to do so[2]. Salah Shahade, one of the leaders of the armed branch of Hamas (Izz ad-Din al Quassam brigades) was killed in a "targeted" Israeli attack on his home in Gaza on July 22, 2002, also killing 15 people in his family, seven of whom were children, and wounding 150 others in the neighborhood. Mahmoud al-Mabhouh, one of the leaders of the movement, was assassinated on June 14, 2010 in a Dubai hotel by Mossad agents using stolen European passports belonging to Israelis with dual nationality[3]. Ahmed al-Jabari, a high Hamas official, held for 13 years in Israeli prison, involved in peace talks with the Israeli administration through Israeli pacifist Gershon Baskin, who acted as mediator, was killed in a targeted attack in November 2012[4]. Mohammed Deif,

---

[1] Cf Ben Hayes, "How the EU subsidies Israel´s military-industrial complex", *openDemocracyy*, March 6, 2013. (*www.opendemoracy.net*).

[2] The antidote probably would have arrived too late to save Mashal, who owes his life to the ability of the Jordanian doctors to properly identify the type of poison used and give him the proper antidote from their own supplies.

[3] One of the agents, an Australian national, Ben Zygier, arrested on February 24, 2010, described the overall operation to Kuwaiti authorities. He was then arrested by Mossad agents and imprisoned *incomunicado* in solitary confinement in the Ayallon prison, where he allegedly committed suicide in December 2013. See Jodi Rudoren, "Prisoner X may be tied to Dubai killing", *International New York Times,* February 16-17, 2013.

[4] Reuven Pedatzur, "Why did Israel Kill Jabari?", *Haaretz*, December 4, 2012.

leader of the Hamas military wing, was also the object of a targeted attack by the Israeli Air Force in August 2014. Also killed were his wife Wilad, his 8-month son Ali and three other children with their mother. Commander of the Israeli Air Force (2000-2004) Dan Halutz boasted to the press that he had supervised between 80 and 100 targeted, extra-judicial assassinations with "*a 90% success rate*"[1].

The massive sales of arms in the region and the summary executions of Hamas leaders are clearly not road signs on the map to peace. According to our contacts, the premises for negotiations can only be achieved by freezing arms sales and including Hamas in the process. After all, the Zionist organizations *Irgun*, directed by Menachem Begin and Eitan Livni[2] and *Lehi* of Avraham Stern and Yitzhak Shamir, the African National Congress of Nelson Mandela, the Provisional Irish Republican Army of Martin McGuiness and Gerry Adams, the Palestine Liberation Organization of Yasser Arafat, and the *Tupamaros* (MLN-T) of José Mujica, incarcerated for 14 years in Uruguayan military prison, elected president of Uruguay (2010-2014), were all classified as terrorist organizations before being considered essential partners in negotiations. Nelson Mandela was not removed from this list until 2008[3].

However, our contacts stress that the real issue is the Palestinian question. Israel has sought to avoid this issue for too long, as illustrated by the slogan: "*A land without people for a people without a land*"[4], the classic concept informing their colonial policy, considering the coveted territories to be *res nullius*, much to the distress of the indigenous population. In 1948, two thirds of the Palestinian population had been expelled from their lands, some 750,000 people, and 500 of their villages had been destroyed. Israel long sought to deny the existence of a Palestinian national movement, branding it as a terrorist organization. It will end up at the negotiating table with Hamas, just as it did with the Palestine Liberation Organization. Refusing to talk to Hamas is to reject the outcome of free elections. The best guarantee of Israel's security is the restored dignity of the Palestinian people and not, as declared by the Minister of Internal Affairs in the Netanyahu government, Eli Yishai, during bombardment of the Gaza Strip, to "*send Gaza back to the Middle Ages*"[5]. The photographs of Heidi Levine, recent winner of the Anja Niedringhaus Prize for courage in photojournalism, clearly illustrate what he means[6]. Levine says that she has never seen scenes of violence and hatred that can equal what she witnessed during the recent Israeli

---

[1] Laura Blumenfeld, "A Divisive Struggle Over Targeted Killing", *The Washington Post*, August 27, 2006.

[2] Father of Tzipi Livni, former Israeli Minister of Foreign Affairs in 2006-2009 and current leader of the Hatnuah party. Sentenced to 15 years in prison in 1946 by the British authorities for acts of terrorism, Eitan Livni served three terms in the Knesset (1973-1985).

[3]. "Mandela Taken Off U.S. Terror List", *BBC News*, July 1, 2008.

[4] Mur Diana, "A land without a People for a People without a land", *Middle Eastern Quarterly*, Spring 2008, Vol. 15, no. 2.

[5]. Mario Augusto Kakobskind, *Pragmatismo Politico*, November 21, 2012.

[6] 2015 Anja Niedringhaus Courage in Photojournalism Award, given by the International Women's Media Foundation with funding from the Howard Buffet Foundation.

offensive[1]. The Brazilian president characterized the offensive as a "*massacre*"[2], the Commissioner General of UNRWA spoke of "*carnage*"[3]. The stories collected from Israeli soldiers and officers by the Israeli NGO Breaking the Silence, founded in March 2004 by a group of Israeli soldiers, are disturbing[4]. Entire neighborhoods and villages, orchards and olive groves were systematically destroyed (Juhar al-Dik, al-Bureij, Shuja ayya...). More than two thirds of the population of Gaza now depends on aid from UNRWA for their survival. The World Health Organization estimates that 20% need psychological care[5].

The destruction of civil infrastructure (electrical power plants, canals, hospitals, mosques, and schools, including those of the United Nations that were used as bomb shelters), and an alarming proportion of women and children killed are all part of the long tradition of violence against the Palestinian people: the Dei-Yassin and al-Dawayima massacres in April and May 1948, the Kafr Kassem massacre in 1956, the El-Tawafiq massacre in 1962, the Sabra and Shatila massacre in September 1982, the Qana massacre in 1996.

In an open letter published by the British newspaper *The Guardian*, six Nobel Peace Prize laureates asked for the cessation of hostilities and an embargo on arms sales. Two of them were South American: Adolfo Pres Esquivel (Argentina) and Rigoberta Mandchu (Guatemala). Brazil, Ecuador, Chile, Peru, and El Salvador recalled their ambassadors from Tel Aviv for consultations (Bolivia and Venezuela had broken off diplomatic relations in January 2009 after the second Israeli offensive on the Gaza Strip, Nicaragua suspended them in February 2010). Cuba broke off diplomatic relations in 1973 after the Yom Kippur War, during which it had dispatched a contingent of 1,300 Cuban soldiers to support the Syrian army. The Mercosur countries (Brazil, Venezuela, Argentina, Uruguay, Bolivia) issued a special declaration at their 46th summit condemning "*the disproportionate use of force by the Israeli army*". Paraguay, temporarily suspended from Mercosur, did not sign. Bolivia revoked the visa exemption for Israeli citizens established in 1972 and President Evo Morales qualified Israel as a "*terrorist state*". Venezuelan President Nicolas Maduro announced the establishment of an immigration center (*Casa de Abrigo*) for orphaned Palestinian children. The Uruguayan president spoke of genocide

---

1 *International New York Times*, March 26, 2015.

2 "*Não acho qué genocídio, mas acho que é um massacre*" (I do not think we can call it genocide, but it is certainly a massacre), Conflito em Israel, "*Não é genocídio, é massacre*" (It is not genocide, it's a massacre), *Folha de São Paulo*, July 28, 2014.

3 "*We have moved beyond the realm of humanitarian action alone. We are in the realm of accountability. I call on the international community to take deliberate international political action to put an immediate end to the continuing carnage*", UNRWA United Nations Relief and Works Agency for Palestine Refugees in the Near East, July 30, 2014 (www.unrwa.org).

4 "This Is How We Fought In Gaza. Soldiers' Testimonies and photographs from Operation Protective Edge", Breaking the Silence, 2014 (www.breakingthesilence.org.il).

5 "Shell-shocked Gazans seek to expand mental health services in wake of conflict", September 2014 (www.who.int).

in Gaza[1]. All Latin American countries that are members of the United Nations Human Rights Council voted in July 2014 to create a Commission of Inquiry to investigate the Israeli attacks. The European countries abstained. The United States was the only country to vote against it.

This brutal repression of the civilian population in Gaza and the worsening of the situation in the West Bank (56 Palestinians killed and 5,868 injured by the Israeli army in 2014) contributed to the decision by Palestine to recognize the jurisdiction of the International Criminal Court (Palestine was admitted on January 20, 2015), a decision that was challenged, with Israel responding by suspending payment of customs duties to the Palestinian National Authority (amounting to a yearly average of 3 billion dollars, one third of its budgetary resources). It is a grotesque situation in which a country is punished for joining an institution of international law which includes 123 member countries (27 of them in Latin America, Brazil joined in June 2002). Among Arab countries, only Jordan, Tunisia, and Palestine are currently parties to the International Criminal Court.

The suspension of payment of customs duties has become a classic retaliatory measure employed by the Israeli government: 2 years starting in October 2000 during the second Intifada; 18 months starting in March 2006 after the Palestinian legislative elections; one month in March 2011 after the reconciliation of the principal Palestinian authorities; four months starting in November 2012 when Palestine was granted non-member status in the United Nations. No compensation is provided for these repeated suspensions of payment that contribute to fiscal instability and discourage investment. This when the Palestinian Authority is required to pay 10% interest if it does not pay its monthly electricity bills within 11 days (an average yearly bill of 660 million dollars with all electricity in the West Bank depending entirely on the Israeli-owned Israel Electric Corporation)[2].

Brazilian diplomacy has evolved as regards the Palestinian question. While the previous administration (the dyad Lula-Amorim) was inclined to think that the solution to the conflict would be found within the framework of international negotiations with all concerned parties to achieve the peaceful coexistence of two sovereign states, convinced that the paradigm of bilateral negotiations championed under the U.S. aegis was obsolete, Brasilia is now more circumspect. The massive expansion of Israeli settlements now makes it nearly impossible to create a Palestinian state. The Netanyahu coalition, in power since March 2015, and the majority of the Israelis do not want it. Israelis named the Occupied Palestinian territories by their biblical words (Judea and Samaria); Justice Minister Ayelet Shaked says that the West Bank and East-

[1] Mujíca qualifies the Gaza attacks: "*Cuando se bombardean hospitales, niños y viejos me parece que es un genocídio*" (When hospitals, children and old people are bombed, I call it genocide), *Página12*, August 5, 2014.

[2] "Report on UNCTAD assistance to the Palestinian people. Developments in the economy of the Occupied Palestinian Territory", July 6, 2015.

Jerusalem are "*an area under dispute*" refusing to acknowledge that there is an occupation. A study funded by the State Department and launched by the Jerusalem based Council for Religious Institutions in the Holy Land, an interfaith association of Jewish, Christian and Muslim leaders and scholars in Israel and the Occupied Territories, revealed that 76% of Israeli textbooks maps fail to distinguish the Palestinian territories and Israel. Most elementary and secondary schoolbooks on either side presented "exclusive unilateral national narratives"[1].

The exceptions are found among a few intellectuals and professors (Gideon Levy, Zeev Sternhel, Amos Oz, Yehoshua, David Grossman, Uri Avnery, Ilan Pappe...), pacifist movements (Shalom Achshav - Peace Now, Gush Shalom, Jewish Voice for Peace, Ta´ayush, Yesh Din, Gisha...), humanitarian organizations (B'Tselem, Zochrot, Physicians for Human Rights...), the newspaper *Haaretz*, and certain tiny political parties. There are only a few hundred conscripts that refuse to serve in the occupied territories each year[2]. Isaac Herzog, the opposition candidate, himself qualified the movement begun in 2005 to boycott Israeli companies situated in the occupied territories as a "*terrorist movement*".

Israel's objective is clear: it wants to extend its settlements into those places, excluding the desert areas, that are the least densely populated by Palestinians, and then proceed with a relocation of the population for security reasons. As Ilan Pappé put it, the Palestinians have the choice between an open-air prison (West Bank) or a high security prison (Gaza)[3], with the Palestinian elite, on its leash, getting to live in the "oasis" of Ramallah.

After the Oslo II Accord (September 28, 1995), the number of Israeli settlements in the West Bank increased fourfold. There are now more Israeli settlers in resource-rich Zone C of the West Bank than there are Palestinians: 341.000 Israeli colonists in 235 settlements as opposed to an estimated 300.000 Palestinians[4]. And there is an increasing number of confrontations and clashes: in 2014, colonists destroyed more than 9.000 Palestinian fruit trees, and another 5.600 in the sole month of January 2015[5].

Brasilia seems to have raised the bar still higher for the resolution of the conflict if one gives credence to Dilma Rousseff's speech before United Nations in September 2014, stating that only an abandonment of arms and a reform of the Security Council can bring an end to the conflict:

---

[1] "Victims of Our Own Narratives? Portrayal of the "Other" in Israeli and Palestinian School Books", February 4, 2013 (www.IsraeliPalestinianSchoolbooks.blogspot.com).

[2] Moriel Rothman-Zecher, "Why I won´t serve Israel", *International New York Times*, January 13, 2015.

[3] "*The [Israeli] government offered two versions of the mega prison to the people in the West Bank and the Gaza Strip. One was an open-air prison and the other a maximum security one. Should they not accept the former, they would get the latter*", in *On Palestine* (Chapter 10), Haymarket Books, Chicago, 2015.

[4] United Nations Office for the Coordination of the Humanitarian Affairs (OCHA), 2014 a.

[5] Report on UNCTAD assistance to the Palestinian people. Developments in the Economy of the Occupied Palestinian Territory", July 6, 2015.

"The use of force is incapable of eliminating the underlying causes of conflict. This is made clear by the persistence of the Question of Palestine; the systematic massacre of the Syrian people; the tragic national destructuring of Iraq; the serious insecurity in Libya; the conflicts in the Sahel; and the clashes in Ukraine. Each military intervention leads not to peace, but to the deterioration of these conflicts. We witness a tragic proliferation in the numbers of civilian victims and humanitarian catastrophes. We cannot allow these barbaric acts to increase, harming our ethical, moral and civilizational values. The Security Council has been having difficulties in promoting peaceful solutions to those conflicts. A genuine reform of the Security Council is necessary to overcome the current paralysis. This process has been dragging on for too long[1]."

Between September 1972 and February 2011, the United States has used its veto in the Security Council 42 times on resolutions regarding Palestine and the occupied territories; this is more than half of the vetoes used by this country in this forum.

Itamaraty diplomats estimate that only the perception of a risk of noticeable change in the United States' support for Israel could lead Tel Aviv to the negotiating table and thus make possible "a Solomonic judgment".

Nothing may be expected of Israeli civil society, which, in spite of the deteriorating image of Israel in its external relations, does not call into question the policy of the government. A survey by the University of Tel Aviv and the think tank Israel Democratic Institute shows that 92% of Israelis approve of the last Gaza offensive[2]. The trend in recent years has been toward increasing extremism, religious orthodoxy, and nationalism. Scenes such as Israelis cheering the bombing of Gaza by the Israeli Air Force, as reported by CNN journalist Diana Magnay, at her own risk[3], were hardly imaginable several decades ago, just as it was hard to conceive of the retribution measures against journalists who gave a relatively balanced treatment of the Palestinian question (Donald Neff, Phil Reeves, Robert Fisk, Suzanne Goldenberg, Ewa Jasiewicz, Jared Malsin, Ayman Mohyeldin, Richard Labevière, John Pilger, etc.). We must also mention the Palestinian journalists who were targeted and killed (Tami Rayan, Sameh Aryan, Najla Alhaj, Khaled Hamad, Abdulrahman Abuhen, Izzat Daher, Baha Garib, Ahed Afif Zaqout, Baha Kamel Alghareib, Imad Eid...) and

---

[1] "*O uso da força é incapaz de eliminar as causas profundas dos conflitos. Isso está claro na persistência da Questão Palestina; no massacre sistemático do povo sírio; na trágica desestruturação nacional do Iraque; na grave insegurança na Líbia; nos conflitos no Sahel e nos embates na Ucrânia. A cada intervenção militar não caminhamos para a Paz mas, sim, assistimos ao acirramento desses conflitos. Verifica-se uma trágica multiplicação do número de vítimas civis e de dramas humanitários. Não podemos aceitar que essas manifestações de barbárie recrudesçam, ferind nossos valores éticos, morais e civilizatórios. O Conselho de Segurança tem encontrado dificuldade em promover a solução pacífica desses conflitos. Para vencer esses impasses será necessária uma verdadeira reforma do Conselho de Segurança, processo que se arrasta há muito tempo*", September 24, 2014 (www2planalto.gov).

[2] Mirren Gida, "Poll: 92% of Israeli Jews Say Operation 'Protective Edge' was justified", *Time*, August 19, 2014.

[3] "CNN Reassigns Reporter Who Called Israelis Cheering Bombs 'Scum' in Tweet", *The New York Times*, July 18, 2014.

Palestinian children rights advocate such as Hashem Abu Maria who worked with Defense for Children international (a Palestine children´s right association) fatally shot by an Israeli soldier sniper in July 2014.

Israeli forces have on numerous occasions used live ammunition against Palestinians who posed no imminent threat during West Bank protests, and the Israeli military has a poor record of bringing soldiers to justice for such acts, Human Rights Watch reported. B'Tselem documented at least 46 cases from 2005 to early 2013 in which Israeli forces killed Palestinians in the West Bank "*by firing live ammunition at stone throwers*". Since September 2000, Israeli forces have killed more than 3.000 Palestinians who did not participate in hostilities in the West Bank and Gaza, according to B'Tselem's data. But the military justice system has convicted only six Israeli soldiers for unlawfully killing Palestinians, with seven-and-a-half months as the longest jail sentence, according to Yesh

Criticism against the Israeli government is illegitimately qualified as being anti-Semitic, even when made by people whose moral stature is unquestioned (Uruguayan president José Mujica, former U.S. president Jimmy Carter, former director general of UNESCO Federico Mayor, and a number of Nobel Peace Prize laureates: the Argentine Adolfo Pérez Esquivel, the Irish Betty Williams and Mairead Maguire, the American Jody Williams, the Guatemalan Rigoberta Menchú, the South African Desmond Tutu). U.S. Secretary of State John Kerry, who remarked during a closed-door meeting of the Trilateral Commission[1] in April 2014 that Israel risked becoming "*an apartheid state*", was forced to retract his comment within 48 hours[2].

By the combined action of predominantly Ashkenazi immigration from Eastern Europe, a religious orthodoxy drawing on the Hebrew Bible, *Tanakh*, a belief in inalienable divine rights on other people's land despite repeated words of caution from Zionists of renown, including the philosopher Ahad Ha'am (Asher Zvi Hirsch Ginsberg, 1856-1927)[3], a sovereign army that holds itself above right and wrong to which every Israeli citizen dedicates 36 months of their life and where every Israeli has a relative who is enlisted or on the payroll, an ethnic approach based on exclusion reminiscent of the worst years of apartheid, as evidenced, among other things, by the prison for undocumented

---

[1] A Washington-based think tank created by David Rockefeller in 1973.

[2] Michael Gordon, "Kerry Expresses Regret after Apartheid Remark", *International New York Times*, April 28, 2014.

[3] "*We must surely learn, from both our past and present history, how careful we must be not to provoke the anger of the native people by doing them wrong, how we should be cautious in our dealings with a foreign people among whom we returned to live, to handle these people with love and respect and, needless to say, with justice and good judgment. And what do our brothers do? Exactly the opposite! They were slaves in their Diasporas, and suddenly they find themselves with unlimited freedom, wild freedom that only a country like Turkey [the Ottoman Empire] can offer. This sudden change has planted despotic tendencies in their hearts, as always happens to former slaves ['eved ki yimlokh – when a slave becomes king – Proverbs 30:22]. They deal with the Arabs with hostility and cruelty, trespass unjustly, beat them shamefully for no sufficient reason, and even boast about their actions. There is no one to stop the flood and put an end to this despicable and dangerous tendency*" in Tony Kushner (ed.), Alisa Solomom (ed.), *Wrestling with Zion*, p. 16, Grove Press, 2003.

asylum seekers arriving from Sudan or Eritrea[1], Israeli society now finds itself diametrically opposed to the nation announced and celebrated some decades ago by many authors and intellectuals, such as Joseph Kessel (Jerusalem, 1948)[2], Arthur Koestler, who shared the communal life of the kibbutz in the 1920s, rendered homage to Israel in his book *Analyse d´un miracle; naissance d'Israel* (1949)[3] and the Brazilian Moacyr Scliar (1937-2011) celebrating "*the socialist ideal of the Zionist odyssey*"[4]. How has a nation that was built "*through those migrations, those expulsions, those proscriptions, those inquisitions, through those massacres, those auto-da-fés and those pogroms, through centuries and centuries of dread, ghettos and tortures*"[5] become such a painful quandary for many Brazilian Jews? The month of October 2015 sum up the tragedy of the Palestinian-Israeli conflict: death-chanting Israeli mob of 70 settlers, captured on a video, lynched 19 year-old Fadi Alloun in the Old City of Jerusalem, later executed by Israeli police forces[6]; the drive-by shooting of an Israeli couple (Eitam and Naamia Henkin) in front of their four children as they drove between settlements in the West Bank[7]; a 13 years old Palestinian Ahmed Manasrah bleeding in the Pisgat Ze´ev neighborhood of East Jerusalem under the insults from Israeli bystanders watching the agony of the child who stabbed with his 15 year-old brother an 13 year-old Israeli boy[8]; six young Palestiniansin killed by Israeli forces in the Gaza strip including a 15 year old boy as they opened fire to quell youths that hurled rocks[9]; an Israeli Jew Uri Rezken stabbed by a Jewish man who believed he was an Arab in Haifa suburb[10]; two ultra-orthodox Jewish men, Nehemia Levi and Aharon Benita-Bennett, fatally stabbed to death and a two year old girl with her mother wounded in Jerusalem Old City by an Arab teenager[11];

---

[1]. Qualified as 'intruders' by the Israeli authorities, there are more than 2.000 detained in a so-called "open" prison, the Holot Residency Center in the Negev desert 65 kilometers from the nearest town (Beersheba). They are forced to sign an attendance ledger three times a day and to spend the night in the facility. The Israeli journalist Lia Tarachansky dedicated a film to the drama here in 2014 (*Ethnocracy in the Promised Land: Israel's African Refugees*) and the humanitarian organization Human Rights Watch published a report in September 2014 ("*Make Their Lives Miserable. Israel's Coercion of Eritrean and Sudanese Asylum Seekers to Leave Israel*"), in spite of the remarkable healthcare work done by Physicians for Human Rights-Israel (Open Clinic).

[2] Joseph Kessel, *La Nouvelle saison* ; *1948, Israël : Il a fallu deux mille ans*.

[3] Arthur Koestler, *Analyse d´un miracle*, Calman-Levy, Paris, 1949.

[4] Moacy Scliar in *Entre o shtetl e o gulag: vozes do judaísmo russo* (www.scliar.org).

[5] Joseph Kessel, "1948, Israël : Il a fallu deux mille ans", in *La Nouvelle Saison. Reportages 1948-1954*, Éditions Taillandier, Paris 2010.

[6] Hasson Nir, "Let the People of Israel Enter the Gates and Kill Arabs", *Haaretz*, October 4, 2015.

[7] Medad Batya, "World Ignores Terror Murder of Henkin Couple", *TheJewishPress.com*, October 2, 2015.

[8] Mackey Robert, Kershner Isabel, "Conflicting Accounts of Jerusalem Strife Surround a Wounded Arab Boy", *New York Times*, October 15, 2015.

[9] Rudoren Jodi, "Israeli Soldiers Kill 6 Palestinians in Gaza as West Bank Unrest Grows, *International New York Times*, October 9, 2015.

[10] Shuttleworth Kate, "Stabbed Israeli Jew mistaken for Arab criticises violence", *The Guardian*, October 15, 2015.

[11] Rudoren Jody, Risen Jonathan, "Palestinian kills 2 Israelis in Jerusalem", *New York Times*, October 3, 2015.

13 years old Palestinian Abdel Rahman Abdullah killed "by mistake" by Israeli soldiers near Bethlehem[1]; aa civil right activist, Richard lakin, fatally shot and stabbed in a Jerusalem bus by Palestinians assaillants[2] an innocent Eritrean asylum seeker, Mulu Habtom Zerhom shot by a security guard because he looks "Arab", then bleeding out on the floor of a bus terminal in the southern city of Beersheba beaten by a lynch mob that includes soldiers[3].

Nothing has changed since March 29, 2002 when Ayat al-Akhras a 16 year-old Palestinian girl suicide bomber killed 17 year-old Rachel Levy in Jerusalem´s Kiryat Ha Yovel main supermarket. As president George W. Bush observed then: "*When a Palestinian girl is induced to blow herself up and in the process kills a 17 year-old Israeli girl, the future itself is dying, the future of the Palestinian people and the future of the Israeli people*[4]".

Those Palestinians children born at time of the Oslo Accords (1993) are now 20 year-old with little hope for their bleak future and in process of radicalization.

Israeli politicians and religious leaders communicate with violence, threats, retaliation and intimidation. The only result is more hatred, more killing, more violence.

Shmuel Eliyahu, the chief rabbi of Safed, a Jewish studies center in the northern of Israel, whose salary is paid by the government, demanded in October 2015 that police officers who do not summarily execute Palestinians after they have been arrested should themselves be put on trial, according to *Haaretz* newspaper[5]. One must remember May 15, 1974, when 105 Israeli Jewish Elementary school children from Safed on a school trip were taken by a Palestinian group (Democratic Front for the Liberation of Palestine), while sleeping in a school in Maalot: 22 of them were among those killed by the hostage takers and 68 more were injured[6].

Ayelet Shaked, member of the Israeli parliament for the far right Jewish Home Party (Habeyiy Hayehudi), Justice Minister since May 2015, called for genocide against the mothers of the "*snakes*" in July 2014, one week after the Palestinian teenager Muhammad Abu Khadeir was snatched and burned alive by six Israeli Jewish youths:

> "*Behind every terrorist stand dozens of men and women, without whom he could not engage in terrorism. They are all enemy combatants, and their blood shall be on all their heads. Now this also includes the mothers of the martyrs, who send them to hell with flowers and kisses. They should follow their sons, nothing would be more just. They should go, as should*

---

[1] "IDF Says Palestinian boy was killed by mistake", *The Times of Israel*, October 6, 2015.

[2] Rudoren Jody, "A Teacher Killed by Palestinians, Recalled as a Man of Peace", *International New York Times,* October 28, 2015.

[3] Malm Sara, "Eritrean asylum seeker shot and lynched in Israel, mistaken for a "terrorist", *Daily Mail,* October 19, 2015.

[4] Hammer Joshua, "How two lives met in death", *Newsweek*, April 15, 2002.

[5] Ettinger Yair, "Safed Rabbi: Terrorists Must Not Be Allowed to Survive Attacks", *Haaretz*, October 15, 2015.

[6] Palestinian president Mahmoud Abbas was born in Safed.

the physical homes in which they raised the snakes. Otherwise, more little snakes will be raised there[1]."

Prime Minister Benjamin Netanyahu contibutes to the demonization of the Arabe people, particularly the Palestinians, when he stated at the 37th Zionist Congress in October 2015 that the grand mufti of Jerusalem Haj Amin al-Husseini, an Arab nationalist and a zealous foe of Zionism, then and now a renowned figure in Palestinian circles, suggested to Hitler in 1941 the "final solution" of the Jewish question.

Each round of negotiations since 2008 (Annapolis Conference, negotiations led by Robert Mitchell, resumption of talks led by John Kerry) has been followed by military operations in Gaza on Israel's initiative. Every Security Council resolution has gone unheeded. The Palestinian economy is an Israeli captive while the Israeli settlements spread inexorably on Palestinian land (there are more than 350.000 Israeli settlers in the West Bank subsidized by the state to the tune of an annual average of 250 million dollars for the past six years, and 300.000 Israelis living in the area of Jerusalem that was unilaterally annexed in 1967[2]).

According to Brasilia, Islamist terrorism derives from and is nourished in large part by the Palestinian question. It regards all nations. It is the "*mother of all evils*" in the expression used by the Franco-American professor Scott Atrari[3]. It is why it must be the object of a multilateral approach, with the participation of nations that do not have interests in the region, instead of being "*kidnapped by a small group of countries*" in the words of President Lula's Minister of Foreign Affairs, Celso Amorim[4].

Mediation in the Iranian Nuclear Issue

The agreement forged on May 17, 2010 during President Lula's official visit to Tehran, modeled on the proposition made in October 2009 in Geneva by the Vienna Group (France, Russia, United States, International Atomic Energy Agency) with the support of Germany, while Iran declined, is unquestionably the most daring initiative of Brazilian diplomacy to date: Iran exports 1.200 kg of Low-Enriched Uranium within one month to be held in escrow in Turkey in exchange for 120 kg of 20%-enriched uranium within one year.

After the visit to Brasilia in May 2009 of Mohammad Nahavandian, president of the Iranian Chamber of Commerce and Industry and adjunct

---

[1] Mira Bar Hillel, "Why I´m on the brink of burning my Israeli passport", *Independent*, July 11, 2014 (www.independent.co.uk).

[2] *International New York Times*, March 13, 2015.

[3] Scott Atrari, *Talking to the Enemy: Faith, Brotherhood and the (Un) making of Terrorists*, Harpers Collins Publishers, 2010.

[4] Celso Amorim, "O Brasil e o Oriente Médio" (p. 132), in "*Teerã, Ramalá e Doha, memórias da politica externa ativa e altiva*", 2015.

secretary of the Iranian National Security Council, who had discussions in Itamaraty with the Secretary General Samuel Pinheiro Guimarães, Brasilia had envisaged the possibility of mediation with the assistance of Turkey.

President Lula took part in the G15 summit in Tehran in May 2010. Created at the Belgrade Conference in September 1989, the G15 includes 18 observers and members of the non-aligned nations[1]. In January 2010, prior to the summit, the Brazilian Minister of Foreign Affairs, Celso Amorim was invited to Ankara. Iranian president Ahmadinejad made an official visit to Brasilia in November 2009. During the nuclear security summit in Washington on April 12 and 13, 2009, President Obama met with President Lula and the Turkish Prime Minister, Recep Tayyip Erdogan. Celso Amorim met again with President Ahmadinejad and the Iranian Minister of Foreign Affairs, Manouchehr Mottaki, in December 2009 and April 2010. The Itamaraty chief was pleased to point out that between November 2009 and May 2010 Brazil and Turkey had dedicated more time, and certainly more energy, to talks with Iran than had the P5+1 (the five members of the Security Council plus Germany).

Brazil sought to prevent a fourth round of sanctions against Iran by the Security Council, believing that they only exacerbated tensions[2]. The U.S. Senate had already adopted a unilateral sanctions plan against Iran on January 29, 2010. Brasilia saw the May 17 agreement as a first step toward a solution to the impasse characterized by distrust, incomprehension, antagonism, and hostility among the parties (excepting China) deriving from a long history of conflict.

And the conflicts were by no means insignificant: CIA coup against the democratically elected government of Prime Minister Mohammed Mosaddegh in 1953 because of his move to nationalize Iranian oil against the interests of the Anglo-Iranian Oil Company, placing Mohammed Reza Shah Pahlavi in power; invasion of the United States embassy and the holding of 52 hostages for 444 days (1979); France-Iran crisis over the EURODIF consortium for the enrichment of uranium and attacks in the French capital in 1985-86 attributed to Iran; U.S. support for the invasion of Iran by Saddam Hussein, a war which caused one million deaths (1980-1988), including 95,000 Iranian children; breaking off of diplomatic relations with the United States in 1980 and with France in 1987; American embargo starting in 1995 and the passage of the D'Amato-Kennedy Act (Iran and Libya Sanctions Act of 1996); the destruction of Iran Air Flight 655 in Iranian airspace over the Strait of Hormuz by surface-to-air missiles fired from the USS Vincennes, killing 290, including 66 children (1988); George W. Bush's 2002 State of the Union address qualifying Iran as part of the "*Axis of Evil*"; the CIA's "Brain Drain" program begun in 2005 (resulting in the defections of the Iranian Vice Minister of Defense, Ali Reza

---

1. Africa is represented by Egypt, Algeria, Kenya, Nigeria, Senegal, and Zimbabwe; Asia by India, Indonesia, Iran, Malaysia, and Sri Lanka; Latin America and the Caribbean by Argentina, Brazil, Chile, Jamaica, Mexico, Peru, and Venezuela.

2. Resolution 1737 (December 2006); Resolution 1747 (March 2007); Resolution 1803 (March 2008).

Asgari, and Iranian scientists); planting of the Stuxnet virus in Iranian computer systems in 2009 in order to delay the country's nuclear program; terrorist attacks on the Iranian army in October 2009 by the Jundallah, a group allegedly funded by the United States; the assassination of five Iranian scientists on the streets of Tehran since 2007 (Adeshir Hosseinpour in January 2007, Massoud Ali Mohammadi in January 2010, Majid Shahriari in November 2010 – with another failed attack that same day against Fereydoun Abbasi Davani, current president of the Atomic Energy Organization of Iran –, Darioush Rezaei Nejad in July 2011, and Mostafa Ahmadi Roshan in January 2012); suspicious explosion at the Bid Kaneh missile base, near Tehran, killing a key figure in Iran's missile program, General Hassan Moqaddam, as well as 17 members of the Revolutionary Guards in November 2011; attacks on Israeli diplomats in February 2012.

In an interview with a Brazilian newspaper published on May 28, 2010, the former director of the International Atomic Energy Agency (1999-2009), Mohamed ElBaradei, agreed that the Agreement of May 17 should be used as the basis for negotiations, constituting an important first step that Iran should seize and not allow to die stillborn[1].

The Security Council voted for sanctions less than one month after the Tehran Agreement (Turkey and Brazil voted against them). The IAEA report on Iran, published in June 2010, did not even make mention of the Agreement. It was later learned, thanks to the information made available by Edward Snowden, that the 14 members of the Security Council that took part in the vote had all been put under surveillance by the National Security Agency (NSA), including Brazil. It was the first time in Brazilian diplomatic history that Brazil voted against a UN Security Council resolution: it was a "*question of honor*" in the words of President Lula, a position echoed by the Turkish Prime Minister, Recep Erdoğan.

Celso Amorim revealed that the U.S. president had justified the hasty adoption of new sanctions because they would preempt an Israeli attack on the Iranian nuclear facilities. He saw it as an admission of the inability of U.S. diplomats to convince or control the actions of its very close ally: "*the guardian that fears its ward*[2]".

Brazil would expect more regard for Turkey, NATO member, one of the United States' foremost arms customers, one of the major recipients of U.S. aid, and the major European source of foreign students in the United States

[1]. "*I would hope that this offer is accepted and marks the beginning of negotiations. Saying that sanctions will be applied regardless of this agreement is, to my mind, totally counter-productive.*" *Jornal do Brasil*, May 29, 2010.

[2] *Folha de São Paulo,* February 22, 2015, interview with journalist Patricia Campos Mello, "*Fiquei estarrecido e comentei com o president Lula: é o protetor com medo do protegido. E o reconhecimento da incapacidade de persuadir um aliado ultra-proximo, que depende de voce para muita coisa*" (I was astonished and commented to President Lula: The protector afraid of the protected. An inability to persuade a very close ally who depends on you for so much). See also Amorim's book, *Teerã, Ramalà e Doha: Memórias da Politica Externa Ativa e Altiva,* published by Davirà-Saraiva (Brazil), March 2015.

over the past ten years[1], then engaged in a policy of detente with its neighbors (until the tragic boarding of the Turkish humanitarian ship Mavi Marmara in May 2010 by the Israeli navy and the brutal repression pursued by the Assad regime in Syria). At the time, Celso Amorim's daughter was married to a senior Turkish diplomat, with whom she has two children.

Unlike its South American neighbors (Argentina, Chile, Uruguay, Venezuela, Bolivia), Brazil has not recognized the Armenian Genocide, anxious to maintain a balanced relationship with Turkey and Armenia and "neutrality" in its relations with Turkish and Armenian communities in Brazil. There are somewhere between 90.000 and 130.000 Armenians in Brazil, most of them in the cities of São Paulo and Osasco. The Turkish Cultural Center, which actively defends Ankara's position on this issue, includes luminaries from Brazilian cultural circles on its Advisory Council (Ana Helena Curti, Claudia Toni, Eduardo Saron, Aurea Leszcynski...). A bill was introduced in the Federal Congress (3190/12) by representative Walter Feldman (Brazilian Social Democratic Party – PSDB, São Paulo) to make it a crime to deny the genocide of the Armenian people perpetrated in 1915-1917 by the troops of the Ottoman Empire. This complex issue is now more easily discussed in Ankara and Brazilian diplomacy hopes to let time do its work, pointing out the slow development of the question among Turkish authorities. Certain once abandoned places of memory of the massacres perpetrated against Armenians and Greeks are now being restored in Turkey.

The approach to these developments, it was observed, unquestionably shapes European foreign relations and governance to some extent and the complex debate on Islamophobia. The Armenians were the first Christians, the Kingdom of Armenia was the first state to adopt Christianity as the national religion (early 4th century, before the Emperor Constantine). On the other hand, for Western countries, the insistence on terming the massacre of the Armenians a genocide (in which the Kurds also took part) contrasts with their discretion on matters of the same tragic scope as the extermination of the Incas and the Aztecs during the Spanish conquest of South and Central America, of the native North Americans while the United States "won the west", of the aborigines in Australia, not to mention the enslavement and massacres perpetrated by the colonial powers in Asia and Africa and, historically closer, the brutal repressions in Franco´s Spain, by Indonesia in Timor, or the Vietnam War, which killed 6 or 7 million Vietnamese. The South African sociologist Stanley Cohen dedicated a book to this amnesia on nations before their misdeeds[2].

In June 2015 the Brazilian Senate approved a solidarity motion with the Armenian people, qualifying the massacres perpetrated under the Ottoman Empire as genocide. Turkey recalled its ambassador for consultation in a sign

---

1. More than the United Kingdom and Germany; some 12.000 students in 2012. Source: *International Herald Tribune*, April 8, 2013.

2 Stanley Cohen, *"States of Denial: Knowing about Atrocities and Suffering"*, Polity Press, Cambridge, 2001.

of protest in spite of the explanations given to the Turkish diplomatic representative by the Secretary General of Itamaraty[1]. The legislatures of certain states in the Brazilian federation had previously recognized the genocide (São Paulo, Ceara). Uruguay was the first Latin American country to acknowledge the Armenian genocide (1965).

The Syrian crisis and the emergence of the Islamic State have led Ankara into a tightrope act on the rigid cord of its sovereignty, its religious schisms, the conflict that has pitted it for 40 years against the armed independence movement of the Kurdistan Workers' Party (PKK), and its membership in NATO, which preceded its probably hopeless application for admission to the European Union.

Turkey joined the Nuclear Non-Proliferation Treaty in 1969 (ratifying it in 1980) and the Additional Protocol in 2001. It ratified the Comprehensive Nuclear-Test-Ban Treaty in 2001.

Celso Amorim notes that the proposals made to Iran entail, implicitly or explicitly, that Iran abandon the enrichment of uranium it needs to operate its research reactor in Tehran (provided by the United States and with the most recent fuel supply provided by Argentina in 1992), when this is its right according to Article IV of the Non-Proliferation Treaty[2]. Brazil enriches uranium by 20% and has had to reckon with the major powers over this decision: in 1974 supplies to Brazil were suspended, similarly to what happened to Tehran in 1979. On February 15, 2012, Iranian public television presented a live broadcast of the insertion of a bar of 20%-enriched uranium into the core of the research reactor in Tehran.

The Iranian nuclear program dates to the 1970s with the United States, Germany, France, and Russia taking part in its development. A number of Iranian nuclear engineers got their training at the Massachusetts Institute of Technology. The Tehran reactor is mainly used to produce radioisotopes for medical and agricultural applications. It was Iran's need for enriched uranium to operate the reactor that prompted the swap proposal by the P5+1. Enrichment would take place in Russia and the fuel preparation in France, a country with which Iran had had a serious dispute in the past[3] which was resolved in a secret agreement on December 29, 1991.

Brazil will not accept the condition, imposed by the United States, that the provision of nuclear technology by the Nuclear Suppliers Group, to which it belongs, be contingent on Brazil's signing of the Additional Protocol to the

---

[1] Adriana Mendes, Christiane Jungblut, "*Itamaraty busca superar impasse diplomátio com a Turquia*" (Itamaraty seeks end to diplomatic impasse with Turkey), *O´Globo*, June 10, 2015.

[2]. Article IV: "*Nothing in this Treaty shall be interpreted as affecting the inalienable right of all the Parties to the Treaty to develop research, production and use of nuclear energy for peaceful purposes without discrimination and in conformity with Articles I and II of this Treaty.*"

[3]. Terrorist attacks in the French capital (February-September 1986) blamed on Iran in retribution for France's withdrawal from a contract involving Tehran's one-billion-dollar loan to the European Gaseous Diffusion Uranium Enrichment Consortium (EURODIF) in return for production rights.

Non-Proliferation Treaty. The signature gives IAEA inspectors the right to inspect, without notice, any nuclear installations in countries that have ratified the Protocol, including those that have not been declared and that might be used for military purposes. Brazil clearly fears that, as part of these guarantees, measures similar to those imposed upon Iran may be applied to it in the future. This is why Brazilian diplomacy and its representative in Vienna, Ambassador Laércio Vinhas, have appeared hesitant about current developments in the policy toward Iran and in the strengthening of guarantees in a state-specific approach called "state-level concept" that they see as discriminatory and influenced by information coming from outside of the missions of the IAEA inspectors.

Iran signed the Additional Protocol in Vienna on December 18, 2003, later reconsidering the decision and annulling its implementation on February 6, 2005. The G77, which includes 130 countries, has recognized Iran's right to enrich uranium for peaceful purposes. It is thus difficult to accept the argument generally put forward by the European Union and the United States of "the opposition of the international community", something which Mostafa Zahrani, director of the Institute for Political and International Studies in Tehran, qualifies as an ethnocentric Western concept.

Celso Amorim points out that he had rarely had the opportunity to observe a decision-making process as compromised as that regarding the Iranian question. It was not so much the type of sanctions, which is a normal process, but the negotiation of exemptions to unilateral sanctions as a carrot to gain support for a resolution, a strategy whose legitimacy and legality he finds questionable[1]. Brazil and Turkey oppose sanctions applied unilaterally by the United States and the European Union. Collective action, particularly within the framework of the Security Council, has been permanently compromised by the unilateral machinations of the United States and the European Union. Brazil's point of view on this point coincides with that of Russia: for Iran, as for Kosovo, the Quartet, Afghanistan or the expansion of NATO, the initiative was unilateral.

Brasilia points out the flagrant disparity between the hostile approach to a country that is seeking to develop its civilian nuclear power capabilities as authorized by the NPT (Article IV) and under surveillance by the IAEA, and the mild one observed to countries that have not signed the treaty (Israel, India, Pakistan), or that have flouted it (North Korea). The proposal by the European Union (EU3) presented to Iran on August 5, 2005 is a very clear example of this double standard. According to our contacts, by bowing to the wishes of Washington, the European Union has bargained away any leadership role it may have had in negotiating a halt to the Iranian uranium enrichment program, which in any case is completely in compliance with the Nuclear Non-Proliferation Treaty.

---

[1] Celso Amorim, *Conversas com jovems diplomatas*, Ed. Benvira, São Paulo, 2011.

Israel joined the OECD in May 2010 and was admitted with observer country status to the European Organization for Nuclear Research (CERN), thus enjoying an upgrade to its relations with the European Union, despite its bombardment in June 1981 of the Osirak nuclear reactor in Iraq (provided by France) and the bombing of the Dair Alzour site in Syria in September 2007, flagrant violations of international law that have gone unpunished.

In September 2008, the embargo imposed by the Nuclear Suppliers Group on India was lifted. Since that date, it has signed nuclear cooperation agreements with a number of other countries. In the period 2002-2005, the United States negotiated the terms of a strategic partnership, the Next Steps in Strategic Partnership (NSSP), with India to lay the groundwork for cooperation in civilian nuclear energy and aerospace research. The India-United States Civil Nuclear Cooperation Initiative, one of the U.S. "123 Agreements", signed in July 2007, has been strongly criticized because it contains trade guarantees that go far beyond anything Washington has ever agreed to with any of its trading partners, not even those that have met all their obligations and responsibilities vis-à-vis the Nuclear Non-Proliferation Treaty. The 123 Agreement allows India to purchase nuclear fuel for civil industrial applications and to keep its own strategic reserves for its nuclear weapons program. By indirectly favoring the expansion of the Indian military program, the United States compromises the regional security equilibrium between India and Pakistan.

One of the statements of policy in the U.S.-India Peaceful Atomic Energy Cooperation Act, better known as the Hyde Act, recommends limiting, dissuading, and, if necessary, sanctioning Iran for its attempts to enrich uranium. This policy met with opposition both in Iran and India. Tehran believes that this act undermines the legitimacy of the Non-Proliferation Treaty. Iran condemned Indian nuclear tests in 1998 and supported the Security Council resolution demanding that India and Pakistan observe the Non-Proliferation Treaty and the Nuclear-Test-Ban Treaty.

In March 2003, as part of negotiations between the United States, Japan, South Korea, Russia, and China, food aid was offered to North Korea (250.000 tons) in exchange for suspension of its uranium enrichment program and the opening of its nuclear facilities in Yongbyon to IAEA inspectors, who Pyongyang expelled in 2009.

Pakistan, which has not signed the NPT, receives two billion dollars in annual military aid from the United States.

The resolution by the International Atomic Energy Agency in October 2009 demanding that Israel join the NPT and open its installations to inspectors has gone unheeded, as has Article 14 of Security Council Resolution 687 (1991) for the institution of a nuclear-free zone in the Middle East. The proposal by the former head of the United Nations Monitoring, Verification and Inspection Commission, Hans Blix, submitted during the five-year NPT review conference in New York in May 2005, for an embargo on enriched uranium destined to the Middle East, whether to Israel or Iran, was ignored by all media with the sole exception of the *Los Angeles Times*[1]. The notion of equidistance is difficult to apply where Israel is concerned.

The final document from the Treaty review conference in 2010 made reference to a meeting on denuclearization of the region in 2012, a concession from the United States to Egypt. The United Nations had planned to hold the meeting in Helsinki, but it was postponed. This issue has been on the UN General Assembly agenda each year since the adoption during the 62nd session in December 1974 of Resolution 3263, promoting the institution of a nuclear-free zone in the Middle East.

Brasilia believes that the inclusion of Iran, a nation in transition, where forces for change wrestle with old orthodoxies, a proud and pugnacious nation, is the best guarantee of non-proliferation, rather than its isolation, containment, or overt threats of military intervention: Israeli Air Force exercises over the eastern Mediterranean in June 2008; deployment of Israeli submarines in the Gulf of Oman in April 2010; transport of 13-ton "bunkerbuster" bombs to the Diego Garcia naval base according to the March 14, 2010 issue of the *Sunday Herald*; supply of these bombs to Israel, according to the *New York Times – International Herald Tribune* of September 26, 2011; delivery of 72 British Typhoon combat aircraft to Saudi Arabia starting in 2009; delivery of F-16 combat aircraft to Saudi Arabia and Iraq for 33 billion dollars (2012).

The Vice Prime Minister of Israel, Moshe Ya'alon, former Chief of Staff of the Israel Defense Forces (IDF), stated during a conference at the Fisher Institute in April 2010: "*We are already engaged in a military confrontation with Iran*" in spite of the still rudimental state of development of the Iranian nuclear capability, as most experts agree, including the former Israeli Defense Minister and chief of the Israeli intelligence agency, Mossad, Meir Dagan, the former Chief of Staff of the Israeli Army, Gabi Ashkenazi, and the current chief of Shin Bet, the Israeli Security Agency, Yuval Diskin[2]. The U.S. National Intelligence Council published a report in November 2007 titled "Iran Nuclear Intentions and Capabilities", which stated that Iran had stopped its military nuclear program at the end of 2003. Experts from IAEA agreed with this analysis.

The current conflict rests to a large extent on an apocalyptical and obsessional vision of the Iranian nuclear capability painted by Israeli authorities that the American administration, under the weight of the powerful American Israel Public Affairs Committee and its own advisors with ties to Israel[3], is struggling to qualify. Yuval Diskin, former chief of the Israeli Intelligence Service, Shin Bet, speaks of a "*messianic sentiment*" in describing this obsession[4]. The Israeli Prime Minister, Benjamin Netanyahu, steps forward as the

---

[1]. Kaveh Afrasiabi, *Iran's Nuclear Program* (p. 101), BookSurge, New York, 2006.

[2]. *Haaretz*, May 14, 2012.

[3]. Dennis Ross, special envoy to the Middle East; Rahm Emanuel, a volunteer in the Israeli Army during the first Gulf War.

[4]. Dan Perry, Diaa Hadid, *Huff PostWorld*, April 28, 2012.

champion of non-proliferation when his country has more than 400 nuclear arms, according to most estimations[1].

A former United Nations inspector assigned to Iraq to investigate allegations of the existence weapons of mass destruction from 1991 to 1999 wrote: "*The conflict currently underway between the United States and Iran is, first and foremost, a conflict born in Israel*"[2]. The coincidence of the fabrication of an Iranian menace by Tel Aviv in 1992 with the thawing of relations between the United States and Iran (illustrated by Iran's neutrality during the Iraqi invasion of Kuwait and cooperation against the Taliban through its positive influence as moderator at the Bonn Conference in December 2001, facilitated by the friendship between the Afghan president, Hamid Karzai, and his Iranian counterpart, Mohammad Khatami, was certainly not fortuitous.

We must recognize that the threat that the USSR may have posed to France in the 1960s, leveraged by French diplomacy to justify deterrence measures, was much more hypothetical than that openly represented by the United States and Israel toward Iran, which is also confronted by a growing militarization of countries in the Persian Gulf. Saudi Arabia, Kuwait, and Oman destine 10% of their Gross Domestic Product to the purchase of weapons, amounting to some 30 billion dollars in 2011. The International Institute for Strategic Studies (IISS), based in London, estimates the Iranian defense budget at seven billion dollars, approximately 2% of the U.S. defense budget, and less than a fourth of Saudi Arabia's. The more Iran feels threatened, the more it will hope to prevail with its nuclear program. The Libyan example may serve as a lesson for Iran: Muammar Gaddafi gave up his nuclear program in 2004.

In the agreement signed on November 14, 2004 with the European troika (France, Germany, Great Britain), Iran agreed to delay its uranium enrichment program if formal commitments were made regarding its security. Our contacts in Brasilia believe that is the fundamental concern for the Islamic Republic of Iran.

It appears that the option of developing a nuclear capacity was envisaged by Ayatollah Khomeini at the end of the war with Iraq (1988), a war that was a veritable bloodbath, cynically fueled by arms sales by Western powers to both sides, in complete disregard for their own legislation[3].

---

[1] Farr Warner, "The Third Temple's Holy of Holies: Israel's Nuclear Weapons", US Air Force Counterproliferation Center, *Future Warfare Series No. 2*, Air War College, September 1999; Abdullah Toukan, Anthony Cordesman, "Study on a Possible Israeli Strike on Iran's Nuclear Development Facilities", *Center for Strategic and International Studies*, March 14, 2009.

[2]. Scott Rider in *Target Iran. The Truth about the US Government's Plans for Regime Change*, Nation Books, New York, 2006.

[3]. *Cf.* The Irangate scheme to covertly fund the *Contras*, based in Honduras, against the democratically elected Sandinista regime in Nicaragua from 1984 to 1986, involved U.S. arms sales to Iran via Israel in spite of their prohibition by the U.S. Congress in 1985 (Boland Amendment introduced in 1982 and becoming public law in 1985). Between 1979 and 1986, Israel sold weapons to the Somoza regime and to the *Contras* (the Israeli Defense Minister visited Managua in December 1982 to facilitate these sales).

Celso Amorim states that it was at the G8 meeting in L'Aquila (Italy) in July 2009 that President Obama expressly requested President Lula's assistance in the Iranian question, a request confirmed in writing with conditions contained in a letter addressed to Lula dated April 20, 2010. The letter was made public. This is why, according to Amorim, he took it upon himself to personally inform his American counterpart, Hillary Clinton, when the presidential airplane made a stopover in Madrid on its way back from Tehran. But on May 27, in a conference at the Brookings Institute, Hillary Clinton criticized the agreement worked out by Brazil and Turkey for "*making the world more dangerous*".

The outcome of the 3rd United Nations Alliance of Civilizations forum[1], taking place in Rio de Janeiro on May 28, expressly underscored, in response to Hillary Clinton, that "*nuclear arms, not the agreement with Iran, make the world more dangerous*". On that occasion, the Foreign Affairs Ministers of Brazil and Turkey presented an article published by the major newspapers that did not shy away from mentioning the "Talk To Iran" manifesto signed by the former Ministers of Foreign Affairs of the United States (Madeleine Albright), the Netherlands (Jozias van Aarsten), Germany (Joschka Fischer), France (Hubert Védrine), Luxembourg (Lydia Polfer), and Poland (Bronislaw Geremek). It was published in the *New York Times* on April 26, 2006 promoting the opening of a dialogue with Iran.

Before the 1979 Iranian revolution there were some 52.000 Americans students studying in Iran; today there are only five. The United States have not had an embassy in Tehran since 1991. The Iranian head of state has not been received in Paris, Berlin, Washington or London, while the presidents of Iraq and Libya have been received and on several occasions. President Lula underscored in an interview with the American magazine *The New Yorker* in November 2011 that he had spoken with Presidents Sarkozy and Obama and with the German Chancellor Angela Merkel at the G20 summit to ask why they refuse to speak directly with the Iranian president[2]. The Under Secretary of State for Political Affairs in the George W. Bush administration, career diplomat, and advisor to Bill Clinton from 1990 to 1995, R. Nicholas Burns, admitted before the Senate Foreign Relations Committee on September 19, 2006 that at no time during his long career had he ever met a single Iranian official. During George W. Bush's second term in office (2005-2008), Burns

---

1. The Alliance of Civilizations was an initiative of the Spanish Prime Minister, José Luís Rodriguez Zapatero, and the Turkish Prime Minister Recep Tayyip Erdogan, presented at the 59th session of the General Assembly of the United Nations in 2005 with the goal of reducing tensions between the Islamic world and the West. It takes inspiration from the proposal presented in 2000 by the Iranian president, Mohammad Khatami, to the United Nations known as the Dialogue Among Civilizations. A High Level Group composed of 20 people was created by the Secretary General Kofi Annan. It is based at the United Nations in New York. The high representative of the committee is the former president of Portugal, Jorge Sampaio. The Alliance met in Madrid in 2008, in Istanbul in 2009, and in Rio de Janeiro in 2010. An action plan for the Mediterranean was implemented for 2011-2015 to strengthen European-Arab cooperation.

2. *The New Yorker*, December 5, 2011. Interview with Nicholas Lemann.

and his colleagues were forbidden from having contact with Iranian officials[1]. No American official has ever met the supreme leader, Ayatollah Ali Khamenei. President Lula met with him on May 16, 2010.

Iran had expressed hopes in the early 1990s for global negotiations with the United States on all issues affecting the region (nuclear, terrorism, Israel, Hamas, Hezbollah...). President Clinton, anxious to please Israel, then engaged in the Oslo Accords, destroyed that willingness by adopting the bill introduced by Senator D'Amato in 1995 (Iran and Libya Sanctions Act), imposing sanctions on businesses that invested more than 40 million dollars in the oil sector in Libya or Iran. Iran had just awarded the exploitation of the Sirri oilfields to Conoco.

Elected in May 1997, Mohammad Khatami renewed the offer of openness to the Bush administration. Ayatollah Ali Khamenei reformulated it in 2003 via the Swiss ambassador to Tehran, the local representative of American interests[2]. In spite of the agreement in principle with the Department of State (Colin Powell, Richard Armitage) and the recommendations of the Iraq Study Group[3], Vice President Dick Cheney and Secretary of Defense Donald Rumsfeld opposed it. In 2005, Ahmadinejad, legitimately elected, put a limit on the suspension of uranium enrichment as agreed in the dialogue with the European troika, and, by adopting a public rhetoric of defiance and provocation against Israel, denying the Shoah, he made it more difficult to achieve a negotiated solution[4].

The appointment in August 2013 of a career diplomat – a scholar in international studies educated in the United States (University of Denver), Permanent Representative of Iran to the United Nations (2002-2007) and current Iranian Minister of Foreign Affairs –, Mohammad Javad Zarif, following the election in June of Hassan Rouhani as president and the designation of a respected legal expert, Elham Aminzadeh as vice president, offered the chance to resume a mutually respectful dialogue free of the threat of additional sanctions. Brasilia sees sanctions as being ineffectual, i.e. counterproductive, whether unilateral (essentially decided by the United States) or multilateral (decided by the United Nations and/or European Union). This was the tenor of the message sent to the American authorities in July 2013 by the Iraqi Prime Minister, Nuri Kamal al-Maliki, working in close contact with Tehran and Damascus (he had taken refuge in Syria and Iran during the years of repression by Saddam Hussein). The U.S. Secretary of State, John Kerry, met his Iranian counterpart, Mohammad Javad Zarif on September 26, 2013 during

[1]. *Boston Globe*, March 15, 2012.

[2]. Trita Parsi, *A Single Roll of the Dice. Obama's diplomacy with Iran*, Yale University Press, New Haven, 2012.

[3]. Created by the U.S. Congress, the group is composed of 10 members and co-chaired by James Baker, former Secretary of State (1989-1992) in the George H. W. Bush administration. Its final report, published on December 6, 2006, recommended direct dialogue with Syrian and Iran.

[4]. For example, in December 2006 he organized a purported "international" conference in Tehran focusing on refuting the Holocaust.

meetings with the P5+1 (the five members of the Security Council plus Germany), held in conjunction with the General Assembly of the United Nations. President Obama had a telephone conversation with his Iranian counterpart, Hassan Rouhani, the first bilateral presidential contact since 1979.

But the sanctions remained: in August 2012 the British bank Standard Chartered was fined 667 million dollars for having violated the American embargo, and in June 2013 the Bank of Tokyo-Mitsubishi was fined 250 million dollars.

Brasilia believes that a nuclear-capable Iran – which seems to be Tehran's ultimate goal – is less dangerous than a military intervention against Iranian nuclear installations. This is similar to the conclusion presented by Jacques Chirac some time earlier during a press conference on January 29, 2007[1]. This is also the view of Trita Parsi, founder and current president of the National Iranian American Council in Washington, who organized a series of focus groups over the two-year period 2008-2010 with the Israeli National Security Research Institute in Tel Aviv, the Carnegie Foundation, the Brookings Institute, and the Aspen Institute (Washington).

Brazilian Defense Minister Celso Amorim criticized this approach to non-proliferation as being "*asymmetrical*", focusing on non-transfer (Articles I, II, III of the NPT) over equally fundamental objectives such as the peaceful use of nuclear power (Article IV) and the initiation of real negotiations on nuclear disarmament (Article VI)[2].

The military option against Iran ("*all options remain on the table*") has been the leitmotif of American policy since the presidency of George H. W. Bush. The public statement to this effect by President George W. Bush in April 2006 triggered a full-page ad in the *New York Times* on February 15, 2007 by American intellectuals and scientists, including twelve Nobel Prize laureates, urging Congress to pass legislation to limit the president's power to use tactical nuclear weapons against non-nuclear states.

Matthew Kroenig, former advisor to the U.S. Secretary of Defense, responsible for the policy toward Iran (July 2010-July 2011), recommended in the February 2012 issues of the journal *Foreign Affairs* a U.S. military attack with a minimum of delay, qualifying it as the "*least bad option*". We find this echoed in articles published in the *New York Times*[3], signed by John Bolton, former United States Ambassador to the United Nations (August 2005-December 2006, Bush administration) and in the *Washington Post*[4], by Joshua Muravchik, former researcher at the George W. Bush Institute and member of the Freedom House, based in Washington (its members include Otto Reich, Donald

---

1. Elaine Sciolino, "Living with a nuclear Iran. Chirac said what many analysts believe", *International Herald Tribune*, February 3, 2007.

2. Speech before the Foreign Affairs and Defense Committee of the Chamber of Deputies on November 27, 2012.

3 John Bolton, "To Stop Iran´s Bomb, Bomb Iran", *New York Times*, March 26, 2015.

4 Joshua Muravchik, "War with Iran is probably our best option", *The Washington Post*, March 13, 2015.

Rumsfeld, Paul Wolfowitz and consorts). The British newspaper *Financial Times* reported that the Freedom House, subsidized by the federal government, had been chosen by the Department of State to review the funds used to finance covert operation in Iran[1].

In January 2012, Israel put forward, through its Defense Minister Ehud Barak, the new concept of an "*immunity zone*", beyond which bombs would be ineffective because the Iranians would move their centrifuges into underground silos deep beneath the mountains. The U.S. Ambassador to Tel Aviv, Dan Shapiro, stressed on May 17, 2012 that the military option was ready to be implemented[2].

The interim agreement signed in Geneva on November 24, 2013 and the continuation of negotiations with the aim of reaching a long-term agreement in the first half of 2015 on the question of enrichment and *in situ* inspections of Iranian nuclear facilities and the pace of rollback of sanctions imposed since 2006, particularly the progressive release of some 100 billion dollars of frozen Iranian assets, was well received in Brasilia. But Celso Amorim observes that the significant increase in Iran's enriched uranium stocks since 2010, now estimated at 7.000 tons, could have been avoided had the agreement of May 17, 2010 been pursued[3]. The agreement signed on July 14, 2015 (Joint Comprehensive Plan of Action) involves a drastic reduction in these stocks (98%) over 15 years.

Our contacts deplore the fact that the Iranian economy has been held hostage by these negotiations, and that the positive outcome could be threatened by the U.S. Senate, as intimated by 46 Republican congressmen in an open letter addressed to President Rouhani in March 2015. The influential Democratic Senator from New York, Chuck Schumer[4], who is Jewish, has rallied to this position, as have many Jewish Democratic Representatives in the House (Brad Scherman, Nita Lowey, Steve Israel, Ted Deutch...) leading to schisms in the Jewish vote, which is generally homogeneous in the United States. Opinion surveys taken in August 2015 show that 60% of the Jews who took the survey were in favor of the agreement, but, with the exception of J Street, all Jewish organizations are opposed to it (Conference of Presidents of Major Jewish Organizations, Jewish Federation, American Israeli Public Affairs Committee – AIPAC, Anti-Defamation League, American Jewish Committee)[5]. AIPAC paid travel and lodging expenses for a trip by 58 U.S. congresspeople (22 Democrats and 36 Republicans) to Israel on August 4-10, 2015 within the framework of the powerful lobby put together by the American Jewish

---

[1] Guy Dinmore, "Bush enters Iran Freedom debate", *Financial Times*, March 31, 2014.

[2]. *O'Globo*, May 18, 2012.

[3] Amorim Celso, *Teerã, Ramalá e Doha, memórias da política externa ativa e altiva,* Benvirá, editora Saraiva, São Paulo, 2015.

[4] Jennifer Steinhauer, Jonathan Weisman, "Chuck Schumer Opposes Iran Nuclear Deal, Shaking Democratic Firewall", *International New York Times,* August 6, 2015.

[5] Michael Wilner, "Key Jewish Democrats in Congress say they Will vote against Iran deal", *The Jerusalem Post,* August 9, 2015.

organizations to block the July 14, 2015 agreement in the House. The Jewish associations cited above announced that they would spend from 20 to 40 million dollars on a campaign to persuade U.S. congresspeople to reject the agreements, even when polls appear to show that a majority of Jews in the United States support it[1].

The negotiations indicate the reestablishment of the influence of Iran in the region (Lebanon, Syria, Iraq, Afghanistan), allied *de facto* with the Kurdish and Iraqi forces against military operations and attacks by the Islamic State of Iraq and the Levant (ISIL)[2] and, probably, the risky anti-Russian strategy of the United States to reduce Europe's need for Russian natural gas, with Iran having the world's second-largest reserves.

The essential question for Brazilian diplomacy, after President Lula's trip to Tel Aviv and Ramallah, and the Brazil-Turkey-Iran agreement of May 17, 2010, is to know whether the "central" powers are truly ready to alter the current system of governance, a legacy of the Second World War, and to include "marginal" players in the decision-making process, whether emerging or allied, on a global chessboard that they consider their exclusive turf, when this association would help alleviate tensions and prevent confusion and, in the words of Amorim, the slippery slope we have seen in Iraq.

Brazilian television gave a great deal of airplay to an American intelligence document revealed by the British newspaper *The Guardian*, leaked by the young IT specialist Edward Snowden, according to which the emergence of Brazil and Turkey onto the global scene will represent a "*challenge*" to U.S. diplomacy over the period 2014-2019 and a "*risk to regional stability*".

---

1 Todd Gitlin, Steven M. Cohen, "On the Iran deal, American Jewish 'leaders' don´t speak for most Jews", *The Washington Post,*, August 14, 2015.

2 Helene Cooper, "U.S. strategy in Iraq relies increasingly on Tehran", *International New York Times*, March 6, 2015.

CONCLUSION

Brazil's foreign policy during the 20th century may be measured by the yardstick of its relations with the United States. Its alignment with the positions of the United States from 1942 to the end of the military dictatorship in 1985, certainly not fully uniform (the Jânio Quadros-João Goulart years, 1961-1964) or without crises (in 1977 Brazil denounced the military cooperation agreement signed in 1952 in the light of President Jimmy Carter's human rights policy; in 1980 the United States revoked a contract signed in 1973 regarding the provision of enriched uranium), is illustrated by the relative constancy of Brazil's pro-Washington voting behavior at the United Nations. This complex relationship is nevertheless marked by a latent anti-Americanism among the Latin American political class, tempered in the 1960s and 1970s by the Cold War and the fear of Communism and Socialism, and again later, following the reestablishment of democratic institutions, by the attractiveness of U.S. university educations for the young Brazilian elites[1], of the North American job market for the middle class, and of the dynamism of the business climate in the United States for Brazilian industrialists and businessmen.

Due to its late entry into the Second World War (involved only in the Italian campaign from September 1944 to May 1945), Brazil was not included in the conferences at Dumbarton Oaks (1944) and Potsdam (1945). The Vargas government (1951-1954) opposed Washington's request for the deployment of Brazilian troops in Korea. Violent mass demonstrations greeted Vice President Richard Nixon on his visit to Brazil in 1958 (and also in Argentina, Uruguay, Ecuador, Colombia, Peru, and Venezuela).

With the support of the Argentine president Arturo Frondizi (1958-1962), Juscelino Kubitschek (1956-1961) initiated Operation Pan America in 1958 and the Latin American Free Trade Association (LAFTA) in 1960, both initiatives geared toward achieving greater autonomy for Latin America with respect to the United States. Kubitschek's successor, Jânio Quadros (1961) implemented a foreign policy aiming at independence (*Politica Exterior Independente*), which was continued by President João Goulart's Minister of External Relations, San Tiago Dantas (September 1961-July 1962). Brazil has been opposed to military intervention against Fidel Castro's regime and to the expulsion of Cuba from the Organization of American States, leading Argentina, Mexico, Chile, Ecuador, and Bolivia in this stance. Brazil restored diplomatic relations with the USSR in November 1961 and signed a trade agreement in April 1963.

1. 9.000 Brazilian students were enrolled in U.S. universities in 2011; compared to 150.000 from China, 100.000 from India, and 70.000 from South Korea.

But the coups d'état in the 1960s, supported by the United States[1] – Argentina and Peru (1962), Guatemala and Ecuador (1963), Brazil (1964), Argentina again (1966), all countries united in the Inter-American Defense Board (IADB) – aligned political and military power against the enemy within (trade unions, students, leftwing political organizations and their leaders, the artistic class...). The business community and the leading corporations put their support behind the neo-liberal policies of the Chicago school (Jacob Viner, Milton Friedman, George Stigler) and adhered to the "Washington Consensus". Meanwhile, Brazil supported or participated in U.S. military interventions in Latin America (Panama, Dominican Republic, Grenada). "*What is good for the United States is good for Brazil*[2]", stated General Juracy Magalhaes, Brazilian ambassador to the United States and later Minister of External Relations (January 1966 - March 1967). Rarely were voices heard within the Brazilian administration in favor of independent diplomacy. Roberto Campos, a minister in the Castelo Branco government, timidly advanced plans for the institution of an Inter-American Peace Force, seeking to subject U.S. military intervention in the region to a continental consensus. After the coup in Chile against Salvador Allende (1973), supported and largely orchestrated by Washington, Brazil, under its military dictatorship, spearheaded the development of Operation Condor, a campaign of kidnappings, assassinations, and terror with the Southern Cone dictatorships.

The first election taking place under universal suffrage, after the fall of the military regime, placed the young governor of the State of Alagoas, one of the Brazilian Federation's poorest and most violent, Fernando Collor de Mello, in the presidency. Alignment with U.S. positions was strengthened (neoliberal Enterprise for the Americas Act of 1990) and emulated in Argentina by Carlos Menem and in Mexico by Carlos Salinas de Gortari. But if Argentina participated in the 1991 Gulf War sending a destroyer and a corvette, Brazil did not. After the impeachment of Collor de Mello on corruption charges and the assumption of office by the Vice President Itamar Franco (1992-1994), with two preeminent Ministers of External Relations, Fernando Henrique Cardoso (1992-1993) and Celso Amorim (1993-1994), Brazil emerged emancipated.

Interest on debt represented an obstacle to greater integration within the sphere of international trade (protectionist tendencies seeking to reduce imports; subsidies to agribusiness and export crops over food crops; edicts from the International Monetary Fund) and to an improvement in the country's international image (hyperinflation and deep social inequalities). The generally ineffectual dialogue among the economically and socially troubled Southern countries contrasted strongly with the hegemony exerted by the United States and the European powers, which consolidated their economies within regional

1. José Passos Meirelles, "*Golpe de 64 : relatórios provam ajuda dos EUA*" (1964 coup, reports show U.S. involvement), *O 'Globo*, July 3, 2007.

2 "*O que for bom para os Estados Unidos é bom para o Brasil*".

integration schemes (the United States and Canada; the European Economic Community).

The election of Fernando Henrique Cardoso as President of Brazil in 1992, a sociologist by training and one of the most brilliant intellectuals of his generation, having spent the years of the military dictatorship in exile in Paris, did not fundamentally alter this complex deferential position, infused with mistrust, submission and enthrallment via-à-vis the United States, partially due to the constraints of the country's economic, financial, and social situation. The Minister of External Relations, Celso Lafer (January 2001-January 2003), who did not come out of the Rio Branco Institute (Itamaraty) but was educated at Cornell University, a close ally of the business community, Minister of Trade and Industry (January 1999-July 1999), represents an example of this ambivalence with respect to the United States.

Following the September 11, 2001 attacks in New York, Lafer startled everyone by calling a meeting of the advisory committee of the Organization of American States in virtue of the Inter-American Treaty of Reciprocal Assistance (*Tratado Interamericano de Asistencia* – TIAR, a.k.a. the Rio Treaty). This obsolete Cold War artifact, dating to 1947, had proven ineffective against the U.S. invasion of Grenada (1983) and Panama (1989), and also as regards the Falklands War (1982). The President of Mexico had demanded its repeal; Celso Lafer sought to resuscitate it.

Lafer also decided drop like a hot potato the diplomat José Mauricio Bustani, elected to head the Organization for the Prohibition of Chemical Weapons (OPCW) in 1997 and again in 2000, who found himself in a standoff with the United States when he sought to bring Iraq into the OPCW. The Bush administration, anxious to have free rein in Iraq, succeeded in ousting Bustani with the promise of allowing a Brazilian to assume the leadership of the Office of the High Commissioner for Human Rights, currently led by Mary Robinson, former President of Ireland, whose criticism of the Guantanamo Bay detention camp had not pleased the U.S. Department of State. The UN Transitional Administrator in East Timor, Sergio Vieira de Mello, was the man chosen to replace Robinson.

Bustani filed a complaint with the Administrative Tribunal of the International Labour Organization (ILO), which ruled in his favor in July 2003, recognizing the illegal nature of his ouster and providing financial compensation, which the Brazilian diplomat generously donated to the OPCW to support its efforts in disadvantaged countries[1]. The OPCW was awarded the Nobel Peace Prize in October 2013. Vieira de Mello accepted UN Secretary General Kofi Annan's proposal to leave the Office of the United Nations High Commissioner for Human Rights and lead the United Nations Assistance Mission for Iraq, in a war that had begun without authorization from the UN

---

[1]. José Mario Bustani, "O Brasil e a OPAQ : Diplomacia e Defesa do Sistema Multilateral sob Attaque" (Brazil and OPCW: Diplomacy and Defense of Multilateralism under Attack), *Estudos Avançados*, vol. 16 (46), December 2002 (www.usp.br/iea/revista).

Security Council, in violation of international law, and that is particularly controversial as regards human rights. On August 19, 2003, he was killed by a suicide bomber along with 21 of his colleagues in the Canal Hotel in Baghdad. August 19 is now celebrated as World Humanitarian Day.

With the election of Luiz Inacio da Silva to the presidency, (January 1, 2003), Brazilian diplomacy began to express stronger ideological positions (multipolarity, South-South dialogue, Latin-American integration) and progressively asserted a more autonomous stance backed by new economic stability and growth, taking its place in an emerging multipolar world (China, Russia, India, European Union).

The weekly magazine *The Economist* underscored that Brazil has never been so important to the United States nor the United States so secondary for Brazil. The fact remains that the U.S. economy is six times larger than Brazil's and the trade deficit with the United States is Brazil's largest (11.89 billion dollars in 2014 according to U.S. sources[1]; 7.9 billion dollars according to Brazilian sources). The only time Brazil has ever had a trade surplus with the United States was between 2002 and 2007. In recent years, Brazil's trade deficit with the United States has consistently remained above 11 billion dollars, if we refer to U.S. data[2]. It is true that China has become Brazil's premier trading partner (78 billion dollars in 2014 as opposed to 62 billion with the United States[3]) and the most significant regional integration initiatives do not include the United States (Mercosur, ALBA, USAN, CELAC). But the United States is still a major trading partner in the region (trade agreements with nine countries, estimated trade in 2014 of 336.7 billion dollars, a growing trade deficit for the region since 2012 on the order of 33.3 billion dollars, not including Mexico[4]) and an indispensable partner in issues regarding the drug trade, immigration, universities, and investment.

Although North American interference is never brought up by the political class or the major Brazilian media, our contacts at Itamaraty have expressed concern regarding U.S. sanctions on Venezuela and the recent statements by President Obama that Venezuela is "*an unusual and extraordinary threat to the national security and foreign policy of the United States*"[5], a nearly verbatim echo of those uttered by former president Reagan in 1985 regarding Nicaragua[6] and leading to the consequences that are now part of the public record. They testify to the constancy of U.S. interventionism in Latin America and the

[1] United States Census Bureau. U.S. Trade in Goods with Brazil 2014 / Brazilian Ministry of Development, Industry and Foreign Trade (www.mdic.gov.br).

[2] 11.89 billion dollars in 2014; 16.46 in 2013; 11.60 in 2012; 11.20 in 2011; 11.40 in 2010. Source: United States Census Bureau. Trade in Goods with Brazil 2015.

[3] Brazilian Ministry of Development, Industry and Foreign Trade (www.mdic.gov.br)

[4] United States Census Bureau. Trade in Goods with South and Central America 2015.

[5] Executive Order 03-09-2015.

[6] "*The policies and actions of the Government of Nicaragua constitute an unusual and extraordinary threat to the national security and foreign policy of the United States*" (Ronald Reagan, May 1, 1985, Federal Register, Executive Order 12513, www.archives.org).

superpower's mistrust of independent, nationalist governments engaged in regional organizations (ALBA, created in 2004; USAN, founded in 2008; CELAC, formed in 2011) that exclude the United States.

Regarding Venezuela, we must also mention that Citgo, a subsidiary of the Venezuelan national oil company, has provided aid since 2005 to thousands of poor American families in the form of subsidized diesel fuel, and via the Petrocaribe program, favorable financing conditions for Central American and Caribbean countries for oil and infrastructure development. Certain academics, venturing into the fertile and perhaps often overly imaginative realm of conjecture[1], go so far as to equate the case of Venezuela with popular protests in São Paulo in March 2015, some demanding the transfer of power to the military, the privatization of the national oil company, and the impeachment of President Dilma Rousseff, reelected to a second 4-year term five months earlier.

While the major powers generally acknowledge Brazil's regional influence, they are still reluctant to recognize it as a global player. The former president, Fernando Henrique Cardoso, approves of the current development of his country's foreign policy: "*It is only natural that Brazil insists on being included at the table with global decision makers*[2]."

One of the key elements in Lula's foreign policy is his challenge to the distribution of power on the international level and his efforts to see it transferred to the major multilateral institutions. The current system of world governance is considered unfavorable to developing countries and unfavorable to Brazilian interests. Hence Brazil's efforts with developing countries and its BRICS partners to work together to replace hegemony and unilateralism with a greater democratization of world governance, to implement truly effective development strategies and lay the groundwork for a financial architecture that better represents the realities of the international community. In Lula's words: "*Multilateralism is to international relations what democracy has represented and still represents for nations*[3]". This objective takes precedence over concerns about human rights or representative democracy, which are issues that must be addressed within multilateral bodies, or, at the least, by each nation according to its specificities, without foreign intervention, sanctions or expeditionary forces. The asymmetries among countries must not produce hegemonies, whether global or regional, but rather lead to a balanced set of actors within a multilateral system, where emerging countries can exercise broader responsibilities and find a fairer and more rightful place.

---

[1] Darío Pignotti, "La prensa usa la corrupción para desgastar a Dilma. Golpismo precoz" (Press cites corruption to weaken Dilma: foretaste of coup), *Página12*, March 3, 2015.

[2]. *O 'Globo*, June 6, 2010.

[3]. Speech at the focus group on multilateralism at the 3rd Latin America-Caribbean-European Union summit in Guadalajara, Mexico on May 28, 2004. *Repertorio de Política Externa: posições do Brasil.*

BIBLIOGRAPHY

Ideological Foundations

Almeida, Paulo Roberto de. "Uma política externa engajada: a diplomacia do governo Lula", *Revista Brasileira de Politica Internacional*, vol. 47, n° 1, Brasilia, 2004.

Almeida, Paulo Roberto de. "La politique internationale du Parti des Travailleurs : de la fondation du parti à la diplomatie du gouvernement Lula", *in* **Rolland Denis, Chassin Joëlle** (coord.). *Pour comprendre le Brésil de Lula*, L'Harmattan, Paris, 2004, pp. 221-238.

Amorim, Celso. *Discurso de posse no Ministerio de Relações Exteriores*, 2003 (www.itamaraty.gov.br). / "Conceitos e Estrategias da Diplomacia do Governo Lula". *Diplomacia, Strategia e Politica*, vol. 1, n° 1, October 2004./ *Tehran, Ramallah, Doha: Memoria de la Politica Externa, Activa e Altiva*, Benvira, Editora Saraiva, Rio de Janeiro, 2015

Bacevich, Andrew (University of Boston). *The Limits of Power. The end of American Excepcionalism*, Henry Holt and Company, New York, 2008.

Cameron, Maxwell; **Hershberg, Eric** (ed.). *Latin America's left Turn. Politics, policies and trajectories of change*, Lynne Reiner, Boulder, 2010.

Cardoso Sandra Aparecida, Miyamoto Shiguenoli,"A politica externa dos governos Geisel e Lula: similitudes e diferenças", *Revista de Economia e Relações Internacionais* (FAAP), Vol. 11, N°21, July 2012

Fonseca, Gelson. *Apontamentos para o estudo da diplomacia multilateral do Brasil : momentos fundadores e temas politicos nas Nações Unidas,* Dissertation, Universidade Federal do Rio Grande do Sul, Porto Alegre, 2014.

Garcia, Marco Aurelio. interview with the magazine *Piaui* (Brazil), April 2009.

Greenway, H.D.S. "The Grand Illusion", about **Bacevich Anrew**'s book *"The Limit of Power: The End of American Exceptionalism", New York Times,* October 21, 2008.

Guimaraes, Samuel Pinheiro. *Quinhentos Anos de periferia: uma contribuição ao estúdio da política internacional*, Universidade Federal do Rio Grande do Sul. Porto Alegre. 1999 / *Desafios Brasileiros na era dos gigantes*, Ed. Contraponto, Rio de Janeiro, 2005.

Hoffmann, Stanley. "Répression américaine", *New York Review of Books*, vol. 1, n° 10, June 12, 2003.

Lafer, Celso. *Mudam-se os tempos: diplomacia brasileira (2001-2002),* Funag, Brasilia. 2002.

Lins da Silva, Carlos Eduardo. "Dilma se Afasta do Itamaraty, e Brasil Perde Espaço no Mundo", *Interesse Nacional*, N°26, July-September 2014.

Sader, Emir. "*The New Mole. Paths of the Latin American Left*", VersoBooks, 2011.

Simon, Roberto. "Entretien avec Samuel Pinheiro Guimarães", *O Estado de São Paulo*, March 10, 2010.

Texeira, Soares. *O Brasil no conflito global ideologico*, Civilização Brasileira, Rio de Janeiro, 1980.

Foreign Policy

Actis Esteban, "Brasil se mueve con ritmo proprio", *La Nación,* November 5, 2013.

Albuquerque, J.A.G. (ed.). *Sessenta Anos de Politica Externa Brasileira (1930-1990). Prioridades, Atores e Politicas*, USP, São Paulo, 2000.

Allison, Graham (Harvard University, Belfer Center for Science and International Affairs). "Second thoughts on foreign wars", *New York Times, International Herald Tribune*, April 9, 2010.

Almeida, Paulo Roberto de. *Relações Internacionais e Politica Externa do Brasil. A Diplomacia Brasileira no contexto da Globalização*, Grupo Editorial Nacional, Rio de Janeiro, 2012 (2nd edition). / "A diplomacia da era Lula: balanço e avaliação", *Politica Externa*, vol. 20, n° 3, February 2012.

Amorim, Celso. *Breves narrativas diplomáticas*, Benvira, São Paulo, 2013.

Alsina, Soares João Paulo. *Politica externa e poder militar no Brasil*, Fundação Getulio Vargas, Rio de Janeiro, 2009.
Altemani, Henrique; Lessa, Antonio Carlos (ed.). *Relações Internacionais do Brasil: temas e agendas*, Ed. Saraiva, São Paulo, 2006.
Amorim, Celso Luiz Nunes. *Politica Externa–Democracia–Desenvolvimento*, Funag-MRE, Brasilia, 1995 / *A diplomacia multilateral do Brasil*. Funag, Brasilia. 2007 / *Entretien de presse*, April 8, 2010 (www.ipea.gov.br) / *Conversas com jovems diplomatas*, Éd. Benvira, São Paulo, 2011 / Interview on the *BBC* (Júla Dias Carneiro), March 24, 2011 (*www.bbc.co.uk*).
Amorim, Neto Octavio. *De Dutra a Lula: a Condução e os Determinantes da Politica Externa Brasileira*, Ed Campus, São Paulo, 2011.
Baena Soares, João Clemente. *Sem Medo de Diplomacia: depoimento* (ed. Maria Celina d´Araujo), Fundação Getulio Vargas, Rio de Janeiro, 2006.
Barros, Octavio; Giambingi, Fabio (ed.). *O Brasil Globalizado. O Brasil em um mundo sorprendente*, Elsevier Editora, 2008.
Benjamin, Daniel; Simon, Steven. "The Failure to prove a Saddam-Qaeda link", *New York Times, International Herald Tribune*, July 21, 2003.
Blum, William. *America´s Deadliest Export: democracy. The Truth about US Foreign Policy*, Zed Books, London, 2013.
Buarque, Cristovam. "As vergonhas que temos" (on Brazil's social indicators), *O´Globo*, April 9, 2011.
Bumiller, Elisabeth. "A decided tilt east for U.S.", *New York Times, International Herald Tribune*, October 26, 2011.
Burges, Sean. *Brazilian Foreign policy after the Cold War*, University Press of Florida, Gainesville, 2009.
Cardoso, Fernando Henrique. *Xadrez Internacional e Social democracia*, Ed. Paz y terra, São Paulo, 2010 / *A Soma e o Resto*, Civilização Brasileira, Rio de Janeiro, 2011 / *Conversas Politicas* (ed. Muanis, Carlos; Fornazieri, Aldo), interview, Chapter 1, Civilização Brasileira, Rio de Janeiro, 2014 / "Diplomacia inerte", *O´Globo*, March 2, 2014.
Debray, Régis. "Américains, si vous saviez", *Le Figaro*, September 6, 2003.
Cervo, Amado Luiz; Lessa, Antonio Carlos. "An assessment of the Lula era. Emerging Brazil under Lula: 2003-2010", *Revista Brasileira de Politica Internacional*, édition spéciale, nov. 2010.
Cervo, Amado Luiz. "A política exterior: de Cardoso a Lula". *Revista Brasileira de Politica Internacional*, vol. 46, n° 1, 2003 / "Brazil´s rise on the international scene: Brazil and the world", in **Denis Rolland, Antônio Carlos Lessa** (vol. 1), *Relations internationales du Brésil, les Chemins de la Puissance*, L´Harmattan, Paris, 2012.
Chomsky, Noam. *Power Systems*, interview with David Barsamian, Metropolitan Books, New York, 2013.
Cintra, Rodrigo. "Politica externa no periodo Fernando Henrique Cardoso: a busca da autonomia pela integração", Revista Tempo Social, vol. 15, n° 2, 2004.
Cohen, Noam; **Stelter, Brian**. "A web site with enemies. With Iraq assault video, Wikileaks shapes role of journalism in digital age", *New York Times, International Herald Tribune*, April 8, 2010.
Coutinho Marcelo, "O Papel do Brasil", *O´Globo*, December 22, 2008.
Danese, Sérgio. *A escola da liderança, Ensaios sobre a politica externa e a inserção internacional do Brasil*, Editora Record, Rio de Janeiro, 2009.
Dangl, Benjamin. *Dancing with Dynamite: Social Movements and States in Latin America*, AK Press, Oakland, 2010.
Dantas, Santiago. *Coletânea de textos sobre política exterior*, Fundação Alexandre de Gusmão, Brasilia, 2009, Ed. Civilização Brasileira, 2010.
Dupas, Gilberto; **Vigevani Tullo** (ed.). *O Brasil e as novas dimensões da Segurança Internacional*, Ed. Alfa Omega, São Paulo, 1999.
Dytz, Nilo. *Crise e Reforma da UNESCO. Reflexões sobre a Promoção do poder Brando do Brasil no Plano Multilateral*, FUNAG, Brasilia, 2014.
Erlanger, Steven. "As Europe spends less on military, NATO struggles to maintain relevance", *New York Times, International Herald Tribune*, April 12, 2013.

Ferreira, O. *A crise na política externa: autonomia o subordinação*, Revan, Rio de Janeiro, 2001.

Fonseca, Gelson. *A Legitimidade. Outras Questões Internacionais*, São Paulo, Ed. Paz y Terra, 2004 / *Diplomacia e Academia: um estudo sobre as análises acadêmicas sobre a politica externa brasileira na década de 70 e sobre as relações entre o Itamaraty e a communidade acadêmica*, Fundação Alexandre de Gusmão, Brasilia, 2011.

Foner, Philip. *The Spanish-Cuban American War and the Birth of American Imperialism* (2 vol.), Monthly Review Press, New York, 1972.

Freixo, Adriano de; **Pedone, Luiz; Rodrigues, Moreira Thiago**; **Alves, Camilo**; **Vagner** (ed.). *Política externa na era Lula: um balanço*, Ed. Apicuri, Rio de Janeiro, 2011.

Garcia, Marco Aurelio (diplomatic advisor to Lula 2003-2010 and to Dilma Rousseff). "Repostas da política externa brasileira as incertezas do mundo atual", Interview with Luis Antônio Araujo and Oliveira de Roseine, *Zero Hora*, Porto Alegre, May 13, 2004.

Gelb, Leslie. *How Common Sense Can rescue American Foreign policy*, Harper Collins, 2009.

Gómez, Alejandro Sergio. "El Foro de São Paulo sobrepaso la prueba del tiempo", *Granma* (Havana), April 26, 2013.

Granick Stisa, Jennifer; **Sprigman, Jon Christopher**. "The Criminal N.S.A." (on covert surveillance), *New York Times, International Herald Tribune*, June 29-30, 2013.

Guaderrama, José; **Otero, Silvia**. "Na América do Sul, à procura dos vizinhos", *O'Globo*, March 10, 2013.

Halimi, Serge. "À quoi sert l'OTAN ?", *Le Monde diplomatique*, n° 660, March 2009.

Hague, William (Secretary of State for Foreign and Commonwealth Affairs for the United Kingdom). "Parceiros para o futuro", *O'Globo*, January 16, 2012.

Hawksley, Humphrey. *Democracy kills: What's So Good About the Vote?* Macmillan, 2009.

Hirst Mônica, "La política exterior de Brasil ya no es tan palaciega", *Clarín*, August 30, 2013.

Hirst, Mônica; Lima, Maria Regina Soares de. "Brazil as an intermediate state and regional power: action, choice and responsabilities", *International Affairs*, vol. 82, n° 1, 2006.

Hrymych, Maryna (ed.). *Ukrainians in Brazil*, Duliby, Kiev, 2011.

Jaber, Hala. *The Flying Carpet of Small miracles: A woman's flight to Save Two Orphans*, Riverhead Books, Macmillan, 2009.

Johnson, Ian; Calmes, Jackie. "U.S. making presence felt in Beijing's backyard", *New York Times, International Herald Tribune*, November 16, 2011.

Lafer, Celso. *Politica Externa Brasileira: Tres Momentos*, Fundação Konrad Adenauer Stiftung, São Paulo, 1993 / *A Identidade internacional do Brasil e a Politica externa Brasileira: passado, presente, futuro*, Ed. Perspectiva. 2007.

Lampreia, Luiz Felipe (Minister of External Relations from 1995 to 2001). *O Brasil e os ventos do mundo: memórias de cinco décadas de cena internacional*, Ed. Objetiva. Rio de Janeiro. 2010 / Agenda para a política externa no Governo Dilma, *Interesse Nacional*, Ano 4, n° 13, April-June 2011. (www.interessenacional.com).

Lee Myers, Steven. "U.S. budget crunch threatens foreign aid", *New York Times, International Herald Tribune*, October 5, 2011.

Lessa, Antonio Carlos, *Relations internationales du Brésil. Les Chemins de la Puissance*, L'Harmattan, Paris, 2012 / *Brazilian Foreign Policy in Changing Times: The Quest for autonomy from Sarney to Lula*, Lexington Books, 2009 (in Portuguese *A Politica Externa Brasileira: a Busca da Autonomia, de Sarney a Lula*, Ed. Unesp, São Paulo)/ *Dois polos das relações internacionais : Estados Unidos e Europa*, Instituto Brasileiro de Relações Internacionais, Funag, Brasilia, 2002 / "Parcerias estratégicas do Brasil: um balanço da era Lula (2003-2006)", *Revista Brasileira de Politica Internacional*, vol. 53, December 2010.

Lessa, Carlos Antonio; **Couto, Leandro Freitas**; **Farias, Rogerio de Souza**. "Política Externa Planejada: Os planos pluriannuais e a ação internacional do Brasil, de Cardoso a Lula (1995-2008)", *Revista Brasileira de Politica Internacional*, vol. 52, n° 1, 2009.

Lima, Maria Regina Soares de (University of the State of Rio de Janeiro). "A política externa brasileira e os desafios da cooperação Sul-Sul", *Revista Brasileira de Politica*, 48, 2005 / "A politização da política exterior e os interesses nacionais", *Correio Braziliense*, June 11, 2009 / "El legado de la política exterior de Lula", *El País*, September 29, 2010 / *Decisões e Indecisões: um balanço da política exterior no primeiro governo do presidente Lula* (www.observatorio.iuperj.br).

Lima, Maria Regina Soares de. *The Political Economy of Brazilian Foreign Policy*, Dissertation, Vanderbilt University, 1986.
Makki, Sami. "Privatisation de la sécurité et transformation de la guerre", *Politique étrangère*, 4/2004.
Malamud, Andrés (University of Lisbon). "Leadership without Followers: The Contested Case for Brazilian Power Status", in **Estevão de Rezende Martins; Miriam Gomes Saraiva**, *Brasil-União Europeia-América do Sul. Anos 2010-2020*, Foundation Konrad Adenauer Stiftung, Rio de Janeiro, 2009.
Marcondes, Danilo de Souza Neto (PUC, Rio). *A política externa brasileira nos oito anos do governo Lula: legados e lições para a inserção do Brasil no mundo,* Heinrich Böll Stiftung, PUC, Rio, 2011.
Mégie, Antoine; Merand, Frédéric (ed.). "L'Union européenne et le nouvel équilibre des puissances", *Politique européenne*, n° 39, Paris, 2013.
Mello, Eduardo Brigidi de. *A nova política externa independente: o governo Lula e a inserção externa brasileira no século XXI*, Dissertation, Federal University of Rio Grande do Sul, Porto Alegre, 2009.
Mora, Frank; Rowman, Hey (ed.). *Latin American and Caribbean Foreign Policy*, Littlefield Publishers, 2002.
Morales, Evo. "Moi, Président de la Bolivie, séquestré en Europe", *Le Monde diplomatique,* August 2013.
Muxagato, Bruno. *Politique Étrangère du Brésil au XXIe siècle. L´action autonomiste et universaliste d´une puissance mondialisée,* L´Harmattan, Paris, 2015.
Oliveira, Eliane. "Na América Latina, PIB do Brasil na lanterna", *O´Globo*, June 24, 2013.
Oliveira, Eliane; Weber, Demetrio. "De igual para igual", *O´Globo*, March 18, 2011.
Oliveira, Henrique Altemani de. *Política externa brasileira,* Ed. Saraiva, São Paulo, 2005.
Oliveira, Henrique Altemani de; Lessa, Antonio Carlos (ed.). *Relações Internacionais do Brasil: temas e agendas*, Saraiva ed., São Paulo, 2006.
Oliveira, Marcelo Fernandes de. "Estratégias internacionais e Diálogo Sul-Sul no governo Lula: Alianças Duradoras ou Coalizões Efêmeras", in **Fabio Villares** (ed.) *India, Brasil e Africa do Sul: Perspectivas e Alianças*, Unesp, São Paulo, 2006.
O'Rourke, Lindsey. "The woman behind the bomb" (on terrorist profiles), *New York Times, International Herald Tribune*, August 5, 2008.
Paseiro Bécquer, Laura. "Foro de São Paulo apuesta por fortalecer la izquierda latinoamericana y caribeña", *Granma* (Havana), April 30, 2013./ "La Integración plena es el objetivo estratégico de Nuestra América", *Granma* (Havana), May 1, 2013.
Passos, José Mereilles. "Necessidade neurótica de ser igual aos EUA", *O´Globo*, January 4, 2011.
Patriota, Antonio de Aguiar (Minister of External Relations). "Sob o comando da 'cacica' Dilma", *O´Globo*, August 7, 2011.
Pecequilo, Cristina. "A Politica Externa do Brasil no século XXI: os eixos combinados de cooperação horizontal e vertical", *Revista Brasileira de Politica Internacional*, vol. 51, n° 2, 2008.
Perrone de Miranda, Samir. *A integração da America do Sul no discurso da política externa brasileira (1992-2010),* Dissertation, Federal University of Rio Grande do Sul, January 7, 2014.
Priest, Dana; Arkin, William. "Inteligência de mais, segurança de menos. Luta anti terror nos EUA envolve sistema gigantesco com 854 000 pessoas", from the *Washington Post, O´Globo*, July 20, 2010.
Reid, Michael, *Brazil: The Troubled Rise of a Global Power,* Yale University Press, 2014.
Rezende Martins, Estevão Chaves de. *Relações internacionais: visões do Brasil e da America latina,* Instituto Brasileiro de Relações Internacionais, Funag, Brasilia, 2003.
Rezende Martins, Estevão C. de; Saraiva, Miriam Gomes (ed.). *Brasil-União Europea-America do Sul,* Anos 2010-2020, Fondation Konrad Adenauer, Rio de Janeiro, 2009, (www.pralmeida.org).
Ricupero, Rubens, "O atacado e o varejo da diplomacia", *Folha de São Paulo*, June 26, 2005 / "A sombra de Charles de Gaulle : uma diplomacia carismática e intransferível. A política externa do governo Luiz Inácio da Silva (2003-2010)", *Revista Novos Estudos*, July 2010, n° 87.

Rohan, Josselin de; Besson, Jean; Piras, Bernard; Pozzo di Borgo, Yves. "Continuités et inflexions en politique étrangère", Travaux parlementaires. Report on a mission to Brazil by the French Senate Commission on Foreign Affairs and Defense (April 11-14, 2011). (www.senat.fr/rap).

Rolland, Denis (ed.) with **José Flavio Sombra Saraiva; Amado Luiz Cervo**. *Le Brésil et le Monde. Pour une histoire des relations internationales des puissances émergentes*, L´Harmattan, Paris, 2004.

Rolland, Denis; Lessa, Antonio Carlos (ed.). *Les relations internationales du Brésil : Les chemins de la puissance*, L´Harmattan, Paris, 2010.

Rouquié, Alain. *Le Brésil au XXIe siècle*, Fayard, Paris, 2006 / "Brazil, a South American State Among the Key Players", in **Christophe Jaffrelot** (ed.), *Emerging States*, Columbia University Press, New York, 2009 (in French, *L´Enjeu mondial. Les Pays émergents.* Presses de la Fondation Nationale des Sciences politiques, 2008).

Sader, Emir. "El Foro de São Paulo y la izquierda latinoamericana hoy", *Granma* (Havana), April 20, 2013.

Sader, Emir; Garcia, Marco Aurelio (ed.). *Brasil entre o Passado e o Futuro*, Ed. Fundação Perseu Abramo, Ed. Boitempo, São Paulo, 2010.

Sanger, David; Shane, Scott. "How technology helps mine data faster", *New York Times, International Herald Tribune*, June 10, 2013.

Sarmento, Claudia. "Premier japonês tenta deixar amarras pacifictas para trás", *O´Globo*, August 25, 2013.

Shanker, Thom. "China warns U.S. on deal with Taiwan", *New York Times, International Herald Tribune*, October 6, 2008.

Silva Santos, Artur Henrique de, "Os Desafios da Politica Externa Brasileira", conference, Conferencia Nacional 2003-2013: Uma Nova Politica Externa, OPSA, UERJ, July 15-18, 2013.

Silva; Amorim; Guimarães. *A política externa do Brasil*, Ipri / Funag, Brasilia, 2003.

Singer, Peter. *Corporate Warriors: the Rise of the privatized Military Industry*, Cornell University Press, 2003.

Soares Alsina Junior, João Paulo. *Politica externa e Poder Militar no Brasil: universos paralelos,* Fundação Getulio Vargas, 2009.

Souza, Amaury. *A agenda internacional do Brasil: um estudo sobre a comunidade brasileira de política externa*, Centro Brasileiro de Relações Internacionais, Rio de Janeiro, 2002 (www.cebri.org)./ "Terrorism and Law. The Obama administration has created yet another parallel system of unlimited detention without rights", Editorial du *New York Times, International Herald Tribune*, July 18, 2011.

Stanger, Allison. *One Nation under contract: the Outsourcing of American Power and the Future of Foreign Policy,* Yale Press, 2009.

Tokatlian, Juan Gabriel. "El desafío de definir el rol como potencia global", *La Nación*, November 6, 2010.

Tucker, Robert (Johns Hopkins University); **Hendrikson, David** (Colorado College), "The Sources of American legitimacy", *Foreign Affairs*, vol. 83, n° 6, November 2004.

Veiga, Pedro da Motta; Rios, Sandra Polônia. A política externa brasileira sob Lula: o fim do "consenso de Brasilia", *Cebri*, vol. 3, ano V, September 2010 (www.cebri.org.br) / "Política externa do governo Dilma: dilemas e desafios", *Pontes*, vol. 7, n° 1, May 2011, www.ictsd.org.

Vieira de Souza, Unaldo Eugenio. *"Aliança de civilizações: conflitos e diálogos. Análise de uma iniciativa pela paz e da relevância do papel a ser exercido pelo Brasil"*, Dissertation (N°620). Itamaraty, Rio Branco Institute, 2011.

Vigevani, Tulio; Cepaluni, Gabriel. "A política externa de Lula da Silva: a estratégia da autonomia pela diversificação", *Contexto Internacional*, vol. 29, n° 2, July-December 2007 / *A Politica Externa Brasileira: a Busca da Autonomia, de Sarney a Lula*, Editora Unesp, São Paulo, 2011.

Viotti, Maria Luiza (Brazilian representative to the United Nations). "Eles tem uma única receita: sanções", Interview with *O´Globo*, January 2, 2012.

Vizentini, Paulo. *Relações internacionais no Brasil, de Vargas a Lula*, Fundação Perseu Abramo, São Paulo, 2003.

Vltchek, André; Chomsky, Noam. *On Western Terrorism: From Hiroshima to Drone Walfare,* Pluto Press, London, 2013.
Weber, Demétrio. "Chanceleres do Brasil e Reino Unido divergem sobre Irã e soberania das Malvinas" (disagreements with the United Kingdom on Iran and the Falklands), *O'Globo,* January 19, 2012.
Woodward, Bob. *Obama's Wars,* Simon & Schuster, New York, 2010.

Brazil-United States Relations

Almeida, Paulo Roberto de; Barbosa, Antonio Rubens (ed.). *Relações Brasil-Estados Unidos. Assimetrias e Convergências,* Ed. Saraiva, São Paulo, 2006.
Ayerbe, Luis Fernando. *EUA e America Latina: a construção da hegemonia,* Ed. Unesp, São Paulo, 2002.
Bacevich, Andrew. *Washington Rules. America's Path to Permanent War,* Metropolitan Books, San Francisco, 2011.
Bandeira, Muniz. *"Brasil-Estados Unidos: A rivalidade emergente",* Ed. Civilizaçaõ Brasileira, Rio de Janeiro, 1989 / *Brasil, Argentina, Estados Unidos: da Triplice Alliança ao Mercosur,* Ed. Revan, Rio de Janeiro, 2003.
Barbosa, Flávia. "Espionagem nos EUA. Sem pedido de desculpas", *O'Globo,* May 17, 2013 / "Na ONU contra os EUA. Dilma acusa país de violação de direitos humanos com espionagem e propõe regulação internacional", *O'Globo,* September 25, 2013.
Barbosa, Antonio Rubens. *O Dissenso de Washington,* Ed. Nova Fronteira, Rio de Janeiro, 2011 / "As perspectivas das relações Brasil-EUA nos próximos dez anos", *Revista Internacional,* 2011.
Battaglino, Jorge (University of Torcuato di Tella). "A reativação da IV frota e o novo paradigma de controle global dos Estados Unidos", *Política Externa,* vol. 17, n° 4, 2009.
Bennett Ladelle, Carolyn. *No Land, No Island, No People Apart,* XLibris, Bloomington, 2012.
Bodman, Samuel; Wolfensohn, James; Sweig, Julia. "Relations Brazil-USA", *Council of Foreign Relations,* n° 66. New York, 2011, *Politica Externa,* vol. 20, n° 2, 2011.
Bonomo Zancan, Diego. "A parceria Brasil-EUA em energia", *Politica Externa,* vol. 20, n° 4, May 2012.
Boutros-Ghali. *Unvanquished: a US-UN Saga,* Random House, New York, 1999.
Cantanhêde, Eliane, "Diplomatas criticam Brasil por omissão diante da crise ucraniana", *Folha de São Paulo,* March 15, 2014.
Carneiro, Lucianne. "Defesa de Cuba pelo Brasil amplia debate", *O'Globo,* April 11, 2012.
Center for Research and Teaching in Economics (Centro de Investigación y Docencia Económicas), *"The Americas and the World: A new Study on Public Opinion in Latin America on Foreign Affairs",* Mexico, 2009.
Chomsky, Noam. *Liberté, Indépendance et Impérialisme au XXIe siècle,* Coll. Futurs proches, Montréal, 2011.
De Luca, Isabel. "Mercosul se articula contra espionagem", *O'Globo,* August 6, 2013.
Eichenberg, Fernando. "Guerra ao terror tem seu preço", *O'Globo,* June 30, 2011 / "Prova de confiança nos mecanismos multilaterais", interview with **José Mauricio Bustani,** Brazilian Ambassador to Paris and former Head of OPCW, *O'Globo,* October 12, 2013.
Fackler, Martin. "Japan retools military plan, with China as top threat", *New York Times, International Herald Tribune,* December 13, 2010.
Figueireido, Janaína. "No alvo dos EUA. Indignação em bloco", *O'Globo,* July 13, 2013 / "Brasil propõe á Argentina aliança para defesa cibernética. Em meio à espionagem dos EUA, Amorim diz que questão é crucial", *O'Globo,* September 13, 2013.
Fontaine, Roger. *Brazil and the USA. Towards a maturing relationship,* Stanford University Press, 1974.
Frechette, Myles; Samolis, Frank. "Uma aproximação hesitante: as relações comerciais e políticas entre Brasil e Estados Unidos", *Politica Externa,* vol. 20, n° 4, May 2012.
Galeano, Eduardo. "Cuba duele", *La Jornada,* April 18, 2003.

Gaspari, Elio. "Me engana que eu gosto" (regarding the interrogation of Brazilian national David Miranda while transiting London – Snowden issue), *O´Globo*, August 21, 2013.
Godoy, Fernanda. "Brasil tenta manter Odebrecht na Flórida", *O´Globo*, April 11, 2012.
Goodman, Melvin. *National Insecurity: The Cost of American Militarism*, City Lights Publishers, San Francisco, 2013.
Gordon, Lincoln (U.S. Ambassador to Brazil from 1961 to 1966). *Brazil´s Second Chance: En Route Toward the First World*, Century Foundation Book, Brookings Institution Press, 2001.
Hakim, Peter. "O Brasil e a agenda da segurança dos EUA", *Politica Externa*, vol. 20, n° 3, February 2013.
Hallinan, Conn. "The Shameful Legacy of the Monroe Doctrine. Militarizing Latin America", *Counterpunch*, January 16, 2013.
Haines, Gerald. *The Americanization of Brazil. A Study of US Cold War Diplomacy with the Thirld World 1945-1964*, SR Books, Wilmington, 1989.
Hennessey, Kathleen; Bevins, Vincent. "Brazil´s president angry about spying cancels state visit to U.S.", *Los Angeles Times*, September 17, 2013.
Hirst, Mônica. *Brasil-Estados Unidos: Desencontros e Afinidades*, FGV Editores, Rio de Janeiro, 2009 / *The United States and Brazil: a long road of unmet expectations*, Routledge, New York, 2005.
Kas, Roberto. "Petrobras na mira. Maior empresa do país foi alvo de espionagem da Agencia de Segurança Nacional dos EUA", *O´Globo*, September 9, 2013.
Keck, Zachary. "Why Did BRICS Back Russia on Crimea?", *The Diplomat*, March 31, 2014.
Khramtchikhine, Alexandre. "L´OTAN sous perfusion", *Izvestia*, in *Courrier international*, November 25, 2010.
Kimber, Stephen. *What lies across the water. The real story of the Cuban Five*, Fernwood Publishing, Halifax, 2013.
Lessa, Antonio Carlos. *Dois pólos de relações Internacionais: Estados Unidos e Europa*, Funag, Brasilia, 2002.
Madar, Chase. "Samantha Power and the Weaponization of Human Rights", *Counterpunch*, Jun 6, 2013.
Malone, David; Foong, Khong Yuen (ed.). *Unilateralism and US Foreign Policy: International Perspectives*, Lynne Rienner Publishers, Boulder, Colorado, 2003.
Mandelbaum, Michael. *The Frugal Superpower, America´s Global Leadership in a Cash-Strapped Era*, Public Affairs, New York, 2010.
Martins, Elisa. "Há tempos o governo Obama tenta criminalizar o jornalismo", interview with *The Guardian* journalist Glenn Greenwald, *O´Globo*, July 2, 2013.
Mearsheimer, John. "Why the Ukraine Crisis is the West's Fault", *Foreign Affairs*, September-October 2014.
Moniz Bandeira, Luiz Alberto. *As Relações perigosas: Brasil-Estados Unidos (de Collor a Lula)*, Civilização Brasileira, 2004.
Nars, Vali. *The Dispensable Nation: American Policy in Retreat*, Random House, KDPG, New York, 2013.
Oliveira, Èliane. "Segurança x privacidade. Explicações insuficientes", *O´Globo*, August 14, 2013.
Oswald, Vivian. "Brasil monitorado. Explicação presidencial. Obama se reúne com Dilma para falar sobre natureza do serviço de espionagem americano", *O´Globo*, September 6, 2013.
Oswald, Vivian; Carvalho, Jackson de. "À espera de explicações. Brasil convoca embaixador britânico para esclarecer detenção de companheiro de jornalista", *O´Globo*, August 20, 2013.
Paraguassu, Lisandra. "Itamaraty reitera apoio ao TPI e recusa acordo bilateral", *O´Globo*, July 2, 2003.
Patriota, Antonio de Aguiar (then Brazilian Ambassador to Washington). "O Brasil e a politica externa dos EUA no governo Obama", *Política Externa*, vol. 18, n° 1, June-July 2009.
Passos, José Meirelles. "Represália americana. Bush corta ajuda militar a 35 paises que apoiaram criação do TPI, inclusive Brasil", *O´Globo*, July 2, 2003 / "Bush autoriza missão secreta em pais aliado", *O´Globo*, February 3, 2005.

Pecequilo, Cristina Soreana. "As Relações bilaterais Brasil-Estados Unidos (1989-2008)", *Revista Nueva Sociedade*, (www.nuso.org), October 2008.
Perlez, Jane; Buckley, Chris. "China paper suggests U.S. is making Asia tenser", *New York Times, International Herald Tribune,* April 17, 2013.
Purcell Kaufman, Susan (University of Miami). "Reinicializando a relação Brasil-Estados Unidos", *Política Externa*, vol. 20, n° 1, August 2011.
Rappoport, Mario; Laufer, Rubén. "Los Estados Unidos ante el Brasil y la Argentina. Los golpes militares de la década del 60", *Estúdios Interdisciplinarios de America latina y el Caribe* (Argentina), Vol. 11, N°2, 2000.
Rebello, Aldo; Fernandes, Luis; Cardim, Luis; Henrique, Carlos (ed.). *Politica externa do Brasil para o século XXI*, Papers of the seminar organized by the Brazilian Chamber of Deputies, Brasília, 2003.
Richman, Sheldon. "How the US Empire Provokes Terrorism", *Counterpunch,* August 9-11, 2013.
Roberts, Paul Craig. "The Cultivation of Hate", *Counterpunch,* July 29, 2014.
Romero, Simon; Calmes, Jackie. "U.S. and Brazil still testing the waters", *New York Times, International Herald Tribune*, April 11, 2012.
Schoultz, Lars. *EUA: poder e submissão. Uma historia da política norte americana em relação* a *America Latina*, Edusc, 2008.
Smith, Joseph. *Brazil and the United States. Convergence and Divergence*, The University of Georgia Press, 2010 / "Brazil and the United States", *Politica Externa*, vol. 20, n° 1, June-July 2011.
Sotero, Paulo. "Brasil-Estados Unidos, uma relação em compasso de espera" *Politica Externa*, vol. 18, n° 4, May 2010.
Tardáguila, Cristina; Gama, Júnia. "EUA espionaram Dilma", *O´Globo,* September 2, 2013.
Victor, Duilo; Milhorance, Flávia. "Caso Snowden. Retaliação britânica", *O´Globo*, August 19, 2013.
Vizentini, Paulo; Wiesebron, Marianne (ed.). *Neo-hegemonia americana ou multipolaridade? Pólos de poder e sistema internacional.* UFRGS, Porto Alegre, 2006.
Weisbrot, Mark. "Brazil´s cancellation of state visit to Washington, a new low for US/Latin American relations", *Counterpunch,* September 19, 2013.
Winter, Brian. "Brazil´s Rousseff targets internet companies after NSA spying", *Reuters,* September 12, 2013.

Mercosur, Latin America and the Caribbean

Abreu, Sérgio; Lima, Florencio. "Modelos de desenvolvimento latino-americanos: um paralelo entre o Brasil e o México", *Politica Externa,* vol. 20, n° 3, February 2012 / "Mercosul e política externa brasileira. NAFTA e comércio exterior mexicano. Crises e desafios", *Politica Externa,* vol. 23, n°3, January-March 2015.
Alencastro, Catarina; Damé, Luiza; Pereira, Celso. "Alliança inabalável. Surdos às contestações. Criticada por apoio incondicional ao chavismo, Dilma recebe Maduro com pompa em Brasilia", *O´Globo*, May 10, 2013.
Almeida, Paulo Roberto. *Le Mercosur : un Marché Commun pour l´Amérique du Sud*, L´Harmattan, 2000.
Barbosa, Rubens. *O Mercosul e a Integração Regional*, Imprensa official do Estado de São Paulo, São Paulo, 2010 / "50 Anos de integração latino-americana", *O´Globo*, September 14, 2010.
Cavlak, Iuri. "A união entre Brasil e Argentina no desenvolvimentismo (1958-1962)", *Fronteiras, Revista Catarinense de Historia,* n° 17, 2009.
Cervo, Amado Luiz. *As relações internacionais da America Latina: velhos e novos paradigmas*, Ibri, Brasilia, 2001.
Coutinho Marcelo, "A America do Sul na politica externa brasileira", *Valor Econômico,* August, 17, 2009.
Economic Commission for Latin America and the Caribbean (ECLAC), " *The European Union and Latin America and the Caribbean in the new economic and social context",* May, 2015. /

"Determinants and home-country effects of FDI outflows: Evidence from Latin American Countries" (Padilla, Ramon; Gomes Nogueira, Caroline), August, 2015.

Ellner, Steve (ed.). *Latin America's Radical Left: Challenges and Complexities of Political Power in the Twenty First Century,* Rowman & Littlefield, Lanham, 2014.

Fadul, Sergio; Gois, Chico de; Gama, Júnia. "Imbróglio Diplomàtico. Fuga derruba Patriota", *O'Globo*, August 27, 2013.

Fernandes, Sujatha. *Who can stop the drums? Urban Social Movements in Chavez's Venezuela,* Duke University Press, 2010.

Figueiredo, Janaína. "Dilma defende acordo da Vale na Argentina", *O'Globo*, April 26, 2013 / "Assessor de Dilma critica saída da Vale da Argentina", *O'Globo,* May 3, 2013.

Frank, Mora; Hey, Rowman (ed.). *Latin American and Caribbean Foreign Policy,* Littlefield Publishers, 2002.

González, Horacio. "Perspectivas de la izquierda progresista en Latinoamerica. Lula, el anfitrión de um debate sin tabúes", *El Pais,* January 27, 2013.

Hirst, Mônica (University of Torcuato di Tella). "Hacia la construcción de um proyecto sud-americano", *La Nación,* November 6, 2010./ "La Argentina y Brasil están condenados a la allianza", *Página12,* May 2, 2011.

Inter-American Development Bank, (Coord. Giordano Paolo), *Trade and Integration Monitor 2015. Latin American and the Caribbean facing the Contraction of World Trade,* October 2015.

Kume, H. (ed.). *Crecimiento económico, instituciones, política comercial y defensa de la competencia em el Mercosur,* Red Mercosur, vol. 11, Montevideo, 2008.

Lambert, Renaud. "Vers la constitution d´un bloc sud-américain. Le Brésil s´empare du rêve de Bolivar", *Le Monde diplomatique,* June 2013.

Laviola, Mauro. "Amor e ódio no Mercosul", *O'Globo,* March 18, 2013.

Lechini, G; Klagsbrunn, V; Gonçalves, W (ed.). *Argentina e Brasil: vencendo os preconceitos, as varias arestas de uma concepção estratégica,* Ed. Revan, UFF, Niterói, Rio de Janeiro, 2009.

Leitão, Míriam. "Pesos do Mercosul", *O'Globo,* July 13, 2013.

Lima, Maria Regina Soares de (University of the State of Rio de Janeiro). "A politização da política exterior e os interesses nacionais", *Correio Braziliense,* June 11, 2009.

Luiz Inácio Lula da Silva. "Latin America after Chávez", *New York Times, International Herald Tribune,* March 8, 2013.

Malamud, Andrés; Sousa, Luis de. *Regional parliaments in Europe and Latin America: between Empowerment and Irrelevance,* in **Andrea Ribeiro Hoffmann** (PUC, Rio), **Anna van der Vleuten** (University of Radboud Nijmegen) (ed.) *Closing or Widening the gap? Legitimacy and Democracy in Regional international Organizations,* Ashgate, 2007.

Malamud, Andrés. "Presidential Diplomacy and the Institutional Underpinnings of Mercosur", *Latin American Research Review*, vol. 40, n° 1, 2005.

Maltais, André. "Militarisation de l´Amérique centrale", *Global Research,* April 14, 2012.

Martins, Antonio. "Oxfam reforça criticas de Amorim", *Wordpress,* July 23, 2008, www.wordpress.com.

Muxagato, Bruno. *Le leadership du Brésil em Amérique du sud. De la contestation à l´émergence d´une hégémonie consensuelle,* L´Harmattan, Paris, 2015.

Nogueira, Danielle; Figueiredo, Janaïna. "Aliança do Pacífico se fortalece e MERCOSUL fica à sua sombra", *O'Globo*, February 24, 2013 / "Mina de problemas. Vale suspende investimento de US$ 6 bi na Argentina, o maior do país, 6 mil perdem emprego", *O'Globo,* March 12, 2013 / "Saída da Vale da Argentina afeta empresas do Brasil", *O'Globo*, March 13, 2013.

O'Globo, (editorial) : "Mais prejuízos impostos pelo 'risco Argentina'", March 13, 2013.

O'Neill, Shannon, "Foreign Direct Investment in Latin America", Council of Foreign Relations, June 4, 2015.

Oliveira, Eliane. "Baixa competitividade faz país perder US$ 7,4 bi em exportação para América do Sul em 3 anos", *O'Globo*, May 19, 2013 / "Com crise no Mercosul, Brasil pode apelar para acordos bilaterais. Especialistas afirmam que limitações no bloco prejudicam recuperação da balança comercial", *O'Globo*, June 10, 2013 / "Na América Latina, PIB do Brasil na lanterna", *O'Globo*, June 24, 2013.

Oliveira, Eliane; Alvarez, Regina. "Patriota : Atenção especial aos Sul-americanos", *O´Globo*, January 4, 2011.
Oliveira, Eliane. "Amorim critica poder excessivo de potências", *O´Globo*, June 16, 2010.
Passos, José Mereilles. "Lula absurdamente brando com Evo", *O´Globo*, December 30, 2010.
Rappoport Mario. "Desglobalización y estratégia internacional de Argentina", *Página12*, May 26, 2015.
Rezende Martins, Chaves Estevão de (ed.). *Relações Internacionais: visões do Brasil e da America Latina*, Funag, Brasília, 2003.
Rezende Martins, Estevão de; Saraiva, Miriam Gomes (ed.). *União Europeia, America do Sul, Anos 2010-2020*, Fundação Konrad Adenauer, Rio de Janeiro, 2009.
Rodrigues Marques da Silva, Roberta. "Dossié: "Argentina e Brasil: Paralelos e divergências", *Revista de Sociologia e Politica* (Brazil), Vol. 17, N°33, June 2009.
Romero, Simon. "Ecuador´s Leader Purges Military and Moves to Expel American Base", *New York Times*, April 21, 2008.
Rouquié, Alain. *Brazil, a South American State Among the Key Players*, in **Christophe Jaffrelot** (ed.), *The Emerging States*, Columbia University Press, New York, 2009.
Santos, Fernanda; Zemansky, Rebekah. "Taking riskier paths to America" (on emigration to the USA via Mexico), *New York Times*, *International Herald Tribune*, May 22, 2013.
Villafañe Santos, Luís Cláudio. *A América do Sul no Discurso Diplomático Brasileiro,* FUNAG, Brasilia, 2014.
Weber, Demétrio. "Brasil e Colômbia fazem acordo militar", *O´Globo*, January 18, 2012.
Zaiat, Alfredo. "Panorama Economico. El riesgo Brasil", *Pagina12*, February 21, 2015.

Africa

Anunciato, Renata Oliveira. *"Politica externa brasileira e a situação da Embrapa no caso do Cotton-4",* Dissertation, Federal University of Rio Grande do Sul, March 25, 2014.
Bangerter, Olivier. "Le CICR et les Groupes armés non-étatiques", in "Exploring Criteria and Conditions for Engaging Armed Non-State Actors to Respect Humanitarian Laws and Human Rights Law", *Conference Report,* United Nations Institute for Disarmament, June 4-5, 2007, Geneva.
Benot, Yves. *Massacres coloniaux, 1944-1950: la IVe République et la mise au pas des colonies françaises,* La Découverte, Paris, 1994.
Boilley, Pierre. *Les Touregs Kel Adagh. Dépendances et révoltes : du Soudan français au Mali contemporain,* Karthala, Paris, 2000.
Campbell, Horace. *Global NATO and the Catastrophic Failure in Libya: lessons for Africa in the forging of African unity,* Monthly Review Press, New York, 2013.
Casado, José. "Paises pobres, presidents ricos. Ditadores perdoados", *O´Globo*, August 4, 2013.
Castro, Juliana; Guandeline, Leonardo. "Governo de Angola suspende atividades da Igreja Universal", *O´Globo*, February 6, 2013.
Coelho, Sergio Motta; Saraiva, José Flavio Sombra (ed.). *Forum Brasil-Africa: política, cooperação e comercio,* Instituto Brasileiro de Relações Internacionais, Brasilia, 2004.
Coning, Cedric; Karlsrud, John; Gelot Linnéa. "Options Stratégiques pour l'Avenir des Opérations de Paix Africaines 2015-2025", Seminar Report (Cape Town, December 17-18, 2014), Norwegian Institute of International Affairs, Oslo, 2015.
Costa e Silva, Alberto de. *A manilha e o libambo. A áfrica e a escravidão de 1500 a 1700,* Nova Fronteira, Rio de Janeiro, 2002.
Costa, Katarina; Veiga, Pedro da Motta. *O Brasil frente à emergência da Africa: comercio e política internacional,* Brevissimos Cindes (Centro de Estudos de Integração e Desenvolvimento), July 29, 2011, www.cindebrasil.org.
Damé, Luiza. "Dilma nomeia Lula para chefiar missão na África", *O´Globo*, June 28, 2011 / "Na Nigéria, Dilma defende cooperação", *O´Globo*, February 24, 2013.
Dampha, Fafa Lang. "*Afrique Subsaharienne*", L'Harmattan, Paris, 2013.

Dianteill, Erwan; Pordens, Ismael; Vatin, Xavier; Gonçalves da Silva, Vagner; Busca, Joëlle; Motta, Roberto. *Brésil, l'héritage africain*, Éditions Dapper, Paris, 2005.
Djereke, Jean-Claude. *Abattre la Françafrique ou périr. Le dilemme de l'Afrique francophone*, L'Harmattan, Paris, 2014.
Doui-Wawaye, Augustin Jeremie. *Repenser la sécurité em République Centreafricaine,* L'Harmattan, Paris, 2014.
Doumbi-Fakoly; Magassa, Hamidou; Bâ, Ciré; Boubacar, Diagana. *L'occupation du nord du Mali*, L'Harmattan, Bamako, 2012.
Galy, Michel. "Les Occidentaux doivent s'attendre à de nouvelles guerres en Afrique. La poussée du djihadisme sur le continent africain s'explique par l'autoritarisme des États et les inégalités sociales qui prolifèrent", *Le Monde*, March 12, 2015.
Gaspari, Elio. "Os ingleses e a morte de Lumumba", *O'Globo*, April 3, 2013.
Gottinger, Paul. "Understanding Kenya's Westgate Mall Attack", *Counterpunch*, September 25, 2013.
Guimaraes, Samuel Pinheiro. *Brasil e Africa do Sul: riscos e opportunidades no tumulto da globalização,* Ipri, Brasilia, 1996.
Jeangène-Vilmer, Jean Baptiste; Gourery, Franck. *Erythrée. Un naufrage totalitaire,* Presses Universitaires de France, 2015.
Krakovics, Fernanda. "Resgate controverso na Africa. Senado tenta barrar perdão de novas dividas", *O'Globo*, August 5, 2013 / "Senado quer novas regras de perdão de dívidas externas", *O'Globo*, August 6, 2013.
Kornblum, Alex. "Can a Costly Campaign to Eradicate Polio From Nigeria Possibly Succeed?" *The Nation,* November 25, 2014.
Lima, Maria Regina Soares de. "Senado aprova o perdã da divida do Congo", *O'Globo*, July 11, 2013.
Louvel, Roland. "*Les ruses de la mondialisation en Afrique noire. Le rôle des intermédiaires*", L'Harmattan, Paris, 2013.
Mary, André. "Le Pentecôtisme brésilien en Terre africaine", *Cahiers d'Études Africaines*, n° 167, 2002, (www.etudesafricaines.revues.org).
Mehenni, Ferhat. *Le siècle identitaire ou la fin des États post-coloniaux*, éditions Michalon, Paris, 2010 / *Afrique, le casse-tête français ou la France a t-elle perdu l'Afrique ?*, Éditions de Passy, Paris, 2013.
Miyamoto Shiguenoli, "A politica Externa Brasileira para Africa no inicio do novo seculo: interesses e motivações", working paper, XI Congresso Luso Afro Brasileiro de Ciências Sociais, Salvador, August 7-10, 2011.
O'Neill, Carrie. "Holder versus Humanitarian Law Project", Harvard Negotiation and Mediation Program, Harvard Law School, July 3, 2011.
Penha Alves, Eli. *Relações Brasil-Africa e geopolítica do Atlantico Sul*, Editora da Universidade Federal da Bahia, Salvador, 2011.
Pérouse de Montclos, Marc Antoine. "Nigeria : l'ombre de Boko Haram", *Politique internationale,* n° 139, Spring 2013.
Romero, Simon. "Brazil Gains Business and Influence as It Offers Aid and Loans in Africa", *New York Times*, August 7, 2012.
Sadia, Antoine. "*Democratic Governance and Foreign Aid in Sub-Saharian* Africa", L'Harmattan, Paris, 2013.
Salles Menezes, Antônio Carlos de. "*Apoio ao setor algodeiro dos paises do Cotton- 4 (Benin, Burkina faso, Chade e Mali), um projeto bem sucedido: perspectivas para o future da cooperação sul-sul brasileiro*", Dissertation (n°672), Itamaraty, Rio Branco Institute, 2013.
Santana, Ivo. "Notas e comentários sobre a dinâmica do comercio Brasil-Africa nas décadas de 1970 a 1990", *Revista Brasileira de Politica Internacional*, anno 46, n° 2, 2006.
Saraiva, José Flavio Sombra. "Politica exterior do governo Lula: desafio africano", *Revista Brasileira de Política Internacional*, vol. 45, n° 2, 2002 / "Communidade dos Paises de Lingua Portuguesa", *Instituto Brasileiro de Relações Internacionais*, Brasilia, 2001.
Schmitt, Eric. "Fresh doubts about Mali's future", *New York Times, International Herald Tribune*, March 19, 2013.

Sengupta, Somini. "Allegations Against French Peacekeepers Highlight Obstacles in Addressing Abuse", *International New York Times,* May 25, 2015.
Sosa Fonseca, Claudia. "Unión Africana. Medio siglo buscando unidad y desarollo", *Granma,* May 24, 2013.
Souza, André de, "Procura por refúgio cresce no Brasil", *O 'Globo*, April 27, 2013.
Thornton, Christophe. "A Dangerous Precedent. The Consequences of prohibiting Engagement with Non-State Armed Groups", *Conflict Trends,* 2010.
Traore Aminata, "*L'Afrique humiliée*", Fayard, Paris 2011 (First édition 2008).
Turse, Nick. *Tomorrow's Battlefield: U.S. proxy Wars and Secret Ops in Africa,* Haymarket Books, Chicago, 2015.
Traoré, Alioune. *Cheikh Hamahoullah. L'Islam face à la colonisation française en Afrique,* Maisonneuve et Larose, Paris, 1983.

MINUSTAH (Haiti)

Carvalho, Cleide. "Acre sofre com invasão de imigrantes do Haiti", *O 'Globo*, January 2. 2012.
Edmond, Kevin. "Restoration of the Haitian Army: Martelly keeps one Campaign Promise", *Nacla-North American Congress on Latin America,* September 19, 2013.
Ensiedel, Sebastian van; Malone, David. "Peace and Democracy for Haiti: a un mission impossible", *International Relations,* vol. 20, n° 2, 2006.
Farmer, Paul. *The Uses of Haiti,* Common Courage Press, Monroe, 2005.
Fontoura, Paulo Roberto Campos. *O Brasil e as Operações de Manutenção da Paz das Nações Unidas,* Funag, Brasilia, 1999.
Figueiredo Façanha, Luisa Café. *As motivações da política exterior brasileira para participar das Missões de Paz das Nações Unidas: O caso do Haïti.* Speech during the 2nd meeting of the Brazilian Association of Defense Studies (ABED), Federal University of Rio de Janeiro, 2008.
Hirst, Mônica. "A intervenção Sul-Americana no Haiti", *Analise de Conjontura,* June 6, 2007.
Johnston, Jake. "Is USAID helping Haiti to Recover, or US Contractors to Make Millions", *The Nation,* January 2, 2015.
Krakovics, Fernanda. "Haitianos voltam a entrar ilegalmente no Acre, diz Senador", *O 'Globo*, April 9, 2013.
Krakovics, Fernanda; Roxo, Sergio. "Acre decreta emergência devido a descontrole na entrada de haitianos", *O 'Globo*, April 10, 2013.
MacFarquhar, Neil. "UN Peacekeeping pushed to brink", *New York Times, International Herald Tribune,* January 11, 2009.
Malone, David. *Decision-making in the UN Security Council: The case of Haïti,* Oxford University Press, 1999.
Marcondes, Danilo de Souza Neto; Herz, Mônica. *A política brasileira para as operações de paz e intervenções humanitárias: norma, ética e regionalização no envolvimento brasileiro na Minutash*, Thesis, PUC, Rio de Janeiro, 2010.
Mello, Valerie de Campos. "Paz e Segurança na ONU: A visão do Brasil", *in* **Clovis Brigagão, Domicio Proença Junior** (ed.), *Brasil e o Mundo,* Rio de Janeiro, 2002.
Quigley, Fran. *How Human Rights Can Build Haiti: Activists, Lawyers and the Grassroot Campaign,* Vanderbilt University Press, Nashville, 2014.
Ribeiro, Marcelle. "Haïti ainda de joelhos dois anos após terremoto", *O 'Globo*, January 12, 2012.
Robles, Frances. "Haitian president presides unchecked. Scandals involving family and friends multiply as Martelly rules by decree", *International New York Times,* March 17, 2015.
Seitenfus, Ricardo. "Elementos para uma Diplomacia Solidaria. A Crise Haitiana e os Desafios da Ordem Internacional Contemporânea", *Carta Internacional,* vol. 1, n° 1, March 2006.
Souza, André de. "Congo : brasileiro chefiará forças da ONU. General que serviu no Haiti comandará 20 mil soldados", *O 'Globo,* April 27, 2013.
Suplicy, Eduardo. "O Haïti dos Haitianos", *Jornal do Brasil,* February 19, 2006.
Vigo, Julian. *Earthquake in Haiti: The pornography of Poverty and the Politics of Development,* Bobab Tree Books, 2015.

The United Nations Security Council

Amorim, Celso. "O Brasil e o Conselho de Segurança das Nações Unidas", *Politica Externa*, vol. 3, n° 4, 1995 / "Entre o desequilibrio unipolar e a multipolaridade: o Conselho de Segurança da ONU no período pos-guerra fria", September 11, 1998. Speech at the Institute of Advanced Studies of the University of São Paulo (www.iea.usp.br/artigos).

Costa Vargas, João Augusto. *Campanha Permanente. O Brasil e a Reforma do Conselho de Segurança da. ONU*, Fundação Getulio Vargas, Rio de Janeiro, 2010.

Garcia Vargas, Eugênio. *O sexto membro permanente. O Brasil e a criação da ONU*, thesis, Rio Branco Institute, Rio de Janeiro, Éd. Contaponto, 2012.

Glinternisc Botelli, Julio. *"A Argentina, o Brasil e a reforma do Conselho de Segurança das Nações Unidas: baliza de parceria stratégica ou trincheira de uma rivalidade minguante"*, Dissertation (N°472), Itamaraty, Rio Branco Institute, 2007.

Gois, Chico de. "Lula critica déficit de legitimidade global", *O'Globo*, November 19, 2010.

Luck, Edward (Columbia University). "Reforming the United Nations: lessons from a History in Progress", *International Relations Studies and the United Nations Occasional Papers*, n° 1, 2003 (www.reform.net).

Malone, David (former Canadian Ambassador to the United Nations) (ed.). *The Future of the UN Council: From the Cold War to the 21st century*, Lynne Rienner Publishers, Boulder, 2004.

Melo Campos, Valeria. *A Reforma da ONU*, Ed. Fundação Konrad Adenauer Stiftung, Brasilia, 2007.

Novosseloff, Alexandra. "The Role of Emerging Countries in the United Nations", in **Christophe Jaffrelot** (ed.) *The Emerging States*, Columbia University Press, New York, 2009 (in French, *L'enjeu mondial, Les Pays émergents*, Presses de la Fondation Nationale des Sciences politiques, Paris, 2008).

Oliveira, Eliane. "China acena com apoio ao Brasil em vaga na ONU", *O'Globo*, April 13, 2011.

Patriota, Antonio de Aguiar (Brazilian Minister of Foreign Affairs 2011-2013), *O Conselho de Segurança após a guerra do Golfo*, Fundag, Brasilia, 1998 / "Hora de reformar", *O'Globo*, April 28, 2013.

Saliba Tuffi, Aziz. *Conselho de Segurança da ONU. Sanções e Limites Jurídicas*, Ed. Juruá, Curitiba, 2009.

Sardenberg, Ronaldo Motta. *O Brasil e as Nações Unidas*, in **J.A.G. Albuquerque** (ed.), *Sessenta Anos de Politica externa brasileira (1930-1990)*, Usp, São Paulo, 2000.

Seitenfus, R. *Le Sud devient le Nord : fondements stratégiques de l'actuelle diplomatie brésilienne*, in **Stéphane Monclaire; Jean-François Deluchey**, *Gouverner l'intégration*, Pepper Éd., Paris, 2006.

Seixas, Corrêa. *O Brasil na ONU*, FUNAG, Brasilia, 2008.

Uziel, Eduardo. "Brasil, Conselho de Segurança e operações de manutenção da paz da ONU", *Politica Externa*, vol. 19, n° 1, August 2010 / *O Conselho de Segurança. As Missões de Paz e o Brasil No mecanismo de Segurança Coletiva das Nações Unidas*, 2nd edition, FUNAG, Brasilia, 2015.

Vargas, Joâo Augusto Costa. *Campanha permanente. O Brasil e a reforma do Conselho de Segurança da ONU*, Fundação Getulio Vargas, Rio de Janeiro, 2010.

Viotti Ribeiro, Maria Luiza; Dunlop Cordeiro, Regina Maria (Brazilian representative and adjoint representative to the United Nations, 2007-2013, respectively), **Fernandes Gorgulho, Leonardo Luís** (ed.). *O Brasil no Conselho de Segurança da ONU*, FUNAG, Brasilia, 2014.

Voeten, Erik (Georgetown University). *Reforming the United Nations for Peace and Security for the Study of Globalization*, Yale Center, New Haven, Connecticut, 2005.

Voeten, Erik; Merdzanoric, Adis. *United Nations General Assembly Voting*, 1946-2008, (http/dvn.iq.harvard.edu).

Weiss, Thomas (Ralph Bunche Institute for International Studies). "The Illusion of UN Security Council Reform", *The Washington Quarterly*, vol. 26, n° 4, 2003. (www.twq.com).

IBSA and BRICS

Abdenur, Adriana Erthal (PUC, Rio de Janeiro). "A reação dos BRICS à crise econômica", *Pontes*, vol. 7, n° 4, November 2011 (www.iestd.org).

Aguiar, Luiza Maria Barroso de. "Posição dos BRICS diante da questão da Palestina", Centro de Estudos e Pesquisas BRICS, BRICS Policy Center, January 2012, (www.bricspolicycenter.org).

Alden, Chris; **Vieira, Marco Antonio**. "The New Diplomacy of the South: South Africa, Brazil, India, and Trilateralism", *Third World Quarterly*, vol. 26, n° 7, 2005 / "India, Brasil e Africa do Sul, uma Parceria Duradoura? Avaliando o papel da identidade na iniciativa IBAS", speech at an international seminar at the University of Rio de Janeiro (IUPERJ) "*Novos Caminhos no Sul? Uma avaliação da importância do Fórum do Diálogo India-Brasil-Africa do sul (IBAS) para as Relações Internacionais*", Rio de Janeiro, 2009.

Almeida, J. G. *O Fórum de Diálogo India, Brasil e Africa do sul (IBAS): Análise e Perspectivas*, Fundação Alexandre de Gusmão, Brasilia, 2009.

Almeida Silvia, Antonio Ruy de. "Os BRICS e a Segurança Internacional". *Centro de Estudos e Pesquisa BRICS*, BRICS Policy Center, October 2011, (www.bricspolicycenter.org).

Amorim, Celso. "Os BRICS e a reorganização do mundo", *Folha de São Paulo*, June 8, 2008 / "Balanço dos BRICS", *O´Globo*, February 3, 2012.

Batista Nogueira, Paulo, "Os Brics em Durban", *O´Globo*, March 30, 2013.

Baumann das Neves, Renato (ed.). *O Brasil e os demais BRICS: commercio e política*, UN Commission for Latin America and the Caribbean (CEPAL)-Institute of Applied Economic Research (IPEA), Brasilia, 2010.

Baumann das Neves, Renato; Gregol de Farias, Tamara (ed.). *VI BRICS Academic Forum*, FUNAG, Brasilia 2014.

Bond, Patrick; **Sharife, Khadija**. "BRICS Lessons from Durban. If you Carve Africa, Africa May Carve You", *Counterpunch*, March 28, 2013.

Bowring, Philip. "A gathering of BRICS", *New York Times*, *International Herald Tribune*, April 21, 2011.

BRICS Policy Center "Os BRICS e as operações de Paz", *Centro de Estudos e Pesquisas BRICS*, May 2011. (www.bricspolicycenter.org).

Carmody, Padraig. *The Rise of the BRICS in Africa. The Geopolitics* of *South-South Relations*, Zed Books, London, 2013.

Carneiro, Lucianne; **Rodrigues, Luciana**. "Emergentes. Risco na periferia", *O´Globo*, September 9, 2013.

Carneiro, Lucianne; Valente, Gabriela. "Dilemas no crescimento. Sem fôlego para crescer", *O´Globo*, May 21, 2013.

Casella Borba, Paulo. *BRICS, Brasil, Rússia, India, China e Africa do Sul: uma perspectiva de cooperação internacional*, Ed. Atlas. São Paulo, 2011.

Chen, Dingding. "Three reasons the BRICS´ bank matters", *Indian Council on Global Relations*, Gateway House, July 23, 2014.

Cohen, Sandra. "A verdadeira Belíndia. Governo cogita implantar o Bolsa Família", *O´Globo*, April 20, 2012.

Corréa, Marcello. "Investimento estrangeiro no bloco triplica desde 2000", *O´Globo*, March 26, 2013.

Joint declaration of the BRICS Vice Ministers of Foreign Relations on the Middle East and North Africa, Moscow, November 24, 2011 (www.itamaraty.gov.br).

Dupas, Gilberto; **Oliveira, Marcello Fernandes de**; **Le Prê, Garth**. *India, Brasil, Africa do Sul*, Unesp Ed. São Paulo, 2006.

FAAP, "*O Brasil, os BRICS e a Agenda Internacional*", round table at the Armando Álvares Penteado University Foundation with the Institute of Research on International Relations (IPRI) on December 6, 2011 in São Paulo, *Qualimetria*, n° 245, January 2012.

Farah, Tatiana. "Proteção anticrise. Em meio à turbulência na EU, Brics vão destinar US$ 100 a fundo mútuo de resgate", *O´Globo*, March 26, 2013 / "Brasil deve injetar US$ 18 bi em fundo dos Brics contra crises", *O´Globo*, March 27, 2013.

Graça Lima, José Alfredo. "VI Cúpula do BRICS: Perspectivas e Resultados", *Cadernos de Politica Exterior*, Ano 1, N°1, FUNAG, Brasilia, 1st semester 2015.
Herz, Monica; Perez, Lucas Florentino. "Os BRICS e as revoltas no Oriente Medio e Norte da África", *Centro de Estudos e Pesquisas BRICS*, BRICS Policy Center, December 2011 (www.bricspolicycenter.org).
Hirst, Mônica (ed.). *Brasil, India, Africa do Sul*, Paz e Terra Ed., 2009.
Hurrel, Andrew; Lima, Maria Regina Soares de; Hirst, Mônica; MacFarlane, Neil; Narlikar, Amrita; Foot, Rosemary. *Os BRICS e a Ordem Global*, Fundação Getulio Vargas, Rio de Janeiro, 2009.
Jaffrelot, C. (ed.). *The Emerging States: The Wellspring of a New World Order*, Columbia University Press, New York, 2009 (in French, *L'Enjeu mondial. Les Pays émergents*, Presses de la Fondation Nationale des Sciences politiques, Paris, 2008).
Kuwayana, M. *Brazil and India: two BRICS as a "building bloc" for South-South cooperation*, CEPAL, 2010.
Kynge, James. "Developing counries challenge dollar", *Financial Times*, Special report "The Future of the Renminbi-Emerging Markets", September 30, 2014.
Ladwig, Walter. "An artificial bloc built on a catchphrase", *New York Times, International Herald Tribune*, March 27, 2012.
Lage, Victor Coutinho. "Os BRICS nas Resoluções sob o Capitulo VII da Carta da ONU após a Guerra Fria", *Centro de Estudos e Pesquisas BRICS*, BRICS Policy Center, August 2011 (www.bricspolicycenter.org).
Leitão, Miriam. "Mudanças nos emergentes", *O'Globo*, July 10, 2013.
Lima, Maria Regina Soares de; Hirst, Mônica. *Brasil, India e Africa do Sul. Desafios e oportunidades para novas parcerias*, Ed. Paz y Terra, 2011.
Lima, Maria Regina Soares de; Castelan, Daniel Ricardo (University of the State of Rio de Janeiro). *O Brasil, os BRICS e a Institucionalização do Conflito Internacional*, Instituto de Estudos Sociais e Políticos, UERJ, Rio de Janeiro, vol. 6, n° 12, 2011 (www.opsa.com.br).
Lima, Maria Regina Soares de. "A política externa brasileira e os desafios da cooperação Sul-Sul", *Revista Brasileira de Politica Internacional*, n° 48. 2005 / *Brasil e Polos Emergentes do Poder Mundial: Rússia, India, China e Africa do Sul. O Brasil e os demais BRICS*, CEPAL, Brasilia, 2010.
Mathur, Akshay. "Mandate for BRICS Bank", *Indian Council on Global Relations*, Gateway House, July 4, 2014.
Moura, G.F.G. "O diálogo India, Brasil, Africa do Sul (IBAS)", in *IBAS III Conferência Nacional de Politica Externa e Politica Internacional*, Fundação Alexandre de Gusmão, Brasilia, 2009.
Nessman, Ravi. "Ambitious India Now World's Largest Arms Importer", *Associated Press*, March 13, 2011.
Oliveira, Eliane. "Balança comercial no vermelho. Buraco de US$ 100 bi na indústria" *O'Globo*, May 6, 2013.
Oswald, Viviane; Beck, Martha; Batista, Henrique; Melo, Liana. "O Bndes dos BRICS: acordo une bancos de desenvolvimento de Brasil, India e China", *O'Globo*, April 15, 2010.
Penna de Almeida Cunha, Maria Dolores. "*Construindo uma Ordem democratica: o apoio do desenvolvimentolocal como Politica Externa – a experiença do Fundo IBAS para Alivio da pobreza e da Fome"*, Dissertation (N°146), Itamaraty, Rio Branco Institute, 2012.
Rodrigues, Diego de Freitas. "Cooperação horizontal Sul-Sul: arranjos de concertação política entre a India e a Africa do Sul", *Revista Brasileira de Politica Internacional*, vol. 53, n° 1, 2010.
Rosa, Bruno. "Carga tributária atinge recorde de 36,27 % do PIB", *O'Globo*, March 5, 2013.
Sikri, Rajiv. *Challenge and Strategy: Rethinking India's Foreign Policy*, Sage Publications, New Delhi, June 3, 2013.
Stuenkel, Olivier. "The Case for Stronger Brazil-India relations", *Indian Foreign Affairs Journal*, Vol. 5 N°3, September 2010.
Tatlow, Kirsten Didi. "BRICS agitate for a seat at the table", *New York Times, International Herald Tribune*, April 20, 2012.
Tokatlian, J. (ed.), *India, Brasil y Sudáfrica: El impacto de las Nuevas Potencias Regionales*, Libros del Zorzal, Buenos Aires, 2007.

Vaz, Alcides Coasta (ed.). *Intermediate States, Regional leadership and Security: India, Brazil and South Africa*, Editora da Unb, Brasilia, 2006.
Villares, Fabio (ed.), *India, Brasil, Africa do Sul: Perspectivas e Allianças*, Ed. Unesp, São Paulo, 2006.
Vogt-Downey, Marilyn. "A Historical Context. Ukrainian nationalism: What is the Real Story", *Counterpunch*, July 8, 2014.
Yardley, Jim. "An alliance in search of unity", *New York Times, International Herald Tribune*, March 29, 2012.
Zhebit, Alexander (ed.). "Brasil-Russia: historia política e cultura", in **Mônica Hirst** (ed.), *Brasil, India, Africa do Sul*, Ed. Paz y Terra, 2009.

China-Brazil Relations

Almeida Gomes, Henrique. "Importação da China ao Brasil dobra em cinco anos, para 14,55 % do total", *O´Globo*, December 28, 2011.
Amorim, Celso; **Rezende, Sergio**. "A cooperação Brasil-China na área espacial", *Folha de São Paulo,* February 19, 2009.
Archibold, Randall. "Flush with cash, Beijing makes Caribbean inroads", *New York Times, International Herald Tribune*, April 9, 2012.
Barbosa, Rubens. "O poder do Pacifico", *O´Globo*, March 23, 2010.
Batista Gomes, Henrique. "China avança e America Latina perde espaço nas exportações de serviços", *O´Globo*, April 24, 2011.
Berlinck, Deborah. "Dilma reclama do cambio chinês e não dara dinheiro a fundo europeu", *O´Globo*, November 5, 2011.
Biato Junior, Oswaldo. *A parceria estratégica sino-brasileira: origens, evolução e perspectivas (1993-2006)*, Fundação Alexandre de Gusmão, Brasilia, 2001.
Bradsher, Keith; **Wang, Hilda**. "A victory rings hollow for strikers in China", *New York Times, International Herald Tribune*, June 14, 2010.
Bradsher, Keith. "China seeks leading role in US rail boom", April 8, 2010 / "Bold moves from China on trade policy", September 27, 2010, *New York Times, International Herald Tribune.*
Brasil de Holanda, Francisco Mauro. "Brasil e China: Inserção na Economia Internacional e Agenda de Cooperação para os Proximos Anos", *Cadernos de Politica Exterior,* Ano1, N°1, FUNAG, Brasilia, 1st semester 2015.
Brautigam, Deborah. "*The Dragon's Gift: The Real Story of China in Africa*", Oxford University Press, Oxford, 2009.
Brito, Agnaldo. "Vale obtém US $ 1,2 bi para supernavios", *Folha de São Paulo*, September 11, 2010.
Chambers, Sam. "China´s ticking time bomb", *New York Times, International Herald Tribune*, August 17, 2010.
Cheng, Leonard; **Ma, Zihui**. "China´s outward FDI: Past and future", Contribution to the Conference on China´s Growing Role in World Trade, *National Bureau of Economic Research*, Cambridge, Massachusetts, October 2006.
Cirilo, Junior. "Invasão chinesa chega para o près-sal", *Folha de São Paulo*, September 13, 2011.
Dyer, Geoff; **Anderlini, Jamil; Sender, Henry**. "China´s lending hits new heights", *Financial Times*, May 17, 2011.
Economic Commission for Latin America and the Caribbean (ECLAC), *"First Forum of China and the Community of Latin American and Caribbean States (CELAC): Exploring Opportunities for Cooperation on Trade and Investment",* January, 2105./ *"Latin America and the Caribbean and China: Towards a New Era in Economic Cooperation",* May, 2015.
Ellis, Ryan Evan. *China in Latin America, The whats and wherefores*, Lynne Rienne Publishers, Boulder, Colorado, 2009.
Frayssinet, Fabiana. "America latina, banco de prueba para la moneda chinesa", *InterPresse Service*, February 2012 (www.psnoticias.net).
Fujita, Edmundo (Brazilian Ambassador to Indonesia and South Korea). *O Brasil e a Asia no século XXI*, Funag, Brasilia, 2003.

Gallagher, Kevin; Porzecanski, Roberto. *The Dragon in the Room: China and the Future of Latin-American Industrialization*, Stanford University Press, 2010.
Gomes, Wagner. "Desvalorização do dolar anula barreira aos brinquedos chineses", *O´Globo*, April 13, 2011.
Haibin, Niu. "Emerging Global Partnership: Brazil and China", *Revista Brasileira de Politica Internacional*, Vol. 53, 2010.
Huguenev, Clodoaldo (Brazilian Ambassador to Beijing). "Um olhar sobre o futuro das relações Brasil-China", *Interesse Nacional*, 2011 (www.interesse nacional.uol.com.br/artigos).
International Herald Tribune, "China, the sweatshop", July 9, 2010.
Jenkins, Rhys; Barbosa, Alexandre de Freitas. "Fear for Manufacturing? China and the Future of Industry in Brazil and Latin America", *The China Quarterly*, n° 209, 2012.
Kaletsky, Anatole. "Blaming China won´t help America", *New York Times, International Herald Tribune*, September 28, 2010.
Kaplinsky, Raphael. "What does the Rise of China do for industrialisation in Sub-saharan Africa?", *Review of African Political Economy*, n° 32, 2009.
Krauss, Clifford; Bradsher, Keith. "China´s Golbal Ambitions, With Loans and Strings Attached", *International New York Times*, July 24, 2015.
Kupfer, David; Hufbauer, Gary; Myers, Margaret; Williamson, John. "How big of an Economic Threat Does China Pose to Brazil", *Latin American Advisor, American Dialogue*, September 21, 2011, (www.thedialogue.org).
Landim, Raquel. "Brasil depende da China para evitar crise", *O Estado de São Paulo*, August 14, 2011.
Leitão, Miriam. "Por dentro do déficit", *O´Globo*, February 4, 2011.
Maisonnave, Fabiano. "China lidera investimento em petróleo", *Folha de São Paulo*, November 2, 2010.
Manriquez, José León; Alvarez, Luis F. "Mao's steps in Monroe's backyard: towards a United States- China hegemonic struggle in Latin America", *Revista Brasileira de Politica Internacional*, Vol. 57, 2014.
Marques, Joseph; Spanakos, Anthony. "South South Relations and the English School of International Relations: Chinese and Brazilian ideas and involvement in Sub-Saharan Africa", *Revista Brasileira de Politica Internacional*, Vol. 57, 2014.
Mauro, Francisco. *Brasil e China: Inserção na Economia Internacional e Agenda de Cooperação para os próximos anos*, FUNAG, Fundação Alexandre de Gusmão, Brasilia, 2015.
Medeiros, Evan. *China´s International Behavior: Activism, Opportunism and Diversification*, Paperback, Rand Corporation monograph series, 2009.
Moyo, Dambisa. "Beijing, a Boon for Africa", *The New York Times*, June 27, 2012.
N´Piénikoua, Serge Felix. "Des Chinois un peu trop encombrants", originally published in *Le Bénin Aujourd´hui*, reproduced in *Courrier International*, n° 1042, 21-October 27, 2010.
Novo, Aguinaldo. "Sem encomendas, Embraer quer sair da China", *O´Globo*, October 8, 2010.
O´Globo, (editorial), "Novo líder reforça presença da China na Àfrica", March 30, 2013.
Oliveira, Eliane; Alvarez, Regina. "Brasil vai pressionar China por compensações", *O´Globo*, January 18, 2011.
Oliveira, Eliane; Scofield, Gilberto. "China acena com apoio ao Brasil em vaga na ONU", *O´Globo*, April 13, 2011.
Oliveira, Henrique Altemani. "Brasil-China: trinta anos de uma parceria estratégica", *Revista Brasileira de Politica Internacional*, vol. 47, n° 1, Brasilia, 2004. (www.scielo.br).
Ordoñez, Ramona. "Sidérurgica chinesa compra parte da MMX de Eike", *O´Globo*, December 1, 2009.
Oswald, Vivian. "Brasil é 9° parceiro comercial da China", *O´Globo*, January 18, 2012 / "China já é o maior fornecedor do Brasil", *O´Globo*, April 29, 2012.
Oswald, Vivian; Alvarez, Regina. "China investe no Brasil o triplo do que revela", *O´Globo*, March 4, 2012.
Porter, Eduardo. "A slowdown in China bruises Latin America", *International New York Times*, December 18, 2014.

Ribeiro, Fabiana; **Setti, Rennan**; **D'Ercole, Ronaldo**. "Quebrando a muralha", *O'Globo*, June 13, 2010.
Rodrigues, Eduardo. "China passa Estados Unidos como principal parceiro comercial do Brasil", *O'Globo*, May 5, 2009.
Rosa, Bruno; **Novo, Aguinaldo**. "Desembarque chinês. Passos de gigante", *O'Globo*, May 22, 2010.
Rosa, Bruno. "Oi leva US $ 1 bi de chineses. Cresce presença da China no Brasil", *O'Globo*, April 14, 2010.
Schott, P. K. *The Relative Competitiveness of China's Exports to the United States vis a vis other Countries in Asia, the Caribbean, Latin American and the OECD*, Ocasional Paper, Buenos Aires, IDB-INTAL, July 2006.
Scofield, Gilberto. "Após emprestar US$ 10 bi à Petrobras, China negocia novo financiamento", *O'Globo*, April 15, 2011.
Soreanu Pecequilo, Cristina. "Brazil and Sino-American relations: triangulations and perceptions", in **Moreira Lima Ségio Eduardo**, *"Global Governance. Crossed Perceptions"*, FUNAG, *Cadernos de Politica Exterior,* Ano1. N°1, Brasilia, 1st semester 2015.
Sorima Neto, Joaquim; **D'Ercole, Ronaldo**. "Brasil já é o quarto destino de investimentos chineses", *O'Globo,* November 10, 2013.
Tatlow, Kirsten Didi. "Out of jail but by no means free", *New York Times, International Herald Tribune*, March 10, 2011.
Tavares, Monica; **Ordoñez, Ramona**; **Novo, Aguinaldo**. "Negocio de Rs 3 bi da China no setor de energia do Brasil terá de passar na Aneel", *O'Globo*, May 19, 2010.
Teng, C.C. "Hegemony or Partnership : China Strategy and Diplomacy Toward Latin America", in **J. Eisenman; E. Heginbotham; D. Mitchell** (ed.), *China and the Developing World: Beijing's Strategy for the Twenty-first Century*, East Gate Books, 2007.
Uri, Dadush; **Shimelse, Ali**. "China's Rise and Latin America: A Global Long Term Perspective", *International Economic Bulletin, American Dialogue,* March 8, 2012.
Villa Bôas, Bruno. "China fica com fatia de 21 % da EDP", *O'Globo*, December 20, 2011.
Walker, Christopher; **Cook, Sarah** (Freedom House). "The dark side of China aid", *New York Times, International Herald Tribune,* March 25, 2010.
Wheatley, Alan. "An appetite that changes the world", April 27, 2010 / "If Beijing fails to play by the rules", *New York Times, International Herald Tribune*, September 28, 2010.
Wong, Edward. "China jails a relative of Nobel peace laureate", *New York Times, International Herald Tribune*, June 10, 2013.
Zerpa, Fabiola. "Revolução chinesa conquista América latina", *El Nacional* (Venezuela), December 18, 2011.

Multilateral Trade Negotiations

Abott Frederick, "The Doha declaration on the Trips Agreement and Public Health and the contradictory trend in bilateral and regional free trade agreements, Quaker United Nations office, *Occasional paper* n°14, April 2004.
Andriolli, Ana Paula. "A parceria estratégica Brasil-União Européia: um caminho de muitas oportunidades", Seminar at the University of Santa Catarina, May 18-20, 2010.
Ayerbe, Luis Fernando. "*Negociações econômicas internacionais: abordagens, atores e perspectivas desde o Brasil*", Editora Unesp, São Paulo, 2011.
Bacha, Edmar. "Por que os brasileiros gastam tanto no exterior", *O'Globo*, May 27, 2013.
Barbosa, Rubens (former Brazilian Ambassador to Washington, president of the Foreign Trade Council of the Federation of Industries of the State of São Paulo - FIESP). "A OMC na encruzilhada", *O'Globo*, April 9, 2013.
Barral, Weber; **Bhorer, Carolina** (Rio Branco Institute). "A politica commercial do governo Dilma Roussef, primeiras impressões", *Politica Externa*, vol. 20, n° 3, February 2012.
Barros, Octavio de; **Giambiagi, Fabio** (ed.). *O Brasil globalizado: O Brasil em um mundo sorprendente*, Elsevier Editora Limitada, 2008.

Batista, Paulo Nogueira. *O Brasil e a economia internacional: recuperação e defesa da autonomia nacional*, Ed. Campus, São Paulo, 2005.
Batista, Paulo Nogueira; Torres, Héctor Rogelio (Brazilian Executive Directors of the IMF). "Um brasileiro na OMC", *O´Globo*, May 11, 2013.
Baumard, Marilyn. "Economie de la connaissance. L´école privée sur le toit du monde", *Le Monde,* September 18, 2014.
Bulard, Martine. "Libre-échange, version Pacifique", *Le Monde Diplomatique*, November 2014.
Beck, Martha; Batista Gomes, Henrique. "Déficit externo do Brasil cresce e preocupa especialistas", *O´Globo*, June 9, 2013.
Berlinck, Deborah. "Todos querem virar a página de Doha" (interview with Roberto Azevêdo, WTO Director General), *O´Globo*, April 27, 2013.
Berlinck, Deborah; Oliveira, Eliane; Carneiro, Lucianne. "Azevêdo: protectionismo está se alastrando. Novo director geral da OMC avalia que instituição vive momento critico e afirma que há uma 'paralisia'", *O´Globo*, April 9, 2005.
Berlinck, Deborah; Oliveira, Eliane; Damé, Luiza. "Comércio Emergente. Vitória brasileira na OMC", *O´Globo*, May 8, 2013.
Blustein, Paul. *Desventuras das nações mais favorecidas: egos em conflito, ambições desmedidas e as grandes confusões do sistema multilateral*, FUNAG, Brasilia, 2011.
Canuto, Otaviano; Reis, José Guilherme (World Bank). *Comércio global e crescimento: perspectivas e desafios para as economias em desenvolvimento*, (www.ictsd.org/i/news/*pontes*/124285).
Cardoso, Fernando Henrique. *Desafios do Brasil no Plano Internacional*, Instituto de Estudos Avançados da Universidade de São Paulo, 2004, (www.iea.usp.br/artigos).
Celestino, Helena. "O Brasil bem na foto" (on the election of the Brazilian candidate to the WTO), *O´Globo*, May 8, 2013.
Cesar, Susan; Sato, Eliti. "Doha Round, changes in the international trade regime and the Brazilian commercial policy", *Revista Brasileira de Politica Internacional*, Vol. 55, 2012.
Conyers, John (Democrat, U.S. Representative for Michigan's 13th congressional district since 1965), "Why the TPP is a Terrible Deal for Most Americans", *The Nation*, June 11, 2015.
Corporate Europe Observatory, Transnational Institute. "Profiting From Injustice: How law Firms, Arbitrators and Financiers Are Fuelling an Investment Arbitration Boom" (in French, "Les profiteurs de l'injustice : comment les cabinets juridiques, les arbitres et les financiers alimentent un boom de l'arbitrage d'investissement"), < corporateeurope.org>, November 27, 2012.
Cyran, Olivier. "A maquina de costura do mundo. Em Bangladesh, o horror", *Le Monde diplomatique* (Brazil), September 30, 2013.
Danaher, Kevin; Burbach Roger (ed.), *Globalize this! The Battle Against the World trade Organization and Corporate Rule,* Common Courage Press, Monroe, 2000.
D´Ercole, Ronaldo. "Brasil anvançou em investimento direto estrangeiro", *O´Globo,* June 27, 2013.
Fuller, Thomas; Bradsher, Keith. "Cambodia factory collapse", *New York Times, International Herald Tribune*, May 17, 2013.
Gallagher, Kevin, "New Sovereign debt management regime should be G20 focus", *Financial Times*, June 21, 2010.
Galvão, Marcos. "O G20 e a transformação da governança internacional", *Politica Externa,* vol. 20, n° 3, February 2012.
Gardiner, Harris. "Cheap drugs trumph as India rejects patent claim", *New York Times, International Herald Tribune*, April 2, 2013.
Giambiagi, Fabio. "Olhem o balance de pagamentos", *O´Globo*, August 12, 2013.
Glennie, Jonathan. "Colombia is latest addition to pantheon of free-trade follies", *The Guardian*, September 19, 2013.
Granville, Kevin. "The Trans-pacific Partnership Trade Deal: What It Would Mean", *International New York Times,* May 11, 2015.
Greenhouse, Steven. "Wal-Mart offers own plan for safe factories", *New York Times, International Herald Tribune*, May 16, 2013.

Jennar, Raoul Marc. "Cinquante États négocient en secret la libéralisation des services", *Le Monde Diplomatique*, September 2014.

Ledeman, Daniel; Maloney, William; Serven, Luis. "Lessons from NAFTA for Latin America and the Caribbean Countries: A Summary of Research Findings", *World Bank Report,* Washington, 2003.

Leitão, Míriam. "Vizinhos saudaveis" (Brazil's growth compared to that of its neighbors), *O´Globo,* March 1, 2013 / "Brasil deu motive", *O´Globo,* April 30, 2013 / "Ciranda cambial", *O´Globo,* August 24, 2014.

Le Monde Diplomatique. "TAFTA, CETA, TISA. Libre-échange, la déferlante", Manière de voir N°141, June-July 2015.

Levy, Daniel. *"Les abus de l´arbitrage commercial international"*, L´Harmattan, Paris, 2015.

Lima, Maria Regina Soares de. "A política externa e os desafios da cooperação Sul-Sul", *Revista Brasileira de Politica Internacional,* vol. 48, n° 1. Brasilia, 2005 (www.scielo.br) / *Misadventures of Most Favored Nations: clashing Egos, Inflated Ambitions, and the Great Shambles of the World Trade System,* New York Public Affairs, 2009.

Macaray, David. "Sweat Shops, Then and Now ", *Counterpunch,* June 4, 2013.

Madrick, Jeff. "Our misplaced faith in free trade", *International New York Times,* October 4-5, 2014.

Mather, Steven. "Colombia Anti-free Trade Strike brings Gains for Left", *Counterpunch,* September 25, 2013.

McNeil, Donald. "Price slashed for cancer vaccine in poor nations", *New York Times, International Herald Tribune,* May 10, 2005.

Montoya Botero, Rodrigo (former Colombian Minister of Finance). "Aliança para o future" (on the Pacific Alliance), *O´Globo,* May 28, 2005.

Narlikar, Amrita; Tussie, Diana. "The G20 at the Cancun Ministerial: developing Countries and their Evolving Coalitions in the WTO", *World Economy,* vol. 27, n° 7. 2004 / *O Brasil e o Contencioso na OMC,* Ed. Saraiva, São Paulo, 2009.

Nogueira, Paulo Batista. "Política comercial", *O´Globo,* March 21, 2014.

O'Brien, Kevin. "Trade rift grows, but at what cost?", *New York Times, International Herald Tribune,* May 27, 2013.

Oliveira, Eliane; Paula, Nice De. "Acordo entre Estados Unidos e Europa põe Mercosul em xeque", *O´Globo,* February 15, 2003.

Organisation for Economic Co-operation and Development (OECD). Annual Report, "Education at a Glance", Paris, September 2014.

Oswald, Vivian. "Brasil é o 10° mais protectionista do mundo", *O´Globo,* May 12, 2013.

Oswald, Vivian; Beck, Martha. "Mais básico e mais vulnerável. Brasil perde US$ 27 bi por exportar menos manufaturas", *O´Globo,* August 8, 2010.

Pereira, Celso de Tarso; Costa Mendes, Valeria; Rocha de Araujo, Leandro. "100 Casos na OMC: a experiência brasileira em solução de controvérsias", *Politica Externa,* May 2012.

Pigeon, Martin; McDonald, David: Hoedeman, Olivier; Kishimoto, Satoko (ed.). *Remunicipalisations: Putting Water back into Public Hands,* Transational Institute, Amsterdam, 2012.

Pollack, Andrew. "Doctors rebuke drug makers over prices", *New York Times, International Herald Tribune,* April 26, 2013.

Porter, Eduardo. "Trade that benefit U.S. workers", *International New York Times,* February 26, 2015.

Postel-Vinay, Karoline. *Le G-20, laboratoire d´un monde émergent,* Presses de la Fondation Nationale des Sciences politiques, Paris, 2011.

Rezende Martins, Estevão de; Saraiva, Miriam Gomes (ed.). *União Europeia, America do Sul, Anos* 2010-2020, Fundação Konrad Adenauer Stiftung, Brasilia, 2009.

Richani, Nazih. "Colombia´s Agrarian National Strike Enters Its Fourth Week", *Cuadernos Colombianos, Nacla-North American Congress on Latin America,* September 11, 2013.

Rosnick, David. "Economic Study Finds Transpacific partnersip Would Have Tiny Impact on Economic Growth but Coninue to Expand Wealth Disparity", *Center for Economic Research,* Washington, September 2013.

Saraiva, Miriam Gomes. "A União européia como ator internacional e os países do Mercosul", *Revista Brasileira de Politica Internacional*, vol. 47, n° 1. Brasilia, June 2004, (www.scielo.br) / "As estratégias de cooperação Sul-Sul nos marcos da política externa brasileira de 1993 a 2007," *Revista Brasileira de Politica Internacional*, vol. 50, n° 2, Brasilia, 2007, (www.scielo.br).

Schaffer, Ellen; Waitzkin, Howard; Jasso-Aguilar, Rebecca; Brenner, Joseph, "Global trade and Public Health", *American Journal of Public Health*, n°95, 2005.

Sinclair, Scott; Mertins-Kirkwood, Hadrian. "The Trade in Services Agreement and the Corporate Agenda", Public Services International, April 28, 2014.

Smith, Richard; Correa, Carlos; Oh, Cecilia,"Trade, TRIPS and Pharmaceuticals", *Lancet*, n°373, 2009.

Sweig, Julia. "Desafio imediato é como manter a OMC relevante", *O'Globo*, May 8, 2013.

Tavares de Araujo, José. "Conversibilidade do real e Inserção internacional da economia brasileira", *Revista Brasileira de Comercio Exterior*, n° 101, Rio de Janeiro, October-December 2009.

Tavares de Araujo, José; Miranda, Pedro. "Antidumping e antitruste : peculiaridades do caso Brasileiro", *Breve Cindes* n° 8. Centro de Estudos de Integração e Desenvolvimento, Rio de Janeiro, 2008 (www.cindesbrasil.org).

Taylor, Paul. "Free trade or fair trade: choose one", *New York Times, International Herald Tribune*, April 3, 2012.

Thomas, Kathie. "Drug makers using U.S safety rules to thwart generic copies", *The New York Times, International Herald Tribune*, April 17, 2013.

Valente, Gabriela. "Mercado perdido. Setor industrial reduziu participação nas exportações, com perdas de US$ 14 bi. Falta investimento", *O'Globo,* February 18, 2013 / "Brasileiro nunca gastou tanto no exterior: US$ 2,3 bi", *O'Globo*, February 23, 2013.

Valle, Marina Valeria. "O peso das relações inter-regionais com a União Européia em relação a outras alternativas de política externa do Mercosul", *Revista Brasileira de Politica Internacional*, vol. 48, n° 1. Brasilia, 2005 (www.scielo.br).

Van Harten, Gus. "*Investment Treaty. Arbitration and Public Law*", Oxford University Press, 2007.

Veiga, Pedro da Motta; Rios, Sandra Polónia. "Politica econômica externa do governo Dilma: dilemas e desafios", *Pontes* (International Center for Trade and Sustainable Development), vol. 7, n° 1, April-May 2011.

Velásquez,German; Correa, Carlos, "*L'accès aux médicaments: entre le droit à la santé et les nouvelles règles du commerce international*", L'Harmattan, Paris, 2009.

Ventura, Enrique. "Le Brésil et l'OMC : Bilan d'une diplomatie volontaire depuis 2003", in **Denis Rolland; Antonio Carlos Lessa**, *Relations internationales du Brésil. Les Chemins de la Puissance,* L'Harmattan, Paris, 2010.

Woll, Cornelia. "Emerging Power strategies in the World trade Organization", in **Christophe Jaffrelo** (ed.), *The Emerging States*, Columbia University Press, New York.

Yardley, Jim. "Weaving a toxic legacy in Bangladesh", *The New York Times, International Herald Tribune,* July 16, 2013.

Zaiat, Alfredo. "Integración", *Pagina12*, March 10, 2013.

Zero, Marcelo (advisor to the Workers' Party, Brazilian Senate), "Aliança do factoide. A Aliança do Pacifico : o novo modismo", *Brasil de Fato*, September 27, 2013.

Zhan, James (coord.). "World Investment Report", UNCTAD, New York, June 2012.

World Governance

Amorim, Celso. "Let's hear from the new kids on the block", *New York Times, International Herald Tribune*, June 15, 2006.

Appelbaum, Binyamin. "IMF creates top post for Chinese official", *New York Times, International Herald Tribune,* July 14, 2011.

Azevedo Ribeiro, Paulo Eduardo de. "*Cúpulas do G-20: o Brasil e a transformação da governance ecnômico-financieira mundial*", Dissertation (N°692), Itamaraty, Rio Branco Institute, 2011.

Barbosa, Flavia. "Brasil cede e admite contribuir para reforçar caixa do FMI contra a crise", *O'Globo*, April 20, 2012 / "FMI garante US $ 430 bi, mas BRICS racha", *O'Globo*, April 21, 2012 / "FMI recomenda a Brasil subir juros", *O'Globo*, July 30, 2013.
Beck, Martha. "Mantega pede ao FMI novo cálculo da divida", *O'Globo*, July 28, 2013.
Beck, Martha; **Bonfanti, Christiane**; **Barbosa, Flavia**; **Almeida, Cassia**; **Spitz, Clarice**. "No Fundo , a divergência", *O'Globo*, August 2, 2013.
Berlinck, Deborah. "Emergentes exigem pressa na reforma do FMI", *O'Globo*, March 30, 2012.
Bollyky, Thomas (Council of Foreign Relations). "How to fix the World Bank", *New York Times, International Herald Tribune*, April 8, 2012.
Brand, Michèle; Herrera, Rémy. "Our Currency, Your Problem. Dollar Imperialism, 2015 Edition", *Counterpunch*, March 6-8, 2015.
Briscoe, John. "O Brasil no futuro do Bird", *O'Globo*, April 8, 2012.
Bugge, Axel; Simões, Eduardo. "Former colonies attract Portugal's jobless", *New York Times, International Herald Tribune*, March 15, 2012.
Burgueño, Carlos. *Los Buitres. Historia oculta de la mayor operación financiera contra la Argentina*, Edhasa, Buenos Aires, 2013.
Dupas, Gilberto; **Vigevani, Tullo** (ed.). *O Brasil e as novas dimensões da Segurança Internacional*, Alfa Omega, São Paulo, 1999.
Galvão, Marcos. "O G20 e a transformação da governancia internacional", *Politica Externa*, vol. 20, n° 3, February 2012.
Granovsky, Martin. "La Triple A de lós buitres", *Página12,* May 24, 2015.
Guélaud, Claire. "Les économies émergentes vacillent. Les incertitudes sur le calendrier de la remontée des taux américains entretiennent les inquiétudes", *Le Monde*, December 18, 2014.
Higgins, Andrew. "Europeans defy U.S. to join China's new bank", *International New York Times,* March 18, 2015.
Knight, W. Andy. *A Changing United Nations: Multilateral Evolution and the Quest for Global Governance*, Palgrave ed., New York, 2000.
Laudonia, Maria. *Los Buitres de la Deuda. El desendeudamento de la Argentina contado a través de sus protagonistas,* Ed. Biblos, Buenos Aires, 2014.
Lowrey, Annie. "World Bank adheres to 'old order' in its new chief", *New York Times, International Herald Tribune*, April 17, 2012.
Moreira Lima, Ségio Eduardo. "Global Governance. Crossed Perceptions", FUNAG, *Cadernos de Politica Exterior*, Ano 1, N°1, Brasilia, 1st semester 2015.
Nogueira, Paulo Batista. "Resistência à mudança", *O'Globo*, April 14, 2012.
Norris, Floyd. "No one wins in ruling on Argentina", *International New York Times,* November 21, 2014.
Oliveira, Eliane. "Amorim critica poder excessivo de potências", *O'Globo*, June 16, 2010.
Parag, Khana (New American Foundation). *The Second World: How Emerging Powers are Redefining Global Competition at the 21st Century*, Random House, New York, 2009.
Paris, Gilles; Bernard, Philippe. "La banque asiatique divise Washington et Londres", *Le Monde,* March 15-16, 2015.
Prasad, Eswar. "Setting a fresh course of the World Bank", *New York Times, International Herald Tribune*, April 20, 2012.
Prashad, Vijay, *The Poorer Nations. A Possible History of The Global South,* VersoBooks, London, 2013.
Rosenthal, Gert. "The Scale of Assessment of the UN budget. A case Study of how the US exercises its leverage in a Multilateral Setting", *Global Governance*, a Review of Multilateralism and International Organizations, vol. 10, n° 3, July-September 2004.
Soares de Lima, Maria Regina, *A Institucionalização do Conflito internacional e a Successão no FMI*, Monitor on South American Politics, Institute for Social and Political Studies, University of the State of Rio de Janeiro (IESP/UERJ), May 31, 2011 (www.opsa.com.br).
Stiglitz, Joseph. "Whose World Bank?", *New York Times, International Herald Tribune*, April 4, 2012.

Toussaint, Éric; and the Committee for the Abolition of Third World Debt (CADTM). *L'Équateur à la croisée des chemins*, Éditions Abya Yala, Quito, 2009.
UNDP – United Nations Development Programme – *Informe sobre Desarollo Humano*, "El ascenso del Sur : progresso humano en un mundo diverso", New York, 2013.
Vilches, Jorge. "Argentina´s 'Me-Toos' Make Sure No Vultures Left Behind", *Counterpunch*, June 11, 2015.
Vivien, Renaud interviews **Hugo Palacio Arias** (Ecuador). "Les traités de protection des investissements sont dangereux pour la souveraineté nationale et les droits humains", *http://cadtm.org/*, November 15, 2011.

Innovative Financing and UNITAID

Attaran, Amir,"How Do Patents and Economic Policies Affect Access to Essencial Medicines in Developping Countries?", *Health Affairs*, n°23, 2004.
Bagcchi Sanjeet, "Indian generic drugs debate heats up", *The Lancet,* vol. 384,n°9951, October 11, 2014.
Bajaj, Vika; Pollack, Andrew. "Crucial test for low-cost drugs", *New York Times, International Herald Tribune*, March 7, 2012.
Bréger Thomas, *L´accès aux médicaments des pays en développement. Enjeu d´une rénovation des politiques de développement*, L´Harmattan, Paris, 2011.
Brill Steven, "Bitter Pill: Why medical Bills Are Killing Us", Ime Magazine, special issue, February 2013.
Bulard Martine, "Les firmes pharmaceutiques organisent l´*apartheid* sanitaire", *Le Monde Diplomatique,* January 2000.
Cash Richard, "Public Health or political Health? *The Lancet,* Vol.383,n°9936, June 28, 2014.
Castle, Stephen. "U.K. accuses Glaxo of interfering with generics", *New York Times, International Herald Tribune*, April 20-21, 2013.
Cepik, Marco; Paes de Sousa, Romulo. *A política externa brasileira e a cooperação internacional em saúde no começo do governo Lula*, Centro de Estudos Internacionais sobre Governo, Universidade Federal do Rio Grande do Sul, 2009, (www.ufrgs.br/cegov).
Duarte, Alessandra. "Justiça Federal quebra patente de principio ativo de remédio anti-Aids", *O´Globo*, April 7, 2012.
Eboko Fred, "Le droit contre la morale? L´accès aux médicaments contre le sida en Afrique", *Revue Internationale de Sciences Sociales,* n°4, November 12, 2014.
Farmer, Paul (Harvard Medical School, Partners in Health). "The Global Fund matters", *New York Times, International Herald Tribune*, February 2, 2012.
Gold Richard (from Mc Gill University and other experts),"Toward a new Era of Intellectual property: from Confrontation to negociation", *A Report from the International Expert Group on Biotechnology, Innovation and Intellectual Property*, Montréal, September 2008 (www.org.casimir.uk).
Homedes, Núria; Ugalde, Antonio; Rovia Forns, Joan, "The World bank, Pharmaceutical Policies and Health reforms in Latin America", *International Journal of Health Services*, vol.35, n°4, 2005.
Jungblut, Cristiane. "Dilma defende quebra de patente", *O´Globo*, September 20, 2011.
Levich Jacob, "The Real Agenda of the Gates Foundation", *Monthly Review*, n° 57, May 2014.
Lowé Gninteden, Patrick Juvet, *L'Obtention des brevets pharmaceutiques en Afrique. Le cas des pays de l'Organisation africaine de Propriété intellectuelle*, L'Harmattan, Paris, 2013.
Mbogo, Stephen. "Africa: futuro dizimado pela Aids", *Jornal do Brasil*, September 28, 2003.
McIntyre Robert, Philips Richard, Baxandall Phineas, "Offshore Shell Games 2015. The Use of Offshore Tax havens by Fortune 500 Companies", Report, October 6, 2015.
Nogueira, Danielle. "Laboratorios receavam política de Lula", *O´Globo*, December 16, 2010.
Oliveira, Eliane. "Brasil e India vão a OMC contra EU por genéricos", *O´Globo*, May 13, 2010.
Rivière, Philippe, "Sous l´influence de Big Pharma", *Le Monde Diplomatique*, February-March 2004.

Sell, Susan, *Private power, Public Law. The Globalization of Intellectual Property Rights,* Cambridge Studies in International Relations, Cambridge University Press, 2003.

Climate and Environment; Climate Change Aid to Poor Countries

Alencar, Emanuel. "Gonzalo Alonso Hernández. Uma paixão fervosa pela natureza do Rio", *O 'Globo*, August 20, 2013.
Alencar, Emanuel; Souza, Dicler de Mello. "Policia vai pedir quebra de sigilo de suspeitos de matar espanhol" (on the murder of Spanish biologist and environmental activist Gonzalo Alonso Hernández), *O 'Globo*, August 20, 2013.
Alencastro, Catarina. "Instituto Chico Mendes sem comando", *O 'Globo*, March 10, 2003 / "Menos desmatamento e queda nas emissões", *O 'Globo*, November 25, 2009 / "Emissões de $C0_2$ no país aumentam 69 %", *O 'Globo*, November 26, 2009 / "'A reforma permite desmatamento desenfreado', Professor da USP afirma que alterações no Codigo Florestal não tem embasamento técnico e são políticas", Interview de Luiz Antonio Martinelli, *O 'Globo*, June 19, 2010.
Alencastro, Catarina; Gois, Chico de; Oswald, Vivian. "Amazônia registra menor desmatamento em 21 anos", *O 'Globo*, November 13, 2009.
Alencastro, Catarina; Éboli, Evandro; Damé, Luiza. "'Emenda da vergonha' é aprovada. Pmdb e ruralistas derrotam governo na votação do Codigo Florestal e anistiam desmatadores", *O 'Globo*, May 25, 2011.
Algranti, Eduardo. "A missão perigosa" (on asbestos), *O 'Globo*, February 16, 2012.
Almeida, Cássia. "Supremo decide suspender lei contra o amianto", *O 'Globo*, December 21, 2007.
Amorim, Silvia. "Pastoral da Terra acusa governo de omissão", *O 'Globo*, June 2, 2011.
Baima, Cesar. "Á beira do abismo. Concentração de CO_2 está perto do ponto que aquecimento do 2ºC é ineviável", *O 'Globo*, April 24, 2013.
Barbosa, Flavia. "O aquecimento, segundo Obama. Presidente apresenta plano americano para reduzir emissões de gases-estufa", *O 'Globo*, June 26, 2013.
Barros-Platiau, Ana Flavia. "Quand les pays émergents réforment la gouvernance globale des changements climatiques : le Brésil sous Lula", in **Denis Rolland; Carlos Antonio Lessa**, *Relations internationales du Brésil. Les chemins de la puissance*, L'Harmattan, Paris, 2010 (in English, "When emergent countries reform global governance of climate change: Brazil under Lula", *Revista Brasileira de Politica Internacional*, n° 53, 2010).
Batista, Henrique Gomes, "Dez anos de transgênicos", *O 'Globo,* July 7, 2013 / "Brasil quer construir hidrelétricas nas Guianas", *O 'Globo,* September 8, 2013.
Berlinck, Deborah; Magalhães-Ruether, Graça. "Lula diz que é possível salvar acordo do clima. Dilma lamenta decisão de EUA e China de fecharem apenas um pacto político em Copenhague", *O 'Globo*, November 17, 2009.
Brandão, Tulio. "Politicos do grupo Verde europeu protestam contra emissões da CSA", *O 'Globo*, December 20, 2009.
Broder, John. "Determined to tackle climate change", *New York Times, International Herald Tribune*, July 30, 2013.
Camargo, Aspasia; Ribeiro Capobianco, João Paulo; Puppim de Oliveira, José Antonio, *Meio Ambiente Brasil: avanços e obstáculos pós Rio-92*, Estaçaõ Libertade Ed., 2008.
Capobianco, João Paulo Ribeiro (former Brazilian Secretary for Biodiversity and Forests, 2003-2007). "A fragilização da política ambiental do Brasil em crescimento econômico na era das mudanças climáticas", Instituto de pesquisas Ambiental da Amazonia, *Interesse Nacional, Vol.2, N°5, 2009* (www.interessenacional.uol.com.br/artigos)/"De Rio a Copenhague, sem escala em Kyoto", *Politica Externa*, vol. 18, n° 4, March-May 2010.
Carvalho, Cleide. "Arrastão na floresta. Ataque à mata amazônica aumentou no rastro das mudanças no Código Florestal", *O 'Globo*, May 29, 2011 / "Madeira da Amazônia sem chancela legal", *O 'Globo*, June 9, 2013 / "Após anistia, desmatamento cresceu 437 % na Amazônia", *O 'Globo*, July 18, 2013.

Carvalho, Jailton de. "Novo Código Florestal anistia desmatadores", *O'Globo*, July 7, 2010 / "Senado aprova plantio de cana na Amazônia e no cerrado", *O'Globo*, May 15, 2013.

Damé, Luiza; Oliveira, Eliane. "A soja da discórdia", *O'Globo*, January 25, 2008.

De Luca, Isabel; Barbosa, Flavia; Grandelle, Renato. "Brasil não assina documento da Cúpula do Clima para zerar desmatamento", *O'Globo*, September 23, 2014.

Doca, Geralda. "Sem acordo no TST para indenizar vítimas de Paulínia", *O'Globo*, February 15, 2013.

Druker, Steven. *Altered Genes, Twisted Truth*, Clear River Press, Salt Lake City, 2015.

Éboli, Evandro. "Attaque á Floresta. Marina desafia produtores rurais", *O'Globo*, January 26, 2008 / "Os radicais nos querem pendurados em árvores", interview with Senator Blairo Maggi, the 'soybean king', *O'Globo*, February 27, 2013 / "Amianto: Eternit é processada em RS 1 bi", *O'Globo*, August 18, 2013.

Estevo, Jefferson dos Santos. "Influência de fatores domésticos na formulação da política externa brasileira para mudanças climáticas", Talk at a seminar at the Federal University of Parana, September 26-28, 2011.
(www.seminariosociologiapolitica.ufpr.br).

Fariello, Danilo. "Depois de longo impasse, governo vai regulamentar acesso à biodiversidade", *O'Globo,* March 17, 2013 / Desmatamento em alta, *O'Globo*, November 12, 2013.

Fearnside, Philip. *Dams in the Amazon: Belo Monte and Brazil's Hydroelectric Development of the Xingu River Basin*, Environmental Management, vol. XX. 2006.

Gasnier, Annie. "Nouvelles menaces contre la forêt amazonienne", *Le Monde*, December 4, 2008.

Giometti, A.B.; Moreira, H.M., "O protocolo de Quioto e as possibilidades de inserção do Brasil no Mecanismo de Desenvolvimento Limpo por meio de projetos em energia limpa", *Revue Contexto Nacional*, vol. 20, n° 1, January 2008.

Global Canopy Program. *The little REDD book: A guide to governmental and non-governmental proposals for reducing emissions for deforestation and degradation*, 2008, (www.thelittleREDDbook.org).

Gois, Chico de. "Lula anistia desmatadores do passado. Ao lançar programa de regularização de terras na Amazônia, presidente também critica ONG", *O'Globo*, June 20, 2009.

Goldemberg, José. "Copenhague: um post-mortari", *Politica Externa*, vol. 18, n° 4, May 2010.

Grandelle, Renato. "Metade dos gases-estufa vem da pecuária", *O'Globo*, December 11, 2009 / "Usinas de energia dependem de florestas", *O'Globo*, May 14, 2013 / "Desmatamento e morte. Ambiente perigoso", *O'Globo*, April 17, 2014.

Ilha, Flávio. "PF prende secretários de Meio Ambiente no RS", *O'Globo*, April 30, 2013.

Ilha, Flávio; Lins, Leticia; Rios, Odilon; Maltchik, Roberto. "Reforma Agrária. Em marcha para a cidade", *O'Globo*, January 27, 2013.

Inoue, Cristina. "Governance of global climate change in the Brazilian Amazon: the case of Amazonian municipalities", *Revista Brasileira de Politica Internacional,* Vol. 55, 2012.

Lago, André Aranha Corrêa do. *Estocolmo, Rio, Joanesburgo: o Brasil e as três conferencias ambientais das Nações Unidas*, FUNAG, Brasilia, 2007.

Latina-America : la menos temerosa an las negociaciones de la Cop 17, vol. 12, n° 5, December 2011, International Center for Trade and Sustainable Development (www.icstd.org).

Le Monde diplomatique (Brazilian edition), special supplement, "Sustentabilidade e desenvolvimento. O que esperar da Rio+20", Ano 4 (48), July 2011

Leitão, Míriam. "Malabarismo verde", *O'Globo*, November 13, 2009. "Desmatamento continua" *O'Globo*, July 17, 2013.

Lisboa, Marijane Vieira, (PUC, São Paulo). *Balanço da política ambiental do governo Lula: grandes e douradouros impactos*, 2009 / *Transgênicos no governo Lula: libertade para contaminar*, October 3, 2007 (www.ecodebate.cpm.br).

Machado Figueiredo, Luiz Alberto. "A conferencia de Cancún e a luta internacional contra a mudança do clima", *Política Externa*, vol. 19 (4), March 2011 / "O Êxito da Conferência do Clima de Durban e o caminho para a Rio+20", *Politica Externa*, vol. 20, n° 4, May 2012.

Marcovitch, Jacques (University of São Paulo). "Desafios do clima no Brasil e no Mundo", *Politica Externa*, vol. 18, n° 4, April 2010 / *A gestão da Amazonia. Ações Empresariais, Politicas Publicas, Estudos e Propostas*, EDUSP, São Paulo, 2011.
Marengo, José. "*Mudanças climáticas globais e seus efeitos sobre a biodiversidade – caracterização do clima atual e definição das alterações climáticas para o território brasileiro ao longo do século XXI*, Ministério do Meio Ambiente, Brasilia, 2007.
Matsuura, Sérgio. "Senado debate fim de ròtulo transgênico", *O 'Globo*, May 23, 2015.
Medeiros de Freitas Francisco Josué, "Código Florestal: Ainda há esquerda e direita no Brasil", Observatorio Politico Sul-Americano OPSA/UERJ, May 31, 2011.
Melo, Liana. "Amazônia nacionalizada. Governo busca verba para assumir 100 % de projeto científico que tem dinheiro da Nasa" *O 'Globo*, October 7, 2007.
Miguez, José Domingos Gonzalez. "A visão para Durban sobre o destino do Protocolo de Kyoto", *Pontes*, vol. 7, n° 4, November-December 2011.
Motta, Claudio; Grandelle, Renato. "Impasse climático", *O 'Globo*, December 10, 2011.
Novaes, Washington (former Secretary of the Environment, Science and Technology of the Federal District of Brasilia, 1991-1992). "Meio Ambiente : a estratégia que falta ao Brasil", *Revue Interesse Nacional*, July 2010.
(www.interessenacional.uol.com.br/artigos).
Piovesan, Flávia. "O conflito se agrava" (on the Indian question), *O 'Globo*, June 27, 2013.
Prolongeau, Hubert; Marie, Béatrice. "L'Amazonie asphyxiée par le soja", *Le Monde*, September 19, 2007.
Ricupero, Rubens. "A Amazônia e a Rio+20 : uma proposta para a revitalização da cooperação amazônica", *Politica Externa*, vol. 20, n° 4, May 2012.
Rodrigues, Délcio. "Estratégia amazônica", *O 'Globo*, March 27, 2013.
Rodrigues, Lino. "Em 11 anos, contaminação já matou 72 pessoas", *O 'Globo,* February 15, 2013.
Sassine, Vinicius. "Verba da Funai para proteção de terra indígena caiu 68 %", *O 'Globo,* June 11, 2013.
Serôa Da Motta, Ronaldo. *A Politica nacional sobre mudança do clima: aspectos regulatórios e de governança*, IPEA, Brasilia, 2011.
Serivano, Roberta. "Rio+20 : sociedade pede seriedade a governo", *O 'Globo*, April 19, 2012.
Silva, André Luiz Reis da; Visentini, Paulo G. Fagundes. "Brazil and Economic, Political and Environmental Multilateralism: the Lula years (2003-2010)", *Revista Brasileira de Politica internacional*, n° 53, 2010.
Souza, André. "Assassinato de índios aumenta 168 % nos governos Lula e Dilma", *O 'Globo,* June 8, 2013./ "Relatório aponta que 60 índios foram assassinados em 2012", *O 'Globo,* June 28, 2013.
Teixeira, Izabella. "Os Novos Caminhos da Política Ambiental no Brasil", *Interesse Nacional*, N° 26, July-September 2014.
Tilio, Neto. *Ecopolitica das mudanças climáticas: o Ipcc e o ecologismo dos pobres*, Pleïade, São Paulo, 2009.
Tinoco, Dandara; Fabrini, Fabio. "Impunidade agrava situação dos marcados para morrer" (on the killing of rural leaders), *O 'Globo*, June 5, 2011.
Uribe, Gustavo; Farah, Tatiana. "No campo, total de 'jurados de morte' sobe 107 %. Dados da Comissão Pastoral da Terra apontam 172 pessoas ameaçadas e 29 assassinadas; este ano, já são 9 mortos", *O 'Globo*, April 6, 2012 / "Violência crescente. Número de mortes em conflitos por terras cresce 10,3 % em todo o país entre 2011 e 2012", *O 'Globo,* March 4, 2013.
Viola, Eduardo; Franchini, Matias (University of Brasilia). *Politicas publicas climáticas no Brasil (2009-2011) / Mudança climática em 2011: a governança global estagnada.* Centro de Estudos de Integração e Desenvolvimento-Cindes, July 2011 (www.cindesbrasil.org).
Wasserman, Julio Cesar; Hacon, Sandra; Wasserman, Maria Angelica. "O ciclo do mercúrio no ambiente amazônico", *Mundo & Vida*, vol. 2, 2001.

Human Rights

Alexandre, Nina. *Action against hunger and poverty. Brazilian foreign policy in Lula's first term* (Working Paper), Center for Brazilian Studies, 2006.
Amorim, Celso. "Brasil e os Direitos Humanos: em busca de uma agenda positiva", *Política Externa*, vol. 18, n° 2, 2009 / "O dedo acusador pode até render aplauso, mas raramente salva", *Folha de São Paulo*, August 15, 2010.
Arbex, Daniela. *Holocausto Brasileiro - Vida, Genocidio e 60 mil mortes no maior hospício do Brasil,* Geração Editorial, São Paulo, 2013.
Arruda, Roldão. "Erundina vê 'jogo' com Comissão da Verdade", *O Estado de São Paulo*, September 8, 2011.
Asano, Camila Lissa; Nader, Lucia, "Reflexões sobre a política externa em direitos humanos do governo Lula", in **Marilene de Paula**, *Nunca antes na historia desse país.Um balanço das políticas do governo Lula,* Fondation Heinrich Böll Stiftung, Rio de Janeiro, 2011.
Ball, Patrick; Spirer, Herbert; Kobrak, Paul. *State Violence in Guatemala. Aquantitative Reflection (1960-1996)*, American Association for the Advancement of Science, Washington, 1999. (http/shr.aaas.org/projects/human_rights/Guatemala/report).
Barbara, Vanessa. "Reform Brazil´s military Police", *International New York Times*, February 20, 2014.
Barbosa, Alexandre de Freitas (ed.). *"O Brasil Real: A Desigualidade para Além dos Indicadores"*, Outras Expressões, São Paulo, 2012.
Barbosa, Flávia. "Comissão de Direitos Humanos da OEA sob ameaça", *O´Globo*, March 8, 2013 / "Na OEA, disputa por controle de comissão", *O´Globo,* March 10, 2013.
Bogalska, Ewa (ed.). *Être Noir au Brésil Aujourd'hui. Identités et mémoires en mutation*, L'Harmattan, Paris 2015.
Bottari, Elenilce. "Vítimas da ditadura terão assistência psicológica", *O´Globo*, April 20, 2013.
Bruno, Cássio; Castro, Juliana. "Em 13 estados não há plano para direitos humanos", *O´Globo*, March 16, 2013.
Carvalho, Cleide. "Policiais do Amazonas são acusados de tortura", *O´Globo*, April 29, 2012 / "Pastoral denuncia tortura em presídio da Paraiba", *O´Globo*, May 1, 2012.
Cassano, Alberto, *Cuba. Coopération internationale et droits de l´Homme*, L´Harmattan, Paris, 2010.
Castro Espin, Alejandro (son of Raul Castro), interview with Greek journalist Lasonas Pipinis Velasco, "The Future of Cuba", *Counterpunch*, February 27-March 1, 2015.
Castro, Juliana. "Tempo para Commissão da Verdade apurar é criticado", *O´Globo*, September 23, 2011.
Cazes, Leonardo. "Visões sobre a miséria e as iniciativas para combatê-la. A luta por comida", *O´Globo*, July 13, 2013 / "Luto em suspensão" (on disappearances in Brazil), *O´Globo*, September 7, 2013.
Ciconello, Alexandre. "Os avanços e contradições das políticas de Direitos Humanos no governo Lula", in **Marilene de Paula**, *Nunca na historia desse país. Um balanço das políticas do governo Lula*, Fondation Heinrich Böll Stiftung, Rio de Janeiro, 2011.
Chomsky, Noam. "The Torture Memos and Historical Amnesia", *The Nation,* June 1, 2009.
Commissão da Verdade no Brasil. Nucleo de Preservação da Memoria política, São Paulo, (www.nucleomemoria.org.br).
Corbyn, Jeremy; Davis, David; Mitchell, Andrew; Slaughter, Andy. "Obama´s Slap in Britain´s face" (British members of parliament act on behalf of Shaker Aamer, held without charges at the Guantanamo detention center for over 13 years), *International New York Times,* June 7, 2015.
Cunha, Luiz Cláudio (former Truth Commission member). "A verdade sobre a Comissão da Verdade", *O´Globo*, July 5, 2013.
Diehl, Jackson. "The end of a freedom fighter", *New York Times*, *International Herald Tribune*, March 4, 2013.
Éboli, Evandro. "Cresce a adesão de militares a manifesto", *O´Globo*, March 3, 2012 / "Tortura no campus. Comissão da Verdade diz que, a partir de 1964, havia porões da ditadura em

universidades e refinarias", *O´Globo*, May 22, 2005 / "Vanucchi: cenário do Brasil é desanimador. Representante na Comissão de Direitos Humanos da OEA cita prisões e indígenas", *O´Globo*, June 11, 2013.

Éboli, Evandro; Camarotti, Gerson. "Amorim manda punir 100 oficiais da reserva", *O´Globo*, March 1, 2012.

Fagundes, Ezequiel. "Policiais são suspeitos de morte de jornalistas", *O´Globo*, April 20, 2013.

Farah, Tatiana; Éboli, Evandro. "Ustra obtém direito de se calar em Comissão", *O´Globo*, May 10, 2013.

Fernandes, Leticia. "Violência contra imprensa cresce 166 % no país", *O´Globo*, October 14, 2013.

Fernandes, Leticia; Ramalho, Sérgio. "Anistia critica violência da PM e acende discussão sobre o tema", *O´Globo*, July 13, 2013.

Figuereido, Janaina. "Futuro da comissão depende da sociedade", Interview with Graciela Meijide, former minister, member of CONADEP (Argentine National Commission on the Disappearance of Persons), *O´Globo*, May 19, 2012 / "Da Argentina para a Comissão da Verdade. Grupo recebe de Cristina Kirchner 66 caixas com material sobre ditadura", *O´Globo,* April 20, 2013.

Foster, Bruce. "Relevés de notes sur les droits des réfugiés", *Migrations Forcées,* n° 37, April 2011.

Godoy, Fernanda. "Amorim apela a Ahmadinejad por americanos", *O´Globo*, September 23, 2010.

Gregori, José (former Secretary of State for Human Rights and former Justice Minister in the Fernando Henrique Cardoso government). "Comissão da Verdade: mais um elo de uma corrente", *Revue Interesse Nacional*, n° 17, June 2012, São Paulo.

Guandeline, Leonardo. "Vítimas de homicídio crescem 40% em São Paulo", *O´Globo*, January 26, 2013.

Hamann, Eduarda Passarelli. *The protection of Civilians in conflict and Brazil´s 'responsibility while protecting"*, NOREF, Norwegian Peacebuilding Resource Center, October 2012.

Herdy, Thiago. "Grupo protesta contra acusados de tortura", *O´Globo*, March 27, 2012 / "Pais querem saber o destino de seus filhos"; "Dilma orientou integrantes da Comissão da Verdade a dar prioridade à busca de informações sobre desaparecidos", *O´Globo*, May 18, 2012 / "Comissão cobra dos EUA explicação sobre visita ao Dops", *O´Globo*, February 19, 2013.

Hermet, Guy. "L´apurement du passé," *L´Amérique latine, Pouvoirs*, n° 98, 2001, Éditions du Seuil, Paris (English edition, "Human Rights Against the Test of Emerging Countries", in **Christophe Jaffrelot** (ed.), *The Emerging States,* Columbia University Press, New York, 2009).

Howlett-Martin, Patrick, *La coopération médicale internationale de Cuba. L´altruisme récompensé,* L´Harmattan, Paris, 2015

Iglesias, Simone; Éboli, Evandro; Brígido, Carolina. "Fonteles deixa Comissão da Verdade em meio a tensão", *O´Globo*, June 19, 2013.

Ilha, Flávio. "Ex-marido de Dilma afirma que empresários assistiam a torturas", *O´Globo*, March 19, 2013 / "Operação Condor sob investigação. Comissão da Verdade pedirá à Argentina informações sobre desaparecimento de 15 brasileiros", *O´Globo,* March 13, 2013.

Jakobskind, Mário Augusto. "Hora da Verdade. Brasil e Uruguai desvendam os crimes da ditadura", *Revue Caros Amigos*, April 2012.

Leech, Garry. "The Bias of Human Rights Watch", *Counterpunch,* March 14, 2013.

Leitão, Míriam. "Convencer os militares", *O´Globo*, June 28, 2014.

Leitão, Miriam; Renato, Claudio. "Procurador reabre casos de desaparecidos", *O´Globo*, March 2, 2012.

Leitão, Miriam. "Círculo Militar", *O´Globo*, March 11, 2012.

Liao, Yi Wu. *For a Song and a Hundred Songs: A Poet's Journey Through a Chinese Prison*, New Harvest, New York, 2013.

Martin, Arnaud (ed.). *Les droits indigènes en Amérique Latine*, L´Harmattan, Paris, 2015.

McCoy, Alfred. *Torture and Impunity: The U.S. Doctrine of Coercitive Interrogation*, University of Wisconsin Press, 2012.

Malkin, Elisabeth. "Guatemalan Mayans describe massacres in ex-dictator's genocide trial", April 16, 2013 / "Guatemala trial leaves out U.S. role", April 18-19, 2013 / "Legal victory for ex-dictator in Guatemala", May 22, 2013, *New York Times, International Herald Tribune.*
Marques da Silva, Ivan Luís. *Crimes da ditadura militar*, Editora Revista dos Tribunais, 2011.
Mello, Liana. "Brasil não aceita convite da OEA sobre a hidrelectrica de Belo Monte", *O´Globo*, October 25, 2011 / "Brasil no rol dos países doadores aos pobres", *O´Globo*, February 12, 2012.
Mendez, Luz. "The Strange Trial of Rios Montt", *Counterpunch*, May 24-26, 2013.
Merlino, Tatiana. "Ditadura. Luzes sobre a operação Condor", *Revue Caros Amigos*, April 2012.
Mitchell, Andrew (UK Secrerary of State for International Development). "Parceria para acabar com a miséria", *O´Globo*, April 20, 2012.
Netto, Marcelo; **Medeiros, Rogério** (testimony on Antônio Guerra, torturer and agent of repression). *Memórias de uma guerra suja*, TopBooks, Rio de Janeiro, 2012.
Nunes, Maria do Rosario (Secretary for Human Rights in the Rousseff administration), "Luta contra a tortura", *O´Globo*, July 21, 2013.
O´Globo, editorial. "Limites da Comissão da Verdade. Rever a lei de Anistia é um revanchismo que tenta o impossível e indesejável: pôr o país numa máquina do tempo e levá-lo para um período de tensãoes já superado", May 21, 2013.
Otavio, Chico. "Brasil entre os piores no ranking da imprensa livre", *O´Globo*, May 4, 2013 / "Exército barra acesso ao DOI; entidades pedem tombamento", *O´Globo*, August 21, 2013 / "Comissão só terá Dipp se superar crise", *O´Globo*, August 28, 2013.
Parry, Robert. "U.S. Sponsored Dictators : Tales of Reagan´s Guatemala genocide", *Global Research*, April 18, 2013.
Payne, Leigh. *A amnistia na era da responsabilização: o Brasil em perspectiva internacional comparada*, 2011, (www.memoriasreveladas.gov.br).
Pereira, Merval. "Em busca da verdade", *O´Globo*, March 31, 2013.
Perez, Ana Candida. *"Evolução da Política Externa de Direitos Humanos: conceitos e discurso"*, Dissertation (N°360), Itamaraty, Rio Branco Institute, 2003.
Pierry, Flávia. "Comissão da Verdade: parentes de vítimas pedem mudanças", *O´Globo*, July 16, 2013.
Piovesan, Flávia. "Lei de Anistia, Direito à Verdade e à Justiça: o Caso Brasileiro", *Revue Interesse Nacional*, Na 5, n° 17, June 2012, São Paulo.
Reis, Daniel Aarão. "A Comissão da Verdade vai ser à brinca ou à vera?", *O´Globo*, May 15, 2012.
Roxo, Sérgio. "Dízimo na igreja, cofre no escritório" (on the president of the Parliamentary Commission on Human Rights), *O´Globo*, March 10, 2013.
Roxo, Sergio; **Herdy, Thiago**. "Tensão urbana. São Paulo sitiada", *O´Globo*, June 14, 2013.
Sagrillo Figueiredo, Cesar Alessandro. *"A política brasileira para refugiados (1998-2012)"*, Dissertation, Universidade Federal do Rio Grande do Sul, April 4, 2013.
Sanches, Mariana. "Imigrantes sofrem com trabalho degradante", *O´Globo,* August 17, 2014.
Sanford, Victoria. "Victory in Guatemala? Not yet", *New York Times*, *International Herald Tribune,* May 15, 2013.
Sassine, Vinicius. "Tortura e abandon em hospitais de custódia", *O´Globo*, February 18, 2013 / "Vergonha internacional. ONU retrata horror em prisões do Brasil", *O´Globo*, March 29, 2013.
Sciolino, Elaine. "A poet's tale from China's gulag", *New York Times*, *International Herald Tribune,* April 11, 2013.
Scrivano, Roberta. "Associações de jornalistas condenam a atuação da PM", *O´Globo*, June 15, 2013.
Senise Paes Leme, João Marcos, *"A responsabilidade de proteger antes e depois da intervenção na Libia: uma perspectiva brasileira"*, Dissertation, (N°686), Itamaraty, Rio Branco Institute, 2011.
Shane, Scott. "Torture. U. S. inflicts pain in a Soviet way", *New York Times*, June 16, 2007.
Sikkink, Kathryn; **Walling, Carrie Booth**. "The impacts of Human Rights trials in America Latina", *Journal of Peace Research*, vol. 44, n° 4, 2007.

Sikkink, Kathryn. "The Justice Cascade: How Human Rights Prosecutions are changing World politics. The case of Human Rights prosecutions", *New York Times, International Herald Tribune*, September 16, 2011.
Soares, Inês Virgínia Prado; **Shimada, Akemi; Kishi, Sandra** (coord.). *Memória e verdade: a justiça de transição no Estado democratico brasileiro*, Forúm, Belo Horizonte, 2009.
Soares, Luiz Eduardo. "Raízes do Imobilismo Político na Segurança Pública", *Interesse Nacional*, nº 20, March 2013.
Souza, André de; **Alencastro, Catarina; Damé, Luiza**. "Verdade sem ressentimento. Dilma instala comissão para apurar crimes da ditadura e destaca política de Estado", *O'Globo*, May 17, 2012.
Stover, Eric; Weinstein, Hervé. *My neighbour, my enemy: justice and community in the aftermath of mass atrocity*, Cambridge University Press, 2004.
Sweig, Julia; Bustamante, Michael (Foreign Affairs Council). *Cuba 2011: nova era, novos desafios*, vol. 19, n° 4, May 2011.
Teles, Edson; Quinalha, Renan. "O trabalho de Sísifo da Comissão Nacional da Verdade", *Le Monde diplomatique* (Brazil), September 2013.
Teófilo, Priscyla Barcelos. *Análise da atuação do Brasil no Conselho de Direitos Humanos das Nações Unidas no período 2006-2010*, Monographs, Catholic University of Brasilia, Brasilia, 2011, (www.pt.scribd.com).
Timoteo da Costa, Mariana; **Farah, Titiana**; **Brigido, Carolina**. "Apontar os responsáveis já será uma punição", O'Globo, May 12, 2012.
UNESCO, *The safety of Journalists and the danger of impunity*, Report by the Director General, 28th session of the International Programme for the Development of Communication (IPDC), Paris, March 22-23, 2012.
Uribe, Gustavo. "Homicídio de índios é o maior desde 1988", *O'Globo,* January 15, 2014.
Uribe, Gustavo; Bruno, Cássio. "Não tem dois lados, o outro lado foi assassinado" (on the Commission of Inquiry), *O'Globo*, May 15, 2012.
Villa, Marco Antonio. "Verdade? Que verdade?", *O'Globo*, May 22, 2012.
Wasserman, Claudia. "A recepção da Revolução Cubana no Brasil: a histriografia brasileira", *Estudios Interdisciplinarios de America Latina y el Caribe,* Vol. 12, N°2, Buenos Aires, 2007.
Weber, Demétrio. "Ministro diz que governo não pedirá revisão da Lei da Anistia. Cardozo desautoriza Comissão da Verdade, que na véspera defendera julgamento para punir torturadores", *O'Globo*, May 23, 2013.
Weichert, Marlon Alberto. "A sentença da Corte Interamericana de Direitos Humanos e a obrigação de instituir uma Comissão da Verdade", in **Luiz Flavio Gomes; Valerio Mazzuoli** (ed.), *Crimes da Ditadura Militar*, Ed. Revista dos Tribunais, 2011.
Weber, Demétrio. "No mundo, um em cada oito sofre com fome crônica. Relatório da ONU diz que Brasil é um dos 62 países que atingiu meta de alimentação", *O'Globo*, October 2, 2013.
Worth, Robert; **Fathi, Nazila**. "*Iranian confirms abuses in prisons*", *New York Times, International Herald Tribune*, August 18, 2009.

The Honduras Crisis

Alexandrov, Nick. "Honduras: the killings Continue", *Counterpunch*, February 26, 2013.
Arce, Alberto. "Dad seeks Justice for Slain Son in Broken Honduras", *Associated Press*, November 12, 2012.
Avila Vianna, Renato de. *"A atuação diplomatic do Brasil na crise de Honduras"*, Dissertation (N° 641), Itamaraty, Rio Branco Institute, 2011.
Bhatt, Keane. "The New York Times on Venezuela and Honduras: A Case of Journalistic Misconduct", *North Amerivan Congress on Latin America* (NACLA), May 8, 2013 / "Noam Chomsky, Scholars Ask NT Times Public Editor to Investigate Bias on Honduras and Venezuela", *North Amerivan Congress on Latin America* (NACLA), May 14, 2013.
Cabral, Otavio; **Teixeira, Duda**. "Honduras: o papel do Brasil nessa confusão", *Veja*, September 30, 2009.

Filgueiras, Fernando. "Justiça constitucional, legitimidade e interesse público", *Revista Brasileira de Ciênça Política*, n° 7, Brasilia, January-April 2012.
Frank, Dana. "Democrats divided over Honduras", *The Nation*, April 16, 2012.
Haugaard, Lisa; Kinosian, Sarah; Hartung, William. "Can the Violence in Honduras be Stopped?", *Counterpunch*, February 20-22, 2015.
Llana, Sara Miller, "Honduras Crisis: Brazil grabs leadership role", *The Christian Science Monitor*, September 22, 2009.
Pagina 12, "El ranking de la violencia", February 16, 2013.
Weisbrot, Mark. "The New Generation of Honduran Death Squads", *Counterpunch*, April 3, 2013.

Disarmament

Baena Soares, Rodrigo de Lima. "A base Industrial de Defesa Brasileira e a Politica Externa" *Cadernos de Politica Exterior*, Ano 1, N°1, Brasilia, September 1, 2015
Baker, Peter; Cooper, Helene. "Nuclear pact is a modest means to bigger ends", *New York Times, International Herald Tribune*, March 27-28, 2010.
Berrigan, Frida. "États-Unis, le premier marchand de canons de la planète", *Los Angeles Times*, in *Courrier International de l'Unesco*, 865, May 31-June 6, 2007.
Bildt, Carl (former Swedish Minister of Foreign Affairs); **Sikorski, Radek** (Polish Minister of Foreign Affairs). "Next, the tactical nukes", *New York Times, International Herald Tribune*, February 2, 2010.
Blair, Bruce (Global Zero); **Bosetti, Damon; Weeden, Brian**. "Bombs Away", *New York Times, International Herald Tribune*, December 8, 2010.
Brown, Andrew. *Keeper of the Nuclear Conscience: The Life and work of Joseph Roblat*, Oxford University Press, 2012.
Bumiller, Elisabeth. "Potentially destabilizing arms buildup by China feared", *New York Times, International Herald Tribune*, August 26, 2011.
Damasceno, Marcio. *Specialistas alemães veem com ceticismo cooperação militar Brasil-França*, October 24, 2010, (www.dw-world.de).
Dupas, Gilberto; Vigevani, Tullo (ed.). *O Brasil e as novas dimensões da segurança internacional*, AlfaOmega Ed., São Paulo, 1999.
Erlanger, Steven, "Panetta urges Nato unity on spending", *New York Times, International Herald Tribune*, October 6, 2011.
Erlanger, Steven; Shanker, Thom. "Gates assails NATO over willingness to share costs", *New York Times, International Herald Tribune*, June 11, 2011.
Folha de São Paulo. "Corrida Armamentista. Gasto militar atinge nível da Guerra Fria", June 10, 2004.
Freitas, Janio de. "O país escondido. Na recusa ao banimento de bombas de fragmentações, o Brasil alinhou-se a Estados Unidos, Israel e Russia", *Folha de São Paulo*, December 7, 2008.
Garcia, Denise. "Contestação de normas e ameaça à paz e à segurança regional e internacional: a facilidade excessiva de accesso as armas" (Norm contestation and threat to regional and international peace and security: excessive ease of access to arms), *Contexto Nacional*, Vol. 33, July-December 2011.
Hirst, M. "Intermediate States, Multilateralism and International Security", in *The Role of Brazil in the Fields of Peace and Security*, Papers for the conference organized with the support of the Ford Foundation at IUPERJ, March 22, 2004, Rio de Janeiro, 2004.
House of Commons. "Scrutiny of Arms Exports and Arms Control", Committee on Arms Export Controls, London, June 1, 2013.
International Herald Tribune (New York Times) "Reshape the arsenal. By cutting its nuclear arms, the US will have more credibility in its effort to contain other´s nuclear ambitions", *International Herald Tribune*, March 13, 2012 / "A Bloated US Arsenal", October 31, 2011.

Kissinger, Henry (Secretary of State under Richard Nixon and Gerald Ford); **Shultz, George** (Secretary of State under Ronald Reagan). "After Georgia: Finding common ground", *New York Times, International Herald Tribune*, October 1, 2008.
Lobato, André. "Tratado de armas alcança quorum no primeiro dia", *O'Globo*, June 4, 2013.
Macfarquhar, Neil. "U.N. backs first treaty on conventional arms Sales", *New York Times, International Herald Tribune*, April 3, 2013.
Melo, Regiane de. *Indústria de Defesa e Desenvolvimento estratégico. Estudo comparado França Brasil*, FUNAG, Brasilia, 2015.
Muggah, Robert; **Risso, Melina**. "É hora de o Brasil liderar o controle de armas", *O'Globo*, March 7, 2013.
O'Globo. "Putin declara moratoria em pacto antiarmas", April 27, 2007.
O Estado de São Paulo. "Londres renovará arsenal nuclear", March 15, 2007.
Perry, William (former Secretary of Defense), **Schultz, George** (former Secretary of State, 1982-1989). "How to build on the SALT Treaty", *New York Times, International Herald Tribune*, April 12, 2010.
Rosa, Rui Namorado (president of the Portuguese Council for Peace and Cooperation). "OTAN, uma maquina de guerra global em movimento", *Vermelho*, August 9, 2008, (www.vermelho.org.br).
Schwartz, Stephen (ed.). *Atomic audit: The cost and consequences of US nuclear weapons since 1940*, Brookings Institution Press, 1998.
Scofield, Gilberto. "Embraer quer investir, mais na área de defesa", *O'Globo*, December 14, 2011.
Shanker, Thom. "Resurgent Russian military marches anew", October 20, 2010 / "Pentagon expresses concern over China's military expansion", October 18, 2010, *New York Times, International Herald Tribune*.
Sifton, John. "Drones. A troubling history", *The Nation*, February 27, 2012.
Souza, André De; **Éboli, Evandro**; **Castro, Juliana**. "Militares reclaman de penúria da Aeronáutica", *O'Globo*, July 28, 2013.
The Economist. "The Anglo-French defence pact. Divided we fall", November 6, 2010.
Vinocur, John. "An E.U. flow of weapons to China?", *New York Times, International Herald Tribune*, January 11, 2011.
Vorobyov, Vladislav. "Russia's rearmament drive is justified", *Russia Now*, April 1, 2011.
White, Nigel; Freeman, John; Dekken, Guido; Asada, Masahito. "Arms control" (seminar), *Journal of Conflict amd security Law*, vol. 9, n° 3, 2004.
Wong, Edward. "Chinese navy reaches far", *New York Times, International Herald Tribune*, June 16, 2011.
Zechini, Laurent. "À Brest, Michèle Alliot-Marie défend la nouvelle génération de missiles nucléaires M51", *Le Monde*, January 13, 2005 / "Les dépenses militaires mondiales ont progressé de 45 % en dix ans", *Le Monde*, June 11, 2008 / "Dépenses militaires. Un réarmement mondial", *Le Monde*, June 20, 2007.

Nuclear Non-Proliferation

Almeida, Paulo Roberto. *A velha questão nuclear e alguns novos atores*, in *Segurança Internacional: um dialogo Europa-America do Sul*, Fundação Konrad Adenauer, Rio de Janeiro, 2008.
Alperovitz, Gar. *The Decision to use the Atomic Bomb*, Random House, New York, 1996.
Baracho Teixeira, Démia. "A influência dos EUA sobre a adesão brasileira ao Tratado de Não-proliferação de Armas Nucleares (TNP)", Dissertation, University of Brasilia, November 2007.
Beilin, Yossi (former Israeli Minister of Justice). "Let Jordan enrich its own uranium", *New York Times, International Herald Tribune*, June 28, 2010.
Bolton, John (former U.S. Ambassador to the United Nations, 2005-2006). "*A fast way to lose the arms race*", *New York Times, International Herald Tribune*, May 26, 2009.
Bolton, John; Yoo, John (University of California, Berkeley). "Why rush to cut nukes?", *New York Times, International Herald Tribune*, November 11, 2010.

Broad, William; Sanger, David. *"Obama's nuclear-free vision"*, *New York Times, International Herald Tribune*, July 6, 2009.
Cohen, Avner (Monterrey Institute of International Studies); **Miller, Marvin** (Massachussetts Institute of Technology). "Bringing Israel's bomb out of the basement", *New York Times, International Herald Tribune*, August 25, 2010.
Cohen, Avner. *The worst kept-secret. Israel's Bargain with the Bomb*, Columbia University Press, 2010.
Chen, Roger. "Dangerous nuclear illusions", *New York Times, International Herald Tribune*, November 12, 2010.
Cohen, Avner. *Israel and the Bomb*, Columbia University Press, New York, 1998.
Da Silva, Fernando Aparicio, *"O Brasil e o TNP. Uma apreciação Critica da Implementação do tratado de Non-proliferação de Armas nucleares após 2000"*, Dissertation (N°401), Itamaraty, Rio Branco Institute, 2005.
Dempsey, Judy. "Hope for arms control if U.S. and Russia lead", December 6, 2008 / "West to seek revival of arms treaty in Europe", April 30, 2010 / "Europe lacks plan on nuclear arms", May 3, 2010 / "NATO to address nuclear disarmament", October 1, 2010, *New York Times, International Herald Tribune*.
Duarte, Sergio (High Representative of the United Nations for Disarmament Affairs). "A VIII Conferencia de Exame do Tratado de Não Proliferação de Armas Nucleares: histórico e perspectivas", *Política Externa*, vol. 19, n° 1, August 2010.
Eberstadt, Nicholas. "North Korea. Talking Only Makes it Worse", *Time*, February 5, 2007.
O'Globo. "EUA liberam pesquisa de novas armas nucleares", *O'Globo*, May 23, 2003.
ElBaradei, Mohamed. *The Age of Deception. Nuclear Diplomacy in Treacherous Times*, Metropolitan Books, New York, 2011.
Evans, Gareth; Kawaguchi, Yonko. *Éliminer les menaces nucléaires. Rapport de la Commission internationale sur la non-prolifération et le désarmement nucléaire*, Canberra, 2009 (www.icnnd.org).
Fahmy, Nabil (University of Cairo); **Lewis, Patricia**. *Éléments possibles d'un traité sur une zone exempte d'armes nucléaires au Moyen-Orient*, Forum on Disarmament, 2011.
Fariello, Danilo. "Energia Polêmica. Reforço atômico", *O'Globo*, February 10, 2013.
Fountain, Henry. "Chernobyl: Capping a Catastrophe", *The New York Times*, April 27, 2014.
Füllgraf, Frederico. *A Bomba Pacifica. O Brasil e outros Cenários da Corrida Nuclear*, Editora Brasiliense, Saõ Paulo, 1988.
Gall, Norman. "Atoms for Brazil, Dangers for All", *O Estado de São Paulo*, June 13, 1976.
Goldemberg, José. *Is Brazil setting a bad example in enriching uranium?* Carnegie Endowment for International Peace, July 16, 2007.
(www.carnegieendowment.org/2007/07/16).
Hak Neto, Ibrahim Abdul. *Armas de Destruição em Massa no Seculo XXI: Novas Regras para um velho Jogo*, FUNDAG, Brasilia, 2011.
Herz, Monica; **Missari, Nizar**. "A politica nuclear na política internacional", *Politica Externa*, vol. 20, n° 3, February 2012.
Hornblum, Allen; **Newman, Judith Lynn**; **Dober, Gregory**. *Against their Will. The Secret History of Medical Experimentation on Children in Cold war America*, Palgrave Macmillan, New York, 2013.
Hounan, Peter. *The Woman from Mossad; the Story of Mordechai Vanunu and the Israeli Nuclear Program*, Frog Books, Berkeley,1999.
Inderfurth, Karl (former Undersecretary of State for South Asia, 1997-2001); **Riedel, Bruce** (former member of the National Security Council, 1997-2002, member of the Brookings Intitute). "A US-Indian partnership against nukes", *New York Times, International Herald Tribune*, November 27, 2007.
International Herald Tribune (New York Times) "Questioning the India US deal", October 8, 2007 / "France signs nuclear deal with India", October 1, 2008 / "New START matters: European foreign ministers urge the U.S. and Russia to ratify New START", December 23, 2010 / "A nuclear retreat: The Obama administration is wrong not to insist on a very non-proliferation provision in nuclear cooperation agreement", February 7, 2012.
International New York Times, (editorial). "Backsliding on nuclear promises", September 24, 2014.

International Physicians for the Prevention of Nuclear War (IPPNW). Critical Analysis of the UNSCEAR Report "Levels and effects of radiation exposure due to the nuclear accident after the 2011 Great East-Japan Earthquake and Tsunami", April 2014 (www.ippnw.de).
Jungblut, Cristiane. "Dilma quer inspeção em arsenais", *O 'Globo*, September 23, 2011.
Kassenova, Togzhan. *"Brazil's Nuclear Kaleidoscope: An Evolving Identity"*, Carnegie Endowment for International Peace, Washington, 2014.
carnegieendowment.com
Klein, Jean. "La France face à la seconde ère nucléaire", *Le Monde diplomatique*, mars 2006.
Krasno, Jean. "Non-proliferation: Brazil's Secret Nuclear program", *Orbis,* Vol 38, N°3, 1994.
Laforge, John. "We are Number One! US Nuclear Weapons Proliferation", *Counterpunch*, April 18-20, 2014.
Lepage, Corinne. *La vérité sur le nucléaire*, Éditions Albin Michel, Paris, 2011.
Lintner, Bertil. "Brazil-North Korea. Brothers in Trade", *Asia Times*, June 3, 2010.
Landau, Emily (University of Tel-Aviv). "Analysis: who is afraid of a nuke-free zone in the Middle East?", *Jerusalem Post*, April 26, 2010.
Landau, Emily, (University of Tel-Aviv), *A weapon-of-mass-destruction-free zone in the Middle East: shaping the contours of discussion towards 2012.* (www.boell.de), Fondation Heinrich Böll Stiftung, July 6, 2010.
Langewiesche, William. *The Atomic Bazaar. The rise of the Nuclear Poor*, Farrar, Strauss and Giroux Books, New York, 2007.
Magalhães-Ruether, Graça. "Acordo 'atomic' com Brasil racha Alemanha", *O 'Globo*, June 27, 2007.
Mampaey, Luc. "Les zones exemptes d'armes nucléaires : état des lieux, bilan et nouveaux enjeux", Group for Research and Information on Peace and Security – GRIP, Brussels (www.grip.org).
Nunn, Sam (former U.S. Senator). "Towards a world without nukes", *New York Times, International Herald Tribune,* April 14, 2012.
O 'Globo, editorial. "Brasil precisa de mais usinas nucleares", February 15, 2013.
Ordoñez, Ramona. "Siñal verde para Angra 3", *O 'Globo*, June 1, 2010.
Ordoñez, Ramona. "Brasil investe quase R$ 1 bi para produzir todo o urânio de Angra 3", *O 'Globo*, January 19, 2011.
Oswald, Vivian. "Clima de Guerra Fria no ar", *O 'Globo*, October 19, 2008 / "Líder russa de construção de usina nuclear quer entrar no Brasil", *O 'Globo*, June 6, 2013.
Patti, Carlo. "Brazil and the Nuclear Issues in the Years of the Luis Inácio da Silva Government (2003-2010)", *Revista Brasileira de Politica Internacional*, vol. 53, n° 2, 2010.
Perkovitch, George. *Abolishing Nuclear weapons: Why the USA should lead*, Carnegie Endowment For International Peace, October 2008.
Perkovich, George; **Acton, Jans**. *Abolishing Nuclear Weapons: A Debate,* Carnegie Endowment for International Peace, 2009.
Poitevin, Cedric; **Tudosia, Manuela**. "Le Groupe des Pays Fournisseurs Nucléaires dans le régime international de non-prolifération", Analysis Note, GRIP, Brussels, June 30, 2008.
Polgreen, Lydia. "US urges India to ease access to nuclear work", *New York Times, International Herald Tribune*, July 20, 2007.
Reed, Thomas; **Stillman, Dany**. *The Nuclear Express. A Political history of the Bomb and its Proliferation*, Zenith Press, Minneapolis, 2009.
Robbins, Carol Anne. "Putting Nuclear Genies Back in Their Bottles", *New York Times, International Herald Tribune*, May 19, 2007.
Rosa, Bruno. "Início de Angra 3 passa de 2016 para 2018", *O 'Globo*, June 8, 2013.
Rouppert, Bérangère. "La conférence d'examen du TNP 2010 : vers un renforcement du régime de non-prolifération", GRIP, Brussels, May 5, 2010.
Sanger, David. "Obama faces new hurdles for nuclear priorities", *New York Times, International Herald Tribune*, December 25, 2010.
Sang-Hun, Choe. "Kim inherits framework on nuclear deal with US", *New York Times, International Herald Tribune*, March 2, 2012.

Schlosser, Eric. "*Command and Control: Nuclear Weapons, the Damascus Accident and the Illusion of Safety*", Penguin Books, New York, 2013.
Scowcroft, Brent; Hadley, Stephen; Miller, Franklin. "NATO-Based Nuclear Weapons are an Advantage in a Dangerous World", *The Washington Post,* August 18, 2014.
Shanker, Thom. "Former chief of U.S. arsenal calls for slashing nuclear arms", *New York Times, International Herald Tribune,* May 16, 2012.
Sheinan, David. "Nuclear Development and the Shaping of an Independent Foreign Policy 1950-1990", *Estudios Interdisciplinarios de America Latina y el Caribe,* Vol.16, N°2, Buenos Aires, 2005.
Shen, Digli. "Can Sanctions Stop Proliferation?", *The Washington Quarterly,* Summer 2008.
Slater, Alice. "New Campaign for a Treaty to Ban Nuclear Weapons Gains Momentum", *Counterpunch,* May 27, 2014.
Sobral Duarte, Carlos Sérgio. "*O Brasil Estado-parte no Tratado de Não Proliferação de Armas Nucleares (TNP): implicação para a ação diplomática brasileira nos campos do desarmamento e da não proliferação nuclear",* Dissertation (N°353), Itamaraty, Rio Branco Institute, 2002.
Stillman, Dany. *The Nuclear Express. A Political History of the Bomb and its Proliferation,* Zenith Press, Minneapolis, 2009.
Tavares, Monica; Alvarez, Regina; Ordoñez, Ramona. "Sinal verde para energia nuclear", *O´Globo,* June 26, 2007.
Ténèze, Nicolas. *Israël et sa dissuasion. Histoire politique d´un paradoxe,* L´Harmattan, Paris, 2015.
Timmons, Heather; Kumar, Hari. "India extends its nuclear reach", *New York Times, International Herald Tribune,* April 20, 2012.
Zajec, Olivier. "T.N.P. Bouclier nucléaire en péril", *Le Monde diplomatique,* May 2010.
Zecchini, Laurent. "Inquiétant commerce nucléaire", *Le Monde,* April 8, 2006.

The Middle East

Akyop, Mustafa (Turkish journalist). "In the Middle East, democracy isn´t enough", *New York Times, International Herald Tribune,* May 14, 2012.
Amorim, Celso, "Brazil and the Middle East", *The Cairo Review of Global Affairs* (American University of Cairo), May 2012.
Barbosa, Flávia; De Luca, Isabel. "Em discurso na ONU, Dilma afirma que intervenções militares acentuam 'barbárie'", *O´Globo,* September 24, 2014.
Barluet, Alain. "Les interventions militaires aident-elles à résoudre les crises?", *Le Monde,* March 17, 2014.
Brun, Élodie. *Les Relations entre l´Amérique du Sud et le Moyen-Orient,* Éd. L´Harmattan, Paris, 2008.
Byrne, Malcolm (ed.) with James Blight, Janet Lang, John Tirman, Hussein Banai, and Bruce Riedel. *Becoming Enemies. U.S.-Iran Relations,* Musgrove Conference Papers, National Security Archive, St. Simons Island, Georgia, 2012.
Chomsky, Noam. *Modern-Day American Imperialism: The Middle East and Beyond,* ZSpace, December 23, 2009, reproduction of a conference at the University of Boston on March 17, 2009.
Cook, Jonathan. *Israel and the Clash of Civilisations: Iraq, Iran and the Plan to Remake the Middle East,* Pluto Press, London, 2008.
Djalili, Mohammad-Reza; Kellner, Thierry. "Iran, l´arbitre du Proche-Orient?", *Le Monde,* September 13, 2014.
Durand, Stefan. "Fascisme, Islam et grossiers amalgames", *Le Monde diplomatique,* November 2006.
Lackner, Helen. *Why Yemen Matters: A Society in Transition,* Saqi Books, London, 2014.
Le Monde Diplomatique. "Vous avez dit Terrorisme ?", Manière de voir (dossier), N°140, April-May 2015.
Passos, José Meirelles. "Acão brasileira no Oriente Médio irritou os EUA", *O´Globo,* February 6, 2011.

Ramos, Murilo. "Viagem de Lula ao Oriente Médio visa estreitar os laços", *Meio Norte*, December 2, 2003.
Raposo Lopes, Marcos Leal. "*Cooperação com os países arábes – o potencial da Liga dos Estados Arabes como parceira do Brasil*", Dissertation (N°459), Itamaraty, Rio Branco Institute, 2006.
Schuessler, Jennifer. "Charlie Hebdo Award at PEN Gala Sparks More Debate", *International New York Times*, May 4, 2015.
Toensing, Chris. "Yemen is Starving and We´re Partly to Blame", *Middle East Research and Information Project*", May-June 1986.
Vigo, Julian. "Islamophobia and the Aegis of Freedom of Speech", *Counterpunch*, May 12, 2015.

Afghanistan

Afghanistan Rights Monitor. "Mid-Year Report Civilian Casualties of Conflict", (January-June 2010).
Ahmed, Azam. "Afghan civilian war casualties rise", July 31, 2013 / "Grim toil at the suicide bombers´ graveyard", August 5, 2013, *New York Times, International Herald Tribune.*
Aikins, Mathieu. "Guerre et trafic d´opium an Afghanistan", *Harper´s Magazine*, in *Courrier International*, n° 1034 of August 26 – September 1, 2010.
Angeli, Claude. "L´Élysée s´inquiète d´une forte poussée de fièvre dans l´armée", *Le Canard enchaîné*, July 21, 2010.
Bowley, Graham. "Afghans brace for the occupation´s end", *New York Times*, *International Herald Tribune*, February 2, 2012.
Bowley, Graham; **Rubin, Alissa**. "Afghan body-part photographs bring condemnation from U. S.", *New York Times*, *International Herald Tribune*, April 19, 2012.
Braithwaite, Rodric. *Afgantsy. The Russians in Afghanistan 1979-89*, Oxford University Press, 2012.
Brenner, Michael. "The CIA´s Dirty Wars", *Counterpunch*, April 22, 2013.
Brothers, Caroline. "Wave of young Afghans crossing Europe. A generation of lone boys on the road and in cities strains protection system", *New York Times*, *International Herald Tribune*, August 26, 2009.
Bumiller, Elisabeth. "U.S. outlines big goals for Afghan forces. High recruitment figures are necessary to cover desertion and resignation", *New York Times*, *International Herald Tribune*, August 25, 2010.
Burns, John. "U.K. war inquiry focuses on Blair", *New York Times*, *International Herald Tribune*, November 25, 2009.
Cahill, Kevin. *Human security for all: a tribute to Sergio Vieira de Mello*, Fordham University Press, New York, 2004.
Caño, Antonio. "Karzai admite receber sacos de dinheiro do Irã" (on corruption of administrators), *El País*, in *O´Globo*, October 26, 2010.
Chivers, C.J.; **Rubin, Alissa; Wesley, Morgan**. "US forces pull back from rugged Afghan ally", *New York Times*, *International Herald Tribune*, February 26-27, 2011.
Cohen, Roger. "Of fruit flies and drones", *New York Times*, *International Herald Tribune*, November 13, 2009.
Cooper, Helene. "Few U.S. options to leverage Karzai", *New York Times*, *International Herald Tribune*, November 12, 2009.
Dalrymple, William. "The ghosts of Gandamak", *New York Times*, *International Herald Tribune*, May 10, 2010.
Dao, James. "Two-edged sword in Afghan fight", *New York Times*, *International Herald Tribune*, August 6, 2009.
DeYoung, Karen; **Londoño, Ernesto**. "In Afghanistan U.S. losing patience as deadline for long-term deals nears", *The Washington Post,* October 11, 2013.
Dempsey, Judy. "German general breaks silence: Afghan mission is a ¨miserable failure¨", December 1, 2008 / "Europe´s Afghan mission still in disarray", November 13, 2009 / "Berlin

to pay Afghan families for fatal attack", August 11, 2010, *New York Times*, *International Herald Tribune.*

Dorronsoro, Gilles (Carnegie Endowment for International Peace). "Face reality: Talk to the Taliban", *New York Times*, *International Herald Tribune*, September 15, 2010.

Dreyfuss, Bob. "How the US War in Afghanistan Fueled the Taliban Insurgency", *The Nation*, October 7, 2013 / "Karzai lashes Out Over Civilian Deaths", *The Nation*, October 8, 2013.

Dreyfuss, Bob; Turse, Nick. "America´s Afghan Victims. Civilian Fatalities 2001-2012", *The Nation*, September 18, 2013.

Duarte, Fernando. "Por quem os sinos britânicos dobram", August 1, 2010 / "Uma conversão embaraçosa para Blair", October 26, 2010, *O´Globo.*

Ellick, Adam. "Choices for Afghans: Bad and worse", *New York Times*, *International Herald Tribune*, July 6, 2009.

Fairweather, Jack. "Give the Taliban a chance", *International New York Times*, November 12, 2014.

Fergusson, James. *Taliban. The Unknown enemy*, Da Capo Press, Perseus Books Group, Philadelphia, 2010.

Filkins, Dexter; **Mazzetti, Mark**. "Karzai aide linked to C.I.A", *New York Times*, *International Herald Tribune*, August 27, 2010.

Filkins, Dexter; **Rubin, Alissa**. "Kabul corruption setback", *New York Times*, *International Herald Tribune*, August 30, 2010.

Filkins, Dexter. "With U.S. help, warlord builds empire", June 7, 2010 / "U.S. is said to fund Afghan warlords", June 23, 2010 / "As Kabul Bank totters, system is feared to be at risk" / "Afghan minorities fear pact with Taliban", June 28, 2010 / "Taliban and corruption are horns of a dilemma for a war-weary people", September 2, 2010 / "Iran buying influence in Kabul with bags of cash", October 25, 2010, *New York Times*, *International Herald Tribune.*

Friedman, Thomas. "This time we really mean it", *New York Times*, *International Herald Tribune*, April 1, 2010.

Gall, Carlotta; **Khapalwak, Ruhullah**. "Afghan leader buries assassinated brother", *New York Times*, *International Herald Tribune*, July 14, 2011.

Gall, Carlotta; Sanger, David. "Killings of Civilians Provoke Afghan Anger", *New York Times*, in *Le Monde*, May 19, 2007.

Gall, Carlotta. "Afghan firms complain not being paid", July 8, 2010 / "Battling to win hearts, minds and a war", October 18, 2010, *New York Times*, *International Herald Tribune.*

Gelb, Leslie (Council on Foreign Relations). "How to leave", *New York Times*, *International Herald Tribune*, March 14, 2009.

Gezari, Vanessa. "How to read Afghanistan", *New York Times*, *International Herald Tribune*, August 12, 2013.

Gorbachev, Mikail. "Soviet lessons from Aghanistan", *New York Times*, *International Herald Tribune*, February 5, 2010.

Greenway, H. "Interpreting Afghanistan", June 2, 2010 / "Karzai´s legitimacy dilemma", *New York Times*, *International Herald Tribune*, May 14, 2011.

Gromov, Boris (governor of the Moscow region, former Commander in Afghanistan); **Rogozin Dmitry** (Russian Ambassador to NATO). "Russian advice on Afghanistan", *New York Times*, *International Herald Tribune*, January 12, 2010.

Halimi, Serge. "Bombons de manhã, napalm á tarde", *Le Monde diplomatique*, (Brazil), November 2009.

Hallinan, Conn. "Afghanistan: Is It Really the End Game", *Counterpunch*, May 30, 2013.

Hastings, Michael. *The Operators: The Wild and Terrifying Story of America´s War in Afghanistan*, Penguin Books, London, 2012.

Hopquin, Benoît. "Guantanamo, la colère des détenus français", *Le Monde*, May 12, 2011.

Imbert, Louis. "D´où vient l´argent des talibans ?", *Le Monde diplomatique*, n° 678, September 2010.

Inderfurth, Karl (George Washington University). "Losing the 'other war'", *New York Times*, *International Herald Tribune*, May 30, 2007.

Jacquette, Rogene Fisher. "Karzai doesn´t budge in saying firms will go. By the end of the year, private contractors must be out of Afghanistan" (on American private security companies), *New York Times, International Herald Tribune*, August 23, 2010.
Jones, Ann. *They Were Soldiers: How the Wounded Return From America´s Wars. The Untold Story*, Haymarket Books, Chicago, 2014.
Kinzer, Stephen. "More troops mean more war", *New York Times, International Herald Tribune*, October 18, 2008.
Knowlton, Brian. "NATO faces a perilous weakening, U.S. warns", *New York Times, International Herald Tribune*, February 24, 2010.
Kraeutler, Kirk. "Even for Taliban, too much opium", *New York Times, International Herald Tribune*, November 28, 2008.
Kristof, Nicholas. "The Afghanistan Abyss. More troops, more blood, more chaos", *New York Times*, September 12, 2009.
Lakshmanan, Indira. "Dutch recognize the limits of their Afghan approach", *New York Times, International Herald Tribune*, April 8, 2009.
Lieven, Anatol (King´s College, London). "Shape a peaceful Afghan exit", *New York Times, International Herald Tribune*, March 15, 2012.
Lohdi, Maleeha (former Pakistani Ambassador to Washington and London); **Anatol, Lieven** (New America Foundation). "Heeding the lessons of another war", *New York Times, International Herald Tribune*, October 2, 2008.
Londoño, Ernesto. "Afghan officials accuse U.S. of snatching Pakistani Taliban leader from their custody", *The Washington Post,* October 11, 2013.
Maley, William. *Rescuing Afghanistan*, University of New South Wales Press, 2006.
Martins, Marilia; Scofield, Gilberto. "De Guantanámo para Nova York", *O´Globo*, June 10, 2010.
Mazzetti, Mark; Schmitt, Eric. "New missions, blurred roles: the Pentagon and the C.I.A", *New York Times, International Herald Tribune,* April 29, 2011.
Nordland, Rod. "NATO looks other way on opium in Marja", March 22, 2010 / "U.S. softens plan for Kandahar operation", June 10, 2010 / "NATO confirms casualties in airstrike", August 8, 2010 / "Afghans seek to end night raids", December 6, 2011 / "Mission to save Afghan orphans", January 3, 2012 / "Perils of Afghan war shift to civilian contractors", January 13, 2012 / "Afghan polio surges, provoking alarm", January 19, 2012 / "Double setback on Afghan pullout", March 16, 2012 / "For 3rd year, Afghan opium cultivation rises, April 17, 2013, *New York Times, International Herald Tribune.*
Mercille, Julien. *Cruel Harvest: US Intervention in the Afghan Drug Trade*, Pluto Books, London, 2013.
O´Globo. "Fotos de soldados com afegãos mortos causam mais embaraço à Casa Branca", (on shocking photos), April 19, 2012.
O Estado de São Paulo. "EUA usaram arma proibida pela ONU", (on the use of white phosphorus), November 17, 2005.
Oppel, Richard. "Shootings of Afghans at checkpoints rise sharply", *New York Times, International Herald Tribune*, May 10, 2005.
Polk, William. "Lições do Vietnã", *Le Monde diplomatique*-Brésil, November 2009.
Rahimi, Sangar; Rubin, Alissa; Sahak, Sharifullah. "U.S. offer apology to Afghans after mishandling of Korans", *New York Times, International Herald Tribune*, February 22, 2012.
Rashid, Ahmed. *Descent into Chaos: The United States and the failure of nation building in Pakistan, Aghanistan and Central Asia,* Penguin Group, New York, *2006.*
Risen, James; Mazzetti, Mark. "Blackwater guards teamed with C.I.A. on raids", *New York Times, International Herald Tribune*, December 12, 2012.
Risen, James. "Reports link brother of Karzai to drug trade", October 6, 2008 / "Business empire grows for a Karzai", March 5, 2009, *New York Times, International Herald Tribune.*
Rivera, Ray; Sahak, Sharifullah; Schmitt, Eric. "A new terror in Afghanistan: Death squads", *New York Times, International Herald Tribune*, November 30, 2011.

Rivera, Ray. "Afghan detainee transfers halted amid abuse allegations", *New York Times, International Herald Tribune*, September 8, 2011.
Rosenberg, Matthew. "For Afghans, a sovereignty test", *New York Times*, *International Herald Tribune*, January 9, 2012.
Rosenberg, Matthew; Ahmed, Azam. "Doubts emerge on Afghan handling of U.S. cash", *International New York Times*, January 31, 2014.
Rubin, Alissa. "Scandal-plagued bank, split by Afghan authorities", April 21, 2011 / "Growing drug problem adds to Afghans´misery", August 26, 2011 / "Afghan street is skeptical that more U.S. troops would help", November 7, 2009 / "Bleak view of Afghan economy after 2014", November 24, 2011 / "A grim Record in Afghanistan: Civilians casualties", February 6, 2012, *New York Times, International Herald Tribune* / "Karzai to Forbid Afhan Forces From Requesting Foreign Airstrikes, *The New York Times,* February 16, 2013.
Ruiz, David Santirso. "Desde que llegó la OTAN aumento 40 veces la produción de heroína en Afganistán", *Granma,* May 17, 2013.
Savage, Charlie. "Judge clears way for U.S. to target radical cleric" (on the legalization of targeted assassination), December 8, 2010 / "Court hears case of army 'kill team' in Afghanistan", October 4, 2011, *New York Times, International Herald Tribune.*
Schmitt, Eric; **Mazzetti, Mark**. "Afghan civilian deaths a threat to U.S. mission" (on civilian casualties), *New York Times, International Herald Tribune*, March 11, 2009.
Schmitt, Eric; **Mazzetti, Mark**. "U.S. officials link Taliban surge to Pakistani agents", *New York Times, International Herald Tribune*, March 26, 2009.
Schmitt, Eric; Shanker, Thom. "U.S. inquiry faults Afghan airstrikes. Airmen failed to follow rules in civilian bombing", *New York Times, International Herald Tribune*, June 3, 2009.
Schorzman, Douglas. "Government Panel in Afghanistan Confirms Widespread Torture of Detainees", *The New York Times,* February 11, 2013.
Shah, Taimoo; **Rubin, Alissa**. "Rogue U.S. soldiers on the hunt" (abuses committed by U.S. soldiers), *New York Times, International Herald Tribune*, October 5, 2010.
Shah, Taimoor; **Bowley, Graham**. "For Afghan family, home becomes a killing field", *New York Times, International Herald Tribune*, March 13, 2012.
Shah, Taimoor; **Nordland, Rod**. "U.S. destroying Afghan buildings", *New York Times, International Herald Tribune*, November 17, 2010.
Shane, Scott; **Mazzetti, Mark; Filkins Dexter**. "Afghan corruption undercuts U.S. efforts", *New York Times, International Herald Tribune*, December 3, 2010.
Shanker, Tom. "Afghan forces falling far behind", November 6, 2009 / "Partners on the front line", May 16, 2013, *New York Times, International Herald Tribune,*
Smale, Alison. "Grim view of Afghan risks and missteps", *New York Times, International Herald Tribune*, September 15, 2008.
Sopko, John. Testimony Before the Senate Caucus on International Narcotics Control: Future U.S.Counternarcotics Efforts in Afghanistan. Special Inspector General for Afghanistan Reconstruction (SIGAR), Washington, January 15, 2014.
Steel, Jonathan. "Ghosts of Afghanistan. The Haunted Battleground", *Counterpoint,* 2012.
Stewart, Rory. "How to save Afghanistan", *Time,* July 28, 2008.
Stewart, Rory. "The 'Good War' isn´t worth fighting", *New York Times, International Herald Tribune*, November 25, 2008.
Tirman, John. *The Deaths of Others: The Fate of Civilians in America´s wars,* Oxford University Press, 2011.
Topping, Seymour. "No Afghan ally left behind", *New York Times, International Herald Tribune*, August 5, 2010.
Turse, Nick. "America´s lethal profiling of Afghan men", *The Nation*, September 18, 2013.
UNAMA (United Nations Assistance Mission in Afghanistan). "Treatment of conflict-related detainees in Afghan custody", *Report,* January 20, 2013.
(www.unama.unmissions.org).
Valle, Sabrina. "Afeganistão e Iraque entre os países mais corruptos do mundo, diz estudo" (on corruption), *O´Globo*, November 18, 2009.

Yardley, William. "Afghan veteran says he is no monster" (on the massacre of civilians), *New York Times*, *International Herald Tribune*, October 5, 2010. See also, "US soldier accused of Afghanistan massacre", *Mail on Line*. (www.dailymail.co.uk).

Iraq

Amstrong, Stephen. "Exército privado tem 20 mil homens no Iraque. Esse é o total de agentes das 16 empresas estrangeiras de segurança supervisionadas por veterano das Malvinas" (on private security personnel), *The Guardian*, in *O Estado de São Paulo*, May 28, 2010.

Arango, Tim. "Visa delays imperil U.S. helpers in Iraq", July 13, 2011 / "U.S. program to train police in Iraq may be canceled", May 14, 2012, *New York Times*, *International Herald Tribune*.

Barbier, Chrystelle. "L´ONU critique le recrutement des mercenaires dans le Tiers-monde", *Le Monde*, February 4-5, 2007.

Bonn International Center for Conversion in Cooperation. Papers and working groups, "Interventions à l´occasion du séminaire sur les sanctions ciblées", organized by the Federal Republic of Germany in Bonn, November 21-23, 1999. (www.bicc.de).

Bowley, Graham; Rubin, Alissa. "Afghan body-part photographs bring condemnation from U.S.", *New York Times*, *International Herald Tribune*, April 19, 2012.

Braut-Hegghammer, Malfrid (Norwegian Defense University College), "Real lessons of Iraq" *New York Times*, *International Herald Tribune*, November 29, 2001.

Celestino, Helena. "Nas escolas, uma ante-sala da guerra no Iraque", *O´Globo*, December 11, 2005.

Chomsky, Noam. "L´autisme de l´Empire", *Le Monde diplomatique*, May 2004 / "John Negroponte, Da America Central para o Iraque", *A Tarde*, August 15, 2004.

Claude, Patrice. "Fraudes en Irak : 23 milliards de dollars ont disparu", *Le Monde*, June 18, 2008.

Cockburn, Patrick. *The Jihadis Return. ISIS and the New Sunni Uprising*, Simon and Schuster, OR Books, London, 2014.

Corm, Georges. "Révoltes et refus au nom de l´Islam", *Le Monde diplomatique*, March 2006.

Cortright, David. *A hard look at Iraq sanctions* (www.thenation.com), 2001.

Duarte, Fernando. "Amnesty International pede que União Europea investigue prisões da CIA", *O´Globo*, November 19, 2005 / "A guerra deu a Bin Laden a sua jihad iraquiana", *O´Globo*, July 21, 2010.

Eichenberg, Fernando. "Nova missão no Iraque", *O´Globo*, August 20, 2010 / "Europa investiga sequestros feitos pela CIA" (on CIA kidnappings), *O´Globo,* March 14, 2005.

Engelhardt, Tom. "The Colossus of Baghdad", *Tomdispatch.com*, May 29, 2007.

Fares, Seme Taleb. "O Pragmatismo do Petróleo: as relações entre o Brasil e o Iraque" (The Oil Pragmatism: the Brazil-Iraq Relations), *Revista Brasileira de Politica Internacional*, Vol. 50, Brasilia, July-December 2007.

Figuereido Padovan, Gisela Maria. *Diplomacia e o uso da Força: os panéis do Iraque*, Brasilia, FUNAG, 2010, June-July 2011.

Fitzgerald, P. "If Property Rights Were treated like Human rights, They Could Never Get Away With This. Blacklisting and due process in US economic sanctions programs", *Hastings Law Journal*, vol. 51, p. 73-169, 1999.

Friedman, Thomas. "Paying for allies", *New York Times*, *International Herald Tribune*, November 5, 2009.

Garcin, Thierry. "Les contradictions de la politique américaine durant la crise irakienne", *Annuaire français de Relations internationales*, Paris, 2004.

Garfield, Richard. *Morbidity and Mortality among Iraqui children from 1990 through 1998*: *assessing the impact of the Gulf war and economic sanctions.*
(kroc.nd.edu/ocpapers).

Genugten, W.J.M. van; Groot, G. A. de (ed.). *United Sanctions; Effectiveness and Effects, Especially in the Field of Human Rights, A Multi-disciplinary Approach*, Insentia, 1999.

Glanz, James. "'Dirty money' trail yields new Iraq fraud cases", *New York Times*, *International Herald Tribune*, March 15, 2010.

Gordon, Joy. "Mauvaise gestion, fraudes, prévarications. En Irak, la reconstruction aussi est un échec", *Le Monde diplomatique*, April 2007.
Greenberg, Karen; Dratel, Joshua. *The torture papers: the road to Abu Ghraib*, Cambridge University Press, 2005.
Hagopian, Amy; Flaxman, Abraham; Takaro, Tim; Al-Shatari, Sahar; Becker, Stan; Levin-Rector, Gilbert. Mortality in Iraq Associated with the 2003-2011 War and Occupation: Findings from a National Cluster Sample Survey by the University Collaborative Iraq Mortality Study, *PLOS Medicine Review,* October 15, 2013.
Harling, Peter. "Dossier : Bilan d´une intervention occidentale. Dix ans après, que devient l´Irak", *Le Monde diplomatique*, March 2013.
Healy, Jack. "Top Iraqi official accused of running death squad", *New York Times, International Herald Tribune*, December 20, 2011.
Human Rights Watch. Report: *"No One is Safe". The Abuse of Women in Iraq´s Criminal Justice System*, February 6, 2014.
Johnston, David. "Blackwater guards offered immunity" (on private security agents), *New York Times, International Herald Tribune*, October 31, 2007.
Jornal do Brasil, "Tortura. Pentágon isenta generais de culpa" (torture, generals exonerated), March 11, 2005.
International Herald Tribune, "The folly of using mercenaries in Iraq", November 6, 2007 / "Trying to contain the disaster in Iraq", October 25, 2006.
Kauffman, Sylvie. "Le dossier irakien (*Wikileaks*)", *Le Monde*, October 24, 2010.
Kramer, Andrew. "U.S. companies get slice of Iraq´s oil", *New York Times, International Herald Tribune*, June 15, 2011.
Leland, John. "New U.S. embassy in Iraq is dubious showoff", *New York Times, International Herald Tribune*, October 28, 2009.
Magnoli, Demétrio. "Leis da tortura", *O´Globo*, December 28, 2006.
Mazzetti, Mark; Risen, James. "Blackwater said to have planned Iraq bribes" (private agents and corruption), *New York Times, International Herald Tribune*, November 12, 2009.
Milan, Ray. *War Plan. Ten reasons against War in Iraq*, Verso Ed., London, 2002 / "ONU legaliza ocupação do Iraque", *O´Globo*, May 23, 2003.
Myers, Lee Steven. "Missing laptops: A tale of Iraqi graft" (on corruption), September 27, 2010 / "A new exodus of Iraqui Christians", December 13, 2010 / "Looking beyond the bloodshed", May 21, 2011, *New York Times, International Herald Tribune.*
Nader, Ralph. "The Sociocide of Iraq by Bush/Cheney", March 22-24, 2013 / "A Lawless Legacy. Obama is Comfortable with Bush´s Inferno", *Counterpunch*. April 22, 2013.
Napoleoni, Loretta. *The Islamist Phoenix: The Islamic State and the Redrawing of the Middle East,* Seven Stories Press, New York, 2014.
Mottadel, David. "Ancestors of the jihadist state", *International New York Times,* September 25, 2014
O´Globo. "França oferece cooperação nuclear à Libya", July 26, 2007 / "Fotos de soldados com afegãos mortos causam mais embaraço à casa Branca", April 19, 2012.
Ourdan, Rémy. "Enquête et reportages au cœur de la guérilla en Irak", *Le Monde*, October 23, 2004.
Padovan, Gisela. *Diplomacia e uso da força: os paneis do Iraque*, FUNAG, Brasilia, 2010.
Passos, José Meirelles. "Embaixador polemico, Negroponte é indicado para comando da Inteligência Nacional dos EUA", *O´Globo,* February 18, 2005.
Prashad, Vijay. "TenYears of Bombs over Baghdad", March 19, 2013 / "Bradley Manning, Crimes Against Humanity and the Values of International Law", *Counterpunch,* August 22, 2013,.
Rangel, Rodrigo. "Os mercenarios brasileiros. Empresa recruta 500 ex-soldados para vigiar instalações militares em território iraquiano" (on the recruitment of former Brazilian soldiers for Iraq), *O´Globo*, February 6, 2005 / "Recrutamento sob investigação", *O´Globo*, February 10, 2005.
Robertson, Campbell; al-Salhy, Suadad. "Iraq legislators scuffle over U.S. security pact. Dispute in Parliament turns physical", *New York Times, International Herald Tribune*, November 20, 2008.

Rohricht, Alyssa. "Soldier Suicide", *Counterpunch*, March 22-24, 2013.
Rubin, Alissa. "Afghan aid splits Nato", *New York Times, International Herald Tribune*, May 17, 2012.
Samaha, Joseph. "Les nouveaux voleurs de Bagdad. As Safir (Beyrouth)", in *Courrier international*, October 23, 2003.
Schmidt, Michael; Schmitt, Eric. "U.S. to sell arms to Iraq despite fears of misuse", *New York Times, International Herald Tribune*, December 29, 2011.
Schmitt, Michael; Ghazi, Yasir. "Scores killed after wave of attacks sweeps Iraq", *New York Times, International Herald Tribune*, August 16, 2011.
Schmitt, Eric; Rohde, David. "U.S. reports criticize oversight of private security in Iraq" (on private security personnel), *New York Times, International Herald Tribune*, October 24, 2007.
Shadid, Anthony. "Anonymous, but not forgotten in Iraq", *New York Times, International Herald Tribune*, August 31, 2010.
Shorrock, Tim. *Spies for Hire: The Secret World of intelligence Outsourcing*, Simon and Schuster, New York, 2008.
Starita, Massimo (University of Palermo). "L´occupation de l´Iraq, le Conseil de Sécurité, le droit de la guerre et le droit des peuples à disposer d´eux-mêmes", *Revue générale de droit international public*, tome 108, n° 4, 2004.
Stiglitz, Joseph; **Bilmes, Linda**. "Bien trop coûteuse guerre d´Irak", *The Washington Post, in Courrier International*, September 9, 2010.
Tavernise, Sabrina; Lehren, Andrew. "Most civilian casualties are attributed to Iraquis", *New York.Times, International Herald Tribune*, October 23, 2010.
Tavernise, Sabrina; **McNeil, Donald**. "Toll as high as 600,000, disputed Iraq study says", October 12, 2006, *New York Times, International Herald Tribune.*
Van Buren, Peter. "Occupying Iraq, State Department style", *The Nation*, June 7, 2011 / "Why the Invasion of Iraq Was the Single Worst Foreign Policy Decision in American History", *The Nation*, March 7, 2013.
Van Buren, Peter. "We cannot Win in Iraq", *The Nation,* September 23, 2014.
Von Sponeck, Hans (former UN Humanitarian Coordinator for Iraq, November 1998-February 2000). *A Different Kind of War : the UN Sanction Regime in Iraque*, Berghahn, New York, 2006 (first published in Germany, *Ein anderer Krieg. Das Sanktionsregimee der UNO im Irak*, Hamburger Edition, 2005)..
Williams, Timothy. "U.S. companies sizing up Iraq opportunities", January 14, 2010 / "Squalor atop Basra´s oil wealth. Few jobs and little hope in area that generates up to 80 % of output", November 9, 2009 / "Major oil companies gaining a foothold in Iraq", December 2, 2009, *New York Times, International Herald Tribune.*
Wimmer, Maria. "Du phosphore blanc sur Fallouja", *Le Monde diplomatique*, January 2006.
Zangana, Haifa. *Dreaming of Baghdad,* Women Unlimited, London, 2012.
Zoepf, Katherine. "U.S. prosecutor pursues Blackwater case in Iraq", *New York Times, International Herald Tribune*, December 8, 2008.

The Drone Question

Ahmed, Akbar. "Drone war´s lasting damage", *The New York Times, International Herald Tribune*, June 1-2, 2013 / *The Thistle and the Drone: How America´s War* on *Terror Became a Global War on Tribal Islam*, Brookings Institution Press. New York. 2013.
Associated Press. "U.S. drone suspected in Yemen strike on militants", in *International Herald Tribune*, May 6, 2011.
Benjamin, Medea. "*Drone Warfare Killing*", ORBooks, New York, 2012.
Bumiller, Elisabeth; Shanker, Thom. "From bugs to blimps, drones reshape war", *New York Times, International Herald Tribune*, June 22, 2011.
Cavendish, Julius. "Intelligence failures led to deaths of Aghan civilians", *The Independent*, March 12, 2011.
Chamayou, Grégoire. *A Theory of The Drone,* The New Press, New York, 2015.

Chatterjee, Pratap. "American Drone Operators Are Quitting in Record Numbers", *The Nation*, March 5, 2015.
Checola, Laurent; Pflimlin, Édouard. "Drones, la mort qui vient du ciel", *Le Monde diplomatique*, December 2009.
Cohn, Marjorie. *Drones and Targeted Killing: legal, Moral, and Geopolitical Issues,* Olive Branch Press, Northampton, 2015.
Cole, Juan. "The Age of American Shadow Power. Covert operations have now become the cutting edge of US foreign policy", *The Nation*, April 30, 2012.
Dreyfuss, Robert. "Challenging US claims on civilian deaths in drone attacks", *The Nation*, August 15, 2011.
Engelhardt, Tom. "When It Comes to Drone Body Counts, Whose Body Counts?", *The Nation*, May 4, 2015.
Flanders, Laura. "Will Drones make General Atomics the next Blackwater?", *The Nation*, August 26, 2009.
Gallais, Sébastien. *Cadre juridique de l'emploi des drones au combat*, L'Harmattan, 2013.
Gharib, Ali. "Human Rights Groups to Obama: Investigate All Civilian Victims of Drone Strikes", *The Nation,* May 13, 2015.
Gordon, Neve. "Drones and the New Ethics of War", *Counterpunch*, January 23-24, 2015.
Hastings, Michael. "The Rise of the Killer Drones: How America Goes to War in Secret", *The Rolling Stone*, April 16, 2012.
Human Rights Watch, "Between a Drone and Al-Quaeda: The Civilian Cost of US Targeted Killings in Yemen ", October 2013. / "A Wedding That Became a Funeral. US Drone Attack on Marriage Procession in Yemen", February 2014.
Jordan, Jenna (Harris School of Public Policy Studies, University of Chicago). *When Heads Roll: Assessing the Effectiveness of Leadership Decapitation*, Securities Studies, December 2009.
Kaplan, Fred. "Attack of the Drones", *Newsweek*, September 28, 2009.
Kasinof, Laura; **Mazzetti, Mark**; **Cowell, Alan**. "U.S. drone strike kills Qaeda leader", *New York Times*, *International Herald Tribune*, October 2, 2011.
Knuckey, Sarah; Mihirig, Balquees; Khawaja, Bassan; Gopalan, Surya. "Ten More Strikes the Obama Administration Should Immediately Acknowledge and Investigate", Justsecurity, April 28, 2015 (www.justsecurity.org).
Masood, Salman. "C.I.A. quits drone base at insistence of Pakistan", *New York Times*, *International Herald Tribune*, November 14, 2011.
Mazzetti, Mark. "Covert airstrikes escalate in Yemen. Amid power vacuum US drone dispatched to hunt Qaeda militants", June 10, 2011 / "Qaeda´s no. 2 leader killed by drone, U.S. official says", August 29, 2011, *New York Times*, *International Herald Tribune* / *The Way of the Knife. The CIA, a secret army, and a war at the ends of the earth*, The Penguin Press, New York, 2013.
Mazzetti, Mark; Schmitt, Eric. First Evidence of a Blunder in Drone Strike: 2 Extra Bodies, *International New York Times,* April 23, 2015.
Medish, Mark; **McCleary, Joel** (former advisors to Presidents Jimmy Carter and Bill Clinton). "Assassination season is open" *New York Times*, *International Herald Tribune*, April 4, 2010.
Migault, Philippe. "Drones et éthique. Un débat d´actualité", *Revue Défense*, IHEDN, n° 162, May-June 2013.
Moraes, Marcio Senne de. "Radicalismo islâmico domina terror global", *O´Globo*, September 26, 2004.
Perlez, Jane. "U.S. general is warned by Pakistan on air attack", *New York Times*, *International Herald Tribune*, November 4, 2008.
Savage, Charlie. "U.S. should limit attacks by drones, U.N. asserts", *New York Times*, *International Herald Tribune*, June 3, 2010.
Scahill, Jeremy. "Inside America´s Dirty Wars", *The Nation,* April 24, 2013.
Schmitt, Eric. "Insurgents regroup amid a U.S. lull in drone strikes", *New York Times*, *International Herald Tribune*, January 9, 2012.
Schmitt, Eric; **Drew, Christopher**. "U.S. to increase drone strikes on rebels", *New York Times*, *International Herald Tribune*, April 8, 2009.

Schmitt, Eric; Perlez, Jane. "Attacks by U.S. drones radicalizing Al Qaeda", *New York Times, International Herald Tribune*, February 25, 2009.

Shahzad, Bashir; Crews, Robert D.; Tarzi, Amin; Dorronsoro, Gilles. *Under the Drones: Modern Lives in the Afghanistan-Pakistan Borderlands*, Kindle Ed., 2012.

Shane, Scott. "Accuracy claims for drones are disputed", August 12, 2008 / "Effective yet controversial, drones are here to stay", December 3, 2009 / "In cleric´s killing, an issue of due process", October 2, 2011 / "Drones Strikes Reveal Uncomfortable Truth: U.S. Is Often Unsure About Who Will Die, April 23, 2015, *New York Times, International Herald Tribune.*

Shane, Scott; Shanker, Thom. "A tilt to drones as cheaper war tool", *New York Times, International Herald Tribune*, October 3, 2011.

Shane, Scott; Mazzetti, Mark; Worth, Robert. "U.S. moves deeper into the shadows on terror war", *New York Times, International Herald Tribune*, August 16, 2010.

Sifton, John. "Drones, a trouble story", *The Nation*, February 27, 2012.

Singer, Peter (Brookings Institution). "Drone strikes on democracy", *New York Times, International Herald Tribune,* January 21-22, 2012.

The Economist. "Drones in Pakistan. A growing controversy over the use of unmanned aerial strikes", July 30, 2011 / "Flight of the drones. Why the future of air power belongs to unmanned systems", October 8, 2011.

Turse, Nick. "America´s Secret Empire of Drone Bases", *The Nation*, October 17, 2011 / "The Life and Death of American Drones", *The Nation*, December 20, 2011 / "The 'Crash and Burn' Future of Drone warfare", *The Nation*, January 17, 2012.

Walsh, Declan. "U.S. drone kills 3 in Pakistan´s tribal belt", April 30, 2012 / "U.S. drone strike said to kill commander of Pakistani Taliban faction", February 10, 2012, *New York Times, International Herald Tribune.*

Wright, Robert (New American Foundation). "The high cost of political killing", *New York Times, International Herald Tribune*, April 15, 2010.

Zubeldia, Océane. "Les drones. La situation de la France et ses perspectives". *Revue Défense*, IHEDN, n° 162, May-June 2013.

The Arab Spring: Bahrain,Tunisia, Yemen, Egypt, Syria

Al-Amin, Essam. "The Arab Awakening Unveiled: Undestanding Transformations and Revolutions in the Middle East" / "Egypt´s Shameful Day. Bloodbath on the Nile", *Counterpunch*, August 16-18, 2013.

Alencastro, Catarina; Damé, Luiza. "Dilma compara Brasil e Egito na redemocratização", *O´Globo*, May 9, 2013.

Ali, Ayaan Hirsi (American Enterprise Institute). "Get ready for the Muslim Brotherhood", February 4, 2011 / "Bahrain: Daughter of jailed activist sent to prison after protests", April 7, 2012, *New York Times, International Herald Tribune.*

Amaral, Rubem Guimarães. "*O Egito no fim da era Mubarak: sociedade, renovação politica e esperanças de democracia. Perspectivas para as relações Brasil-Egito e a politica externa brasileira para o oriente Medio*", Dissertation (N°621), Itamaraty, Rio Branco Institute, 2011.

Attalah, Lina. "A Beast That Took a Break and Came Back. Prison Torture in Egypt", *Middle East Research and Information Project*", Vol. 45, Spring 2015.

Bachega, Hugo. "Fim da Primavera egípcia. Exército sufoca protestos em batalha campal", *O´Globo*, August 15, 2013 / "Golpe militar. Mesquita da morte", *O´Globo*, August 16, 2013 / "Golpe militar. Massacre sem contestação", *O´Globo*, August 18, 2013.

Bailey, Pam; Benjamin, Medea. "Egypt Joins Israel as Gaza´s Jailer", *Counterpunch*, September 19, 2013.

Barnard, Anne. "Battle zone of a different kind mires Syria in debt", *New York Times, International Herald Tribune*, July 15, 2013.

Barnard, Anne; Schmitt, Eric. "Syria risks being extremist haven as fighters flow in", *New York Times, International Herald Tribune,* August 10-11, 2013.

Berlinck, Deborah. "Sob o commando de Alá. As muitas vozes do Islã. Pesquisa em 39 países mostra que maioria quer lei islâmica, mas rejeita autocracias", *O´Globo*, May 4, 2013 / 'Bombas químicas na Síria. Investigação liderada por brasileiro aponta indícios razoáveis do uso de arsenal proibido", *O´Globo*, June 5, 2013.

Bonnefoy, Laurent; Mermier, Franck; Poirier, Marine. *Yémen. Le tournant révolutionnaire*, Karthala, Paris, 2012.

Burdy, Jean Paul; Dal, Emel Parlar. "*Syrie*", Eurorient n° 41, L´Harmattan, Paris, May 2013.

Calvert, John. *Sayyid Qutb and the origins of Radical Islamism*, Hurst and Co., Columbia University Press, New York, 2010.

Cambanis, Thanassis. "Egypt´s Muslim Brotherhood stands alone", *New York Times, International Herald Tribune*, September 7, 2010.

Celestino, Helena. "ONU procura. O ministro Celso Amorim é um dos nomes considerados para assumir o papel de mediador da ONU na interminável guerra da Síria", *O´Globo*, July 6, 2014.

Chambraud, Cécile. "'Daech est un produit de notre modernité'. La tentation du djihad a saisi des milliers de jeunes Européens", *Le Monde*, January 10, 2015.

Chivers, C. "Rebels´ brutality poses dilemma for West", *The New York Times, International Herald Tribune*, September 6, 2013.

Cohn, Marjorie; Mirer, Jeanne. "Agent Orange: the Struggle Continues", *Counterpunch*, August 9-11, 2013.

Cowell, Alan; Myers, Steven Lee. "U.N. panel sees 'gross' rights crimes by Syria", *New York Times, International Herald Tribune*, February 24, 2012.

Cumming-Bruce, Nick. "U.N. raises Estimate of Dead in Syrian Conflict to 191,000", *International New York Times*, August 22, 2014.

Day, Stephen. *Regionalism and Rebellion in Yemen: A Troubled National Union*, (Cambridge Middle East Studies), Cambridge University Press, New York, 2012.

Delgado, Dalia González. "Hacia dónde va Egipto", *Granma* (Havana), August 16, 2013.

Dempsey, Judy. "The hazards in Turkey´s new strategy", *New York Times, International Herald Tribune*, October 25, 2011.

Dot-Puoillard, Nicolas. *Tunisie : la Révolution et ses passés*, L´Harmattan, Paris, 2013.

El Sheikh, Mavy. "Egypt´s hunger strikers", *International New York Times*, September 25, 2014.

El Sheikh, Mavy; Kilpatrick, David. "Egypt court controls voice of Morsi with a glass Cage", *International New York Times*, January 29, 2014.

Fagundes, Alvaro; Rossi, Clovis. "Onda de revoltas. Resolução da ONU poupa mercenários", *Folha de São Paulo*, February 28, 2011.

Fahim, Kareem; Kirkpatrick, David. "Saudis push for a Gulf Federation", *New York Times, International Herald Tribune*, May 16, 2012.

Friedman, Thomas. "Egypt´s step backward", *New York Times, International Herald Tribune*, February 23, 2012.

Gettleman, Jeffrey. "Somali president assails U.N. report", March 18, 2010 / "In Somalia, bright kids compete for firepower", September 24, 2011 / "In Somalia, true crisis is hunger, not pirates", October 11, 2008, *New York Times, International Herald Tribune.*

González Rodríguez, José Luis. "Egipto. La demência de un Ejército", *Juventud Rebelde* (Havana), August 16, 2013.

Gresh, Alan. "Don´t Exclude the Muslim Brotherhood. Shadow of the Army Over Egypt´s Revolution", *Counterpunch*, August 1, 2013 / "Confusão diplomatica no Egito", *Le Monde Diplomatique* (Brazil), September 2013.

Halimi, Serge. "Polarisation politique en Tunisie. Islamistes au pied du mur", *Le Monde diplomatique*, April 2013.

Hashemi, Nader; Postel, Danny (ed.). "*The Syria Dilemma*", The MIT Press, London, 2013.

Howlett-Martin, Patrick. "Viet-Nam. Un printemps sans oiseaux. Neuf ans de guerre chimique", *Le Nouvel Observateur*, n° 321, January 4, 1971.

Hubbard, Ben. "In taking control, military looks out for itself. Unshackled by ideology, generals aim to maintain their realm of privilege", *The New York Times, International Herald Tribune*, July 5, 2013.

Human Rights Watch. "All According to Plan. The Rab´a Massacre and Mass Killings of Protesters in Egypt", August 12, 2014.

International New York Times. "Political Executions in Egypt", editorial, April 28, 2014.

Karabell, Zachary. "Economic insularity imperils change in Arab world", *New York Times, International Herald Tribune*, May 26, 2011.

Kasinof, Laura. "Yemen cleric joins revolt with call for Islamic state", *New York Times, International Herald Tribune*, March 2, 2011 / *Don´t be Afraid of the Bullets. An Accidental War Correspondent in Yemen,* Arcade Publishing, New York , 2014.

Khouri, Rami. "The Arab Awakening", *The Nation*, September 12, 2011.

Kirkpatrick, David. "Egypt´s unfinished revolution", *New York Times, International Herald Tribune*, January 11, 2012 / "Egypt Accuses Human Rights Watch of Breaking the Law", *International New York Times*, August 12, 2014.

Kirkpatrick, David; Fahim, Kareem. "Dozens killed as troops fire on Morsi vigil", *The New York Times, International Herald Tribune*, July 9, 2013.

Kirkpatrick, David; Myers, Steven Lee. "U.S. reversal on Egyptian Islamists is historic shift", *New York times, International Herald Tribune*, January 5, 2012.

Klare, Mikael. "Why the Push for Syrian Intervention is about More Than Just Assad", *The Nation*, September 10, 2013.

Kouddous, Sharif Abdel. "Chaos and Bloodshed in the Streets of Cairo", *The Nation*, August 14, 2013.

Kristoff, Nicholas. "In Egypt, an Islamist at odds with his party", June 21, 2011 / "Somalia, unspeakable violence", September 26, 2011, *New York Times, International Herald Tribune.*

Lackner, Helen. *Why Yemen matters: A Society in Transition,* Saqi Books, London, 2014.

Lampreia, Luiz Felipe (former Brazilian Minister of Foreign Affairs, 1995-2001). "Egito: Sem luz no caminho", *O´Globo*, July 17, 2013.

Landler, Mark; Sanger, David. "U.S. tries to parse Mideast tumult", *New York Times, International Herald Tribune*, February 7, 2011.

Leparmentier, Arnaud. "Questions sur la laïcité. Le modèle français de laïcité s´est déréglé avec l´irruption de l´Islam", *Le Monde*, January 15, 2015.

Leupp, Gary. "What motivated the Boston Bombers", *Counterpunch*, April 25, 2013.

Levine, Andrew. "Balancing Freedom and Security. Insults to Our Intelligence", *Counterpunch*, August 9-11, 2013.

Lindorff, David. "We don´t Gas Children, We Shred Them. Obama´s Grotesque Hypocrisy Over Cluster Munitions", *Counterpunch*, September 20-22, 2013.

Malkes, Renata. "Egito. Golpe military. Um país brutalizado", *O´Globo,* August 17, 2013.

Malik, Mohamed; **Omar, Mohamad**. "Egypt During the Reign of the Lunatics", *Counterpunch*, August 19, 2013.

Malsin, Jared; Yeginsu, Ceylan. "Egyptian Court Sentences Ousted President Morsi to Death", *International New York Times*, May 16, 2005

Mercier, Gilbert. "The Rise of ISIS", *Counterpunch,* June 24, 2014.

Miranda, André. Interview with **Kofi Annan**, "Eu queria mais a paz do que os protagonistas do conflito", *O´Globo*, May 16, 2013.

Mountain, Thomas. "The UN and 250,000 Dead Somalis", *Counterpunch*, May 7, 2013.

Nossiter, Adam. "Corpses stack high in Nigeria conflict", May 8, 2013 / "As Nigeria pursues Islamists, civilians are wary", May 17, 2013, *The New York Times, International Herald Tribune.*

O´Globo. "Atiradores matam 46 no Iemen. Oposição fala de massacre e presidente nega envolvimento" (repression and massacre in Yemen), March 19, 2011./"Forças ponderosas apoiam ditadura no Egito", editorial, August 21, 2013./"Escalada na guerra civil. Horror químico", dossier, August 22, 2013.

Patriota, Antonio de Aguiar (Brazilian Minister of Foreign Affairs, 2011-2013). "Tempos de mudança no Mundo Arabe", *Politica Externa*, vol. 20, n° 1, June-August 2011.

Pollack, Norman. "Egypt is Bleeding, Thanks to US Dollars for Military Thugs", *Counterpunch,* August 16-18, 2013.
Porter, Gareth. "Houthi Arms bonanza Came from Saleh, not Iran", *The Nation,* April 23, 2015.
Ramadan, Tariq. "Wither the Muslim Brotherhood?", *New York Times, International Herald Tribune*, February 9, 2011.
Roston, Aram; Rohde, David. "Egypt´s for-profit military appears to divert U.S. aid", *New York Times, International Herald Tribune*, March 7, 2011.
Sardenberg, Ronaldo; Duarte, Sergio (Brazilian diplomats, members of the Latin American and Caribbean Leadership Network for Nuclear Disarmament and Non-Proliferation). "O uso de armas químicas e a consciência", *O´Globo,* September 7, 2013.
Scahill, Jeremy. "The CIA´s Secret Sites in Somalia", *The Nation,* August 1-8, 2011.
Schmitt, Eric. "Syrian war lures more Western Muslims", *New York Times, International Herald Tribune*, July 29, 2013.
Schmitt, Eric; Schmidt, Michael; Alderman, Liz. "Western nations struggle to halt flow of citizens who want to fight abroad", *International New York Times,* January 13, 2015.
Schmitt, Eric; **Shane, Scott**. "Idea of escalating military aid to Yemen divides U.S. officials", *New York Times, International Herald Tribune*, September 16, 2010.
Shadid, Anthony. "Surging Turkey seeks alliance with Egypt", *New York Times, International Herald Tribune*, September 20, 2011.
Shane, Scott. "Al Qaeda left out in Arab sea changes", *New York Times, International Herald Tribune*, March 1, 2011.
Siddiqa, Ayesha. "Where armies rule. Pakistan and Egypt show that once the military is entrenched in power, it keeps democracy at bay", *New York Times, International Herald Tribune,* July 17, 2013.
Slackman, Michael. "Egypt cracks down early on Islamic movement", *New York Times, International Herald Tribune*, March 12, 2010.
Solvang Ole, "The Tragic Civilian Toll of Airstrikes in Yemen", *Newsweek*, October 12, 2015.
Sprejer, Pedro. "O vigor da poesia, da praça Tahrir aos destroços da Guerra na Síria. Ecos da primavera" (interview with Tamin al-Barghouti), *O´Globo*, April 27, 2013.
Thompson, Andrew; Suri, Jeremi. "How America helped ISIS", *International New York Times,* October 2, 2014.
Tlass, Manaf (former general in the Syrian Republican Guard). Interview with **Isabelle Lasserre**, "Le régime syrien vu de l´intérieur", *Politique Internationale*, n° 139, Spring 2013.
United Nations Human Rights Council. "Report of the Independent International Commission of Inquiry on the Syrian Arab Republic", (Resolution S-17, 19th session), February 22, 2012.
Vinocur, John. "Syria tests U.S. resolve to do right", *New York Times, International Herald Tribune,* July 19, 2011.
Wezeman, Pieter. *Arms transfers to Syria*, Oxford University Press, SIPRI Yearbook, Stockhom, 2013.
Worth, Robert. "West faces a morass of obstacles in Yemen", *New York Times, International Herald Tribune,* January 27, 2009.

Libya

Agence France Presse (AFP). "Kadhafi : les contrats qu´il a signés", December 11, 2007.
Burns, John. "Cameron tells military to stay out of politics", *New York Times, International Herald Tribune,* June 22, 2011.
Campbell, Horace. *Global NATO and the Catastrophic failure in Libya: Lessons for Africa in the Forging of African Unity*, Monthly Review Press, 2013.
Forte, Maximilian. *Slouching Towards Sirte: NATO´s War on Libya and Africa*, Baraka Books, Montreal, 2012.
Francis, David. "Libya may be Nato´s last mission", *The Fiscal Times,* June 22, 2011.

Haimzadeh, Patrick. "En Libye, ce n´est pas le chaos, c´est la guerre", *Le Monde Diplomatique*, April 2015.
Kirkpatrick, David. "Libya: Tribal war or a democratic conflict?", *New York Times*, *International Herald Tribune*, March 23, 2011.
Kouddous, Sharif Abdel. "Report From the Front: Libya's Descent Into Chaos", *The Nation*, February 25, 2015.
Lichtblau, Eric; **Rohde, David**; **Risen, James**; **Walsh, Barclay.** "The price of business in Libya", *New York Times*, *International Herald Tribune*, March 24, 2011.
Maltchik, Roberto; **Oliveira, Eliane**. "Ataques a civis são motivo de preocupação para o Brasil", *O´Globo*, March 21, 2011.
Mekhennet, Souad. "Out of Libya, and telling of its horrors. The Female factor", *New York Times*, *International Herald Tribune*, April 6, 2011.
Mekhennet, Souad; **Schmitt, Eric**. "Libyan rebels seek to shed Qaeda past", *New York Times*, *International Herald Tribune*, July 19, 2011.
Nordland, Rod. "Files note close C.I.A. ties with Gaddafi spy unit", *New York Times*, *International Herald Tribune*, September 5, 2011.
Nordland, Rod; **Kirkpatrick, David**. "Islamists´ role fuels a debate among Libyans", *New York Times*, *International Herald Tribune*, September 15, 2011.
Prashad, Vijay. *Arab Spring Libyan Winter*, AK Press, Oakland, 2012.
Rémy, Jean-Philippe. "Le fantôme de l'Etat islamique plane sur Tripoli", *Le Monde*, January 29, 2015 / "Tripoli capitale d'un pays déchiré", *Le Monde*, February 5, 2015.
Schmitt, Eric. "NATO report details crucial shortcomings of air campaign over Libya", *New York Times*, *International Herald Tribune*, April 16, 2012.
Yardley, Jim. "Survivors of a ruthless trade", *International New York Times*, October 21, 2014.
Zuckoff, Mitchell. *13 Hours. The Inside Account of What really happened in Benghazi*, Hachette Book group, 2014.

Israel and Palestine

Abuelaish, Izzeldin. *I shall not hate: a Gaza doctor´s journey on the road to Peace and human dignity*, Bloomsbury, New York, 2010.
Ashton, Catherine (High Representative of the EU for Foreign Affairs and Security Policy). "Lessons from a Gaza trip", *New York Times*, *International Herald Tribune*, March 22, 2010.
Avnery, Uri. "Obama´s Empathy Deficit in Palestine", *Counterpunch*, April 5-7, 2013.
Baeza, Cecilia. "Palestinians and Latin America´s Indigenous Peoples. Coexistence, Convergence, Solidarity", *Middle East Research and Information Project*, Vol. 45, Spring 2005.
Bannelier, Karine (ed.). *L´intervention en Irak et le droit international*, Pedone, Paris, 2004.
Beinart, Peter. *The Crisis of Zionism*, Times Books, Henry Holt and Company, New York, 2012.
Beit-Hallahmi, Benjamin. *The Israeli Connection: Who Israel Arms and Why*, Pantheon Books, New York, 1987.
Ben-Ami, Shlomo (Israeli diplomat). *Scars of War, Wounds of Peace: the Israeli-Arab Tragedy*, Oxford University Press, 2006.
Black, George. "Israeli Connection: Not Just Guns for Guatemala", *NACLA report on the Americas*, May-June 1993.
Blumenfeld, Laura. "A Divisive Struggle Over Targeted Killing", *The Washington Post*, August 27, 2006.
Bôle-Richard, Michel. "Hypocrisie internationale autour de Gaza", *Le Monde*, June 16, 2007 / "Des militants anti-apartheid juifs sud-africains 'choqués' par leur visite en Cisjordanie occupée", *Le Monde*, July 20-21, 2008.
Booth, William. "In blow to Gaza´s economy, Israeli strikes have left industries hard-hit", *The Washington Post*, August 21, 2014.
Brahimi, Lakhdar (former Special Advisor and Undersecretary General of the United Nations, United Nations and Arab League Special Envoy for Syria). interview with **Deborah Berlinck**, "*Le mouvement islamique va se renforcer*", *O´Globo*, January 13, 2009.

Breaking the Silence (Israeli NGO). *Our Harsh Logic: Israeli Soldiers´ Testimonies From The Occupied Territories*, Metropolitan Books, New York, 2012 / *"This is How We Fought in Gaza: Soldiers´s Testimonies and photographs from Operation 'Protective Edge'"*, 2014 (www.breakingthesilence.org.il).
Brenner Lenni, *"Zionism in the Age of the Dictators"*, ooabooks, 2014.
Bronner, Ethan; **Taghreed, El-khodary**. "Hamas leader reaches the West", *New York Times, International Herald Tribune*, May 6, 2009.
Bronner, Ethan. "Olmert urges Israel to leave West Bank", September 30, 2008 / "Family´s horror laid to phosphorus", January 22, 2009 / "In Gaza, nothing to do but get angrier", May 29, 2009 / "Bending to reality at Mideast talks", December 9, 2010 / "Jobless rate in Gaza hits a record high", June 15, 2011, *New York Times, International Herald Tribune.*
Burston, Bradley. "Gaza sera notre Vietnam", *Haaretz*, in *Courrier de l'Unesco* 1022, June 3-9, 2010.
Caraciki Leonel, "A aposta antisionista e a equação do sionismo como racismo na resolução 3379 da Assembleia Geral das Nações Unidas (1975)", thesis, Federal University of Rio de Janeiro, 2013.
Carey, Roane (ed.); **Shainin, Jonathan** (ed.). *The Other Israel. Voices of Refusal and Dissent,* The New Press, New York, 2002.
Carter, Jimmy (former president of the United States, director of the Carter Foundation). *Palestine: Peace not Apartheid,* Simon & Schuster, New York, 2006 / "Don´t give up on Mideast peace", *New York Times, International Herald Tribune*, April 13, 2012.
Casarões Guilherme, Vigevani Tullo, "O lugar de Israel e da Palestina na politica externa brasileira: antisemitismo, voto majoritário ou promotor de paz?", *Historia*, Vol.33, N°2, July-December 2014
Cher-Leparrain, Marc. "Ces Français volontaires dans l´armée israélienne", *Orient* XXI, March 18, 2014.
Chomsky, Noam; Pappé, Ilan. *Gaza in Crisis: Reflections on Israel's War Against The Palestinians*, Haymarket Books, Chicago, 2010 / *On Palestine*, Haymarket Books, Chicago, 2015.
Cockburn Alexander, St. Clair Jeffrey, *"The Politics of Anti-semitism"*, Counterpunch, 2003.
Cohen, Roger. "Middle East reality check", March 9, 2009 / *"The fierce urgency of peace"*, March 26, 2009 / "The Israel-Turkey imbroglio", July 9, 2010 / "The 'real Jew' debate", December 10, 2010 / "Fayyad steps down, not out", May 4-5, 2013 / "The two-state imperative", July 23, 2013, *New York Times, International Herald Tribune.*
Combanis, Thanassis. *A privilege to die. Inside Hezbollah´s Legions and their endless War against Israel*, Simon and Schuster, New York, 2010.
Cook, Jonathan. *Israel and the Clash of Civilisations: Irak, Iran and the Plan to Remake the Middle East*, Pluto Press, London, 2008 / *"Disappearing Palestine: Israel´s Experiments in Human Despair"*, Zed Books, London, 2008.
Cronin, David. *Europe´s Alliance With Israel: Aiding the Occupation,* Pluto Press, London, 2010.
Davila Jerry, Lesser Jeffrey, "Brasil, Israel y el voto sionismo= racismo en los Naciones Unidas", in **Rein Ranan, Cano Pérez María José, Molina Rueda Beatriz** (ed.), *"Más allá del Medio Oriente. Las diásporas júdias y árabe en America Latina"*, Eirena, Granada, 2012.
Delmotte, Paul (Institut des Hautes Études de Communication Sociale - Brussels). "Le Hamas et la reconnaissance d´Israël", *Le Monde diplomatique*, January 2007.
Dempsey, Judy. "Embracing Israel costs Merkel clout", *New York Times, International Herald Tribune*, January 21, 2010.
Dobry Hernán, *"Operación Israel. El rearme argentino durante la dictadura (1976-1983)"*, Lumiere, Buenos Aires, 2011.
Dreyfuss, Bob. "Israel Making itself irrelevant to the Iran debate?", *The Nation*, October 2. 2013.
Eddé, Dominique. "Logique de purification ethnique à Gaza", *Le Monde*, January 6, 2009.
Feiner, Schmuel. *"The Jewish Enlightenment"*, Jewish Culture and Contexts, University of Pennsylvania Press, 2011.
Friedman, Thomas. "Reality check. The failed attempt by the U.S. to bribe Israel", *New York Times, International Herald Tribune*, December 13, 2010.

Galeano, Eduardo. "Quem deu a Israel o direito de negar todos os direitos?", *Pragmatismo Politico*, November 22, 2012.
Gheur, Charles (University of Liège). *L'Union européenne face au conflit israélo-palestinien*, Études, 3993, September 2003.
Goldberg, Jeffrey (The Atlantic); **Ibish, Hussein** (American Task force on Palestine). "Good news from the Middle East (really)", *New York Times*, *International Herald Tribune*, January 28, 2001.
Goldsmith, Jack (former U.S. Assistant Attorney General in the George W. Bush administration). "Don't try terrorists, lock them up", *New York Times*, *International Herald Tribune*, October 11, 2010.
Gresh, Alain. "Demain l'État palestinien, toujours demain", *Le Monde diplomatique*, October 2011 / *"De quoi la Palestine est-elle le nom?"*, Actes Sud, Paris, 2012.
Gunning, Jeroen. *Hamas in Politics*, Columbia University Press, New York, 2009.
Haaretz. "Changing World" (on Gaza), editorial reprinted in the *International Herald Tribune* on June 10, 2010.
Hamid, Sônia Cristina. "(Des) Integrado Refugiados. Os Processos de Reassentamento de Palestinos no Brasil". Doctoral dissertation in Social Anthropology, University of Brasilia, 2012.
Human Rights Watch. *Israel, The Occupied West Bank and Gaza and The Palestinian Authorithy*, Vol. 14, N° 2, New York, 2002.
Hunter, Jane. *Israeli Foreign Policy: South Africa and Central America,* South End Press, Boston, 1987.
Jackson, Willy. "Israël est-il menacé par une campagne de désinvestissement?", *Le Monde Diplomatique*, September 2009.
Jakobskind, Mário Augusto. "Extrema direita israelense usa como chantagem emocional o Holocausto da II Guerra Mundial para desrespeitar os direitos humanos com as constantes incursões contra palestinos", *Pragmatismo Politico*, November 21, 2012.
Jornal do Commercio. "Pobreza aumenta entre palestinos", November 24, 2004.
Kapelik, Amon. "Israël: o peso dos generais", *Le Monde diplomatique* (Brazil), November 2007.
Keenan, Thomas (Human Rights Project); **Weizman, Eyal** (Goldsmith Institute). "À la recherche d'un nouvel ennemi. Israël et la troisième menace", *Le Monde diplomatique*, July 2010.
Kershner, Isabel. "Israelis fire on protesters near Golan Heights", June 6, 2011 / "U.N. condemns Israel for firing on unarmed protesters", July 8, 2011, *New York Times*, *International Herald Tribune*./ "Stabbings, and Deadly Responses, Add to Israel's Decurity Challenge, *International New York Times*, October 12, 2015.
Khalidi, Rachid. *L'identité palestinienne. La construction d'une conscience nationale moderne*, La Fabrique, Paris, 2005.
Kodmani, Bassma (Arab Reform Initiative). "Une génération arabe traumatisée par la défaite", *Le Monde diplomatique*, June 2007.
Kreach, Daniela. "Palestina vira realidade na America do Sul", *O'Globo*, January 17, 2011 / "Brasil doa quase US $ 1 milhão para a ONU em Gaza", *O'Globo*, December 16, 2011.
Kresch, Daniela. "Israel escapa de pressão para ratificar Convenção de Armas Quimicas", *O'Globo*, September 17, 2013.
Kristof, Nicholas. "The Gaza boomerang", January 9, 2009 / "Saving Israel from itself", June 4, 2010, *New York Times*, *International Herald Tribune* / "Winds of war in Gaza", *International New York Times*, March 9, 2015.
Kushner, Tony (ed.); **Solomon, Alisa** (ed.). *Wrestling with Zion: Progressive jewish-American Responses to the Israeli-palestinian Conflict,* Grove Press, New York, 2003.
Lasurdo Domenico, "O Sionismo e a tragedia do povo palestino", *Crítica Marxista* (www.ifch.unicamp)
Lemieux, Jacques. "Le rôle d'Israël: Encerclement du régime sandiniste", *Le Monde Diplomatique,* October 1984.
Lemoine, Maurice. "L'Amérique latine s'invite en Palestine", *Le Monde diplomatique*, February 2001.
Le Monde. "Proche-Orient. Hamas. L'Union européenne prête à couper l'aide à l'Autorité palestinienne", April 10, 2006.

Lessa Antonio Carlos, "Israel e o mundo árabe no cruzamento das escolhas internacionais do Brasil", in Santos Norma Breda dos (org.), *"Brasil e Israel: diplomacia e sociedades"*, Brasilia, UNB, 2000.
Lesser, Jeffrey. *Welcoming the Undesirables. Brazil and the Jewish Question*, University of California Press, 1995 (Brazilian edition titled *O Brasil e a questão judaica: imigração, diplomacia e preconceito,* Imago, Rio de Janeiro, 1995).
Lewin Helena (Coord.), *"Identidade e cidadania, como se expressa o judaismo brasileiro"*, Centro Edelstein de Pesquisas Sociais, Scielo Books, Rio de Janeiro, 2009.
Lichfield, Gideon (correspondent for *The Economist* in Jerusalem from 2005 to 2008), "Gaza War. Fighting to preserve a myth", *New York Times, International Herald Tribune*, January 9, 2009.
Losardo Domenico, "O sionismo e a tragedia do povo palestino", Crítica Marxista (www.ifch.unicamp), translated from Italian by Modesto Florenzano, L'Ernesto N°4, 2001, July 1rst, 2001.
Lotersztain Gabriela, *"Los Judios bajo el terror. Argentina 1976-1983"*, Ejercitar la mémoria editores, Buenos Aires, 2008.
Makdisi, Saree. "Israel and the Palestinians. Occupation by bureaucracy", *New York Times, International Herald Tribune*, June 25, 2008.
Masalha, Nur. *A Land without a People: Israel, Transfer and the Palestinians 1949-1996*, Faber & Faber, London, 1996.
Marten, Kimberly. "The bane of Palestinian infighting", *The New York Times, International Herald Tribune*, June 27, 2013.
Mattar, Marisa. "Guerra ou massacre, o que está acontecendo na Faixa de Gaza?", *Pragmatismo Politico*, November 20, 2012.
Mearsheimer, John; Walt, Stephen. *The Israel Lobby and US Foreign Policy*, Penguin Books, London, 2007.
Menuhim, Moshe. *The Decadence of Judaism in Our Time,* Exposition Press, 1965.
Milton, Jamail; Margo, Gutierez. "Israel in Central America", *Middle East Research and Information Project*, May-June 1986.
Molkes, Renata. "A batalha silenciosa dos árabes-Israëlenses", *O'Globo*, January 18, 2009.
Neiman, Oper; Shapira, Yonatan. "A vergonha de Caetano e Gil em Israel", (free opinions of two Israelis in favor of the boycott, published in a newspaper that is generally supportive of the Jewish state), *O'Globo,* July 29, 2015.
Neve, Gordon. *Israel's Occupation,* University of California Press, Berkeley, 2008.
Nirenberg David, *"Anti-Judaism. The Western Tradition*", W.W.Norton & Company, New York, 2014.
Ousset-Krief, Annie. *Les juifs américains et Israël. De l'AIPAC à Jstreet*, Coll. L'Aire anglophone, L'Harmattan, Paris, 2012.
Pappe, Ilan. *The Ethnic Cleansing of Palestine,* Oneworld Publications, Oxford, 2006.
Parag, Khana (New America Foundation). "Listen to the Arabs", *New York Times, International Herald Tribune*, March 26, 2010.
Passos, José Meirelles. "Pobreza absoluta espreita palestinos" (on the misery in Palestine), *O'Globo*, November 23, 2004.
Pellet, Alain. "The declaration of Palestine and the jurisdiction of the International Criminal Court", *Journal of International Criminal Justice*, N°4, 2010.
Petras, James; Henry, Veltmeyer. *The Power of Israel in the United States,* Clarity Press, Atlanta, 2006.
Prates, Daniele Regina Abilas. "O Fio do Ariadne: deslocamento, heterotopia e memória entre refugiados palestinos em Mogi das Cruzes, Brasil e Burj al-Barajneh, Libano. Master's thesis in Anthropology, Federal University of Fluminense, Niteroi, 2012.
Raja, Shehadeh. *Palestinian walks. Forays into a vanishing landscape*, Scribner, Simon and Schuster, New York, 2008.
Rapoport, Menon (journalist for *Haaretz*). "Comment l'occupation a transformé Israël", *Le Monde diplomatique*, June 2007.

Raz-Krakotzkin, Amnon. *Exil et souveraineté : judaïsme, sionisme et pensée binationale,* La Fabrique Éd., Paris, 2007.
Reed, John. "Israeli 'refuseniks' denounced as criminals", *Financial Times,* September 16, 2014.
Rose, Jacqueline. *The Question of Zion,* Princeton University Press, 2005.
Ross, Dennis; Makovsky, David. *Myths, illusions and Peace: Finding a New Direction for America* in *the Middle East,* Viking, Penguin Group, New York, 2009.
Rothman-Zecher. Moriel. "Why I won´t serve Israel", *International New York Times,* January 13, 2015.
Rubenberg, Cheryl, *"Israel and Guatemala. Arms, Advice and Counterinsurgency"*, Middle East Research and Information Project, May-June 1986.
Rudoren, Jody. "In trying to revive Mideast peace talks, Kerry finds a conflicted Israel", June 19, 2013 / "Israel criticizes E.U. on bilateral guidelines", July 17, 2013, *New York Times, International Herald Tribune* / "Battered, but Gazans still embrace Hamas", *International New York Times,* September 5, 2014.
Ruebner, Josh. *Shattered Hopes: Obama´s Failure to Broker Israeli-Palestinian Peace*, VersoBooks, London, 2013.
Scheer, Robert. "Israel´s Dependency on the Drug of Militarism", *The Nation,* August 2, 2006, (www.thenation.com).
Segal, Jerome (Peace Consultancy Project). "Declare a Palestinian State", *New York Times, International Herald Tribune,* January 24, 2010.
Shtrasler, Nehemia. "Israël. La Shoah ne protègera pas éternellement l´État hébreu", *Haaretz,* in *Courrier international,* n° 1018, May 6, 2010.
Shulamit, Aloni. "Sadly, Israel is no longer democratic", *Haaretz,* May 1, 2009.
Siegman, Henry (director of the US Middle East Project). "Israelis and Obama", *New York Times, International Herald Tribune,* November 2, 2009.
Simon, Roberto. "Brasil reconstroi pontes destruidas por Israël" (Brazilian aid to Palestine), *O Estado de São Paulo,* November 6, 2011.
Sochaczewski Monique, "O fim das equidistância: o veto brasileiro ao sionismo en politica exterior do governo Geisel para o Oriente Médio (1974-1979), Thesis, State University of Rio de Janeiro, 2004.
Sponeck, Hans von. "*A Different Kind of War. The UN Sanctions in Iraq"*, Berghahn Books, New York, 2006. First published in Germany in 2005 (*"Ein andere krieg. Das Sanktions regime der UNO im Irak"*. Hamburger Edition)
St Clair, Jeffrey. "Israeli Gears", *Counterpunch,* May 22-24, 2015.
Tarazi, Monica. "Planning Apartheid in the Naquab", in "Apartheid and Beyond", *Middle East Research and Information Project,* Vol. 39, Winter 2009.
Tavernise, Sabrina. "Rebuilding where even cement is political", *New York Times, International Herald Tribune,* January 27, 2009.
Tibi, Ahmad (Knesset member), "A Palestinian and an Israeli", *New York Times, International Herald Tribune,* April 7, 2009.
Tolan, Sandy. "As the UN debates Its Bid for Statehood, Palestine Disappears", *The Nation,* September 22, 2011.
Vidal, Dominique. "Boycott: la contre-offensive d´Israël et de ses amis", *Le Monde Diplomatique,* February 2010.
Yossi, Alpher (co-editor of bitterlemons.org). "Who rules Israel?", *New York Times, International Herald Tribune,* December 23, 2010.
Zahar, Mahmoud (member of the Hamas Policy Office in Gaza). Interview with **Aude Marcovitch**, "Le Hamas dans la bataille", *Politique Internationale,* n° 139, Spring 2013.
Zertal, Idith; Eldar, Akiva, *Lords of the Land: The War for Israel´s Settlements in the Occupied Territories 1967-2007*, Nation Books, Philadelphie, 2007, translated from the Hebrew, Dvir Publishing House, Tel Aviv, 2005.

Mediation in the Iranian nuclear question

Afrasiabi, Kaveh. *Iran´s Nuclear program. Debating facts versus fiction*, BookSurge, New York, 2006.

Amorim, Celso. "Bobagem pensar que país ficou amiguinho do Iran", interview with the newspaper *O´Globo*, August 10, 2011.

Ansari, Ali. *Confronting Iran,* Basic Books, New York, 2006.

Baima, Cesar. "Independencia nuclear. Reator para uso médico e pesquisas sai do papel e tornara país autosuficiente na área", *O´Globo*, February 7, 2012.

Barrionuevo, Alexei. "Obama Writes to Brazil´s leader About Irak", *New York Times,* November 24, 2009.

Bergman, Ronen. *The Secret War with Iran. Clandestine Struggle Against the World´s Most Dangerous Terrorist Power*, Free Press, Simon and Schuster, New York, 2008. (Original edition, *Nekudat Halal Chazor*, Kinneret, Zmora-Bitan, Dvir-Publishing House Ltd. Tel-Aviv, 2007) / "For Israel, decision time looms on striking Iran", *New York Times*, *International Herald Tribune*, January 28-29, 2012.

Berlinck, Deborah. Interview with the Iranian author **Marina Nemat**, exiled to Canada, "Quantos mais terão de morrer até regime cair ?", *O´Globo*, June 10, 2006.

Berlinck, Deborah; Oliveira, Eliane. "Brasil se afasta do Iran em direitos humanos" (human rights and Iran-Brazil relations), *O´Globo*, March 25, 2011.

Bilevsky, Daniel. "Europe approves more sanctions against Iran", *New York Times*, *International Herald Tribune*, April 24, 2007.

Bildt, Carl (Swedish Minister of Foreign Affairs); **Erkki, Tuomioja** (Finnish Minister of Foreign Affairs). "The only option on Iran", *New York Times*, *International Herald Tribune*, March 21, 2011.

Bonnet, Yves. *Nucléaire iranien*, Éd. Michel Lafon, Paris, 2008.

Burns, Nicholas. "Obama delivers a clear message to Iran", *Boston Globe*, March 15, 2012.

Cagaptay, Soner. "The Empires strike back", *New York Times*, *International Herald Tribune*, January 16, 2012.

Carroll, James. "Options on the table", *New York Times*, *International Herald Tribune*, December 14, 2012.

Carvalho, Cleide. "Amorim condenou apoio a ONU sobre Irã", *O´Globo*, August 9, 2011.

Chade, Jamil. "Para Brasil, não houve fraude" (on Iranian elections), *O Estado de São Paulo*, June 15, 2009.

Cohen, Roger. "The Making of an Iran Policy", August 2, 2009 / "An ordinary Israel", October 16, 2009, *The New York Times*, *International Herald Tribune*.

Cooper, Helen. "West looks at how it could live without a nuclear Iran", *New York Times*, *International Herald Tribune*, January 26, 2012.

Delpech, Thérèse. *Iran and the Bomb*, Hurst and Company, London, 2007.

Djalili, Mohammad-Reza; Therme. "L´Iran en Amérique latine : la République islamique dans le pré-carré des États-Unis", *Revue Maghreb-Makrek*, n° 197, October 2008.

Ebadi, Shirin (Nobel Peace Prize in 2003); **Sahimi, Muhammad** (University of Southern California), "The follies of Bush´s policy", *New York Times*, May 30, 2007.

Emirates Center for Strategic studies and Research. "Iran´s nuclear program. Realities and Repercussions", Papers of the conference on the Iranian nuclear program in Abu Dhabi on February 26, 2006.

Erdbring, Thomas. "Iran sees success in its atom strategy", May 16, 2012 / "From Tehran, hints of new directions", July 27-28, 2013, *New York Times*, *International Herald Tribune*,

Erlanger, Steven. "In talks with Iran, a new reading of motives", April 13, 2012. / "Iran passes test in 7-nation nuclear talks", April 16, 2012, *New York Times*, *International Herald Tribune*.

Farah, Tatiana. "Empresa do Brasil na lista negra dos EUA" (threat of retaliation against Brazilian companies doing business with Iran), *O´Globo*, January 16, 2011.

Farr, Warner. "The Third Temple´s Holy of Holies: Israel´s Nuclear Weapons", US Air Force Counter Proliferation Center, Future Warfare N°2, Air War College, September 1999.

Gladstone, Rick. "U.S. increases Iranian sanctions for 4th time in a week", New *York Times, International Herald Tribune*, June 6, 2013.
Gois, Chico de. "Sanções ao amigo Ahmadinejad", *O´Globo*, August 11, 2010.
Gordon, Michael. "Iran is said to be open to nuclear talks with U.S.", *New York Times, International Herald Tribune*, July 27-28, 2013.
Haggai, Ram. *Iranophobia. The logic of an Israeli obsession*, Stanford University Press, California, 2009.
Hakim, Peter (Inter American Dialogue). "O Brasil e a agenda de segurança dos Estados Unidos", *Política Externa*, vol. 20 (3), February 2012.
Helev, Mark (Institute of National Security Studies, Tel Aviv), "A Europe-Iran war", *New York Times, International Herald Tribune*, January 26, 2012.
Hibbs, Mark; **Levite, Ariel**; **Perkovich, George** (Nuclear Policy Program of the Carnegie Endowment for International Peace), "How to tell if the Iran talks are working", *New York Times, International Herald Tribune*, April 14, 2012.
Jesus, Diego Santos Vieira de (PUC, Rio). "Building trust and flexibility: a Brazilian view of the fuel swap with Iran", *The Washington Quarterly*, Winter 2011 / "Setting fire to the rain: Brazil´s strategic postures, goals and perceptions towards Iran", in Makinsky Michel (ed.), *L´Iran et les grands acteurs régionaux et globaux*, L´Harmattan, Paris, 2012.
Kaye, Dalia Dassa; **Wehrey, Frederic** (Rand Corporation). "Avoiding a Two-Dimensional Strategy in a Four Dimensional Region", *The Washington Quarterly*, July 2009.
Keller, Bill. "Bomb, bomb, bomb Iran", *New York Times, International Herald Tribune*, January 24, 2012.
Kemenade, Willem van. "China vs. the Western campaign for Iran sanctions", *The Washington Quarterly*, July 2010.
Kibaroglu, Mustafa. "Uma perspective turca sobre a iniciativa nuclear Brasil-Turquia em relação ao Irã", *Politica Externa*, vol. 20, nº 3, February 2012.
Kourlandsky, Jean Jacques. "L´Iran et l´Amérique latine de langue espagnole" in **Makinsky, Michel** (ed.), *L´Iran et les grands acteurs régionaux et globaux*, L´Harmattan, Paris, 2012.
Krauss, Clifford. "Oil market vulnerable if Iran cuts off Gulf", *New York Times, International Herald Tribune*, January 6, 2012.
Kresh, Daniela. "Irã moderado racha Israel", *O´Globo*, September 26, 2013.
Landau, Emily (University of Tel-Aviv). "Too confrontational on Iran?", *The Jerusalem Post*, February 6, 2012.
Lampreia, Luiz Felipe. *Aposta em Teerã: o Acordo Nuclear entre Brasil, Turquia e Irã*, Editora Objetiva, São Paulo, 2004.
Landler, Mark; **Sanger, David**. "US and Israel at odds over Iran´s atomic 'immunity zone'", *New York Times, International Herald Tribune*, February 10, 2012.
Levaillant, Melissa. *La politique étrangère de l´Inde envers l´Iran. Entre politique de responsabilité et autonomie stratégique (1993-2010)*, L´Iran en transition Collection, L´Harmattan, Paris, 2012.
Leverett, Flynt; Leverett, Hilary Mann. *Going to Tehran: Why America Must Accept the Islamic Republic of Iran*, Metropolitan Books, New York, 2014.
Lorentz, Dominique. *Une guerre atomique : la bombe iranienne ou la terrible histoire des otages français au Liban*, Éd. Des Arènes, Paris, 2002.
Lorentz, Dominique; **Car-Brown, David**. *La République atomique. France-Iran, le pacte nucléaire*, Paris, 2001.
Luers, William; **Pickering, Thomas**. "Envisioning a deal with Teheran", *New York Times, International Herald Tribune*, February 4-5, 2012.
Majd, Hooman. "Starving Iran won´t free it", March 5, 2012 / "In Iran, hints of hope and change", June 19, 2013, *New York Times, International Herald Tribune*,
Makinsky, Michel (ed.). *L´Iran et les grands acteurs régionaux et globaux*, L´Harmattan, Paris, 2012.
Maloney, Suzanne (Brookings Institution). "Sanctioning Iran: if only it were so simple", *The Washington Quarterly*, January 2010.
Maltchik, Roberto. "O Brasil oficializa convite de abrigo a Sakineh" (on right to asylum for the Iranian Sakineh), *O´Globo*, August 10, 2010.

Mazzetti, Mark; Broad, William. "Uncertainty on reality of Iranian missiles", *Wikileaks*, in the *International Herald Tribune*, December 4, 2010.
Mekdour, Mehdi. "Les craintes et motivations liées au programme nucléaire iranien", Group for Research and Information on Peace and Security - GRIP, September 8, 2009 / "Les sanctions isolent-elles vraiment l'Iran ?", Group for Research and Information on Peace and Security - GRIP, Analysis Note, September 24, 2010, Brussels.
Melikian, Souren. "Turkey Rewakening to Its Vast Iranian Ties", *New York Times*, November 24, 2009.
Nahavandi, Firouzeh (coord.). *L'Iran dans le monde*, L'Harmattan, Paris, 2013.
Nader, Bazin. *L'Iran nucléaire*, L'Harmattan, Paris, 2007.
O'Globo. "Estados Unidos grampearam telephones de El Baradei", December 13, 2004 / "A política externa das más companhias" (a critique of Brazilian policy toward Iran), July 6, 2010.
Oliveira, Eliane. "Uma diplomacia que despertou polêmica" (a critique of Brazilian diplomacy toward Iran), *O'Globo,* December 19, 2010 / "Previsão é de uma relação fria com governo brasileiro", *O'Globo*, June 11, 2013.
Ottolenghi, Emanuele (Foundation for Defense of Democracies). "Only crippling sanctions will stop Iran", *New York Times, International Herald Tribune,* March 5, 2012.
Pant, Harsh (King's College of London). "India's relations with Iran: much ado about nothing", *The Washington Quarterly*, Winter 2011.
Parsi, Trita (Iran/United States National Council). "A declaração de Teerã e o futuro da mediação turco-brasileira", *Politica Externa*, vol. 20 (3), February 2012. / "War fever over Iran", *The Nation*, February 27, 2012 / *A Single Roll of the Dice. Obama's diplomacy with Iran*, Yale University Press, New Haven, 2012.
Perthes, Volker (Stiftung Wissenschaft un Politik, German institute of international studies), "If at first Iran says no, try, try again", *New York Times*, *International Herald Tribune*, April 12, 2012.
Piovesan, Flavia. "Mudança de rumo com o Iran", *O'Globo*, April 21, 2011.
Plessis, Laurent Athur de. *L'Iran dans la troisième guerre mondiale*, Jean Cyrille Godefroy Éd., Paris, 2005.
Poitevin, Cedric. "Le rapport des services secrets américains. Une victoire pour l'Iran", Group for Research and Information on Peace and Security - GRIP, December 14, 2007, Brussels.
Polk, William. *Understanding Iran*, Macmillan, New York, 2009.
Pollack, Kenneth. *Unthinkable: Iran, the Bomb and American Strategy*, Simon & Schuster, New York, 2013.
Porter, Gareth. "Les dessous des négociations avec l'Iran", *Le Monde diplomatique*, December 2009 / *Manufactured Crisis: The Untold Story of the Iran Nuclear Scare*, Just World Books, Charlottesville, 2014.
Posen, Barry. *A nuclear armed Iran; a difficult but not impossible policy problem*, Century Foundation, Washington D.C., 2006 / "We can live with a nuclear Iran", *New York Times*, *International Herald Tribune*, February 26, 2006.
Ray, Takeyh (Council of Foreign Relations). "Iran's missing moderates", *New York Times*, *International Herald Tribune*, March 20, 2012.
Ritter, Scott (UN inspector on weapons of mass destruction, 1991-1998). *Target Iran. The Truth about the US Government's plans for regime change*, Nation Books, New York, 2006.
Rouppert, Bérangère. "La crise du nucléaire iranien : vers un retour des négociations", Group for Research and Information on Peace and Security - GRIP, Analysis Note, February 24, 2012, Brussels.
Rubin, Alisssa; Rahimi, Sangar. "NATO issues apology for deaths of Afghan boys", *New York Times*, *International Herald tribune*, March 3, 2011.
Sanger, David. "Shadow war with Tehran appears set to get dirtier", *New York Times*, *International Herald Tribune*, November 7, 2011.
Sanger, David; Broad, William. "U.N. team finds evidence of an Iran bomb plan", November 9, 2011 / "Iran missile site blast is seen as big setback", December 6, 2011, *New York Times*, *International Herald Tribune*.

Sanger, David; Healy, Jack. "Tehran to enrich fuel at higher level", December 3, 2009 / "Iran appears set for a nuclear shift", September 2, 2011, *New York Times, International Herald Tribune.*
Shane, Scott. "After two wars, drums again beat over Iran", *New York Times, International Herald Tribune*, January 22, 2012.
Schell, Jonathan. "Thinking the Unthinkable. A war on Iran to stop its nuclear program would bring on a proliferation catastrophe", *The Nation*, April 23, 2012.
Shen, Dingli (Fudan University, Shanghai). "Can sanctions stop proliferation?", *The Washington Quarterly*, Summer 2008.
Silver-Greenberg, Jessica; Protess, Ben. "Japanese lender fined for sanctions violations", *New York Times, International Herald Tribune*, June 21, 2006.
Slackman, Michael. "Bombing in Iran kills commanders of elite force", *New York Times, International Herald Tribune*, October 19, 2009.
Sotero, Paulo. "EUA espionaram chefe da AIEA. Washington Post revela que telefones do egípcio El-Baradei foram grampeados", *O Estado de São Paulo*, December 13, 2004 / "Uma reflexão sobre a frustrada iniciativa Brasil - Turquia para superar o impasse nuclear entre o Irã e a comunidade internacional", *Politica Externa,* vol. 20, n° 3, February 2012.
Stein, Shimon; Feldman, Shai; Brom, Shlomo. "The public discussion of Israel´s strategy regarding a nuclear Iran", *The Institute for National Security Studies*, n° 310, January 31, 2012.
Tavernise, Sabrina. "Turkey speaks up in Mideast", June 9, 2010 / "Turkey´s risky bridging of East and West", June 14, 2010, *New York Times, International Herald Tribune.*
Telhami, Shibley (University of Maryland); **Kull Steven** (International Policy Attitude). "Preventing a nuclear Iran, peacefully", *New York Times, International Herald Tribune*, January 16, 2012.
Torbati, Yeganeh. "Iran´s banks holding in London", *New York Times, International Herald Tribune*, December 29, 2011.
Toukan, Abdullah; Cordesman, Anthony. "Study on a Possible Israeli Strike on Iran´s Nuclear Development Facilities", Center for Strategic and International Studies, March 14, 2009.
Von Kemenade, Willem, *Iran´s relations with China and the West: cooperation and confrontation in Asia*, Clingendael, Netherland Institute of International Relations and the West, November 1, 2009 (www.clingendael.nl).
Vinocur, John. "West´s time to act on Iran is narrowing", *New York Times, International Herald Tribune*, December 30, 2012.
Waltz, Kenneth. "Why Iran Should Get the Bomb. Nuclear balancing Would Mean Stability", *Foreign Affairs*, July-August 2012.
Worth, Robert. "Iran´s top leader threatens retaliation over U.S. sanctions", *New York Times, International Herald Tribune*, February 4, 2012.

Conclusions

Bimbaum, Jeffrey; Mufson, Steven. "Is Citgo Program for Poor or for Chàvez?", *Washington Post,* February 24, 2007.
Maduro, Nicolas. "An Open letter to the People of the United States, Venezuela is Not a Threat", *Counterpunch*, March 20-22, 2015

L'HARMATTAN ITALIA
Via Degli Artisti 15; 10124 Torino
harmattan.italia@gmail.com

L'HARMATTAN HONGRIE
Könyvesbolt ; Kossuth L. u. 14-16
1053 Budapest

L'HARMATTAN KINSHASA
185, avenue Nyangwe
Commune de Lingwala
Kinshasa, R.D. Congo
(00243) 998697603 ou (00243) 999229662

L'HARMATTAN CONGO
67, av. E. P. Lumumba
Bât. – Congo Pharmacie (Bib. Nat.)
BP2874 Brazzaville
harmattan.congo@yahoo.fr

L'HARMATTAN GUINÉE
Almamya Rue KA 028, en face
du restaurant Le Cèdre
OKB agency BP 3470 Conakry
(00224) 657 20 85 08 / 664 28 91 96
harmattanguinee@yahoo.fr

L'HARMATTAN MALI
Rue 73, Porte 536, Niamakoro,
Cité Unicef, Bamako
Tél. 00 (223) 20205724 / +(223) 76378082
poudiougopaul@yahoo.fr
pp.harmattan@gmail.com

L'HARMATTAN CAMEROUN
BP 11486
Face à la SNI, immeuble Don Bosco
Yaoundé
(00237) 99 76 61 66
harmattancam@yahoo.fr

L'HARMATTAN CÔTE D'IVOIRE
Résidence Karl / cité des arts
Abidjan-Cocody 03 BP 1588 Abidjan 03
(00225) 05 77 87 31
etien_nda@yahoo.fr

L'HARMATTAN BURKINA
Penou Achille Some
Ouagadougou
(+226) 70 26 88 27

L'HARMATTAN SÉNÉGAL
10 VDN en face Mermoz, après le pont de Fann
BP 45034 Dakar Fann
33 825 98 58 / 33 860 9858
senharmattan@gmail.com / senlibraire@gmail.com
www.harmattansenegal.com

L'HARMATTAN BÉNIN
ISOR-BENIN
01 BP 359 COTONOU-RP
Quartier Gbèdjromèdé,
Rue Agbélenco, Lot 1247 I
Tél : 00 229 21 32 53 79
christian_dablaka123@yahoo.fr

Achevé d'imprimer par Corlet Numérique - 14110 Condé-sur-Noireau
N° d'Imprimeur : 124228 - Dépôt légal : décembre 2015 - *Imprimé en France*